THE FAITHFUL SIXTH

To Gerald -
Best Wishes
Harry Moses
28. 8. 95.

Harry Moses

Published by
County Durham Books

DEDICATION

This book is dedicated to all officers and men, past members of
the 6th Battalion The Durham Light Infantry and in memory of
those who made the supreme sacrifice in both World Wars, and to
the widows and families of all who have served with the Battalion.

Text © Harry Moses, 1995

Published by County Durham Books, 1995

County Durham Books is the imprint of Durham County Council:
Arts, Libraries & Museums Department

ISBN 1 897585 19 5

FOREWORD

BRIGADIER P.J. JEFFREYS DSO & BAR, OBE.

The children of Aycliffe Village in County Durham have been fortunate to be taught and led by Harry Moses. And how lucky are we to have him, born and bred at Tow Law, to record so well the great history of the Sixth Battalion of The Durham Light Infantry.

And what a story it is. It stretches from the early days as part of the Durham Rifle Volunteers in 1859 and then on through the two Great Wars until finally its end in 1968 with the other battalions of the Regiment.

Harry's research has taken him several years and deserves high praise; its detail, accuracy, and thoroughness binds the story into a great work.

I hope it will be read by all those still living who served in the Battalion as well as by members of the families and friends of the descendents. Drawn mostly from the West and South West of the County it has all through its life been very much based on families and local close-knit communities. For example, I am so proud of my father, John, who was the Regular Adjutant in 1914 during its mobilization and entry into action at Ypres and who commanded it frequently thereafter between sickness and wounds in the first years of the War; proud too of my own service, strangely in exactly the same appointments at the start of the Second World War - including Arras and the retreat to Dunkirk.

The Battalion, through all its long life, has been characterised by a notable spirit of comradeship and this, with cheerful toughness has generated that base of courage which combats so well the changes and discomforts of the battlefield and has brought glory to so many grim scenes.

This book shows well how this spirit has been nurtured in its old strongholds of Bishop Auckland, Barnard Castle, Crook, Consett and Spennymoor and their neighbouring smaller townships and villages. It will surely now continue, through its successor, the 7th Battalion of The (Durham) Light Infantry, to produce FAITHFUL service.

County Durham *Recruitment Area for the Volunteers and 6th Battalion The Durham Light Infantry.*

CHAPTER 1
DEFENCE NOT DEFIANCE
1859 -1908

The Volunteer Rifle Corps movement, forerunner of the Territorial Army, owed its inception in 1859 to what were perceived as threats from continental powers to the security of our country. The French press in particular advocated periodically an invasion of these islands. Real or imagined these threats were seen to be a danger to our security.

The threats themselves were not new in the history of our relationship with our nearest continental neighbour and would not have raised much alarm in earlier times. After all the Royal Navy ruled the seas and had proved in the past to be an insurmountable barrier to any power bent on landing an invasion force on our shores - a factor Napoleon Bonaparte had found to his cost. However in the late 1850s naval technology was rapidly narrowing the gap between British and French sea power. The French challenge to our traditional naval shield was seen in some quarters as one to be taken very seriously. It was believed that French application of steam to her new warships would seriously test the ability of the Royal Navy to deny the Channel to a hostile French fleet. These new warships were protected and strengthened with iron (the Ironclads) and being armed with the new rifled guns could throw more powerful and effective shells longer distances. Britain, too, was introducing the new technology to her fleet, but it was feared that France had a narrow head start and would be more than capable of challenging our naval supremacy. The outcome of any naval engagement in the Channel would be very much in doubt and a French victory would open up the real possibility of a successful invasion.

If the French navy could gain supremacy in the Channel and land an invasion force upon our shores, many people with military experience were concerned about our ability to defeat such a force after it had landed. Traditional antipathy towards a large standing army, as much to do with the cost of maintenance as any threats against our liberties, meant that immediately a major war was over the regular army underwent a series of cutbacks. An estimated quarter of a million strong in 1816, the regular army was reduced to under 100,000 by 1841. This force had to protect a widening empire as well as these islands. In 1850 the size of the French army was estimated at over 400,000 regulars with the back-up of a Garde Nationale of some 2 million men.

The British military organisation creaked and groaned under the successive demands of the 1850s. The Crimean War revealed the country's weaknesses. The lessons of this war had revealed a total lack of a reserve force which could either reinforce the regular forces abroad, or defend the country in their absence. Events which followed this war only served to highlight the country's military weakness. The Indian Mutiny only added to our problems. At the outbreak of the Mutiny there were less than 40,000 British troops in India. They were very widely dispersed and thin on the ground, barely sufficient to contain the Mutiny. The military and naval actions in China between 1858 and 1860 stretched resources even further. The small regular forces at home were considered, in some quarters, to be insufficient to face the threat of an invasion from across the English Channel. With a Bonaparte once again as head of state who displayed ambitions towards reviving the glories of his illustrious forebear by extending French boundaries and power, there were influential people who were becoming more and more concerned at our ability to defend ourselves against any threat from France.

Those people concerned with the defence of our country sought possible solutions to the problems we now faced. There were several approaches to these difficulties. The regular army and the militia could be expanded together with increased expenditure to improve fortifications, supplies and weapons. The increased taxation necessary to pay for these expansions together with the demands on employers to release men for the militia would be most unpopular. There were growing demands for the formation of rifle volunteer units. Their supporters saw them as a possible solution but there were also detractors.

Opposition to the volunteer movement was strong. Some leading politicians felt that they would be too costly to raise and maintain. Furthermore as part-time soldiers, hence only partly trained, they would not be able to meet the physical demands of campaigning. The opposition not only came from government and politicians. The Duke of Cambridge, Commander-in-Chief from 1855 - 1895, thought that the volunteer corps would be a 'very dangerous rabble', ill-disciplined, and would have an adverse affect upon the army. There were many other objections on similar lines. Yet the use of volunteers fired by patriotic zeal had already been seen during the Napoleonic Wars. Localities had raised their volunteer units for home and local defence against the threat of invasion from France. It was estimated that some 400,000 men had been raised in this way throughout the country. The County of Durham had taken a prominent part in this movement with units, infantry and horsed, raised in areas such as Sunderland, Stockton, Darlington and elsewhere. These volunteer units had remained in being for the periods of hostility between France and Britain and were disbanded when peace was made.

There were, indeed, many people who feared that a volunteer movement would put weapons into the hands of the working classes who might use them to threaten state and employer power and seek improved social conditions. Yet there were also many who saw the volunteer movement as an opportunity for professional and skilled workers, led by the local gentry, to exercise their patriotic duty to defend their country when threatened by any foreign power. These people would certainly not join the regular army or the militia. The press orchestrated a campaign in support of the movement. Leading newspapers like *The Times* gave support, during the 1850s, to those people who were demanding the establishment of Volunteer Corps, which they saw as a means of meeting our military weaknesses. Both Queen Victoria and Prince Albert were now taking an increasing interest in and giving support to the volunteer movement.

The volunteer movement of 1859 was an attempt to strengthen the armed forces in Britain which might be called upon to defend the country from any invader. It was considered that the raising of volunteers would satisfy strong public opinion and, at the same time, would cost the government very little in the way of financial outlay. The volunteer units would be largely self-supporting, though not entirely so, as was first envisaged. The government supplied rifles and a capitation fee based on the number of effectives - men who had attained their training targets - each unit held on roll. A circular letter dated 12th May, 1859, from General Sir John Peel, Secretary of State at the War Office, to Lords Lieutenants authorised the latter to raise Volunteer Rifle Corps under the powers obtained from the Yeoman and Volunteers Consolidation Act of 1804. This was superseded by an Act of 1863 which met the new conditions more effectively and efficiently than those of the Napoleonic Wars for which the 1804 Act had been designed.

So much for an outline of the background to the factors which influenced the formation of the volunteer movement. We are concerned with the raising of those Volunteer Corps which were to be disbanded in 1908 and reformed as the 6th Battalion The Durham Light Infantry (Territorial Force).

'A meeting was held in Barrington School, Bishop Auckland, in August, 1859, to consider the formation of a Company of Volunteers. Colonel Stobart, Durham Artillery Militia, presided. It was proposed to form a company of Volunteers and soon over a hundred names were taken. A Company was formed and was called the 4th Durham Rifle Volunteers. They appeared for the first time in uniform on Whit Monday, 1860 under the command of Captain W. Trotter.' *(Watson Papers)*

A second company of the 4th Durham Rifle Volunteers was raised at Black Boy and Coundon in 1861, commanded by Captain C.L. Wood. By February, 1861, the 4th Rifle Volunteer Corps was one of eighteen Corps formed in the County of Durham.

Number	Place	Commanding Officer
1st	Stockton	Captain R. Thompson
3rd	Sunderland	Captain T.E. Chapman
4th	Bishop Auckland	Captain W. Trotter
6th	South Shields	Captain J. Williamson
7th	Durham	Captain J. Fogg-Elliott
8th	Gateshead	Captain G.H.L. Hawks
9th	Blaydon	Captain J. Cowen
10th	Beamish	Captain J. Joicey
11th	Chester-le-Street	Captain P.S. Reid
12th	Middleton-in-Teesdale	Captain H.G. Bainbridge
13th	Birtley	Captain E.M. Perkins
14th	Felling	Captain W.W. Pattinson
15th	Darlington	Captain J.J. Scurfield
16th	Castle Eden	Captain R.C. Bewicke
17th	Wolsingham	Captain T.H. Bates.
18th	Shotley Bridge	Captain J.B. Richardson
19th	Hartlepool	Captain J.W. Jeffrey
20th	Stanhope	Captain J.T. Roddam

In August, 1861, corps were grouped into Administrative Battalions and 1st, 4th, 12th, 15th, 16th, 17th, 18th, 19th and 20th were formed into the 2nd Administrative Battalion, Durham Rifle Volunteers, commanded by Lieutenant-Colonel W. Trotter, with headquarters at Bishop Auckland. Further changes to the composition of the Administrative Battalion quickly followed.

1st, 15th, 16th and 19th Durham Rifle Volunteers left the 2nd Administrative Battalion and formed the 4th Administrative Battalion. This Battalion appeared in the Army List for the first time in January, 1862. On the 1st April, 1862, the 2nd Administrative Battalion consisted of the 4th (Bishop Auckland), 12th (Middleton-in-Teesdale), 17th (Wolsingham), 18th (Shotley Bridge) and the 20th (Stanhope) Durham Rifle Volunteers. There were a total of seven companies and an enrolled membership of four hundred and seven. Over the years to 1908, the composition of the administrative battalions changed as the popularity of the

Captain Jobson, *Bishop Auckland, 4th Durham Rifle Volunteers. In his uniform: light grey with scarlet facings, 1861*

Group of officers of the 4th Durham Rifle Volunteers *taken in Captain Jobson's garden, Market Place, Bishop Auckland, 1861.*

movement waned or increased. The 7th North Yorkshire Rifle Volunteers was formed in 1860 with headquarters at Startforth. This corps was transferred to the 2nd Administrative Battalion and appeared for the first time in the Army List for January, 1864, as the 21st Durham Rifle Volunteers with headquarters at Barnard Castle. The 18th DRV based at Shotley Bridge appeared for the last time in the Army List for July 1865. In the same year the Shildon Company of the 4th (Bishop Auckland) DRV came into existence. The 17th (Wolsingham) DRV was disbanded in

1866. For the next twenty years the 2nd Administrative Battalion consisted of 4th (Bishop Auckland), 12th (Middleton-in-Teesdale), 20th (Stanhope) and 21st (Barnard Castle) Durham Rifle Volunteers with an overall total of six companies.

The Shildon Company had an interesting early history. It was raised in 1865 with an initial membership of over one hundred volunteers. The first commanding officer was Captain S. Fielden. A drill hall was provided in a large railway shed. About 1872, Captain W. Davison commanded the company. He had business interests in Darlington and moved the company to that town where it became part of the 1st Durham Rifle Volunteers with an armoury in Alliance Street, Hopetown. In Darlington they were obviously considered interlopers and caused much discontent in the local corps. This was clearly shown in a letter to the editor of the *North Star* from John Smith of Bulmer Street, Darlington:

> 'Sir - Please allow me, as an old member of the 15th Durham RV (The Darlington Corps) now the 'D' and 'E' Companies of the 1st Durham Rifle Volunteers, to inform the inhabitants of the town and neighbourhood that the volunteers commanded by Captain W.N. Davison is the Shildon or 'C' Company of the Bishop Auckland Battalion, who, a short time ago, embarked at Shildon (which is their proper station), and after tossing about and being shipwrecked on the ocean of life, were cast ashore at the Wagon Company Works, at Albert Hill. They now strive to usurp and supplant the original corps by misrepresentation, stating that they are the Darlington Volunteers. Let the public judge for themselves, and at the same time allow me to inform Captain Davison that the Darlington Corps simply look upon these Shildon emigrants as very good fellows, but they are poaching.'

In 1884 the Shildon Company was disbanded and many of its members joined the Woodland Company under Captain Metcalfe-Gibson and Lieutenant Dowdswell. This company was formed in 1885 and achieved some local fame through its excellent Woodland Band. This was not the end of the company's wanderings. At some point it moved to Copley, then Butterknowle. In 1900 it moved to Evenwood and then on to West Auckland. Finally in 1903 it moved back to Shildon where it remained until it disbanded in March, 1908.

The 12th Durham Rifle Volunteers was raised in 1860 at Middleton-in-Teesdale after two public meetings with an initial membership of fifty men. Most of the volunteers worked for the London Lead Company, managed by the Bainbridge family. The first Commanding Officer was Captain H.G. Bainbridge. The Lead Company gave financial support to the corps for much of its existence. The decline of lead mining towards the end of the century led to a drastic fall in membership and the corps was disbanded in 1899.

The 20th (Stanhope) Rifle Volunteer Corps was formed in 1861 with an initial membership of nine men. By the end of the year this had risen to over sixty volunteers, commanded by Captain J.T. Roddam. The 21st DRV (formally 7th North Yorks) commenced in 1860 with sixty-three members on roll. The first Commanding Officer was W.J.S. Morritt of Rokeby Hall with Morley Headlam of Whorlton Hall as second in command.

The next major change in the structure of the Rifle Volunteer Corps Movement occurred in 1880. The local independence which the corps had enjoyed under the pre-1880 structure was, in theory, dispensed with. In the Army List of April, 1880, the corps which formed the 2nd Administrative Battalion were now grouped together and were given a new title: 4th Durham Rifle Volunteers. In the Army List of July, 1880, this title was again changed to 2nd Durham Rifle Volunteers. On the 6th March, 1886, the establishment of the battalion was increased from six to eight companies by the addition of two companies raised at Spennymoor, both lettered 'G' and 'H' and commanded by Captain F. Badcock and Captain P.B. Junor respectively. The Battalion now comprised:

'A' Company	Bishop Auckland Raised 1860.
'B' Company	Black Boy and Coundon Raised 1861.
'C' Company	Woodland and Butterknowle Raised 1885.
'D' Company	Middleton-in-Teesdale Raised 1861.
'E' Company	Stanhope Raised 1861.
'F' Company	Barnard Castle Raised 1860.
'G' Company	Spennymoor Raised 1886.
'H' Company	Spennymoor Raised 1886.

Further changes in the title followed with the policy of linking the volunteers to the County Regiment. The Army List of January, 1888, listed the volunteers under the title: 'The 2nd Volunteer Battalion, The Durham Light Infantry.'

In 1899, following the demise of the Middleton-in-Teesdale Company, a new 'D' Company was raised at Crook to replace it. This company had a difficult start as it inherited the debts of its predecessor. A bazaar was held in Crook Board School in September, 1900, and the amount raised was sufficient to meet the debts. The first Commanding Office was Captain W. Wilkinson.

In 1900 the Battalion was again increased from eight to eleven companies. Two companies were raised at Consett and a third was raised as a cycling company. These were lettered 'K', 'L' and 'I' respectively. Some controversy arose as to which battalion the two Consett companies should be attached. Whilst other battalion commanders hesitated, Colonel D. Armstrong of the 2nd Volunteer Battalion stepped in and accepted these companies. 'K' Company was commanded by Captain J. Pertherick and 'L' Company by Captain L. Parker. The cyclist company was raised in May, 1900, with headquarters at Bishop Auckland and detachments in other towns such as Barnard Castle and Consett. Its first Commanding Officer was Captain .A. York. Recruits for this company were drawn from the whole of the Battalion's recruiting area. This company was disbanded on the 31st March, 1908, and did not join the territorial unit. The composition of the Battalion was now as follows:

'A' Company	Bishop Auckland and Shildon.
'B' Company	Bishop Auckland.
'C' Company	Bishop Auckland.
'D' Company	Crook.
'E' Company	Wolsingham and Stanhope.
'F' Company	Barnard Castle.
'G' Company	Spennymoor.
'H' Company	Spennymoor.

'K' Company	Consett.
'L' Company	Consett.
'I' Company	Cyclists.

In 1907 as a result of the Haldane Reforms, the Territorial and Reserve Forces Act became law and brought an end to the Volunteer Force. This took effect from the 1st April, 1908, when a new battalion of eight companies with an establishment of twenty-nine officers and nine hundred and eighty men was brought into being. The old 2nd Volunteer Battalion was disbanded and thirty officers and seven hundred and seventeen men from that unit transferred to the new 6th Battalion The Durham Light Infantry. The eight companies of the 6th Battalion were as follows:

'A' Company	Bishop Auckland (Det. at Coundon)
	Captain C.E. Cummins.
'B' Company	Bishop Auckland (Det. at West Auckland)
	Capt.W. Wilkinson.
'C' Company	Spennymoor
	Captain S.E. Badcock.
'D' Company	Crook (Det. at Willington)
	Captain J.H. Ramsey.
'E' Company	Stanhope (Dets. at Wolsingham, Frosterley and St. John's Chapel)
	Captain J. Gray.
'F' Company	Barnard Castle (Dets. at Staindrop, Gainford and Winston)
	Captain J.W.B. Heslop.
'G' Company	Consett
	Commanding: Captain J. Petherick.
'H' Company	Consett
	Commanding: Captain J.E. Parker.

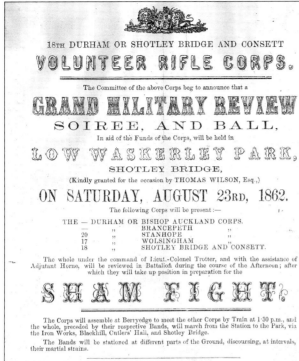

Events such as these gave the Volunteers an opportunity to show themselves to the public and to raise much needed funds.

The local gentry, leaders in successful commercial and industrial undertakings and members of the professions, took a leading role in raising and, in many cases, commanding the Volunteer Corps. The first commanding officer of the 4th Durham Rifle Volunteers was William Trotter of Byers Green Hall, Spennymoor. He was already a Captain in the South Durham Militia. His father had raised the Darlington Legion and the 1st Durham Local Militia. Local gentry involved in raising other corps included the Wood family of Howletch Hall (Black Boy and Coundon Company); W.J.S. Morritt of Rokeby Hall and Morley Headlam of Whorlton Hall (7th North Yorkshire, later 21st Durham Rifle Volunteers). The Bainbridge family who managed the London Lead Company raised the 12th DRV. The Bates family who owned large areas of land in Weardale helped raise the 17th DRV. In addition to the influence of persons of position and substance in the community in persuading men to join, the local vicar often took an active part and added a religious dimension to the proceedings.

The background of the men who joined the movement over the years, represented a cross-section of the local society. In Barnard Castle, a market town, shopkeepers, tailors, carpenters, stone masons, plumbers, engineers, gardeners, spinners and weavers were represented among the volunteers of the 7th North Yorkshire. Bishop Auckland, Spennymoor and Crook volunteers included small businessmen, skilled and semi-skilled workmen, many of the latter from the coal mines which made up so much of the industry of these areas. Shildon Corps drew on the railways and coal mines for many of its members. The burgeoning steelworks provided many of the volunteers for the Consett companies. Stanhope and Middleton-in-Teesdale Corps found the majority of members from their mainly agricultural and lead mining communities.

What attracted these men to the movement? Patriotism probably remained high amongst the factors which attracted and motivated the officers, allied to a sense of responsibility and duty towards the community which looked upon them as the natural leaders of local society. It was deemed appropriate that male members of the families of the local hierarchy should seek commissions in the volunteers as part of their responsibility and

Battalion headquarters was at Bishop Auckland. Battalion Commander was Colonel The Hon. W.L. Vane.

So much for the changing structure of the Volunteer Corps from 1859 to 1908; what were the backgrounds of the volunteers themselves?

duty to family and community. The motives of the other ranks for joining were probably more basic and it is doubtful that patriotism figured large in their decision. The attraction and prestige of wearing a uniform which added glamour and colour and appealed to the ladies were motivating factors. Joining friends already in the corps ensured a very strong group identity and loyalty. This group empathy so often strengthened each individual's loyalty and resolve during moments of intense crisis and danger when in action in later wars. The emphasis on fitness and recreation increased as years went by and these attracted many young men to the movement. Later when annual camps were introduced the attraction of a fortnight away from home with all of its boredom and drudgeries, the opportunity to see other places and the bounty payment, seemed most attractive. The pressure to join exerted by employers, who officered the corps, upon their employees was also a significant factor.

Drilling with rifles and firing on a local range seem to have been the basic activities of the early volunteers. To show the volunteers skill with the rifle and to encourage popular support for the movement the National Rifle Association organised the first of its annual shooting competitions in 1860. This took place on Wimbledon Common and was officially opened by Queen Victoria. Representatives of Volunteer Rifle Corps throughout the country competed for the Queen's Medal. The first winner of this medal was a member of the 7th North Yorkshire RVC (later 21st Durham RVC), named Edward Ross. He was nineteen years of age and lived at Whorlton. His father was a deer stalker of some repute and it was obvious that he had taught his son from a young age to use the rifle. The news of his success was received

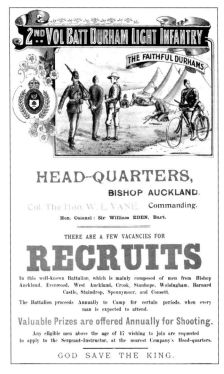

Recruiting Poster - *2nd Volunteer Battalion, The Durham Light Infantry, 1902*

with much excitement and jubilation not only by his fellow volunteers in the corps but also by the town of Barnard Castle at large. Ross was met at the railway station by the Corps Band and carried shoulder high through the town. The 6th Battalion The Durham Light Infantry had its own winner of the Queen's Prize in 1957, when the medal was won by Corporal J.W. Meynall. He won the Queen's Prize for a second time in 1964

Inspections were necessary to measure the efficiency of corps and battalions. Government grants were based upon the attainment of a minimum standard of drill, manoeuvre and skill with the rifle. On the 8th September, 1883, for example, the 2nd Durham Rifle Volunteers paraded in the grounds of Auckland Park. Five hundred and fifty two men were on parade and inspected by Colonel Nevin, the Commander of the Northern District. He found the Battalion to be in good order but there was, 'Too much talking in the ranks.' A large review and inspection took place in 1885 at Gosforth Park, Newcastle-upon-Tyne, in which several battalions of volunteers took part. The 2nd Durham Rifle Volunteers were represented by sixteen officers and four hundred and eighteen NCOs and men. It formed part of an attacking force of three thousand eight hundred and five men who manoeuvred against a defending force of one thousand five hundred and fifty. At the end of the review the whole contingent marched past the inspecting officer, General Willis, GOC-in-C, Northern Command.

The Battalion was represented in London on 22nd June, 1897, on the occasion of Queen Victoria's Jubilee. A party of NCOs and men commanded by Captain H.C. Watson were members of the lining party on London Bridge. Captain Watson was awarded the

Jubilee Medal. A small group of volunteers from the Battalion commanded by Lieutenant C.E. Cummins was part of a street lining party at the coronation of King Edward VII held in London on the 9th August, 1902. Lieutenant Cummins and Colour Sergeant G.W. Egglestone were awarded the Coronation Medal.

The Boer War which broke out in 1899 found the regular army woefully weak in numbers. The expectation was that a war against the Boers, whose image in the eyes of our military leaders was that of untrained farmers, would not last long as it was considered well within the ability of our small regular army to bring it to a swift conclusion. Leaders in the volunteer movement saw the war as an opportunity to prove the military worth of their officers and men. Initially they were to be disappointed. From the beginning of the war the policy of the War Office was to turn down offers from volunteers to serve in South Africa. The disasters of Black Week, 9th to 15th December, when the regular forces suffered humiliating defeats at the hands of the Boer farmers, changed the official attitude to offers of service overseas from the volunteers. Special Army Order dated 2nd January, 1900, authorised the raising of volunteer service companies by county regiments. Each to contain 116 men aged 25 - 35, first class shots, physically fit, of good character, passed as 'efficient' for the last two years and preferably unmarried. To overcome the obstacle presented by the Volunteer Act which laid down that volunteers were for local defence and were not to serve abroad, men were allowed to enlist in the regular army for one year. Each volunteer battalion of a regiment could raise a company which, upon arrival in South Africa, was attached to its affiliated regiment and placed under the command of the latter's commanding officer.

The volunteers who joined the 1st Battalion The Durham Light Infantry in South Africa were drawn from the five volunteer battalions of the regiment and were formed into service companies. These companies were raised, in turn, at the Regimental Depot, Newcastle-upon-Tyne. Their period of training was for three weeks before being sent to South Africa. They were clothed and equipped by grant from the War Office. Four officers and one hundred and thirty NCOs and men volunteered from the 2nd Volunteer Battalion The Durham Light Infantry. None of these men were killed in action but one volunteer, Private Armstrong, was killed on railway duty whilst in South Africa.

The 1st Volunteer Service Company which included twenty five NCOs and men of the Battalion left Southampton on the 23rd February, 1900. It arrived at Cape Town on the 17th March. Two days later it sailed on to Durban, disembarked there and moved on to join 1st Battalion The Durham Light Infantry, at a place called Elandslaagte. Here, on the 10th April, the volunteers came under fire for the first time when they were shelled out of their positions by Boer artillery. They took part in operations on the Biggarsberg and those which forced the Botha Pass and prevented the Boer leader De Wet from linking up with Botha. In August, 1900, they left the 1st Battalion and arrived at Pietermaritzburg on the 10th October. The Company stayed here for a few days and then moved into Orange Free State where it remained until April, 1901. Here it spent its time working on the blockhouse line. It left Durban on the 8th May and arrived at Southampton on the 30th May, 1901.

The 2nd Volunteer Service Company left England for South Africa on the 15th March, 1901. This company included twenty six NCOs and men of the 2nd Volunteer Battalion. It also joined the 1st Battalion of the Regiment. Corporal Appleby of the volunteers wrote the following letter to Major H.C. Watson. It was published in a local newspaper on the 23rd April, 1902, and is an account of the company's activities:

'...After reaching the regiment we were kept on line patrols for a few weeks, keeping small bodies of the enemy from crossing or damaging the railways, as just at that time the derailing of trains by the enemy were of rather frequent occurrence. In June we were placed in blockhouses (one non-commissioned officer and six men in each). Blockhouse life was very dull and the monotony was only broken by the attempts on the part of the enemy to break through. These attempts, owing to the excellent system with which the line was guarded, generally resulted in complete failure and often with loss to the Boers. After about five months of this work we were sent on the trek, being attached to Colonel Campbell's column. We marched with him during his operations for clearing the Bethel district and remained with him until he was relieved of command and

Major H.C. Watson, Sergeants and Other Ranks, *1898. Note the change in uniform to rifle green.*

Photograph shows: (left to right)

Sergeant Welford   Private F. Beer   Lance Corporal Barnes   Private Johnstone   Private Culley   Private Routledge

Colour Sergeant   Major H.C. Watson   Sergeant Instructor Burtonwood

allowed home on leave. We were then attached to Colonel Wing, under General Bruce Hamilton, and assisted in the capture of a whole Boer Laager at Trichardsfontein. Shortly after this (December) we reached Ermelo, at which place Major Vane was commandant. We were concerned in the capture of General Erasmus and his commando and, shortly after, of Major Wolmarans and several of the Staats artillery. We then became escorts to convoys running between Standerton and Ermelo under the command of Major Saunders and whilst we often had small skirmishes with the enemy they were never of a serious nature...'

Blockhouse duty near the Swazi border followed. On the 26th April, 1902, the Company left this area and moved to Cape Town, which was reached on the 7th May. It embarked for home and reached Southampton on the 5th June.

Church parade group, *Bishop Auckland, 25th April, 1905.*
Note the slouch hats which were part of the uniform for a short period

The 3rd Volunteer Service Battalion contained twenty-two NCOs and men of the Battalion. It left England in March, 1902. This Company saw very little active service. It joined the 1st Battlion of the Regiment and was used in blockhouse duty until peace was declared, following which it returned to England in August, 1902.

The 4th Volunteer Service Company, in which there were twenty seven NCOs and men of the Battalion, was linked with the Northumberland Fusiliers. It left England on 15th March, 1901, and arrived in South Africa on the 19th April. Several months of blockhouse duty in various locations followed until it left Cape Town in May, 1902, and arrived home in the following month.

The balance of the men of the Battalion who went to South Africa served with the Imperial Yeomanry, whilst Sergeant Castling, Corporal J.G. Hardacre and Corporal S. Harper served in both the 1st and 3rd Special Companies.

At the end of the Boer War or at the end of their service commitment the volunteers returned to their normal duties and to their training. In 1905, in recognition of their role in the war, the battle honour 'South Africa' was granted to volunteer battalions who had raised service companies.

Bishop Auckland was the headquarters of the 2nd Volunteer Battalion. The names of all of the men who served in the Boer War are recorded on a bronze tablet in the Town Hall. This was unveiled in 1903 by Colonel A.L. Woodland, CB, who commanded the 5th and 68th Regimental Districts. It remains a unique record of the first rifle volunteers of the Battalion to see active service abroad.

CHAPTER 2
THE TERRITORIAL YEARS
1908 - 1914

The weaknesses in our military structure which surfaced so quickly during the Boer War triggered off a searching examination of the system. An invasion panic had swept the country following the movement of the regular army to South Africa. It was quite clear that the public had little or no confidence in the skill and ability of part-time volunteers and militia to defend these islands against any foreign aggressor who might take advantage of the country denuded of its professional army. Questions were raised about the efficiency of the volunteers to meet any threat. The volunteers were raised for home defence only and their availability for future overseas service was also seen as a problem. As has been seen in the case of the Boer War, volunteers had signed on with the regular army for one year thus enabling them to serve abroad. Certainly three weeks initial training given to those who had gone to South Africa was found to be grossly insufficient and in no way made a part-time volunteer into a skilled and fully prepared combat soldier.

These concerns enabled the Secretary of State for War to demand more in the way of training and service from volunteers. Resources were made available by the government to increase the number of volunteers in training. Units were encouraged to recruit above their establishments. It was proposed to extend annual camps to four weeks in each year, but this was bitterly opposed by employers and had to be dropped. It was finally agreed that camps be of a fortnight's duration. A capitation grant of £2 2s 0d was implemented plus army rates of pay for all who remained in camp for the full fourteen days, provided a minimum of 50 per cent of the battalion attended for that period. Non-attendance at camp was penalised.

These changes only went so far in bringing about an increase in the efficiency and effectiveness of the volunteers. The burning question to be addressed was, 'What was to become of the Volunteer Force itself?' Its role had simply been seen as that of a home defence force supporting the regular army against any invader. The experience of the Boer War led to support for its use as an army reserve, available for service throughout the Empire. Home defence of this country or army reserve - what was its role to be? Both views on the future use of the volunteers had their vociferous supporters which led to prolonged and bitter debate following the Boer War. The situation enabled Richard Haldane, Secretary of State for War, to bring in his reform of the Volunteer Movement in 1907.

There were two hundred and twenty-one battalions of volunteers in existence throughout the country in 1907. Haldane's Territorial and Reserve Forces Act became law on the 1st April, 1908. The yeomanry and volunteer forces were combined into one organisation which took the title of 'Territorial Force.' Fourteen territorial divisions were established, each made up of three brigades with four battalions to each brigade. The new territorial battalions were still linked to their regular regiment but, along with the militia units, were renumbered. In The Durham Light Infantry the regular battalions numbered 1st and 2nd and were followed by the militia battalions numbered 3rd and 4th. These latter battalions were established as Special

An early photograph of officers of the Battalion following the change to Territorial status in April, 1908. The uniform is khaki. Note the Volunteer cap badge, shortly to be changed to the black bugle badge

Reserve units. The new territorial battalions in the regiment were numbered and given the title 5th, 6th, 7th, 8th and 9th Battalions The Durham Light Infantry (TF). The 6th Battalion was formerly our own 2nd Volunteer Battalion. The battalions were brigaded as part of a new Northumbrian Division. The 5th Battalion was brigaded with the Yorkshire and Durham Brigade of the Division. The other four battalions were brigaded as the Durham Brigade. The third and final brigade of the Division was the Northumberland Brigade which consisted of territorial battalions of the Northumberland Fusiliers.

In an attempt to overcome the problem of the new territorials only serving at home and to make the system more flexible in time of need a man could volunteer for service abroad. If a territorial agreed to do this he was entitled to wear above his right breast a badge inscribed 'Imperial Service' surmounted by a crown. If ninety per cent of a battalion volunteered for service abroad the words 'Imperial Service' could be placed below the unit's title in the Army List. In fact very few men volunteered to serve abroad and very few units attained the above target.

The Territorial and Reserve Forces Act also brought changes to the uniform worn by the territorials. Khaki became the service dress. In 1910 all territorial battalions of the regiment changed to the uniform and badges of the regular or line battalions, except the 6th Battalion. The Commanding Officer, Colonel the Hon.

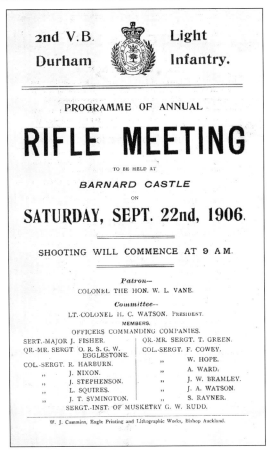

2nd V.B. Durham **Light Infantry.**

PROGRAMME OF ANNUAL

RIFLE MEETING

TO BE HELD AT

BARNARD CASTLE

ON

SATURDAY, SEPT. 22nd, 1906.

SHOOTING WILL COMMENCE AT 9 A.M.

Patron—
COLONEL THE HON. W. L. VANE.

Committee—
LT.-COLONEL H. C. WATSON. PRESIDENT.
MEMBERS.
OFFICERS COMMANDING COMPANIES.

SERT.-MAJOR J. FISHER.	QR.-MR. SERGT. T. GREEN.
QR.-MR. SERGT O. R. S. G. W. EGGLESTONE.	COL.-SERGT. F. COWEY.
COL.-SERGT. R. HARBURN.	,, W. HOPE.
,, J. NIXON.	,, A. WARD.
,, J. STEPHENSON.	,, J. W. BRAMLEY.
,, L. SQUIRES.	,, J. A. WATSON.
,, J. T. SYMINGTON.	,, S. RAYNER.
SERGT.-INST. OF MUSKETRY G. W. RUDD.	

W. J. Cummins, Eagle Printing and Lithographic Works, Bishop Auckland.

Rifle meetings were held regularly between battalions and companies. Prizes were awarded to winners and runners-up

W.L. Vane, strongly opposed this change, so the unit did not drop its old connection with the volunteers as a rifle unit. All badges and buttons were black. The officers still wear black boots and belts. The cross belt badge remains the same. Although the other badges, except in the case of full dress when the Maltese Cross is still worn, are those of The Durham Light Infantry, the uniform is the same as that of the King's Royal Rifle Corps. As with other rifle battalions, the 6th have no colours. Its members are intensely proud of their connection with the old rifle volunteers and are equally proud to wear their black badges and buttons.

On the 1st April, 1908, thirty officers and seven hundred and seventeen men transferred from the old 2nd Volunteers to 6th Battalion The Durham Light Infantry. By the October of 1909 there was a total of nine hundred and sixty-nine on roll, made up of twenty-eight officers and nine hundred and forty-one NCOs and men.

1909 also saw the beginning of weekend camps under the command of captains. On the 11th to the 13th June, the very first weekend camp was held at Fitches Farm, near Witton-le-Wear. This was commanded by Captain J.H. Ramsey, and thirty men from 'D' Company and thirty from 'E' Company attended. During the remainder of June and July a number of these weekend camps were held and proved to be quite popular with officers and men. In addition the established annual camps continued to be held, usually in late July and early August. In

1909, a Durham Brigade camp was held at Blackhall Rocks, near Castle Eden. Between 1888 and 1909 sixteen brigade camps had been held with a further six battalion camps. In 1910 a brigade camp was held at Rothbury from the 24th July to the 7th August. In 1911, the annual camp was held at Bisley, in 1912 and 1913 at Scarborough. On the eve of the First World War in 1914, the annual camp was held at Conway.

1911 was the year of the coronation of King George V. The 6th Battalion was well represented amongst the parties of troops lining the ceremonial route. The following group of one officer and twenty-five NCOs and men journeyed to London on the 20th June where they became part of 'B' Composite Battalion of the 23rd Provisional Brigade:

Captain W. Wilkinson	Sergeant H. McNair
Corporal F. Lodge	Corporal A. Chandler
Lance-Corporal J. Johnson	Lance-Corporal W. Mitchell
Bugler T. Buckle	Private W. Castle
Private J. Dent	Private C. Davison
Private J. Ellwood	Private J. Golightly
Private J. Hodges	Private F. Hooper
Private G. Foster	Private T. Moore
Private C. Nixon	Private J. Pattison
Private J. Pearson	Private N. Sayer
Private W. Sanderson	Private C. Sherwood
Private R. Siddle	Private J. Suddes
Private G. Taylor	Private A. Travis

A second group of four officers and eight NCOs and men also joined 'B' Composite Battalion, all except one of whom were from 6th Battalion:

Colonel The Hon. W.L. Vane	Commanding Officer
Captain A.H. Bowen (8th Bn.)	Adjutant
Major W.J. Anderson	Quartermaster
Captain W. Mackay	Medical-Officer
Sergeant-Major H. Sherwood	Sergeant-Major
QMS W. Hope	Quartermaster-Sergeant
Sergeant J. Dixon	Stretcher-Bearer
Private J. Bell	Stretcher-Bearer
Private O. Hann	Stretcher-Bearer
Private J. Tait	Stretcher-Bearer
Private H. Howard	Cook
Private T. Vayro	Pioneer

'B' Composite Company of 23rd Brigade comprised twenty-three officers and four hundred and eighty-nine ORs representing nineteen territorial battalions of Northern Command. Encamped in Kensington Gardens, the unit was on duty in Pall Mall on the 22nd June and in The Strand on the following day. It must have been a very exciting experience for many of the men who had never been to London. The Coronation Medal was awarded to the following:

Colonel The Hon. W.L. Vane

Sergeant-Major H. Sherwood

Private W. Harris (the oldest private in 6DLI)

Captain W. Wilkinson

Major & Quartermaster W.J. Anderson

In 1911, The Hon. W.L. Vane was succeeded as commanding officer of the 6th Battalion by Lieutenant-Colonel H.C. Watson. The Battalion strength was thirty one officers and nine hundred and forty-six NCOs and men, one officer over strength and forty three NCOs and men short of a full complement. The officers and men settled very quickly into the new territorial organisation as, for the most part, very little had changed from the original volunteer system. Drills and weapon training filled most of the drill nights with the weekend camps giving an opportunity for

Battalion football team, *Scarborough Camp, 1913. Sport was of considerable importance. Not only did it keep men fit it built team spirit.*

section, platoon and even company training. Parades and inspections took place from time to time. Shooting competitions within and between battalions were organised and medals awarded to the winners. Annual camps gave further opportunity for training on a much larger scale on a battalion or brigade basis when more ambitious manoeuvres could be practised. There seemed little to disturb the routine and yet as the second decade of the century was entered storm clouds were gathering. The territorials were about to be called upon to prove their worth in a war the likes of which the world had never witnessed.

CHAPTER 3
MOBILISATION & PREPARATION
1914

On Saturday 25th July, 1914, the Northumbrian Division moved to its annual camp in North Wales. 6th Battalion The Durham Light Infantry, was encamped at Conway and quickly settled in to the usual training routine of drills, route marches and exercises. A small minority of men who had an interest in or understanding of foreign affairs were possibly aware that relations between our country and Germany were deteriorating. The belief that war was imminent never occurred to the great majority of officers and men who looked forward to enjoying a period away from the responsibilities of work, home and families. The Battalion had barely settled into camp when the first indications that all was not well became apparent. Military trains were observed moving troops along the main railway line which ran past the camp site.

On the 2nd August, a small group of men left the camp and returned to Battalion Headquarters at Bishop Auckland to prepare for the return of the Battalion. On Monday, 3rd August, the men packed up and travelled back to Bishop Auckland by rail. On reaching Darlington a message was received by Lieutenant-Colonel H.C. Watson, Commanding Officer, that the Battalion was to stay the night in Bishop Auckland where accommodation was available in the Drill Hall and the Town Hall. The following morning the companies were sent to their own headquarters in the various towns and the men were then dismissed and went to their homes. This was in accordance with those regulations which governed the mobilization of territorial forces for home defence. At 8 p.m. on this same day, Tuesday, 4th August, 1914, the telegram to mobilise was received by

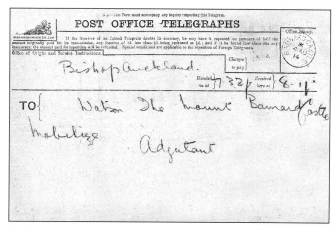

The historical telegram to Lieutenant Colonel H.C. Watson ordering him to mobilise the Battalion for war.

Lieutenant-Colonel Watson at his home in Barnard Castle.

On Wednesday, 5th August, the Companies of the Battalion were recalled and proceeded to Bishop Auckland where they were billeted in the Drill Hall, Town Hall and the Edgar Hall. Over the next few days equipment was cleaned and checked and transport organised. These were days of hard work with many inspections which tested the patience of both officers and men. On Saturday, 8th August, the Battalion was paraded at 11 a.m. in Bishop Auckland market place and then marched to the grounds of the Bishop of Durham's Palace where it was addressed by

Last Church Parade before the outbreak of war, *Conway, 1914. Whilst the officers are in service dress (khaki) all the other ranks are, for the last time in the history of the Battalion, wearing full dress.*

their Honorary Colonel, Sir W. Eden. The somewhat bored indifference of the population to the territorials in peacetime was now replaced by a new enthusiasm and many people gathered to watch the parade. The affect of this interest must have filled the men on parade that morning with confidence and pride.

At 12 noon on Sunday 9th August, the Battalion proceeded to its war station in the Boldon area of County Durham. It was billeted in schools and the Miners' Hall. For the whole of the following week the Battalion was employed in building and preparing defences, not least of which involved the digging of trenches. On Sunday 16th August, the Battalion proceeded to billets in schools and halls in the Sunderland Road area of Gateshead. Three days were spent on inspections and drills until

Snowy scene at Bensham *where the Battalion was billeted during the winter of 1914-15. The officers occupied houses, the men were in various halls.*

the following Wednesday 19th August, when a move was made to Ravensworth Park, where the Battalion was to spend the next two and a half months. This was a large tented camp in the grounds surrounding Ravensworth Castle. It was not to be a pleasant experience as the onset of a wet and windy winter turned the ground into a sea of mud and conditions quickly deteriorated. It was difficult to keep warm and dry. Route marches up the steep Lobley Hill and Chowdene Banks in low temperatures and driving rain were not pleasant yet were recalled with some nostalgia when serving during the winters of the Western Front. Exercises, tactical training on the moors, route marches and digging trenches filled the days. It was during this period that the territorials were asked to volunteer for service overseas. The great majority of men agreed to do so.

At the beginning of November the Battalion was moved into winter billets in the Bensham area and remained here until moving overseas in April, 1915. The men were quartered in the local schools which proved to be dry and comfortable. The officers seemed to have been somewhat unlucky and one or two of them experienced a cultural shock on moving into their billets. Second-Lieutenant Hugh Lyon wrote:

> 'The 6th Battalion of the DLI was ... billeted in that peculiarly unattractive suburb of Newcastle which is known as Bensham. In this unsavoury district of dingy streets and drab houses we had been training assiduously for five months, ever since the first rains of a wet and windy winter had driven us out of our camp at Ravensworth. The men were certainly fortunate in having the best schools of the town to live in ... Of the officers' billets the less said the better, even in this area, where the ideal of a home could not have been very high, the two houses which were allotted to us had not found tenants for some years. As a result the sick list was, as late as March, very considerable, and I was not the only one to visit the Newcastle Infirmary...'

In December, 1914, the eight company organisation of the territorial Battalion was changed to four companies, so matching those of the regular Battalion. This was done by combining the companies in the following way:

'A' & 'B' Companies became 'A' Company

'C' & 'D' Companies became 'B' Company

'E' & 'F' Companies became 'C' Company

'G' & 'H' Companies became 'D' Company

The Commanding Officers of the Battalion and its companies were now as follows:

Commanding Officer:	Lieutenant-Colonel H.C. Watson
2nd in Command:	Major J.E. Hawdon
Adjutant:	Capt. J.W. Jeffreys
Medical Officer:	Major W.E. Mackay
'A' Company:	Captain A.P. Cummins

No. 13 Platoon at bayonet drill, *1915.*

'B' Company:	Major S.E. Badcock
'C' Company:	Captain W.D.H. Devey
'D' Company:	Captain J. Townend

Intensive training took place at Bensham and in the surrounding countryside. Tactical training and exercises, rifle and bayonet drills, shooting on the ranges and the interminable inspections took up most of each day, added to which were guard duties at bridges, railway junctions and similar places considered to be of importance to the community or military.

Captain F. Walton left the Battalion for Le Havre on the 10th April, 1915, to make arrangements for the arrival of the Transport and Machine-Gun Sections which followed him on the 17th April. These sections moved abroad under the command of

Major Hawdon and Lieutenant H.T. Bircham who was the Transport Officer.

The rumours and counter rumours which had inundated the Battalion over a number of weeks came to an end with the news that it was to move to France. Second-Lieutenant Lyon wrote:

'...the official news came as a tremendous relief. The last days were spent in an orgy of packing; the inevitable abandonment of many cherished articles to conform to the minimum of 35 lbs per officer occupied much thought and many searchings of heart. The men, who for months had been perforce content with old and worn-out equipment, suddenly discovered that there was enough and to spare of 'new parts' waiting for them. This unprecedented liberality of the Quartermaster General convinced the last doubters that this time we were really "for it".'

Nine months since the Battalion had been raised to 'full-time' status with the outbreak of the war, what state of efficiency had it reached by April, 1915? Second-Lieutenant Lyon wrote in his record compiled in 1916:

'At the date of embarkation the Battalion had reached a pitch of efficiency, in the opinion of independent critics, which, while still lacking that absolute sureness which only comes with long years of training or with experience of active service, was considerably higher than most of us had expected when we first joined. The discipline and steadiness acquired were in very large part due to our adjutant (Captain Jeffreys) - our only 'Regular' officer, and our Regimental Sergeant-Major (Regimental Sergeant-Major Perry) who added to an imposing presence and prestige of 33 years service in the line a very considerable power over men - These two were destined to guide us through many vicissitudes with the same zeal which they displayed in our training. But even their power and energy might have been in vain had not

The Battalion Transport Section at Bensham, *winter 1914/15. The sign to the right of the group is an advertisement for the Coatsworth Cinema.*

they found to their hand such splendid material. The miners of Durham are some of the finest fighters the country possesses ... rough in manner, they possess a power of endurance and a courageous spirit, very admirable in adversity.'

The Northumbrian Division began the move to France on the 16th April, 1915, and the days immediately following. The 6th Battalion The Durham Light Infantry, left its billets early in the morning of the 19th April and marched to Newcastle Central Station. The route was lined by crowds of excited and enthusiastic people. Hats and handkerchiefs were waved as the troops marched past and cheers and counter cheers broke out. At the station dense crowds waited and as the troops arrived the Reserve Battalion band played the men onto the platform. The soldiers were in great spirits. Private J.H. Clarey wrote to his parents who lived at Crook:

'It was on Monday morning when we left Bensham and

marched to Newcastle Central Station to go to the front. Everyone of us was happy and singing. There were tears as well as joy when we left Newcastle. There was a great shout of "Good Luck" and the flags were flying. We had a very pleasant ride. We were taken on board a fine ship and guarded by others.'

The Battalion left the Central Station at 8.15 a.m. in two trains, one commanded by Lieutenant-Colonel Watson comprised Brigade Headquarters, Battalion Headquarters and 'A' and 'D' Companies. The remainder of the Battalion followed in the second train commanded by the Adjutant, Captain Jeffreys. Folkestone was reached at 8 p.m. Second-Lieutenant Lyon wrote:

'At Folkestone we embarked with speed and an almost officious orderliness, and started on what must have been the first journey across sea for most of the men. Fortunately it was a calm night. The presence of a lean silent destroyer which accompanied us like a shadow all the way brought a thrill of adventure into the peaceful expedition.'

The steamship *Invicta* carried the Battalion towards what most of the men saw as an exciting adventure in a foreign land. It was an adventure which was to turn into a horrifying nightmare and many of the men would suffer violent death or painful wounds within a very few days of landing in France.

CHAPTER 4

THE SECOND BATTLE OF YPRES

1915

The 6th Battalion landed at Boulogne at about 11.30 p.m. on Monday, 19th April, 1915. Fully laden with packs and rifles the men were marched up the steep hill out of the town to the tented camp known as St. Martin's Camp, Ostrovhe. They arrived at the camp, somewhat tired, at about 12.30 a.m. after an exciting journey and the long march. The camp was quite full and the men had to be crammed tightly into the tents which were made available to them. It was a cold night and being tightly packed helped to keep them warm.

Reveille the next morning, 20th April, was at 5.30 a.m. Bedding issued to them was returned to the camp store. There was no information as to where they were going or what was to happen to them. The result was the usual soldiers' response to uncertainty. Rumours grew and flew round the men to be received very often with irritation. The army will not leave soldiers idle for long and the men soon found themselves cleaning kit, preparing for inspections and being inspected. None of these activities were received with enthusiasm by the Battalion. Time was set aside to enable the men to send their first field service postcards to their families informing them that they had landed in France. Civilians ever mindful that soldiers have money arrived at the camp with their various wares. The Boulogne women who sold oranges

Some members of No. 13 Platoon at St. Martin's Camp, Ostrovhe, Boulogne. 21st April, 1915

gave the men the opportunity to converse and exchange compliments which, even if not understood, added some excitement to the occasion. The uncertainty came to an end later in the day when orders were given to fall in and the Battalion marched out of camp, a distance of some three miles, to the railway station at Pont de Briques. Here, at about 6 p.m. a train from Le Havre pulled into the station. On board were the Transport and Machine-Gun Sections and the rest of the Battalion entrained in cattle trucks each of which held forty men. The officers were accommodated in drab passenger carriages through which the cold night wind blew to their great discomfort. It was a long, slow and uncomfortable journey of some four hours' duration before the train reached Cassel, reputedly the place where the Grand Old Duke of York marched his men up the hill and down again.

The journey was still not completed and some time was to elapse before the Battalion reached its immediate destination. Second-Lieutenant Lyon of 'D' Company wrote:

> 'A most unaccountable delay followed, hardly anyone seemed to know where we were going, and even those who did know seemed ignorant of the best route to travel. At length, somewhere between 2 a.m. and 5.30 a.m. on the morning of Wednesday, April 21st, we marched eight miles to the minute village of Hardifort, where we were left to our devices in the matter of lodgement. Poor old D Company was, as usual, left till the last - But in the end I found good accommodation for over 100 men in a small farm about $1/2$ mile out of the village. Once everyone was under cover we abandoned ourselves to sleep.'

A few hours sleep was allowed to the men followed by breakfast at 12 noon. They awoke to their new surroundings, full of curiosity. Colpaert Farm was typically French, built around three sides of a square with a pool and open ground in the centre. Pigs rutted about the centre space, all of whom seemed to have a voracious appetite and ate anything or everything, including parts of the men's webbing left carelessly lying around. The other half of 'D' Company , under Second-Lieutenant Favell, was billeted in a nearby farm. The two officers were accommodated in the farmhouses, the men in the barns lying on hay or straw. The senior officers of the Battalion found houses in the village and the remaining companies in farmhouses and barns similar to those described above.

The Battalion began to settle into its new surroundings. The French on the whole were quite hospitable, the majority of whom were women, children and a few men, the latter too old for the forces. Young men were away fighting the Germans. Officers of the Battalion negotiated prices for farm produce and the men supplemented army rations by purchasing eggs, milk and other items available to them. The general opinion of the French people was that they were quite nice but 'tarked funny'. Cleaning up was the order of the day, both equipment and personal. The inevitable kit and equipment inspections took place to which the men submitted with their usual stoicism. Their main concern was to obtain cigarettes.

At this point it is opportune to outline what was expected of a division newly arrived from England. On moving into its concentration area - Cassel in the case of the Northumbrian Division - a period of time was spent in cleaning up and checking equipment. A training programme was undertaken away from the battle zone to prepare officers and men for what lay ahead. After a few weeks of this a division would be moved closer to the front line, invariably to a quiet area. It would be linked to a division in the front line and would begin to learn the lessons of trench life from the more experienced units. Ultimately the division itself would move into a quiet sector of the front line to complete the learning process. This was not to be the experience of the Northumbrian Division. Within a few short days the officers and men, who had not had a shot fired at them in anger, were rushed into a cauldron of frightening violence and sudden death.

Thursday, 22nd April, was very much like the previous day, only with more cleaning and inspections. To the east could be heard the dull rumble of the guns, but not sufficient in concentration to disturb the Battalion's activities, nor the men's minds as they went about their tasks. In the late afternoon the rumble of the guns increased considerably which, whilst it caused some to comment, still failed to disturb the routine. The increased volume of gun fire signalled the beginning of the German use of gas against the Allied troops manning the Ypres Salient. There is a need to describe briefly how this came about, in order to place the movements and actions of the 6th Battalion into their proper context.

The day began with quite lovely spring weather. There was hardly any breeze and the sun shone from an almost cloudless

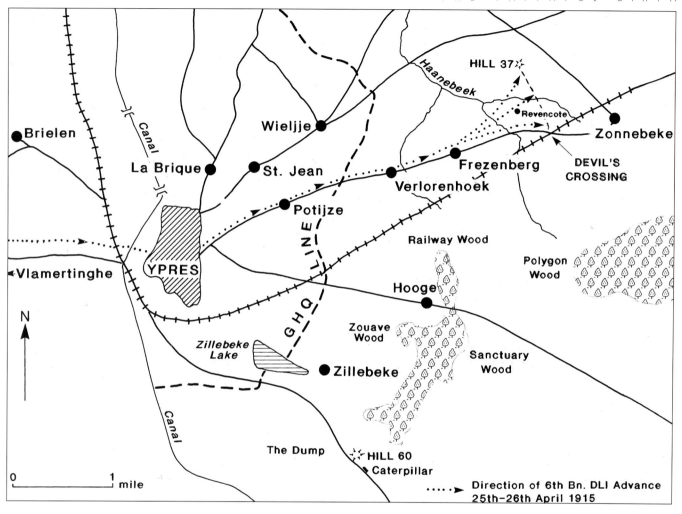

Ypres Salient 1915-16. *Battalion advance and attack of the 26th April, 1915 is shown*

sky. There was very little warlike activity. Some sporadic shelling by the Germans fell on the roads and villages in front of Ypres but did little to disturb what was becoming a relatively peaceful day. In the late afternoon, a soft south-westerly breeze arose. At about 5 p.m. the Germans commenced a violent bombardment of the roads leading into and out of Ypres and of the villages and isolated farm buildings inside the salient itself. Shortly afterwards, the Germans released gas from their trenches on both sides of the village of Langemarck. This chlorine gas was slowly carried by the south-westerly breeze onto the trenches held by unsuspecting French and Canadian troops. The worst concentration of gas fell upon the 45th Algerian Division and 87th French Territorial Division and affected the extreme left flank of the Canadian Division on the French right. Choking and gasping for breath the terrified French colonial and second line territorial troops broke and streamed into the back areas. Many died in the trenches and others dropped dead on the sides of roads and tracks leading to the rear. A gap of several miles was torn in the French lines, through which the following up German troops advanced. The position was extremely serious. The Canadians and those French troops remaining in the line fought with great gallantry but with flanks turned and threatened from the rear they had to give way. Over the next few days the story of the Second Battle of Ypres was one of the greatest soldiers' actions of history. Units were poured piecemeal into the gaps created by the Germans, and officers and men fought to the death in almost hopeless counter-attacks in an attempt to rebuild a solid defense line to contain the German advance. The Northumbrian Division was called forward on the 23rd April, its brigades and battalions split and handed over to various commands and pushed into action. It was less than a week since its arrival in France.

At Colpaert Farm, Second-Lieutenant Lyons and his men were still settling into their routine. He wrote:

'Here we remained till the morning of Friday, April 23rd. Then, just as we had finished our morning manoevres, Jeffreys galloped round and ordered an alarm parade in half an hour. The reason was as yet concealed by some higher authority, and the rendezvous was appointed at a village some miles away - we consumed hasty dinners, and lumbered away about one o'clock to an unknown destination.'

The Durham Light Infantry Brigade had been ordered to concentrate at the village of Ryveld a few miles from Hardifort. The companies of the 6th Battalion concentrated in Hardifort, then quickly marched off to their destination, leaving behind officers' baggage and the men's blankets. From Ryveld the Brigade marched to Steenvoorde where the battalions were marched into a large field on the outskirts of the village. Here they rested and had tea. The guns ahead were now much louder and more disturbing. The road past the field was crammed with troop reinforcements marching and carried in all types of wheeled transport on their way to the front. Dressings and iodine were issued to each man, a distribution which sobered the tense high spirits of many. Some men wrote their wills. At about seven o'clock in the evening, the men's curiosity was raised by the approach of a long line of London double-decker buses. The 8th and 6th Battalions boarded these buses and set off up the road to Vlamertinghe. 7th and 9th Battalions of the Brigade marched off on foot. The route lay through Abeele on the French-Belgium frontier, on to Poperinghe and reached Vlamertinghe late in the evening, officers and men tired and hungry. The 6th Battalion was billeted in huts except unlucky 'D' Company for which there was no room. The Company slept out in the open. One hut was left for the officers. The guns sounded unpleasantly close and an arc of star-shells mapped out the boundaries of the Salient. Ahead of them Ypres was burning.

Most of Saturday, 24th April was spent standing-to in Vlamertinghe awaiting orders to move forward. The men were able to wash and clean-up and fill their water bottles. There was enormous activity in the town. Troops were still pouring forward along the road to Ypres. French and Canadian wounded and gassed, were coming down from the front line to a Canadian hospital close to the Battalion position. Refugees streamed westward with their few belongings. Rumours and counter rumours travelled amongst the officers and men. At 6 p.m. orders were received to move at once. The companies paraded, an activity which lifted the men's spirits after a day of depressing inactivity and speculation and the Battalion marched off singing along the road towards Ypres. Second-Lieutenant Lyons described that march through Ypres:

'Of all the experiences which attended these weeks there is not one of which I have so vivid a recollection as that march through the perishing city. For three days it had suffered an intense bombardment. A shell came shrieking in to it as we went through (our hearts jumped at this first experience), and several rumbled over our heads after we had passed beyond. There were ruins along every street, fresh gaping holes, and the roads were choked with debris. We moved in a thin serpent line through the confusion, adjusting our ideas of war as best we could to this shattered reality, which lay about our path, clear-cut in the bright moon. By the muttered exclamations of the men I judged the sight had a very profound effect upon them.'

Buildings burned, here and there a dead civilian lay at the roadside or in some ruin. The Cloth Hall, still recognisable though damaged, lay on their immediate left as they marched across the square and into the short street leading to the Menin Gate. They marched out onto the road to Zonnebeke and came upon the then ruined village of Potijze and beyond to the GHQ Line where, at midnight, they relieved the 2nd Battalion The Shropshire Light Infantry under Colonel Bridgford. 'A' Company took up position on the south side of the road. The remaining companies were on the north side, 'B' Company next to the road itself, 'D' Company in the centre and 'C' Company on the left. The Battalion was now under the command of Brigadier Chapman, 85th Brigade, 28th Division.

The GHQ Line was a support line built by the French. It ran northwards from Zillebeke Lake to half a mile east of Wieltje where it turned gradually north-west to Boesinghe village. It was well sited with a good field of fire and comprised a number of well built redoubts, some four to five hundred yards apart, connected to each other by fire trenches. The Battalion remained here during most of Sunday, 25th April, under heavy shell fire, and had three men slightly wounded. This was the second day of the Battle of St. Julien, to give the official name to the confused and bitter fighting which went on till the end of April. On this same day, a short distance away at Boetleer's Farm on Gravenstafel Ridge, the 8th Battalion was experiencing its baptism of fire and suffering grievous losses. The 5th Battalion was in action for the first time with the Yorkshire and Durham Brigade in front of St. Julien.

At 9 p.m. on the 25th April, the 6th Battalion left the trenches and lined up on the Zonnebeke road. It was dark and raining. An occasional shell came over from the enemy positions and exploded in Ypres adding to its ruin and desolation. Officers and men were pleased to be active again having experienced for the first time in their lives the fear and stress of lying still for several hours as shells rained down around them. Fortunately no one

was injured and it was with feelings of great relief all round as the Battalion marched down the road towards Zonnebeke. It was stopped outside Verlorenhoek where it lay in the hedgerows until 3 a.m. when it again moved and took up positions behind more hedgerows and in hastily dug trenches some three hundred yards beyond the village. Wet, covered in clay, the men spent a miserable night trying to sleep. They had been ordered not to move about in the early morning light in case of being spotted by German aircraft which would bring shell fire down upon them. At 10 a.m. Lieutenant-Colonel Watson and his adjutant, Captain Jeffreys, were ordered forward to confer with Brigadier-General Martin, commanding the Durham Brigade. Captain Jeffreys diary records:

'With him was General Chapman, who is commanding 85th Bde, to which the DLI Brigade is attached. General Chapman pointed out to the CO Shropshire LI and CO 6th DLI, the hill on the left of the watershed line and directed the CO 6th DLI on the right, by naming a level crossing on the map. The order was to move in great haste to occupy the line - level crossing - Hill 37 - and drive back the Germans who had broken through...by bringing flanking fire upon them as they crossed our front.'

The Battalion lined up with 'A' Company on the right, directed on to the crossing. 'D' Company was directed to advance to Hill 37. 'B' and 'C' Companies were to take position between these two. Second-Lieutenant Lyon takes up the story:

'At about 10 o'clock came the order to advance. As far as can be gathered, our instructions were vague in the extreme. No information was given us of any troops in front of us - and from what the Brigadier had told our colonel he understood there were none. The direction of advance was indicated by a wave of the hand, and the final objective was completely unknown. As far as I can make out, we were really intended to advance into reserve positions, in readiness to reinforce our front line in the event of another attack.

'We advanced roughly in two lines of companies, in extended order. As soon as we showed ourselves the German batteries opened a heavy fire on us, which was maintained for some time. Almost at once central control, difficult at all times with so broad a formation, was completely lost. I myself with my platoon was on the extreme right of the second line. I saw the whole line to my left swinging more and more to the left, and finally facing almost at right angles from our original direction of advance. Thinking, naturally, that the various company commanders had orders to that effect, I began to conform. However hearing a shout, I looked round, and saw Colonel Watson signalling me to maintain the original direction. I did so, as far as was in my power; but whistle and voice would not carry far in the confusion, and so only about two thirds of my platoon heard me and corrected their line of march. At this point I lost touch with the remainder of the company, who did not see the Colonel's signal.'

There was no time for written orders from Brigade to reconnoitre, nor to give precise orders to companies and platoons. The boundaries of the Battalion objective had been indicated by pointing in their direction with the added instruction of filling the gap in between. There were no maps for the officers to guide them to their objective. The order given was to move immediately. The vagueness of the orders were confirmed by Captain Walton:

'To me at this late date, the orders for the advance on 26th April are most interesting as my Company Commander ('D') appeared to have no orders other than to follow 'A' Company. We started in artillery formation and I went to HQ to find out what we were supposed to be doing, but even the CO could give me no information. We passed through a a battery of 13 pounders with only one gun firing, as they had little or no ammunition, and on over Hill 37 where we got rifle and machine-gun fire in addition to the shelling that had followed us from the start.

'There was a trench down the forward slope of the Hill and with fire and movement many of the men got into it, but they were not welcome as they drew fire onto the occupants. A machine-gun took heavy toll and every time fire ceased on its position it opened up again and eventually got me in the knee before I could reach the trench, so I had to lie down in the open until things calmed down towards evening. The rigid training and strict discipline that Jeffreys had instilled into the Battalion were reflected in the marvellous behaviour of the men under that baptism of fire, and it was only with the greatest difficulty that I could prevent them from leaving their cover to come for me. The slightest movement drew fire from the accurate machine-gun.'

The men, carrying their packs and 170 rounds of ammunition,

advanced as quickly as they could. Under the storm of enemy artillery and machine-gun fire some lost direction and with vague orders and resulting confusion officers were unable to act with speed and decisiveness. The men advanced on the understanding that there was no one in front of them. The confusion was increased when they came upon men of other regiments holding out in isolated trenches and shell holes. Their appearance on these positions was not welcomed as it brought down German shell fire. Some platoons and companies became intermingled adding to the difficulty of control. As we shall see later, Lieutenant-Colonel Watson became an early casualty. The courage of the officers and men was not in doubt as they resolutely advanced but disaster was not far off unless control was reasserted.

At the moment of worst confusion Captain Jeffreys galloped up on his horse and proceeded to organise the line. Starting at the level crossing - which became known as Devil's Crossing - he rode along the line to Hill 37 sorting out entangled units, placing them in position and giving clear and precise orders, all of this whilst under extremely heavy shell and machine-gun fire. He wrote in a letter home to his wife:

'...we sallied forth under a most unpleasant rain of shrapnel and Black Marias. We lost heavily (8 officers and about 140 men) but we did well, all we were told to do - Had a rough time - I lost my horse and saddlebag - infernal nuisance. It's all most interesting. The Colonel became in a dreadful state owing to the losses and strain...Had a most exciting time on 26th. Galloped about amongst all these missiles until my horse was stone cold. Then shifted my saddle on to another brute, and he's lost.'

The line was taken up. 'B' Company had taken station on the right with Second-Lieutenants Hare and Haythornthwaite and their platoons doing particularly well. No. 5 Platoon under Second-Lieutenant A.B. Hare reached the crossing safely and occupied a trench on the right of the line. No. 11 Platoon and part of No. 9 under Lieutenant T.B. Heslop joined men of the London Rifle Brigade. No. 10 Platoon under Lieutenant R.B. Hare joined units of the Shropshire Light Infantry. The balance of No. 9 Platoon under Second-Lieutenant Angus took up a position of support on Hill 37. With a line sorted out, Captain Jeffreys visited

The Battalion had suffered severely. Captain Monkhouse and Second-Lieutenant Kynock were dead. Major S.E. Badcock had received severe wounds from which he had died lying out on the battlefield. Captains Walton and Devey were wounded along with Lieutenant Thorpe and Second-Lieutenants Nicholson, Kirkhouse and Leighton. Lieutenant Badcock, brother of Major Badcock, was slightly wounded. Major Mackay, Battalion Medical Officer, was also wounded. Casualties in NCOs and men numbered over one hundred.

At 6 p.m. on the 26th April, the Battalion was ordered to move in support of 7 DLI and a Battalion of The Shropshire Light Infantry who were to attack a hill held by the enemy. The advance was made through the usual heavy enemy bombardment. On reaching the ridge, 'B' Company was ordered forward to fill a gap in the front line alongside 1st Battalion The Hampshire Regiment. 'A' and 'D' Companies were warned to stand by in case they were needed to give further support to the Hampshires. For 'B' Company this was the beginning of a five day ordeal in front line trenches. Constantly shelled by the Germans during the day, repairing and improving their trenches during the night and with little food and sleep the Company held the position until relieved on the 30th April. It had no periscopes for observing the enemy positions under cover. There were no flare pistols for calling for assistance and illuminating No Man's Land and, it must be remembered, the Company had no experience of trench warfare. The Company's casualties were fourteen NCOs and men killed, including three sergeants, and one officer and fifty-five men wounded.

Second-Lieutenant Lyon described the movements of the Battalion and the fog of war which enveloped the battlefield:

> 'We now had orders to reinforce the front line under cover of darkness. We reached a road along a high ridge safely. Then we advanced still further Eastwards and eventually came to a kind of No Man's Land. Here we were handed over to a regular colonel, who seemed to have assumed command of all detachments in the vicinity. One company (B) was sent to occupy a gap in the front line. The remainder of 'A' and 'D' Companys, we were about 90 in all, were left at this colonel's disposal. At this time no one knew exactly where our line was,

In 1914, **Captain Jeffreys** *was the adjutant of the Battalion. He rose to command the Battalion on a number of occasions during the First World War.*

every company and platoon. He was surprised to find Lieutenant Lyon and his No. 13 Platoon of 'D' Company dug in as he had been informed that the young officer was dead. Lyon and his men had moved forward through the violent bombardment and '...none suffered more severe casualty than accidents to caps and clothing'.

or where the Germans were. A sudden increase of activity to the North made the colonel think there was a massed attack about to pierce our line at this point, and we were lined along a hedge with fixed bayonets and told to expect the Hun at any minute. I confess that now for the first time I completely gave up speculating on my chances of getting out alive, and made up my mind to die with some distinction.'

'C' Company had remained in support and was used during the night to take rations up to the other three companies of the Battalion.

During the night of the 26th-27th April, 'A' and 'D' Companies remained in the hedge as described by Second-Lieutenant Lyon. No attack materialised and the colonel - probably commanding 1st Hampshires - told the two companies that he no longer needed them. Second-Lieutenant Lyon takes up the story:

'At which we suddenly discovered that we didn't know where to go. After waking up the detachment (who had fallen fast asleep as they lay waiting for the main attack with fixed bayonets!) and being reinforced by a party of 'C' Company under Angus, who was returning from a most adventurous expedition with the rations, we decided to try and find our way back. In single file we trailed slowly over the country. From where we were the star-shells marking the salient, formed almost a complete circle round us, so that it was not a little difficult to decide which way would bring us back to the Ypres road. But before dawn found ourselves back at Zevenkote Farm, and eventually came to a halt in a field - honeycombed with ditches - which we were assured were a favourite German target. After trying to induce my dog-tired platoon to take some better shelter than that afforded by their greatcoats, I chose the deepest, wettest ditch and went asleep sitting crouched up on two sandbags.'

Gradually over the next few hours the Battalion, less 'B' Company, assembled in the vicinity of Zevenkote Farm, just north of the Ypres - Zonnebeke road.

It was during the evening of the 26th April that Lieutenant-Colonel Watson left the Battalion. He had started the day leading his men into their first action and had been prominent in the advance. However the activities of the last three days were taking their toll. Colonel Watson, now over fifty years of age, had joined the Volunteer Battalion as a very young subaltern. He had commanded the Battalion since 1911 and knew every officer and man. He was a strict commanding officer with no great sense of humour. He did not suffer fools lightly and many officers and men felt the lash of his tongue. However, it was his Battalion and he had a great attachment to it. On this day as he advanced he saw his officers and men falling around him, heard the cries of the wounded and the dying. He had had little sleep for three days, exhaustion was not far away. The losses, the frightening shell fire and the stress of the last hours proved too much and he collapsed, unable to give commands and make decisions. In the early hours of the 27th April, Lieutenant-Colonel Watson walked into Brigade Headquarters. He returned to England where, after rest, he assumed command of the training battalion of the Regiment which supplied officers and men for the front line units. He was so successful in this capacity that in 1917 he was Mentioned in Despatches. Captain Jeffreys assumed temporary command of the Battalion. As adjutant he was a regular soldier whose energy and courage were invaluable to the Battalion.

On 27th April, 'A' Company was sent forward to fill a gap in the front line between the Hampshires and Northumberland Fusiliers. They, too, were without periscopes or other trench appliances. They were to remain in the trenches for four nights under heavy daylight bombardment. Captains Cummins and Park were severely wounded and Second-Lieutenant Blenkinsopp took command of the company. On the evening of the 28th April, Lieutenant Blenkinsopp sent a runner back to Battalion Headquarters with the following message:

'Are we to be relieved from these trenches tonight? Captain Cummins and Captain Park have been severely wounded, and we have been shelled all day. We have had a small number of wounded. The trenches are 1 foot deep in water, and we had to make them ourselves from improvised ones, with no picks or shovels. The men got rations last night for 65, while our strength is 120. Many have had little to eat for three days. If I must stay here tonight, can you send full rations, spades and reinforcements in officers?'

Later that night Second-Lieutenant R.B. Hare was sent forward to 'A' Company with the rations and supplies as requested. The wounded were brought back by the ration party. Many of the wounded were in a poor state having laid in the trenches with what little medical attention their comrades could provide until they could be moved to safety.

On the 29th April, the Battalion, less the two companies in the front line, marched back across the ground they had attacked over three days previously, to Verlorenhoek. They arrived at 8.00 p.m. and proceeded to dig themselves in so as to be out of sight before daybreak and to prevent observation by German spotter aircraft. Tired though they were, the Battalion paraded at 2.30 a.m. and, under the supervision of Royal Engineers, spent the remainder of the night digging trenches to form a new defensive line.

Letters were received on the 30th April, from Lieutenant Welch (commanding 'B' Company) and Second-Lieutenant Hare (commanding 'A' Company), stating that their men were very tired, shaken and short of food and water. These two companies were relieved that night, having done extremely well. They were commended by Brigadier Prouse (11th Brigade) for the stout defense of their positions. The two companies rejoined the Battalion on 1st May.

The morning of the 2nd May was relatively quiet. At about 4.30 p.m. the Germans commenced a violent bombardment of the front line and released gas. The Battalion was ordered to stand to and remained so until 7.00 p.m. The violence of the bombardment and the effects of the gas were such that the nerve of some of the units of other regiments in the support line broke and batches of thirty or forty men streamed past the Durhams' position. Captain Jeffreys' diary records that: 'They had a bad look when they came back, in fact were almost a rabble'. In these early days of the use of gas the means of protection against this frightful weapon were primitive and not particularly effective. Cloths soaked in any liquid available in the trench - urine if no other liquid available - held or fastened over the mouth and nose, were the only protection until the arrival of more effective respirators. Soldiers choked and gasped for breath. Shells poured down upon them and behind the bombardment came the German infantry. The great majority of our soldiers fought to the death or till the attack was stopped, but at some point, it proved too much and some men gave way. Every man has a limit to his endurance.

At 7.00 p.m. the Battalion stood down as the front line had obviously held.

At 10.30 p.m. the Battalion marched off as the rear battalion of The Durham Light Infantry Brigade, through Ypres and into huts near Vlamertinghe and into rest. The total losses suffered by the Battalion in the five days fighting were: three officers killed, twelve wounded and two sent home suffering from shock. Twenty seven NCO's and men were killed, two hundred and eighteen wounded, thirty four were missing. The casualties were heavy but they had fought well and earned the praise of their own Brigade Commander, Brigadier Martin, and that of Brigadier Prouse.

The wounded wrote home and had their letters published in the local press. Private J.J. Davidson had been volunteer and territorial for fourteen years, three of them as holder of the Battalion Cup for the best soldier in the unit. He wrote to his mother who lived at Frosterley:

'I have been suffering more from gas poisoning. I am no worse for the bat I got with a piece of shrapnel on the left foot. It cut my boot through and knocked the sole off one side. I am in a base hospital now 'Somewhere in France.' I am only sorry I didn't get a shot at the German scoundrels before I was knocked out. I didn't even see one ... I think the 6th Durhams went into action as brave and as game as any regiment could go.'

A number of letters commented on the invisible enemy. The shell and the machine-gun dominated the battlefield and there was rare opportunity to come to close quarters with the enemy.

Private J. Cosgrove wrote to his brother who lived at Crook telling of his lucky escape and his experiences in the trenches:

'I got wounded on the left breast and another on the right thigh, but it is not serious yet as I can walk about. Had it not been for an oil tin which I found in my top coat pocket I would have had a serious wound in my thigh, for it went clean through the tin. We were in the worst part of the firing line, holding some trenches, but we only had to fire in case of an attack which they (we) did not like. It was just like a horse-shoe and our trenches were the most advanced. They were shelling us from the front, on both sides, with awful things called trench mortars and "Jack Johnsons". We were told to hold our position at any cost, which we did. After shelling us they used to put asphyxiating fire on us, expecting us to run out. It was awful. No words can describe what it was like. Some had their heads and arms blown off. The most touching point was when we had to steal out and bury 14 of the boys and carry the wounded out to a safer place. We had to creep for the snipers were all around and sending stray shots about. Some more got wounded. I escaped all that...'

The journey to safety and treatment for the wounded was often fraught with danger. Private J.F. Loughron of Witton Park wrote:

"I am on my way to England, but I don't know what hospital I will get into. I have been hit on the foot by shrapnel, but am not seriously hurt ... We had it rather hot, I can tell you. I was shelled out of one dressing station and I had to make my way as best I could for two or three miles with shells flying all around me..."

Corporal John Quinn wrote to his parents who lived in Coundon, near Bishop Auckland and described the morale of the Battalion:

'I am going on champion, but I am still in bed. I was wounded in the left foot, a bullet entered just at the bottom of the second toe and going right through. I don't know whether it broke the bone or not, but anyway they have not taken my toe off, so I think it is not broken. Jimmy (a brother) went through the battle without a scratch. He is as jolly as ever. We had not many killed in the 6th, but we had a lot wounded. We went into battle just as if we were going to dinner. Oh! they were splendid, the 6th. The shells and "Jack Johnsons" were flying all roads, but they might as well have thrown coconuts, for all the 6th cared, and they were still holding the line when I came away ... We had only one Captain killed - Captain Monkhouse. He was killed going into the attack, poor chap. He was a fine officer. You are never downhearted in the trenches, someone is always joking and we are always having a laugh. I was smoking my pipe when a bullet came and nearly knocked it out, but a miss is as good as a mile, and the 6th Durhams are as jolly as ever...'

If there was relief at receiving news that family loved ones had survived, others were not so lucky. The dead included Sergeant Thomas Venn, 'B' Company, of Willington, killed by a shell which landed on his trench. A member of the Battalion for sixteen years,

he possessed the Long Service Medal. He was married with eight children. Private Alfred Emerson of Coundon who in civilian life assisted his stepfather, Mr Bell, as sexton and caretaker of schools in the town was killed. Sergeant Linsley wrote to Emerson's mother:

'My task is not a very pleasant one, but you must know some time. I deeply regret to tell you that Alfred was killed by a fragment of shell on April 27th. We buried him beside some of our men and put up a cross at the head of his grave.'

A simple note which conveys the poignant image of men burying their comrades. Platoon and company commanders were having their first experience of writing to inform families of the death of loved ones, an experience which was to become all too common in the months and years ahead. An officer of the Battalion wrote to the wife of Lance-Corporal Joseph Southan of Bishop Auckland who was killed on the first day of action.

'It is with the most profound regret that I write to inform you that your husband was killed in action on April 26th. You have undoubtedly suffered an irreparable loss, but in this your hour of trial you have the consolation of knowing that your husband died a hero's death. The horrors and cruelty of this war are unspeakable, and its tragedies almost beyond description, but the power of the unhuman, soulless beast opposed to us must be crushed, or he will establish a perfect hell on earth. Victory must be ours, for we are fighting for the right, and this being so the relatives and dear ones of those who fall in the fray will assuredly receive Divine comfort and compassion.'

A number of letters refer to the pride in their Battalion which the men felt so strongly. It had done well in its first action. It had not let its recruiting area down. They had gone into action like men. An unnamed sergeant writing home touched upon the peacetime attitudes towards the territorials so often displayed by the civilian population:

'I am still in the land of the living ... there are a good few of our chaps gone under. Poor little "Buller" [Private Francis of Crook] and Burnip and a few more I knew. Little Mat Cunningham went under too. Surely the folks cannot call us "fireside soldiers" now.'

'Fireside soldiers', 'Toy soldiers', 'Playing soldiers', names shouted at them as they had made their way to the drill hall in peacetime. The labels rankled even though they largely ignored them. Now in the cauldron of the Ypres Salient they had come of age. They were soldiers now.

Many brave deeds went unrecorded but a number were brought to the attention of senior officers. Second-Lieutenant Favell of 'D' Company wrote to the Battalion Commander on 27th April:

'Sir: I beg to record the extremely gallant conduct of Private McCrone (J) of D coy. On the 26th April after the attack of 6th DLI under heavy artillery fire, I had taken cover with a number of D coy men on a line of trenches. Private McCrone, hearing two wounded men calling out, rushed back immediately and remained with them for an hour dressing their wounds, and brought them to cover under a very heavy artillery and rifle fire. He acted entirely on his own initiative having been advised by Sergeant D. Malpass not to go out. The above was witnessed by Sergeant D. Malpass and Sergeants J. Seymour and Cuthbertson.'

There appears to have been no award for this action as Second-Lieutenant Lyon, platoon commander, wrote to McCrone's family:

'I am proud to have such a man in my platoon, and I think it is right you should know, even though he does not get the medal he deserves.'

Second-Lieutenant Blenkinsopp wrote to the Battalion Commander on another incident:

'Sir: I have the honour to report that on Monday Ap[ril] 26th I witnessed an act of great presence of mind and bravery, whereby Company Sergeant-Major Bousfield brought a number of men through a devastating fire to a place of safety. He acted on his own initiative and undoubtedly saved a large number of lives. This act was witnessed by Captains Cummins, Park, Walton, and myself and would have been reported by these, had they not been wounded soon after the occurrence.'

Again there appears to have been no award made at this time.

A retrospective award of the Military Cross was made to Lieutenant T. Welch who commanded 'B' Company during its stay in the trenches. The citation reads as follows:

'For conspicuous gallantry and tenacity at Zonnebeke from

April, 26th to 30th when he with his company held a trench under heavy shell fire. His company was short of rations and water and he had no flare pistols or periscopes and no previous experience of trench warfare. The losses of his company in killed and wounded were 45 out of a total of 120.'

'B' Company was separated from the Germans by a trench block some ten yards wide. It was subjected to heavy mortar and sniper fire. A number of posts held by the Company were blown in and several men wounded and buried. Lance-Corporal J.J. Robinson was sitting with others in a post which was hit by a shell and a number of the occupants were buried. Robinson crossed open ground under heavy fire to a nearby sergeants' post to seek assistance. He was ordered to stay there as the artillery fire was too heavy. Unable to obtain help he returned, again under heavy fire, and using his hands and entrenching tool succeeded in digging out the three other occupants of the post, so saving their lives. He was awarded the Croix de Guerre by the French and this medal was pinned to his chest at a ceremony held in Darlington on Sunday 5th December, 1915. In March, 1916, the London Gazette announced the award of the Distinguished Conduct Medal to Lance-Corporal Robinson for this same courageous act.

The actions of the Battalion and its sacrifice had not gone unnoticed back home. A letter dated the 8th May, 1915, to Lieutenant-Colonel Watson, was received from Harold Jevons, Clerk to Durham County Council:-

'At the request of the Chairman of the Durham County Council, I beg to convey to you the following resolution unanimously passed at the Meeting of the Council on the 5th instant:-

"That this Council place on record its proud appreciation of the gallant fighting of The Durham Light Infantry in the Ypres engagement, and their profound sorrow at the losses incurred, accompanied with their deep sympathy with the relatives and friends of the fallen.'

No more eminent newspaper than *The Times* should have the last word on the exploits of the Northumbrian Division of which 6th Battalion The Durham Light Infantry was a part. The article appeared in the issue of the newspaper dated the 24th May, 1915:

'Consider what is meant by the fight of these Northern

Privates Jackson and Pattison, *Shrapnel Corner, 1915. Standards of dress were much relaxed in the trenches where keeping clean was always a problem*

The situation in the Ypres Salient continued to be quite serious. The inroads made by the Germans threatened the flank and even the rear of the British front line positions. The French had failed to counterattack and regain the lost ground in the north and west of the Salient. Whilst this remained the case, the British, despite fierce attempts to hold their lines, were in an almost untenable position. There was an obvious case for shortening and straightening the line. These movements would remove the danger of enemy outflanking attacks and enable troops to be less thinly spread on the ground. A decision was taken to withdraw to a new defensive line and this was completed by the British on the night of the 3rd May, 1915. The new line ran from near Hill 60, through Sanctuary Wood, in front of Hooge, Frezenberg, Mouse Trap Farm, and on to Turco Farm where it joined the old line.

On the 3rd May, the Battalion moved to St. Jan Ter Biezen, between Ypres and Watou, where it remained for five days. New drafts were received and the days taken up with refitting and inspections. The village was full of refugees. On the 9th May, the Battalion marched with the Brigade through Poperinghe to a wood about a mile north of Brandhoek where bivouacs and temporary shelters were erected. No fires were allowed after sunset and before sunrise. Hot meals were brought up from Steenvoorde by the cooks. Except for the sound of guns from the front this proved to be a quiet and delightful area. The trees had received their new foliage. The weather was fine and warm. The whole environment of the camp helped to restore the men's

Territorials. Men only lately out from home, most of whom had never seen a shot fired in battle, were plunged suddenly into the most nerve racking kind of engagement. They had to face one of the worst artillery bombardments of the war and the new devilry of the poison gas. There was no time for adequate staff preparation, the whole was a wild rush, a crowding up of every available man to fill the gap and reinforce the thin lines. They were led by officers who, a year ago, were architects, solicitors and business men. The result was a soldiers' battle like Albuera, where we escaped the annihilation, which, by all the rules, were our due, by the sheer, dogged fighting quality of our men and their leaders. The miners of the North are a sturdy race in peace, both in work and sport. The second battle of Ypres has proved them to be one of the finest fighting stocks on earth.'

energies and morale. The interminable inspections continued and a number of men on fatigue duties were detailed to move a 9.2in. gun.

On the 11th May, the Brigade was ordered to relieve the 1st Cavalry Division in the GHQ Line astride the Potijze - Menin road. From the right, 7th, 6th and 9th Battalions took up position from Zillebeke Lake, across the Ypres - Menin road at the level crossing, and then west to a point 500 yds. east of Potijze Village. The men carried the next day's rations and the move was made in darkness. Second-Lieutenant Lyon wrote:

'On the evening of Tuesday, May 11th, we again moved up to the trenches - This time, as Ypres was in flames, and being shelled without cessation, we had to move to our posts in single file along the railway which skirts the city on the South. We had to man the second line trenches on either side of the Menin road. 'D' Company was perhaps the worst situated as our position consisted of a very muddy ditch (originally a bad communication trench) just North of "Shrapnel Corner". The whole line was a notorious bad one, as it was ill-constructed and frequently shelled - we were destined to carry away many memories of it before the month was over.'

Second-Lieutenant Lyon's 'D' Company was not the only one of the Battalion which had its difficulties. The exact position of the trenches was not known and it was difficult to find the way forward in the dark. At one point the Battalion was halted and patrols sent forward to find the trenches, which they did.

Most of the Battalion was involved in digging trenches close to the front line during the night of the 11th-12th May. It was during this period that the Durhams' reputation for digging splendid trenches was established. One Cavalry officer was heard to

Some members of 13 Platoon, *Shrapnel Corner, 1915. The stresses of war were beginning to show on some of the faces*

remark on hearing that men of the DLI Brigade were digging trenches for them: 'Thank God, we'll get some decent trenches.'

On the 12th May, information was received that the Division was redesignated, 50th Northumbrian Division. The 6th, 7th, 8th and 9th Battalions were now to form 151 Brigade.

On Wednesday, 13th May, the British front and reserve trenches were subjected to a violent bombardment from German artillery. It lasted from 3.30 a.m. to 6.00 p.m. with little respite. The men of the 6th Battalion kept low in their trenches throughout the ordeal. The German gun fire was very accurate and two shells exploded in the Battalion's trenches, killing two men and wounding several others. The two men killed were Sergeant Coates and Corporal Bell. Thomas Coates, from Shildon, was Second-Lieutenant Lyon's platoon sergeant, a competent and much respected NCO. Henry Bell was from Blackhill.

There was little opportunity to recover from this severe bombardment. Trenches had to be dug and that night the Battalion was marched out to a position in advance of the front line to dig a new trench covering a gap made by the enemy as a result of their attacks during the day. Captain Jeffreys wrote this description of the night's activities, in a letter to his wife, dated the 16th May, 1915:

> 'That night (13th May) I had to take 800 men out to dig - split them into two parties. I took one and was told that Major Pollard would show me where to dig ... He was a terrier RE Major and was from Newcastle ... He has already got the DSO in the war and is marvellously cool and collected. When we went out to dig, he was to show me where the trench was to be made, did not exactly know which were our trenches and which Bosche. There was one that we could see every now and then, in the light of the flares about 120 yards from us. I asked if that was all right. "I'll go and find out," he said. I managed to dissuade him from going himself (of course not his job) and he eventually consented to send 4 sappers. They had gone 10 minutes when they came running back saying neither side held the trench, but that they had taken a prisoner! Anyhow we got down and dug till 2 a.m. with nobody between us and the German trenches except 6 men on picquet.'

The Battalion continued to find working parties over the next two days. On the 16th May it was moved to a hutted

Sergeant Coates and family. *He was killed along with Corporal Bell on 13th May, 1915*

encampment, north-west of Ypres, where the men settled in and began to clean up and looked forward to a few days out of the line. It was not to be. At 8.00 p.m. on the 17th May they marched, in heavy rain, to Potijze where they came under the command of General Chetwode, 5th Cavalry Brigade. Their role again was one of improving trenches held by cavalry units. It was at this point that higher authority thought it was time that 151 Brigade should commence the usual practice followed by new units just out from England, of being attached to a more experienced front line brigade, to gradually learn how things were managed in the trenches. Two officers from each company in the 6th Battalion were sent into the line. Those from 'A' and 'B' Companies were attached to the Scots Greys. The officers of 'C' Company were attached to XII Lancers and those of 'D' Company to the XX Hussars. It was an exercise which, in the light of the experiences of late April, was looked upon with some surprise. The Battalion felt it had already learned these lessons the hard way.

The move into the trenches and subsequent activities were described by Second-Lieutenant Lyon:

> 'That night, accordingly, we moved up in single file; an old enemy sniper in the wood gave us some trouble, but we arrived safely. My platoon had, I think, come to the conclusion that they were about to come to close quarters with the Germans, and had spent most of the day sharpening their bayonets. They were somewhat disgusted when they found they had come to trenches at no place less than knee deep in liquid mud, with the German lines out of sight, and with more work to do than they had yet dreamt of. For the rest of the night they were kept hard at work draining a trench and building a dug-out under the direction of the cavalry men, who were only to pleased to have some one to assist them at the uncongenial task - At dawn they took over a part of trench and did sentry duty all day, the "reliefs" being commandeered for further drainage and revetting purposes. When night fell again they were still kept on sentry duty, with the avowed purpose that they should see what it was like - and once again when not actually looking over the parapet they were set to various fatigues.'

Major W.E. Taylor, York and Lancaster Regiment and Calcutta Light Horse (Indian Volunteer Corps), joined the Battalion as Commanding Officer, replacing Captain Jeffreys who had been in temporary command since Lieutenant-Colonel Watson had left at the end of April. Captain Jeffreys reverted to his previous position as Battalion Adjutant. At 9.30 p.m. on the 21st May, the Battalion left the trenches and marched back to a hutted camp near Brandhoek, arriving at 3.00 a.m. on Saturday, 22nd May. Groups of hutted camps were scattered around the area of Vlamertinghe. They were quite comfortable in dry weather, but were known to leak, and the ground surrounding them turn to seas of mud, when wet. The occasional shell dropped amongst them and all were within the sound of the guns. The usual activities were undertaken when in rest: cleaning clothing and equipment followed by inspections, hopefully a bath and change of clothing to rid themselves, temporarily, of the ubiquitous lice. Practice trenches were dug, supervised by the Battalion Bombing Officer, Second-Lieutenant Lyon, and 'dummy' bombs thrown with great energy and enthusiasm. The weather was fine, and it seemed as though a calm had settled over the battlefield. Officers and men settled into, what they hoped would be, a less troubled time in the future.

Sunday evening, 23rd May, was lovely and calm. As night fell, the stars came out, and everyone was in a peaceful frame of mind. Back at headquarters orders were received that 151 Brigade was to be attached to the 28th Division which was holding the line from the left of the Cavalry Corps, just west of Bellewaarde, to the right of 4th Division. At 2.45 a.m. on the morning of 24th May, a fierce German bombardment broke out and gas was released, which drifted over the British positions. German infantry followed behind the gas cloud and attacked our lines from near Hooge almost to Turco Farm. At 3.30 a.m. the gas fumes reached the huts where the sleeping Durhams lay. British guns in the vicinity of the camp were by now blasting away for all they were worth. The first sign of gas was the pungent smell, followed by smarting and weeping eyes and breathing difficulties. At 4.30 a.m. the Battalion was moved from the huts to dug-outs west of the camp, situated on higher ground, and almost free of the gas. At 6.45 a.m. the Brigade Major arrived with orders for the Battalion to march to Potijze and report to Brigadier General Periera, GOC 85th Brigade. The Battalion marched through Ypres, and passed many dead men and horses lying about. It took up the following positions: 'A' Company (Lieutenant Gill) with machine-guns in GHQ Trench Line, south of the Verlorenhoek road. 'B' Company (Lieutenant

Waiting to move to counter-attack *on the 24th May, 1915. This action was cancelled. Private Perry is facing the camera holding the biscuit*

Haythornthwaite), 'C' Company (Lieutenant Heslop), and 'D' Company (Captain Livesay), in Potijze Chateau grounds.

Second-Lieutenant Lyon's 'D' Company was again allocated a hot spot in the line:

'Unfortunately the position allotted to our company was the NE corner of Potijze wood, one of the most unhealthy of the many notorious woods round Ypres. The only dug-outs available were rendered untenable by gas fumes, and so we had to make the best of the scanty shelter afforded by shell holes and various excavations, all half full of water. As soon as we were established there, the Germans began conscientiously bombarding it with gas shells, and for two hours we lay on our faces and wondered how soon we should be hit - another Sergeant in my platoon and a private were killed (Sergeant Hunter and Private Perry, both from Consett) and buried by one shell, and two or three were wounded. I tried to distract my mind by the scientific bullying of worms. In the hole next to me

Following the cancellation of the counter-attack, the Battalion marched back towards Ypres. CQMS Bennison leads the column. Private Perry, on the right, was killed by a shell one hour after this photograph was taken.

as to what might have happened to him. His body was found three days later in a corner of the wood.

The 25th May was spent in dug-outs in the GHQ Line. At 8.30 p.m. the Battalion, now three hundred strong, collected sandbags and shovels and marched to dig a new trench to connect up the right of the line by the railway, with the left, so closing a gap created by the Germans in their attack of the day before. It was a very dangerous spot and a very unpleasant job with the Germans holding the wood just ahead of them. Second-Lieutenant Lyon has left a description of this task which shows the problems of and dangers to units carrying out such necessary work:

was a private of my company, who looked anxiously over the dividing wall after each unusual near one to see if I was still alive: the effort to make my reassuring replies cheery and nonchalant in tone needed considerable self-possession.'

The shelling went on from 8.00 a.m. till 7.00 p.m. The men had little food and no rest. At 10.00 a.m. the Battalion was ordered to advance in file along the GHQ Trench and deploy on reaching the railway to counter-attack. Fortunately the order was cancelled at midday, and 84th Brigade ordered to carry it out. Major Taylor was severely wounded by shrapnel and Captain Jeffreys again resumed command of the Battalion. A further twenty-seven NCOs and men were killed, wounded and gassed. Lieutenant J.M. Hare was missing and there was some conjecture

'As soon as it was dark we paraded as strong as possible and wound our way in single file up to our front line. Our object was to dig a trench to connect our original second line just by Railway Wood with the front line which faced East. This had been made necessary by the occupation of the front line in Railway Wood by the Germans on Whit Monday (24th May). The Battalion of the Buffs which was to occupy this trench was in waiting when we came - the fact that we were commandeered to dig their trench was a distinct compliment to our digging qualities. An attack was expected by dawn and so this new trench had to be made defensible in time for it; so the men dug, as even they, hardened miners though they were, had never dug before. Possibly the desirability of our being able to return to our own trench before it grew too light may have added a spur to their energies!

'With the exception of a few snipers we were not troubled by the enemy, though he must have been at some points very close to

Lieutenant Hugh Lyon, *13 Platoon. Later Headmaster of Rugby School*

Here Brigadier General Martin, GOC 151 Brigade, inspected the Battalion on the following day. Battalion strength was twenty officers and five hundred and eleven men. On the morning of the 4th June, the Battalion marched off to join the Brigade on the Renninghelst road, and then marched on to Dickebusche into a combination of billets in farms and bivouacs. On the 5th June, the Brigades, 149, 150, and 151, came under the command of 50th Division for the first time since they had marched into the attack at the end of April. Orders were received that the 6th and 8th Battalions were to amalgamate, and this was carried out on the 8th June much to the unhappiness of officers and men of both Battalions who were great rivals. The organisation of the new Composite Battalion was as follows:-

Commanding Officer:	Lieutenant-Colonel J. Turnbull (8th Battalion).
Second in Command:	Major J.H. Smeddle (8th Battalion).
Adjutant:	Captain G.A. Stevens (8th Battalion).
Quartermaster:	Lieutenant Hope (6th Battalion).
'A' Company	Captain T.A. Bradford (8th Battalion) (8th DLI men).
'B' Company	Lieutenant W.P. Gill (6th Battalion) (6th DLI men)
'C' Company	Lieutenant T.B. Heslop (6th Battalion) (6th DLI men)
'D' Company	Captain F.H. Livsay (6th Battalion) (6th DLI men)

Total strength of the composite Battalion was forty nine officers and eight hundred and three men.

Captain Jeffreys was transferred and took over as temporary adjutant to the 2/5th Lancashire Fusiliers. Several officers surplus to requirement were sent to 35th Infantry Base Camp at Harfleur, near Le Havre. 1/5th Battalion Loyal North Lancashire Regiment joined 151 Brigade to bring it up to four battalion strength.

us. And it was not until the work was finished, to the complete satisfaction of all concerned, that any trouble arose. Then, in a fit of nervousness, someone on the right opened on the German trenches with a machine-gun: the alarm appeared to spread. The Germans caught the infection and sent up star-shells, which revealed us. A hail of bullets followed, but we and the Buffs were by now low down in the new dug trench and we lost only one man, who was shot through the heart. Fortunately the firing died down as quickly as it had begun, and we made our way back to the trenches with only the usual attention from the snipers.'

For the remaining days until and including the 28th May, the Battalion remained in the GHQ Line, improving dug-outs and digging trenches. One man was wounded on the 26th and one killed on the 28th May. The Battalion was congratulated by Brigadier General Periera, GOC 85th Brigade, for its digging carried out on the 25th. On the 28th of the month, the Battalion was relieved by one company of The Royal Scots, and one company of The Northumberland Fusiliers. A night march was made back to bivouacs in a wood near Oosthoek. This rest period lasted until the 2nd June. On this day the Battalion moved to the southern edge of Poperinghe where the men were accommodated in bivouacs and the officers in two small farms.

Lieutenant T.B. Heslop and fellow officers, *1915*
L to R: Brock, Heslop, Angus (seated), Mann, McNair

From the 9th to the 11th June, the Battalion lay at rest, time taken to clean themselves and their equipment. On the evening of the 11th June, the Battalion marched to Kruistraat and into dugouts in the grounds of the chateau and unexpected luxury. Many of the dugouts were panelled with wood and fitted out with furniture obtained from the houses of neighbouring Ypres.

On the 12th June, the Battalion was ordered to Sanctuary Wood a place which had already obtained an unenviable name for danger and sacrifice. The march route followed by the Battalion at dusk on this day was over the canal south of Ypres to the Lille Gate, then south of Zillebeke Lake to Maple Copse and into Sanctuary Wood. There was great difficulty in finding sufficient dugouts for all of the men and a number of them had to sleep out in the open, not the most relaxing of experiences as there was a little shelling and a large number of bullets screaming through the wood. Fortunately casualties were confined to one man only,

Private T.H. Fletcher of 'A' Company being wounded.

The Battalion came under the orders of 149 Brigade on the 13th June and was set to work on the Hooge defences. Whilst there was very little shelling from the Germans there was considerable rifle and machine-gun fire coming over. Again casualties were extremely light, namely Private Charlton wounded. Rations came up to the men from Maple Copse but could only be moved at night as it was far too dangerous to move during daylight. Work continued on these defences the following day during which Corporal Longridge and Lance-Corporal Neasham were both wounded by enemy fire.

The Battalion was ordered to support 149 Brigade which was to attack the German positions on the 16th June. To hide their presence from the Germans, no fires were allowed in Sanctuary Wood. At 2.30 a.m. on 16th June, the Battalion moved into the second line trenches and the switch line running east and west through the wood. The British bombardment in support of 149 Brigade attack commenced at 2.50 a.m. but German retaliation was both instant and severe and a heavy counter bombardment fell on both front and second line British trenches. The attack commenced at 4.15 p.m. and appeared to be going well, as viewed from the Battalion positions. At 6.30 a.m. a request was received from the Commanding Officer of forces due to attack north of Hooge for support in this action. Two companies, commanded by Major Hawdon, were sent to assist whilst two more companies were collected and held ready to move into Zouave Wood. At 7.30 a.m. these orders were cancelled and the companies returned to the Battalion. Throughout the whole of the day the Battalion was under heavy German artillery fire as part of a more comprehensive bombardment which raked the area of the British attack. This increased in severity between 3.00 and 4.00 p.m. as the enemy counter-attacked. Towards dusk the artillery fire died down. Orders to provide working parties to repair and reinforce the Hooge defences were cancelled and at 8.00 p.m. the Battalion stood to, ready to man the front line trenches at short notice. At 9.00 p.m. the Battalion relieved 7th Battalion The Northumberland Fusiliers, in trenches in Hooge Chateau. 'A' and 'B' Companies were in trenches up to the chateau stables, 'C' Company were in the stables, and 'D'

Company was in support. The Germans were in possession of the chateau itself. At the end of an exhausting and stressful day the Battalion spent much of the night repairing the trenches which had been badly knocked about by the German bombardment. Casualties included Lieutenant Hawthornthwaite of the 6th Battalion who had a gunshot wound in the right shoulder and two 8th Battalion men, Sergeant Bugler Miles, wounded, and Private Dent, killed.

The 17th June continued to be a day of heavy shelling of our trenches. Part of 'B' Company trench was so severely damaged as to become untenable and the communication trench from Zouave Wood badly knocked about. Lieutenant Saint (8th DLI), Battalion Bombing Officer, with his bombers carried out a successful attack on the German sap in front of 'C' Company's trenches. In this attack he was supported by the Battalion machine-guns under Lieutenant Howe (6th DLI). Casualties for the day were Sergeant Masters killed and Sergeant Makepeace and one other rank wounded, all 8th Battalion men. The day's endeavours were spent in trying to repair the trenches as they were damaged by enemy gun fire, and in bringing up supplies and ammunition. At night one hundred and fifty men of the 7th Battalion The Northumberland Fusiliers were sent forward to assist in repairing trenches.

Hard digging and repair work on damaged trenches continued throughout the 18th June. The Battalion also partly excavated a second communication trench from Zouve Wood to Hooge but were unable to complete the task before the end of the day. At dark it was relieved by 7th Battalion Northumberland Fusiliers and a Battalion of the Wiltshire Regiment. The Machine-Gun Section was not relieved and remained in Armagh Wood for a further eighteen days before rejoining the Battalion at Locre. The Battalion march to the rear was via Maple Copse and Kruisstraat and experienced only mild shell fire. Heavy rifle fire on the other hand resulted in one man killed and two wounded as they left Zouave Wood. The 6th Battalion's first tour of duty in the Ypres Salient was completed. It had experienced its first action. Many friends had been lost. The final words on this episode are best left to Second-Lieutenant Lyon who wrote the following poem:

THE ROAD

There runs a road from Poperinghe,
 Through Ypres to Zonnebeke,
Where winter, spring and summer time
 Are one unending trek,
For eastward lies the enemy,
 And westward shines the sea;
And west and east the men march on
 To keep their homeland free.

The maps all mark it yellow,
 And the lorries dust it white,
But it's black that road and bloody,
 To the men that know it right;
For the trees are torn with shrapnel,
 And the pavé's splashed with red,
With gaping wounds by the ditches side,
 Where the guns have claimed their dead.

On runs the battered highway,
 Past broken walls and bare,
Through the city of all sorrows
 To the lone cathedral square;
But never a man that lingers,
 Where the feet of kings have trod,
But on he steps with awe-struck eyes
 And a prayer in his heart to God.

And over the bridge of Menin,
 And past the Menin Road,
Where the Red Cross vans come down from Hooge

With their pitiful shattered load;
On to the Potijze crossroads
 Or northward to St. Jean,
And heaven help your transport
 If the big guns catch it then.

But this side of Verlorenhoek
 The marching feet stop still,
For a thin brown breastwork holds them,
 At the gates of a water-mill;
But the desolate road runs onward,
 Barren and overgrown,
Where death, the wanton, beckoning, beckoning,
 Walks in the night alone.

What of the men who trod it?
 Who will tread no road again?
The wind in the nodding Poplars
 Whispers their message plain;
Still eastward lies the enemy,
 And westward shines the sea;
March on from west to east, march on,
 To keep our homeland free.

Hugh Lyon

CHAPTER 5
THE QUIET FRONT - KEMMEL AND ARMENTIÈRES
1915

'F' Huts near Vlamertinghe were reached in the early hours of the 19th June and the remainder of the day was spent resting. On Sunday, 20th June, 151 Brigade was transferred from V Corps to II Corps, which was commanded by Sir Charles Ferguson. The move commenced at 8.30 a.m. and the Battalion marched via Ouderdam and Locre to Dranoutre and bivouacced at Corunna Farm, west of this village. The following day the Composite Battalion, along with the 9th Battalion, were addressed by the Corps Commander who told all ranks that he was pleased to have them under his command. They would now find themselves in a quiet area. The trenches were good and he expected that they would keep them that way - the rapidly spreading reputation of the Durhams for digging and maintaining excellent trenches did not appear to have reached General Ferguson. In the evening the Battalion relieved the 4th Battalion The Lincolnshire Regiment in trenches in front of Lindenhoek crossroads, with Battalion Headquarters in a small villa on the east slopes of Kemmel Hill. It was quickly discovered that there was no regular support line and the Battalion's first task was to remedy this weakness by digging support trenches completed, as usual, in record time. The German trenches were some forty yards from our lines on the right, to two hundred yards distant on the left. They were on higher and drier ground and so dominated our trenches making movement during the day difficult as snipers had a good field of fire. Our trenches faced Messines Ridge and were approached from Lindenhoek crossroads by a long communication trench named Regent Street. Behind the trench lines was Kemmel Hill, very steep and high,

which afforded an excellent view of the German positions, not only in the immediate area but also as far as Ypres. After the Salient, this was an extremely pleasant area. The country was quite beautiful; poppies and flax covered the fields with splashes of brilliant colour. Small farmers still worked their farms and some civilians remained in Kemmel Village. Days were relatively quiet, only disturbed by the brief but lively 'stonks' from both artilleries at stand to and stand down, and the enemy snipers on the higher ground, which made it dangerous to raise one's head above the parapet, and kept the Battalion casualty lists fairly high. The first man killed in these positions was Private A. Patterson who had enlisted at Bishop Auckland. Battalion strength was twenty-seven officers and eight hundred and twenty-six other ranks.

The 23rd June, was a quiet day except for the usual artillery fire referred to above. The Battalion commenced work pushing out a mine towards the enemy lines. At 5.00 p.m. the enemy held a placard above their parapet which bore the words, 'Lemberg is taken,' followed by much cheering and firing of rifles and flares. The Battalion response was to give them five rounds rapid - for luck! Mail arrived and a rum ration was issued. Lieutenant Lyon who was now the Brigade Bombing Officer, arrived in the trenches to organise a bomb attack on the enemy opposite. He wrote:

> I arranged with Saint [the bomb officer of the 6th/8th Battalion] to send out eight men from one of our advanced works [40 yards from the German lines] with two bombs each. Angus, who was in command of the breastwork in question, assisted us with rifle

fire before and after the event, and with flares to light up the objective. I will not guarantee that any Germans were killed, but I think we may have woken some of them up!'

The following two days were quiet and on the 27th June the Battalion, with the exception of 'C' Company, was relieved by elements of the 7 DLI and 5th Battalion The Loyal North Lancs. The men marched to huts at Locre about three and a half miles from Bailleul. Access to Bailleul enabled the Battalion to enjoy good shops and its one excellent hotel *The Faucon*. The month ended in these pleasant surroundings, with baths to wash off the accumulated dirt of the trenches and laundered uniforms to rid them of that most troublesome of afflictions of trench life - body lice. For the next five days, drills and marches were the order of the day to toughen up the men's feet, softened by the period of time spent in the trenches.

On the 3rd July, the Battalion returned to the trenches they had occupied previously. The relief was completed by midnight. The companies were disposed from right to left as follows: 'C' Company (Lieutenant Heslop), 'A' Company (Captain J.S. Ritson), 'B' Company (Lieutenant Blenkinsop), 'D' Company (Captain Livsay). The latter company was in support in Regent Street dugouts. The Battalion roll was twenty seven officers and eight hundred and seventy two other ranks, of whom thirteen officers and three hundred and twenty-men were of the 8th Battalion.

The next day, the Battalion was informed that Brigadier General Martin had been replaced by Brigadier General Shea, CB, DSO, from 6th Division. The new 151 Brigade Commander made an instant impression on both officers and men. He was quite young with a commanding personality. He had considerable organising ability. His officers always found him willing to advise and help them and he showed a clear understanding of their problems. He visited the trenches every day and very quickly displayed a growing affection and respect for his Durham soldiers which was reciprocated by the men.

This tour of duty in the trenches lasted until the 8th July. The Battalion provided working parties at night and although it was thought that the Germans were preparing positions for installing gas, nothing happened and the routine remained normal for the length of stay in these positions. Lance-Corporal Robinson and Private H.G. Scott, the latter of the 8th Battalion, were both wounded.

Relieved by 7th Battalion The Durham Light Infantry, at 9.30 p.m. on 9th July, the Battalion marched back to dugouts and shelters in the Kemmel Hill area. It was now in Brigade support. For five days, time was taken up with cleaning, inspections and providing working parties at night. Working parties were the curse of officers and men when out of the line, particularly if the line occupied had been very active and it had been difficult to obtain adequate rest. 'At Rest' was very often a misnomer and very little relaxation and sleep were possible. On coming out of the front line trenches, the immediate demand was for cleaning themselves, weapons and equipment. Drills and training had to be recommenced and, to add to these, frequent calls for working parties were made, invariably at night, the only time it was possible to dig and repair trenches in the front line. It is sometimes difficult to escape from the thought that the Durhams paid a price for their reputation as excellent diggers of trenches by being constantly in demand. The result was very tired soldiers. Working in front line trenches and in No Man's Land was a very dangerous occupation. On 13th July, working parties near Lindenhoek crossroads were shelled by the enemy and one man was killed and five wounded.

The advance party of 28th Division arrived on 15th July to take over the sector from the 50th Division. Home leave was commenced on this day and two officers and three other ranks were sent back to England, the officers for six days, the other ranks for four days. Meanwhile the 50th Division moved to Armentières. The Battalion set off at 7.30 p.m. and marched, in rain, via Locre, Bailleul, Pont de Nieppe, some of it along cobbled roads which tried and tested soft feet. The journey was made in full marching order and before Armentières was reached there were a number of stragglers. Armentières was reached at 1.00 a.m. on the 17th July and the companies went into billets at Blue Blind Factory, with Battalion Headquarters in Rue Sadi Carnot. After a hurried breakfast, officers were sent forward to reconnoitre the trenches which the Battalion would occupy in front of Chapelle d'Armentières. Here the Battalion relieved companies of the Royal Scots and Monmouthshires. These were the best trenches which the Battalion had occupied so far. Leith Walk and Lothian Avenue were communication trenches wide enough to allow fully laden soldiers to pass each other quite easily. Enough dugouts to go round were indeed a pleasant surprise, and these were most comfortable compared with any others they had occupied. At the entrance to each communication trench, newly baked bread, eggs and butter could be bought. The family living at Pigot's Farm, now ruined, had evacuated, leaving fields of vegetables which could be picked by the troops with very little risk from enemy fire. It was, indeed, a very quiet sector. However, a reminder that war was not far away and none were immune from its horrors, lay behind one of the trenches close to the abandoned farm. A baby had been laid to rest in a grave with a tiny shoe tied to the marker. The German trenches lay between two hundred and fifty and three hundred yards away.

Quiet sector, in First World War terms, is not one which is completely inactive. Desultory artillery fire may be experienced. The early morning and dusk 'hate' bombardment were invariably fired on both lines. Snipers were always active and a soldier needed to keep his head down when going about his daily tasks in the trenches. From the 18th to 23rd July, the companies strengthened the front line by building shell shelter trenches and worked in the second line improving supporting positions. Snipers wounded four men; Corporal R.B. Tuck, Private H. Taylor, Private J. Fletcher and Private Pinkney. Second-Lieutenant G.C. Robertson was killed.

Two companies of the Battalion were relieved by 5th Battalion TheLoyal North Lancs, and moved to the Hospice in Armentieres, with Battalion Headquarters at Rue Nationale. Two companies remained, one in the support line, and the other at Lille Post, until relieved by 9 DLI on the 29th July. Armentieres was shelled every day, usually with shrapnel. Even so some inhabitants remained. A number of shops and estaminets were open. Prices were high. The inevitable working parties were found and casualties suffered. Private T. Thomas of Spennymoor was killed on the 25th July. Private J. Hayton and Private Rourke were wounded on the following days. Second-Lieutenant J.C.

Miller (brother of Lieutenant-Colonel H. Miller who commanded 6 DLI from 1934 to 1940) went to the front line trenches on 27th July to do some sniping. He was shot through the head and killed when in the act of firing through the loophole.

News was received on 1st August, 1915, that the composite Battalion was to be split up and revert to their original and separate identities. During the time the two Battalions had been combined they had worked very well together but both now looked forward to the separation. Major-General P.S. Wilkinson succeeded Lord Cavan as GOC 50th Division. On the 7th August, the composite Battalion was broken up and the 6th and 8th resumed their separate identities. Lieutenant-Colonel Turnbull remained in overall control of both Battalions for administrative purposes until Major Borritt, DSO, arrived on 11th August to take command of the 6th Battalion. Captain Jeffreys returned to the Battalion on the 13th August and took up the position of Adjutant.

The 6th relieved the 8th Battalion in the front line trenches on the night of the 13th/14th August. Much of the time during this tour was taken up in improving the trenches. Brigadier General Shea inspected the work. Captain Jeffreys wrote, 'He does this daily and is a real good commander.' The greatest nuisance suffered by the men in the trenches was the enormous numbers of flies which fed on the trench refuse and were a considerable danger to health and hygiene. Trenches were sprayed regularly with creosote in an attempt to control their numbers and stringent discipline was enforced to get rid of refuse and maintain cleanliness. On the 15th August, Major Borritt left the Battalion to take command of the 5th Battalion Shropshire Light Infantry. Captain Jeffreys succeeded him in command of the Battalion. The following day Private G. Hayton of Stanhope, was killed by a shell whilst cooking in the rear of the trench. Even in quiet sectors, death was not far away. The Battalion remained in the line till relieved on 19th August by the 7th Battalion The Northumberland Fusiliers. The relief took place at 8.30 p.m. and it then marched to billets at Pont de Nieppe. Headquarters was in a very pleasant house, with clean sheets and bedding available and comfortable beds to lay them on. The men were not so lucky as their billets were very crowded.

The usual routine of cleaning, drills and working parties followed. In addition, new drafts of officers and men were received from the second line depots of the Regiment. A move to the Asylum in Armentières was welcomed as it meant a considerable improvement in the men's billets. Armentières experienced its usual dose of shelling from enemy guns but no casualties were suffered in the Battalion. During this time the four Companies were re-named 'W', 'X', 'Y' and 'Z'.

A particularly unpleasant situation was experienced by one company following the relief of 5 The Loyal North Lancs on the evening of 31st August. Royal Engineers in the line thought they could detect German mining under a trench named *The Mushroom*, and were of the opinion that it might be blown up at any time. For the first night of the relief the company of the Loyal North Lancs., already in the trench, were told to remain in position. It was relieved at 5.00 a.m. by 'W' Company of the 6th Battalion under Lieutenant W.F.E. Badcock, who had just returned to the Battalion after recovering from wounds received at the end of April, 1915. For four days this company held 'The Mushroom', wrestling with the fear that their narrow world might disintegrate around them at any moment. The reader can only imagine the fear of officers and men, yet marvel at their discipline. They were heartened by the appearance of Brigadier-General Shea who continued to visit the trenches daily. Lieutenant Badcock's company was partly withdrawn from 'The Mushroom' on 4th September, leaving only three groups of sentries at the right, centre and left of their sector. At night, patrols were sent out in front of the trench to protect it against sudden attack from the Germans. There must have been a great sigh of relief when the Battalion moved back to billets in the Hospice and Grand College in Armentières and the 5th Battalion The Border Regiment and 7th Battalion The Northumberland Fusiliers took over the line on 6th September.

Billets were cleaned up, parades and drills held, and the usual working parties found. One of these working parties was hit by a shell and fourteen men were wounded, six of them seriously. Private E. Brown from Crook died of his wounds in the Casualty Clearing Station. Higher authority asked for a list of names of men recommended for gallantry awards. The following list was forwarded on 15th September: Captain Welsh, Lieutenant Gill, Lieutenant R.V. Hare, Lieutenant A.L. Blenkinsopp, Privates Robinson, McCrome, Captain G.A. Hardy, Company Sergeant-Major Bousfield, Corporal Turton, Sergeant Malpass and Sergeant Hall. A further list was forwarded on 17th September: Captain Heslop, Lieutenant Angus, Lieutenant Badcock, Regimental Sergeant-Major Perry, Sergeant-Major McNair, Sergeant Linsley, Private A. Taylor, Sergeant Bland, Sergeant Elliott, Sergeant Johnson, Company Quartermaster Sergeant Walton, and Company Quartermaster Sergeant Bennison.

The Battalion relieved the 8th Battalion in the front line, on 18th September. The Battle of Loos was about to begin and to divert the enemy's attention from this area and to cause him to retain reserves supporting his lines in the Armentières sector, the Division was ordered to make a demonstration against enemy trenches opposite. This took the form of a heavy bombardment by the Divisional artillery and bundles of burning straw released into No Man's Land, to simulate an impending attack on the enemy lines. Well aware that the Germans would retaliate with a fierce bombardment of our lines, the Battalion front line trenches were evacuated for shell shelter trenches. These were narrow and deep trenches dug a short distance behind the fire trenches, with a strong overhead cover of heavy timbers. Six sentries were left in the fire trench, again in splinter-proof shelters. The enemy retaliated as expected and subjected the fire trenches to a storm of shells of all calibre. Private Redshaw was buried alive. His comrades rushed to release him, which they did after frantic digging under this sustained fire. He was suffering from shock and a broken leg and he died in the Casualty Clearing Station on the following day. He was a Cumberland man who had enlisted at Leadgate, near Consett. The nosecap of another shell went clean through Private Harwood, killing him instantly. He hailed from Consett. The trenches were left in quite a mess and the next three days were spent in carrying out urgent repairs.

The Battalion was relieved by the 5th Battalion The Northumberland Fusiliers on the 23rd September and marched into billets near Armentières Station. The Division was now in reserve for VI Corps. On the 26th September, the Battalion relieved the 11th Battalion The Middlesex Regiment in the

Houplines sector. Houplines was a suburb of Armentières and lay very close to the front line. It still provided good billets and though lying very close to the enemy it was, at this period, not greatly damaged. All civilians had left the town. The days until 29th September were spent cleaning up and improving the trenches they now occupied. Three companies of the Battalion were relieved by the 8th Battalion, and moved into billets at the Tissage in Houplines. 'Y' Company (Captain Heslop) remained in the front line.

Life in the trenches was hard. Whilst some were well built with good dug-outs, others were in a very poor state, and required a great deal of repairing and improving to make life in them even tolerable. Fortunately the digging skills of the Battalion enabled poor trenches to be improved with speed. However, even the best trenches were still holes in the ground. Rain, snow and ice, not to mention German artillery and mortar fire, destroyed much of the skilful work which had gone into construction of a trench. Constant maintenance had to be undertaken. Much thought was spent on ways of alleviating these conditions to make men's lives as comfortable as possible, especially in the winter. Not least of these were the ladies' committees set up at home to raise funds for the purchase of items which were either non-existant or in very short supply, the receipt of which, did so much to make life more comfortable at the front, and showed the men they were in the thoughts of people back home. Invariably organised and chaired by a lady of some standing in the community, often wives or mothers of serving officers, the committees raised funds by a variety of means. Flag Day Fund Committees were set up to raise money to purchase items for the troops. Prisoner of War Fund Committees raised money to purchase items required by those men incarcerated in German POW camps. A letter, dated August 23rd, 1915, from Captain Jeffreys to Mrs Watson, wife of Lieutenant-Colonel Watson, outlined the items considered necessary for the men's welfare:

'I have been thinking about your ladies committee and socks and shirts and other valuable articles of underclothing and have come to this conclusion. It is the business of the Government to supply soldiers with these things, and they seem to manage it all right. So will you save your money for woolly gloves, cardigans etc. when the cold weather comes on. The men love lots of tobacco and if you have £3 knocking about that you would like to spend, please send some footballs, spare bladders, and a pump to blow them out."

These requested items were added to in the course of time to include football kit, books, band instruments and so on. Families provided their men-folk serving in the forces with necessities. An officer wrote to his wife in September, 1915:

'...Cigarettes and chocolate are the two most needed items out here. You can send me both at any time. After the two aforementioned I think soap and toilet necessaries would rank next in order of importance. A cake like the last one you sent will always be acceptable and I can assure you that socks in any numbers will be found very useful during the coming cold weather.'

Letters and parcels from home were eagerly looked forward to by officers and men, and did so much to raise spirits and morale.

From 1st to 4th October, 1915, the Battalion remained in billets in Houplines, cleaning person and equipment, and making up deficiencies in kit. Early in the evening of 4th October, a group of men in the Battalion returned to the billets with a supply of brandy, eau de vie, absinthe etc., which they had found in a cellar in the village. As the War Diary goes on to state: 'There was a certain amount of trouble which was soon checked by the Battalion and Company Sergeant-Majors.' The diary is silent on any punishments given out.

On the 5th October, the Battalion relieved the 8th Battalion in Trenches 81, 82 and 83, where it was to remain until the 14th of the month. On the 8th October, Private W. Hutchinson of Crook, a member of 'Z' Company, was killed when walking up the fire trench. The following night, a patrol comprising Corporal Moyle and Privates Coglan, Pybus, Brown and Fairhurst, all of 'W' Company, set out from our lines, first to call at a listening post in front of Trench 83. Having done so, they moved off to find another listening post in front of Trench 82. They never arrived at this post and it is probable that they stumbled into the German lines and were taken prisoner. Navigation in No Man's Land at night was never easy, particularly without the assistance of a moon or stars, and identifiable landmarks. On the 10th October, a company of the 15th Battalion The Durham Light Infantry which had suffered heavy losses at Loos in September, was attached to the Battalion for instruction in trench warfare. On the 13th of the month, the Divisional artillery bombarded the German trenches from 2.00 to 3.30 p.m. When this ceased troops threw smoke bombs over the parapet to cause the enemy to think an attack was about to take place, and so tie his reserves to our front, whilst First Army carried out offensive activities elsewhere. Enemy retaliation was immediate with a bombardment which did little damage and caused no casualties. The Battalion continued to fire on the enemy parapet during the night and about midnight the Germans fired three or four Whizz Bangs at Trench 81 where one man was wounded. The morning of 14th October was misty and, under its cover, a patrol was sent out to ascertain the amount of damage done to the German wire following the previous day's activity. This patrol comprised Second-Lieutenant McLellan, Sergeant T.W. Firbank and Private Hutchinson. On getting close to the enemy parapet the patrol was fired on and Sergeant Firbank, who came from Shildon, was killed instantly. His body had to be left inside the enemy wire when the other two members of the patrol returned to our trenches. The Battalion was relieved by the 7th Battalion DLI, and marched to billets in the Hospice Civil and the Collège des Garçons, Armentières.

The Battalion remained in these billets until 19th October. On this date it took over Trenches 84 to 87, inclusive, from the 9th Battalion. A quiet spell of duty ensued until 26th of the month, when the Battalion was relieved by the 7th Battalion DLI and billets were again occupied in Armentieres. A detachment comprising Lieutenant McNair, Second-Lieutenant Brock, Regimental Sergeant-Major Perry and fifty one men of the Battalion, paraded with other detachments of 50th Division at Bailleul, on 27th October, to be inspected by HM King George V.

On 30th October, 1915, the Battalion again moved into the line occupying Trenches 81 to 83, inclusive. It relieved the 9th Battalion DLI. Six platoons of the 8th Battalion The Somerset Light Infantry were attached for training in trench warfare and, to accommodate them, four platoons of the Battalion under Lieutenant Angus moved into billets in Houplines. The Battalion remained in these front line trenches until 7th November. Company Commanders at this time were:

'W' Company:	Captain W.F.E. Badcock.
'X' Company:	Captain G.E. Cardew.
'Y' Company:	Captain T.B. Heslop.
'Z' Company:	Captain R.A. Howe.

After two days' rain on the 2nd and the 3rd of November, the front line, support and communication trenches partially collapsed, with two feet of water in the bottom of most of them, adding to the misery of the soldiers. Fine weather on the 4th of the month, enabled work to commence on clearing and repairing the damage. The platoons of The Somerset Light Infantry were replaced by some of the 8th Battalion The Lincolnshire Regiment, again for trench training. Repairs to trenches continued on the 5th November. Lance-Corporal Lowe was severely wounded in the head. One of the Lincolnshires was shot through the brain. Lieutenant McNair was injured when he stepped on a bayonet and he had to be taken to hospital. Repairs and revetting of the trenches continued until relieved by the 7th Battalion DLI on the 7th November. 'W' and 'X' Companies were billeted in The Hospice Civil, and 'Y' and 'Z' Companies in the Collège des Garçons. Battalion HQ was in the Rue Nationale; all, of course, in Armentières. For the next two days, time was taken up cleaning arms, equipment and clothing caked with mud.

CHAPTER 6

RETURN TO THE SALIENT - SANCTUARY WOOD - THE BLUFF - HILL 60

1915-1916

The Battalion marched to La Maison Blanche, near Bailleul, on the 10th November, to begin a month's rest in huts which, at first, were overcrowded until additional buildings were erected. The time was taken up with daily training. The inevitable working parties were found. A Battalion band and bugles were set up and urgent requests sent home to the ladies' committees for additional musical instruments. Football and boxing tournaments were arranged. The weather fluctuated with days of rain followed by fine and frosty spells. On the 22nd November the Brigade was inspected by Sir Hubert Plumer, Army Commander, and General Sir Charles Ferguson, Corps Commander, both of whom commented favourably on the high standard of turn-out. There was now a spring in the step of the men which showed that the period of rest was helping to diminish the strain they had experienced in the trenches. Queen Alexandra's Fund supplied eight bales of gifts which were distributed amongst the men on the 25th November. Baths were provided at Bailleul on the 2nd December and blankets disinfected on the 10th of the month. The following day numerous cases of scabies were identified amongst the men and the people infected were evacuated to hospital for treatment. Towards the end of the period of rest, the Division was informed that it was to be transferred from II Corps to V Corps and would be returning to the Salient. The first indication of this move was on the 16th December, when the Machine-Gun Section under Second-Lieutenant Brock was moved to Dickebusch where it was billeted for one night before moving into the trenches. The Battalion set off in full marching order at 11.15 a.m. on the 17th

December. The march to Steenwerck was carried out in heavy rain. On arriving at Steenwerck, officers and men entrained for Poperinghe. The Battalion left Poperinghe and marched off to occupy huts at Dickebusch and into an environment which tested even the most tolerant of men. The camp was in a disgraceful state. The huts were completely surrounded by knee deep mud. It had rained all day and the men were already soaked on arrival. One factor which helped to alleviate the conditions were visits to nearby Dickebusch Village. Though partially destroyed and damaged, a few civilians remained and two or three shops sold food and wine.

The stay in the camp was short and on the 18th December the Battalion moved into Maple Copse, and relieved the 6th Battalion The Royal Scots in the reserve positions. The move was made with the loss of Sergeant F. Lodge, who was wounded on the railway track going into Zillebeke. Company positions were: 'W' Company, Canal Dugouts; 'X' Company, Maple Copse; 'Y' Company, Sanctuary Wood; 'Z' Company, Redoubts, 2,3 and 4 on the right of Sanctuary Wood. The trenches were in a very bad state consisting of holes and ditches. Fortunately it proved to be a quiet day, and the Battalion, with its usual vigour, set about improving the line and making it more safe and comfortable.

At 5.00 a.m. on the 19th December, the Germans opened a heavy bombardment and infantry attack north of Hooge. This bombardment gradually spread to the front line held by the 12th Battalion The Royal Scots to whom the 6th Battalion were in reserve. The shells included both gas and lachrymatory (tear gas) projectiles. Sergeant J. Grainger of Scarborough and Private R. Gardiner of Coundon, both in 'W' Company, were killed and five men wounded in Canal Dugouts. 'W' Company was attached to 21st Brigade and moved up to Railway Dugouts. Captain Heslop's 'Y' Company in reserve trenches in Sanctuary Wood began to suffer casualties and was withdrawn to dugouts where there was better shelter against the enormous amount of shrapnel flying about. Over two hundred shells fell upon the Battalion positions on the right of Sanctuary Wood. Fortunately little damage was done and there were few casualties. In the dark hours of the night the Battalion relieved the 12th Battalion The Royal Scots in the front line and this was accomplished despite heavy enemy shelling. The trenches occupied were numbered A7 to A12. The enemy shelling continued through the night. It must not be forgotten that Battalion transport had to bring up much needed food and supplies every night after dark, and in doing so, had to run the gauntlet of the Menin road which was constantly under accurate enemy gunfire. The journey was made to the Zillebeke Dump. From here a light trench railway carried the rations to the front line.

The enemy bombardment continued during the 20th December. 'X' Company (Captain Cardew) in Trenches A10 and A11 was particularly hard hit, losing six men killed and a dozen wounded. Lieutenant-Colonel Jeffreys was wounded and evacuated. His loss to the Battalion was described by Brigadier General Shea in a letter to the Colonel's wife dated 21st December:

> 'I am thankful to say that your husband's wounds are not serious and that he will, please God, be soon well and hearty again. He was wounded in both thighs and in the right hand, but not seriously. He was in one of the forward trenches with the Engineer Officer and the doctor. There were two men also there who were killed by the same shell which wounded your husband and the Engineer. It was a great mercy that they both were saved. I cannot tell you how I shall miss your husband until he comes back again ... He was always so splendid in spite of the very many difficulties with which he had to contend and he is such a fierce soldier and has done so much since he got command of the 6th...'

The difficulty in getting wounded men out of the trenches

when under fire is described by Lieutenant Hope (Quartermaster) in a letter to Lieutenant-Colonel Watson dated 21st December. He also describes the conditions they were now experiencing:

> '...We are back in Ypres again and we have received a warm reception. Colonel Jeffreys was wounded yesterday. I carried him out to the ambulance and an awful journey I had. I had 2 miles to go to get to the car (Shrapnel Corner) but you rarely get that far down. I was hit rather hard on the thigh by a lump of flying timber just after I got the Colonel into he car, but so far I am alright except for a little bruise. We had a good few casualties yesterday ... The gas was dreadful last night. My eyes were fairly closed up. My store is in a sea of mud nine miles away from the dump. Old Ypres is still a lively spot. We were the only people to get through with the rations last night without a casualty. Walker the cook from B[arnard] C[astle] ... was hit rather badly in the leg last night. The mud is fearful. Ravensworth at its worst was nothing like this. The stamp of recruits which we have had are not at all bad, but every man Jack of them were dreadfully clothed and booted and not one man was in possession of a complete small kit ... The clothing they have come in has been disgraceful ... The socks and muffler I have given to a machine-gunner, the cigs I have divided between 2 men, the cake will do for me...'

The Battalion was not without its heroes. The following citation refers to the award of the Distinguished Conduct Medal to Sergeant J. Malpass, from Stanley:

> 'For conspicuous gallantry near Zillebeke on the night of 19/20 December, 1915, when he went out under heavy shell fire and rendered first aid to two wounded men in the open. He carried one to an ambulance and, returning, got the other away into safety. Sergeant Malpass had previously distinguished himself in action.'

Major G. A. Stevens succeeded Colonel Jeffreys in command of the Battalion. The Battalion was fortunate in that one fine soldier was replaced by another. Major Stevens had come over to France as Adjutant with the 8th Battalion DLI He had distinguished himself in action and had gained the reputation of a first class leader of men. On the 21st December, Captain R. B. Bradford, MC was transferred from the 7th DLI, and became Battalion Adjutant. Captain Bradford was to win the Victoria Cross on the

Somme when commanding 9th DLI, and in late 1917 became the youngest Brigadier General in the British army, at the age of 25 years. He was killed at Cambrai on the 30th November, 1917.

It rained all day on the 21st December, but if the weather was dreary, conditions improved as the enemy bombardment, which had lasted two days, ceased, and things quietened down. An interesting entry occurs in the Battalion war diary on 22nd December:

'Considerable excitement was caused in Trench A12 by the sight of a man waving a white handkerchief and approaching our trench. Several shots were fired at him and one entered his shoulder. The man, however, managed to reach our trenches and turned out to be an escaped Russian prisoner. He had been employed by the Germans on their subsidiary line. A few minutes later another man was seen running towards the same trench, which he managed to reach. He evinced the greatest ecstasy on finding that the occupants of the trench were British. He was sent to Brigade Headquarters under escort, whilst his comrade, after being medically attended was sent to the Field Ambulance...'

On this same day, Lieutenant Peberdy was mortally wounded whilst out on patrol. Corporal Layton and Lance-Corporal Conlon went out from the trenches, under heavy enemy fire, and brought in the wounded officer. They were promoted to sergeant and corporal respectively for this action.

The Battalion was relieved by the 5th Battalion The Border Regiment which had been transferred from 150 to 151 Brigade to replace the Loyal North Lancashires. The relief was carried out on the 23rd December, without enemy interference. Officers and men had experienced the most appalling weather conditions during this tour of the trenches. They were covered from head to toe with thick, clinging mud which had reached between knee and waist deep in the trenches. It was an aching, shivering column which made its weary way into reserve and to the huts at Dickebusch. Total casualties during the period of time in the trenches were; one officer and eight other ranks killed; one officer and forty-five other ranks wounded.

On the 25th December, the Divisional Commander, Major-General Wilkinson visited the huts and wished the men a Merry Christmas. Plum puddings came up with the rations and the Expeditionary Force Canteen in Poperinghe provided a few more delicacies. Undisturbed by enemy guns the Battalion was able to celebrate its first Christmas on active service. It remained in reserve until the 27th December when it relieved the 5th Battalion The Border Regiment in trenches A7 to A12. The 28th to 30th December were fairly quiet days, except for some enemy artillery activity, and the opportunity was taken to improve the drainage and to repair trenches. The enemy shelled Trench A7 and one of our machine-gun emplacements on the 31st December. Private C. Riley of New Shildon, was killed. Private Greenwood was wounded. Both were in 'Z' Company. On this day relief was carried out by the 5 Border Regiment, and the Battalion moved back into reserve in Maple Copse. 'Y' Company went into Redoubts, 2,3 and 4. 'Z' Company were in dugouts in Sanctuary Wood. 'X' Company remained in Maple Copse, with 'W' Company in the Canal Dugouts. The New Year was signalled in by a five minute artillery strafe of the enemy positions by the divisional artillery.

The 6th Battalion remained in Brigade Reserve for the first three days of January, 1916. There was the usual enemy artillery activity, none of which disturbed the Battalion to any degree. Captain R.B. Bradford left the Battalion to take up the appointment of 151 Brigade Major. Second-Lieutenant C.E. Yaldwyn became adjutant in his place. It was about this time that the Battalion trench magazine *The Whizz Bang* was created, edited by Second-Lieutenant Yaldwyn, illustrations by Lieutenant C.H.B. Catford. A monthly issue, it was to run for the whole of 1916, when publication ceased. Written in a somewhat light hearted vein, nevertheless it gives an insight into the activities of the Battalion and the conditions in which it served. A mixture of articles, letters, poems and sketch drawings of officers, its publication was looked forward to with keen anticipation by officers and men and it did much to relieve the monotony of trench life.

One of *The Whizz Bang* early issues contained the following description of Sanctuary Wood where the Battalion now lay:

'...In one corner of the wood is a cemetery, with rows of wooden crosses to mark the graves of fallen heroes ... Strange and often ground all around, sending up great columns of black smoke and earth, and flinging death-dealing pieces of shell case screaming and hissing in all directions, snapping the branches of the trees, hitting their trunks with sickening thud, or falling with sudden noise into the ground. The wood has become a kind of inferno full of fire, and moans, and strange noises, which echo and re-echo through the long columns of trees ... There is not a tree in the wood but has the scars of war upon it. Often the upper part of the tree has broken off, the branches are rent away, the trunks are full of holes made by bullets and shell fragments, and in many places are splintered in such a way that the splinters stand out as though in imitation of a bursting shell. At night bullets whistle and crack through the air, and innumerable rats run about the ground squeaking and scratching, and the trees sigh in the wind as though bemoaning the folly of man which has wrought such destruction beneath their shade, and sorrowing for the brave dead round whose brainless skulls their roots entwine.'

A draft of fifty men was received on the 2nd January, from the 3rd Entrenching Battalion. Although fit-looking specimens, six of them were found to have scabies and had to be sent to hospital. Captain F. Walton and Lieutenant S.D. Thorpe arrived from England and rejoined the Battalion after recovering from wounds received on 26th April, 1915.

On the 4th January, the Battalion relieved the 5th Border Regiment in Trenches A7 to A12. It remained in these trenches until the 9th January when relieved by the 5th Borders, and returned to Dickebusch. This tour was marked by intermittent, yet accurate enemy artillery fire. Private R. Robinson was wounded and Private M. Vickerstaffe of Spennymoor was killed in Trench A7, both on the 5th January. Private G.W. Whitfield was wounded on the 7th of the month and Private M. Lowes of Lanchester was killed the following day. Casualties remained low largely due to the heightening of the trenches and the rebuilding of traverses which strengthened the positions.

Until the 13th January when the Battalion was back in the front line trenches, much of the time was taken up by inspections of clothing, equipment and weapons. On this day, Lieutenants W.P. Gill and H.H. Nicholson rejoined after recovery from sickness and wounds respectively, and Second-Lieutenant Freeman

Appeared in the Battalion trench magazine, **The Whizz Bang***, drawn by Lieutenant C.H.B. Catford who was later killed in action*

horrible sounds re-echo through that wood now. Shells shriek and moan through the air, and the roar of guns rumbles through the wood like terrible thunder ... The air is full of awful noises, the ground is continually vibrating, shells are bursting in the reported on joining the Battalion. Private H. Coulthard, from Stanhope, was wounded by a sniper on the 14th January. He died of his wounds shortly afterwards. Crab Crawl Communication Trench, which was no more than a very wet ditch in December, was deepened and improved by Battalion working parties. A draft of sixty-seven other ranks under Second-Lieutenant V.J.R. Clarke arrived at Dickebusch Huts on the 15th of the month.

The following day, notification was received of honours and awards made to members of the Battalion. These included:

Lieutenant-Colonel J.W. Jeffreys	*Distinguished Service Order.*
Lieutenant-Colonel G.A. Stevens	*Distinguished Service Order.*
Lieutenant W.P. Gill	*Military Cross.*
Lieutenant (ex CSM) H. McNair	*Distinguished Conduct Medal.*
Regimental Sergeant-Major G. Perry	
	Distinguished Conduct Medal.
Regimental Sergeant-Major F.H. Bousfield	
	Distinguished Conduct Medal.
Lance-Corporal J.J. Robinson	*Distinguished Conduct Medal.*

Lance-Corporal Robinson's deed is described in the previous chapter. Lieutenant Colonels Jeffreys' and Stevens' awards were for leadership qualities and courageous deeds in many a hot corner in 1915, the latter mainly with the 8th Battalion. Lieutenant Gill's award was for gallant and distinguished conduct during the period 26th to 30th April, 1915; ex-Company Sergeant-Majors McNair and Bousfield for distinguished conduct and good example over the period that the Battalion had been in France. McNair took a commission and Bousfield became Regimental Sergeant-Major to the 9th Battalion. Regimental Sergeant-Major Perry's citation read:

'For conspicuous good and efficient work as Sergeant-Major throughout the campaign, always displaying great coolness,

courage and devotion to duty, and giving a fine example to all ranks.'

Regimental Sergeant-Major Perry had been a tower of strength to all ranks. Always cool in the most dangerous situations he was the very epitome of the British regular sergeant-major. His commanding presence was an example and source of comfort to all ranks. He was of the opinion that the Battalion held the record of having the oldest soldier with continuous service in France, namely himself, with thirty-two years' soldiering behind him.

Company Sergeant-Major B. Bennison was informed on 17th January, that his promotion to Second-Lieutenant had been approved. In anticipation of the enemy's artillery reply to a British bombardment which was about to begin, the front line trenches were thinned out. This precaution saved many casualties as the German response to our bombardment was vigorous and severe. The whole of our front line including Sanctuary Wood was heavily shelled. Captain Cardew was wounded. Captain E. White, the Battalion Medical Officer, braved the heavy enemy shellfire to go to him and bind his wound. Casualties were surprisingly light. Private J. Cranney of Gateshead was killed, and four men wounded, all of 'Z' Company. As night drew in, the Battalion was relieved by the 5th Borders.

The Battalion was now in reserve in the Maple Copse area. It was far from safe here. On the 19th January, a platoon of 'W' Company in No. 2 Redoubt was heavily shelled. Private W. Stephenson of Bishop Auckland, was killed. Sergeant Hogg, Lance-Corporal Quickmire, and two other ranks were wounded. Second-Lieutenant Wilson, Company Sergeant-Major Walton and Bugler Scrafton showed complete disregard for their own safety during the enemy bombardment by attending to the wounded and rallying the men. Evidently, the British artillery's reply to the enemy fire was relatively ineffective due to a large percentage of duds among its 8in. shells.

The Battalion relieved the 5th Borders in Trenches A7 to A12 on the 21st January. Private Appleby was killed by a shell on the following day. Except for the usual shelling, this four day tour was surprisingly quiet and the men were put to work repairing and strengthening the trenches. At the end of their four days in the line, the Battalion was relieved by the 5th Borders and went into Divisional Reserve at Dickebusch. Over the next four days there were medical inspections and the companies were marched to baths in Poperinghe. Two officers and forty-one other ranks went on leave to England. When a territorial soldier reached the end of his engagement he could elect to return to England and civilian life. No doubt a number of men did so, though with the institution of conscription in January, 1916, they would find themselves back in the forces, probably in another unit and away from their friends. However, when their engagements were completed, men were encouraged to re-engage. On the 25th January, twenty-three NCOs and men were granted one month's special leave for signing on to stay with the Battalion.

The Battalion went back into Sanctuary Wood and Trenches A7 to A12, on the 29th January, again relieving the 5th Borders. It was damp and foggy weather with an easterly wind blowing from the German lines opposite. Whenever a wind blew from this direction gas precautions had to be taken. However the Germans remained relatively quiet. Private Atkinson of 'X' Company and Private Blackburn of 'Y' Company, were both wounded whilst wiring in front of the trenches. Life in the trenches in winter was far from comfortable and tested the morale and discipline of all ranks. Biting winds, heavy rain or snowfalls, and severe frosts made for the most trying conditions with which the men had to cope. However the British soldier in general, and the Durham soldier in particular,

Another Catford Cartoon for the **Whizz Bang**

seem to have a genius for minimising the worst effects of difficult conditions. A combination of humour, copious cups of hot tea, and the occasional issue of rum, together with a hot meal, did wonders in raising the spirits of the men. Each group of men seemed to have at least one 'scrounger' - a member with the innate ability to find materials for making dugouts more safe and comfortable, and finding food and fuel. The comfort of letters and parcels from home, the latter shared with close comrades, did much for personal and unit morale. Officers, on the whole, seemed to fare a little better than the men. The following is a letter from Lieutenant Cyril Catford, Battalion Sniper Officer, to his mother dated 1st February, 1916:

'We are having much colder weather out here now as the wind is in the East. The situation is pretty quiet for the part of the line. Last night we had quite a "do" in my dug-out. One of the Gunner Officers came round to dinner and for the Front Line Trenches in the most deadly sector in the line. Turtle Soup, meat and two vegetables and Apricots and Cream washed down with Whiskey and Perrier consumed from glasses isn't bad is it?

'Of course this was one of the occasions when my Mess Sergeant managed to buy me some stuff at P[operinghe] and sent it up to the trenches ... The greatest nuisance out here is the lack of fuel. However I get a couple of my men chopping up wood and manage to burn logs in my stove when it is very cold...'

The Battalion remained in the trenches until 2nd February when, relieved by the 5th Borders, it moved into support. 'W' Company had one platoon in R1, central, and three platoons in dugouts supporting A4 and A5. 'X' Company moved into dugouts in Vigo Street Communication Trench. 'Z' Company were in R2 to R4. The 50th Divisional sector was now divided into two sub-sectors, with 'W' and 'X' Companies in the right one under the direct command of Colonel Hedley of the 5th Borders. 'Y' Company was in the left sub-sector under the direct command of Colonel Henderson, 9th DLI. Battalion Headquarters was in Maple Copse. Working parties were found both day and night. Lance-Corporal T. Brown and Private A. Long of 'W' Company were both wounded whilst on working parties. The weather improved and this encouraged enemy aircraft to appear above the British lines, spotting for their artillery. On the 5th February, Privates R. Grant, J. Rutherford, G.T. Johnson, and H. Reed were slightly wounded by enemy shell fire whilst in Sanctuary Wood. Their position had been given away by smoking fires, spotted by circling enemy aircraft. Sergeant A.R. Bainbridge who enlisted at Stanley, Crook, was shot and killed by a sniper. Private J.R. Stafford, 'Z' Company, from Consett, was shot through the head and killed whilst working on a light railway at Maple Copse Dump.

The Battalion relieved the 5th Borders on the 6th February and the companies took up the following positions: 'W' Company in trenches A4 and A5; 'Z' Company in A6 to A7; 'Y' Company in A8 to A9; 'X' Company in A10 to A11. On the following day, enemy shelling caused the inevitable casualties. Private R.H. Adamson, 'Y' Company, of Rookhope, was killed. Corporal Denham and Private N. Coulthard were wounded. The 8th February was a day of heavy enemy shelling, falling very largely on the support areas. Gas shells were fired into Ypres and Zillebeke. Enemy aircraft were most audacious, flying very low over the trenches and positions, spotting for their artillery. Rifle and machine-gun fire failed to drive them off. Private J. J. Gill, 'Y' Company, of Alston, Cumberland, and Private W. Marley, 'X' Company, of Tow Law, were killed whilst sitting in a dugout in Sanctuary Wood. Private J. Angus was wounded. Private W.D. Parry was wounded whilst on guard near Battalion Headquarters. Enemy artillery remained very active throughout the night. On this same day, 8th February, Battalion Orders contained the following announcement:

> 'The Commanding Officer [Lieutenant-Colonel G.A. Stevens] has much pleasure in bringing to the notice of the Battalion, the gallant conduct of Corporal Hann. During this afternoon, when Sanctuary Wood was heavily shelled, Corporal Hann, with total disregard for his own safety, thinking some of the dugouts might have been hit, went round the dugouts to ascertain if there were any casualties.'

Corporal Hann, a Battalion stretcher-bearer, was from Bishop Auckland and had come over to France in April, 1915. He had been wounded twice, though recovering from these in France, and had only been home to England once on seven days' leave.

Artillery fire continued at intervals from both sides throughout the 9th February. German guns seemed to be concentrating on the back areas. Lieutenant Catford wrote to his mother on this day:

> '...We have been indulging in a good deal of "Strafing" lately and owing to the most unfortunate fact that for the moment the Bosche has superiority in the Air we have had a very bad time, the worst since our first few days up here. Their wretched planes are an awful nuisance and the wonder is they don't land in our dug-out and the Bosche airmen get out and come in and have tea...'

Enemy artillery fire continued on the following day, again seeking out the back areas. The Battalion was relieved by the 5th Borders and went into Brigade Reserve with 'W' Company in Maple Copse, and 'X', 'Y' and 'Z' Companies, and Battalion HQ, in Railway Dugouts. At this stage of the war these dugouts had been improved until they offered good and comfortable shelter. They were dug into the embankment of the Ypres - Comines Railway, a short distance south of Zillebeke Lake, close to Shrapnel Corner. The 11th February was a relatively quiet day with working parties out in Sanctuary Wood and at Brigade HQ. A German gun nicknamed 'Silent Susie' by the troops, fired on Battalion Headquarters. Colonel Stevens and Regimental Sergeant-Major Perry had a lucky escape when a piece of shrapnel flew between them. A very heavy German bombardment was opened on the following day, to the left of the Hooge sector, lasting from the afternoon till dusk. No infantry attacks were made. The Battalion was relieved by a Northumberland Fusiliers Battalion of 149 Brigade, and the companies marched to Canada Huts at Dickebusche.

The effects of stress after long periods in the line were touched upon by Lieutenant Catford in a letter to his mother dated 11th February:

'...After a time war gets on one's nerves a little, anyway in this place. The incessant row, the constant and terrific shocks of shells bursting close by and the strain of being always on the "qui vive" are bound to tell in time even on the strongest of us...'

Courage is not unlimited. A great deal of it is used up in the initial drive and enthusiasm of the soldier facing his first actions. As men survive successive actions and, having seen their comrades killed and wounded, they begin to temper outright boldness with caution. The feeling that the longer they survived the more chance of being killed or wounded became strong with some men. A kind of 'battlefield law of averages' held sway. Yet, on the other hand, some men untouched by bullet or shell, began to feel they were invincible. Caution did not mean that a man had used up his supply of courage. It meant that he became more aware of what was possible; experience had taught him when to drop, for example, and when to move. But move he did. However the amount of courage a soldier had to draw on, differed from man to man and some cracked under the strain before others. The army in the First World War could deal harshly with those who did crack, in contrast with their comrades who, though stronger, invariably understood and sympathised.

On the 13th February, the Battalion rest was disturbed, first, by enemy aircraft who bombed their camp. Colonel Stevens had yet another narrow escape from a 13-pounder bomb which dropped near him and failed to explode. In the evening the Battalion was ordered to 'Stand To' and be ready to move at half an hour's notice. The Germans were making every effort to capture 'The Bluff', an artificial hill constructed from the spoil dug out when building the Ypres - Comines Canal. The enemy's main assault against this strong point went in on the 14th and 15th February and was successful. 151 Brigade was in V Corps Reserve, and from the 14th to 17th February, was standing to, ready to counter-attack if needed. It was a difficult time for the 6th Battalion, which was below strength. Absences due to leave, wounds and sickness placed additional burdens on officers and men. Lieutenant Catford's letter to his mother dated 15th February, 1916, stated:

'...I think I shall have to add the word "Ubique" after my name. Today the CO sent for me and told me that I should be placed in Command of the machine-guns in case of an attack. The machine-gun Officer is away on leave and so I am let in for it ... I get a lot of extra work and that means less rest. I have now under my command (1) a platoon, (2) 21 snipers, and (3) 4 machine-guns and a machine-gun Section of 35 men. I doubt there is another officer in France who has such a varied command...'

Relieved by 149 Brigade on the 18th February, the Battalion moved into Trenches 48, 49, 50 and A1 to A5 and Armagh Dugouts. Further relieved on the night of 18-19th by the 4th Battalion The Yorkshire Regiment, it moved to Mount Sorrell and into Trenches 49 to A3. Armagh Wood and Trenches A1 to A3 were heavily bombarded by enemy guns on the 20th February. Captain Gill was slightly wounded by a piece of periscope glass which was hit by a sniper's bullet as he used it. Enemy aircraft were again active. An ominous entry appeared in the Battalion war diary: 'The health of the men shows signs of deterioration.' A very long spell in or close to the front line in an evil area of the Salient was beginning to have its toll. Private A. Best, Lewis Gunner, was wounded on the 21st of the month. Private Gibson, Lewis Gunner, was wounded on the following day. The Battalion was relieved by the 5th Borders and went into close support. It remained in support until it relieved the 5th Borders on Mount Sorrell on the 26th February. The weather was cold and frosty with some falls of snow. A draft of seventy-one other ranks, commanded by Lieutenant Angus, was received from the Base. Fifteen of these were sick or wounded who were returning from Base or hospitals in England. The physique of these men was fairly good. The fighting strength of the Battalion was now twenty-four officers and seven hundred and forty-two NCOs and other ranks.

The relief was carried out, as usual, at night, and was not completed until the early hours of the morning of the 27th February. On the Battalion right was the 8th DLI, and on its left,

4th Battalion The Yorkshire Regiment. News was received of the German offensive at Verdun and that they had suffered huge losses in the first hours of their attack against the French. The Salient remained unusually quiet. It did not last long. Very heavy enemy mortaring of the trenches broke out on the following day, which did serious damage to trenches and caused casualties. Sergeant W.E. Johnson of Low Hartforth, who enlisted at Barnard Castle, was killed. Others killed were Private M. Duffy, who enlisted at Bishop Auckland and was a member of the draft received on the 25th February; Private C.H. Gill of Consett, a Battalion grenadier, and Private A. Adamson who had enlisted at Crook. The wounded were Sergeant R. Dixon; Lance-Corporal R. Newton; Privates E. Jones (grenadier); P. Robinson; D. Fitzgerald; J.A. Hunter, and M. Hunter. British artillery retaliated and both sides' bombardments quietened towards evening, only to break out with renewed violence about 8.30 p.m. A report was received that the enemy were massing behind Sanctuary Wood and might attack. The 8.30 p.m. bombardment was thought to indicate that an attack by the Germans was about to start and, as Zillebeke and area was receiving the greatest enemy attention, this could be where the attack would come in. The attack did not materialise but Battalion casualties for the day increased when Private J. Marsh of Crook was killed whilst working on the light railway. Private J. Carter of 'Z' Company was wounded. The artillery contest was renewed on the 29th, fortunately without further casualties and by nightfall, quietness had descended and held throughout the hours of darkness.

The Battalion, along with the others of 151 Brigade and indeed the 50th Division, was showing its customary stubbornness and stamina after a long spell in the line, support and reserve positions under winter conditions and subjected to German artillery and mortar bombardments as outlined above. Snipers were ever present and casualties built up. On the 1st March, 1916, Brigadier General Shea sent the following message to Lieutenant-Colonel Stevens:

> 'I congratulate you on the admirable spirit which is being displayed by your Battalion under very trying circumstances. Please tell all ranks how very pleased I am with them all round.'

It was most imperative that The Bluff, captured by the Germans on 15th February, 1916, should be recaptured. This task was assigned to the 17th Division, the attack to take place on the 2nd March. The 6th Battalion was ordered to concentrate during the night 1st-2nd March, on Mount Sorrell and, along with the rest of the 151 Brigade, make it appear that an attack was to be made on the German trenches opposite. A preliminary bombardment of the German trenches commenced at 5.00 p.m., to which the enemy guns immediately retaliated. This continued for two hours when all activity ceased. Battalion casualties were one killed and thirteen wounded. At 3.45 a.m., on the 2nd March, with the 17th Division attack on The Bluff due, the Battalion stood to. At 4.00 a.m. a bombardment of the enemy positions in front began and trench mortars were fired off at the German Salient, The Snout, The Caterpillar and Hill 60. The Germans predictably retaliated but casualties were light, and only three men were wounded. The artillery of both sides were still active as the Battalion was relieved by 6th Battalion Northumberland Fusiliers, and marched back to Canada Huts, Dickebusch, completed at 11.30 p.m.

The Battalion remained in Canada Huts for the next two days. On the 5th March, the whole Brigade was ordered to move into close support and the companies of the 6th Battalion were distributed as follows: HQ and 'Y' Company in Armagh Wood; 'W' Company and half of 'X' Company at Blauwepoort Farm; the other half of 'X' Company in Railway Dugouts; 'Z' Company were accommodated in dugouts. The Battalion remained in close support until the 8th March. It had a quiet time. The weather was cold and dry except for the odd heavy snowstorm. Relieved by the 8th Durhams, the Battalion moved to 'B' Huts, Dickebusch. The next five days passed quietly. Captains Townend and Barkas returned from England on the 10th of the month and on the 13th a Brigade concert was held with the 6th and 8th Battalions providing the entertainment and the 7th Battalion band played. The onset of spring weather lifted everyone's spirits. On the 14th of the month, the Battalion relieved the 5th Northumberland Fusiliers in the Mount Sorrell trenches, which were found to be in a very bad state of repair following recent enemy bombardments. The four day spell in the trenches were quiet and uneventful and allowed essential repairs to be undertaken. Relieved by the 5th

Battalion The Yorkshire Regiment on the 17th March, the Battalion entrained for Poperinghe where headquarters and companies were billeted in the Rue de Ypres, Rue de Messines and Rue de Cemetière. Three days were spent in cleaning themselves and equipment until, on the 23rd March, the Battalion again entrained at 6.45 p.m. and moved to the Asylum in Ypres where it marched on to relieve the 10th Royal Welsh Fusiliers in the Bluff trenches. Relief was completed by 11.00 p.m. The companies were disposed as follows: 'Z' Company was in The Bean; 'X' Company was in International and New Year Trenches; 'W' Company was in The Loop; 'Y' Company was in the support lines and Gordon Post.

The Bluff measured some thirty to forty feet high and three hundred yards in length. Captured by the Germans on 15th February, it had been recaptured on the 2nd March. Peace time trees had been torn by shot and shell and reduced to stumps. The thickly tangled undergrowth hid bodies of the dead of both sides. Hurriedly dug trenches criss-crossed the surface, which was heavily pock-marked by shell and mine craters. The main crater site was situated at the north-eastern corner of The Bluff, close to The Bean. This mine had been blown by the Germans on the 14th February when they made their successful attack and drove the British off The Bluff. Dugouts had been blown in along with the men occupying them. Bodies were still being removed from this area when the Battalion took over. The trenches were in a very bad state and immediate repair, cleaning up and strengthening was ordered. Bodies discovered were removed and buried. The Battalion grenadiers occupied several bombing posts at the crater from which they exacted retribution upon the German occupants of nearby trenches. These bombing posts could only be relieved at night. The enemy, in fact, was actively employed in repairing and strengthening his own positions and remained quiet during the Battalion's tour. Only snipers were active and care had to be taken in moving around in daylight. On relief by the 8th Durhams on the 26th March, the Battalion, less 'Y' Company, went into Brigade Reserve and occupied Kingsway and Gordon Terrace Dugouts. 'Y' Company remained with the 8th Battalion. In reserve for the next four days, the Battalion had a quiet time in fine spring weather. On the 30th March, it relieved the 8th Battalion in the same front line positions.

Enemy bombardments over the next three days reached a crescendo on the 2nd April. The German guns had the exact range of the Brigade positions and from 2.00 p.m. onwards subjected the trenches and dugouts to a severe pounding. Gordon Post and Brigade HQ suffered particularly. All dugouts except those occupied by the signallers and the dressing station, were either very badly damaged or destroyed. Captain Harter, Brigade-Major, out and about the trenches with Brigadier-General Shea, was mortally wounded. Brigadier General Shea escaped unscathed. The trenches held by the Battalion were wrecked and casualties were kept to a minimum by skilful evacuation organised by company commanders. The Battalion lost six men killed or wounded at The Dump and Langhof Chateau. A great deal of kit was lost either by direct hit, or by the killed or wounded, or because it was not possible to reach it due to the heavy and continuous bombardment. On the night 2nd-3rd April, the Battalion was relieved by 1st Battalion, 1st Division, Canadian Corps. The movement of headquarters from the line was delayed as the relief could not reach them for some time. After the relief, it was only with the very greatest difficulty that Lieutenant-Colonel Stevens, Major F. Walton, (second in command), Captain E. White (Medical Officer), and the acting adjutant, were able to make their way through the wrecked dugouts of Kingsway, and the severely damaged trench tramway to Langhof Chateau, and then via The Dump to Dickebusch.

On the 4th April, the Battalion moved to Scottish Lines arriving at 10.00 a.m. Brigadier General Shea sent his congratulations to the Battalion for the manner in which it had held its position and its bearing during the time it had been in the Ypres Salient, which dated from 17th December, 1915. His message stated that he would give them the highest compliment which any soldier could receive 'Men, you are good soldiers'.

CHAPTER 7
MONT DES CATS - VIERSTRAAT - KEMMELL
1916

The following day, the Battalion moved to La Clytte, which was a divisional rest area. This village lay on the main road between Reninghelst and Kemmel. Behind the lines, the area was largely under cultivation and some of the farms were still occupied by the farmers. The Brigade reserve position was in Ridgewood which, though only just over a mile from the front, was a relatively quiet area, and experienced very little shelling. The trees were little damaged and enabled men to move about in relative safety. Dugouts were comfortable and clean and the YMCA had even set up a canteen in a large dugout in the middle of the wood.

Kit inspections and the replacement of lost items took up most of the 6th and 7th April. The Bois Carre and Brasserie defences, the trenches numbered N3 to O4, were taken over on the 8th April, with 8th Battalion on the right and the Canadians on the left at St. Eloi. The trenches were breastworks and were found to be in very poor condition and not even bullet proof. The parados hardly existed to protect against back blast from shells which just cleared the trench. There were few dugouts and those that did exist were in very poor condition. Once again the Durhams were faced with an urgent trench construction problem which they took on with their usual skill and enthusiasm. It was as well that they did. In the early hours of the 9th April, the Canadians on the left attacked the St. Eloi Ridge and craters. The Battalion Lewis guns joined in and fired on the German trenches in front. The Germans retaliated with artillery and mortar fire on the front line supports and communication trenches. Considerable damage was done and a number of men were wounded. British artillery replied with some success, causing damage to German trenches opposite. Canadian attacks at St. Eloi continued until the 16th April. As what appeared to be part of the German retaliation for this action the enemy artillery continued to shell the front line held by 151 Brigade. This sector had always been considered a quiet area and it was most unfortunate that the Brigade suffered in this way.

The Battalion was relieved by the 9th Battalion at about 11.00 p.m. on the 11th April, and moved into Brigade reserve in Ridgewood. One company under Captain S. Thorpe was in dugouts between the GHQ Line and the Dickebusch-Vierstraat road. The 12th and 13th April were relatively quiet, disturbed occasionally by some enemy shelling. The weather was exceedingly good and encouraged German aircraft to put in an appearance over the British positions. These were chased off by our aeroplanes on the 14th April. At 9.00 p.m. on this date, the Battalion relieved the 8th Battalion and moved into divisional reserve at La Clytte. Three days' rest and quiet followed and on 17th April, the Battalion moved to Brigade reserve in Ridgewood. On the night of 20th-21st April, it relieved the 9th Battalion in N to O Trenches. The Germans commenced a bombardment of Battalion Headquarters, near Brasserie. Sergeant W. O'Dair, Orderly Room Sergeant, was severely wounded. Private Ryder, stretcher-bearer, dressed his wounds and took him to the dressing station. There were nine casualties in total. The Canadians lost almost all of the gains at St. Eloi in severe fighting on the 21st April. The enemy continued to shell Bois Carre and M, N and O Trenches, as part of this counter action. This heavy shelling continued the next day, with British artillery countering with vigour. The Battalion was relieved by the 7th Battalion The King's Shropshire Light Infantry, 3rd Division, and moved to Ridge Wood. The following night, relieved by 8th Battalion The East Yorkshire Regiment, also of the 3rd Division, the Battalion marched to billets in the area east and south-east of Berthen. Here, on the 24th of the month, an intensive training programme was commenced, which was to last until the 8th of May. On the 26th April, Lieutenant-Colonel Stevens was transferred to 8th Canadian Brigade as Brigade Major Lieutenant-Colonel Jeffreys resumed command of the Battalion on recovering from his wounds sustained the previous December.

For the first seven days of May the Battalion continued its training. This included a route march on the 2nd of the month. The distance was over eight miles and, as some of the route was cobbled, it turned out to be not only strenuous but painful on the feet. Six or seven men fell out. After a very long spell in the trenches, it was now obvious that the Battalion was not fit for marching. On the 8th May, the Battalion marched, in rain, to La Clytte. It remained here until the 12th May, providing two parties of one hundred and thirty men each to work on the Vierstraat Switch. The parties were paraded for 7.30 p.m. and 8.15 p.m., and were out digging until 2.30 a.m. This work was continued until 12th May, when the Battalion marched eight miles to billets round Mont des Cats, close to Berthen, and in the Bailleul area. It was a hot day and the march proved too much for fifteen men, who had to drop out. On arrival, all officers were ordered to attend a brigade riding school.

The Mont des Cats was one of the prominent hills which reached from Cassel in the west to Kemmel in the east. A Trappist Monastery crowned the top of the hill and was still occupied by the monks too old to serve in their country's army. On the south and west sides, the walls bore the marks of shell and bullet, resulting from the actions of 1914. The view from the top of the hill stretched across the Flanders Plain and, on a clear day, the view stretched to the coast from Boulogne to Ostend. The Salient lay in the foreground with the smoke from exploding shells drifting in the air. British and enemy lines could be clearly seen. The village of Berthen lay at the foot of the hill, with

Bailleul some three miles distant. It was, in the spring of 1916, a quiet and pleasant area which had recovered from any damage sustained in 1914.

The Battalion rested in this area until the 28th of the month. It was training, marching, relaxing and playing inter-Battalion football, which resulted in it winning the Brigade football competition. On the 16th May, the Battalion lost Brigadier General Shea who left to command the 30th New Army Division. A strict, though very fair disciplinarian, Brigadier-General Shea was highly respected by all ranks. He had led from the front and could almost always be found in the tightest of spots, encouraging officers and men. On this day, he came to say farewell to the Brigade. He had called his men 'Tigers' and it was a name to which every man in the Brigade was proud to answer. Sergeant Smith won the heavyweight title at the Brigade boxing tournament on 20th May, with Sergeant Malpass taking the middleweight title both, of course, 6th Battalion men. Brigadier-General P.T. Westmorland arrived to take over command of the Brigade on the 21st of the month. Lieutenant-General Sir Hubert Plumer, GOC Second Army, gave medals to officers and men of 50th Division, awarded for distinguished service. This took place on the 23rd May. On the 28th of the month, the Battalion marched to Ridge Wood and relieved the 7th Battalion The Kings Shropshire Light Infantry, in Brigade reserve. The trenches held stretched from near St. Eloi to opposite Vierstraat. The following day, three hundred and fifty men of the Battalion were provided for parties to work on the trenches. Privates Brown and Chapman were wounded whilst out on a working party in Trench N11. In Ridgewood, which was some eleven miles from the German lines, the Battalion was billeted in wooden huts which protected them from the weather but were not bullet-proof. Excellent dugouts, with French steel framework, were dug here during the Battalion's stay.

The Battalion remained in reserve until the 2nd June. This day commenced with a very heavy enemy bombardment of the Ypres Salient, which commenced at about 8.30 a.m. and ceased about 1.30 p.m. During the evening, the Battalion was relieved by 5th Battalion Border Regiment and, in its turn, relieved the 9th Battlion DLI in the front line trenches N3 to O4. HQ was close to

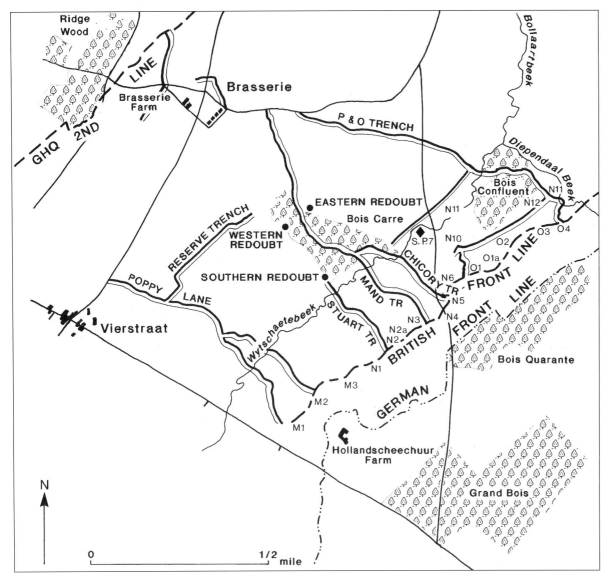

Ridge Wood

LINE

Brasserie

Brasserie Farm

GHQ 2ND

P & O TRENCH

Bollaartbeek

Diependaal Beek

Bois Confluent

N11

N12

RESERVE TRENCH

EASTERN REDOUBT

Bois Carre

N11

N10

O2 O3 O4

WESTERN REDOUBT

S. P.7

O1a

O1

FRONT LINE

SOUTHERN REDOUBT

CHICORY TR

N6

POPPY

LANE

MAND TR

N5

Wytschaetebeek

STUART TR

N4

N3

FRONT

Vierstraat

N2a

N2

BRITISH

LINE

N1

Bois Quarante

M3

GERMAN

M2

M1

Hollandscheechuur Farm

Grand Bois

N

0   1/2 mile

Vierstraat Sector - 1916.

the Brasserie and the companies disposed as follows: 'Y' Company N3 to O1 with one platoon in N12 bombers post; 'X' Company O1A to O4 with one platoon in N12 left; 'W' Company in Bois Carre; 'Z' Company in the Brasserie N11 to SP7. A heavy enemy bombardment of the Salient commenced just after midnight and lasted for one hour. A tremendous enemy artillery and mortar bombardment was opened on the 2nd June on the Canadian positions in Sanctuary Wood and on Mount Sorrell. In the ensuing German infantry attack most of the Wood and the Mount Sorrell position were lost: a setback of some interest to the Durhams who had held these positions in the recent past. They were, in fact, recaptured by the Canadians on the 13th June.

On the 3rd June, Second-Lieutenants Barnet, Du Mosch, Harvey, D.F. Charlton, W.F. Charlton and Appleby arrived on draft from England. The following day Second-Lieutenant Ebsworth, of the East Lancashire Regiment, joined the Battalion and took over as Adjutant. He was to serve the Battalion with distinction. Corporal Lean, Second Battalion King Edward's Horse, was transferred to the Battalion as a Second-Lieutenant. He was immediately sent off to England to get officer's clothing. Second-Lieutenant Meyer joined the Battalion on the 6th June. He had come over from South Africa where he had seen action against the Germans in the West African campaign. Second-Lieutenant G.B. Wilson joined the following day.

The Battalion was relieved by the 9th Battalion, the relief being completed by 10.30 p.m. The men marched to Durham Huts, La Clytte, in pouring rain. In reserve, once again the usual working parties had to be found each night. The parties were between one hundred and forty and two hundred and forty strong. The weather over the period was wet and digging under these conditions during the major part of each night, was particularly hard on the men - and there were casualties. Second-Lieutenant Meyer, who had joined the Battalion on the 6th June, was killed whilst in charge of a working party just behind the front line. He was buried the following day in the soldiers' cemetery, with full military honours. Lieutenant-Colonel Jeffreys wrote to Colonel Watson on the 14th June:

> '...We are jogging along quite well. Abominably weak. 300 under strength and an awful amount of digging to be done.

'Have had nine officers sent out lately. Ebsworth, late drill sergeant in the Grenadier Guards, Regimental Sergeant-Major and later Second-Lieutenant in the East Lancashire Regt. is doing adjutant, since 4th June. 7 boys came out from your 2nd Line. Very good chaps. About the best of them - Meyer - was shot through the head 3 days after when on a working party ... The first time he had been in rifle range of the enemy. Bad business wasn't it ... We have been in Divisional Reserve for 6 days and go back to the front line tonight. They tell me the trenches are all falling in on account of the down pour of rain we've had in the last 6 days.'

The Battalion did move up to the front line on the 14th June, relieving the 9th Battalion in Trenches N3 to N6, O1 to O4; Southern, Eastern and Western Redoubts; S.P.7; Bois Carre dugouts and the Brasserie defences. The relief was completed by 10.30 p.m. Half an hour later, in accordance with the provisions of the Daylight Saving Bill, all watches were put forward one hour.

Whilst casualties and sickness amongst the officers and men had caused many changes to personnel there were still a number of the original complement of the Batt[alion] present. One of these, Private T. Parkin of Barnard Castle, wrote to Mrs Watson on the 16th June, 1916. In it he described his experiences and hopes:

> '...I was highly pleased with the contents of the parcel, it was just the right sort of parcel for a fellow in the line, a piece of cake and a few tabs. I was in the trenches when I got it so you see it came at a right time ... I have now been out here about 14 months. I came out with the Battalion of which your husband Mrs Watson was in command and I can honestly tell you that I have seen a lot of changes since we left old England. I have never missed a trench with the Batt[alion], only one and that was when I got my leave to Bd. Castle after been 12 months out here. I have never been sick while I have been out and I have been very lucky. I have had the experience of being blown up by the Germans while doing some night work in a crater. I was buried up in earth, so you see I have had a share. All I pray for now is that the Lord above will watch over me in the future like what he has done in the past and bring me safely back to my wife and little one at home which I hope will not be long...'

Although enemy bombardments continued in the Salient and

on positions to the south, the Battalion front had a relatively quiet time until the 18th June. German guns and trench mortars opened up on the area just behind N and O Trenches and the Battalion bombers' positions. Four men were wounded, fortunately not seriously. The 5th Battalion East Yorkshires on the Battalion left had a desperate time when their positions were almost destroyed by 'Rum Jars', a nickname given by the troops to particularly heavy missiles fired from German trench mortars. Corporal Davison of the Battalion was seriously wounded when in Chicory Communication Trench. A ten-minute enemy bombardment of the front line and communication trenches occurred about midday on the 19th June. No casualties were reported and very little damage was done. The 9th Battalion took over the line on the 20th and the Battalion marched to Ridgewood. The relief was completed by midnight. The officers and men were exceedingly tired. The enemy trench mortars had prevented any sleep by day, and the nights were largely taken up with carrying out repairs to and strengthening trenches damaged by the weather and enemy fire.

At Ridge Wood the inevitable working parties, invariably out at night, made a further claim on the men's depleted energies. The nature of the front line soldier on both sides of No Man's Land was turned around. Sleep had usually to be found during the day. During the hours of darkness the trenches became alive with activities such as trench digging and repairs, wiring, bringing up supplies, patroling and other tasks which could only be carried out under the blanket of darkness. As has been seen so often, working parties worked under dangerous conditions. The sudden flare may reveal them to an alert enemy, and they would be immediately fired on. Experience taught that, once caught in a flare, the soldier should freeze, making no movement, for it is movement which attracts the attention and draws enemy fire. A sudden bombardment might catch a working party unaware and unable to take cover. Noise can give away a working group and bring down fire upon it. Dumps, roads and railways are usual working places, and when sites are identified by the enemy, artillery, rifle and machine-gun fire are brought down upon them. On the 25th June, Private W. Rowe, 'W' Company, who had enlisted at Crook, was killed on a working party. Private Lawson

and Private Wilson were badly wounded. Private Wilson, who enlisted at Coundon Grange, died of his wounds the following day. Private Frank Lawson, who had enlisted at Ferryhill, died of his wounds on the 6th July.

The 9th Battlion was relieved on the 26th June and positions taken up in Trenches N3 to O4. The relief was completed by 11.50 p.m. The Divisional artillery bombarded the enemy lines from 1.30 to 2.30 a.m. and again at 2.45 to 3.15 a.m. on the 27th. The enemy reaction was slight. The Divisional bombardment continued throughout the next day. The following day, mortars of both sides were active as they attempted to silence each other. The last day of the month ended quietly with the wind blowing south and south-west, hence, there was no danger of a gas attack.

On the 24th June one of the greatest artillery bombardments in British military history opened on the Somme. A five day bombardment, extended to seven, it heralded a campaign of fierce fighting which did not cease until the middle of November, 1916. 50th Division's involvement in the battle did not commence until September. Meanwhile the 6th Battalion continued to operate in the Vierstraat sector. The first two days of July were fairly quiet, disturbed only by intermittent mortaring by both sides. On the 2nd July, the Battalion was relieved by the 9th Battalion The Durham Light Infantry, and returned to Durham Huts at La Clytte, which it reached at 2.00 a.m. on the the following morning. Officers and men must have been very tired. The Battalion had spent the last thirty-six days either in the trenches or providing working parties of between two hundred and three hundred men. No digging parties were asked for on the 3rd July, news which was received with much relief and delight by all. However there was no place for idle hands in the Battalion, and cleaning equipment and clothing, and inspections kept all ranks busy. A small number were to be kept even more busy over the next few days.

General Wilkinson, GOC 50th Division, informed Colonel Jeffreys that he wanted the Battalion to make a raid on the enemy positions opposite Trench N4. Here the lines were 80 yards apart. The aim of the raid was to get into the enemy trenches, kill Germans, and bring back prisoners. The party to carry out this most dangerous venture was selected and put under the command of Second-Lieutenant Arnett. The ground, over which the raiding party was to move to reach the German lines, was reconnoitred with considerable care. The raid was fixed for 11.30 p.m on the 6th July. During the intervening two days the raiders practised, watched on the 5th of the month, by the Brigade Commander, Brigadier General Westmorland. The raiding party consisted of Second-Lieutenant Arnett (commanding), Second-Lieutenant Aubin, eighteen NCOs and men of 'Y' Company, and fourteen bombers. At 11.15 p.m. on the 6th July, the party left our lines with the intention of surprising the enemy and breaking into the crater, held by him, on the west side of Bois Carre. The raiders returned at 2.00 a.m. having failed to reach their objective. The enemy were found to be on the alert and manning their parapet. The Battalion relieved the 9th DLI, on the 8th July, and took over Trenches N3 to O4. German minnenwerfers bombarded the trenches on the 9th July, wounding Captain Bennison and three men of 'W' Company. The signallers' dugout was blown in though, fortunately, the occupants escaped without injury. The raiding party made another attempt to reach the enemy positions, leaving Trench N4 at 11.20 p.m. The party bumped into an enemy patrol just in front of our wire. One German was taken prisoner before his patrol made its escape. He was a private in the 215th Reserve Regiment and a painter by trade. Second-Lieutenant Arnett decided to return with the raiding party to his own trench, as he felt that the escaped patrol would give the alarm and the enemy would be very much on the alert. On the following day, congratulations on taking a prisoner were received from Second Army, V Corps and 50th Division. Prisoners were highly prized as they often had vital information on the enemy formations facing our troops.

The next three days were quiet except for an enemy minnenwerfer attack on our trenches on the 11th July. One of these heavy mortar shells exploded unexpectedly and close behind Captain McNair, who fainted in the trench. On the 14th of the month, enemy shell fire on Trench O4 killed Privates J. Corns, who enlisted at Bishop Auckland; E. Lauder, who enlisted at Crook, and T.A. Stokeld, of East Hartlepool; all of 'Y' Company. Sergeant Watson of the same company was wounded. An

officers' patrol was selected to raid the enemy trench opposite N5. It consisted of Second-Lieutenant Arnett (commanding), Second-Lieutenant Aubin, Sergeant Gough, Sergeant Smith, Sergeant Bryant, Lance-Sergeant Thirling, ten bombers, and ten riflemen. The patrol were successful and entered the German trenches. Second-Lieutenant Arnett turned to the left and moved down the trench with a group of the patrol. This section of the trench was in disrepair and unoccupied. Second-Lieutenant Aubin and his group turned right and found themselves face to face with the enemy occupants. A fierce struggle ensued with both sides using bomb, rifle and bayonet. Sergeant Gough was slightly wounded, but there were no other casualties to our soldiers. It was estimated that the Germans suffered four or five casualties. The patrol returned to our trenches highly elated with their success. The Battalion was relieved by 6th Battalion Northumberland Fusiliers, and marched to a camp near Brulooze and Sherpenberg, where it arrived at 3 a.m.

The tented camp was comfortable. A small draft of thirteen other ranks was received from Base on the 16th of the month. On the 17th, Lieutenant-Colonel Jeffreys was sent home on ten days' leave due to ill-health. Major Walton took over as Commanding Officer during the Colonel's absence. A working party of four officers and four hundred and fifty other ranks was found and marched off at 7.15 p.m. The Brigade informed the Battalion on the 18th July that Corporal Dixon of the Signal Section had been awarded the Military Medal. There were no working parties on the following day, and on the 20th the Battalion relieved the 3rd Battalion Rifle Brigade, in reserve at Aircraft Farm. The relief was carried out in daylight. Later in the day the Battalion marched past Brigadier-General Westmorland, at Brigade headquarters at Dranoutre. Band and bugles played *Marching Through Georgia* at the head of a fit looking body of men.

The following six days were spent in repairing and erecting huts at Aircraft Farm, together with the usual working parties, and cleaning and inspections. On the 26th July the Battalion relieved the 8th Durhams in Trenches G1 to G4, in the Kemmel area. The companies were located as follows: 'Z' Company, front line; 'X' Company, SP11 and Albert Dugouts; Two platoons of 'W' Company and the whole of 'Y' Company in Kemmel Chateau.

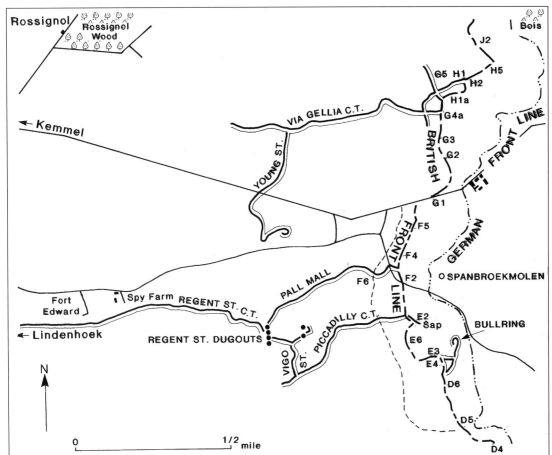

Rossignol

Rossignol Wood

Bois

J2

G5 H1 H5

H2

H1a

VIA GELLIA C.T.

← Kemmel

G4a

BRITISH

G3

G2

FRONT LINE

YOUNG ST.

G1

FRONT LINE

F5

F4

GERMAN

O SPANBROEKMOLEN

PALL MALL

F6

F2

Fort Edward

Spy Farm REGENT ST. C.T.

PICCADILLY C.T.

E2 Sap

BULLRING

← Lindenhoek

REGENT ST. DUGOUTS

E6

E3

E4

VIGO ST.

D6

N

D5

D4

0   1/2 mile

Kemmel Sector
1916.

Captain McNair had continued with his duties following his shock on the 11th July, described above. However in spite of all of his efforts it proved too much for him, and at 2.00 p.m. on the 27th, he collapsed with shock and was taken to hospital. At 2.45 p.m. the Germans launched a heavy trench mortar bombardment on G Trenches, which lasted till 5.15 p.m. It was a particularly trying time for officers and men. Private J. Goodfellow, who had enlisted at Bishop Auckland, was killed, along with Private J.W. Pears of Crook. Both men were Lewis gunners with 'X' Company. Corporal Jackson, Private Mulholland and Lance-Corporal Dodds were wounded. 'X' Company headquarters was blown in, and the support trenches were very badly damaged. Fortunately the front fire trenches received few direct hits and were only slightly damaged. On the 28th July, 'Z' Company were withdrawn from the front line except for two Lewis gunners, one bombing post, and a sniper post which remained occupied, and one sentry group in position. All others were moved back to Kitchen Avenue and Young Street. During the hours of darkness 'Z' Company was relieved in the front line by 'Y' Company. The last three days of the month were quiet. The weather was hot. An expected draft of one hundred and ninety men did not arrive. The opportunity was taken to repair the trenches which had received German attention recently. Private J.G. Carter, who had enlisted at Willington, was killed by a rifle bullet when out on patrol. He was a bomber with 'Y' Company. The company and two platoons at Kemmel Chateau, had a much less active time and made use of the moat which surrounded the house and had water in it, by bathing every day.

When relieved in Trenches G1 to G4 by the 8th DLI, the Battalion had lost three men killed and four wounded during the seven days it occupied the sector. Several men had suffered from shell-shock, particularly from the heavy trench mortar bombardment of the 27th July. The relief was completed at 11.45 p.m., on the 1st August, and the Battalion marched to Wakefield Huts between Westoutre and Locre. The last of the men reached the huts at 2.45 a.m. on the following day. The draft of one hundred and ninety men, expected at the end of the previous month, reached the Battalion on this same day. All of them were Durhams from the second line 6th, 7th, 8th and 9th Battalions. On

the 4th August, secret orders were received at Headquarters that the 50th Division was going into rest, prior to moving down to the Somme front. On this day a further draft of one hundred and fourteen other ranks was received from the 2nd and 3rd line depots. The Battalion remained in Wakefield Huts until the 7th August, when it marched to billets near Mont des Cats and Berthen, the same area it had occupied the previous May. It remained here in pleasant and comfortable billets until the 10th of the month when it marched along a slow and dusty route to Godwaersvelde station which it reached at dusk. At 10.30 p.m. it entrained for Flienvillers-Candas, arriving at about 7.30 p.m. Battalion strength was thirty officers and nine hundred and fifty-four other ranks. On arrival at its destination the Battalion marched to Heauzecourt, arriving at 3.15 p.m. - another hot and dusty route.

The billets in Heauzecourt were quite comfortable and the companies could bathe in the nearby River Outhie. A letter, dated 13th August, from Lieutenant W.P. Tattersall to Colonel Watson, gives a picture of the village after two years of war, and the suffering of the French people:

> '...The village is small, the houses with the exception of one or two are composed mostly of mud!! The church is rickety in the extreme, while its tower vies with that of 'Pisa' almost. The grave-yard is a mass of weeds and tumbledown grave-stones. The inhabitants are wizened and the youngest seems to be quite 75!!! - in short desolation is written all over the place!! Here if anywhere one sees the results of war. The house in which 3 others and myself live is quite comfortable and beautifully clean inside - which is quite a change from the Belgium dwellings. The good lady of the house is a refugee. She lived, as a matter of fact, somewhere in the district which is now the scene of our present operations. The Bosch came suddenly, her house was raised to the ground! her husband killed! and her cattle and poultry stolen! Since then both her sons have fallen - fighting for France - How difficult it is for we British to realise the awfulness of war - !!!...'

CHAPTER 8
THE SOMME
1916

At 3 o'clock on the morning of the 15th August, the Battalion left Heauzecourt and marched fourteen and a half miles to Villers Bocage. The following day it completed an eight-mile march to billets, *en route* to a wood near Baizieux. This wood was reached the following day after marching a further eleven miles. The weather was hot and several men fell out along the route. Brigadier General N.J.G. Cameron took command of 51 Brigade on the 6th September. The Battalion remained in Baizieux Wood until the 10th September. It was a good training area and platoon, company and brigade exercises filled up much of the time. The officers were in tents and the rest of the Battalion on bivouacs made of sticks and waterproof sheets. Heavy rainfall at the end of August interfered with the training programme and made life somewhat uncomfortable for the men in bivouacs. The Adjutant, Lieutenant Ebsworth, injured his left arm when his horse fell on him whilst on parade. He had to be evacuated to hospital. Second Lieutenant Kirkhouse took his place as acting Adjutant. Much of the training involved practising attacks on trenches, which seemed to indicate a much more aggressive role for the Battalion in the days ahead. At 5.00 a.m. on the 10th September, the Battalion left Baizieux Wood and marched nearer to the front line, to Becourt Wood. It was here that each member of the Battalion began to wear the red diamond which became an important part of the uniform. All ranks were under bivouacs. Working parties were out on the 12th September. On the 14th of the month, a night march was made to Shelter Wood, captured by the 23rd Division on the 3rd July. It was here that final preparations were made prior to the Battalion going into the front line on the 15th. Twenty officers and six hundred and fifty other ranks would go into action. The remainder were left out of battle in order to form a foundation for reorganising the Battalion, should losses in action prove considerable. Lieutenant Ebsworth rejoined from sick-leave in England.

A brief outline at the progress made by the British on the Somme since 1st of July, would seem appropriate. The result of the battle, on this day, was considered afterwards to be the greatest disaster visited on the British Army in the whole of its history to that date. Fifty seven thousand four hundred and seventy casualties resulted, of which nineteen thousand two hundred and forty were killed. North of the Albert - Bapaume road success was slight and losses extremely heavy. The attacks carried out south of this road were increasingly successful. On the extreme right, 30th and 18th Divisions of XIII Corps, attained their first day objectives. 30th Division was commanded by Major-General Shea, late Brigadier General commanding 151 Brigade.

A combination of delay, due to an emphasis on consolidation, stiffening German opposition and bad weather, resulted in slow progress over the next few days. At dawn on the 14th July, after a night assembly, a brilliant attack was carried out by four divisions on the German Second Line on the Longueval - Bazentin Ridge. At this point, with High Wood empty and the Germans streaming away in retreat, attacking British Divisions, particularly the 3rd and the 7th, were refused permission to advance and take High Wood and the ridge on which it stands. It would be two months and many casualties before this position was taken.

In the early days of September, a general relief of the divisions already holding the line, was carried out. On the left, 15th Division held on to its front with the exception of its left hand brigade, which was relieved by the 50th Division. The 50th Division boundary was as follows: 47th London Division on the right, whose task it was to clear High Wood, already the scene of bitter and costly fighting. On the left was the 15th Highland Division, south-west of Martinpuich. The 50th Division held a salient, with the 47th Division some three hundred yards in the rear of the right flank of 149 Brigade and the 15th Division about 250 yards in the rear of the left flank of 150 Brigade; a very dangerous position from whence to commence an attack, with the Germans able to enfilade each flank of the attacking brigades. Major-General Wilkinson had to come to an early decision; to let the flanking divisions attack and, hopefully, come up level with his own division before moving forward himself, or, attack immediately and, by threatening the German flanks, assist the 47th and 15th Divisions in their tasks. He decided on the latter. The Division was to attack on a front of one thousand one hundred yards. This would increase to one thousand eight hundred yards when the final objectives were reached. 151 Brigade was in divisional reserve to 149 and 150 Brigades in the front line. Two of the new tanks were allocated to 150 Brigade and were of considerable assistance in the initial stages of the attack. The line in which the 50th Division found itself was a confused maze of trenches and tracks. On the right, Sutherland Alley was taken over. This was a communication trench running north and south and joined Clarks-Trench at the Bazentin-le-Petit - High Wood road. Here the line turned westward along Clarks and Swansea Trenches. Ahead of this line was Hook Trench which was held by the enemy and was the Division's first objective on the 15th September.

Under the umbrella title of 'The Battle of the Somme', a series of subtitles were given to each particularly violent engagement, for which special plans and arrangements had been made. The battle, which began on the morning of the 15th September and lasted until the 22nd of the month, went under the title, 'The Battle of Flers - Courcelette.' Following a three-day bombardment of the German positions, the British attack went in at 6.20 a.m. 149 Brigade attacked on the right of the Divisional front with the 4th and 7th Battalions Northumberland Fusiliers. Hook Trench was captured about 7.00 a.m. As the Battalions moved forward to attack the Starfish Line, they suffered heavy losses from enfilade fire from the German positions in High Wood, where very little progress had been made by the 47th Division, against fanatical enemy resistance. By mid-morning, entry had been made to the sunken road south of the enemy strongpoint - The Bow. Later in the morning, a few men entered the Starfish Line at a number of points. Casualties in the battalions of the Northumberland Fusiliers had been exceptionally heavy. At 12.50 p.m. the 9th Battalion The Durham Light Infantry, 151 Brigade, was loaned to 149 Brigade, to reinforce the attack on the Starfish Line and effect its capture. The German shelling had by now reached a crescendo and included strong enemy counter-attacks to regain lost ground. By 3.30 p.m., the Northumberland Fusiliers could hold on no longer and withdrew to Hook Trench, leaving survivors of the 7th Battalion Northumberland Fusiliers in the sunken road south of The Bow.

As the attack started at 6.20 a.m., the 6th Durhams, moved from Shelter Wood to the south west corner of Mametz Wood. The journey was made over the twisted, shell torn landscape of previous actions, when man seemed intent not only on destroying his fellows but the very earth itself. Craters covered the ground in profusion. The refuse of war had been hurled into the air and lay all over the place - equipment, wire, timber and other debris. Trenches and dugouts had been obliterated. Mametz Wood had already achieved an evil reputation. Its blasted stumps and undergrowth continued to receive the attention of the German artillery, which would be well aware that these afforded some protection for troops moving up to and coming down from the line. Later in the day the Battalion moved into Mametz Wood itself. At about 4.00 p.m. on the 15th September, a message was received from Divisional Headquarters that it was to move up to the line at once. Lieutenant-Colonel Jeffreys immediately called his company

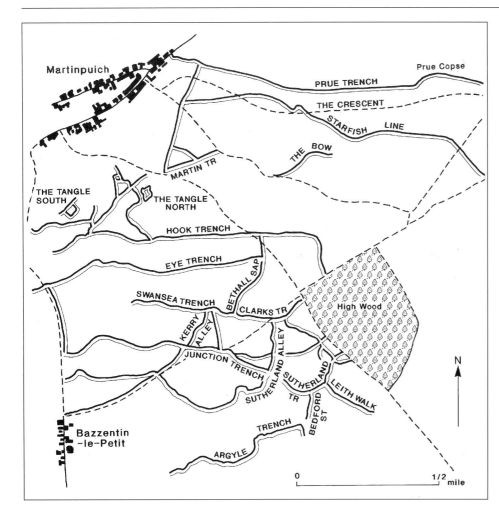

Battle of the Somme - *15th September, 1916: The attack at High Wood*

Wood by the 47th Division at about 1.00 p.m. These successes, for which the 47th Division, in particular, had paid a heavy price, must have been due in part to the threat to the German flanks by the advance of 50th Division. The enemy's flank threat to 151 Brigade, therefore, was no longer a problem.

The 9th and 6th Battalions moved into Hook Trench, but the 5th Battalion Border Regiment was delayed and did not reach the assembly positions in time to join in the attack. The attack on Prue Trench underwent a number of delays which did not help matters. It was first ordered for 7.30 p.m., altered to 8.00 p.m. then 8.30 p.m. and finally went in at 9.40 p.m. It failed. The two Battalions went forward in four waves, with considerable energy and spirit. 'W' Company (Captain J. Cook) was on the left of the first wave, 'X' Company (Captain W.E. Badcock) was on the right. 'Z' Company (left) and 'Y' Company (right) followed in support. Early in the advance, Second-Lieutenant Arnett, commanding 'Y' Company was killed. Second-Lieutenant B.J. Harvey, though wounded, took over command of this company. The advance was made down the slope towards Prue and Starfish Trenches under heavy machine-gun and rifle fire. Captain Badcock was wounded. The enemy fire became so accurate and fierce, that the advance came to a halt and men took cover in shell holes and ditches. A few men, who had reached Prue and Starfish, quickly became casualties and were driven out

commanders to a conference to discuss the situation and give out orders. At 6.05 p.m. orders came down from Division that 151 Brigade was to attack Pru Trench. Martinpuich on the left had been taken by 15th Division as early as 10.00 a.m. and High by German counter-attacks. At about 3.30 a.m. on the 16th September, Lieutenant-Colonel Jeffreys took 'Z' Company forward to reinforce the front line. By this time the 5th Borders had appeared on the left. The Battalion was by now very scattered and Lieutenant-Colonel Jeffreys set about reuniting the various elements, so far as that was possible. On the 17th September, he had the following under his control once more: half of 'W' Company under Captain Cook, part of 'X' Company under Lieutenant Harris, a platoon of 'Z' Company under Lieutenant Hansell. 'Y' Company was in reserve in a sunken road, under Second-Lieutenants McVicker and Richardson. Isolated groups lay out in front. One of these was organised for defence under the orders of Private B. McLinden of 'X' Company who was to receive a Military Medal for his actions.

The remnants of the Battalion dug in behind the Northumberland Fusiliers who were holding the sunken road south of the Bow. On the 17th September, an assault was made upon the German strongpoint known as the Crescent. It was carried out by two bombing parties, one each from the 6th and 8th Battalions under the command of the Brigade Bombing Officer, Second-Lieutenant J.F.G. Aubin. The parties left Crescent Alley about 6.00 p.m. but became considerably disorganised on coming under severe enemy artillery fire and were driven back. A further attempt was made a little later with the same end result. The Germans were reported to be evacuating the Starfish Line on the 18th September and plans were made to occupy it. The 6th and 9th Battalions provided one hundred men each for this attack. The Battalion contingent in the front wave comprised fifty men of 'W' Company, under Second-Lieutenant W. Little, with a supporting wave, which included the other fifty men from 'Z' Company, under Second-Lieutenant W.F. Charlton. The Starfish Line proved to be strongly held and casualties, from enemy fire, were heavy.

The heavy artillery of both sides hammered away at each other. Second-Lieutenant Harris was killed and Second-Lieutenant Ramsay wounded. These casualties resulted in 'X' Company being left without any officers and the senior NCOs were left in command. The casualty list from the 15th to the 18th September, in addition to those already named above, included Lieutenant

W.F. Charlton killed, Captain Cook, Second-Lieutenants Harvey, Tattersall and D.F. Charlton wounded. Forty other ranks were killed, and twenty wounded. The Battalion was relieved on the 18th by the 8th Battalion and moved into brigade reserve in 6th Avenue, 6th Avenue East, Intermediate Trench and Jutland Avenue. The rains came from the 18th of the month. As the rain fell, the craters and holes filled rapidly with water covering the dead and drowning the wounded who were unable to move. Trenches became muddy ditches, so deep in mud it was difficult to move. No fires could be lit and ration parties laboured under their loads to reach half-starved men in the front line.

The 18th September was used by the Battalion to improve dugouts in the trenches and this work went ahead in spite of enemy shell fire. There was plenty of debris lying about, which could be used to do this work. On the 20th, the Battalion moved to the north-west corner of Mametz Wood. Here it remained until the 24th of the month. It received a draft of fifty other ranks from the second line 6th Battalion Essex Regiment. Baths were allocated and working parties found. On the 23rd, a working party, comprising the entire Battalion, undertook road repairs at the edge of Bazentin-le-Petit Wood. On this day Major G.E. Wilkinson, officer commanding 149 Machine-Gun Company, joined the Battalion as Second in Command. The whole Battalion again formed a working party at 7.00 a.m. till 12 noon on the 24th and then moved at 3.00 p.m. to 6th Avenue East and Intermediate Trench. Lieutenant Catford wrote to his family on the 25th as follows:

'Surely truth is stranger than fiction! Last night I had a most excellent sleep in No Mans Land, during a fairly heavy bombardment such as is practically continuous in this the greatest battle of the War!!

'Had I not the testimony of some of the most gallant fellows who ever walked God's earth, even to you, I should hardly care to relate the facts of an episode which sounds so improbable of having occurred. There was another big attack yesterday. After it was over my Battalion had to go up to the front line - we were in reserve - and dig what is called a "jumping off trench" to be dug in advance of our own front line mid-way between that trench and the Germans. Arrived in No Mans Land after a tiring march, including many falls into "Crump" holes etc, we were absolutely unable to find any Officer, NCO or man of the Brigade in the front line who knew exactly where the trench had to be dug. The Adjutant roamed about until challenged by Bosches and it is a thousand wonders we were not all wiped out by machine-gun fire. Tired of waiting and rather exhausted after the long march I must have fallen off to sleep as the next thing I knew was that one of my Sergeants who was lying next to me woke me up and told me that we had to return as the exact location of the site of the trench had not been defined.

'I am pleased to say that I got the whole company back without a single casualty. As a matter of fact up to the present my Company, "Y" proverbial for their luck in the Battalion have had only 15 casualties whereas other Companies have lost at least 50 per cent of their personnel...

'...There is very little to say about this big show except the Artillery is awful and the flies are worse, whilst conditions of living are worse still. All the same we are exceptionally cheerful. We bear everything I hope like good soldiers proud to have beaten thoroughly the reputed "Invincible German Army." The men are absolutely wonderful. My Company are in the best of spirits. I think you might send out 1000 Woodbines for them.

'Well I think I have given you some idea of what it is like out here. Men live and die like heroes and face with the greatest of courage that which no men ought to be called upon to face. I can say no more.'

On the 25th September, the second of the Somme battles commenced. 'The Battle of Morval' lasted from this date until the 28th of the month. This battle commenced with the usual intense bombardment from our guns on the German lines stretching from Morval to north of Martinpuich. 151 Brigade took no part in this battle but relieved 150 Brigade in the front line trenches on the 28th. On the 26th September, Lieutenant-Colonel Jeffreys was sent on sick-leave to England. Writing to Mrs. Watson on the 21st October, he showed his displeasure with the order:

'They sent me home on sick leave at the end of September. I tried to maintain that I was no more sick than the next but they insisted that I hadn't got over my wounds in Sanctuary Wood so here I am in England recouperating. I hated leaving the Battalion in such an abominable place as they were in - between High Wood and Martinpuich - but there was no way out.'

The 6th Battalion was in the Starfish Line with two companies in Hook Trench. It remained here under constant and heavy bombardment from enemy guns until the 30th September, when it relieved the 9th Battalion in forward trenches. The Battalion must have been very low on experienced officers as the companies, at this time, were commanded by the following young officers: 'W' Company, Second-Lieutenant Barnett; 'X' Company, Second-Lieutenant Lean; 'Y' Company, Lieutenant Catford; 'Z' Company, Captain Peberdy. 'Y' Company had lost some of its good luck. Lieutenant Catford wrote home on the 30th as follows:

'...I have only one officer left in my Company. One left last night with shell-shock. I do not wonder at it seeing what we have to put up with ... Tomorrow we go into our final big attack. Do not worry if you don't hear for a day or two from me. I shall not have very much opportunity of writing to you for a bit.'

Lieutenant Catford was a little premature. It was, in effect, the penultimate battle for the Battalion on the Somme. One final trial of strength was to follow in early November.

On the 29th September, the 23rd Division captured Destremont Farm, south west of Le Sars. The assault on the Flers Line was to be undertaken, from the right of the line, by the New Zealand Division, 47th London Division, 50th Division and the 23rd Division. The 50th Division, which would attack in the centre, placed the 6th Battalion on the right and the Composite Battalion, made up of the 8th Durhams and 5th Battalion Border Regiment, in the centre of the assault. Two Battalions of 149 Brigade were attached: the 5th Northumberland Fusiliers would attack on the right, with the 4th Battalion of this regiment in close support. The 9th Durhams were was in close support to the 6th Battalion, on the right of the attack. Due to the non arrival of the 47th Division on the right of the brigade, delayed by fierce German resistance, the 6th Battalion would attack with its right flank in the air, from which direction it would be subjected to enemy enfilade fire and flank attack.

British artillery concentrated on cutting the enemy wire during the 30th September. Enemy guns were very active during the evening of this day but eased off during the night. On the night of 30th September-1st October, the British artillery bombarded enemy trenches and communications. Pioneers and infantry dug jumping-off trenches, which were given the names, North Durham Trench, South Durham Trench, Blaydon Trench and Rutherford Avenue. Bombs, ammunition and water supplies were stacked in the attacking trenches. The assault was planned to take place at 3.15 p.m. on the 1st October. It was a fine autumn day.

Final arrangements were put in hand prior to the attack. At 3.00 a.m., the Commanding Officer of the 6th Battalion, Major Wilkinson, held an officers' group meeting to discuss details of the forthcoming advance. The attacking Battalions had occupied the jumping off trenches by 6.00 a.m. Sixty men, composed of a new draft and people from the transport lines, were organised as a carrying party for the Battalion, to ensure a flow of supplies to the trenches. Enemy shelling was intermittent until about 9.00 a.m., when it increased in volume and the jumping-off trenches, front line and support positions were targeted. The closely packed men, already facing a long wait for the attack to start, had to crouch there and take everything the Germans threw at them. There were a number of casualties. Second-Lieutenant Yaldwyn, Battalion Sniper Officer, was wounded. He had been attached to 'Y' Company for the duration of the action. The most serious loss was Major Wilkinson himself, who was wounded about 1.30 p.m., less than two hours before the attack commenced. On making his way to the casualty clearing station, Major Wilkinson met Lieutenant-Colonel Bradford of the 9th Battalion. He asked Lieutenant-Colonel Bradford to take command of the 6th Battalion for the attack, and confirmation was sought from the Brigade Commander, which was given.

An intense bombardment of the enemy wire and trenches had

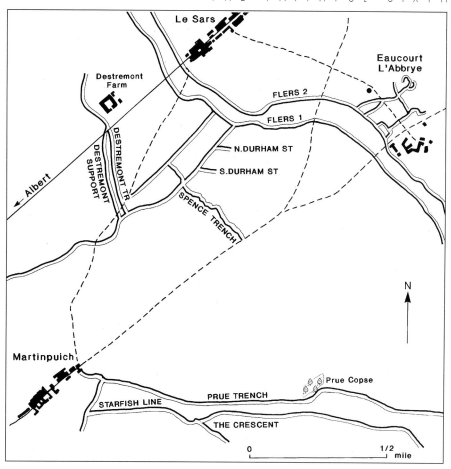

The Battle of the Somme - 1st/2nd October, 1916

commenced at 7.00 a.m., and continued up to 3.15 p.m., when the troops left the jumping off trenches. At this time the barrage reached a crescendo of fire and the attacking Battalions moved behind a wall of exploding shells. It was one of the most effective barrages of the war. Even so, some sections of the wire in front of the enemy trenches had not been cut and there was some delay as the assaulting troops searched for and found gaps. Usually this would have led to heavy losses from enemy counter fire, but the British barrage was so intense, and the lines of advancing troops so close to the exploding shells, that effective German retaliation could not be formed before our troops were into their trenches. The Composite Battalion of the 8th DLI and 5th Borders quickly gained their first objective. Due very largely to the fact that 47th Division had not come up on its right, so leaving an open flank, the 6th Battalion had a much harder task. Second-Lieutenants T. Little and C.L. Tyerman got three Lewis gun teams of 'X' Company, and Second-Lieutenant Barnett got a Lewis gun team of 'W' Company into the first objective, where they organised resistance and carried out bombing attacks. Lieutenant Little was killed at this time. Heavy rifle and machine-gun fire poured into the Battalion's exposed right flank and progress ground to a halt. At this moment, Lieutenant-Colonel Bradford arrived and rallied the men. He was everywhere, organising, encouraging, issuing clear and precise instructions. The first objective was taken and a block established between the Durhams and the Germans on the right flank. 'A' Company of the 9th Battalion arrived to reinforce the troops holding the first objective. The second objective was taken about 1.00 a.m. on the 2nd October, and a block was also established there, between the British and the enemy. The fighting between the bombers of both adversaries around the trench blocks, was extremely severe and raged on for most of the next twenty-four hours. The Germans realised that to break through at this point would have serious implications, not only for turning our troops out of the captured trenches, but for 151 Brigade which, in turn, would be in danger of having its right flank rolled up, with a 'knock-on' effect on the divisions fighting on the brigade left. However, the enemy did not succeed in rushing the blocks, despite many gallant efforts, nor could our troops make progress in this area. Severe though the fighting was, a stalemate occurred with neither side able to advance. Enemy artillery was active throughout the day and the following night, but it left the captured trenches alone and concentrated on the support lines. The rains came and the relief of both 6th and 9th Battalions, which commenced on the night of 2nd-3rd October, was slow and added to the weariness of the men. Relief was carried out by the 7th Northumberland Fusiliers. Lieutenant-Colonel Bradford handed over command of the 6th Battalion to Lieutenant Ebsworth, and it moved into the Starfish Line.

Casualties were heavy and included, in addition to Lieutenant Little: Second-Lieutenant Peacock killed; Captain Peberdy, Lieutenant Cotching, Second-Lieutenants Lean, Barnett and Appleby wounded. Lieutenant-Colonel Bradford received the Victoria Cross for his coolness, resourcefulness, courage and leadership. Military Medals were awarded to Corporal Dixon, Privates Rushworth and Atkinson, all signallers, and Private Turnbull of 'Y' Company. Outstanding work was carried out by Sergeants Gowland and Winslow. Lieutenant Ebsworth wrote to Mrs Watson on the 20th October:

'The officers, NCOs and men of the Battalion, in common with the Brigade, assaulted and carried the German 1st and 2nd line of trenches with the utmost gallantry, as their losses will testify. When we were relieved on 3rd October only four officers remained, the A[cting] Adj[utant], Signal Officer, one Second-Lieutenant and self. 3 Company Sergeant-Majors commanded companies...'

At 1.00 p.m. on the 3rd October, the Battalion marched to Becourt Wood and into the same camp it had occupied on the way up to the Somme. It remained here for one night only and at 11.45 on the following morning moved on to Henencourt Wood. This was a very good tented camp. The Battalion remained here until the 23rd October. The time was taken up with cleaning, making up deficiencies and training. Inter-company and Battalion football commenced; officers received several lectures on such subjects as; 'Morale', 'Trench Attacks' and 'Supplies'. Towards the end of the stay, working parties were found for erecting huts and roadmaking. On the morning of the 23rd October the Battalion, as part of the Brigade, moved to Becourt Wood. The whole Brigade was accommodated in a tented camp. Two hundred and fifty men were occupied on roadmaking tasks on the following day. In the afternoon, a tragic accident occurred when Private H.O. Thompson, who had enlisted at Blaydon, was accidentally killed by the explosion of a bomb. No additional details are given in the war diary although a court of inquiry into the accident was held a few days later.

On the morning of the 25th October, the Battalion moved to the south-west corner of Mametz Wood, relieving the 11th Royal Scots. Though accommodation was in tents, the conditions were extremely wet and muddy. The Battalion remained here until the 3rd November. Working parties were found every day for a variety of tasks. The Commanding Officer, Company and Specialist Officers reconnoitred the support and forward trenches they were expected to occupy when the Battalion moved into the line. Conditions were now deteriorating to a considerable extent. Rain churned up the ground and turned it into a thick mud. The mud on the Somme seemed to be different from any other experienced elsewhere. It clung to boots like glue, each succeeding layer adhering to the previous one, until men seemed to have large mud packs on the end of their legs. This mud fiercely resisted any attempts by the men to pull their boots clear and movement was not only extremely difficult, under such conditions, but also sapped the troops' energies. Add to this, the working parties being found for both day and night, and it is not difficult to imagine how tired men became - and this immediately before a major battle. The working parties, out on the 30th October, were so soaked and cold that they had to be issued with a rum ration on return to camp. The same working parties had to have their feet rubbed with whale oil, to protect them against frostbite. Conditions were so bad on the 31st October that the camp had to be moved to better ground. The working parties continued for the first two days in November. On the 2nd of the month extra small arms ammunition, bombs and flares were issued. At 1.00 p.m. on the 4th November, the Battalion moved, along with the Brigade, into the front and support line. 'W' Company was in Snag Trench in the front line, 'X' and 'Y' Companies were in the Flers Line. 'Z' Company and the Raiding Party were in Flers Switch. The Battalion relieved the 4th Yorkshire Regiment. During the relief, 'Y' Company lost one man killed and three wounded. In front lay the Butte de Warlencourt.

By the end of October, Le Sars and Snag Trench were in British hands. Attempts had been made to take the Butte and the Gird Line, but these had failed. The Butte de Warlencourt, estimated at

over forty feet high, lay just to the east of the Albert - Bapaume road. It was reputed to have been an ancient burial mound. Its cover of trees and close undergrowth had been blasted away by the intense artillery fire and it now lay before our troops, a white, cratered chalk mass. In the soldiers' minds it had taken on a power of its own. They felt that their every move was mapped by the enemy, established on its summit. The machine-gun positions built into its sides dominated the battlefield. In the words of Lieutenant-Colonel Bradford, commanding the 9th Durhams, whose task it was to take the Butte, it had:

> '...become an obsession. Everybody wanted it. It loomed large in the minds of the soldiers in the forward area and they attributed many of their misfortunes to it. The newspaper correspondents talked about "that miniature Gibraltar". So it had to be taken.
>
> 'It seems that the attack was one of those tempting and unfortunately at one time frequent, local operations which are so costly and which are rarely worthwhile.
>
> 'But perhaps that is only the narrow view of the Regimental Officer.'

Bradford, and others, were of the opinion that the Butte gave little tactical advantage, even if taken. It would be difficult to hold and even if retained by the Germans, its worth as an observation point would be much lessened now that the British trenches were so close to it. Artillery and mortars could quite easily deny its use to the enemy. However it had to be assaulted and 151 Brigade was given the task of its capture, together with the Gird and Gird Support Trenches.

The weather and ground conditions were now appalling. The trenches were at least knee deep in mud. The ground over which the attack would proceed was cratered with shell holes which, in turn, were full of water. Heavy rain, at the end of October, had deepened the mud of the battlefield to such an extent that the attack had had to be postponed until drier weather made the ground firm enough for men to move across. A series of postponements took place until, on the 3rd November, the date of the attack was finally fixed for two days later, the 5th of the month. The Brigade would attack with all three Durham Battalions in the line. The 8th Battalion was on the right, the 6th Battalion was in the centre and the 9th Battalion, attacking the

Butte itself, was on the left. The Battalions assembled in Snag Trench, Snag Support, Maxwell Trench and Tail Trench. The objectives of the 6th and 8th Battalions were Gird and Gird Support Trenches. On the right of the Brigade, the Australians would attack at the same time. The 46th Division, on the left of the Brigade, would not attack but would assist the advance by flank covering fire. The Germans facing were first class troops of the Guard and Guard Reserve Divisions, holding very strong positions.

On the 4th November, the men were withdrawn from the front line, leaving only a few posts in position. This was to safeguard against any casualties resulting from the expected enemy retaliation to the preparatory British bombardment of their front line. Brigadier Cameron saw his Battalion Commanders at 3.00 p.m. to make final arrangements for the attack and give out necessary orders. In turn, Battalion Commanders met their Company Commanders to explain details of the attack and, again, give out orders. The hope that the fine weather might hold was dashed. During the night of the 4th/5th November, heavy rain and gale force winds blew, filling holes and deepening the mud. The conditions were now dreadful in the extreme, but no postponement was considered, or ordered. The companies moved into their assembly positions, the men struggling under the weight of their loads of weapons, extra ammunition and equipment. Mud was now thigh deep in places. Movement could only be made with immense physical effort. From dawn till zero hour for the attack at 9.10 a.m. on the 5th November, the battalions moved up and took over their assault positions. Drenched to the skin, caked with the heavy, glutinous

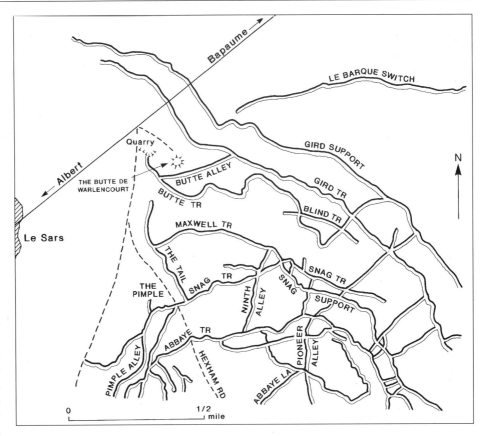

The Battle of the Somme - *5th November, 1916:*
The Butte de Warlencourt

mud, standing in mud and water, cold and miserable, they waited for hours in the front line positions. There were reports that a number of 6th Battalion men had drowned as they made their way into the trenches.

The 6th Battalion disposed its companies as follows: 'X' Company on the right, 'Y' in the centre, 'Z' on the left and 'W' Company in support. Due to the terrible conditions 'Z' Company were late in arriving, being in position as late as 9.00 a.m., ten minutes before the attack was due to start. At 9.10 a.m. the advance began. The mud was so deep that the first men to get out of the trenches turned to assist those who followed by pulling them over the parapet. The lines formed as best they could and set off dragging their increasingly weary legs out of the thick mud. Movement was, at best, painfully slow and in some areas at a standstill. The enemy counter-barrage fell largely on Snag Trench and was not particularly heavy. However, machine-gun fire was immediate and intense, both from the front and the flanks. On the right of the Brigade-attack, the Australians made no progress, men falling dead or wounded as soon as they showed themselves above the parapet, or fell in the mud within the first few yards of leaving the trenches. This had a dire affect upon the 8th Battalion on their left. Enfiladed by enemy machine-guns, the Battalion struggled forward and survivors of the first waves reached to within thirty yards of the enemy in Butte Trench. A withdrawal was ordered and the remnants got back to the trenches from whence they had started.

The failure of the 8th Battalion, in turn, affected the progress of the right wing of the 6th Battalion, which suffered a similar fate. The left of the 6th Battalion made progress, largely due to the initial success of the 9th Battalion on its left, which had captured the Butte de Warlencourt. At 10.00 a.m., 'W' Company was sent forward from support to reinforce 'X' Company on the right of the Battalion front, where the open flank referred to above ensured very little progress. With the 9th Battalion now over the Butte and the left of the 6th Battalion in possession of its objectives in Gird Trench at 11.35 a.m., the latter Battalion was placed under the command of Lieutenant-Colonel Bradford of the 9th, when it was considered that the unification of command would help ensure the protection of his right flank. At 11.50 a.m., Second-Lieutenant G.W. Robson was ordered to bring forward his raiding party and establish a double block on the right of the Battalion in Gird Trench. and so ensure some protection against enemy counter-measures from the open right flank. Enemy counter-attacks were strong and persevered with. The artillery of both sides was extremely active. Due to the lack of information as to the positions held by both sides and the adversaries being locked in close combat, shells from the guns of both sides sometimes fell upon their own men.

Desperate hand-to-hand fighting continued throughout the afternoon, with the Germans striving every sinew to drive out the persistent Durhams. At 12.30 p.m. Major Ebsworth, Commanding Officer of the 6th Battalion, went into Maxwell Trench and moved up the remaining reserves to re-inforce the companies locked in battle at the front. Losses on both sides were extremely heavy. By late afternoon it was becoming increasingly

Lieutenant H. Miller *served on the Somme and subsequent actions. He commanded the Battalion from 1934 to 1940*

obvious that German opposition was hardening and, hence, more difficult to hold onto the positions captured. At 4.20 p.m., Sergeant Young arrived back at Battlion HQ with the survivors of the raiding party, who had established the blocks in Gird Trench. He reported that Second-Lieutenant Robson had been killed. The magnificent effort of the 9th Battalion was in jeopardy due to heavy losses and the lack of reinforcements. At 8.00 p.m. Second-Lieutenants K.B. Stuart and R.H.C. Wharrier moved out of Maxwell Trench with about one hundred and fifty men to attempt to reach the 9th Battalion. In the attempt - the war diary is silent on whether they succeeded in reaching the Battalion - Second-Lieutenant Stuart was amongst those killed. At about

12.20 a.m. on the 6th November, both the 6th and 9th Battalions were back in Maxwell Trench. Those objectives which had been reached, could not be held against fierce and strengthening enemy resistance.

The appalling conditions, fierce artillery and machine-gun fire and the open right flank, had proved too much despite the courage and tenacity of the Durhams. Yet their sacrifices have lived down through the years to become part of the Regimental lore. An example of these virtues lies in the following description of the action written by Lance-Corporal H. Cruddace, who received a Military Medal for his part in the battle and who was finally to hold three of these medals by the end of the war:

'...I was a Lance-Corporal in 'X' Company in command of two Lewis Gun sections composed of seven men per section carrying gun, spare parts and old fashioned paniers holding four magazines each. Lieutenant Ludgate was acting Captain in command of my company. Owing to the slow progress of the troops it was daylight when we reached the front line trench to be greeted by the gallant 'W' Company. The trench was in such a deplorable state that we marched along the parados in order to reach our places quicker. As we were in full view of the enemy he met us with a terrible hail of shell, machine-gun and rifle fire, and we were glad to take advantage of the slimey trench and reach our places as best we could. By this time we had suffered numerous casualties. On arrival at our destination in the trench, I found myself with my sections linked up with 8th DLI on the right. ...Every man then looking to the loading of his rifle and the fixing of his bayonet as the zero hour was almost upon us. Serious men gazed eagerly into one another's faces and some muttered thoughts of "God" and their loved ones at home. Chums clasped hands and said "Cheerio," not knowing what the day held in store for them. Officers were in eager conversation with the senior NCO's regarding the readiness of the men. The enemy kept up a ceaseless bombardment of our trenches in conjunction with the merciless rain and cold. The attack was to be made in the wave system and everyone knew his own place and held himself in readiness. At last the zero hour arrived and the officers' whistles sounded the advance. Immediately the first wave mounted the trench and made off in the direction of the enemy trenches. They were met by terrific and annihilating fire and crumbled up like snow in summer. The second wave was by this time on its way. I was in that wave and placed my gun and sections in single file to make a less target. The enemy barrage was doing enormous damage and our fighting strength was fast diminishing ... We had suffered terrible casualties when our company commander Lieutenant Ludgate was wounded and fell into a shell hole. By this time the whole line was held up and Lieutenant Ludgate ordered me to proceed and engage the enemy machine-guns, a task almost impossible. Out of my two sections of 14 men there were two of us left, a No.1 on the gun by name Private Allen, and myself. I pushed on with one gun and a quantity of ammunition to about 30 yards of the German trench and took up a position in a shell hole and we opened fire on the opposing troops who formed an excellent target owing to the fact that they had us at a disadvantage. In taking up my position in the excitement I placed myself on the right side of the gun instead of on the left which was fortunate for me. After firing off one or two mags the enemy found us with a machine-gun and succeeded in wounding my No.1 in four places down his left side. Thinking him dead I pushed him aside and carried on until want of ammunition forced me to withdraw to our troops in the rear. I took back my gun and spare parts and came in contact with an officer of another company to whom I made my report. A few minutes later I saw my No. 1 who was out in front lift an arm in an appealing manner and I knew he whom I had thought dead was still alive. I immediately ran out in a zig zag method and brought him back to the shelter of the shell hole we were then manning. After attending to his wounds we set about organising and consolidating in preparation for a counter-attack from the enemy ... As night drew on we were made stronger by our comrades from 'W' Company in linking up and gathering the Lewis Guns from men who had fallen. The expected happened and the enemy counter-attacked under cover of darkness, but we stayed off the assault at a great price. Despite our weakened condition we held on till the night of the 6th Nov when we were relieved by another Brigade of our Div...'

Lance-Corporal Cruddace's citation for the award of his Military Medal for this action is worth recording here:

'After the attack on the morning of the 5th November, had been held up, he collected his two Lewis Guns (He was NCO in charge of the detachment) and established them in a strongpoint about 50 yards from the German trench and succeeded in keeping down the German snipers in the opposite trench to a very great extent. He showed a splendid example of coolness and courage to his men and rendered invaluable assistance to his officer in most trying circumstances. Later succeeded in bringing both his guns out of action.'

Orders were received at 8.00 a.m. on the 6th November, that the attack must be carried out again. It is not difficult to imagine the sinking hearts this news caused amongst the survivors of the previous day's action. However, sanity ruled and the order was cancelled later in the day. The Battalion was relieved during the night of the 6th-7th November and moved back to its old camp in Mametz Wood. Casualties had been extremely heavy, particularly those of the junior officers amongst whom the following were numbered:

Killed: Second-Lieutenant K.B.Stuart.
              Second-Lieutenant G.W.Robson.
              Second-Lieutenant A.S. Robson.
Wounded: Second-Lieutenant Ludgate.
              Second-Lieutenant Tyerman.
              Second-Lieutenant R.H. Stewart.
              Second-Lieutenant T. Burton.
              Lieutenant G. Corbett..
Missing: Second-Lieutenant H.Fell.
              Second-Lieutenant Applegarth.
              Second-Lieutenant A.S. Ritson.

Total casualties for other ranks were about one hundred and fifty men.

The 7th November, was a wet day. Lieutenant-Colonel H.M. Allen, DSO, CMG, of the Black Watch, assumed command of the Battalion. Lieutenant T.B. Heslop took over command of 'X' Company and Second-Lieutenant McVicker, the command of 'Y' Company. The Battalion stayed in Mametz Wood for the rest of November. During this period it was employed on numerous working parties and received drafts of both officers and other ranks. On the 21st of the month, notification was received of the awards of Military Medals to Sergeant H. Cruddace - he had been promoted to sergeant immediately after the battle - Private T. Tindle and Private R. Parker. A few men went on leave to England. The weather was largely dull, with some rain and snow. On the 30th November the Battalion moved to Becourt and spent the night in huts.

The Battalion marched to Warloy on the 1st December. Here it stayed until the 28th December. Cleaning up, refitting, receiving drafts and training up to brigade level, filled most of the days. On Christmas Day, Divine Service was held in the morning and Battalion sports in the afternoon. The usual Christmas Dinner was held with whatever additions to the basic rations could be found on neighbouring farms, largely pigs and hens, which were purchased and added to the menu. Fortunately there was no shortage of beer and cigarettes. On the 28th of the month, the Battalion moved to Albert, where it relieved the 5th Warwickshire Regiment. Working parties were found to work on the Albert-Bapaume road. Clothing and equipment were inspected to ensure that all of the men had a complete kit prior to moving once again into the forward area. A final draft of one hundred and eighty men was received, of whom eighty were moved to Baizieux for training. On New Year's Eve, the Battalion marched via La Boiselle and Contalmaison, to Bazentin-le-Petit, where it relieved the 8th Berkshire Regiment. Losses had been very heavy from September to November, 1916. Many friends figured among the casualties and were no longer with the Battalion. Those who had served during this period were tired men, badly in need of rest. Recent drafts had brought the Battalion up to strength. The New Year would bring additional challenges and demands upon officers and men, which they would meet with their usual stubbornness and grit.

Bazentin-le-Petit had been destroyed in the Somme fighting. On its ruins a military town had grown, built of huts and shelters. Hidden from German eyes by the High Wood ridge, a railhead had been established, from which a 60cm railway took supplies up to High Wood itself. The whole area was a hive of activity. Troops were constantly moving up to and coming down from the front. Small tractors pulled the wagons, laden with supplies, along the 60cm railway, which ran up the slope to High Wood. Surprisingly the area suffered only from light shelling. Increasing activity by German aircraft, particularly at night, which bombed and strafed any lighted areas, caused orders to be given that all fires must be sheltered in such a way as to ensure that they could not be spotted from above. The heavy frosts which began to grip the area made for bright, bracing days, but intense cold at night.

For the first three days of January, 1917 the usual working parties were found. Much of the work involved laying water-pipes and improving the camp drainage. All of the Battalion seemed to have been on these parties, with the exception of the specialist sections, who commenced a heavy training programme. In the afternoon of the 3rd January, the Battalion moved up to High Wood West Camp, relieving the 4th East Yorkshire Regiment. This camp was both dreary and dangerous. Shelter was provided in huts made of black tarpaulin. Being on the top of the ridge it was in view of German observers and subjected to shelling. On the following day, the Battalion moved into the support line in the Flers sector. Four days in this position were taken up with working parties, with quite heavy enemy shelling throughout the night. The days were quiet, cold and frosty, the nights bitterly cold. On the 8th of the month, a move was made back to High Wood West Camp, where it remained until the 12th. On this day, the Battalion moved into the front line trenches, with Battalion HQ at Factory Corner. The line consisted of detached posts which could only be relieved during the night. It remained extremely cold and the men suffered greatly. On the 13th of the month, enemy artillery was very active during day and night. Our artillery subjected the German front line to a heavy bombardment, which did much damage. There were two casualties suffered during the day. The following night, patrols were sent out. A German patrol was spotted and annhililated by the Battalion Lewis guns. A wounded German officer was taken but he died shortly after reaching the Battalion lines. Heavy enemy shelling fell on Factory Corner, the front line and communication tracks. On the 15th January, enemy shelling reached back to the camp at High Wood, where several details had been left, and one other rank was killed and eight wounded. Enemy gunfire continued the following day, with high explosive and shrapnel shells. The Battalion was relieved by the 9th Battalion DLI and moved to huts in Bazentin-le-Petit. The next three days were spent cleaning up and finding working parties

until, on the 20th of the month, the Battalion moved back into the support line. Enemy artillery remained active. Working parties improved trenches and shelters and laid new duckboard tracks. A direct hit by enemy guns on one of the Battalion shelters, on the 24th, killed five men and wounded four others. On the 25th January, relieved by the 9th Durhams a move was made to a camp in Bazentin-le-Petit. The following day the Battalion moved to 'B' Camp at Becourt. It remained here until the 29th, when it moved to Ribemont and took over comfortable billets from units of the 4th Australian Division. A pleasant area, three miles from the pretty village of Heilly, fully inhabited by French civilians and served by estaminets, the Battalion hoped it would be left there for some time. Its hopes were not dashed and it stayed here until the 16th of February. Training included bayonet fighting, bombing practice, supervised by the bombing officer, Second-Lieutenant Adamson, and squad and company drills. Frosts were extremely severe and the men were thankful to be out of the line.

In the middle of February, 1917, the British Army took over an additional stretch of the front from the French. The 50th Division relieved the French 35th and 36th Divisions, south west of Peronne, in front of Belloy-en-Sauterre and Berny-en-Sauterre. On the 17th the Battalion marched to Hamel, a few miles north of Amiens. On the 19th February it moved to Proyart, where it stayed for three or four days. It was whilst the Battalion was here, that Lieutenant-Colonel Jeffreys returned to take command once more. After this brief stay in Proyart the Battalion moved to Foucaucourt, a village which had been totally destroyed. Accommodation was in huts, built by the French for their own men. These were large enough to accommodate one hundred and fifty men to a hut and were fairly comfortable. The Battalion was now in divisional reserve. Conditions were deteriorating considerably. Warmer weather was melting the frosts rapidly and trenches were turning into streams of water and mud, the latter waist deep in places. The route to the front line trenches was by way of the long French communication trenches, deep in mud, with crumbling walls. Very often they were beyond negotiating and movement could only be carried out 'over the top'. Reliefs often took far longer than planned, because of the difficulty of moving through the mud, laden down with arms and equipment. 'X' Company had a terrible experience which, if extreme, gives a picture of the difficulties being met. It left the camp at 5 p.m. to carry out a relief. The company strength, on setting out, was one hundred and thirty officers and men. The guides who met them soon lost their way and it was not till dawn on the following morning that the front line was reached. Company strength was down to thirty men, one hundred being lost on the way in. The missing were stuck in the mud, somewhere between the camp and the front line. It took a total of twenty-four hours for the company to assemble and complete the relief. Moving through the trench systems in these conditions, it was not unusual for men to lose their boots in the deep, sucking mud, and, it is reputed, that a few even lost their trousers. Many men went sick living under these conditions. No matter what safeguards were practiced, trench feet remained a major problem when in the trenches. Officers and NCOs had to ensure that the men rubbed their feet regularly with whale oil, and dry socks were worn. Easier said than done, as often spare dry socks carried in the men's packs, were soaked by rain and snow before taken out for use. Whale oil, used from the early days in the trenches to combat trench feet, had proved not to be a complete safeguard against the affliction. It was most effective for frying potatoes, in a mess tin over a small fire. Thigh length gum boots were worn, but the ubiquitous mud and rain found a way through to soak and freeze feet. Added to the conditions were enemy snipers, who were very active, and made movement during daylight hours very precarious.

On the 27th February, the 6th Battalion went into reserve and, three days later, moved into the front line to relieve the 8th Battalion. Enemy artillery quietened down somewhat over the next few days. On the 1st March, Lieutenant-Colonel Jeffreys, DSO, was evacuated to hospital. Major E. Crouch, second in command of the 9th Durhams, took over temporary command of the Battalion. On the 3rd of the month, Major Crouch returned to his Battalion and Major W.B. Little, then with the 5th Battalion The Border Regiment, took over temporary command. Relieved by the 5th Borders on the 4th March, the Battalion moved into support at Berny. On the 5th, Major Little was replaced as temporary commanding officer, by Major W.D.C. Hunt, MC, of the 7th Durhams. Second-Lieutenant H.V. Taylor, with a draft of forty four other ranks, joined the Battalion on this day. The enemy artillery and aircraft were very active and shelled Berny and surrounds. This quietened down on the 7th of the month, giving the Battalion the opportunity to clean and repair their trenches. The following day, 50th Division was relieved by the 59th Division. The 6th Battalion was, in turn, relieved by 5th The South Staffordshire Regiment, and marched to Foucaucourt. Lieutenant-Colonel Jeffreys returned from hospital and took the Battalion out of the trenches. On the 9th March, the Battalion marched to Morcourt, in the valley of the Somme, where it was to remain until the end of the month. After initial cleaning up, regular training was undertaken. As usual, wherever the Durhams found themselves, camp improvements were initiated. A recreational committee was formed, comprising Second-Lieutenant Greener and one NCO from each company. A Battalion concert was held in the Recreation Hut on the evening of the 14th March. Football competitions started. In the Brigade boxing competition, held on the 25th March, Sergeant Young, Privates Nimney and Moody won the Middleweight, Lightweight and Featherweight titles for the Battalion. On the 27th of the month, Lieutenant-Colonel Jeffreys was evacuated sick once more. Wounds and illness had taken their toll and Lieutenant-Colonel Jeffreys left the Battalion for the last time. He had commanded it throughout some terrific battles and he was much admired and respected by both officers and men, for his leadership qualities and aggressive fighting spirit. Major W.C. Hunt resumed in temporary command. On the 31st March, the Battalion paraded at 7.30 a.m. and marched to Talmas where it embussed for Wargnies. 'W', 'X' and 'Y' Companies moved on to Havernas. 50th Division was beginning its move towards the Arras front, where a major offensive action was to be undertaken in the near future.

CHAPTER 9
ARRAS
1917

Divine Service, taken on the morning of Sunday 1st April, was the one and only service involving the temporary commanding officer, Major Hunt, who preached the sermon. Tragically, he was to die of a heart attack on the 5th April, whilst reconnoitring the forward area. The move to the Arras front continued on the 2nd April. The Battalion marched through a heavy snowstorm to Longueville. The following day the route took the Battalion to Vacquerie-le-Boucq where it was billeted in the village. The next day it marched to Blangerval and Blangermont, where it was difficult to find billets in these two villages, due to the large numbers of troops already there. Major Ebsworth rejoined from a Commanding Officers Course in England. Major Hunt was buried at St. Pol on the 6th April, with all of the officers and representative parties of NCOs and other ranks. The move to the Arras front continued over the next few days, until Fauberge de Ronville was reached on the 11th April. On this same date, Major F.W. Robson, DSO, assumed command of the Battalion. The march to Ronville was undertaken in a snowstorm. The men had been ordered to leave greatcoats and all surplus kit behind but carried their blankets. It was a miserable march. On arrival they were billeted in the caves of Ronville. These caves were a remarkable sight for the troops. They covered a large area and were capable of holding thousands of men. Reputed to have been dug by Flemish labour in the Middle Ages to provide material for building work in the city of Arras, the French had used them to provide cover for their troops during the war. The British had added electricity for lighting and ventilation to improve the atmosphere. Whilst they provided safe shelter they were not pleasant places. Despite improvements they were cold, foul-smelling and damp, and a slimy liquid ran down the walls and dripped from the roofs, soaking the men huddled together for warmth on the floor underneath.

The Battalion remained in the caves for one night only. Additional troops were pouring into the area and these took over the caves, whilst the 6th Battalion moved out into the cellars of Ronville. The stay here was very short and in the afternoon of the 12th April, the Battalion marched via Beaurains and Neuville-Vitasse towards Wancourt. Dusk was beginning to fall when it reached a sunken road. From this position a relief of the 14th Division, VII Corps, was arranged and put into operation. 'W', 'X' and 'Y' Companies moved in to Niger and Nepal Trenches, which lay behind the front line. 'Z' Company were ordered forward to dig and occupy a trench near Wancourt cemetery. The Battalion stayed in these positions throughout the 13th April. Orders were received that the Battalion was to attack at dawn on the following day.

The position held by 151 Brigade was as follows: the 9th Battalion was holding the front line from Wancourt Tower, now a ruin, northwards, with two companies, a distance of six to seven hundred yards. The two other companies of this Battalion were in a sunken road, east of the River Cojeul. The 6th Battalion had moved at 1.00 a.m. on the 14th, from Niger and Nepal Trenches, into the dried-up bed of the Cojeul on the right of the 9th Battalion. It had with it one section of the 151st machine-gun Company and was to attack alongside 169 Brigade of the 56th

Division, which was on its right. In the forthcoming attack, the 9th Battalion would not move, but be prepared to meet any enemy counter-attack from Guemappe, which was still in German hands. Immediately before zero hour at 5.30 a.m., the 6th Battalion was ordered to deploy with its left on Wancourt Tower and this late manoeuvre was completed at 5.20 a.m. The 8th Battalion was in support of the attack and moved into the bed of the River Cojeul, when the 6th moved out to the attack. The 8th Battalion, in turn, would be followed into the river bed by the 5th Border Regiment, when it moved out to support the advance of the 6th. Due to lack of information on the progress of the attack, the Borders did not move beyond the river bed. Another weakness which hampered the Battalion's attack, was information as to the exact whereabouts of the German lines. Only an estimation of the position of the German Lines could be given to the attacking companies.

At 5.30 p.m. the 6th Battalion left the river bed and advanced up the ridge about five hundred yards ahead. It was preceded by a heavy artillery barrage and attacked in four company waves. 'W' Company led the way, followed by 'X', 'Y' and 'Z' Companies in that order. Immediately they moved from cover the German artillery bombardment struck and heavy machine-gun fire came from the front and from Guemappe in the right rear. 'W' and 'X' Companies crested the top of the ridge and moved down the other side and out of sight of observers. They were not seen again for the rest of the day. 'Y' and 'Z' Companies reached the top of the ridge but could get no further. Here they were joined by the 8th Battalion. On the left, units of the 56th Division had lost direction and men of the London Regiment

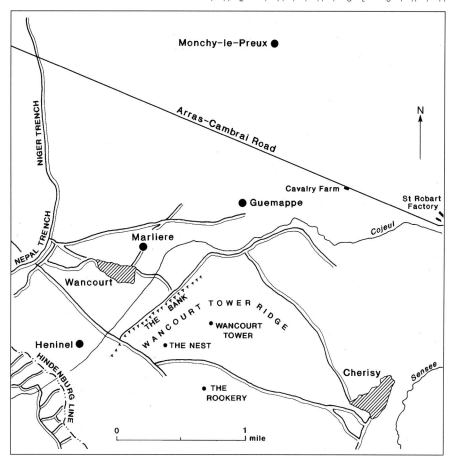

Arras *1917 - Wancourt. The Tower and the Valley of the River Cojeul*

became mixed up with the Durhams. Reorganisation was made virtually impossible by the severity of the enemy fire. There was great concern as to the whereabouts of 'W' and 'X' Companies. Later in the day, they were reported to be holding a tangle of trenches south of Wancourt Tower, where they had beaten off a number of fierce enemy counter-attacks. At this time the survivors of both companies totalled four officers and about twenty men. The remainder of the Battalion were stretched along a sunken road running approximately west to east, south-west of the Tower. Casualties amongst junior officers, always at the sharp end of any assault, were heavy. Captain A.L. Brock, Second-Lieutenants W.L. Newton, H. Greener, J.W. Payne and W.H. Richardson were killed. Captain R.S. Johnson, Second-Lieutenants C. Reed, E.R. Appleton, F.C.D. Scott, D.F. Charlton, H.H. Nicholson, R. Ainsworth and G.R. Roberts were wounded. Fourteen other ranks were killed, with a further ninety-two wounded and sixty-six missing. Captains R.S. Johnson and H. Walton were awarded the Military Cross. They had commanded 'W' and 'X' Companies respectively. Corporal Betts was awarded the Distinguished Conduct Medal and the Croix de Guerre. The remnants of the Battalion were relieved that night by the London Rifle Brigade and moved to dugouts in the Hindenburg Line on Telegraph Hill, reaching there by dawn on the 15th April. Brigadier Cameron sent the following message to the Battalion commander:

> 'The 6th and 8th Battalions DLI had a very difficult task, namely to deploy at very short notice on a mission, and in a direction, for which they were not prepared. The brunt of the difficulty fell on the 6th Battalion DLI and the section of the 151st machine-gun Company attached to it, as they led the advancing portion of the Brigade and had to deploy in the dark, and the Brigade Commander asks the remainder of the Brigade to join with him in congratulating them on the dash and spirit with which they carried out the task allotted to them.'

The following day, the 16th April, the Battalion moved back to the caves in Ronville, and remained there until the 20th of the month, resting, reorganising and re-equipping. On the 21st, the Battalion moved into dugouts in the trenches on the slope of Telegraph Hill, known as The Harp. Here it was in support to the Brigade. The Quartermaster Stores were in Arras which was shelled on the 22nd April, and Second-Lieutenant D.D.R. Lewis, acting Quartermaster, was killed by a direct hit on the stores. The stay in The Harp was brief and in the early hours of the 24th April, the Battalion moved to Niger and Nepal Trenches. On the 26th, it moved again to Telegraph Hill. The following day, it moved to Arras where it entrained for Mondicourt. On arrival it marched into rest, occupying billets in Humbercourt. Again the

stay was a short one and on the 1st May, the Battalion moved to Berles-au-Bois, a ruined and desolate village. The next day, it moved to Rivière-Grosseville, arriving at 6.50 p.m. The billets occupied were in good condition and quite comfortable. Two days rest and reorganising ended when a further move was made back to Humbercourt. The stay here was most pleasant and lasted until the 17th May. After initial cleaning up, training became the order of the day. This encompassed route marches, field training and firing, the latter at the ranges in Lucheux Forest. On the 18th, the Battalion marched off at 8.45 a.m., via Couterelle - Grombremetz-Humberscamp -Pommier - Bienvillers, to Monchy-au-Bois, where it arrived at 2.45 p.m. The accommodation at Monchy was sparse in the extreme. An open field with a trench and wire was the site of the Battalion's billets. These were contrived from the few tents available, the rest being made from shelters made from the men's ground sheets. Five days of training followed, and on the 23rd the Battalion moved to Laherlière. The following day, it moved to Souastre, arriving at 5.50 p.m.

Souastre village had been within a couple of miles of the German lines, until the March retreat. It had hardly suffered from such proximity to the front line. The Battalion was billeted in huts built, by the French, around a parade and sports ground. It was to stay here until the 14th June and enjoy possibly the best time since its arrival in France, a time to build up the morale and strength of the Battalion. Training and recreation was organised, drafts were received. Company, battalion and brigade exercises took place throughout the period. On the 28th May, news was received that Captains R.S. Johnson and H. Walton had been awarded the Military Cross. The Battalion held a sports afternoon on the 31st of the month, and companies practiced night operations, returning to billets about 5 a.m. the next morning, 1st June. On the 2nd June, a poignant journey was made, by a group of eight officers and twelve other ranks, to the Butte-de-Warlencourt, scene of the bitter Somme fighting on the previous 5th November. Included in the visit was a search of the nearby cemetery for the graves of fallen comrades. During this period of time at Souastre, Battalion pioneers built the memorial cross, which was erected on the Butte on the 12th June, by

Warrant Officers and Sergeants at Souastre *resting out of the line in 1917. Armourer Sergeant Osbourne, 3rd from left, middle row, was in the Ordnance Corps and sneaked out to France with the Battalion in 1915 and remained with it almost throughout the war. Sergeant Lowe holds the bat.*

Second-Lieutenant R.H. Stewart and a party of other ranks. It took its place alongside those erected by the 8th and 9th Battalions. In the mid 1920s this cross was brought back to England where it now reposes to this day, in St. Andrew's Church, South Close, Bishop Auckland.

A much refreshed Battalion marched to Henin-sur-Cojeul on the 15th June, a very hot day. The march began at 7.15 a.m. and was made via Bienvillers - Monchy-au-Bois - Adinfer, where there was a stop for dinner at Boislieux-Boiry-Becquerelle and then on to Henin, arriving at 8.00 p.m. The Battalion moved into

the front line and relieved the 10th Essex Regiment, of the 53rd Infantry Brigade, 18th Division. The fighting of April had died down and normal trench activities had replaced it. The 50th Division front now stretched from about one thousand yards west of Fontaines-lez-Croisilles on the right, to the village of Cherisy on the left. The latter was still held by the Germans, although Guemappes was in British hands. The enemy positions lay out of sight, on the reverse slope of the ridge west of the Sensée Valley. 151 and 150 Brigades held the line. The 6th Battalion held the front line for 151 Brigade, with 'Y' Company right, 'W' Company Centre, 'X' Company left and 'Z' Company in support in Mallard Trench.

The Battalion's entry into the front line was not to be a quiet one. On the 17th June, the positions held by 'W' and 'X' Companies were heavily shelled by the enemy. Second-Lieutenant Richardson led a patrol of one NCO and thirteen men to ascertain whether an isolated enemy trench was occupied. As soon as they left the sap, it came under enemy fire and this continued until it reached the isolated trench. At this point a Very light was fired and two Germans were seen running along the trench. The patrol entered the trench and found it to be in poor condition. It had four small dugouts in which there were no enemy occupants. As the patrol returned to our lines, it was again fired on by enemy artillery but there were no casualties. Later the enemy mortared the isolated trench, obviously under the impression that it was now occupied by our troops. At 9.00 p.m. on the 18th June, the enemy began to shell Mallard Trench and Foster Avenue. This bombardment increased in volume at about 9.30 p.m., with the addition of mortar and machine-gun fire. About thirty Germans left their trenches and took up position round a sap head, lying just outside the British wire. Bombs were hurled into the sap and its garrison wounded. Two men also were listed as missing. The Battalion reaction was swift. A bombing counter-attack was organised up the sap but this failed due to strong enemy resistance. Stokes Mortars and rifle grenades were fired into the sap, now occupied by the enemy force. Lewis guns swept No Man's Land on both flanks of the sap. A second counter-attack was organised and led by Second-Lieutenants Aubin and Richardson. This force worked its way up the sap with flanking squads some twenty-five yards away. When the sap was reached it was to discover that the enemy had gone leaving two dead inside, and a further two dead outside. All four of these men were identified to be members of the 457 Infantry Reserve Regiment. The events of the 18th were not yet over. At 10.30 p.m. a patrol of two NCOs and four men, under Second-Lieutenant Druery, left our line to reconnoitre a small enemy trench. They heard a working party, which they understood to be linking and consolidating shell holes in front of Narrow Trench. The patrol failed to get close to this working party, which was protected by a covering party and, in addition, machine-gun fire was brought down upon them. The patrol returned to our trenches without loss.

At 12.30 a.m. on the 19th June, a patrol of one sergeant and four men, under Second-Lieutenant Stewart left a sap to look at a shell hole immediately in front of our positions, which was thought to be occupied by the enemy. The patrol had just reached the shell hole, when it was challenged from the left rear. Four of the enemy were seen in the rear. Shots were immediately exchanged by both sides, and bombs were thrown at one of the patrol who was mortally wounded. The reminder of the patrol withdrew, bringing their wounded member with them, and reached our trenches at 1.30 a.m. Intermittent mortar fire from both sides occupied most of the rest of the day. Battalion patrols remained very active. At 10.00 p.m. a patrol went out and, hearing sounds of an enemy working party, sought to discover the position of this party. It failed to do so. Another patrol, under Second-Lieutenant D.B. Scott, went out from Bullfinch Trench and heard the unmistakable sounds of a large enemy working party. The patrol returned to the trench and artillery fire was brought to bear on the reported position of the enemy party. It was believed that the working party lost some men and ceased activity. Two further patrols, led by NCOs, set out to reconnoitre a sap, which was found to be occupied by the enemy. Stokes Mortars fired into this position and a number of hits were claimed.

The British Army believed in aggressive patrolling as a means of denying No Man's Land to the enemy and so blinding him as to what was going on in our trenches. At the same time it was considered that aggressive patrolling enabled us to get vital information on the enemy's activities in the trenches opposite. Patrolling was a very stressful activity. There were officers and men who were good patrollers and others who viewed the activity with considerable anxiety and reluctance. New officers to a unit often found one of their earliest duties was to take out a night patrol. It seemed to be an accepted way of discovering what they were 'made of'. A patrol described in the *Whizz Bang* of March, 1916, gives an indication of what it was like to be on patrol:

'...So, armed with four bombs and our revolvers, over the parapet we go, having, of course, previously warned the people on each side that a patrol is going out, where it is going to, and which direction we hope to return in. So carefully picking our way through our own wire, we go down the side of a hedge until we come to a friendly embankment that gives us cover from view over where the Bosches send up flares. Following the embankment, we come across some old dugouts, and looking round these find the only recent sign of occupation have been left by our own men, most likely previous patrols. On we go again, and come to an opening. This we were told was our way in. So in we get; drop into an old communication trench, which is partly covered in. Follow this for about 12 yards, then out into a path. This we follow until pulled up by Hunswire. Damnably tough stuff it is, too, as we quickly find while trying to cut through it. What a beastly noise the twigs make, cracking like an eighteen pounder. By this time we are only about 15 yards from the Bosches' trench. Have they heard us? We wonder. Now turn to the right for that rotten sap. Why do people want to push out saps? They're a damned nuisance. It's a very unpleasant thing getting so miserably wet and grubby, and all for the sake of a beastly ditch. Hello! here's the sap. Let's follow it up. We do and find that, at any rate, it is not being used now. So on we crawl to have a look at the German parapet. Get to their wire when Suggins coughs. Never heard such a noise in my life. Up go the flares. We're seen. "Ping, ping," sing the bullets, and we, as one man, make tracks for home. They continue sending up the fireworks, and looking round I see Ritson standing up."Get down, man." "I can't," he replies. "My d____leg is fastened in the wire." He quickly gets his leg out, and we all make possible speed for the cover of the embankment. Reaching there, we stop for a much needed rest. It's hard work trying to beat the speed limit on your hands and knees. After resting a short time, we wend our way back to our line, then to report, and a drink on the strength of it.'

Many patrols must have ended with a similar result.

On the 20th June, the Battalion was relieved by the 8th DLI and moved back to a camp near Boisleux-au-Mont, and into reserve. Casualties, during these hectic activities, had been light. Private W. Hall, born at Marley Hill, who enlisted at Stanley, was killed on the 19th. There were fifteen wounded other ranks and two men, Privates H. Garbett and G.H. Bennett were missing.

The Battalion remained in this area until the 2nd July. It was a period of rest, training and finding working parties. The Battalion, minus 'Y' Company, on detachment to the Corps artillery as a working party, was inspected by the Divisional Commander, Major-General Sir P.S. Wilkinson, on the 27th June. It then moved into Brigade support on the 2nd July. This was a beginning of a regular period of reliefs, whereby the Battalion had two periods of four days in the front line, interspersed by a period of four days in support at Henin or Neuville-Vitesse. These were followed by eight days in reserve.

The companies' positions in the support role were as follows: 'W' Company in Egret Trench, 'Y' Company in Duck and Curlew Trenches and 'Z' Company in Lion and Lion Switch Trenches. 'X' Company was in caves in Marlière, a hamlet lying close to Wancourt, on the road to Monchy-le-Preux. These caves afforded protection from enemy artillery but were on a much smaller scale than those in Ronville. Battalion Headquarters was in Puttee Lane. The relief of the 12th Battalion London Regiment (1st Battalion The Rangers), was completed by 8.00 p.m. Over the next four days, the companies were subjected to intermittent shelling, with little else of note reported. The Battalion moved into the front line during the night of 7th-8th July, and relieved the 9th DLI in Jackdaw and Ape Trenches. 'W' Company held the left position, with 'Z' Company in the Centre and 'X' Company on the right. 'Y' Company was in support in Bison, Boar and Buck Trenches. On the night of the 8th July, a patrol led by Second-Lieutenant Rushworth, observed a small enemy working party near Nut Trench. A few Minnenwerfers were exploded over the Battalion positions during the night. Patrol activity continued over the next three nights when the enemy were occasionally sighted, but disappeared too quickly to be engaged by our men. At 10.00 p.m. on the 11th July, the Battalion was relieved by the 9th Battalion and moved to Neuville-Vitesse and into the camp vacated by the 8th Battalion, who had moved into support. Casualties during this tour of the trenches were three other ranks killed and nine wounded.

The Battalion remained in Brigade reserve until the night of 15th-16th July, when it relieved the 9th Battalion in the front line trenches. The companies dispositions were: 'Y' Company left, 'X'

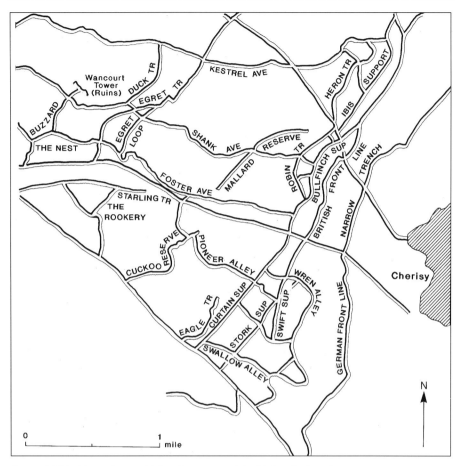

Arras *1917 - Cherisy Sector - 6th Battalion supported the 9th Battalion's raid on Narrow Trench on the 15th September*

command of 151 Brigade, and Major F. Walton replaced him in command of the Battalion. Some shelling by both sides occurred on the 16th and 18th July and this became quite intense on the 19th of the month. For the most part, the period of time in the front line was taken up by active patrolling. It was quickly discovered that No Man's Land was empty of the enemy, except for a working party spotted on the night of the 17th July, which was dispersed by Lewis gun fire. The Battalion was relieved by the 4th Northumberland Fusiliers on the night of the 19th July, and it moved into divisional reserve and into a camp near Neuville-Vitesse. Here it stayed over the next eight days, resting and training. Lieutenant-Colonel Robson returned to take over command on the 24th of the month. On the 27th, the Battalion returned to the support positions, with the companies disposed as follows: 'W' Company on the right in Egret Loop, 'X' Company on the left in Egret Trench and Egret Loop and 'Y' Company in the centre in Egret Trench. 'Z' Company was in support in The Nest and Albatross Trench. One man was wounded during the relief. The Battalion remained in support until it relieved the 9th Battalion in the front line in Swift and Martin Trenches. 'Y' Company was on the left, 'W' Company in the centre and 'Z' Company on the right. 'X' Company was in support with Battalion Headquarters in Avenue Trench.

For the next four days of its stay in the line, there was little enemy activity. The usual patrolling was carried out and, on occasions, the enemy was spotted and fired upon. These were usually working parties but an occasional enemy listening post was discovered. Invariably when a listening post was discovered,

Company right and 'Z' Company in the centre. 'W' Company was in support. As the relief was being carried out, a party of Germans was spotted approaching 'X' Company's positions. Lewis guns were fired at them, resulting in one of the enemy being killed. A patrol under Second-Lieutenant T. Peat went out to examine the condition of the wire in front of 'Y' Company's positions. Lieutenant-Colonel Robson took over temporary its position was noted and shell and mortar fire brought down upon it, or a fighting patrol would be sent to raid the post and, hopefully, take a prisoner. The patrols suffered losses. Second-Lieutenant P.E. Watson was wounded by enemy machine-gun fire when out on patrol on the 3rd August. In the front line, movement during the day was very restricted, and food and supplies were invariably brought up to the companies during the night. Carrying parties performed this task, bearing their heavy loads along the narrow, winding trenches in all weathers and under all conditions. This, too, was a dangerous task, as every night enemy artillery and machine-gun fire sought out the routes used by these parties. On the 1st August, a carrying party led by Second-Lieutenant W.F. Dunne from 'X' Company, was fired on and the officer wounded and evacuated to hospital. Relief was carried out by the 9th Battalion on the 4th August. The 6th Battalion moved back into divisional reserve and into a camp near Henin-sur-Cojeul. Major A.E. Ebsworth returned to the Battalion from the 50th Division Depot Battalion.

Four days in reserve ended on the 8th August, when the 9th Battalion was relieved in the front line. Three companies occupied Swift, Wood and Dodo Trenches, with 'X' Company on the left, 'W' Company in the centre and 'Y' Company on the right. 'Z' Company was in support in the Sunken Road and Battalion HQ in Avenue Trench. Patrolling was immediately initiated. On the first two nights, there were no signs of the enemy. Success was gained on the 10th August. A German soldier, one of a rationing party, lost his way and was captured in front of our wire. The capture of an enemy soldier was always considered a great success and invariably brought congratulations from higher command. Important information could be gained from a prisoner. Enemy units opposite could be identified, their fighting quality established and the strength and conditions of enemy positions verified. On occasions, a prisoner might have knowledge which revealed enemy plans to British intelligence staff. The same, of course, was true of Allied prisoners taken by the Germans. The Battalion organised a raiding party, which went out on the 11th August, led by Second-Lieutenant Leatherbarrow. The objective was a number of shell holes linked together to form an enemy strong point. No enemy troops were found to be in occupation and, though the party remained in the position for twenty minutes, no enemy appeared. A raiding party was usually much stronger in number than a patrol. Its objective was to enter an enemy position to kill and capture Germans and destroy the position. As raiding parties grew in strength and objectives became more ambitious, raids were accompanied by preliminary artillery and mortar support, with the infantry undergoing a period of training prior to the raid. On the 12th August, the Battalion was relieved by the 4th Battalion Northumberland Fusiliers and it moved back to the divisional reserve camp, for rest and training. VI Corps held a horse show on the 18th of the month, when Bugler Sergeant J. Jackson of the Battalion, was in charge of the massed buglers.

The relief of the 4th East Yorkshire Regiment and two companies of the 4th Yorkshire Regiment, was carried out on the 20th August. 'Z' Company was in Lion and Panther Trenches, 'X' Company in Egret Trench and 'Y' Company in Curlew Trench. 'W' Company was in the caves in Marlière Village. These were support positions and four quiet days were spent in these lines. The 9th Battalion was relieved in the front line on the 24th.

Patrols were out that night, on one of which Second-Lieutenant T.J. Burton was wounded though he remained on duty. machine-gun bursts in No Man's Land were heard, along with the sounds of an enemy working party in Nut Trench, but no contact was made. These patrols continued throughout the Battalion's stay in the line. Some enemy activity was reported and Lewis gun and mortar fire searched the area, but no one was actually seen. Relief by the 9th Battalion was carried out during the 28th August, and the Battalion moved into brigade reserve. For the next four days the Battalion was busy cleaning equipment, clothing and providing working parties.

The Battalion relieved the 9th Battalion on the 1st September, with 'X', 'Y' and 'Z' Companies in the front line and 'W' Company in close support. Two men of 'Z' Company were wounded during the relief. This period of time in the line was spent in widening and deepening the communication trenches and in patrolling. No Germans were seen though sounds of digging indicated that they too, were improving their defences. The only activity of note occurred on the night of the 2nd-3rd

Aerial view of the Cherisy Sector, *1917. The straight trench in front of Cherisy is Narrow Trench, one of the objectives of the raid made by the 9th Battalion on 15th September, 1917*

September. An enemy minnenwerfer had been firing intermittently over a period of time into our front line trenches, causing damage. It was eventually located in St. Rohart's Quarry and a decision was taken to put it out of action. On this night, four Stokes Mortars of the 151 Trench Mortar Battery protected by two patrols of the 6th Battalion comprising ten men each and an officer, together with four patrols of the 8th Battalion, went out into No Man's Land and into a previously reconnoitred position. At about midnight, the mortars opened fire at a rate of fifteen rounds a minute, on the enemy minnenwerfer. At the same time two machine-guns fired on the area round St. Rohart's Factory. The action lasted for fifteen minutes when a withdrawal was made to the safety of our trenches, under a protecting barrage. Patrols were sent out to evaluate the success of the action and reported back that there were no sign of the enemy. The minnenwerfer was also silenced. Trench improvements continued and with the exception of some sniping, all was quiet. On the 5th September, the Battalion was relieved by the 4th Northumberland Fusiliers. This relief was completed at 8.30 p.m. One NCO was wounded whilst the relief was taking place. The Battalion moved into Northumberland Lines, a comfortable hutted camp near Mercatel.

The Battalion remained in reserve from the 6th-12th September. Most of the men were on working parties. On the 13th of the month, it relieved the 5th DLI in the Cherisy Sector. Patrols were sent out and the strength and condition of the wire in front of our trenches was inspected. Artillery and mortars on both sides were active but there were no casualties.

A meticulously planned trench raid was carried out by the 9th DLI on the 15th September. The sector of the enemy line to be raided had been carefully identified and located - Narrow Trench. This area was then cut off from any contact with and support from flank and rear enemy units by a wall of fire provided by our artillery, mortars and machine-guns. At 4.00 p.m. three companies of the 9th Battalion crossed No Man's Land and entered the enemy trenches. A number of German soldiers were killed or captured and dugouts destroyed. 9th Battalion casualties were extremely light and the raid was a considerable success. The role of the 6th Battalion in this action was to attract enemy attention by providing a diversion and give the enemy the impression that an attack was to be made from the Battalion's front line. A number of 'dummies,' of men and a tank had been placed in position in No Man's Land during the night preceding the raid. Second-Lieutenant Leatherbarrow and ten men of the Battalion worked these dummies. These attracted the enemy attention and he proceeded to bombard the positions of the dummies with artillery and machine-gun fire. The enemy fire also fell on the Battalion's front and support trenches, killing one man and wounding four others. Seven men also suffered from shell-shock. The second phase of the raid was carried out by 'C' Company, 8th DLI who entered the enemy trenches at 7.40 p.m. Two enemy machine-guns were captured together with three prisoners. Twelve Germans were killed. At 4.00 a.m. on the 16th, the third phase was carried out by releasing gas over the enemy positions. Later, patrols went out and found the German front line empty. Sergeant P. Finn who had assisted Second-Lieutenant Leatherbarrow with the dummies, was awarded the Military Medal. Two other Military Medals were awarded to Corporal Nesbitt and Private Allison of 'X' Company, for digging out a man buried by enemy shellfire whilst they, too, were under enemy artillery and machine-gun fire.

The 9th Battalion relieved the Battalion in the afternoon of the 17th September. 'X' Company moved to Concrete Trench as reserve company to the front line Battalion. The other companies of the Battalion marched into brigade reserve and into a camp near Henin. The Battalion was back in the front line on the 21st September. Headquarters was in Avenue Trench. 'Z' Company was in the Sunken Road and 'X', 'W' and 'Y' Companies were in the front line. Patrols reported that the enemy positions opposite were very strong and he was busy strengthening them even further. Active patrolling over the next few days confirmed the increasing strength of the enemy positions. The raids of the 15th of the month, had obviously made the enemy very alert and he was seeing to his defences. On the 25th of the month, the Battalion moved into support. 'Y' Company was in Cuckoo Reserve Trench, 'X' Company was in Egret Loop, 'W' Company was in The Nest and Albatross Trench and Battalion Headquarters was also in The Nest. During the next four days, the trenches held were systematically improved and strengthened until they ranked amongst the best in the line. Relief arrived on the 29th September and the Battalion went into divisional reserve at Northumberland Lines, where it spent the time cleaning up and providing working parties.

CHAPTER 10
THE THIRD BATTLE OF YPRES
1917

On the 4th October, the Battalion moved to Leeds Camp at Gommiecourt, just off the Bapaume - Arras road. Hugh Lyon (newly appointed Captain) rejoined after recovering from his injuries sustained in December, 1915. A long period of training ensued. Lieutenant-General Haldane, VI Corps Commander, presented Military Medals on the 9th October to Sergeant P. Finn, Corporal Nesbitt and Private Allison. At 1.45 a.m. on the 17th of the month, the Battalion marched off to Bapaume where it entrained for Esquelbecq, north west of Cassel. It arrived here at 2.45 p.m. and marched to billets at Eringhem. On the 20th, the Battalion marched to billets in Arnèke. Brigadier General N.J.G. Cameron left the brigade to take over command of the 49th Division. He was succeeded by Brigadier-General C. Martin. The next day, the Battalion moved to Wormhoudt where it entrained for Proven, just inside the Belgian border. Here it went into Piddington Camp off the Poperinghe road, where it spent the night. Sarawak Camp, in woods north of Poperinghe, was reached on the 22nd. This was described as the dirtiest camp ever occupied by the Battalion. Fortunately the stay was not a long one. On the 24th of the month, the Battalion marched to Proven, entrained for Boesinghe and marched to Hull's Farm Camp, near Brielen. Whilst waiting to get into the camp, still occupied by the 4th Battalion The Northumberland Fusiliers, it lay in a nearby field where it was bombed by German aeroplanes. Second-Lieutenant Ragg and sixteen other ranks were wounded. Over the next three days, German aircraft attacked the camp and its vicinity and bombs were dropped. No casualties were suffered as a result of these raids. Carrying and working parties were supplied over the next six days. The area in which these worked proved to be very dangerous indeed. Six other ranks were wounded on the 25th October. A carrying party for the 151 machine-gun Company provided by 'Z' Company and under the command of Second-Lieutenant E.A. Ambrister, was called upon to support the machine-gunners in an attack carried out on the 26th. Seven other ranks of the party were wounded and twelve reported missing. On the 29th of the month, Lieutenant F.W. Tee in command of a working party, was wounded. The Battalion had arrived in the infamous Salient. The Third Battle of Ypres - Passchendaele to give it its more familiar and emotive title - had some four weeks to run before grinding to a halt shortly after the village of that name was taken by the Canadians.

The 50th Division had relieved the 34th Division on the night of the 24th-25th October, in the sector of the front line which lay south of Houthulst Forest and astride the Ypres - Staden railway. 149 Brigade was in the line on the left and centre of the sector, part of which lay on the edge of the forest. The bitter fighting which had taken place since the Division was last in the Salient, had changed the area beyond recognition. Countless shell holes which in places overlapped each other, were filled with filthy, polluted water. These were a constant source of danger to men carrying their heavy loads along muddy, slippery duckboard tracks, which were the only means of communication between the lines and the back areas. Many soldiers had fallen into these holes and drowned before they could be pulled out. The smell of cordite, gas and putrified flesh hung over the landscape. The wreckage and waste of war lay everywhere. Destroyed and abandoned tanks, tractors, guns and limbers covered the area. The roar of hate from the guns of both sides filled the ears. The troops lived in some of these shell holes which passed for a front line during the period of their tour of duty, covered by a blanket and ground sheet in a pitiful attempt to keep out the wet. Mud stretched as far as the eye could see. Immensely strong concrete German pillboxes dominated the landscape. These were capable of resisting all but a direct hit from the heaviest of shells. Sited so that they gave mutual support as well as covering the ground within the range of their machine-guns, they were formidable obstacles to the advancing British troops and were the cause of very heavy casualties. The more experienced British troops did find two ways of dealing with them. The loopholes were so constructed that the enemy machine-guns could not be sufficiently depressed to cover the ground immediately adjoining the pillboxes. This enabled men of aggression and courage to crawl up to the loopholes and throw in grenades. The second way of dealing with the pillboxes was provided by the extremely muddy conditions. Violent bombardment by British artillery caused mud to be flung up and over the pillboxes, This could cover the loopholes, or even the strongpoints themselves. Captured pillboxes could be turned against the enemy and used as shelters or strongpoints by the British.

The Battalion moved into the front line and relieved the 5th East Yorkshire Regiment on the 31st October. The sector occupied

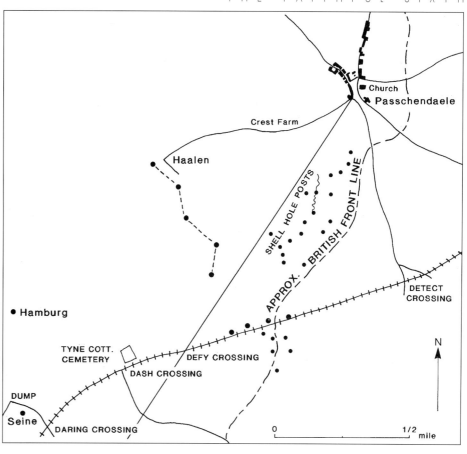

The Third Battle of Ypres - *Passchandaele. In the sodden, desolate battlefield only shell holes could be held as a front line*

was on the left, just inside the Houthulst Forest. Battalion Headquarters was in Egypt House, a captured German pillbox, which became a target for the enemy artillery. The route to the line lay across the canal and along a six mile length of duckboard track. Each man carried four days' rations. The terrain was totally devastated. It was covered by enemy artillery which was very active and under observation and attack from low flying enemy aircraft. The relief was carried out without loss. The positions occupied were a series of water-logged shell holes. On the right of the Battalion's positions was the 4th Yorkshire Regiment and on the left, the 15th Notts and Derby Regiment. The enemy infantry were found to be quiet in this area. During the succeeding nights, the Battalion pushed its posts forward and by doing so gained about two hundred yards, with very light casualties. It was relieved on the 5th November. The following awards were made to officers and men who performed well in these actions: Bar to the Military Cross, Captain J.F.G. Aubin, MC, who commanded 'Y' Company; Military Cross, Captain P.B.H. Lyon, who commanded 'X' Company. Bars to the Military Medal were awarded to Sergeants Britton MM, and Cruddace MM.

When relieved, the Battalion moved to Marsouin Farm Camp on Pilkem Ridge, arriving there about 3 a.m. This desolate and uninviting camp lay in an exposed position on the ridge and was heavily shelled, fortunately without casualties. A further move was made to White Mill

RSM Perry, DCM, and his wife.

Camp, Elverdinghe, which was both safer and more comfortable. The Battalion remained here until the 10th November when it entrained for Watten, north of St. Omer. On reaching this destination it marched to Houlle and into very good billets, particularly 'W' and 'X' Companies who found themselves in the maltery. These billets provided a home for the Battalion until the 11th December. Following initial refitting and cleaning up, comprehensive training was undertaken. Divisional, Brigade and Battalion sports were organised. The Battalion won the Brigade Football and Cross Country Championships and the Divisional Cross Country Shield. On the 11th December, it lost the services of long-serving Regimental Sergeant-Major Perry DCM. He had

been ill for some time and went to hospital, from whence he returned to England. Regimental Sergeant-Major Perry had been a tower of strength to both officers and men. A strict but fair disciplinarian, he was much respected. His place was taken by Company Sergeant-Major J. Taylor, of 'X' Company.

On the 12th December, the Battalion marched from Houlle to Watten where it entrained for Brandhoek. On arrival at the latter it moved into Erie Camp. Three days' training followed and on the 16th final preparations were made prior to moving into the line. Buses arrived on the 17th and the Battalion moved up to a camp west of Potijze Wood. The following day it moved into the support position in the area of the Salient known as Seine, two miles south west of Passchendaele. This area comprised a number of shelters occupied by 5th Border Regiment, which the Battalion relieved. Battalion Headquarters was in a dugout named India Rubber. Lieutenant Rudge, Signalling Officer, and two other ranks were wounded whilst the relief was being carried out. The enemy welcomed the Battalion with considerable shelling which died out during the course of the night. The weather during the Battalion's stay in the line alternated between rain, frost and fog. The conditions were harsh: the land, one vast swamp with numerous water-filled shell holes. There were very few signs of the villages and farmhouses which the Battalion had marched through or passed by in 1915.

The 5th Northumberland Fusiliers was relieved in the front line on the 20th December. These were largely shell hole positions reached by duckboard tracks, marked on the trench maps as H, K, RAMC Tracks etc. The positions were extremely difficult to locate in the darkness, a difficulty made worse by the almost total lack of landmarks. These tracks were well known to the enemy and were under constant shelling. Once in position no movement was possible during daylight. Carrying parties could only operate at night and under the most trying and dangerous circumstances. Battalion Headquarters was at Hamburg Pillbox. The companies were distributed as follows: two companies were in Passchendaele Village itself, with 'Z' Company (Captain Walton), on the left and 'W' Company (Captain Johnson), on the right. 'X' Company (Captain Peberdy), was behind the front line at Crest Farm and 'Y' Company (Captain Aubin) was in its rear at Haalen. A battalion of the 14th Division was on the left of the 6th Battalion. 8th DLI was on the right. The artillery of both sides was active. Except for the shelling the days remained fairly quiet. The 5th Yorkshire Regiment relieved the Battalion on the 24th December. This relief was carried out in record time and without casualties. During the stay in the line the Battalion had one man who died of wounds, Lieutenant Wilson wounded, though he remained on duty, and seven other ranks wounded. A move was made back to Potijze Camp and, knowing they were out of the line for Christmas, the men were in high spirits.

Snow was falling heavily on the morning of Christmas Day 1917. In the afternoon, the Battalion moved by bus to Erie Camp at Brandhoek. Too late to prepare Christmas dinner for the 25th it was decided to do this on the following day, Boxing Day. After spending the morning cleaning up, the men enjoyed a first class Christmas dinner of turkey, roast beef, vegetables, fruit and sweets, plum pudding, beer, port wine and cigarettes. The NCOs served whilst the officers carved. The following morning, a church parade was held. The Battalion was inspected by the Corps Commander, General Sir Hunter Weston, who congratulated it on its smart appearance.

The strain of living, more accurately existing in the line, was terrific. Moving into rest did nothing to bring relief to the men as working parties were found to assist the Royal Engineers to consolidate and strengthen the defensive lines - urgent work in case of enemy counter-attacks. This work, in the appalling conditions of the Salient, was heavy and dangerous and a considerable strain. Lack of sleep was another problem. Officers and men were extremely tired. To counteract this the British

Army decreed that divisions would spend a month in the line, support and reserve positions followed by a month out at rest. 50th Division now went into its month's rest. The Battalion found working parties on the 28th December. It moved to English Farm Camp near St. Jean on the 29th, only to find overcrowded conditions and very bad shelters. On the 30th it moved into St. Jean Camp, sharing this with the 5th Northumberland Fusiliers. Everyone was living in tents. On this day and the last day of the year working parties were again found. 1917 ended as it had started with the Battalion in the Salient and no apparent signs of the ending of the conflict.

The first five days of January, 1918, were spent in St. Jean Camp. The Division formed part of VIII Corps and held the Passchendaele Sector of the front. Working parties were found as usual and undertaken in extremely difficult conditions. The men were wet and numb with cold. The ever present danger of coming under shell or machine-gun fire was a constant strain. On the 6th January, the Battalion moved into a camp at the side of the Menin Road. On the following day, it moved into the Grand Place, Ypres, where it embussed at 10.00 a.m. and proceeded to Steenvoorde and into billets. It remained here for a week. The weather was bitterly cold with snow and hard frosts. A draft of ninety-six arrived from the Depot. Most were aged nineteen to twenty years. On the 17th of the month, the Battalion marched to Caestre Station and entrained for Wizernes, arriving about 6.00 p.m. It then marched to Acquin, a march of two and a half hours, in rain and along very bad roads. Fortunately the billets were good and it was an excellent training area. One section of the training area was adapted to represent Passchendaele Ridge. The Battalion remained here for a fortnight until the 30th January when it marched to Wizerne and entrained for Brandhoek, arriving at 5.30 p.m. It was billeted in the huts at Toronto Camp. The last day of the month was spent in kit and equipment inspections and making final preparations to go up to the front line.

On the 2nd February, the Battalion moved by light railway to Sunderland Camp, near Potijze. It provided working parties during the morning of the 3rd and in the afternoon moved back into cellars in Ypres. A draft of five officers and one hundred other ranks was received the following day. These came from the 10th DLI. A number of them who were due for leave, were immediately sent home. The 4th Yorkshire Regiment was relieved in the Hamburg support position on the 5th February. The next day, the 5th DLI was relieved in the Passchendaele sector. 'W' Company held the right front position. 'Z' Company was the left front company. 'X' Company was at Crest Farm and 'Y' Company at Haalen Switch. The following night, the Battalion position was extended to take over two posts held by the 8th Battalion on its immediate right. No Man's Land was both water-logged and empty. There was no sign of the enemy. On the 9th February, the enemy did make his presence felt. During the day, Second-Lieutenant G.H. King was slightly wounded. Worse followed. A ration party, provided by 'W' Company and led by Second-Lieutenant W. Watkin, was attacked by a small German raiding party. Second-Lieutenant Watkin was wounded and Private Attewell was taken prisoner. The ration party had not reached the front line positions. The Germans had somehow infiltrated between the front line posts without being detected - a skill they were to use with great effect during the forthcoming spring offensive.

CHAPTER 11
THE GERMAN SPRING OFFENSIVE
1918

The Battalion was relieved by the 5th Yorkshire Regiment on the 10th February and moved back to Sunderland Camp. At this time brigades were being reorganised and reduced from four to three Battalions. The 5th DLI was transferred from 150 to 151 Brigade. On the 12th February, 9th DLI was transferred to 62nd Division as the Pioneer Battalion. The following day, the 5th Border Regiment was transferred to the 66th Division, also as Pioneers. 151 Brigade now comprised 5th, 6th and 8th Battalions The Durham Light Infantry. From the 10th to the 14th February, the Battalion provided working parties. On the latter date, it marched off to relieve the 4th ast Yorkshire Regiment in the Hamburg sector. A quiet four days ensued which were taken up supplying carrying parties for the front line Battalions. On the 18th of the month, the Battalion moved to Maiden Camp, to clean up and prepare for the next move. The next day, it entrained at Ypres and travelled to Wizernes where it detrained and marched to St. Martin-au-Laert, a suburb of St. Omer. The billets here were dirty but in good condition and were soon cleaned and improved to provide a comfortable stay for the men. The Battalion remained here until the 8th March. The band and bugles played in St. Omer each day at 'Retreat.' The Battalion concert party, the 'Red Diamonds, which was trained by Captains Cardew and Lyon, entertained officers and men. After initial cleaning up training occupied the time spent in St. Martin, although this was often interrupted by the bad weather.

The Battalion move on the 8th March was made at short notice. It left St. Martin at 8.30 p.m. and marched to Arques where it entrained for Longeau, near Amiens, arriving at 9.30 a.m. on the following day. A march followed to La Neuville, near Corbie and into billets at about 4.00 p.m., having had dinners on route. On the 11th of the month, the Battalion left La Neuville at 8.30 a.m. and marched through Villers Bretoneux to Marcelcave, south of the Amiens - St. Quentin road, arriving at 11.30 a.m. Here it became part of 5th Army reserve.

Information had been reaching the High Command for some time that the enemy was concentrating his forces for a major offensive. The collapse of Russia had released German divisions from the east and these had been moving onto the Western Front to give the enemy a superiority in numbers for the first time in over two years. This superiority gave the Germans the opportunity of breaking the deadlock of trench warfare in the west and bringing a successful conclusion to the war before the full might of America would begin to make itself felt in 1919. It was clearly seen to be Germany's last chance of getting anything out of the war. The British High Command knew that if the impending offensive was held, Germany would have shot its last bolt and would lose the war. Field Marshal Haig retained his main strength in those areas he considered vital to the continuing safety of his forces, namely the Ypres area and Arras - Vimy. The situation had not been helped by an extension of the British line, on the request of the French, which now meant that the fifty-nine divisions under Haig's command had to hold a frontage of some one hundred and twenty-six miles. The dispositions left the 5th Army in the worst position of any of the British armies holding the line. It held a frontage of about forty-two miles with ten infantry divisions and three of cavalry. These were reinforced by four additional infantry divisions as the possibility of the Germans attacking on the Army's front became more apparent. The 50th Division was one of the reinforcements and went into Army reserve. 151 Brigade was placed at the disposal of VII Corps in a counter-attacking role. During the next few days, it undertook training schemes which aimed to prepare it for this task. At 4.40 a.m., on the morning of the 21st March, a tremendous German artillery bombardment broke out along a frontage of over fifty miles. The German offensive had begun.

Immediately following stand to on this morning, the Battalion was ordered to move at short notice. It entrained at Guillaucourt at about 5.00 p.m. and detrained at Brie, south of Péronne, on a very dark night after a long, slow and tiring journey in horse boxes. Lewis guns and other items of equipment were placed on waiting lorries and orders were received to move into billets near Peronne. However, the situation in the front line was desperate and a staff officer arrived with new orders. The Battalion was to move immediately towards Boucly and occupy the Green Line in support of the 66th Division (XIX Corps) which had been under heavy attack all day. The Lewis guns were taken from the lorries and replaced with the men's blankets. The Green Line was a reserve system of partially dug trenches on the crest of a hill. The sector occupied by the Battalion was south of Tincourt - Boucly and in front of Beuzy. The 8th DLI, was on the right. During the course of the night, elements of the 66th Division withdrew through the Battalion's positions. German tactics were to infiltrate defensive positions using Storm Troops especially trained for this work. In addition the enemy sought to turn the flanks of the British positions. Once in the rear and with the flanks turned the only recourse left to the defenders was to retire which, in turn, caused the retirement of adjoining companies and battalions.

On the morning of the 21st March and subsequent mornings, dense fog covered much of the battle front and this weather assisted the enemy infiltrators. Very often by the time the fog cleared the enemy were into, if not through, the defenders' positions. British tanks watched by the men of the Battalion, moved into counter-attack on the morning of the 22nd. They were not successful. On the whole, the morning situation on the Battalion front was quiet. In the afternoon, a heavy enemy bombardment from guns of all calibres commenced. A Battalion patrol captured a wounded enemy scout who was passed on to Brigade Headquarters. Orders were received that the position must be held at all costs. Although partially dug, it was of sufficient strength to give officers and men the confidence that it could be held. However, the withdrawal of divisions and brigades on the flanks brought orders at 9.00 p.m. to move back to the ridge in the rear and in front of Cartigny. This was successfully accomplished by dawn on the 23rd. At 7.00 a.m. information was received that the 5th Army was about to withdraw to the west bank of the River Somme and companies received instructions as to the rearguard actions expected of them. The Battalion was given the task of covering the retirement of the 5th DLI which, in its turn, would cover the withdrawal of the 6th Battalion. The Battalion occupied the village of Cartigny and sought to deny the enemy entry until the withdrawal across the river had been completed. Positions had just been taken up when the enemy arrived on the outskirts of the village and snipers and machine-guns began to cause trouble. The enemy, using his successful infiltration tactics, soon made the positions untenable and the Battalion obtained permission for a withdrawal to be made. This was completed without loss, largely due to the courageous action of 'Y' Company under Captain Aubin MC who held the enemy at bay in a successful rearguard action. A defensive position was taken up in a trench system on a ridge near Le Mesnil. Here a quiet period followed but if this was the situation on the Battalion front, the enemy was very active seeking out the flanks of units in the Péronne area on the left and Le Mesnil on the right. It was imperative to make a stand in this position if transport, still east of the river, was to make its escape.

The nearest bridge available which would allow the Battalion to cross the Somme, was the footbridge at Eterpigny. Orders were received that it should cross the river at this point. The countryside here was wooded with marshes and thick undergrowth as the river was approached. The Battalion marched about a mile across country until the marshes and thick undergrowth were reached and found it was unable to penetrate this area. It was forced to turn off and move through the long, straggling village of Le Mesnil. This march was made under a light shrapnel barrage. 'Z' Company got through the village without any enemy interference. The following companies were attacked. All of these companies and in particular 'Y' Company put up a splendid fight. A fighting withdrawal was made through the village and towards the footbridge over the river. The enemy was held and the three companies crossed the footbridge which was three hundred yards long and partially destroyed. Lieutenant D.F. Charlton was killed in this action. Second-Lieutenant Dobson was captured and a further twenty men were casualties. On reaching the west bank of the river the companies of the Battalion formed a line with remnants of another division. The positions taken up overlooked the marshes which had caused problems during the retreat and, it was hoped, would cause difficulties also to the advancing enemy. Fighting died down and a quiet night followed giving some respite to very weary officers and men. Captain Aubin MC was ultimately awarded the Distinguished Service Order for his courageous leadership of 'Y' Company which had performed so well in the rearguard action.

Any plans of holding the enemy on the line of the River Somme, were quickly dashed on the 24th March. The enemy had crossed the river near Bray and was already threatening the rear of troops on the west bank. Orders were received for the Battalion to withdraw through Barleux to Foucaucourt, to the old POW Camp near the latter village on the main Amiens - Péronne road. The men rested and tried to snatch some sleep but after two hours orders were received to march up to the line again. At 4.00 p.m. the Battalion marched to Estrées and took up reserve positions for the night, north-east of the village. A desperate situation arose on the morning of the following day. The enemy was advancing rapidly and in an attempt to stem the tide, the Battalion marched to Genermont and took up positions south of the main road. Here it came under the orders of the 8th Divison's 24th Brigade. As the situation became more serious and without definite orders, the Battalion moved in artillery formation towards Marchélepot. It moved in the best traditions of the British Army - towards the sound of the guns. Before reaching the village it was learned that 8th Division holding the line, had

retired to the railway embankment behind the village. Gaps in this line were filled by 'W', 'Z' and 'Y' Companies. At 5.00 p.m. a further withdrawal was made by the 24th Division, on the right of 'Y' Company. This company formed a defensive flank and 'X' Company moved to the north-east of Hyencourt and prepared to deliver a counter-attack if it became necessary to do so. A desperate situation was eased when the enemy failed to follow up the advantage he had gained. At 7.00 p.m. orders were received to withdraw to a line of old trenches, south-east of Pressoir. The enemy satisfied himself by shelling these positions which caused a few casualties.

A heavy mist formed at dawn on the 26th March and the enemy took full advantage of the lack of observation by once again using infiltration tactics followed by frontal assaults on the British positions. In the resulting confusion contradictory orders served only to worsen the situation. At 9.00 a.m. the 8th Division quickly withdrew and the Battalion, along with those of the 24th Brigade, moved in artillery formation through the ruins of Lihons which was suffering from heavy German shelling. The withdrawal continued until Rosières was reached and a line taken up about a mile south-east of the village. The Battalion stayed here for the night with the 2nd Northants Regiment on its left and a Labour Battalion on its right. The enemy remained quiet and no attacks were made. A heavy mist again on the 27th enabled the enemy to renew his attacks against the line. The Labour Battalion on the right was forced to withdraw and the Battalion had to fall back also. An immediate counter-attack was put in by 'W', 'X' and 'Z' Companies and this succeeded in restoring the line. Captain H. Walton, MC who commanded 'Z' Company, was killed in this action. Heavy German shelling continued throughout the day with very little response from the British artillery.

The 28th March activities followed the pattern of preceding days. The enemy launched early morning attacks which caused a general withdrawal by the British forces. The first withdrawal by the Battalion was to Warvillers. This was followed by a further move to a line near Caix - a move covered, yet again, by 'Y' Company. During these movements the Battalion suffered a heavy loss when its commanding officer, Lieutenant-Colonel F.W.

Robson, DSO, was killed by machine-gun fire. A territorial officer, he was held in much regard by both officers and men. The line now occupied had some semblance of defensive qualities as it was wired in and the Battalion felt it could be held. Information had been received that troops withdrawing in front of them would reinforce the line. However, on arrival the troops who were retreating moved straight through the positions which necessitated a general withdrawal to the wood south-east of Caix. The remnants of three companies were rallied by Captain Cardew who led them in a counter-attack which succeeded in reoccupying the Caix Line. Captain Cardew and Second-Lieutenant R. Wilson received the Military Cross for this action. However, enemy pressure increased and it was found impossible to hold on to this line. About 4.00 p.m. the Battalion withdrew along the Beaucourt road and on to Moreuil. The heavy losses suffered by 151 Brigade since the 21st March had been such that the cooks, storemen, buglers etc. had become part of a composite Battalion and had already seen some action. They were collected by Major T.B. Heslop along with some stragglers and were now at Ailly-sur-Noye. They were ordered up to the line on the 29th of the month and moved to Demuin Wood, a march of thirty kilometres which took them twenty hours over very congested roads. They remained in these positions for several days and suffered some casualties through enemy action.

The Battalion was becoming somewhat fragmented. On the

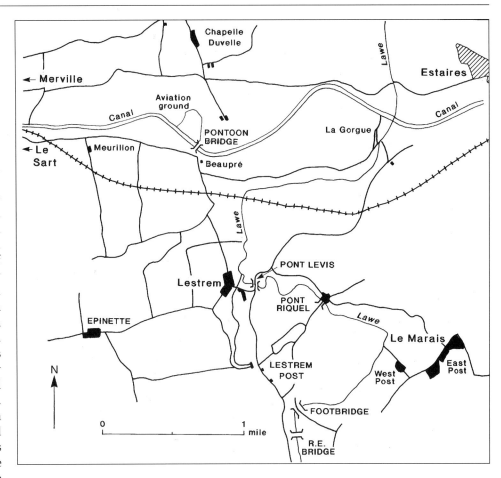

The German Spring Offensive, *1918. The Battles of the Lys and Lawe.*

29th, part of it under Major Heslop moved to Point 90, south of Demuin. When it arrived here, it found that it was not required and moved to Berteaucourt, where it stayed the night. It had suffered several casualties due to shelling, during these moves. The transport moved to Boves where Captain Aubin had collected about two hundred men of the Battalion. Transport and men moved in stages to Saleux, reaching the village on the 31st of the month and passing on the way French troops moving up in an attempt to check the enemy advance. On the 30th of the month, this party moved to Hourges where it went into support north of the village. On the 31st March, Major Heslop's party held its positions in support until all the troops in front had passed through. It then marched to the River Luce when it took up position on the far bank. A night move was made to a point north-west of Domart where the party remained until the next morning.

The casualties suffered by the Battalion from the 21st to 31st March were as follows: six officers and thirty-five other ranks killed; five officers and one hundred and eighty-seven other ranks wounded; two officers and ninety other ranks missing. The total was eleven officers and three hundred and twelve other ranks.

On the 1st April, a party under Major Heslop moved to positions south of Gentelles and in the afternoon it moved into the Bois de Gentelles. At 9.00 p.m. it marched to Longeau. On the evening of this same day, Captain Aubin's party entrained for Rue which it reached in the early hours of the 2nd April. Major Heslop's party marched to Saleux on the 2nd and entrained there for Rue which it reached on the morning of the 3rd. Rue is on the coast and lies between Abbeville and Boulogne. Captain Aubin's party marched to Vron on the 2nd April and was joined there on the following day, by Major Heslop's group. Vron lies three miles from Rue. Hopes of a good rest were soon dashed. The Battalion now concentrated, embussed on the 4th and moved to Beuvry near Béthune, about four miles behind one of the quietest sectors on the British front. A draft of four hundred men arrived. Orders were received to prepare to relieve the 55th Division near La Bassée. This move was not carried out and the Battalion remained in Beuvry for a few days before moving to Estaires, on the 7th April. This town, though only a short distance from the front line, was quite active and flourishing. Civilians remained in possession of their homes and businesses. The officers of the Battalion with the exception of the Commanding Officer, Major Heslop, the Adjutant, Transport Officer and Captain Cardew, were billetted in the Convent. Stand to was carried out at 4.30 a.m. on the 8th as it was expected that the enemy were about to attack the Portuguese battalion on the right. The day remained quiet. Instructions were received to relieve the Portuguese on the following night.

The 9th April, was a disastrous day for the Battalion. The enemy commenced an extremely heavy bombardment of the town of Estaires, beginning at 4.00 a.m. Casualties amongst soldiers and civilians were very considerable. Early in the bombardment a shell hit the Convent where most of the Battalion officers were billeted. The casualties amongst these officers were horrendous. Captain J.F.G. Aubin, MC, DSO, Captain G. Kirkhouse, Lieutenant C.L. Tyreman, Lieutenant D.B. Scott, Second-Lieutenant F. Shirtliffe and Captain R.A. Mackenzie (RAMC) were killed or died of wounds. The Battalion was left with three company officers. These with the magnificent assistance of the NCOs, got the men out of their billets and to safety in double quick time. When this was achieved the Battalion was moved into its battle positions in Cockshy, Marais East and West and Drumiez Posts. A misty morning assisted the Germans once more and the Portuguese troops were driven back, leaving the Battalion's companies fighting with an uncovered right flank. All was confusion, with the fog of war almost complete. No definite news was received of the companies. Major Heslop was first informed that 'W', 'X' and 'Z' Companies had been overwhelmed with two of his three company commanders casualties, namely, Captain Cardew who was killed and Second-Lieutenant Railton who was captured. The survivors of the Battalion held on under the command of Lieutenant A.N. Brown. However, in the afternoon the position became so critical that a withdrawal was ordered to the railway near La Gorgue. Further orders at dusk, sent the Battalion across the River Lawe to hold the west bank. This was successfully accomplished and in this position opportunity was taken to reorganise the Battalion on a two company basis, one under Lieutenant Brown, with Sergeant Finn, MM and Sergeant Field and the other under Company Sergeant-Major T. Sordy, MC, with Sergeants Bell and Cooper.

Heavy fighting continued throughout the 10th April. A company of the 7th DLI reinforced the Battalion. A line readjustment was necessary when troops of the 51st Highland

Division withdrew on the right. The line, now held by the 6th and 8th Battalions, stretched along the west bank of the River Lawe from a little south of the railway bridge where it was in touch with the 51st Division. From here it crossed open ground to the canal and along the north bank of this to the Estaires - Chapelle - Duvelle road, where contact was made with the 5th Durhams. This open ground was dominated by German machine-guns. Over the next two days the Battalion was involved in a fighting withdrawal through Merville, Le Sart, Pont Tournant, to a line about a thousand yards of the edge of the Fôret de Nieppe. On the 13th of the month, the Battalion was relieved by the 5th Battalion and moved to La Motte Chateau. Here it was heavily shelled and moved on to Steenbecque and into reserve. It remained here for two days for much needed rest. The troops were absolutely exhausted. Yet the ubiquitous working parties had to be found to dig trenches in the Fôret-de-Nieppe. On the 16th, the Battalion marched to Cohem near Aire. Here on the following day, it was inspected by the GOC of the Division who thanked all ranks for their efforts during the recent difficult operations. Refitting took place over the next three days. Training commenced and a draft of two hundred men and nine officers was received on the 20th. An indication of the extremely difficult manpower situation which had arisen could be seen in that the draft was largely comprised of men from the Inland Water Transport Companies, Army Service Corps and other corps troops, all of whom needed hard training to fit them up as infantrymen. Inspections, training and refitting took up the next few days. Lieutenant-Colonel F. Walton, MC took over command of the Battalion on the 23rd April. On the 26th of the month, the Battalion embussed for La Pugnoy near Béthune, where it entrained for Serzy, near Soissons. After a twenty-four hour journey in horse trucks it reached Serzy and marched from there to a hutted camp at Arcis-le-Ponsart, near the line on the Chemin des Dames. It was now in the 6th French Army.

CHAPTER 12
THE AISNE - THE LAST BATTLE
1918

The whole of 151 Brigade was in a hutted camp at Arcis-le-Ponsart and all ranks looked forward to a period of rest and much needed training on a front reputed to be very quiet. The 29th was a day put aside for refitting and resting in the new camp. Training commenced on the 30th April. Men not up to standard, which included a number from the Inland Water Transport sections of the Royal Engineers and Army Service Corps, were given separate instruction and eventually were sent away to form a Divisional Training School.

On the 4th May, the Battalion was on the move again. It marched to billets in Glennes, a small village in a deep valley two miles from the Aisne Canal. It remained here and prepared to go into the line. It moved into a support area of the line on the 7th May. This lay south of Corbeny with Craonne on the left flank. The Battalion relieved the 73rd Regiment, 51st French Division. The 50th Division, along with the 8th and 21st Divisions, formed an all British XI Corps of the French 6th Army. The positions taken up were in woods immediately east of the Craonne Plateau. They were in marked contrast to those occupied prior to joining the French. The trees were green, with full foliage. There was little indication that an enemy faced them. Hostilities were confined to odd and extremely light and short bouts of shelling. There was very little going on and the understanding between the opposing forces seemed to be one of live and let live. Rations came direct to Battalion Headquarters by light railway and carrying parties could move about quite safely. All three brigades of the division were in the front line. On the right, 149 Brigade occupied the Buttes. In the centre, 151 Brigade held the line along

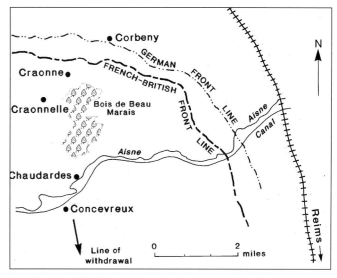

The Aisne, *1918. The last battle for the Battalion in World War I*

the northern edge of the Bois de Beau Marais with Craonne touching its left flank. 150 Brigade held the Calafornie Plateau on the left. Partly across the front lay the River Ailette. The Germans facing held the village of Corbeny. No Man's Land was about one mile wide. 151 Brigade had one Battalion in the line, the 5th Battalion. The 6th Battalion was in close support and the 8th Battalion in reserve in the partly ruined village of Chaudardes, south of the Bois de Beau Marais. The Battalion remained in support for four days. On the 12th May, it relieved the 5th

Battalion with two companies in the front line, one in support and one in reserve. A live and let live policy was never to the liking of the British High Command and active patrolling was instantly instituted on taking over the line from the French. The Battalion was in the line for the next four days. It was relieved by the 5th Battalion on the 18th May and moved into reserve in Chaudardes Village. This village was deserted and held only by troops. Concerts were organised and given by the Jesmond Jesters, the band played and bathing took place in the nearby Aisne Canal. The trees were green, the flowers bloomed and birds sang, all in all, a delightfully pleasant sector. Active patrolling had chased the Germans from No Man's Land which now remained a British preserve. On the 24th May, the Battalion relieved the 5th Battalion with three companies in the front line and one in reserve. The 8th Battalion was on its left. It looked like another quiet occupation of the front line.

Disquieting information filtered through to Battalion Headquarters during the 25th and 26th May. Battalion Headquarters was ordered to withdraw to a position further back if it were attacked as, in its present position, it would find it difficult to control the situation. A further most disquieting order was received, to the effect that no further reinforcements would be sent to this front if the Germans did attack. French airmen reported seeing enemy tank concentrations opposite French 6th Army positions. A German prisoner had given the information that the enemy would attack on the 27th of the month, at 1.00 a.m. in the morning. A message was received on the 26th May that defence precautions be taken immediately. Whilst doubting the seriousness of the situation these precautions were put in hand. Reserves of ammunition were brought up to the front line positions. Surplus personnel were sent down to the transport lines and everybody was warned to be on the alert.

Captain Lyon wrote the following in his diary:

'This was my second day with my company ['X' Company] in this part of the line and the fine weather and peaceful conditions made the business of settling in and keeping everything in good order much easier than I had expected. I had one platoon holding a small area in the front line under G - T. Two other platoon commanders were in support, and G - S was near my HQ in reserve ... The men were happy, and I think pleasantly surprised at the quietness of the line, many of them being in the trenches for the 1st time, and in the majority for the 2nd and 3rd only. The food came up to them quite hot, and the accommodation was excellent ... The support line was the only line at all strongly held, and on a less healthy front we might well have had misgivings on the possible result of an attack in force. We had a shrewd idea that behind us was nothing, or practically nothing.'

Following the warning received at 10.30 p.m. on the 26th May, Captain Lyon wrote his orders to his platoon commanders as follows:-

'Prisoner states attack coming at 4 a.m. Bombardment probably with gas at 1 a.m. Tanks may be used. Troops must fire at infantry and not at tanks. No fighting men to carry wounded. Issue 50 extra rounds per man, and inspect pouches to see number is complete. All Lewis gunners over 4 per team to come to Company HQ at once. Destroy all maps and important documents.'

Captain Lyon then wrote:

'...I went round the men, who seemed cheery and confident, and saw that they understood their orders. I thought their cheerfulness sufficiently marked to mention to our HQ and sent down a message: "All serene. Men cheery as cuckoos."'

At 1.00 a.m. on the 27th May, one of the most concentrated barrages the Battalion had ever faced fell on its positions. It was obvious that though seemingly quiet over a long period of time, the enemy had carefully pinpointed with considerable accuracy, the British and French positions and these were now subjected to a storm of accurate shell and mortar fire on a scale few men in the Battalion had experienced. The enemy bombardment covered an area of three thousand yards in depth and almost every foot of it was blasted with high explosive, shrapnel and gas shells. The whole countryside seemed to be heaving and bubbling like the surface of a lake of boiling volcanic lava. Two thousand batteries of artillery, over half of which were heavies, concentrated on the destruction of the French and British guns. Most of 50th Division's artillery support was lost. The transport was shelled out of Muscourt, many miles south of the Aisne. By 3.30 a.m. the

Band and Bugles. *This photograph was taken two days before the last German offensive of the war began.*

front line trenches had been almost obliterated. The survivors fought on till the last round. Communications broke down. Only two runners were able to reach 151 Brigade Headquarters. At about 8.00 a.m. it was decided to withdraw the Brigade Headquarters to a safer position but on attempting to do so it was found to be surrounded by the enemy. An exploding shell killed Brigadier General Martin, Brigade Commander. The scene was one of utter confusion.

Captain Lyon described what was happening in the front line:

'...When I came into the open [from his company headquarters], I found to my dismay and surprise files of Germans immediately to our front and level with our line on the right. I had been reckoning on the customary pause before an infantry line can follow a barrage. But the German tactics here - well justified by success - were to place their advance troops almost in the skirts of their barrage, thus giving the defence no time to recover ... The intense bombardment, heavy beyond all precedent, had split the line into small isolated groups of sadly shaken men, who fell an easy prey to the first German line. A large number must have surrendered without resistance ... The speed and method of the advance - nowhere did I see the slightest confusion or hurry - filled us with a despairing admiration - I certainly am prepared to regard the preparation and execution of the whole attack as one of the best things an army has ever done.'

The forward positions were overrun. The losses in officers and men were considerable. Captain Lyon reported to Battalion Headquarters that his company ('X') had been wiped out and that the enemy was advancing rapidly. 'Z' Company, as reserve company under Captain R. Green, MC, was in position close to the Battalion Headquarters. Captain Green reported that the enemy was on top of them. Enemy machine-guns were firing into their position from the rear of his right flank and enemy bombers were attacking behind his left flank. Withdrawal of Battalion Headquarters was essential if it was to survive but this was fraught with danger as enemy troops were found to be in its rear. An initial withdrawal of five hundred yards was made down the communication trench. At this point Lieutenant-Colonel Walton, his Adjutant, Signals Officer and Captain Lyon collected about forty men of the Battalion and prepared to make a stand. Heavy enemy shelling and the smoke from exploding shells made this extremely difficult to organise. The Battalion had been almost annihilated. It soon became obvious that a defence could not be organised in this position and the group made its way back to the bridge over the River Aisne at Concevreux. A bridgehead was held here with elements of the 6th and 8th DLI and 5th Northumberland Fusiliers. Lieutenant T. Rushworth of the 6th Battalion was awarded the Military Cross for his actions at the bridge on this day. In command of a small group of men, he held the bridgehead whilst under very heavy machine-gun fire until the Germans outflanked his position. He withdrew his men through the village which the Germans had also entered. Holding a position in the rear of the village he successfully patrolled the area, always under severe machine-gun fire, and maintained contact with the division on his right.

It was now a case of every man, every round. Men of the Battalion in the Transport Lines were collected together under Major Heslop and placed under the orders of the GOC 74th Brigade, 25th Division. They occupied a number of positions during the day and were in touch with the enemy. They also suffered casualties. Men of the 50th Division who had been away attending courses were hastily returned and sent up towards Thery where they joined the Transport Lines. Here, on the 29th May, they were moved forward to Baslieux-sous-Chatillon. Before they reached this place, they were collected and formed part of a company under Major Heslop which represented 151 Brigade in a battalion to which every brigade in the division contributed one company. The night was spent in Quisles Chateau and then this Composite Battalion moved towards Ville-en-Tardenois in support of 74th Brigade. Orders were given to advance and seize the high ground north-east of Romigny. This the Battalion achieved but the Germans attacked in force and the position was lost. The transport, meanwhile, moved back to Broyes, near Sezanne, where they were joined by members of the composite Battalion. Another Composite Battalion was formed on the 30th May, from the Brigade at Broyes and although orders were received to go into the line, these were eventually cancelled. On the 31st of May, the transport arrived at Vert-La-Gravelle where a few stragglers collected and Lieutenant-Colonel Walton rejoined the few who were left of his Battalion. Total casualties suffered from the 27th to 31st May were, thirty officers and four hundred and ninety-nine other ranks, killed wounded or missing. Amongst the missing who were later found to be prisoners, was Captain Lyon. Awards for individual actions during this period of operations in addition to Lieutenant T. Rushworth described above, were as follows: the Military Cross was awarded to Captain A.B. Hare, Second-Lieutenant J. Woodhead and Regimental Sergeant-Major Taylor. Regimental Sergeant-Major Taylor was wounded and replaced by Company Sergeant-Major T. Sordy, MC. The Military Medal was awarded to Sergeant Malone, Lance-Corporal Ripley and Private Dinsley, and the French Croix de Guerre was awarded to Corporal Nield. The Battalion's casualties for the three months March, April and May, were sixty officers and one thousand two hundred other ranks.

The remnants of the Battalion at Vert La Gravelle, about thirty-five men, were inspected by the GOC 50th Division, on the 1st June. A further group of about the same number under Captain

Hare was in the line in action with the French near Bois de Bonval. On the following day, Captain Hare's party moved to the Bois de Courton. The composite Battalion remained at Vert-La-Gravelle until the 5th June, when it moved by bus to Cormoyeux. They then marched to a wood east of the village of Nanteuil and bivouacked for the night. The following day two companies of the Battalion moved to Les Haies and one to Estilly. At night the Battalion relieved the 9th Cheshire Regiment in Montagne de Bligny. Here, facing the Germans, they were organised so as to fill gaps in the line. On the 8th June, the Battalion moved back to Chaumuzy, where it was joined by Captain Hare's party. Positions taken up north and west of the village were far from pleasant. The whole area was under the observation of the enemy and the Battalion was shelled throughout the 10th and 11th June. It was relieved by the 58th Composite Battalion on the 12th. This relief was completed at dawn on the 13th and the Battalion moved into bivouacs in the Bois de Courton. Baths were organised and the men were issued with clean clothing. Training was organised over the next four days. On the 18th June, Italian officers of the Brescia Division came up to to arrange the relief, which was carried out at 9.30 p.m. The Battalion moved to the Bois de Gouffre. The following day, a move was made by train from Germaine to Sezanne. From the latter place the Battalion marched into billets at Broyes on the Marne where they were reunited with the transport and stores. On this day, officers and men rejoined their original units. The next three days were spent cleaning and re-equipping. On the 23rd of the month, a Composite Brigade was formed from 149, 150 and 151 Brigades Composite Battalions. The 151 Composite Battalion was commanded by Lieutenant-Colonel P. Kirkup, DSO, MC, of the 8th DLI. The 6th Battalion provided one company and the transport. Training followed and orders were received to relieve the French on the Marne at Dormans. These orders were cancelled on the 26th. On the 29th June, the composite Battalion was paraded before the GOC of the Division and medals presented to those who had won them. It was at this parade that the GOC announced the possibility of the Battalion being disbanded. On the following day, the 6th Battalion was reformed under the command of Lieutenant-Colonel Walton.

The Battalion had fought its last battle. Along with the 50th Division it was to be broken up. An element would form a cadre to train new recruits for the front. Others would provide drafts for other units. With sufficient reinforcements from England being refused by the Lloyd George Government, GHQ had no alternative but to break up divisions and use their personnel as drafts to reinforce others. The manpower situation was acute. 50th Division had suffered horrendous losses over more than four years of fierce fighting. It would not, tragically, be in at the kill but it had set a standard of stubborn courage and devotion which few other divisions would surpass. It was a standard which would be passed on to its successor in World War II when the sons of its members would prove worthy of their fathers' sacrifice. The 6th Durhams, along with other units of the Division, had been flung into a desperate battle in April, 1915, to stay the advance of a numerical superior German force which threatened to break through and destroy the French and British Armies in the Salient. In the last few days of May 1918, the Battalion once again was fighting with our French allies to stay an even more desperate situation. It had suffered grievous losses but had played its part in slowing down the enemy and inflicting heavy casualties on him until he was finally stopped. When this happened Germany had lost the war.

During July, 1918, the Battalion gradually moved back westward. On the 4th of the month, it had reached Caumont, near Abbeville. On the 15th surplus personnel amounting to one officer and one hundred and seventy other ranks were entrained at Pont Remy and moved to the Base Camp at Étaples. The training cadre of ten officers and fifty other ranks moved to Rouxmesnil, near Dieppe, on the 19th. It remained here until the 16th August, training officers and NCOs. On this date a move was made to Rouen and training continued. The Battalion was finally demobilised on the 6th November, 1918, five days before the end of the war and personnel despatched to the Base Camp.

CHAPTER 13

THE SECOND LINE 6th BATTALION, DURHAM LIGHT INFANTRY

1914 - 1918

The 2nd/6th Battalion The Durham Light Infantry, was formed at Ravensworth Partk, near Gateshead, in September, 1914. In early 1915 it moved to Leam Camp, Heworth, also near Gateshead, as part of the 190th Brigade, 63rd Division. In November, 1915, the Battalion moved to Doncaster. The 63rd Division was broken up in July, 1916, and the 190th Brigade moved to Catterick. The 63rd Division, reconstituted, became the Royal Naval Division. On the 29th November, 1916, the 2nd/6th Battalion became part of the 214th Brigade of the 71st Division and moved to Andover. In March, 1917, the Battalion was at Colchester. In September, 1917, it formed part of the 226th Brigade and was stationed at Frinton-on-Sea, Essex. Here it was designated a Garrison Guard Battalion and comprised men of B1 and B2 medical grade considered unfit for active service. The acute shortage of manpower in 1918 meant that units like the 2nd/6th were sent to France. The Battalion concentrated at Clacton and moved to Dover where it embarked for France, landing at Calais on the 6th May, 1918. It moved to Hestrus where it became part of the 177th Brigade of the 59th Division. This brigade also included the 11th Battalion The Somerset Light Infantry and the 15th The Battalion Essex Regiment.

The 59th (North Midlands) Division had been in France since early 1917 and had seen action on the Western Front. In early 1918, it fell victim to changes which, due to the acute shortage of manpower, saw brigades cut from four Battalions to three Battalions each. This was followed by the breakup of some divisions to provide reinforcements for retained divisions. We

have seen that the 50th Division suffered this fate. The 59th Division lost its North Midlands identity with the transfer of its Battalions comprised of regiments from this region. The Division was now designated a 'B' Division, made up of second line Battalions of low medical grades. It concentrated in the St. Omer area, weeding out men who were obviously unfit for any kind of active service. Whilst this was being done time was spent in digging reserve defences, training and improving efficiency.

At the end of July, 1918, the 59th Division moved into the line and went into its first action on the 30th September in the Aubers Ridge - Laventie area. The final German retreat was taking place and there was no static front line as such. A series of strong points were held by both sides. The enemy rear was covered by Uhlans, German cavalry, whilst British cavalry roamed ahead of the advancing infantry. Overhead British aircraft spotted for the artillery and infantry, charted the enemy withdraawl and attacked the retreating columns. This could and did lead to identity problems. Lance-Corporal G. Thorpe, Lewis gun platoon of the 2nd/6th Battalion, who came from Leicester, has left this record:-

> 'A trooper of the King Edward's Horse (assigned to 59th Division), a unit entirely composed of colonials, whom I met in hospital, described how British spotting aircraft had mistaken Khaki for Field Grey once or twice with unpleasant results. This difficulty was overcome by our troops putting a large white patch on their respirators.'

Initially the advance was through the trench lines until the open country beyond was reached. When the enemy halted and took up defensive positions, careful patrolling and scouting forward had to be undertaken to ascertain the positions and strength of the enemy strong points. This was a dangerous task as the Germans were past masters at concealment of their machine-guns which opened up on the unwary. Lance-Corporal Thorpe wrote:

'The enemy was in full retreat and the old trench system abandoned as they retired.

'It was an eerie experience following up through the deep belt of the old battlefield, every inch of which had been converted times without number over the years of comparatively static warfare.

'The diverse criss-cross pattern of the trenches; the aprons of rusty barbed wire, fouled by growth of four years weeds; the pools of slimey water here and there, made by the rain-filled shell craters, and often coloured by poison gas; a few scattered rough hewn wooden crosses, showing the last resting place of the dead; an ammunition dump of heavy shells; an abandoned rifle leaning against the side of a trench; scattered clips of cartridges; all of these made a picture of desolation, heightened by the few remaining stumps of trees, slashed and pitted by the merciless artillery fire of both sides.

'And over all - a deadly quiet.

'Too quiet for the comfort of the advancing Durhams, moved forward in extended order - rifles at the ready with safety catches on - expecting anything. For even in retreat, the enemy rearguard was still a force to reckon with ... The troops reach a road and bear right, passing what had been an ammunition convoy. It had been spotted by our artillery by the look of the wreckage.

'The Battalion moves down the road, which the enemy had mined at intervals to delay pursuit...'

The Fifth Army, of which the 59th division was a part, followed the retreating Germans. On the 10th October, 1918, the Division entered Wez Mocquart. By the 17th of the month, the Germans were pushed back towards Lille and the Division crossed the Haute Deule Canal and river, north of Lille. The following day, Lille was entirely encircled by the victorious British. The entry into Lille was yet another experience the men never forgot. Lance-Corporal Thorpe took part and wrote as follows:

'The Durhams fell in and marched along the road for an hour or so. Then, suddenly, turning a corner, they came to houses, intact and inhabited. their occupants paused to stare at the Khaki clad troops unbelievingly - some with tears in their eyes. The British looked back at them, wondering ... and then they understood. These folk had been under foreign rule for over four years, cut off from contact with many of their kith and kin by that 'fighting line' which divided their native land ... The reception for the British lads was terrific - women hugged and kissed them in the ranks and everywhere cheers greeted them as the Battalion marched steadily to their billets.'

On the 18th and 19th October, the Germans were driven back to the River Scheldt and the outskirts of Tournai were reached. On the 20th, the 59th Division was the first Allied division to cross the Scheldt. On the 11th November, 1918, when the armistice took effect, the advance elements of the Division were in front of Lessines.

The 59th Division had started the final campaign as a 'B' Division, comprised of men of doubtful physical fitness for war. Manpower shortage had caused it to be thrown into the battle. It distinguished itself over the final weeks of the war, so much so that its Corps Commander ordered that the designation 'B' be struck from its title. The officers and men found themselves in a war of movement, for which they neither had the experience or the training. They learned quickly as they went along. In the short period of actual fighting several men won gallantry awards. One such was Lance-Corporal Thorpe's Platoon - Sergeant, an ex-Hull dockyard worker and veteran of the Boer War, by name J.R. Griffin. He won the Distinguished Conduct Medal within four weeks of going into the line. His citation read:

'For conspicuous gallantry and devotion to duty. He went out with a battle patrol on the night of the 22nd August and occupied an important post in the front of our line in No Man's Land, near Mercatel. During the whole of the forty hours the post was occupied he greatly assisted in the post being held until an attack was launched through the Battalion by another division on the 24th August, after which the patrol was called in. His soldierly conduct and unselfish devotion to duty was a fine example to all around him.'

Sgt G.H. Dowdall also won a DCM. Several men won Military Medals. These included Private W.H. Barnes from Belper, Private

A. Brown from Hinckley, Private J.L. Cawthorne from East Boldon, Co. Durham, Private T. Clarke from East Leake, Corporal F. Clowes from Stoke, Private W. Cook from Oldham and Private F. Cowburn from Crossfields. From this it will be gathered that most of the men of the Battalion came from beyond the boundaries of Durham County. They always referred to themselves as and were proud to be 'Durhams'. Some forty men of the Battalion, from many areas of England, were killed or died of wounds in France. The men of the 2nd/6th Battalion The Durham Light Infantry, may have been of a lower physical grade than that of their senior comrades in the first line Battalion, but they proved to be worthy successors and carried the name of the 6th Battalion with distinction, to the end of the war.

CHAPTER 14
BETWEEN THE WARS
1919 -1939

The end of the Great War in November, 1918, was followed by the demobilisation of a huge citizen army. There was no great urge to put on a uniform and this reluctance was shown by the initial response to recruitment when the Territorial Army was reformed in 1920. The five Territorial Battalions of the county were amongst those units who reformed in that year, namely, the 5th, 6th, 7th, 8th and 9th Battalions, The Durham Light Infantry. The 7th Battlion became an air defence unit in 1936 and took the title 47th (DLI) AA Battalion, RA (TA). The 5th Battalion also became an air defence unit providing, in 1938, two Battalions. The 1/5th became the 54th Searchlight Regiment, and the 2/5th the 55th Searchlight Regiment.

Recruitment for the 6th Battalion was slow to pick up. In early 1921, the Battalion had twenty officers and three hundred and sixty other ranks on role. The first commander was Lieutenant-Colonel G.H. Stobart CBE, DSO. The annual camp held at Scarborough in

TERRITORIAL ARMY

VACANCIES

for suitable YOUNG MEN of 17 years of age and over in the

6th Battalion
The DURHAM LIGHT INFANTRY

A FORTNIGHT'S ANNUAL CAMP WITH PAY
including marriage allowance for men of 21 years of age and over

Uniform provided.   Sports.   Recreation Room.

ANNUAL PROFICIENCY GRANT
£3 10s.—RISING TO £5.

Travelling Expenses paid for attendance at Drills.

FOR FULL PARTICULARS APPLY AT THE
DRILL HALL, UNION STREET, BISHOP AUCKLAND.

G. B. & S.

Battalion recruitment poster

late July, 1921, was attended by fourteen officers and five hundred and seventy other ranks. The depression which followed the war provided an incentive to join the Territorials, for by doing so an annual break away from home was available and the bounty and camp pay provided an additional income. In 1923, recruitment reached a total of twenty officers and six hundred and four other ranks. The permanent staff of the Battalion was: Adjutant, Captain E.T. Heslop; Acting Regimental Sergeant-Major W. Benson; Sergeant Instructors, Company Sergeant-Major Sculthorpe, Sergeants M. Diggins, H.B. Verrier and P. Fitzgerald. Lieutenant-Colonel Stobart was succeeded as Commanding Officer of the Battalion by Lieutenant-Colonel The Lord Barnard in 1926. Recruitment remained high and reached a peak in 1927, when at Ripon Camp, the role was eighteen officers and six hundred and twenty-six men. The Battalion won the Daily Telegraph Cup for the Territorial unit with the highest percentage of its total numbers present at annual camp. It was the first

Jubilee Parade, *1935. Part of 'S' Company and 'HQ' Section at Bishop Auckland*

infantry unit to have its name inscribed on the cup. During the inter-war years recruitment never fell below five hundred officers and men, drawn largely from the mines, quarries, agriculture, shops and offices and, of course, the unemployed. In 1931, The Lord Barnard was succeeded as Commanding Officer of the Battalion by Lieutenant-Colonel H.R. McCullagh, DSO. He, in turn, was succeeded by Lieutenant-Colonel T.H. Miller in 1934.

Annual camps were held every summer, except that of 1932 which was cancelled for economic reasons when it appeared that

Dedicating the Crook War Memorial.

incorporating artillery, machine-guns and mortars and the use of smoke to conceal the advancing forces seemed to have won the day over more flexible methods. Weekend camps were held within the county boundaries, usually for company training. The annual weapons course was fired at Whitburn Camp, near Sunderland. Training nights were held in the drill halls during the week.

The Battalion record in the sporting field during the inter-war years was outstanding, particularly in football. In four out of six seasons between 1924 and 1930, the Battalion won the Territorial Army Cup. It won the trophy in three consecutive seasons; 1924-25, 1925-26, 1926-27. For this feat it was awarded a replica of the cup for its retention. It won the trophy for a fourth time in 1929-30.

In 1927, a Battalion ceremony was held at the Church of St. Andrew, South Church, Bishop Auckland, when the memorial cross, previously erected on the Butte de Warlencourt on the Somme, was unveiled in remembrance of those who had died in that battle in 1916. The cross remains in the Church of St. Andrew to this day.

The Coronation of King George VI and Queen Elizabeth in 1937, was attended by detachments of the Battalion. The processional party was under the command of Lieutenant-Colonel T.H. Miller and the street lining detachment under Major J.H. Curry and Captain W.I. Watson. The late Colonel Bill Watson has left the following description of the event:

cost cutting in the deep depression won the day. Over the years 1921 to 1938, annual camps were held at Catterick and Ripon, four occasions each; Marske on three occasions; Scarborough; Whitby; Alnwick; Lancaster and Pwllehli ; on one occasion each. The 1928 camp held at Marske was attended by Lieutenant le Vicomte Du Jeu, an observer from the French Army. Training in drill, weapons skills, field work and manoeuvres took up most of the time in camp, starting at section and platoon level and working up to battalion and brigade exercises. Night exercises were included - weather permitting. Gas drill remained an important component of camp training. World War I experience influenced the type of training. At one camp it was noted that fire and movement in attack seemed to have suffered from the experiences of WWI, as it was believed that modern weapons would make these manoeuvres too costly. The Fire Plan

Battalion football team *before the game against the 7th Bn. Royal Welch Fusilers, in the Territorial Army Cup. The 6th Battalion won this national competition four seasons out of six in the 1920s*

was going on, immaculately turned out ... We were fed, incidentally, by the Royal Army Service Corps. They came right down Regent Street one side and gave us a package of sandwiches ... which were particularly stale and some of us gave them to the crowd behind us and they discarded them and said they weren't worth eating and the lorry came round again and picked up all the empty paper ... Cigarettes came down like snow from the windows and if you had been ill-disciplined you could have put out your hand and got a packet of cigarettes in no time.'

The 1937 camp included early training in truck loading though, at this point in time, few vehicles were available. What vehicles available were named 'Beetles' by the troops and were brutes to drive. The 50th Division was earmarked as a Motorised Division but in pre-war years titles were given before equipment and materials arrived to make possible effective training for the tasks such a division would have to perform. A critical shortage of vehicles, even in the early days of the war, meant that deficiencies had to be made up by requisitioning civilian transport. In 1937, the first 15 cwt trucks were received at Bishop Auckland. Second-Lieutenant Mike Lockhart, newly commissioned into the 6th Battalion, records:

'I had a ride round the town on one of them. At Whitby Camp, I told Hugh Vaux our Adjutant of this and he asked me to become Motor Transport Officer.'

Again at the 1937 camp, the new Bren guns were demonstrated but were not available to handle in tactical training. As war clouds with Hitler's Germany gathered, the government belatedly made funds available for a five years' rearmament programme. The Territorial Army, as part of this programme, was to be equipped with up-to-date equipment to enable it to fight a modern war. It was a painfully slow procedure. The Czechoslovakian crisis in 1938 brought war so much closer that all TA units received orders to prepare for mobilization. Frantic diplomatic

'...The crowd was absolutely tense. To think that if you gave a command to be heard on the other side was quite impossible, out of the question, and the soldiers on the other side, we had so many on one side and so many on the other side, just had to watch to see what we did and we had to salute with our swords and present arms if any royalty went past ... The windows were absolutely packed in all the buildings and the troops in their dress uniforms ... I remember the band of the Scots Greys passing and the drummer in front had broken the skin of one of his side drums ... The Australians were an extremely bad advertisement. They sat down while waiting to proceed around the lampposts, which was shocking. The best detachment, I reckon, and I still think it was the best, was the Canadian Mounted Police. Every single horse was exactly the same colour and shape and every single trooper sat there quite oblivious of what

Recruitment poster

Each company held its own children's Christmas Party in peacetime

activity delayed war for another year during which rearmament was speeded up and the TA reorganised. This reorganisation included the alteration of the composition of infantry battalions to four rifle companies in place of the three rifle companies and one Support or Machine-Gun Company as hitherto. This now meant that TA Battalions conformed with those in the regular army. Drills were simplified by moving to three ranks instead of four. In April, 1939, the Secretary of State for War, Hore Belisha, appealed for recruitment to double the size of the Territorial Army, from thirteen to twenty-six divisions. Each battalion was asked to double its recruitment and throw off a second line battalion. As a result of this appeal the 6th Battalion raised the 10th Battalion, the 8th Battalion raised the 11th Battalion and the 9th Battalion raised the 12th Battalion which was known as the 1st Battalion. Tyneside Scottish and became attached to the Black Watch. A final reorganisation in the 6th Battalion occurred on the 21st January, 1939, when 'B' Company, the Consett Company, became the 268th AA Battery, Royal Artillery. In its place a company was again raised at Barnard Castle. The companies of the 6th Battalion were now as follows:

HQ and 'A' Companies	Bishop Auckland.
'B' Company	Barnard Castle.
'C' Company	Spennymoor.
'D' Company	Crook.

The 6th, 8th and 9th Battalions formed 151 Brigade of the 50th (Northumbrian) Division. Being a Motorised Division, the 50th was organised as two brigades: 151 and the 150 Brigades. The Northumberland Fusiliers had ceased to be infantry and the former 149 Brigade had been disbanded. This was the organisation of the Division when it went to war in September, 1939.

CHAPTER 15
THE SECOND WORLD WAR
1939
Mobilization - The West Country

The Military Training Act of May, 1939, introduced registration and six months training for men between the ages of twenty and twenty-one years. This training commenced in early June, 1939. The National Service (Armed Forces) Act, came into operation on the first day of the war and introduced conscription. A number of men brought into the army by these two acts found themselves, after initial training, members of the Territorial Battalions of The Durham Light Infantry. Meanwhile, as Hitler prepared to march into Poland, key men of the 6th Battalion were mobilized at the end of August, 1939. These men were the administrative core of the Battalion and it was their task to prepare to receive the influx of the Battalion's members when they, in turn, were mobilized. The tasks were wide and varied and had to be completed in a very short time. These included sleeping, washing and eating arrangements in billets to be found in each company area. Drill halls had to be supplemented by miners' welfare halls and other suitable buildings. The supply of bedding, clothing and equipment and many other tasks filled the long working hours of the administrative staff of the Battalion. At 2.50 p.m. on the 1st September, 1939, a telephone call was received from 151 Brigade, to mobilize and this was followed at 8.10 p.m., by a telegram which simply stated, 'Mobilize.'

The 50th (Northumbrian) Division at the outset of the war was commanded by Lieutenant-General Sir Giffard Le Q. Martel, KCB, KBE, DSO, MC. He had served in France in World War I, where he had won his DSO and MC and was Mentioned in Despatches on five occasions. He was one of the small band of tank enthusiasts who between the wars pressed for more tank research and development and to build up large tank formations. He believed that the tank would spearhead victory in war. He now commanded one of the three motorised divisions in the British Army. The Division was made up of two Brigades, 150 and 151, with a motor reconnaissance unit of The Royal Northumberland Fusiliers in motor cycles and scout cars, in addition to medical, artillery, Royal Army Service Corps and other support services. 151 Brigade was commanded by Brigadier Jackie Churchill, a regular officer of the regiment who had also served in the First World War, where he had won a Military Cross. The 6th Battalion DLI was commanded by Lieutenant-Colonel T.H. Miller, a World War I veteran. Captain (later Brig) Peter Jeffreys, a regular officer of the 1st DLI, was appointed Adjutant of the 6th in 1938. Coincidentally, his father John had been appointed Adjutant to the Battalion in 1913, some twelve months prior to the outbreak of World War I.

On the 1st September, the men of the Battalion reported to their drill halls: 'A' and 'HQ' Companies at Bishop Auckland; 'B' Company at Barnard Castle; 'C' Company at Spennymoor and 'D' Company at Crook. On the following day, in accordance with the provisions of the Civil Defence Scheme, 'D' Company was moved from Crook to Darlington, where it was billeted in the Plaza Cinema. The embodiment of the Battalion was completed with a total of thirty-one officers and five hundred and sixty two other ranks. It is of interest to note that the 10th DLI formed from the 6th Battalion, had a total of ten officers and three hundred and fifty-one other ranks when its embodiment was completed

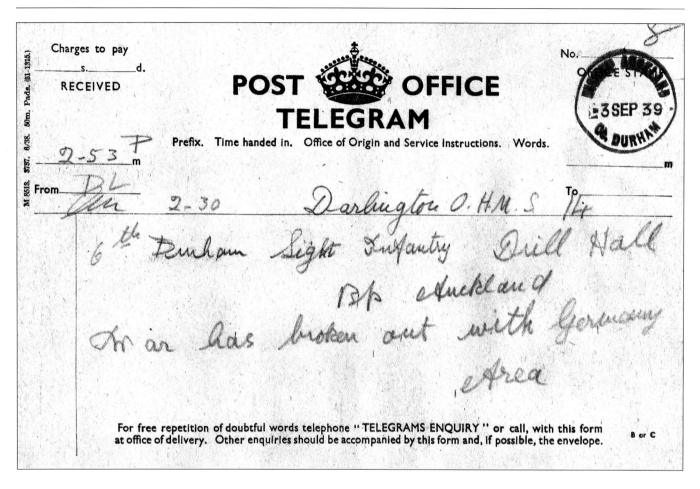

Telegram *announcing the outbreak of World War II*

on the same day. On Sunday the 3rd September, 1939, Mr. Chamberlain, British Prime Minister, spoke to the nation on radio, stating that war had been declared with Germany.

As the companies were sorted out, a small number of officers and men were posted to the Infantry Training Centre (ITC) which was forming at Brancepeth Castle, to help form a training cadre for the large numbers of conscripts coming into the Regiment. Medical examinations commenced immediately and these resulted in a number of men of the Battalion being found to be unfit for active service. Replacements were found amongst the conscripts coming into the ITC Brancepeth. These men, new to army life, found the move from home to Brancepeth, which had almost no facilities at this time, very traumatic. Private Sandersfield of the Battalion wrote of his experience on moving to Brancepeth:

'On 15th September, which was a Friday, I arrived at the Castle which had only been occupied by the army a month earlier and the whole camp was in chaos. On arrival we were checked in and given a conscription number ... Next we were kitted out with uniform and all service clothing plus rifle and gas mask. After this we were given our first meal and what a shock after leaving home! We had been given a mess tin ... a knife, fork and spoon ... As I stepped into the mess tent I was told to take my turn in the line in front of the tables which had all the food laid out in metal containers, into the first half of my mess tin went carrots, peas, potatoes, turnip, then thick meat stew; moving along to the next table the other half of the mess tin was filled with currant pudding, custard and prunes ... must say that most of it went into the swill bins but after a couple of days there was never any food wasted again ... That evening we were all given three blankets then the squad was taken to one of the rooms in the castle where on the floor were beds made out of square biscuits [when they were laid out in a line they formed a six feet by two feet bed]. On these you put one blanket as a sheet then covered yourself with the other two, for the pillow you used your army haversack and gas mask and folded clothing. From then onwards this was called our barrack room, it was completely devoid of all furniture, it had no electric lights, and in the evening we had to use candles and these were snuffed out at 10 p.m. as this was lights out ... I must include the following amusing incident. After lights out one of the lads lit a match to light a cigarette, suddenly there was a yell from the Lance-Corporal, "Put that bloody light out," out goes the light then a voice replies, "Get stuffed," well I think a lot of us went to sleep a lot happier.'

When the camp, centred on the castle, was completed it became one of the most important and efficient ITCs in the country. Conscripts received initial and specialised training in places like Willington, Esh Winning, Brandon Colliery, Medomsley and other mining villages where they were billeted in miners' welfare halls, dance halls, cinemas and various other buildings. Here they were taken into the hearts and homes of the local people. From these centres the men moved as drafts to the Battalion to which they were posted.

On the 5th September, intensive individual training commenced. This included drill, weapon training, route marches and some training in the digging of trenches. A strenuous physical training programme commenced, encouraged by Brigadier Churchill who demanded a very fit Brigade. The most intensive activity centred on bringing the companies up to full and healthy complements. For example, on the 12th of the month, four other ranks were rejected as unfit, eight other ranks were passed for home service only and three officers and sixteen other ranks were posted to the ITC Brancepeth. On the 26th of the month forty-six other ranks were discharged 'Free' as being urgently required for civilian employment, that is, key men in industry. The discharge of key men required for civilian employment was to bedevil the Division over the following months and cause many angry letters between the Divisional Commander and higher authority. Such rejections and postings continued for most of September. Officers and men were sent on a variety of courses, for example, physical training at Aldershot, weapons course at Hythe, gas course, senior officers course and brigade training exercises without troops (TEWTs).

On the 18th September, 'A' Company relieved 'D' Company on civil defence duties in Darlington. Brigadier Churchill visited all companies on the 19th. The Battalion moved to the Whitburn Ranges on the 9th October. The movement was made by a combination of marching and embussing, long remembered by the men who took part. 'A' and 'B' Companies marched to Bishop Auckland from Darlington and Barnard Castle respectively. They were then embussed to Whitburn. 'HQ', 'C' and 'D' Companies embussed to Belmont, Durham, and then marched the remainder of the journey to Whitburn. A week was spent at Whitburn firing a full weapon's course. The Battalion returned to Bishop Auckland on the 16th of the month, again by a combination of marching and embussing. On reaching Bishop Auckland 'HQ' Company was billeted in the Edgar and Jubilee Halls, 'D' Company in the Gymnasium, 'C' Company in the old Gazette Offices and 'A' Company, provisionally, in West Auckland Hall. 'B' Company continued their journey by marching back to Barnard Castle.

On the 21st October, the Battalion entrained for the west country. 'A' and 'B' Companies were brought to Bishop Auckland railway station by bus. The move was made by two trains. The first carried 'B' and 'C' Companies, the Carrier and Mortar

Platoons, under Lieutenant-Colonel Miller. The train left Bishop Auckland at 11.25 p.m. and arrived at Chipping Norton at 7.51 a.m. on the 22nd. The second train carried 'A', 'D' and 'HQ' Companies, less the Carrier and Mortar Platoons, under Lieutenant Mike Ferens. It departed Bishop Auckland at 3.05 a.m. on the 22nd October and arrived at Chipping Norton at 11.50 a.m. The Battalion transport had left a few days earlier. It was a journey not without incident for Lieutenant Vernon Ferens who stated:

'...we marched from Durham to Whitburn to range fire and whilst we were there Peter Jeffreys sent for me, highly secret and said, "I want you to take your car to take the Battalion transport down to a place which is highly hush, hush. You mustn't mention it to a soul. The place you are going to is Chipping Norton. You can have the after-noon off and get ready." Being a member of the AA I thought I would be able to get a route. I rang them up in the midday and said I wanted a route to Chipping Norton and it arrived the next morning at home ... I was leading (the transport) and I had a Rover 10. I kept asking, "Are they behind? Are they still behind?" They were. We got to somewhere just north of Doncaster and he (Avery - batman) said, "I think something's gone wrong, Sir, because the man driving the 8cwt behind us has bright buttons," and, of course, we had black. So I pulled over to the side of the road and this whole convoy which happened to be the 8th Battalion, went past. So I waited thinking, "Good God! My first job and I've gone and lost the whole bloody thing. However, eventually, they came up and I got through ... The 8th and 9th didn't arrive until it was dark ... they got utterly lost on the way. My AA map and route had really done the trick.'

The 6th Battalion was billeted in Chipping Norton, Hook Norton and Kingham. Headquarters was in Chipping Norton. The Division was motorised, although not completely so. Second-Lieutenant Mike Lockhart, Battalion Motor Transport Officer, stated:

'...we moved down to Chipping Norton which was the Battalion HQ and I was billeted in the Blue Boar with Vernon Ferens and the MT had an office and workshop in the old brewery there. The Mess was down a little side-street in quite a nice cottage type of house and one of the things I remember about MT was that we had a teacup and, I think for a penny, an old penny that

is, one could have a cup of tea and a biscuit. Whilst we were there I was sent to Chilwell or that district to buy about twenty cars to teach the various drivers in the Battalion to drive and we got a good selection of cars. I think the maximum price that one was allowed to pay was something about twenty pounds per car. I remember this included a large Vauxhall, a Humber Saloon which I earmarked for myself, and various other vehicles and these were distributed round the companies. Drivers could have experience of driving. Eventually we received, I suppose during this period, our regular 15 cwt vehicles and 3 ton Bedford lorries. During this time whilst we were there, I remember, we had a course for motor cyclists and we were loaned a field where one could learn cross-country riding.'

Officers were billeted in pubs and houses, the men in the brewery and barns. The civilian population was, at first, on its guard. Private George Iceton - Motor Transport Section - stated:

'The people when we first went to Kingham weren't very happy with us but they created a great canteen before we left. It was run by the vicar's wife who had condemned us before we got there ... He stood in his pulpit before we arrived and said that the women had got to be wary because the 'wild men' from the North are coming down and they'd better protect their daughters.'

It was a suspicion which quickly disappeared as the friendly 'Geordies' moved amongst them. Captain Peter Jeffreys stated:

'The people of Chipping Norton were marvellous. The troops' billets were pretty uncomfortable...many of them were in the upper storeys of barns, granaries and that sort of thing, not warm but, of course, you get a platoon in a not very big area generates a certain amount of warmth for themselves. But I think everyone was happy and the relationships with the Chipping Norton people...they were marvellous and, I think, our men were marvellous too. They behaved perfectly. We never had, what you might call, a civil offence ... It was super and after the war a lot of old chaps who had been at Chipping Norton used to go back to Chipping Norton to see old friends there ... Several of them married Chipping Norton girls.'

The men slept on the top floors of the brewery and barns in the area. They were not too comfortable. Dining facilities were on benches and tables on the ground floor with the company cookhouse nearby. Washing and toilet facilities were outside.

Private Alf Bailey - MT Section - remembered the conditions:

'I remember we used to pay two shillings a week for a bucket of warm water, we all used to wash in that. Most of us had scabies. We used to go to hospital at Tidworth ... two or three of us used to wash in one bucket of water. I don't think it was very hygienic at all. We should have gone outside to wash in the place [erected] but it was too cold. We were buying the hot water from the cookhouse.'

On reporting sick with scabies the sufferer was painted with a blue solution which sufficed for most cases. A number of the worst cases went to hospital.

The usual training was continued with the addition of initial training as a motorised unit as vehicles arrived. Officers and NCOs attended courses. Lieutenant-Colonel Miller and Captains Jeffrey and Roddam attended a two day Divisional exercise on the 14th and 15th November. At the beginning of December, companies began to use the firing ranges at Castle Bromwich. The issue of Bren and anti-tank guns was finally made up to war establishment on the 8th December. Platoon and company exercises were held daily throughout the latter half of December.

The movement of key men back into industry had left the Battalion below strength. A number of replacements came from the ITC Brancepeth. Over a hundred officers and men were posted to the Battalion on the 31st October and a further large draft arrived on the 23rd November. A large proportion of these came from the King's Shropshire Light Infantry. Initially, quite upset at having to change regiments, they quickly settled down and were completely integrated into the Battalion where they became more 'Durham' than the Durhams themselves. During December, Battalion transport was made up to strength with the arrival on the 4th of the month of one Humber car, nine 8 cwt trucks, one office truck and twelve 30 cwt trucks. Five carriers had arrived on the 1st December. On the 12th of the month, the first party proceeded on seven days leave. Company exercises took up most of December. A second leave party left on the 21st December, again for seven days and largely made up of married men with families, who got home for Christmas. A third leave party left for the same period of leave on the 29th December. For those left behind with the Battalion, Christmas Day was a special occasion. Officers undertook duties and served the Christmas dinner of turkey, vegetables, pudding and a beer ration: a pleasant first wartime Christmas celebrated by the men of the Battalion.

CHAPTER 16
FRANCE & BELGIUM - THE BATTLE OF ARRAS
1940

The onset of one of the country's severest winters curtailed the training planned for January, though Company and Battalion exercises did take place and a Divisional movement exercise took place on the 11th of the month. On the 17th of the month, King George VI visited the Division. He inspected 151 Brigade at 10.00 a.m. The companies marched into Chipping Norton from the outlying villages and lined the square. It was a cold, yet fine winter's day and the red faces of the men must have enhanced their healthy appearance. Captain Bill Watson wrote:

> '...The whole ceremony passes off without incident, apart from the piquet at the Officers' Mess at Divisional Headquarters which had been found by the Battalion. An attack of nerves or the intense cold caused a member to pull the trigger of his loaded rifle with the result that the bullet narrowly missed the head of the deputy Assistant Provost Marshal and then flattened itself on a chimney of Bury Barns, in which the Mess was housed.'

On the 22nd January, 1940, the advance party of all motor transport and its personnel left Chipping Norton by road for Southampton for embarkation to France on the SS *Fenela*. The extremely harsh winter conditions made the preparations for the move extremely difficult. The thermometer had registered many degrees below freezing and Lieutenant Lockhart and his drivers were constantly faced with the problem of ensuring that the vehicles did not freeze up. On the night of the 21st, the drivers had little sleep as the vehicles' engines had to be run every half hour to prevent freezing up. It was a tired group of drivers who left Chipping Norton early on the following morning, to travel the eighty miles by road to Southampton Docks. Despite the icy conditions on the roads the journey was completed without mishap and all vehicles arrived safely to be taken onboard. The SS *Fenela* sailed on the evening of the 25th January and arrived at Cherbourg at 8.15 a.m. the next day.

The main body of the Battalion had to assemble at Chipping Norton in time to entrain at 8.00 a.m. on the 28th January. The weather conditions were appalling. A blizzard had blown up during the previous evening and the companies stationed at Hook Norton and Kingham were faced with a march of some five miles to the railway station. Hook Norton company had a particularly difficult march and left the village at 5.00 a.m. to give itself enough time to reach its destination. It took one hour to march one mile through deepening drifts and snow blown into the men's faces by the high winds. In full marching order the men pushed on, though it soon became obvious that it would be difficult to reach Chipping Norton in time. Captain Ronnie Roddom, therefore, went ahead alone, reached Chipping Norton in an almost exhausted state but in sufficient time for a requisitioned bus and what remained of HQ transport to pick up the company and ferry it back to the railway station. Private Bert Davies wrote:

> 'After spending a delightful Christmas there, the first Christmas I had had away from home, it came to the crunch and a move was on the agenda. In January we were told we were going to march to Chipping Norton which was five miles away and meet the rest of the regiment there, to be transported to France for

duties there. Of course this was very hush hush! ... I think it was snow and ice and we had to march five miles...full kit to Chipping Norton ... One of the officers fell out and was picked up by transport. Two more fell out. I'll never forget that march.'

It was a cold, wet and shivering Battalion which left Chipping Norton for Southampton where it went onboard the SS *Ulster*. Battalion strength was six hundred and seventy-nine officers and men. Cherbourg was reached early on the morning of the 29th January. It was very cold and pouring with rain. The men had the opportunity of walking round the city for the rest of the day. First impressions were not favourable. The French civilians were indifferent. They had seen many British units coming through the port. One or two French soldiers lounging around the port area did not equate with the mens' understanding of the military prowess of the French Army. Most were pleased to entrain in the evening and begin the move to the Divisional concentration area near Le Mans. The carriages of the train in which the officers travelled, were uncomfortable and draughty. The men travelled in the same style as their fathers who went to war in 1914. They were packed into trucks marked '40 hommes 8 chevaux'. The train crawled through the night via Carentin, Bayeux and Caen to La Hutte, which it reached at 5.15 a.m. on the morning of the 30th January. The Battalion then moved into billets in and around the small town of Fresnay-sur-Sarthe and a first lesson on French drinks.

Promoted Major Peter Jeffreys, as his father had done on going to France in 1915, became second-in-command of the Battalion on the 9th January, with Lieutenant Vernon Ferens taking over as Adjutant. He remembered the experience of the men's first visits to the local estaminets:

'Our wonderfully behaved chaps went into the local pubs, why not? ... they had a terrible rough cider and no beer. Went to a local estaminet and you either got wine or cider and the cider was terrible. It was a most bitter, horrible drink but worst of it was, it absolutely knocked you out and a chap who was used to drinking three pints of beer who drank three pints of that cider, it absolutely floored him.'

If there was excitement and a spirit of adventure at coming abroad for the first time in the lives of many of the men of the Battalion - the same feelings expressed by their fathers in 1915 - in quiet moments thoughts turned to home and the families left behind. Private Sandersfield had the following experience in Fresnay-sur-Sarthe:

'This small village has a special memory for me about a soldier's feeling for home sickness. On the second night there was a large group of our company who had gathered round a large fire in the brewery yard, after a while after having a chin-wag they started singing as there were some good entertainers amongst them. Suddenly someone started playing a radio and it was a Vera Lynn Show and she sang some songs. Naturally all of the men joined in and then at the end Vera sang "The White Cliffs Of Dover" and nearly all of them started to cry. I suppose as nearly all of them were Terriers that meant that most of them were missing their wives and children.'

The response of the local population towards the British troops who had descended upon them swung between friendliness and co-operation and disinterest. Far away from the battlefields of the First World War, they had never experienced the rule of an invader. Furthermore they had a complete belief in the strength of the Maginot Line to hold off any German invasion.

Many of the troops were billeted in the old brewery. Cold and uncomfortable in the freezing winter conditions, it was also infested with rats. Private George Iceton remembered the conditions:

'The Shropshire lads were rural people like ourselves and one had been a gamekeeper and every night the rafters were running with rats and they were dropping off the rafters on to the beds and this lad got so sick. One night he just up with his rifle and shot this rat and it fell down. Unfortunately the rifle bullet went through the roof, so the rain came in as well.'

The Battalion was not intended to stay in the Fresnay area for more than a few days and orders were received from Division that it should prepare to move forward on the 7th February. Unfortunately the winter weather took a hand. Roads were either impassable or so frost-bound that the French authorities refused to allow the movement of vehicles, which they thought would seriously damage the highway. Over the next fortnight the Division became strung out between the Le Mans area and that of Amiens as stop-start orders came down from the French. It was not until the 19th February after two cancellations that the Battalion commenced its move northwards. This move was not without its problems. Captain Mike Ferens was in command of the rear party whose task it was to ensure that the Battalion billeting areas were clean and tidy and to sort out any problems with the civilians. He remembered the following incident:

> 'At Fresnay-sur-Sarthe I was in command of 'B' Company and when the Battalion moved from Fresnay up to Molliens-Vidame, I was left behind in command of the rear party and to sort out all the trouble. I remember very well 'A' Company, commanded by Captain Proud, being conscious of leaving their billets clean and tidy, had piled all the rubbish into the fireplace and set fire to it and then left. The fire fell out and set fire to the house. I had to sort out the compensation for the damage that was done.'

The Battalion reached Tourouvre at 2.00 p.m. on the 19th February. This was to be an overnight stop. The weather closed in and the stay lasted for over a week. Battalion strength dropped to six hundred and thirty-six as a number of men became ill and were sent to hospital to recover. On the 28th February, the Battalion moved on to Molliens-Vidame, near Amiens. This was earmarked as the 50th Divisional training area and the Battalion stayed here for one month during which it got down to strenuous training as a motorised unit. 'HQ' and 'A' Companies were billeted in Molliens-Vidame along with Battalion Headquarters. 'B' Company was billeted in the small village of Dreuil. 'C' and 'D' Companies were billeted in camps nearby. As usual, barns, stables, estaminets, town halls and so on were used to house the men, never comfortable, but being the traditional homes of the soldier, accepted with the stoicism and not a little humour of the Durhams.

Brigadier Churchill drove his Brigade hard and with great personal energy. A Royal Army Service Corps platoon of 3 ton trucks was attached to each Battalion and the men practised embussing and debussing into and out of these, until they got the time for carrying out these drills down to a few seconds. It was a time also for experimentation. Lieutenant Mike Lockhart, Battalion Transport Officer, remembered:

> 'Exercises were carried out to try a new French method of moving at night using two lights facing backwards, which when you were the right distance away you could see as two crosses and, if you were too far away, these blurred into one. In theory it should work pretty well but, I think if I remember rightly, there were one or two prangs during the night exercise.'

From the 9th March onwards, company, battalion or brigade exercises were organised for each day. It was a long, hard and exhausting period; embussing at speed into trucks, followed by a long journey; on stopping, debussing at speed and fanning out into a formation to carry out an attack against a defending force and consolidating ground gained. Battalion strength dropped to as low as six hundred and seven through sickness and transfers to other units. On the 21st March, drafts were received which increased the strength to seven hundred and three. One hundred of these men came from the Infantry Base Depot. The local French population had been well used to seeing British troops, in both world wars, and were very friendly and helpful. On the 29th March, the Battalion left Molliens-Vidame, not a little pleased after the hard work they had been put through and moved to Emmerin, a few miles south of Lille.

Prior to the move to Emmerin, Lieutenant-Colonel Harry Miller decided to carry out a reconnaissance of the new area. He was with the 6th Battalion at the Butte de Wallencourt in November, 1916, and as part of the reconnaissance he took his party to the scene of the battle. Captain Vernon Ferens, who went with him, remembered the journey:

> 'We did a reconnaissance ... so we went in his [Lieutenant-Colonel Miller's] Humber car, Mike Lockhart, the Transport Officer and Frank Robson, QM, the CO and his driver ... We went down from Vimy Ridge, down into the valley and went up towards the Butte de Wallencourt and quite near it was a war graves cemetery and sure enough found these four platoon commanders' and platoon sergeants' graves. I thought to myself, "Here's a man in a lifetime fighting the same enemy on the same ground."'

These were the graves of Lieutenant-Colonel Miller's former platoon officers and sergeants with whom he had fought on the Somme in 1916.

'A' and 'D' Companies were billeted in Ancoisne, a village near Emmerin. 'B', 'C' and 'HQ' Companies were billeted in Emmerin.

The Battalion transport was parked in the market square of Emmerin, with the Transport Section billeted in the room above the café opposite. The Officers' Mess was in a large house just off the square. This area had suffered in the First World War and the inhabitants were used to British soldiers. Private Alf Bailey remembered the welcome:

> 'The people of the North were good, they were very friendly and kind ... They'd experienced war, the older people, they didn't want it again, didn't want it. They were pleased we were there ... They were lovely towards us...We went back there the second time, on the second trip back. It was when we invaded France. We were first back in the same village ... We were last away, we were first back. They were all excited. They were crying.'

The organisation of the Battalion at this time was as follows:

Commanding Officer:	Lieutenant-Colonel T.H. Miller.
Second-in-Command:	Major P.J. Jeffreys.
Adjutant:	Captain V. Ferens.
Intelligence Officer:	Second-Lieutenant C.W. Surtees.
Medical Officer:	Captain J.R. Heslop.
Padre:	Captain P. Wild.
Quartermaster:	Lieutenant F.R. Robson.

'HQ' Company:

Commanding:	Captain B. Holroyde.
Second-in-Command:	Captain M.R. Ferens.
Carrier Platoon:	Second-Lieutenant D.R. Prince.
Signal Platoon:	Second-Lieutenant A.D. Scotson.
Mortar Platoon:	Second-Lieutenant B. Ellett.
MTO	Lieutenant M.A. Lockhart.

Rifle Companies:

'A' Company - Commanding: Captain E.L. Proud.

'B' Company - Commanding: Major J.G. Perry, MC.

'C' Company - Commanding: Major G.R. Roddam.

'D' Company - Commanding: Captain R.L. Cummins.

It is opportune at this point to look at the movement of the British Expeditionary Force since the outbreak of war. Within the first month of the war four regular divisions moved over to France and were in position in front of and south of Lille. 1 Corps, comprising 1st and 2nd Divisions and commanded by Lieutenant-General Sir John Dill, was on the right of the line held by the British II Corps, comprising 3rd and 4th Divisions and commanded by Lieutenant-General A.F. Brooke, was on the left of the line. The immediate task was to reinforce and extend a defensive system of trenches, anti-tank ditches and strong points, commenced by the French. Throughout the bitter winter of 1939-40, the men of the BEF laboured on this task. The build-up of the BEF followed. The first eight months of what came to be called the Phoney War was a period of unexpected calm. The 5th Division was in the line by the end of the year. In January, 1940, the 48th (South Midland), 50th (Northumbrian) and 51st (Highland) Divisions, all Territorial, moved into France. The 42nd (East Lancashire) and 44th (Home Counties) Divisions followed some two months later. The 12th, 23rd - which included the 10th, 11th and 12th Battalions The Durham Light Infantry - and the 46th Divisions followed at the end of April, 1940. These three divisions were very badly equipped and not fully trained and were used on lines of communication work.

On reaching Emmerin, 151 Brigade was employed in digging the anti-tank ditch which was part of the reserve line on the II Corps front. This work started on the 8th April. Two supervision parties were organised, one under Second-Lieutenant H.E. Walton and Corporal Bell of 'D' Company and the other under Second-Lieutenant D.Y. Caldwell and Platoon-Sergeant-Major Hayes of 'HQ' Company. The rifle companies and 'HQ' Company had to find two working parties of about forty-five men in each, with the available NCOs divided equally between the parties. There were two daily shifts; first shift, 8.00 a.m. to 1.00 p.m. and the second shift, 1.00 pm. to 6.00 p.m. Battalion transport moved the working parties to the digging site. The parties were protected by two anti-aircraft light machine-guns and one gas sentry, with siren. Four stretcher-bearers and two stretchers were on duty with each party. The men wore field service marching order, helmets and carried their gas capes along with arms and equipment. The measurements of the ditch were: twenty feet wide at the top, fourteen and a half wide at the bottom and eight feet deep. One side had a sheer face, the other sloping. Each completed section had to be revetted to avoid falling in. It was a formidable task, wet and dirty, but with the strong mining experience in the Battalions, the Brigade section of the line was tackled with speed and skill.

In addition to digging the anti-tank ditch, training was commenced - a continuation of that undertaken at Molliens-Vidame. Battalion movement and debussing practice took place whilst normal French civilian life followed the usual peacetime activities. Army transport shared the roads with civilian traffic and, as normal farming activities went on, the fields could not be used. However, in spite of difficulties, training went ahead and an impressive debussing demonstration was given for Lieutenant-General Brooke, the Corps Commander, on the 3rd May. Weapons were fired on ranges on the coast. Private George Iceton, Major Jeffreys' driver, went with this officer to prepare one range:

> 'During the stay there (Emmerin), Major Jeffreys and I went to Etaples to prepare an anti-tank gun range ... our anti-tank weapon was a 0.5 anti-tank rifle which hardly damaged our carriers never mind a tank. But the scheme was that we prepared these cardboard tanks on wheels and I would pull them between the sand dunes and, as they came out of the sand dunes, they fired at the tank, not me, hopefully. I used to drive between the sand dunes and pull this tank and they had to fire at the tank with this anti-tank rifle. Now, it was a beast of a thing. I think quite a lot of people never even bothered to fire it. We used to get some marks on the target.'

However some aspects of the training or lack of it caused some concern. Major Peter Jeffreys commented:

> '...we trained fairly well but I would say that the preparations made particularly for Territorial Battalions were not good during that period of time of the Phoney War. I think we should have been trained very hard and made physically as hard as possible. Of course nobody foresaw the shape of coming operations. As a result, I don't think we trained quite hard enough. We trained as hard as we could as a Battalion and everyone was becoming much more efficient. The handling of weapons became good.

There was a battle training area near the coast where everybody did field firing and so forth, it was fairly good. But, for example, I remember when Germany invaded we had no grenades and grenades were rushed out to us and we spent two days teaching chaps to throw grenades ... I think that, on the whole, the training as done by the Battalion was as good as they could have possibly done ... Directly we got to Emmerin our main job was digging a trench that went across somewhere east of Lens and, I think, a greater part of the BEF was engaged in digging this damned thing which was absolutely useless ... but anyway, instead of training, everybody got into lorries early in the morning, went out to this place, dug, and at evening time, came back to billets ... So coupled with that fact a motorised division and all this digging we had to do when we were at Emmerin, the Battalion was not marching fit.'

This lack of marching fitness was shortly to bear heavily on the Brigade. It must be remembered that the Division was motorised and, as well as digging the ditch, much training was taken up carrying the Battalions on trucks. It was never envisaged that the men would have to march long distances.

On the 26th April, two officers including the Commanding Officer and twenty seven-men went on ten days' leave to the United Kingdom. This left Major Jeffreys in temporary command of the Battalion. These were followed by a further two officers and twenty-seven men on the 30th of the month. The nearby city of Lille provided a variety of leisure activities for officers and men. 'Oeufs avec pommes frites' - eggs and chips - were available in the local estaminets. On the 7th May, the first length of the anti-tank trap was completed and inspected by Lieutenant-General Brooke. Another leave party left for England that day. The Divisional Boxing Tournament was held on the 8th and 9th May, in which the 6th Battalion gained third place. In the early hours of the morning of the 10th May, 1940, the message 'Birch Six' was received at Battalion Headquarters. The German invasion of Holland and Belgium had begun.

At 7.30 a.m. the Battalion stood to and, on standing down, working parties again went out to dig the next section of the anti-tank ditch. At 8.00 a.m. a route regulation party consisting of Captain Mike Ferens, Lieutenant G.H.A. Percival-Maxwell, Second-Lieutenant R.W. Dennis and twelve other ranks proceeded to the area of Roubaix where they undertook traffic control duties as the main force of the BEF advanced into Belgium. At 3.00 p.m. a German aircraft was shot down in flames near 8th Battalion Headquarters. 'D' Company of the 6th Durhams mounted guard round the wreckage.

When the Germans invaded Belgium and Holland, Plan D was implemented by the Allied forces. This involved an immediate movement into Belgium by the French and British to link up with the Dutch and Belgian forces. On the right, the French Seventh Army dashed for Antwerp and the mouth of the River Escaut. On its right were Dutch and Belgian forces. On their right was the BEF, along the line of the River Dyle, with the French First Army on its right, covering the Gembloux Gap, between the Dyle and the Meuse. Next in line the French Ninth Army covered the exits from the Ardennes, thought to be the least likely line of a German advance. The Second French Army was on the right of the Ninth, with its centre at Sedan. The moves into Belgium were completed by the 11th May, with an excited Belgian population cheering the troops forward as their transport past through village and town. As the French and British moved forward towards what they hoped were defences already prepared by the Belgians and found woefully weak when reached, the Germans initiated their plan to move through the Ardennes, cross the River Meuse on either side of Dinant and Sedan and race for the Somme and coast via Abbeville. This would cut off the main allied armies in the north from the French forces south of the Somme. There have been few more brilliantly conceived plans and more efficiently and effectively executed than this and it succeeded with - almost - disastrous results to the Allies.

The main German assaults fell upon the French though the BEF were heavily engaged on the Dyle. The French armies on both sides of the British were forced back, a manoeuvre which caused the BEF, in turn, to make a retirement. In the action on the Dyle, the Regiment's 2nd Battalion, 6th Brigade, 2nd Division, beat off a fierce German attack and Second-Lieutenant Richard Annand won the first Victoria Cross awarded to a British soldier in the war. On the 15th May, the Dutch capitulated and the French Ninth Army crumbled in front of the unexpected German assault through the Ardennes. A huge gap of some fifty miles appeared in this sector and the German armour poured through and headed for the Somme and the coast. This threat to the rear by the German Army Group A, together with frontal pressure from their Army Group B, was to prove, over the next two weeks, more than the Allies could contain. On the 16th May, orders were received by the BEF to withdraw to the line of the River Escaut and these were carried out.

To return to 151 Brigade and the 6th Battalion, the first few days following the German invasion were spent responding to reports of aircraft shot down, rumours of parachutists dropping in the area and digging the ditch. On the 12th May, Second-Lieutenant H.E. Walton, one NCO and four men went to Coutrai, in Belgium, to collect and bring back gold bars and securities - a novel assignment. The Battalion also continued to fire on the ranges at Bully Grenay and the mortar range at Vendin-le-Vicil. Long expected orders to move into Belgium were received on the 15th of the month and the following day the move commenced. The journey was made in troop carrying lorries of the RASC from Ancoisne via Seclin, Tournai, Rennaix, Nederbrakel, Grammont and Idegem. The Battalion orders were to prepare and occupy bridgeheads over the Dendre Canal on their frontage, to protect the river crossings here and create time to allow the demolition of bridges should this become necessary. In addition a careful lookout was maintained against any attempt to sabotage the bridges by infiltration of enemy groups. There were many rumours of Germans dressed as refugees infiltrating Allied positions to cause mayhem and to cross and attack bridges from the rear. In addition, rumours abounded of spies and Fifth-Columnists operating against the Allies.

'D' Company took up position astride the canal between Santbergen and Idegem in the late afternoon of the 16th May. 'B' Company was positioned between Idegem and Grammont. 'A' and 'C' Companies were behind the canal at Smeerchebbevloersegem. Battalion Headquarters were in and around Moenebreck. The immediate task was to dig in and create defensive positions. Unaware of the serious situation developing on the French front, though rumours were rife that things were not well with our Allies, the Battalion was surprised and somewhat concerned to see Belgian troops moving back in large numbers with no apparent discipline or organisation. At 9.59 p.m. ten shots were fired from a wood as a patrol of 'D' Company's 18 Platoon left it. Five further shots were heard as another patrol of 'D' Company left woods at 5.00 a.m. on the following morning. Whether these shots were fired by Fifth-Columnists or German infiltrators or, indeed, by our own forces, was never established. Already the fog of war was beginning to influence events. Telephoned orders from the 50th Division, were received on the morning of the 17th May, to the effect that anti-tank weapons be placed in position to cover the bridges over the canalised River Dendre. German armoured fighting vehicles were expected at any time. At 5.15 p.m. a warning order was received that 151 Brigade was to prepare to move at half hour's notice at midnight or early morning. A few minutes later three German aircraft flew very low over 'D' Company billets. Sergeant Makepeace probably became the first man in the Battalion to fire at a German in the Second World War, when he opened up with his Bren gun on one of the planes. It appears that he hit the plane before his gun jammed. The third plane returned the fire though no casualties were inflicted.

At 9.30 p.m. on the 17th, a Commanding Officers' Conference was held at Brigade Headquarters at Nederbrakel. Attended by all company commanders, Brigadier Churchill discussed the impending move with the officers and final arrangements were made. It was clear from the outset that only Battalion transport would be available and the men would have to march. The company commanders returned to their units at 2.30 a.m. and the withdrawal to the line of the River Escaut commenced at 6.00 a.m. on the 18th. The order of march was as follows: 'HQ', 'D', 'C', 'A' and 'B' Companies. The route followed was from Nederbrakel, Audenaude, Leupegem, Melden, Berchem, turning right to cross the River Escaut at Kerkhove, then it turned left at Avelghem and on to Bossuyt. A stream of refugees had been met moving into Belgium. This had now turned into a flood and made a marked impression on every man in the Battalion. They hindered the march as far as Leupegem, whereafter the Battalion's route took it away from the refugee packed road. The plight of these innocent victims of war, torn from their homes and moving they knew not where and the march on that first day,

was described by Major Peter Jeffreys:

> '...the refugee problem was quite awful. There were still the cars of the rich covered in their belongings but tragic, unbelievable, hundreds and hundreds and hundreds of poor people on their feet. "Ou est les Bosches?" they said. Poor people, they crammed the road and in addition to this ... in those days the streets were cobbled and cobbles are the devils to march on. Cobbles, full of refugees, it was an absolute nightmare that march but, somehow, one's spirits more than being sorry for oneself and one's chaps ... the whole well of your feelings were full of pity for these poor beggars, women, children, old men, young men, all trudging this way, trudging that way. You could come to a road junction, a lot of people were coming out that way, a lot of people were going down that way and all they would be saying was, "Ou est les Bosches?"'

Major Jeffreys spoke for the whole Battalion.

Lieutenant-Colonel Henry Miller, who had been on leave in England and had then gone on to a staff course, returned and rejoined the Battalion as it completed its march to billets in the Moen area, which were reached about midnight on the 18th May. The march distance had been thirty-five miles. A good night's rest followed.

The advance of the German Army Group A continued unabated. On the 18th May, Cambrai had been reached. Doullens and Amiens had fallen on the 19th of the month. On the 20th the 10th and 11th Battalions DLI and 12th Battalion - the latter now called The Tyneside Scottish and linked with the Black Watch - badly equipped and trained, were attacked by the German Panzers near Wancourt, off the Arras Cambrai road and at Neuville Vitasse, Ficheux and Mercatel. There could only be one result and, in the one-sided fighting, all three Battalions suffered grievous losses. Abbeville fell on the 20th May and the coast was reached on the same day. The Allied armies in the north were now cut off from the French forces south of the Somme. Unless the long German flank could be breached and contact regained with the French armies south of the Somme, a major disaster faced the BEF and its Allies in the north, now increasingly hemmed in on three sides. The scene was set for the only major counter-attack carried out by the British in France in 1940 and this role fell to 151 Brigade. The plan was for the French, south of the Somme, to mount an attack against the German flank in conjunction with the British attack from both sides of Arras. These would link up and thus cut the German flank and split the enemy advance, with most of the armoured spearhead of the attacking Panzers now trapped to the west. This was the plan which was pushed upon Lord Gort, GOC, by General Ironside, CIGS, and higher French command. The French proved not to be ready for such an offensive and the final plan was scaled down from this original one.

151 Brigade task was defined in Frankforce Operation Instruction No. 2, dated 21st May, 1940, in three phases: first, to clear and capture the area south of the River Scarpe from the southern outskirts of Arras; this advance would include the capture of Pelves, Monchy and the line of the River Cojeul as far west as the Arras - Bapaume road. The second phase was to clear and occupy the area south of Arras - Cambrai road, between the Rivers Cojeul and Sensée. During the third phase, 13th Infantry Brigade, 5th Division would attack across the River Scarpe, east of Arras between Fampoux and Biache and clear and occupy the area north of the Arras - Cambrai road as far as the line of the streams between Biache - Lecluse - River Sensée and link up with 151 Brigade.

At 12.30 p.m. on the 19th May, the Battalion was on the move again. It marched via St. Genois, Dries, Hoigem, Hading, turned right to St. Leger where it ran into refugee congestion, on through Belver to Leos Nord where it had a short halt for tea at the side of the road. It then moved on to Lys and arrived at Lannoy at 8.00 p.m. and into billets in a large wool factory. It was a march of over twenty miles. This 'motorised' Battalion had marched over fifty miles in two days, in very warm weather and often over roads crowded with refugees. The men were extremely tired and footsore. On this day, 50th Division was ordered to move to the La Bassée Canal and 151 Brigade's task was to man the bridges over the canal between La Bassée and the Carvin - Lens road. There was little rest for the Battalion. After a hastily arranged meal, the Battalion was made ready to move and at 10.30 p.m. it embussed on RASC troop carrying lorries for its new destination via Hem, Seclin and Ancoisne. It arrived at La Bassée at 3.30 a.m. on the 20th May. and was billeted in an

evacuated hospital. It was obvious that instead of facing east, they were now facing south. What was happening? Why were they there? They were about to find out.

The city of Arras had assumed a position of great importance. On the 20th May, the German XXXIX Corps led by Rommel's 7th Panzer Division were advancing directly from Cambrai. They bumped into the Allied positions. The city was defended by Petreforce - 1st Welsh Guards and a hastily raised mixed force of Base Troops, commanded by Major-General R.L. Petre, commander of the 12th Division. The German armoured spearhead took Beaurains and clashed with the Arras defences during the course of the day. A Battalion of the 150 Brigade was sent to reinforce the city's garrison. General Sir Harold Franklyn, KCB, DSO, MC, commanding 5th Division, was ordered to ensure the security of Arras and initiate an attack south of the city to relieve the German pressure and cut his supply route between his armoured forces pressing west and north and the motorised infantry and supplies following behind. He was given the 50th Division and the 1st Army Brigade of tanks. The whole became known as 'Frankforce.' His operational order to 151 Brigade appears above. The attack was commanded by Major-General Le Q. Martel, GOC, 50th Division.

Lieutenant-Colonel Miller and his company commanders carried out a reconnaissance at 4.30 a.m. on the 20th May, of the canal position, with the intention of taking up defensive positions on it. As the events outlined above began to take effect, there was to be no rest for the Brigade. Previous orders were amended and a move to Vimy Ridge to carry out offensive actions was ordered at 5.15 a.m. This move was to be made by trucks and Second-Lieutenant T.A. Cookson and four men went to Neuve-Chapelle to collect the transport. There was none to be had, though a promise was made that it would be sent on to the Battalion as soon as it arrived at Brigade. In view of the increasingly critical position at Arras, it was decided at 11.05 a.m., to send an advanced group up to Vimy Ridge to reconnoitre and hold positions which the Battalion would move to when transport arrived to carry them. 'D' Company and the Carrier Platoon, under Major Jeffreys, reached Thélus on the ridge at about noon. 'D' Company took up position between the Lens -

Arras road and Thélus - Roclincourt road, with the carriers patrolling between the right of the company and Neuville-St.-Vaast. Whilst 'D' Company dug in, Major Jeffreys carried out a reconnaissance with one of the carriers. A lot of smoke was coming out of Arras and there was occasional shelling but no sign of a German advance towards the ridge. It was a warm, summer day. 'D' Company had dug three weapon pits per platoon, connected up with communication trenches, camouflaged and wired, using wire left over from the last war. As night set in, the men were allowed to rest.

At 2.00 p.m. a company of the 4th Northumberland Fusiliers reached the Battalion. It was to act as a reconnaissance and screening force and at 4.00 p.m. two scout cars of this company began to patrol the front between Thélus and Roclincourt. The Battalion marched to Hulluch where it was ordered to wait until the La Bassée Canal position was relieved by 25 Brigade. This Brigade had joined the 50th Division a short time before and was originally intended for the Arras action. It was replaced by 151 Brigade when transport failed to appear to bring it to La Bassée in time. Troop carrying transport arrived at Hulloch at 10.00 p.m. and the tired troops climbed aboard to seek protection from the cold night air but there was very little sleep. The transport moved off at 3.00 a.m. on the 21st May and reached Petit Vimy - Thélus at 3.30 a.m. as 'D' Company were standing to. The companies took up the following positions: 'D' Company (Captain Cummins) astride the Lens - Arras road with its left flank on Thelus. 'B' Company (Major Perry) was in Thelus itself. 'C' Company (Major Roddam) was between Thelus and Farbus. 'A' Company (Captain E.L. Proud) was in front of Thélus. Battalion Headquarters, Headquarter Company and 'B' Echelon were in Thélus Wood. Orders from the Divisional Commander were that the men were to get as much rest as possible. At 7.30 a.m. cows grazing in the fields were milked to provide breakfast. At 9.30 a.m. the Battalion was warned to be ready to move off at a half hour's notice. Fifteen minutes later Lieutenant-Colonel Miller proceeded to Brigade Headquarters to receive final orders for the proposed attack.

The area to be cleared by the attack of the 6th Battalion on the left and the 8th Battalion on the right was about ten miles deep and four miles wide. General Martel decided that this was too large to be taken by a set piece attack on a broad front with the units he had available. It must be remembered that 25 Brigade was in position on the La Bassée Canal and 150 Brigade had been used to strengthen the Arras defences and to extend these to the east along the River Scarpe. The General decided to attack in two columns on a narrow front. There were further difficulties. There was little information about the enemy. It was not known, for instance, that Rommel's 7th Panzer Division tanks had moved across the front towards the west and the attack would fall upon the soft topped vehicles carrying his supporting infantry and supplies. This attack with tanks was the first combined infantry/tank attack since the end of the First World War and the two Battalions had never worked with tanks. The tanks had travelled throughout the retreat on their tracks and these were in dire need of repair and maintenance. No reconnaissance was possible and no contact had been made with the tank commanders before the attack commenced. Once everyone started moving there was a great difficulty with communications as there were no wirelesses and contact could only be made by runner or by motor cycle or carrier. In addition, maps were scarce. The officers and men were already very tired having marched long distances and had little sleep over the last three days.

The two columns comprised the following:

1. Left hand column:

    6th The Durham Light Infantry.

    4th Royal Tank Regiment with ten Mark II tanks armed with a 2-pounder gun and a 7.9mm machine-gun, and twenty-three Mark I tanks, slow, heavily armoured and armed with one 7.9 mm machine-gun.

    368 Battery, 92nd Field Regiment, Royal Artillery with 18-pounder guns.

    206 Battery, 65th Anti-Tank Regiment, Royal Artillery.

    One platoon 151 Brigade Anti-Tank Company.

    One company, motor cycles and one platoon Scout cars.

    4th Royal Northumberland Fusiliers.

2. Right hand column:

8th The Durham Light Infantry.

7th Royal Tank Regiment with six Mark II tanks and thirty-five Mark I tanks.

365 Battery, 92nd Field Regiment, Royal Artillery.

260th Battery, 65th Anti-Tank Regiment, Royal Artillery.

One platoon 151 Brigade Anti-Tank Company.

One scout platoon - motor cycles.

4th Royal Northumberland Fusiliers.

The 9th Battalion was in reserve and moved behind the 8th to the area of Maroeuil.

The 8th Battalion had an open right flank and this was to be covered by tanks of General Prioux's French Cavalry Corps. The Start Line was to be the Arras - Doullens road. Strong enemy forces were already operating north of this road in front of the 8th Battalion's advance and this Battalion became embroiled in heavy fighting, particularly in the villages of Berneville, Warlus and Duisans and did not reach the Start Line. Tanks of the 7th Royal Tank Regiment were never seen again by the infantry of the 8th Battalion after leaving the assembly area. They had made off with great élan, caused widespread damage to the Germans and heavy losses, but had lost direction. The Battalion's anti-tank gun screen on the right flank did cause heavy losses to German tanks. With the help of French tanks the Battalion was able to extricate itself from a very difficult situation. The full

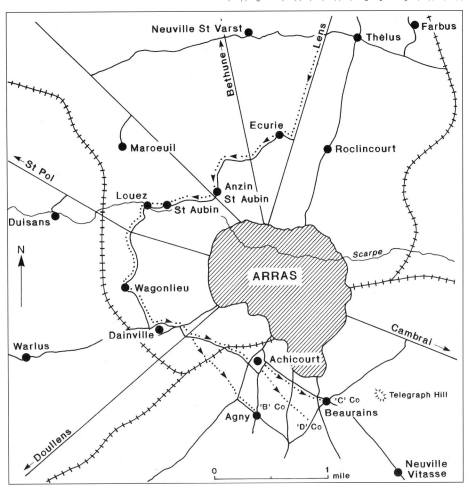

The Battle of Arras, *21st May, 1940. The route followed by the 6th Battalion from Thelus to Beaurains*

story of this gallant action of the 8th Battalion can be read in that excellent book, *Into Battle With The Durhams*, by Majors P.J. Lewis, MC and I.R. English, MC.

The axis of the 6th Battalion advance was Ecurie, Anzin St. Aubin, Wagonlieu, Dainville, Achicourt, Beaurains, Henin-sur-

Cojeul and Croisilles. The plan laid down that the Start Line on the Arras - Doullens road would be crossed at 2.00 p.m. Due to delays in getting out the necessary orders this timescale could not be met. Lieutenant-Colonel Miller, on his return from Brigade Headquarters, issued his orders to the company commanders and these were not completed until 10.55 a.m. To reach the Start Line, the Battalion was confronted with a march of about ten miles to be covered in two and a half hours. It was to set off at 11.30 a.m. into the unknown, with the possibility of meeting enemy forces on the way. In the event, the Start Line was not reached until 3.00 p.m.

Although dinners were being prepared for the men there was not time to wait for them and haversack rations were issued. Unfortunately there was not time to ensure that every man got his rations. At 11.30 a.m. the head of the marching column moved off from the Thélus crossroads, in the following order: 'D' Company, Advanced Battalion Headquarters, 'B' Company, 'C' Company, Carrier Platoon, Mortar Platoon, Rear Battalion Headquarters, RA Battery, Anti-Tank Battery, 'A' Company. 'B' Echelon and elements of Headquarter Company with the transport were left behind in the woods between Thélus and Petit Vimy with Captain Holroyde, Captain M. Ferens and Captain (Quartermaster) Robson. The first two officers and a number of men were left out of battle to form the basis of a reorganised Battalion should heavy losses occur. It was a hot summer day and the roads were very dusty. The men had not had sufficient rest to overcome their weariness and a long march lay ahead. However their spirits were high and there were very few stragglers.

'D' Company led the column and Major Peter Jeffreys, second in command of the Battalion, joined Captain Ronnie Cummins at its head. The column left Thélus and marched down the Lens - Arras road to the Ecurie crossroads where it turned right, on through Anzin-St.-Aubin, with the first German shells falling on the ridge two hundred yards to the north and in the village of Maroeuil. Anzin-St.-Aubin cemetery was the forming up area. With the infantry late, the tanks had gone on though their guns could be heard over the ridge ahead. On forming up, the column moved through St.-Aubin to Louez where it turned left and crossed the River Scarpe. At this point the Battalion transport drew to a halt and the Bren guns and other weapons were taken off from platoon trucks. It was now 1.25 p.m. The column continued its way up the slope towards Wagonlieu. Lieutenant-Colonel Harry Miller wrote:

'Continuing the advance we made good progress in spite of heavy and accurate shelling on the crest at Wagonlieu. I was very pleased at the way in which the forward companies met this shelling and it seemed to me they automatically adopted artillery formation and deployed on each side of the road as ordered, 'D' Company right, 'C' Company left with 'B' behind astride the road. The effect of the enemy fire on the troops seemed to hearten them and they appeared to lose all their previous signs of fatigue. By this time the tanks in front of us were really getting busy and although we could not see much of their activities, we could hear their two pounders and MG's rattling away. Between Wagonlieu and Dainville we were followed by accurate artillery fire, mostly HEs from 5.9s and it was obvious that the Germans were really stirred up and that they had all our movements under careful observation. The companies kept their formations well and advanced steadily, circumventing areas of enemy defensive fire and using ground wherever possible. Due to this our casualties were fortunately only slight. Through Dainville the shelling was particularly severe, but the men went through like veterans with very little loss...'

At 3.30 p.m. the Battalion continued the advance through Dainville and Achicourt. The Battalion Bren carriers were sent on ahead to make contact with the tanks. Lieutenant-Colonel Miller took Battalion Headquarters to the crossroads south-west of Achicourt. Captain Vernon Ferens was not happy with this position:

'Then we went forward and we finally arrived at a crossroads and the CO took up positions on the crossroads, I think foolishly. As, you see, crossroads are found on a map and they had spotter planes which were looking out for us and were giving their gunners instructions where to fire. He sent me forward to see what was going on and I went up to Peter [Jeffreys] and he had got up to the forward companies alright. Then we met some German soldiers whom we had taken prisoner and they were brought back and we sent them under escort, back to our Brigade Headquarters where they were taken care of.'

Christmas card *drawn by Private T. Cairns. It shows 'D' Company holding a ditch line near Achicourt crossroads south west of Arras, 21st May, 1940*

In fact this position did prove to be too hot and the Battalion headquarters had to move back.

Major Jeffreys had moved forward with Advanced Battalion Headquarters. He remembered what followed:

'...The CO was back with main Battalion Headquarters and I was forward with this Forward Battalion Headquarters. So I deployed the chaps ... and I put 'D' Company on the main axis in front, 'B' Company to the right, 'C' to the left and 'A' was back in reserve. We pushed on in open artillery formation. Then as we pushed on the shells came down harder and harder ... When we got passed Dainville, we saw the tanks in action for the first time. There did not seem to be many of them about but they were firing and there were some of them on fire when they had been hit ... there were a few dead Germans and a lot of smashed

up German vehicles ... The route which we had come had these villages on it and open corn land between. The tanks obviously, had played hell with the German infantry which they had met. They had not met German tanks. They had just met German infantry ... The German 7th Armoured Division was moving across the front upon which we attacked. Their tanks had gone on past our right as if to go round the flank and what the 4th Royal Tanks had run into was the soft infantry in vehicles, following the German tanks and, of course, they bashed into them in tremendous form ... we found a lot of German dead and took a lot of German prisoners. They came forward surrendering and very correct they were. I remember a German officer came up to me and he said,"Are you the senior officer round here?" in broken English. "Yes," I said. He said, "I would like personally to surrender to you." "Well," I said, "You can do what you like." And he said, "I and my men would like to lay down our arms and surrender." "Alright. Throw all your stuff down there. Give me your map," and I handed them over to a Lance-Corporal to take back and off we went.'

Major Jeffreys sent 'B' Company into Agny, a village on the right flank. It was involved in clearing this village over the next few hours and a number of prisoners were taken there and sent back for interrogation and the POW cages. Major Jeffreys and 'C' and 'D' Companies pushed on to Achicourt which had been very badly damaged by continuous enemy shell fire and proved difficult to get through. On reaching the railway embankment beyond Achicourt the companies were able to look across open country for quite some distance upon a scene of death and destruction. Many of our tanks had been knocked out, some were on fire. Some of the crews lay inside or had been thrown out and the men were shocked by these fearful scenes of dead and injured. Many tanks had broken down, the tracks no longer able to run after the mauling of the retreat from Belgium. The crews of those tanks still running had not lost their spirits and pressed on full of aggression, seeking more German targets.

Contact had been lost between Battalion Headquarters and the forward companies. There had also been some loss of cohesion and direction as they advanced beyond Achicourt and Agny, now coming under enemy small arms fire as well as increasingly severe shell fire. One platoon of 'B' Company under Lieutenant Jackson found itself with 'C' Company, with whom it remained for a time before rejoining its own company. 'A' Company, in reserve, was following the road that linked these two villages together. At this point the long arm of coincidence was revealed. On the 26th April, 1914, twenty-six years previous, Major Jeffreys' father, up with the forward companies of the Battalion in its first action of that war, had brought order to a confused situation at a time when communications with Battalion Headquarters had almost broken down. Major Jeffreys found himself in a similar role:

'...I had no touch by this time with Battalion Headquarters and the CO. It seemed to me that the only thing we could do was to press on, so we pressed on. We pressed on to a village called Beaurains. When we got to Beaurains I pushed 'C' Company, Ronnie Roddom, up through Beaurains. I said, "Get to the far end of Beaurains and take up a defensive position there ... 'D' Company, I put along the road south, stretching south from Beaurains. I had a marvellous driver, a chap called Iceton, and I had this 15 cwt truck. I said to Iceton, "Come on we'll go and try and find 'B' Company off to the right." So I got in the truck and off we went. I tried to find 'B' Company but couldn't locate them. ['B' Company, after clearing up Agny, had taken up position east of the village]. Trying to find them to the south, I ran into a lot of trouble. Lot of shelling, bit of long distance machine-gun fire, and a good many casualties from 'D' Company who were on this road running south of Beaurains. I and Iceton picked up all the wounded we could, put them in the 15 cwt I said to Iceton, "Drive back and get all these people into an RAP (Regimental Aid Post) ... Do that and come back to me at the crossroads at Beaurains. Well, there I was on my feet by myself. So I walked up to 'C' Company at Beaurains ... they were in good heart but extremely tired ... They had all this marching through the previous days, had had little rest, now they'd come up and they'd been marching since this early morning, fighting a bit, but march, march, march. I told Ronnie, "You sit out here, I'll go back to 'D' Company at the crossroads south-west of the village..."'

Private George Iceton, Major Jeffreys' driver, had followed 'D' Company from Thelus as it marched at the head of the column. He had orders to seek out his officer. He remembered many events of the day:

'Rightly or wrongly I took the asphalt road and could see the attack going on below me and the tanks had done a good job. The enemy we reached at this stage surrendered rather than were captured ... They were shattered. It was the first time it had ever happened to them and they just gave up ... Through Dainville and going towards Achicourt I was trying to keep Major Jeffreys in my sights and he was usually easy to see because he was a tall fellow...I had a good idea where he should be ... I looked across the fields below me and I saw someone with a rifle in the air pointing in the direction of the advance. This is an army signal for the enemy being in the direction of the muzzle ... This fellow was also dancing, so he looked more like a

Red Indian doing a war dance ... In the end I thought he was probably trying to signal me, probably Major Jeffreys had left a message or something. As soon as possible I got off the tarmac road and into the fields. I saw a very energetic corporal from 'C' Company and at this time there were two or three men trying to hold him down and when I got near all I could hear was, "Let me get at the bastards. Let me get at the bastards!" ... I realised then that he was going beserk ... His cheek was hanging beneath his chin and all I could see was the red and white walls of the cheek and the teeth all hanging down ... I got a couple of the lads to put him in the truck and whipped him back to where the M.O. was.'

On dropping off the wounded man with the doctor, Private Iceton set off to find Major Jeffreys. His story went on:

'...I found myself in front of the advancing company ... and I saw what looked like a railway embankment and with shooting coming from all directions I thought that it was a good place to get under. I dashed down into the railway embankment and turned west to get back in amongst our lads. I thought it was a railway embankment at first but apparently ... it was a sunken road ... I was somewhere between Beaurains and Agny ... I was going along the road and it veered off to the left, south a little bit. When I got round the corner I bumped into a German artillery position and it was the first Germans I had seen face-to-face ... There were two men behind the gun in the firing position, there were five standing round it with their rifles on their shoulders with bayonets on. I drove in among them, parked my truck and started waving my hands about to tell them to get up and away down the road. Then I realised I was naked! My rifle was behind the seat in the truck. So I turned round, turned my back on them. I had to get the rifle. Seven Germans there and I turned my back and went and got my rifle. I must admit they were shattered. more shattered than I was...Anyway I managed to get hold of my rifle and made a point of ramming a bullet down the breach and made sure they saw what I was doing and then I started pointing with the muzzle and they decided to get up and move. Now I don't know if you can imagine trying to turn a truck round in a narrow sunken road with one hand pointing (a rifle) at seven prisoners going down the road in front of you. Eventually I got the truck turned round. By this time infantry had come into the sunken road ... they (the Germans) were dejected, they were beat. They wanted to be taken prisoner ... I gave them over to the company..."

Private Iceton came up with Major Jeffreys and collected the wounded as described above. He made several journeys during the day collecting and returning wounded, under fire at all times. For this he was awarded the Military Medal. The citation reads:

'On 21 May, 40, Private. Iceton drove the Battalion 2nd in Comd's truck to Beaurains through heavy shelling. He was sent to find the MO and ambulance and successfully guided them forward to deal with casualties. He then collected wounded men until he himself was wounded. Throughout he showed great coolness and initiative under heavy fire.'

Sergeant Tommy Pallas of 'B' Company was awarded the Military Medal. His citation reads:

'On 21 May near Arras, Sergeant Pallas showed conspicuous courage and powers of leadership gaining the objective given to his platoon although his men were very tired and shaken. In the course of this operation he assisted in the capture of a building containing 25 Germans.'

Lance-Corporal John Boustead, No 17 Platoon, 'D' Company, was awarded a third Military Medal on that fateful day. His citation reads:

'On 21 May, 1940, Lance-Corporal Boustead's section occupied a defensive position under heavy shell fire. His platoon commander and sergeant were casualties but Lance-Corporal Boustead assisted in evacuating the wounded and then remained on his post until relieved.'

Second-Lieutenant D.W. Blackman commanded No 17 Platoon. He was severely wounded in the thigh and arm yet continued to command his men with great coolness and held his position under very heavy enemy fire. He continued to encourage his men until he was evacuated and Lance-Corporal Boustead took charge of the platoon and continued to hold the position. Second-Lieutenant Blackman was awarded the Military Cross.

Private R L Puddle won a fourth Military Medal. His citation reads:

'On 21 May, 1940, Private Puddle and a companion were separated from their comrades. They took shelter in a house to escape attack by an enemy tank. Private Puddle's companion was wounded so he carried him across the open under fire, to a truck and drove it to safety although he had never driven before.'

What was the position in the early evening of the 21st May? 'B' Company had cleared Agny and, following this, took up positions east of that village. 'C' Company was established on the southern edge of Beaurains, whilst 'D' Company was in the village and in the sunken road to the south-west. 'A' Company remained in reserve. The 8th Battalion had been unable to move as quickly as planned on the right due to unexpected heavy enemy opposition met short of the start line. Orders had been given, therefore, for the 6th Battalion to make Beaurains a tank-proof locality until further orders. Beaurains had been cleared by 6.00 p.m. by 'C' and 'D' Companies. Total number of prisoners sent back to Brigade was in the region of two hundred. The Germans had lost heavily in men, guns and vehicles.

Rommel's 7th Panzer Division moved off at 3.00 p.m. in the afternoon of the 21st, just as the 1st Army Tank Brigade commenced its attack on the Division's 6th Infantry Regiment. The Panzer Division's objective was to wheel round Arras and aim at Lille via Acq. As usual Rommel himself was at the head of his armoured spearhead. It appears that he was totally unaware of the danger to his following infantry and it was by luck that he arrived back in time to organise the German response to the British action and, at the same time, save his 7th Infantry Regiment from the same fate as his 6th. The advance of the Division had to be stopped and the 25th Panzer Regiment was recalled to deal with the British threat. The tanks of this unit suffered heavy losses on the anti-tank gun screen on 8th Battalion's right flank. The 7th Panzer Division's 105mm field artillery and 88mm anti-aircraft guns, the latter used in an anti-tank role for probably the first time, stopped the advance of the British tanks and caused heavy losses, including the commander of the 4th Royal Tank Regiment, Lieutenant-Colonel Fitzmaurice, who was killed. The German anti-tank guns had been unable to penetrate the armour of the Mark I and Mark II tanks. The Germans, themselves, now went onto the attack. Increasingly from 6.00 p.m onwards Achicourt, Agny and Beaurains were subjected to severe dive-bombing raids from the notorious Stukas. It was the troops first experience of Stukas and they found it very unnerving. As much a psychological weapon as one of destruction, the scream of plane and bomb had

considerable effect on the forward companies. It was the first and probably the only time that the Stuka gained an ascendancy over the men of 151 Brigade. They soon discovered that it takes a lot of bombs to kill one man and the aircraft's bark was far worse than its bite. But on this occasion, it was a new experience and they could not fight back. Private Bert Davies of the anti-tank platoon wrote:

> 'You felt so helpless. You haven't enough strength to retaliate. As long as you can retaliate a bit you feel alright, but when you can't retaliate, the dive-bombers you see, you can't retaliate to them, you lie down and take it. It was pretty disheartening ... You've got no protection whatsoever.'

With a German counter-attack obviously about to come in, it was extremely difficult to get the exhausted and dazed men back into action. At 8.00 p.m. the shelling on Beaurains increased. Fifteen minutes later a report came through to Battalion Headquarters from 'C' and 'D' Companies stating that enemy tanks were working round their left flank. German machine-guns and infantry on cycles were working round the right flank between them and 'B' Company at Agny. Enemy artillery observers were as close as six hundred yards east of the village. Those tanks of the 4th RTR still running were fighting isolated battles but they now began to withdraw in an attempt to rally farther back. There was now an increasing shortage of ammunition.

Communications were a constant problem throughout the action and Major Jeffreys had to act largely on his own initiative. Captain Vernon Ferens, as Adjutant, was one of the people who had to try to get messages through to the leading companies. He had his own motor bike and has given the following description of his task:

> 'It was quite exciting up on a motor bike getting up to the forward companies, because you had no idea whether there were still snipers about. You just had to take your chance and go. I went and did what the CO asked me to do and went up to the forward companies. They were holding the enemy only for a very short time and he sent me forward again to tell the company commanders to withdraw, to consolidate back on the Scarpe because we had come up against an absolute solid wall. So we went back. I remember going back to these damned

crossroads and getting off the motor bike and at that moment there was a barrage in the fields close to us and I thought, "Good God, we had better get out of this, this is too dangerous altogether." So we moved back and got away. There was a little house, a farmhouse near this crossroads which we made into a Regimental Aid Post and one of our officers, who had been drafted to us, came from London, a man called Ellett. He was brought back very severely wounded in the face. But funny enough, you know, once you got involved and helping, it didn't appear to be as bad as it was.'

Major Peter Jeffreys, who had been in effective command of the three forward companies during most of the operation, did receive a message from Lieutenant-Colonel Harry Miller at Battalion Headquarters at 8.30 p.m., to the effect that Brigade had ordered a withdrawal to Achicourt and to consolidate on the railway embankment east of that village. This must have been the message referred to above by Captain Vernon Ferens. The Major set off to get the orders through to 'C' and 'D' Companies:

'...I had no communication. I had nobody with me. So I went up to Ronnie, at the east end of Beaurains and I said, "You must withdraw." ... He said, "Well, I'll try." I went back to the other end of Beaurains to 'D' Company and when I got there a runner came back from Ronnie saying that there were enemy tanks working round both flanks and he would try and gradually withdraw. There was nothing else he could do ... By this time darkness had started to fall.'

The 5th Panzer Division had been pushed forward from Cambrai at all speed to come to the rescue of the badly mauled German infantry and its tanks began to appear on the battlefield. As darkness set in, the scene was depressing. 4th RTR tanks were scattered about the open country, many of them disabled, some smouldering and burning. German tanks and artillery were creeping ever closer and hammering shell after shell into the Durhams' positions. 'D' Company began to move back towards Achicourt. The darkness made it difficult to identify friend or foe. Major Jeffreys had a narrow escape:

'...the Intelligence Officer of the 4th Royal Tanks came along on a motor bike. I said we were going to withdraw to Achicourt ... At this moment we heard some tanks coming down the road from 'C' Company on the other side of Beaurains towards us. I said to this chap, "Whose tanks are these? Yours?" We could see them

up the road after a bit, about two hundred yards away. "Yes," he said, "That's alright. They're our Matildas." The leading tank came on to the crossroad.This tank man and I walked up to the leading tank and in the gloom at about ten paces, I looked straight at the man with his head out of the top of the tank and he was a German. He had these things on his collar. Then he realised that I was an Englishman so he shut the top of his tank like hell and I ran across the front of his tank, for I realised what was going to happen was that he was going to open up on us. But I thought that the thing to do was to get down in front of his tank so he couldn't depress his guns at me. I nipped across the front of the tank and got into the ditch on the far side of him. There were a couple of more tanks behind him and they opened up ... but behind us were two or three of our own tanks and they engaged the German tanks.'

Both groups of tanks engaged each other in the darkness with their shells screeching above the heads of the cowering infantry until, unable to see their targets clearly, both sides withdrew and allowed the infantry to make its way back to Achicourt as ordered. 'B' Company was moving towards Achicourt from the Agny area. 'D' Company, followed by 'C' Company, was moving in this direction from the Beaurains area. Enemy tanks were very active and inflicting heavy losses on the infantry now caught in the open. Men were firing back at the Germans using their rifles hoping to hit the heads of the tank commanders protruding from the turrets. Major Ronnie Roddom and Lieutenant Perceval Maxwell had remained with a rear party of 'C' Company giving cover whilst the rest of the company got away. One platoon had gone off earlier escorting about one hundred German prisoners. Both of these officers and a number of their men were taken prisoner by a German Armoured Reconnaissance Unit, which in the darkness was mistaken for French. They were both put onto the back of a tank and carried into battle against their own men, a frightening experience indeed.

Captain Vernon Ferens' luck also ran out:

'The CO sent me back to Brigade Headquarters to say that we were going to withdraw behind the Scarpe and I set off in a carrier with a man called Corporal Heslop. I didn't know what had happened to the despatch riders, they had all disappeared. The CO said, "You go back Vernon and inform Brigade that we are going to withdraw behind the River Scarpe." So I set off in this carrier and went to where Brigade Headquarters should be but they weren't there. So we set off to go to the next known position and we ran into an ambush. We were just surrounded by Germans. Corporal Heslop had got a grenade in his hand and he pulled the pin out, so we thought the best thing he could do was to throw it away as he couldn't put the pin back in again. So he threw it out the front when we were stopped. I thought we were all going to be shot, the Germans looked so excited at who threw the grenade but nobody asked of course. So that was it we were put in the bag.'

At 9.00 p.m. the remnants of 'C' and 'D' Companies had reached the crossroads between Achicourt and Beaurains, formerly the site of Battalion Headquarters, which had already moved back into Achicourt itself. There was to be no respite as German tanks appeared and began to systematically brew up a line of parked scout cars of the 4th Northumberland Fusiliers. Throughout the action, the motor bikes and scout cars of this Battalion had provided cover for the 6th Battalion's left flank and a reconnaissance screen as the advance continued. The Fusiliers now, with great gallantry, sought to provide a protective screen between the retreating infantry and the enemy tanks. They, too, suffered heavy losses.

A number of 4th RTR tanks appeared at the crossroads and engaged the German tanks and for a period of time both sides hammered away at each other as the infantry sought shelter in between. The noise was terrific and it was now quite obvious that if a disaster was to be avoided the remnants of 'C' and 'D' Companies would have to get away as best they could. Some men scattered and individually or in small groups made their way back towards Achicourt, over the ground they had marched that morning, and back to Petit Vimy. Officers searched for men and led them back. Captain Ronnie Cummins crawled up a ditch and took with him as many men as he could find. He was awarded the Military Cross for his gallant leadership of 'D' Company throughout the day. Major Jeffreys recalled his journey:

'...in the darkness and this fight, it was a pretty disorganised scene. So I started to walk back across country towards Achicourt and there were men scattered about. Some of them kept shooting towards the German tanks and that sort of thing. I kept shouting out saying, "Hey! Hey! Any 6th DLI about?" After

a bit I got hold of a few chaps who laid down and could not do anymore, were so exhausted. Rest we did, two or three hours, I suppose and then I got them up and we started marching back up the road through Achicourt. We got through Achicourt, to the other side of it. I said,"Well we'd better march on back up towards Vimy," hoping to find some of the British Army. By extraordinary luck I found a 15cwt which had been abandoned and, miracles, the damned thing started. I put every man I could think of in it and the rest I told to start marching and I would dump the first load and go back and get some more, and so on. Eventually later that day [22nd May], I got a good many chaps back to Vimy Ridge.'

It was obvious that the Battalion was in no condition to make a stand at Achicourt. Lieutenant-Colonel Miller and Battalion Headquarters had joined in the retreat which continued until Vimy was reached. He had given up his Humber car which had taken wounded men back and he marched with the men. During the early and subsequent hours of the 22nd May, the remnants of the companies struggled back to Brigade Headquarters at Petit Vimy. Battalion transport which had not been damaged or destroyed was used to bring back some of the men from Achicourt. Many marched back almost out on their feet with exhaustion.

A final blow awaited the Battalion on the 22nd May. Lieutenant-Colonel Miller arrived back on the Ridge and, due to a combination of extreme tiredness, darkness, confusion and incorrect or misunderstood orders, was directed back towards Hulloch and La Bassée, followed by elements of 'A', 'B' and Headquarter Companies, 'B' Echelon and men left out of battle. A further split occurred in La Bassée which had suffered considerable bomb damage from German air raids. In the confusion, Lieutenant-Colonel Miller went off in one direction searching for Brigade Headquarters, whilst the major portion of the column, about one hundred and eighty men in all, with Major Perry, Lieutenant Widdas, Captain Mike Ferens, Captain (Quartermaster) Robson, Transport Officer Lieutenant Lockhart and the Medical Officer Captain Heslop, lost their way and ultimately headed for the coast at Boulogne. Here, after joining with the newly landed Welsh Guards, they took part in the defence of that port and were eventually taken off by destroyer and returned to England and Durham, where they arrived tired, dishevelled and under the impression that the rest of the Battalion was lost. Lieutenant-Colonel Miller, meanwhile, with a small column of officers and men continued to search for Brigade Headquarters which, in fact, had never left Petit Vimy. He searched the countryside north of La Bassée making enquiries as to the whereabouts of the Brigade which no one seemed to know. At last on the 23rd he was told the Brigade was still at Vimy and returned there. Lieutenant-Colonel Miller was in a similar condition to Lieutenant-Colonel Harry Watson who commanded the Battalion at Ypres in late April, 1915. He also was over fifty years of age and had seen the Battalion he had commanded in peacetime for a number of years decimated. He was totally exhausted after long journeys on foot and by truck and very little sleep over the last five days. It was thought best that he return to England, which he did.

Major Jeffreys took command of the Battalion in France on the 22nd May. He organised the companies as follows:

'HQ' Company: Second-Lieutenant D.R. Prince.

'A' Company: Second-Lieutenant D.Y. Caldwell.

'B' Company: Second-Lieutenant H.E. Walton.

'C' Company: Second-Lieutenants T. Allison and T.J. Black.

'D' Company: Captain R.L. Cummins.

Officers and men continued to come into Vimy. On the 23rd, Captain E L Proud, Second-Lieutenants Chamberlain and Dennis and twenty other ranks rejoined, being part of Lieutenant-Colonel Miller's column. Captain Holroyd returned later in the day. He had been at the rear of the Boulogne column, lost contact with it and after a search rejoined Major Jeffreys at Vimy. Losses to the Battalion were estimated at about two hundred killed, wounded or captured. Nearly two hundred, as we have seen, went on to Boulogne and about two hundred remained with Major Jeffreys.

What did the Battle of Arras achieve? In material terms the Germans lost about four hundred prisoners to both attacking Battalions. These were sent back to Brigade Headquarters and thence, under Military Police escort, on to Division and, ultimately, prisoner of war camp in England. The dead and wounded suffered by the enemy are not recorded but must have been heavy as the British tanks got amongst them when they were most vulnerable. The enemy suffered equally heavily in destroyed and damaged vehicles, guns and tanks. Rommel is said to have thought he was confronted by several British divisions.

In terms of morale, the enemy suffered considerably. It must be remembered that the Germans had not experienced any reverse of note since the beginning of hostilities. There was an air of invulnerability about them. The actions of British infantry and tanks at Arras were a major blow to their morale. It has been noted that the enemy infantry was surrendering to our troops, often without a fight. It must also be remembered that these were the cream of the German Army, men of the Panzer Divisions, who had carried all before them since the 10th May. Man for man this action proved that the British soldier could measure up to his German counterpart, a belief which never left the Durhams throughout the war, whether in retreat or advance.

Already tired by its exertions during the moves of the previous five days, the Battalion had now marched a further twelve miles, advancing under fire for much of the way. The Germans had complete air supremacy and were much stronger than the British in tanks and artillery. The withdrawal during darkness from the area of the Brigade's long advance and attack resulted in some confusion and loss of direction. It was a weary party that eventually collected itself at Vimy Ridge next day but it had met Rommel and had, with 4th and 7th Royal Tanks, earned from that formidable General a respect he was always to retain.

During the advance of the Panzers across France the German High Command had been sensitive to any attack on their long, tenuous lines of support and supply to their armoured spearhead. This advance by the Durham Battalions sent a shudder of apprehension through the German Generals which even reached Hitler. A delay was called to allow the infantry to catch up with the armoured spearhead and this, it has been argued, may well have been a contributary factor to the ultimate successful withdrawal from the Dunkirk beaches. Caution crept into the minds of the German High Command. This may well have been conjecture but Arras proved to the Germans that the British soldier had not lost his courage and tenacity.

CHAPTER 17
THE WITHDRAWAL TO DUNKIRK
1940

General Weygand had succeeded General Gamelin as the French supreme commander on the 19th May. He was over seventy years of age and had earned his reputation as General Foch's Chief of staff in the First World War. He immediately initiated the Weygand Plan which aimed to send eight Allied divisions on a counter-attack southwards on the 23rd May, to meet up with an attack northwards from the River Somme by the French Third Army. This attack failed. The 5th and 50th Divisions were still holding the Arras Salient on the 22nd and 23rd May, as part of Frankforce. The Allied defence positions called the Canal Line were established and stretched from Gravelines on the coast, through St. Omer, Béthune and La Bassée. It followed the canalised rivers and canals which linked Gravelines, Aire, St. Venant and Béthune and was held by a number of hastily raised forces which went under the names of their commanders, for example, Polforce, Woodforce and Usherforce. On the east of the pocket the BEF still held the line of the River Escaut on the 22nd May. Troops of the French 1st Army held the bottom of the pocket and the ultimate sacrifice of this army as it stubbornly fought on when all hope was lost, did much to contain German forces and assist in the Dunkirk embarkation.

The reorganised 6th Battalion was able to get a little rest on Vimy Ridge on the 22nd May. Weapons and equipment were checked along with ammunition. At 3.30 p.m. it moved into reserve behind the 9th Battalion, to the left of the track running south from Petit Vimy, with 'B' Company on the right and 'A', 'C' and 'D' Companies on the left of the track. Battalion Headquarters was in Petit Vimy itself. During the afternoon many French troops and vehicles came into the woods behind the 9th Battalion. The Brigade was now in reserve to the 17th Brigade, 5th Division, which held the line of the River Scarpe to the west of Arras. In the afternoon, the Battalion relieved elements of the 4th Royal Northumberland Fusiliers on the left of the road to Lens and the edge of the wood running along Vimy Ridge. German aircraft and artillery had been active throughout the day. Stukas and two engined Dorniers bombed and strafed the Battalion positions. These did little damage in contrast to the enemy artillery which was both accurate and severe. As dusk fell a group of men at a time moved back to the cooks' area and received two sandwiches and a mug of hot tea, a welcome respite for tired and hungry men.

At 4.30 a.m. on the 23rd May, the Battalion took up new positions as follows: 'C' Company on the right of the track, 'A' Company on the left. 'B' Company was on the right of the main road to Lens, with 'D' Company on the left. At 7.00 a.m. a warning order was received from Frankforce that the Germans had used gas bombs with their mortars fired on the 21st May. These had given off a black liquid smelling of garlic which caused sensations of burning. It appears that these reports were never confirmed. Enemy air raids continued throughout the day. Some of the Battalion buried dead refugees and horses caught in the air raids at Vimy, a sad and unpleasant task. Little knowledge was available of enemy activities and moves and when news came to the Battalion it was invariably of the worst kind. This was the case at 10.00 a.m. when news was received that the enemy 5th and 7th Panzers had forced a crossing of the River Scarpe west of Arras and the companies were ordered to push on with digging and preparing defences. Bitter fighting was going on around Maroeuil which was still held by the 17th Brigade. Unknown to the Battalion the news further back on the Canal Line was far from good. The Germans had crossed the canal in front of St. Omer and had extended their bridgehead through Aire to Robecq. Reports also came in from the 3rd French Cavalry Corps that enemy tanks and infantry were about to attack St. Eloi from the west. This constituted a grave threat to the Brigade flank.

In the early afternoon of the 23rd, the Battalion again moved to take up new positions and relieved the 4th RNFs. 'D' Company moved right of the Petit Vimy - Lens road with 'C', 'B' and 'A' Companies on the left. Enemy ranging shells fell on the crest of the ridge in front of the Battalion positions. At 5.00 p.m. Major-General Martel, the Divisional Commander, arrived at Brigade Headquarters and ordered that positions now occupied by the battalions of the Brigade, must be held to the last man and the last round. These orders were passed on to the battalions. The general response of officers and men to these orders was a resolve to make the enemy suffer before that last round was fired. Meanwhile, information was received from Brigade that the French had failed to put their evacuation scheme into effect and, as a consequence, there was the possibility of starvation as essential supplies of food may not be available. Arrangements were immediately made, at a conference of company commanders at Battalion Headquarters, to conserve the food held in the Battalion. Within a few days, rations to officers and men were halved. News was received that the Battalion would be relieved by the 2nd Cameronians at about 10.00 p.m. and it would go into reserve at Petit Vimy, behind the 9th Battalion. Within half an hour this relief was cancelled. At 7.30 p.m., shelling and fires were seen behind Vimy, towards the north-east. Shortly afterwards the enemy attacked the 4th RNFs holding the right flank with machine-guns and using searchlights. They were beaten off. At 8.30 p.m., the 2nd Cameronians started to arrive having received verbal orders to relieve the Battalion. It was with a great sense of relief that the Battalion learned it was not to fight to the last man and last round. The night of the 23rd May ended with instructions for the Brigade to withdraw to the area Ancoisne - Don - Provin. Before the Battalion left, the men received their two sandwiches and mug of hot tea.

The 24th May was a day of great significance in the campaign, played out as the 6th Battalion moved to its new positions unaware, of course, of what was going on. General Weygand planned a new counter-attack southwards by eight divisions, to take place on the 26th May. By the 24th, the only troops available were two British divisions, including the 50th, and three French divisions, all of them very depleted in strength. As the position of the BEF worsened over the next three days and the success of any French led counter-attack became more remote, Lord Gort cancelled the use of the British divisions, now needed urgently elsewhere. The 50th Division was ordered, along with the 5th, to defend Ypres where a widening gap was beginning to appear on the Belgian right. On the 24th, the German armour, attacking the Canal Line, which they had already breached, was halted on orders from the highest authority. The attack by 151 Brigade on the 21st May, had reinforced the German High Command's sensitivity to threats to cut the long supply lines of the rapidly advancing Panzers. The need to close up these mobile forces was in the view of the High Command vital. Furthermore, it was felt that the armoured forces must be conserved for the ultimate operations south of the Somme. The Luftwaffe was flexing its muscles and demanding that it be given the opportunity to commit the final *coup de grâce* on what was seen to be a defeated enemy. It would shut off the Channel to the trapped BEF and bomb it into submission. Army Group B, mainly infantry, would mop up and the precious armour would be available for future operations. The next few hours gave the British and French the opportunity to reorganise their defences which held long enough for the Dunkirk embarkation to succeed beyond all expectation. The Salient occupied by the Allies on the 24th, was seventy miles south from the coast, twenty miles at its widest point and thirteen miles wide at its narrowest. On the 27th May, a final decision was made to withdraw from France through Dunkirk. At midnight, the Belgians capitulated and a huge gap appeared in the east of the Salient.

Just after midnight on the 24th, Captain Ronnie Cummins was sent out to reconnoitre the route via Lens, which the Battalion would take on its way to Don. Many bridges had already been destroyed. The route ran through towns and villages severely damaged by enemy air action, with resultant destruction to houses, blocked roads, dead and injured animals and civilians. At 1.20 a.m. the Battalion moved off in RASC trucks through Billy Montigny and Harnes. Battalion strength was ten officers and one hundred and ninety-two other ranks. The front group completed the journey without incident. The rear party comprising 'A' and 'B' Companies, travelling in tightly packed trucks and more slowly than the front group, fell behind. It found the bomb damaged streets of Lens difficult barriers to pass. Fortunately, an officer in an Austin 7 car led them through goods yards and over railway crossings between Avion and Touquiers and across the canal at Harnes. Even then the adventure was not over. 'B' Company, passing 'B' Echelon transport of many units moving nose-to-tail, rejoined the Battalion at 5.00 a.m. 'A' Company (Captain Leslie Proud and Second-Lieutenant Tim Chamberlain) had found the bridges at La Bassée, Bercleau, Beauvin and Pont-à-Vendin blown and had crossed the canal by boat, after storing kit in a house in Beauvin. They then marched to Ancoisne. A truck was sent to them to bring them to the Battalion, now at Don and their kit was collected by truck from Beauvin.

Whilst at Don on the 24th May, Major Peter Jeffreys reorganised the Battalion as follows:

Second-in-Command and MTO: Captain Holroyde.

Adjutant: Second-Lieutenant Dennis.

Brigade Contact Officer: Second-Lieutenant Ellett.

HQ Company: Second-Lieutenant Prince.

No.1 Company (Captain Leslie Proud): No. 1 Platoon:
Second-Lieutenant Black.

(Consisting of 'A' and 'C' Companys) No.2 Platoon:
Second-Lieutenant Allison.

No.3 Platoon:

Second-Lieutenant Chamberlain.

No.2 Company (Capt. Cummins): No.1 Platoon:
Second-Lieutenant Walton

(Consisting of 'B' and 'D' Companys) No.2 Platoon:
Second-Lieutenant Caldwell.

The Battalion got a good day's rest during the morning and afternoon, much welcomed by all ranks. However, the inevitable heavy enemy air raid occurred at 6.00 p.m. There was much dissatisfaction openly expressed towards the non-appearance of the Royal Air Force as the Germans retained complete mastery of the air. Fortunately casualties remained low.

At 9.25 a.m. on the 25th May, rations were cut by a half. Later in the day Second-Lieutenant Caldwell and Second-Lieutenant Allison were sent into Lille in search of bread and rations. French civilians, who remained in their homes and shops, invariably handed food to the troops though often it could not be paid for. From now on the officers and men remained hungry as well as weary.

At 2.30 p.m. on the 25th, Major Jeffreys attended a Brigade conference and heard for the first time of the proposed Weygand Plan, referred to above, to attack southwards on the following day. The 5th and 50th Divisions were earmarked to join four French divisions in this action. Objectives were: Epinoy, Abincourt, Bantigny, Haynecourt, Blancourt and Gavillers and the advance would commence with a river crossing in the face of enemy opposition. 151 Brigade had never practised river crossings and the prospect was, at the least, daunting. Fortunately the operation was cancelled by GHQ and at 5.00 p.m. the Brigade was put on two hours' notice to move. Orders were received by both the 5th and 50th Divisions to move between the Belgian and British forces on the east of the Salient. Here three German divisions were striving to break through a widening gap between Comines and Ypres.

At 9.20 p.m. Major Jeffreys was informed that he had been promoted to Lieutant-Colonel along with Major Percy (9th Battalion) and Major McLaren (8th Battalion). It was found impossible for the whole Brigade to break away to its new positions as both the 8th and 9th Battalions were heavily involved in fighting in the Cavin and Provin areas, during the 25th and 26th May. The 6th Battalion was able to move ahead at 10.00 a.m. on the 26th. It moved on RASC Transport via Wavrin, Radinghem and Erquinghem-sur-Lys, to a farm between the canal and the main road to Sailly-sur-La-Lys, where the canal bulged northwards. It was a difficult move due to large numbers of French troops on motor transport overtaking at every opportunity. The farm at Erquinghem was reached at 1.00 p.m. and a welcome rest followed. Shortly after midnight, a warning order was received from 151 Brigade to be ready to move to Ypres. The Battalion stood to from 2.00 a.m. at half an hour's notice to move. The roads in the area were heavily congested with motorised and horsed traffic. The Battalion move started at 11.00 a.m. on the 27th May, the column being continually stopped and redirected by the British Military Police and the French. A halt was called near Strazeele at midday and, whilst everyone took the opportunity to rest at the roadside, Lieutenant-Colonel Jeffreys, accompanied by his driver and Orderly Room Sergeant, went on ahead to try to clear up the situation. It was a beautiful, hot, cloudless day and all ranks enjoyed the respite, lying in the sun watching German bombers on their way to attack Ypres. At 1.30 p.m. a number of despatch riders and French armoured vehicles came down the road from the direction of Straleele with the news that a number of enemy tanks had filtered through the line and were causing damage at the north end of the town. Captain Leslie Proud ordered the Battalion to embus immediately and proceeded round Strazeele and on through Bailleul and Dickebusch to Vlamertinghe. *En route*, fires were seen to be burning in Strazeele. Vlamertinghe Chateau was reached by 2.30 p.m. and within half an hour a meal of biscuits and tinned fish was issued to the troops. A reconnaissance party was sent forward to the Yser Canal where the Battalion was to relieve the French 1st Dragoon Regiment. There was some artillery activity and in late afternoon there was an enemy air raid on the chateau.

Lieutenant-Colonel Jeffreys' small party had a narrow escape. As they approached Strazeele they met an enemy tank coming from the opposite direction. The three men took to the ditch

seconds before the tank destroyed their truck. Fortunately it did not see them although, on turning round and coming back, it got so close that it ran over the Orderly Sergeant's rifle lying on the edge of the road. When everything quietened down, the three of them marched towards the village and came across wounded and dead British soldiers who had been attacked by the German tanks. The situation was desperate. Lieutenant-Colonel Jeffreys had lost his transport and his Battalion. In the town, he saw a 15 cwt truck at the side of the road. It belonged to a group of sappers with a young lieutenant in command. The CO approached the young officer and asked if he could possibly borrow the vehicle to enable him to rejoin his Battalion. The officer gave him his truck and driver and Lieutenant-Colonel Jeffreys rejoined the Battalion at 9.00 p.m. at the Vlamertinghe Chateau.

At 11.30 p.m. the relief of the French troops on the Yser Canal started and was completed without incident. The machine-guns of the 2nd Royal Northumberland Fusiliers were in support. The 9th DLI were on the left and the 8th Battalion in reserve. The men were in position by 1.30 a.m. There was slight machine-gun fire on both sides of the canal during the night. Enemy reconnaissance planes dropped parachute flares. The Battalion stood to at 3.00 a.m. At 8.00 a.m. on this day, 28th May, news was received that the Belgians had capitulated. At 9.00 a.m. a group of refugees were seen to be moving up and down the road eight hundred yards away on the opposite side of the canal. It was believed that the group contained a number of German soldiers intermingled amongst the civilians. The 2nd RNFs fired a few warning bursts in front of the group, causing great consternation. During the morning the Brigadier informed Lieutenant-Colonel Jeffreys of the proposed evacuation of the BEF from the Dunkirk area. As the morning wore on, the enemy became more and more active and the shelling and mortaring of the Battalion positions increased in intensity. Heavy rain and a thunder storm drenched the area and added to the discomfort. The shelling caused several casualties. At 3.30 p.m. movement in the 2nd RNF positions seemed to indicate that they were withdrawing and urgent messages were sent to Brigade to clarify the situation. The message came back that the movement was not a withdrawal but a local relief of the men who had been in the line for most of the day. Under cover of heavy enemy machine-gun and mortar fire small parties of enemy troops moved to within two hundred yards of the canal. Brigade was informed of this enemy activity.

At 5.00 p.m. orders were received to withdraw during the night. The Battalion was also ordered to destroy all of its 2in. and 3" mortars before leaving the positions. The men had the satisfaction of knowing that the 3in. mortars, which had been in action all day, had been very effective and had caused the enemy much discomfort. Unfortunately the 2in. mortars had no high explosive bombs and, except for laying down smoke, were of no use. However it was an order which caused much dissatisfaction and concern to the Battalion. To lose weapons in this way, which had the ability to hit back at the enemy, was an indication of the desperate situation facing the BEF. The situation became more desperate by the hour. At 5.45 p.m. a message was received from the 2nd RNFs that a gap had appeared between the 6th Battalion's No. 2 Company on the left and the village of Boesinghe. This gap was being covered by machine-gun fire only. The gap was due to the withdrawal of the French forces holding it and the non-arrival of their relief, the Royal Ulster Rifles of the 3rd Division. Lieutenant-Colonel Jeffreys was satisfied that the gap could be held by the machine-guns. In case of need, the 3rd Division informed the 6th that it had a battalion in Boesinghe ready to counter-attack and that carriers were available some five hundred yards behind the canal. Additional information was also received that the planned withdrawal via Poperinghe and Woesten was not to commence until 4.00 a.m. on the 29th May. Meanwhile enemy shelling increased along with heavy sniping. At 6.30 p.m. No. 1 Company reported that its 1st Platoon had had to withdraw from its position on the canal due to intense enemy shell-fire and German troops were attempting to commence bridging in this area. Second-Lieutenant Prince with his carriers and one platoon from HQ Company were ordered to counter-attack and restore the position. This was successfully achieved but Nos. 1 and 2 Companies were pulled back slightly to enable our artillery to fire on enemy troops now close to the canal. Following this bombardment, difficulty was experienced in getting the companies back into their original positions and one

officer and several men were wounded doing so. By 9.15 p.m. the situation was restored and fifteen minutes later 'A' Company of the 8th Battalion was sent forward to reinforce the 6th on the canal. As midnight approached a thunderstorm broke followed by heavy rain which fell throughout the night.

At 1.30 a.m. on the 29th May, a company of the 8th Battalion attempted to relieve No. 2 Company but was unable to get forward due to heavy enemy shell fire. The two companies of the 6th Battalion commenced their withdrawal from the canal at 4.00 a.m., embussed on RASC transport and moved off to Woesten. Yet another withdrawal and the heavy rain dampened the troops' spirits, summed up in the simple words of Private Alf Bailey of the Transport Section:

> 'You always feel frustrated when you're retreating. When you're retreating you feel that sad. When you're winning...you always feel good.'

The Battalion had experienced very heavy shelling as well as machine-gun and sniper fire during its stay on the Yser Canal. There had been a number of casualties but it had stuck to its task well and it felt confident that it could have held on a little longer and make the enemy suffer. However the evacuation to the Dunkirk bridgehead was now fully underway. The final defence of the perimeter was being organised. It ran from Gravelines, south-east to the Canal de la Colme, along the Canal to Bergues and across the Belgian frontier by Furnes to Nieuport and the coast. The French held the western half of the perimeter as far as and including Bergues, and the British held from there to the coast. Most of the formations of the BEF were now inside the perimeter. The major formations outside and moving towards it were the 5th and 50th Divisions, still delaying the enemy in a number of gallant rearguard actions.

At 7.30 a.m. on the 29th, the Battalion arrived at Woesten and rested for the day in the woods in the area. There was considerable enemy air activity but the Battalion's positions were not spotted and the men got a few hours' sleep. A meal was prepared of biscuits and stew, all that was available to the cooks. Towards evening, artillery and machine-gun fire increased in volume and picquets were placed on all sides of the woods to guard against sudden attack. Enemy air activity increased during the course of the evening. Orders were received that surplus kit, with the exception of equipment and packs, was to be destroyed along with all signalling apparatus. At 8.15 p.m. the Battalion moved off towards the Dunkirk perimeter. The scene, as they travelled along the roads, was one which upset even the strongest of men and was depressing in the extreme. The fields that lined the roads were filled with groups of wrecked guns and transport, some burning and smouldering in the evening light. White flags of truce had been put up by Belgian soldiers and civilians on every home and farm. Defeat and destruction lay on every side but the spirit and discipline of the men held firm. The Durham soldier was renowned for his strength in adversity. The harsh demands of pit, steel works and quarries had forged a strong character which looked upon adversity as something to overcome and not to succumb to. Though in retreat, he still felt that given the opportunity he could give the Germans a good drubbing. At 10.30 p.m. the Battalion crossed the Bergues - Furnes Canal and into the perimeter. The transport was run off into a field on the west side of the road and the men began to dig positions in slit trenches behind the canal. The positions taken ran from Houthem to the railway bridge to the east. The 9th DLI was on the Battalion's left with the 8th Battalion in support on a subsidiary canal about one thousand yards behind the main one.

The enemy had quickly followed the withdrawal and mortar and small arms fire soon opened up on No.1 Company's positions on the left flank. The leading German troops were in Bulscamp by 9.15 a.m. on the 30th May. At 10.30 a.m. Battalion headquarters were moved into Moeres Chateau, one mile behind the Furnes Canal. Lieutenant-Colonel Jeffreys remembered the move:

> 'We took up our position on this Furnes Canal with our HQ close to Brigade HQ at the Moeres Chateau. This would be in Belgium ... Brigade HQ office was in the dining room of this chateau ... There were some steps at the end of the office to the cellars and when you went near the cellar stairs you could hear the Dutch farmer's women weeping. Well we had a very unsettling day defending what was the Furnes Canal ... The other Battalions' headquarters were also adjacent to the Moeres Chateau. It wasn't tactically very sensible because, of course, the German OPs spotted that this chateau was the centre of

communications, central communications for a brigade it was. There was another Battalion attached to the Brigade, 3rd Battalion Grenadier Guards, which helped a bit ... During the afternoon the chateau became a target and drew a tremendous amount of artillery fire. I moved my small headquarters out, considerably to the right hand side ... The shells continued to fall around the chateau grounds and did a lot of damage. Brigade HQ had a terrible time.'

2nd RNF placed their machine-guns in support of the Brigade. Sniping occurred throughout the day as the enemy held the east bank of the canal which overlooked our positions at Bulscamp. No serious attempt was made by the Germans to cross the canal during the night, which was quiet. A message had been received by Lord Gort from the King and it was passed on to the Battalions of the BEF:

> 'All your countrymen have been following with pride and admiration the courageous resistance of the BEF during the continuous fighting of the last fortnight. Placed by circumstances outside their control in a position of extreme difficulty they have displayed a gallantry that has never been surpassed in the annals of the British Army. The hearts of every one of us at home are with you and your troops in this hour of peril.'

Royal Engineers came up to the Battalion positions just before midnight to assist with digging and wiring. Little could be done because the wire never arrived. Information was received to the effect that, if the Dunkirk evacuation went badly, the positions now occupied would have to be held for a further five days. It is not difficult to imagine how this news was received. With evacuation home going on a few short miles behind them and an enemy, superior in numbers and equipment and with almost complete air supremacy pressing them in front, it is to their greatest credit that the troops' spirit and discipline held. The fighting round the canal was intense.

At 3.00 a.m. on the 31st May, enemy small arms fire and sniping commenced. It was followed by very heavy shelling which lasted all day. At 9.00 a.m. information was received that the 9th Battalion had been driven back and the enemy was crossing the canal. A counter-attack was immediately arranged by Brigadier Churchill and, for a time, the enemy was driven back. The 6th Battalion came under heavy shell fire from the rear at 12.50 p.m. This was at first thought to be from our naval guns but it was later confirmed that the shelling was from the enemy firing from the north-east. In the late afternoon, Lieutenant-Colonel Jeffreys went round the companies' positions and informed them that a withdrawal would take place, probably during the night. However the situation on the canal worsened. At 4.15 p.m. the 9th Battalion informed the 6th that it had had to withdraw to the Ringsloot Canal. The 6th Battalion was ordered to conform and withdraw also. A difficult manoeuvre was carried out under heavy enemy shelling and completed not without some casualties. The 4th RNFs filled a gap which had now opened on the Brigade's right with 150 Brigade. Enemy ranging shells began to fall on the new positions. A supply of Bren guns was received. They had been collected from as far back as Dunkirk. Vehicles were on fire, ammunition was exploding and the avalanche of enemy shells rained down on the Brigade's positions. At 7.00 p.m. orders were given to destroy the Battalion transport except one 30 cwt truck and an Austin 7 car. The Brigade front was divided into three sectors by the Brigadier. The right sector under Lieutenant-Colonel Mclaren consisted of the two companies of the 6th DLI, the 8th less one company, one company of the 4th RNFs, one platoon 151 Brigade Anti-Tank Company and one company 9th DLI. Verbal orders were received by the Battalions at 8 p.m. that a withdrawal to Zuydcoot would take place that night, commencing at 2.30 a.m. For the remainder of the night enemy mortar fire fell on the positions.

At 1.30 a.m. on the 1st June, the 8th and 9th Durhams and the RNFs withdrew, followed by the 6th Battalion at 2.30 a.m. The 6th Battalion crossed the fields and then marched by road to the village of Moeres. Here it turned left along the canal and across this obstacle and on to the Furnes - Dunkirk road through woods which were under occasional enemy shelling. Traffic on the road was heavy and subjected to a little bombing. After nearly three hours' marching, the Battalion turned right over the canal to Zuydcoot having marched ten miles. Captain Holroyde, who had gone on ahead to discover the Battalion's lying up place, was there to meet it and direct it to a position behind large sand dunes. The men took shelter under some railway trucks filled with sand, alongside 8th Battalion who had arrived earlier. It lay here and dug a little deeper. Sporadic enemy shelling fell close by and enemy reconnaissance planes put in an appearance from time to time. In the middle of the morning enemy air activity increased with bombing and strafing particularly closer to the shore in front of the Battalion's positions where later two cargo ships were to be sunk. A scene which cheered the men enormously developed above their heads as an air battle broke out between about fifty British fighters and a similar number of enemy planes. The men had a noon meal of corned beef and biscuits though no tea or water was available. Lieutenant-Colonel Jeffreys attended a conference at Brigade Headquarters which was situated in the sand dunes two hundred yards closer to the sea. Here a bombshell was dropped. The Brigadier informed his Battalion Commanders that it was possible that the Brigade may have to move out to meet and hold the enemy once more, to earn more time for embarkation to take place. For tired hungry men, now praying for embarkation themselves, it was an almost devastating blow and surely a suicidal mission. At 12.15 p.m., weapons and ammunition were distributed evenly within the Battalion. It was with a sense of enormous relief that a runner arrived from Brigade Headquarters with the news that the proposed move had been cancelled and the Battalion was to proceed to Dunkirk for embarkation to England.

The Battalion started to move along the beach to Dunkirk at 1.30 p.m.. German planes were bombing the quay. Two of these returned from the attack and passed over the marching men. As they flew very low over the beach they threw hand grenades out which wounded two men of 'C' Company. After moving through the outskirts of Dunkirk the Battalion moved on to the beach, where it lay up in holes and trenches which were found there and awaited orders to move on to the Mole. Private Bert Davies remembered the scene:

'All you could see was men. A lot of them had greatcoats on although it was hot in June ... I can't see us getting away in a ship - too many men here. It looks as if we will become prisoners or get killed. There was a rumour that went round saying that our division was selected as a suicide division. How true that was I don't know ... Durhams again, that was the thing,

Durhams again. Are there no other regiments taking part in this battle? It was cancelled apparently.'

Many British troops were moving towards the Mole. At 8.00 p.m. on the 1st June, the embarkation of the Battalion commenced. Shell fire fell near the Mole and a number of troops were wounded. The 6th Battalion moved along the side of the quay to get cover from the shelling and then on to the Mole in file. Movement was now very slow. The scene was described by Lieutenant-Colonel Peter Jeffreys:

'...As darkness began to fall we closed on the Mole. At the head of the Mole ... the landward end of the Mole, were some staff and some ambulances and the troops, as they approached the Mole were dispersed as much as possible and the shells continued to fall ... but the Mole, I don't think was ever hit or if it was it didn't do any damage to it. A frightful thing at this moment, of course, was if you got wounded you were left behind ... So you didn't want to get wounded ... darkness and then a queue. We got onto the Mole and, by God, just like a bus stop, you hoped that bus would arrive and that you would get on it before the morning. And you gradually got to the head of the queue at the end of the Mole. ... There was one chap not far ahead of me, not in the 6th Battalion ... this chap was hit, shrapnel, I don't know. I suppose a shell hit the edge of the Mole or something like that and he was not badly wounded and we all thought, "By God, you lucky beggar, you're close enough to us to get you into the boat when one comes up. Sure enough these ships came up to the Mole and the 6th Battalion. Most of us embarked on a Royal Navy Minesweeper. One ceased then to be in charge of anything. The naval officers and men just told you where you were to go. "Push up now and lie down. Push up and lie down," and we did, we laid down. The ship went off, arrived at Dover the next morning.'

Private Bert Davies had his memories:

'On the night of 1st-2nd June, we were ordered to get our sections together and quickly and quietly march to get aboard ship waiting at the Mole. Not knowing where we were going, after a struggle we got aboard, packing tightly, we eventually got underway. I remember a sailor came to me and said,"Here's a mug of cocoa and a slice of bread and butter, it was just like nectar and I'll never forget it. After that I just slumped down on the deck and fell fast asleep too tired to worry about anything."

Four French guns close to the Mole opened fire in the direction of the German advance. This caused the enemy artillery to retaliate and shells fell around the Mole, on the beach and in the water. It was 11.00 p.m. and the oil stores across the harbour towards St.-Pol-Sur-Mer, on fire belched flames and dense black smoke into the air. The Battalion embarked with a company of the RNFs and a few French onboard. The crossing was without incident and the minesweeper arrived at Dover at 4.00 a.m. on the morning of the 2nd June. All rifles had to be handed over to the navy, an action which annoyed many of the men. Within fifteen minutes they were on trains to transit camps where they were sorted out and sent on again to the north.

Not all men of the Battalion got home on the minesweeper. Captain Holroyde, Company Quartermaster Sergeant Andell and about thirty-five men of the Division got onto a small Dutch pleasure cruiser sailed by a crew of men from the Royal Navy Volunteer Reserve. It was bombed and strafed on the crossing before arriving at Margate. Private Reg Haseley used his own initiative to get away:

'...On the beach at Dunkirk we waited a few nights. I waded out up to my neck in water and got on board a small boat with different regiments and landed in Dover on 3rd June.'

The final word on the Dunkirk evacuation lies with Lieutenant-Colonel Jeffreys who had commanded the Battalion in the retreat from Arras:

'We felt we'd done rather well really to get back, and still to be a coordinated unit. We were marvellously relieved of course to be back alive ... I don't think we felt we were a defeated army at that time but later, of course, one began to wonder about it a bit. I think the general mood in England was that it was a great thing to have got its divisions back in some sort of order ... We were amongst the last of the BEF to get back.'

CHAPTER 18
DEFENDING THE BEACHES
1940 - 1941

The officers and men of the Battalion, who had come back from France through Boulogne, had arrived in Durham City on the 26th May. Here they were billeted in Crossgate and Shakespeare Halls and the Regal Cinema. Major Bill Watson, who had been on the 50th Division Staff in France and had been invalided home prior to the outbreak of hostilities, took command of the mixed group and immediately organised training, route marches, sports and physical training to lick the men into shape and help raise their spirits. Picquets were established based on Durham Station. These acted as guides to the personnel of the 42nd Division arriving from the BEF. They worked under the supervision and orders of Captain Mike Ferens, who had been appointed Rail Transport Officer. On the 3rd June, half of the men proceeded on forty-eight hours' leave. At about the same time, after staying overnight at the transit camp near Aldershot, the Battalion just back from Dunkirk proceeded to Knutsford and to Tatten Hill Camp. The Durham contingent joined them on the 5th and 6th June. The Battalion which totalled five officers and two hundred and thirty-eight men, moved into the tents allotted to them. Captain Holroyde and Company Quartermaster Sergeant Andell reported from Catterick on the 8th June and personnel who had had no leave from Durham were sent on forty-eight hours' leave. Over the next two days men who had had no leave were sent home for forty-eight hours. A short break for men who had been through so much but it must be remembered that the threat of invasion was a serious one and pressure was on to get units reorganised as quickly as possible.

On the 13th June, the Battalion moved to Rugeley in Staffordshire. Major C.R. Battiscombe was posted to the Battalion from the 9th DLI and took over command from Acting Lieutenant-Colonel Peter Jeffreys who reverted to the rank of Acting Major and second-in-command. Captain Holroyde left the Battalion and was posted to the 8th Battalion as a company commander. It was at Rugeley that the Battalion was completely reorganised. A large draft was received from the Argyll and Sutherland Highlanders, a small number from the King's Shropshire Light Infantry and, over the next few weeks, drafts were received from the DLI Holding Battalion at West Hartlepool. Trouble could be expected when a Scot was ordered to leave his own regiment and join an English one. However, there were a surprisingly small number of difficulties and over a few weeks these men of Scotland settled into the Battalion and their highland head-dress disappeared, to be replaced with that of The Durham Light Infantry. They became fiercely proud of the Durhams and were first class soldiers. Officers posted to the Battalion on the 20th June, were: Second-Lieutenants J. Jackson to 'C' Company, Derek Tomlinson to 'A' Company, A. Jackson to 'D' Company, Druiff to 'B' Company and Bentham to 'HQ' Company. The following day, postings included: Lieutenants Rice to 'B' Company and Ovenden to 'D' Company and Second-Lieutenants Rodway to 'C' Company, Burrough to 'HQ' Company, Halse to 'HQ' Company and Simpson to 'D' Company.

The Battalion left Rugeley Station by special train for Maiden Newton on the 22nd June, arriving there at 5.00 p.m. The following day, the Battalion left Maiden Newton for Bridport,

Officers and sergeants of 'B' Company, *Devon, 1940*

arriving at 6.00 p.m. On the 26th June, Battalion Headquarters moved to Litton Cheney and the rifle companies moved onto the beach between Abbotsbury and Burton Bradstock with from the left; 'A' Company, 'B' Company, 'C' Company and with 'D' Company at Burton Bradstock. Over the next few weeks supporting elements arrived: 'B' Company 2nd RNFs (machine-guns); 386 Battery, Royal Artillery; detachments of the LDV (Later Home Guard); 3-6 pounder Naval Guns; 2-4 inch Naval Guns; sections of 505 Field Company, Royal Engineers.

The move to the beaches had not been made without some anxiety. The state of equipment of the forces guarding the beaches on the south-west coast of the country was desperate. The men had rifles, very few if any Bren guns and they lacked almost all types of support weapons and equipment. This was the situation when the possibility of invasion was at its greatest. What the men did have was great spirit and as the supplies of weapons and equipment improved so their morale increased. The days ahead were hard, with an enormous amount to do and little time to do it in. Private Sandersfield wrote:

'The three field companies [one went into reserve] built

fortifications along the beaches and started to live in slit trenches, covered with one-man tents. Now their lives became a monotonous round of digging, drilling and guard duties and a daily stand to at dawn [and at dusk] in case of invasion.'

Initially the men of the rifle companies and some of their officers lived in their tents, close to the beach defences. The 'HQ' Company, billeted in Litton Cheney, without adequate weapons and equipment to train with, helped with the digging. The digging of the coastal defences went on apace. Slit trenches were dug, wire erected and mines laid. The aim was to have pillboxes at intervals of five hundred yards, six to each forward company. Two standing patrols were to be out each night and one by day. Orders were issued that rifle companies should be in their tents and no more than fifteen minutes from their battle positions from 10.00 p.m. to 5.00 a.m. the next day. For the rest of the day only a quarter of each company needed to be so positioned. In case of attack, sentries were ordered to fire two shots in the air. Posts were to be wired round and camouflaged. Dummy pillboxes were to be erected every one hundred yards. The Local Defence Volunteers (later the Home Guard) had an important role to play in the defence of the coast, manning observation posts, road blocks and being responsible for the local defence of the villages. In addition, they were to support the troops in rounding up parachutists. Officers and men of the Battalion became actively involved in training the LDV.

On the 27th June, Lieutenant Dennis was appointed Transport Officer. Major Watson who had gone to Fenham Barracks to organise the reception of the BEF and then returned to the Depot at Brancepeth, joined the Battalion and was placed in command of 'HQ' Company. Lieutenant David Joy, RAMC, joined the Battalion on the 29th of the month as Medical Officer. He wrote:-

'There was a dairy in the village which I took over as an MI Room. I was allotted an MI Room Clerk. He was a stretcher-bearer ... I was given a truck, there were about two trucks to each company. They were mostly civilian trucks and mine was a baker's van.

'I had virtually no equipment and the men had rifles and virtually no other weapons. There were one or two anti-tank rifles and a few Brens ... We put up minefields to restrict the exits from the beach. A bull escaped into a field which was full of a minefield. The mines were laid close to each other and when the bull trod on one the whole field went off with sympathetic detonation! The beef was very good! Two or three soldiers were injured in the incident - one with a broken leg and a damaged eye.'

Battle Headquarters was sited on the Knoll at Puncknowle and posts were dug on top of this feature to accommodate headquarter staff. The area which the Battalion held was one of the prettiest in the country. Litton Cheney was a lovely village with many thatched buildings. In early July, 1940, 'HQ' Company was digging light machine-gun posts for anti-aircraft defence and slit trenches around the village. On the 7th July, parachutists were reported to have been dropped in the area and a patrol went out to seek them out. It returned in the early hours of the morning having seen no sign of the enemy. This was the first of many false alarms, every one of which had to be checked out. The only parachutists who did land were either German or British airmen who bailed out of destroyed aircraft as the air war hotted up during the Battle of Britain. On many of the hot summer days of 1940, the troops watched the fantastic shapes etched in the blue sky by the slipstreams of the aircraft of both sides locked in mortal combat, each British victory greeted with an enthusiastic cheer.

Further reorganisation took place on the 8th July. Second-Lieutenant Chamberlain transferred from 'A' Company to 'HQ' Company as Mortar Platoon and Gas Officer. Lieutenant Ovenden was transferred from 'D' Company to 'HQ' Company and took over the duties of Carrier Platoon and Training Officer. Second-Lieutenant Ellett moved to 151 Brigade Headquarters for special duties. Second-Lieutenant Benthall was transferred from 'HQ' Company to 'A' Company, Second-Lieutenant Walton transferred from 'HQ' Company to 'D' Company and Second-Lieutenant Burrough took over duties of Intelligence Officer. Two days later Second-Lieutenant Ireland was posted to 'A' Company and Second-Lieutenant Freeman joined 'B' Company.

At 4.00 a.m. on the 11th July, orders were received to stand to and 'HQ' Company and Advanced Battalion Headquarters were moved onto the Knoll. The rifle companies manned the beach defences. This turned out to be a false alarm and four hours later the Battalion stood down. There was a repeat at 4.00 p.m. on the 13th and again 'HQ' Company and Advanced Battalion Headquarters moved to the Knoll with the rifle companies in their defences on the beach; another false alarm and everyone stood down at 5.50 p.m. General Montgomery, the Corps Commander, inspected the Divisional Front from Lyme Regis to Abbotsbury on the 14th July. This was the first contact between the Division and the General who was to command it in the Middle East and North West Europe.

The digging and strengthening of the beach defences went on. 'HQ' Company relieved 'A' Company on the beaches on the 17th July. The latter went into reserve for training and rest. A number of Operational Instructions were issued to the Battalion, dealing with a number of subjects such as 'Tank Defence', 'Artillery Support', and 'Holding The Line'. Conferences and lectures were held for officers of the Battalion, the latter to discuss the lessons learnt in France and Belgium. Towards the end of July, Second-Lieutenant Burrough became Battalion Gas Officer and Second-Lieutenant Druiff proceeded to the Special Air Service at Netheraven. Periods of eight days leave started for the Battalion on the 22nd July.

The supply of weapons and equipment slowly improved, yet were still desperately short by the end of July. Carriers and Bren guns were amongst the first to arrive. To attempt to fill some of the gaps, innovative ideas were called for. On the 24th July, Major Bill Watson wrote in his diary:

> 'Today the gun was fired. This gun has given a great deal of amusement to us. A naval 4in. from one of the old ships and one of a pair, was within two weeks mounted on a large diesel oil motor and chassis, armoured round the driver and completely fitted out and handed over to the 65th A/T with fifty gallons of petrol and given stretchers and fire exstinguishers. A wonderful performance ... The site (for the gun) on the front was chosen by the General, ie: the garage of an old woman ... So without delay the garage was dismantled and rebuilt round the gun ... [The old lady] was so upset and rightly so as she was convinced her house would be blown to bits to which one and all concurred. But a Gen's word is law. Today, therefore, two half-charged rounds were fired. The result: Round 1: Two slates dislodged off main roof, an ominous crack in the wall. Coal House roof almost blown off and doors blown in. Round 2: Twenty slates dislodged off main roof. Crack made very much larger. Coal House demolished, doors blown to bits and plaster off ceilings of five rooms!'

Evidently, on her return, the old lady was pleased to see her house still in one piece. There were more innovations of questionable success. Whilst there was some army transport available to each company, civilian buses had been requisitioned, somewhat old and unreliable. Private Joe Wear remembered:

> 'We had a 30 cwt wagon, our company wagon, but if we were going anywhere we had buses, but when you came to a hill you had to get out because it would not take you up the hill.'

Air raid warnings were sounded most nights as German aircraft flew overhead on their way westwards to Plymouth and other targets. On the 26th July, two bombs fell near Burton Bradstock. As a result, two rabbits were killed, one of which was edible, a few panes of glass were damaged, twenty yards of fencing was down and a crater was blown in a meadow. The latter was filled in by members of 'HQ' Company the following day under the gaze of several curious civilians.

'HQ' Company was increased in numbers to include a motorcycle platoon and a tank hunting platoon. The latter was mounted on bicycles and carried its road mines and home-made bottle bombs in a small impressed tradesman's van. Of greater success was the formation of a Battalion cricket team. There were a number of fine cricketers in the Battalion. These included: Captain E.L. Proud, who played for Chaterhouse, Oxford and Durham. His brother, Lieutenant R.B. Proud, who played for Winchester, Oxford and Hampshire. Lieutenant D. Burroughs, late Somerset Light Infantry, played for Somerset. Captain (QM) Robson had played for the Northern Command. Other fine players included Captain M.R. Ferens, Major P. Jeffreys , Captain Black, Lieutenant Tomlinson and Sergeant Fairly. The first game was played against Long Bredy, the second against Dorchester when Major Jeffreys scored one hundred and fifteen. Both games were won. As the beach defences were completed there was more time for sport; soccer, rugby and so on.

Corporal Bert Davies and a small group of men got some unexpected exercise one day. Corporal Davies described the event:

'There was a barrage balloon and that was floating and broke free from its moorings and was floating out to sea. Now we got to it and grabbed it (the hauser) and it burnt our hands ... dragged us along until five of us took hold of it and, as luck happened, there were no trees around. As luck happened we'd dug a trench and it went under a wall. We ran forward to the end of the hauser before the balloon could get grip of it, dived down the trench, under the wall and tied it to the wall, got a loop around and that was how we halted it.'

The fine, hot weather continued into August and as the beach defences neared completion there was time now for training. On the 4th of the month, 151 Brigade Anti-Tank Company took over from 8th Battalion DLI the sector of the front on the left of 'C' Company, and was placed under the command of the 6th Battalion.

On the same day, shoulder flashes, red cloth with DLI in black, were issued to companies to be worn by all ranks. Battalion exercises commenced on the 10th August, with a scheme aimed at driving an enemy landing into the sea. These were held at regular intervals and, at this stage, enabled the units to practice ways of throwing an invader back into the sea, or to deal with enemy parachutists. On the 19th of the month, a Reinforcement Company was formed from the surplus men held by each company with Lieutenant Rice commanding. Amongst the scares and false alarms with which the Battalion had to deal were reports of spies and fifth-columnists in the area, not least of which were those suspected of signalling to German aircraft. Whilst none were discovered, the Battalion was warned to be on the alert. On the 20th August, Lieutenant Rome was posted to 'B' Company, Second-Lieutenant Chapman to 'D' Company and Second-Lieutenant Smith to 'A' Company. Lieutenant-Colonel V.A.C. Yate, MC, arrived on the 23rd of the month to take command of the Battalion. Major Battiscombe reverted to second-in-command.

On the 1st September, the code word 'Cromwell' was received. This indicated to the Battalion that a German invasion was imminent. The Battle of Britain was at its height and this warning was no scare or false alarm as it was known that Hitler was finalising preparations for an invasion of this country. The defeat of the Luftwaffe would change his plans but that still lay in the future. On the 3rd and 5th of the month, exercises were held by the Battalion. On the 6th, bombs were dropped near Puncknowle village. A further warning order of imminent invasion was received on the 7th September and 'HQ' Company and Advanced Battle Headquarters moved up onto the Knoll with the rifle companies in their beach positions. The order was cancelled on the 19th September and companies reverted to normal activities. Meanwhile, Major Jeffreys left the Battalion to attend the 4th Junior War Staff Course at the Staff College, Camberley, which commenced on the 12th September.

The innovatory activities continued. 5th Corps Camouflage Officer came up with a scheme to bemuse the enemy reconnaissance aircraft. Major Watson wrote:

'...shallow mock posts were dug in the shingle into which were placed plaster representatives of the fully equipped soldier, from the bust upwards, the face being an excellent likeness of Mr. Neville Chamberlain, the former Prime Minister: all in the hope that the enemy would at any rate be deceived by numbers.'

The plaster casts were provided by Denham Film Studios. There was no evidence to suggest that the enemy was bemused. On the 10th September a Battalion exercise was arranged for the 9th Battalion and the 6th supplied the umpires. It appears that the main interest on the scheme was centred on yet another innovation. Major Watson wrote:

'On the scheme much more interest was shown in a quantity of armoured 30 cwts for issue to A/T Companies. Hurriedly put together, they are very top heavy and when the brakes are put on quickly and suddenly the shackles snap. The GOC takes them away for trial and has them shot at to test the plating. A 1/8in. impression against rifle fire but quite unproof against the anti-tank rifle. These vehicles are ordinary 30 cwt chassis with an enormous heavy body quite incapable of being driven at speed.'

All these innovations indicate the weakness of the forces defending the coastline of Southern England in the months following Dunkirk. Fortunately, as time went by, weapons and equipment supplies improved and, with the beach defences completed and Germany defeated in the Battle of Britain, training to enable our forces to face a powerful and dangerous enemy became the order of the day.

On the 19th September, the code word 'Cromwell' was cancelled and the forward companies reverted to normal. 'HQ' Company and Advanced Battalion Headquarters returned from the Knoll to Litton Cheney on the 20th of the month, only to return two days later on what proved to be a false alarm. They reverted to normal activities on the following day. The 9th Battalion relieved the 6th on the beaches on the 30th September and the Battalion moved into Brigade reserve and into billets at Maiden Newton, Rampisham, Frampton and Cattistock.

A period of intense training commenced on the 1st October with operation instructions issued for a Divisional exercise on the 3rd and 4th of the month. A German airman, who was killed when his plane was shot down, was buried by the Padre in Maiden Newton Cemetery on the 2nd October. On the same day the Battalion went to West Bay for a demonstration of and to practice the use of reconnaissance and assault boats. In the Divisional exercise which commenced at 7.15 a.m. on the 3rd of the month, the Battalion moved by bus to the River Frome where the task of two companies was to cross the river by assault boats. On the 7th October, the Battalion was witness to some of the heaviest air battles since their arrival on the south west coast. German and British planes fought it out overhead in a bitter contest. Several enemy planes were brought down in the vicinity of the Battalion area. Four enemy airman, who baled out, were taken by the Home Guard and local police. A Spitfire broke into pieces and its pilot baled out and landed safely though injured. He was taken to hospital at Dorchester. 'B' and 'C' Companies provided guards over the wreckage of crashed aeroplanes.

In the middle of October a draft of one hundred and thirty men was received from the Infantry Training Centre at Brancepeth. From the beginning of the war there had been an almost constant movement of people into and out of the Battalions of the 50th Division. Some of these, of course, were due to losses in action. Quite a number were due to unfitness and age, transfers and key personnel urgently required back in industry. General Martel had protested on a number of occasions to a point of an angry exchange of letters between himself and the Adjutant-General. In July, August and September, 1940, a total of one hundred and eleven officers and six hundred and thirty-six other ranks, in addition to those lost in France, moved out of the Division. The great majority of these were transfers or key men. Many of these men were experienced and promotion material. The shortage of leaders and instructors was, for a time, worrying. It must be clearly stated that many of the replacements were of first class quality and served the Battalion with distinction - men of the Argyll and Sutherland Highlanders and Shropshire Light Infantry, for example. The draft received in the middle of the month was to fill vacancies such as these.

Training exercises were now frequent. Higher authority was confident that a German invasion could not now take place as the late autumn and winter weather in the channel would make such an enterprise exceedingly difficult. Heavy enemy air raids would continue but he had lost the Battle of Britain for command of the skies over this country. The emphasis was now on training to make units fighting fit. Supplies of equipment and weapons were improving. On the 24th October, the Tank Hunting Platoon was disbanded and the officer and men returned to their original units, with the exception of one NCO and five other ranks who formed a Sniping Section and joined the Intelligence Section. On the 26th of the month, the Motorcycle Platoon was merged with the Carrier Platoon under the command of Lieutenant Chamberlain and Second-Lieutenant Allison. His Royal Highness The Duke of Gloucester made a flying visit to the Battalion on the 30th October. It poured with rain which curtailed the visit.

Major-General Martel, the Divisional Commander, visited the Battalion on a tour of inspection on the 5th November. Lieutenant-General Montgomery arrived on the 7th of the month and inspected the Battalion and its positions and seems to have found little to fault on this occasion. On the 21st November, the Battalion left Maiden Newton and moved to the Uffculme area of Devon. The companies were situated as follows:

'HQ' and 'R' Companies at Uffculme.

Signal Platoon at Willand.

'A' Company at Wellington.

'B', 'C' and 'D' Companies at Cullompton.

Carrier Platoon at Culmstock.

The move of the Division inland was due to a change of role, emphasis now placed on counter-attacking an invasion force rather than trying to defeat it on the beaches. 50th Division was now in this attacking role should an enemy force land on the beaches or parachute troops attempt to land in its area of operation. Training exercises were planned for Brigade, Division and Corps and executed with this role in mind. These included night exercises. As the weather deteriorated, exercises held on Exmoor were far from comfortable to all who took part. Snow and biting winds made conditions extremely difficult and, at least on one occasion, groups were cut off on the moor and had to stay out until the weather improved slightly. Lectures and courses for officers and men covered many topics which included those on leadership, the German Army, training and administration. In a Special Order of the Day issued by Major-General G. Le Q. Martel, CB, DSO, MC, on the 10th December, the Divisional Commander announced that he was leaving to take command of the Royal Armoured Corps. Major-General Martel was an armoured expert and, whilst he regretted leaving the Division, this new and immense challenge gave full scope to his views and expertise on the development of armoured forces in the British Army. He was succeeded by Major-General W.H.C. Ramsden CBE, DSO, MC.

The people of Uffculme and district received the Battalion with some caution at first but quickly warmed to these friendly warriors from the north. Some close liaisons with local young ladies resulted in marriage at a later date. Local homes welcomed the men, and baths and meals were offered and gratefully accepted. In return, the Battalion organised entertainment for the men and the people of the area. The band played at dances and concerts, a dance a week at least was held somewhere in the area. The Concert party, 'Durham Review,' was very popular with soldiers and civilians. In addition one or two ENSA concerts were held for the troops. It was a time of very hard work and these leisure activities were a welcome break in a very active military timetable.

Early in December, information was received that the Battalion should hold itself ready to move abroad. The first draft of embarkation leave personnel left on the 19th December, followed by a second draft on the 30th December. The new Divisional Commander, Major-General Ramsden, visited the Battalion on the 22nd of the month. The year ended with the Battalion preparing for embarkation though, of course, it knew not where. Rumours were rife with Iceland, the Middle East and India, the most frequently mentioned. The Division and its Brigades and Battalions were in fine shape, fully equipped and well trained. It looked towards a better future than that which it had faced almost twelve months ago.

CHAPTER 19
EMBARKATION - EGYPT - CYPRUS - IRAQ
1941

Preparation by the Battalion for embarkation for overseas service continued into the new year. The third group of officers and men were sent on embarkation leave on the 8th January, 1941. Lieutenant David Joy, the Medical Officer, commenced examining personnel to ascertain their fitness for overseas service. A number failed the medical tests and these included men who had long service with the Battalion. Some men with long experience still managed to remain with the Battalion, though how they hoodwinked the MO was never revealed. Amongst those who had to leave was Captain (QM) Robson who was considered too old for service abroad. He had served the Battalion for many years. His replacement was Lieutenant (QM) J. Runciman who joined the Battalion from the Regimental Depot where he was Regimental Sergeant-Major.

A Special order of the Day from Lieutenant-General The Hon. H.R.L.G. Alexander, CB, DSO, MC, Commander-in-Chief, Southern Command, was received on the 2nd January. It stated as follows:

> 'The name of the undermentioned has been brought to notice in recognition of distinguished services in connection with operations in the field: March - June, 1940 Captain E.L. Proud.'

The Colonel of the Regiment, Colonel C.L. Matthews, DSO, visited the Battalion on the 23rd January and was very impressed with all he saw. Iceland dropped out of the rumours of potential overseas stations when tropical kit was issued on the 27th of the month. Khaki drill and walking out dress were issued along with the topee. Ladies of the district sewed regimental flashes onto the topees. A Brigade Exercise was held on the 29th January, with the Battalion practising the counter-attack against 'enemy' forces provided by the rest of the Brigade. On the last day of the month, Lieutenant-Colonel Yate inspected the Battalion which paraded in tropical kit. It was a wet and cold day and there was general relief when the parade was over.

Battalion, Brigade and Corps Exercises continued throughout February. The Battalion learned that embarkation had been postponed and would not take place for some time. On the 20th of the month, a three-day Corps Exercise was commenced on Exmoor. A blizzard blew up on the third day, so intense that some of the units were stuck out on the moor and experienced a very uncomfortable time. Whilst in Devon the Battalion had become involved in the training of the Home Guard. On the 25th February, Major Watson attended a meeting with the local Home Guard officers to plan an exercise. He wrote afterwards:-

> 'Everyone likes helping the Home Guard ... At one meeting at Hele having offered to provide instructors for the village of Cadbury, I was told it would be no good sending one of the fellows there as the inhabitants would never understand what he was saying and he would never understand what they were talking about! ... But despite being so foreign the instructors got on very well.'

A farewell message was received from Brigadier Churchill on leaving the Brigade which he had commanded through the difficult days of France and Belgium in 1940. Brigadier Churchill's life was the Army and The Durham Light Infantry. He had done exceedingly well to bring the Brigade out of France under such trying conditions, for which he was awarded the DSO. He was succeeded by Brigadier Redman, ex-King's Yorkshire Light Infantry. During March intense training continued. At the end of the month, more definite information was received that the Battalion was to go abroad shortly. On the 21st of the month, one third of the Battalion proceeded on six days' embarkation leave, followed by a further third on the 28th.

Their Majesties the King and Queen, visited a 50th Division Demonstration on the 2nd April, in which three platoons of the 6th Battalion took part. The final third of the Battalion, who had not had embarkation leave, were despatched for their six days on the 5th of the month. On the 21st, the advance party for overseas, consisting of the Intelligence Officer, Lieutenant Caldwell and twelve other ranks, left for the port of embarkation. On the same day, the following members of the Battalion were mentioned in despatches as a result of actions in France in May, 1940: Major Battiscombe (then 9th Battalion), Major Jeffreys, Lieutenant T. Allison, Company-Sergeant Andell and Private G.R. Wood. A German bomber, presumably fleeing from chasing British fighters, dropped thirty-two bombs on the Battalion area on the night of the 30th April. These all fell in open country and neither damage nor casualties were inflicted. All baggage was packed and loaded and sent to the railway station on the 16th May. Early on the morning of the 18th, the baggage train and baggage party left Cullompton for the port of embarkation. Major Watson described the day of departure, the 20th May:

'...All the men are very fit - The rifle companies with a few of 'HQ' personnel have all done a 50 mile march and exercise in three days periods since the last false alarm. There is no trouble amongst them but they are very quiet and all appreciate that no small adventure is in store for them. The whole of the personnel are being conveyed to the port of embarkation in 2 trains as follows:

(1) Depart Cullompton at 12.50. Bde HQ, 'HQ' Company. and the remainder of 'R' Company. The CO is in charge.

(2) Depart Cullompton at 19.20. All 4 rifle coys. Self as OC train with Second-Lieutenant Thomlinson as Adjutant and Company Sergeant-Major McMahon as Regimental Sergeant-Major.'

'A vast crowd to see us off ... The civilian police rope off the entrance to the station but when we are all in they let the people through and there is one gigantic stampede to the railings to give a last farewell. One piece of luggage is not left behind and that is 'B' Company's duck which has been their mascot for almost ten months.'

The train left Cullompton at 7.25 p.m. It arrived at Carlisle between 6.00 and 7.00 a.m. on the following morning when all personnel got out and were given a cup of tea on the platform and breakfasts were issued. Off again within twenty minutes, Gourock was reached about 11.45 a.m. Here the Battalion embarked on the *Duchess of Windsor* of the Canadian Pacific Line. She was nicknamed the 'Drunken Duchess' as she possessed a permanent roll even in calm water. Also on board were the 8th Battalion, 151 Brigade Headquarters and an assorted group of RAF personnel, with a few Free French and Greeks - a total of around three thousand people. The convoy escort comprised HMS *Exeter* of River Plate fame, HM Aircraft Carrier *Argus*, HMS *Cardiff*, an anti-aircraft cruiser and nine destroyers. There were seven troop carrying vessels. The whole convoy set sail on the evening of the 23rd May and, as it passed the harbour boom, the boom ships crews gave it a hearty cheer. Officers and Senior NCOs were allotted cabins, the men were accommodated on decks used for both sleeping and eating. The latter were tightly packed and as the temperature increased during the voyage, these decks became hot, smelly and very uncomfortable. The food was good and a canteen provided amongst its amenities, cheap beer.

The convoy sailed out into the Atlantic and followed a zig-zag course as a means of countering the interest of any enemy submarines in the neighbourhood. Fortunately none appeared. The 6th and 8th Battalions manned a number of Bren guns for anti-aircraft defence of the ship. In the crowded conditions it was not easy to retain the fitness and training of the Battalion but wherever an area of deck could be utilised, officers and men would be found on physical training, listening to lectures and taking part in a Battalion scheme as a paper exercise. Within a few days at sea the disturbing news arrived of the sinking of HMS *Hood* by the German battleship, the *Bismark*. On the 27th May, the convoy escort, with the exception of the *Exeter*, left to join the chase after the *Bismark*.

On the 1st June, everyone changed into khaki drill for the first time. The weather was warmer as the convoy neared the coast of Africa. As many men as possible were seeking sleeping space on deck at night to be free of the suffocating conditions below deck. It was becoming a long and tedious journey in these cramped conditions. The men relaxed playing 'Housey-Housey,' 'Crown and Anchor,' drinking and talking in small groups in the twilight hours on deck. Boxing tournaments were held. Some men found themselves on picquet duties and a number on fatigues. Decks were inspected regularly by ship's officers. Boat drills were practiced with men paraded in their lifejackets. Many watched with some interest and excitement as the old Walrus aircraft was launched by catapult from the *Exeter* when it proceeded to carry out observation and protection duties over the convoy. On its return to the cruiser it was picked out of the sea by crane. 'B' Company's farmyard duck aroused some amusement as it strutted across the deck. On one occasion, it got at some of the men's beer and was found to be drunk. The ship's captain turned a blind eye to its presence.

On the 4th June, the convoy entered Freetown harbour. No one was allowed off the ship which was quickly surrounded by the natives in bum-boats. Some dived for coins thrown into the sea by the men. Their knowledge of the somewhat crude words picked up from British soldiers who had visited the harbour in years gone by, showed in the replies and entreaties exchanged with the men on board. Some natives offered bananas, pineapples, mangoes, coconuts, baskets and sandals. They were all experts in the art of bartering and traded in money and items such as caps, knives, shoes and trousers. Whilst in the harbour taking on water and oil, a Vichy France reconnaissance plane showed overhead on one of its regular visits. A number of guns opened up on it, which provided some excitement but no hits. The 5th June was a day of torrential rainfall and all ranks spent the time bathing in it, washing and enjoying the refreshing conditions it brought. The convoy sailed on, heading for Durban. On the 9th June, the ship crossed the line and the usual ceremonies took place. Before reaching Durban, the next port of call, the duck, mascot of 'B' Company, affected by the heat and salt air, died and was buried at sea.

Durban was reached on the 20th June and shore leave was granted. The kindness of the people of Durban to all of the troops was to live in the memory for many years afterwards and today's surviving veterans of the Battalion still speak of it. Officers and men were met at the dockyard gates by civilians in cars, who took them to see the sights of the city and the surrounding countryside and entertained them in their homes. For a few days prior to the arrival in the port, the men had been warned to be on their very best behaviour. They did not let themselves or the regiment down. Happy they got, drunk they got, but caused no problems to anyone. Major Watson wrote:

'...On the morning of the 22nd [June], a Divisional Church parade was held in the King's Mead, at which the band of the 9th Battalion played, followed by a March Past, the Lord Mayor of Durban taking the salute and despite having been cooped up for so long, the Brigade looked an inspiring sight as it went by to the strains of the "Light Barque".'

The convoy sailed on the 23rd June. On the 27th, a terrible accident occurred. At 5.00 pm, the Walrus aircraft of HMS *Exeter*, took off on anti-aircraft aiming practice for the convoy. In one of its dives both wings dropped off and the aircraft crashed into the sea, killing the pilot and observer. They were buried at sea. Aden was reached on the 4th July but no one was allowed off the ship. The *Exeter* left the convoy and sailed east. The troopships were now on their own but in safe waters. The heat of the Red Sea was quite exceptional. On the 6th July, a crew member died of heat stroke. He, too, was buried at sea after a church service. Packing, getting equipment together and drawing items from store took up most of the 7th July. On the 8th of the month, Port Suez was reached and the following morning disembarkation onto lighters took place and the men were ferried ashore. First impressions of Egypt were of the terrific heat and the smell. On disembarkation, the Battalion had to march a mile to the railway station. Weighed down with full kit it was a most unpleasant march in the heat. On reaching the station water, tea and buns were given to everyone whilst they waited the arrival of a train to take them on the next stage of their journey. After a two-hour wait in the blazing sun, a train slowly pushed into the station to the accompaniment of a great deal of whistling from the men. A long and slow journey of four hours followed, up the Canal and past Genifa and Ismalia to the transit camp at El Qassassin. The train arrived at El Qassassin station at about 9.00 p.m. where transport waited to ferry the Battalion to Camp 41, some four miles distant.

El Qassassin was a huge tented camp covering about twelve square miles. To the north lay open desert, whilst south of the camp lay the Sweet Water Canal. The latter was anything but sweet, being highly polluted and foul smelling. The camp amenities were good. Excellent showers for washing, a NAAFI, the YMCA and a camp cinema provided places for the men to relax. The discomforts of Egypt were also present. Within the short period of time spent there, the men got their first experience of a sandstorm, the flies, the great heat and, most unpleasant of all, 'Gypsy tummy' and dysentery, which caused great discomfort. Reveille was at 5.45 a.m. In the cool of the morning PT was at 6.15 a.m. This was followed by breakfast in two sittings. Work commenced at 8.45 a.m. until 11.30 a.m., when most activities ceased during the hottest part of the day. In the late afternoon, there was a shower bath parade. Short marches into the desert were undertaken by the companies. On the 15th July, the Battalion marched about two and a half miles into the desert. On the following day, weapon training took place outside the camp.

The stay at El Qassassin was a short one. The war news remained bad. Greece had fallen, followed by the island of Crete. It was now thought possible that the Germans would move on Cyprus. This island was garrisoned by the 1st Battalion Sherwood Foresters, a small group of Australian carriers and armoured cars with a little artillery support. A decision was taken to reinforce the island and strengthen its defences against any German threat. 151 Brigade was sent to carry out this task.

At 6.00 p.m. on the evening of the 23rd July, the Battalion moved to the railway station, where it spent the night before entraining for Port Said. The Reinforcement Company had to be left behind with the following officers; Rice, Allison, Jackson, Druiff, Redway and Butler. The Arab reputation for pilfering was well known and during the night a guard had to be mounted to

Corporal Ramsby *with heliograph, Egypt, July, 1941*

prevent the loss of weapons and equipment. No thieves appeared but one sentry, very alert and excited, almost ran through a wandering goat with his bayonet. At 7.00 a.m. the Battalion left by the usual slow moving train and arrived at Port Said about 1.00 p.m. on the 24th. The Royal Navy was anxious to reach Cyprus during the hours of darkness and get away from the island before dawn and any prospect of being attacked by enemy aircraft. The result was a frantic dash to get the Battalion onto the destroyer, HMS *Kimberley* and the minelaying cruiser, HMS *Abdiel*. HMS *Neptune* carried the 2nd Battalion Cheshire Regiment, the Divisional machine-gun Battalion. All three vessels left Port Said at about 2.30 p.m. The ships were crammed with men and when the Navy learned that the men had had no lunch, they made room for the Company Quartermaster-Sergeant to issue rations and provided an excellent brew of tea. The sight of the three ships travelling at about thirty knots, cutting a bow wave throught the calm sea, was one which lasted in the memory of many men for years afterwards. At 1.15 a.m. on the 25th, the men assembled with their kit and shortly afterwards the ships sailed into Famagusta harbour in complete darkness. The Battalion immediately disembarked at speed and, at about 3.30 a.m., moved off in an assortment of vehicles for Larnaca on the south coast of the island.

The camp, which was reached by dawn, was in an area of scrub on the banks of the salt lake outside the town. Here the Battalion remained out of sight under the trees until the 12th August. During this time it provided working parties on the defences of the nearby aerodrome. The ground was hard and defences had to be blasted out by explosives as well as dug by hand. Fortunately the mining experience of many of the men ensured that the tasks were carried out quickly and efficiently. The climate was a great improvement on Egypt. The countryside was attractive with excellent swimming about half a mile from the camp. Groups of men were allowed into Larnaca each night where entertainment and good meals could be obtained. Fruit was cheap and a soldier could get his helmet filled with grapes for a small sum. Water was in plentiful supply. Italian aircraft made the odd raid but caused little damage.

At 9.00 p.m. on the 12th August, the Battalion embussed and moved to the small hamlet of Kokinni Trimithea, on the Plain of Nicosia in the centre of the island. It arrived at 11.30 p.m. and was again scattered and concealed under olive and fruit trees around the village. The Battalion's role was that of mobile reserve, available to move quickly to any threatened area. The first few days in the area were taken up by the digging and

camouflaging of slit trenches. A start was made on digging a large underground base for use in the event of invasion and work on this continued for most of the time that the Battalion was on the island. It was intended to hold stores and personnel and was protected by pillboxes, trenches, wire and mines. Battalion training commenced with the emphasis on defeating an air or sea borne landing. Support weapons were in short supply. The Battalion possessed one of the only two small anti-tank guns on the island. One company was stood to each day at half an hours notice, supported by two detachments of mortars and one section of carriers. There was the usual stand to each evening and morning.

There was very little entertainment in the area itself. A small group of men were transported into Larnaca each evening. Sunday afternoons were free, following church parade in the morning. There was some dissatisfaction with the Army Postal Service as it took a fortnight for mail to arrive on the island from Cairo. Letters from home are essential to a man's morale and emotional well-being. He longs for news of home and becomes uneasy if there is no mail. A NAAFI opened in an empty house on the outskirts of the village. A Divisional Leave Centre was opened at Troodos in the mountain area of the island, to which men were sent for a few days' rest and relaxation away from the heat of the plains. Whilst at Kokinni Trimithea, Lieutenant-Colonel Yate was succeeded by Lieutenant-Colonel Battiscombe, as Commanding Officer of the Battalion. Lieutenant-Colonel Yate had not been in the best of health. Major P.B. Robinson, ex 10th and 9th Battalions DLI, joined as second-in-command. Major Watson returned from a course held in Egypt and took over 'B' Company.

Company, Battalion and Brigade training filled most days, with the addition of the occasional night exercise. On the 31st October, information was received that the Brigade would be leaving the island and would move to Haifa in Palestine prior to a further move to the Caucasus Region. What had brought this about? The German attack on Russia in June, 1941, was followed by a rapid advance towards the Caucasus and the perceived threat to the Middle East and the Iraq and Iran oilfields. It was to combat this threat that the 50th Division was ordered to the area. The

Battalion moved on the 3rd November, by the narrow gauge railway from Kokinni Trimithea to Famagusta, for yet another sea trip in darkness. At the station, Major Watson noted the mood of the men:

> '...The men appear very cheerful and have been singing lustily in their various platform areas. I believe they don't want to go but any move makes them excited. There has been a very definite sentimental air - for such tunes as "Loch Lomond", "Just A Song At Twilight" etc., with old war tunes have been drifting across the air.'

On arriving at Famagusta, the men changed into battle dress, wore their steel helmets and PT shoes. It was a cold night. A speedy embarkation on HM Destroyers; *Nizam*, *Napier* and *Jackal* followed and at 4.00 a.m. set sail for Haifa. Buses took the Battalion to a new transit camp between Acre and the Lebanon frontier, near the village of Az Zib. Tents were erected and the men moved in. Bathing parades were organised with the sea close at hand. The next few days were busy ones. Stores had to be drawn and preparations made for the long journey to Kirkuk, north of Baghdad. The Divisional transport had been left behind in Cyprus and that of the 5th Indian Division was collected for the journey. This transport was not in the best of condition as the vehicles had been driven thousands of miles during the East African campaign. Captain Lockhart and the Transport Section had an extremely busy time ensuring that the vehicles were in sound running order for the long journey ahead. Their skills were such that every vehicle reached its destination in spite of the long distances travelled over, at times, very difficult terrain. Whilst all this preparation was going ahead the Battalion went on route marches, tested automatic weapons just issued, on the ranges at Acre and enjoyed bathing in the sea.

Reveille was at 3.00 a.m. on the morning of the 12th November, 1941. Breakfasts was at 4.00 a.m. Departure was 6.30 a.m. Haifa was bypassed and the column turned towards the River Jordan. Near the river, a train load of Australian troops was passed and they greeted the column by firing their rifles out of the windows. The Jordan was crossed at Gesher and the column began to climb the hills beyond into Trans jordan by a road with numerous hairpin bends. The countryside passed through was fertile and

well cultivated. On through Ma'ad and Irbid, Mafrak was reached at the end of the first stage at about 3.30 p.m.. The distance travelled was about one hundred and twenty-five miles. After a bitterly cold night in their tents, the journey began again. The route followed a long line of telegraph poles which marked the oil pipe line which carried the crude oil from Iraq to the refineries at Haifa. The countryside was now a desolate desert of black stony and rocky ground. Arab herdsmen with their camels stared with amazement at the long columns of vehicles. Later, a patrol of the Arab Legion passed by. Each hour, after the first two, had a ten minute stop, then one hour for the midday meal, during which the men started a game of baseball on a sandy patch of desert. Shortly before the second day's destination the desert changed to that of sand and stone. The second staging camp was in the vicinity of an Anglo-Iranian Oil Company Station. The distance travelled was again in the order of one hundred and twenty-five miles. On the 14th November, the Battalion moved through a hard, flat terrain, until the road gave out and the vehicles spread out in arrow formation across the desert. So the journey went on until, on the 16th November, the River Euphrates was reached and camp was pitched near Habbanyia airfield. The next day was taken up with cleaning both vehicles and men and carrying out essential maintenance. Later in the day, the Battalion went into the RAF Station to a film show, one of the amenities of this large aerodrome with its shops, churches, houses, swimming pools and gardens.

The Battalion left at 7.30 a.m. on the 18th November, crossed the Euphrates and on to Bagdad. The population was known to be hostile and such proved to be the case. As the vehicles moved through the city, the sullen population made inverted victory signs, spit and threw the odd stone. The troops were ordered to sit upright in the vehicles, wore their steel helmets and held their rifles pointed outwards, in a show of some force. After a run of about one hundred miles, Diltawa was reached and camp pitched. Kirkuk was reached on the 19th of the month, after an unpleasant journey over bad roads and with a sandstorm blowing. Weariness of the journey was beginning to show and men were soon in bed. The journey so far had been over eight hundred miles. The stay in the Kirkuk area lasted for two weeks

Christmas dinner, Iraq, *1941. The men are dressed and huddled up against the bleak winter*

until, on the 5th December, the move to the village of Eski Kellek on the Great Zab River was commenced. The Brigade ordered that the eighty-five mile journey be carried out on foot by the 8th and 9th Battalions, and 'A' and 'C' Companies of the 6th Battalion, under Major Ferens. The rest of the Battalion would complete the journey on transport. By the 13th December the

Brigade was in position.

The camp at Eski Kellek, which was to be the Battalion's home for more than two months, was on the high windswept ground above the village. Many of the inhabitants of the area were Kurds. Most had never seen a British soldier before. Defensive positions were to be dug overlooking the village and the crossings of the Great Zab. Digging and training became the routine. The men settled down to their tasks. Holes were dug and tents were placed in them so that the men were sleeping slightly below ground. In the quite harsh environment, innovation came into its own again and creative minds were put to much use in seeking solutions to the problems of keeping warm, dry and clean. A plentiful supply of crude oil was available at Kirkuk and used for heating water and tents, though some of the innovations bordered on the dangerous. Inter-platoon, company and Battalion football competitions were organised. Game in the area was hunted, particularly by the officers. The game included sand grouse, wild duck, teal and woodcock and an occasional black partridge. Wild pig and gazelle were stalked by members of the Intelligence Section as part of their training.

When darkness fell on Christmas Eve, a large bonfire was lit on the high ground above the camp. The band of the 505 Field Company, Royal Engineers, played carols and the men gathered round and sang. No doubt their thoughts and feelings were for home and their loved ones hundreds of miles away. The elements proved too harsh for most of the men, as an icy wind swept down from the mountains and drove them into their tents, where they continued their singing, talked quietly or lay silent with their thoughts. Christmas Day was cold but the festive spirit won the day. Sandbags and boards were lent by the Sappers and were used to construct tables and benches. The Battalion huddled in great coats and scarfs and ate the turkeys obtained by Captain Chamberlain from the local inhabitants and fowls brought from the Field Bakery at Kirkuk. Private D. Gilliland, an Ayreshire farm worker, sat in the back of the 30 cwt truck plucking the birds on the return journey. In addition parcels were received from the women of India. These contained a small plum pudding, sweets and cigarettes. A ration of plum puddings also arrived just in time for the meal. Each man received an issue of half a pint of beer. A visit to Mosul was arranged for all ranks between Christmas and New Year. The town had a cinema, shops and a bazaar, which provided an interesting break. By the end of 1941, the Battalion had travelled great distances and seen a wide variety of places, people and terrain. There were few who were not curious as to what 1942 would bring.

The weather in the first few days of 1942 continued to deteriorate with low temperatures which registered between 17 and 20 degrees of frost. There were heavy falls of snow and biting winds. At times ice had to be melted to provide water for the cookhouse. The meagre ration of charcoal used for heating purposes gave out. Oil for heating was in plentiful supply but great care had to be exercised in its use. Fumes given off by both charcoal and oil added to the discomfort experienced in the tents. Keeping warm in such conditions was not easy. Major Bill Watson wrote:

> 'So, when darkness fell, apart from the sentries who kept their lonely vigil in company with the howling jackals, all the troops, dressed in as many clothes as possible and huddled together for warmth under their blankets, fell asleep in their tents while their sodden boots froze, until the cold dawn broke on the following day. Later, as if to increase the discomfort, this intense cold was followed by a thaw accompanied by torrential rain, which converted the whole camp into a sea of mud and ruined much of the digging operations.'

However, the men remained cheerful with plenty of physical exercise, digging defences and playing games. Football leagues were organised with games between sections, platoons and companies. An inter-Battalion Competition was held between the 6th, 8th and 9th Battalions. At night a rum ration was issued. Exercises and weapon firing courses were held. On the 11th January, 1942, Captain R.B. Proud left the camp with an advance party, for an unknown destination in the Middle East. This was later revealed to be Baalbek in Syria, a first indication that a move may be in the offing. It was also an indication that the Germans were not going to succeed in breaking through the Caucasus and the immediate threat to the oilfields of the Persian Gulf was lifted. On the 25th January, Brigadier J.S. Nichols, DSO, MC. assumed command of 151 Infantry Brigade. On the 30th of the month, he brought the good news that the Brigade was to move to Syria where it would join the 69 Infantry Brigade of the 50th Division.

At 8.30 a.m. on the 6th February, the Battalion moved off in motor transport and travelled via Erbil, Altun Kopru to Camp K1, Kirkuk, a distance of eighty-seven miles. About three quarters of the Battalion debussed from the transport at a point five miles from K1 and marched the remaining distance. This exercise was carried out near the end of each daily journey so as to give the men some activity after the confinement in the vehicles. The return route followed that which the Battalion had made on the way up to Eski Kellek the previous November. Sixty five miles were covered on the second day of the journey and a further eighty miles on the third, when Diltawa was reached. On the 9th February, the Battalion arrived at Habbaniya. Major Watson wrote:

'On arrival a warning was received that a raid by rifle thieves could be expected, whose cunning far exceeded that of the tribesmen of the North West Frontier of India, and whose methods knew no bounds, so every conceivable precaution was taken. Lamps were lit in every tent and one occupant remained awake all night; sentries prowled the lines with loaded rifles and every rifle was secured by the sling to its owner, who slept with it rolled up in his blankets. Despite all this the inevitable happened. Round about midnight a tent orderly perceived a horrible face peering through the bottom of the tent and one of the sleeping soldiers subconsciously felt his rifle being slowly pulled away. Instantly the alarm was given, shots rang out and figures in the darkness could be seen running into the 'wadis' surrounding the camp, but it was too late, five rifles had been cut from their sleeping owners and slowly drawn out under the flaps of the tents. This was truly an unfortunate stain on the reputation of the Battalion, but few can realise the inordinate cunning of the Iraqi thief.'

The following day the Battalion rested and attended a specially arranged cinema show in the RAF Station. It moved off on the 11th February and travelled via the Air Landing Ground, LG5, H3 Pumping Station, the Iraq-Trans jordan frontier to H4 Pumping Station and arrived at Mafraq on the 14th of the month. Here, Captain R.B. Proud and the advance party, which had left Eski Kellek for Syria on the 11th January, rejoined the Battalion with orders from 151 Brigade that it was now to go on to Egypt. Moving on in beautiful spring weather and through picturesque countryside it reached Affula in Palestine on the following day. On the 16th, the Battalion transport under Captain Mike Lockhart, Transport Officer, left Affula and proceeded independently by road, to rejoin the unit at a later date. With Nazareth nearby, Colonel Battiscombe took a party of other ranks to visit the town. On their return, the remainder of the Battalion proceeded to Tulkarm where it entrained for El Kantara.

CHAPTER 20
THE GAZALA BOX
1942

The Battalion crossed the Suez Canal by ferry on the 17th. It again entrained and continued the journey westward, passing through Ismailia and Tanta and travelling on through the night. At 6.00 p.m. on the 18th February, the Battalion arrived at the railhead at Sidi-Mohammad-El-Gerari and moved into the nearby transit camp, where it remained for three days. Three German fighters attacked a railway engine standing some four hundred yards away from the Battalion positions, wounding the driver and fireman. An enemy reconnaissance plane was shot down. This excitement was offset by the unexpected heavy showers of rain and, on the 20th, the Battalion's first experience of a sandstorm, which made life most uncomfortable. Major Watson described a typical sandstorm which became a feature of life in the desert for the Battalion:

> '...after a sultry morning the fierce Khamseen wind would blow and a huge grey cloud of sand towering into the sky would roll up from the west, blotting out the sun and covering everything with a deep layer of dust. It was then that the sand choked the men, their weapons and vehicles and so charged the last with that strange phenomenon - static electricity, that to touch any part produced an instant shock, it was then, too, that the atmosphere became so depressing that every soldier moved as a listless automaton but mostly lay in their dug-outs or posts hiding their faces until the storm passed.'

On the 22nd February, the Battalion embussed in troop carrying lorries and moved westward for eight miles to Thalata where the motor transport under Captain Lockhart rejoined. The transit camp here was full and the Battalion marched five hundred yards into the desert, brewed tea and ate what rations remained, then rolled into blankets and slept. At 7.45 a.m. on the following day, the Battalion left Thalata and travelled on, crossing the frontier into Lybia at 2.00 p.m. At 4.30 p.m. it stopped and camped for the night. On the 24th, it moved on to Acroma and experienced another sandstorm. The following day, instructions were issued for the move to the forward area. For the purposes of air identification, the St. Andrew's cross was painted on the top of all vehicles. Lieutenant-Colonel Battiscombe, Lieutenant D.E.I. Thomlinson, who was Intelligence Officer, the second in command of the rifle companies, and an advanced party proceeded to the forward area which the Battalion was to occupy. This was held by the 4th Rajputana Rifles of the 5th Indian Brigade, 4th Indian Division. The area occupied lay between Bir Hacheim in the south and Gazala in the north. The Battalion moved from Acroma on the 26th February. It debussed at a point two miles in the rear of the area to be occupied and marched forward in small groups to the respective positions. 'B' Echelon took up its position beside Rear Headquarters, 151 Brigade. The Battalion was now part of the Brigade Box in the Gazala Line and, as usual when entering a new position, set about improving and camouflaging the defences it had inherited.

The Libyan Desert is one of the great arid regions on earth. In outline it is roughly the shape and size of India. Rainfall is scant and usually occurs in the north, nearer the coast. When it does fall, the floor of the desert is covered with brightly coloured flowers which disappear as quickly as they appear, adding a brief splash of colour to the parched landscape. The romantic picture of the desert composed entirely of rolling sand dunes is far from reality. These do exist in areas but very largely the desert is a mixture of grey plateaux of broken stones, plains of brown pebbles and, here and there, flat-topped hills of black and white rock. In the north, the desert stretches twelve hundred miles to the west from Cairo, through Egypt, Cyrenaica, Tripolitania to the foothills of Tunisia. To the south it stretches about one thousand miles to the Sudan. At no point does it reach much above a thousand feet. For mile after mile, the surface is flat and firm until, suddenly, it gives way to soft sand which is churned up by the wheels of the transport and causes a cloud of dust which can be easily seen by spotting aircraft or artillery observers.

Steep escarpments run for between one hundred and two hundred miles, from which fall a series of terraces to a vast area of sand dunes. Here and there depressions occur, with names made famous during the fighting and manoeuvring of the armies: Qattara, Munassib, and Siwa. Some appear as vast craters in the desert with sides almost as sheer as cliffs and range from fifty to one hundred miles in length. The escarpments and sand dunes create a barrier to movement and were difficult to traverse by most of the fighting vehicles of the opposing armies. These armies faced each other on the wider plains of the desert and manoeuvred across the open expanse like fleets of ships at sea.

A coastal road in the north follows the Mediterranean coastline and was the only road of any description capable of taking heavy vehicles. The Italians had improved this road with a tarmac surface from Sollum on the Egyptian frontier to Tripoli. Following their advance into Egypt in late 1940, they had begun to extend this road to their front line positions near Sidi Barrani. Both sides sought to improve the road as the war in the desert continued. Communications in the desert itself were primitive. Ancient caravan tracks such as Trigh el Abd and Trigh Capuzzo, crossed the interior. A single line railway ran from Alexandria to Mersa Matruh and this was extended to Thalata and onward during the course of the war.

There were no towns south of the coast road. Even on the coast these were few and far between and usually very small. Many of them were to achieve a degree of fame as the war went on. Travelling westward from Alexandria, there was no port of any size capable of supplying an army until Benghazi was reached in Cyrenaica, three hundred miles from the Egyptian frontier. Names on the map of the area indicated a ruined fort, a well or water hole - a Bir in Arabic. A pile or mound of stones, marking the final resting place of a holy man, appeared on the map. Sidi is the Arabic title for holy man, followed by the name, such as: Sidi Abd el Rahman, Sidi Breghisc, and Sidi Rezegh. A name given to a pile of stones or an empty oil drum which marked the route of a caravan track, appeared on the map. Many were to become well known to the men who lived and fought in the desert.

The climate in the desert is harsh and unrelenting. The fierce heat of the of the scorching sun during the day gives way to a beautiful sunset and the cold of the nights. High winds can reach storm strength. In the winter these are bitterly cold and penetrate even the warmest clothing available to the troops. In the summer is the dreaded Khamseen which blows the sand into almost impenetrable clouds of thick, choking, dust. Isolated clumps of scrub and the odd tamarisk tree provide what little shade and pasture there is for the camel and gazelle which can be occasionally seen by those who travel in this wilderness.

With the scorching heat of the day came the innumerable flies - the persistent scourge of the soldier. They covered the food prepared for and eaten by the men and settled on the rim of the mugs of tea or water. Attempts to cover food and drinks taken to the mouth were only partially successful and it was not unusual for some flies to be swallowed. The only release from the flies came at dusk and nightfall when they disappeared only to return with the rising sun. Yet the health of the men remained good. The most common complaint was the desert sore. Even the slightest scratch or break in the skin attracted the flies and these caused unpleasant and painful sores which required immediate treatment.

Warfare came to the Western Desert in earnest in the September of 1940, when the Italian Army advanced into Egypt as far as Sidi Barrani, where it halted. In the December, General Wavel's Desert Force attacked the Italians and over the next few weeks drove them back to El Agheila. The arrival of Rommel and the German Afrika Corps rescued the Italians and in the spring of 1941, the Axis drove the Western Desert Force, depleted by calls for assistance to Greece, back to the Egyptian Frontier. General Auchinleck succeeded General Wavel and he launched 'Operation Crusader'against the Axis, with the aim of relieving Tobruk and driving the enemy out of Cyrenaica and out of the whole of Libya. The entry of Japan into the war in December, 1941, diverted reinforcements for the Desert Force, now renamed the Eighth Army, to Singapore and the Far East. On driving the Germans and Italians back to El Agheila, urgent reorganisation and maintenance needed to be carried out on the attacking British forces. A newly arrived and inexperienced 1st Armoured Division relieved most of the British armoured forces at El Agheila. In late January, 1942, Rommel attacked and surprised the British forces before him. The Eighth Army commander, General Neil Ritchie, decided to pull out of Benghazi in late January and retreated to Gazala, where both armies stopped to reorganise, reinforce and prepare for the next offensive. It became a question of who would be ready first to launch the attack.

Meanwhile both adversaries dug in and prepared defensive positions. The Gazala Line was organised in a series of 'Boxes' which stretched from Gazala on the coast to Bir Hacheim in the south, a distance of about fifty miles. The northern end of the line was held by the 1st South African Division with its right flank resting on the coast. The three Brigade Boxes of the 50th Division lay to the left of the South Africans. On the right and next to the South Africans was the 151 Brigade Box, 69 Brigade Box in the centre and the 150 Brigade Box on the left. At the extreme southern end of the Gazala Line was the 1st Free French Brigade Box at Bir Hacheim. There was a six mile gap between the 69 Brigade and the 150 Brigade and a ten mile gap between the latter and the Free French. Southward beyond Bir Hacheim was the open desert, in effect, a vulnerable open flank. Generals Auchinleck and Ritchie were well aware of the vulnerability of this open flank. Behind the Boxes and to the east were a series of strongpoints surrounded by deep minefields, the most important of which was Knightsbridge, about seventeen miles west of El Adem. A junction of desert tracks, this was an important position held by the 200 Guards Brigade and would attract any enemy advance round the open flank. Such an advance would leave the enemy open to counter-attack from the Boxes to the west and from the various armoured units disposed tactically to attack from the east.

Each Box was surrounded by a strong minefield with well marked gaps to enable movement into and out of the Box both to the west and the east. 9th Battalion held the right of the Box, facing north and north-west. 6th Battalion was in the centre, with 8th Battalion on the left. Also in the Box were the Brigade Headquarters, 74th Regiment Field Artillery, 505 Field Company Royal Engineers, 'A' Company Cheshire Regiment with its machine-guns, a battery of the 65th Anti-Tank Regiment (Norfolk Yeomanry), a battery of Bofors of the 25th Light Anti-Aircraft Regiment (Northumberland Yeomanry), a battery of the 149th Anti-Tank Regiment, and 'B' Company of 149 Field Ambulance. Each Box was capable of its own all round defence with supplies of ammunition, food and water buried into the ground in the rear, sufficient to last two weeks of siege. Behind the frontal positions of the infantry companies the guns of the 74th Field Regiment Royal Artillery were dug in and camouflaged and prepared to fire on any targets which presented themselves. Close to them lay the dugouts of the Sappers of 505 Field Company and the underground dressing station of the 149 Field Ambulance. Strongpoints were constructed by each Battalion about three miles in front of the Box and manned by a rifle platoon, a section of carriers, the Gunner Observation Post and a section of machine-guns of the Cheshire Regiment. Each strongpoint was given a distinctive name by its Battalion. That of the 6th Battalion was named Ambulance Post, taking its name from a destroyed ambulance which lay nearby. Brigade Echelon was situated about fifteen miles to the east of the Box. It was here that the Battalion Quartermasters and Motor Transport Officers had their HQ.

The troops lived below ground in their weapon pits which the men, in time, made as comfortable as possible. Dugouts were constructed for Battalion and Company HQ, Officers' Mess, and the cookhouse. Transport allowed in the Box was run into deep pits and camouflaged. Reserve supplies of ammunition, food and water were buried close to section and platoon positions with the main reserve supplies buried, as we have seen, in the rear of the Box. The 6th Battalion lay on the reverse side of a long and almost imperceptible slope. A large minefield stretched from the top of the slope down the other side to No Man's Land. The positions were dug in level with the ground without parapet or parados (mound of excavated soil at the rear of the trench), so making them difficult to see on the flat surface. In this featureless terrain it was easy to lose direction, particularly at night when to move even a few yards from a dugout to relieve a call of nature could cause trouble finding the way back. It became vital to read a compass or the stars with some proficiency. In time the men gained 'desert sense' which enabled them to move about in confidence.

The main problem in the Box was the supply of water. This was brought over a considerable distance across the desert to a filling point behind the line by the RASC water tankers. Here the Battalion water trucks replenished their supplies and brought the precious liquid into the Box. The water was severely rationed to half a gallon a man per day. Two pints of this was handed over to the cooks to prepare the meals sent to the platoon areas in containers. The remaining two pints were used for filling the water bottle and washing and shaving. An ingenious filter made with a sand filled petrol tin made it possible to collect a reasonable amount of water to be used over and over again for washing and shaving. An early morning, midday and evening cup of tea was eagerly looked forward to. Bully beef and tinned food usually provided the main meal. The tinned food included steak, meat and vegetables, processed cheese, together with a weekly supplement of tinned peaches and pears from the NAAFI stores. Occasionally, the arrival of bottled Canadian and American beer from the NAAFI was especially looked forward to by the troops. These were buried in the ground for several days to cool and issued after stand down. Unfortunately, the average per man was only one bottle per week. Sealed cans of food and water were carried on every truck and carrier which went out into the desert. A free issue of cigarettes was issued each week to every man. On one occasion only, during the stay in the Box, there was a visit from the mobile bath unit. This luxury allowed each man to stay for three minutes under the shower. After a two and a half minute warning by the attendant each man was able to wash off the soap suds before the water was cut off.

The enemy positions opposite the Gazala Line were echeloned back, running southwards to include Mekili. No Man's land in the north was comparatively narrow whereas in the south it reached a distance of some forty miles. Opposite 151 Brigade Box, the distance was about thirty miles. This wide area was a challenge the British, who were noted for aggressive patrolling, could not resist. Daylight patrols codenamed 'Apat' were sent out. Each consisted of a section of carriers, a detachment of mortars and a troop of the anti-tank platoon with 2-pounder guns. It is of interest to note that the two troops of the anti-tank platoon of the 6th Battalion were subsequently named 'The Raby Hunt Troop' and 'The Lambton Hunt Troop' respectively, after the well known Durham packs of foxhounds. The carriers of the carrier platoon were each named after a castle in the Battalion's home area, for example, Auckland Castle, Raby Castle etc. Each Apat assembled at dawn near the minefield gap, appropriately named 'Auckland Gap' and moved out into the desert whilst the nights dew still on the ground dampened the dust sufficient to lessen the tell tail cloud, a give away to vehicle movement.

About twelve miles beyond Ambulance Post lay Sidi Breghisc, an ancient tomb of a holy follower of the Prophet Mohammed. Further away, a slight ridge ran north and south across the front with a similar ridge about a thousand yards beyond. This distant ridge was named Heinkel Ridge after the remains of a Heinkel bomber which lay upon it. The nearer ridge was named Lancer Ridge. In between lay a flat sandy area which became a No Man's Land between the patrols of both sides. At dawn, the 6th South African Armoured Car Regiment took up position on Lancer Ridge. Its role was that of Divisional Reconnaissance Regiment and it worked in close cooperation with the Brigade. This armoured car regiment gained a well earned reputation and respect for its audacity as it carried out its role as the eyes and ears of the Brigade. On the ridge, it watched for enemy movement and covered the Apats which pushed on beyond. Brief moments of activity broke the monotony of the days spent out in the searing heat of the desert, where shelter was almost non existent and the flies a constant source of irritation. An enemy armoured car might drive slowly along Heinkel Ridge or a mobile gun drive up to do some shooting. On occasions the Apat or South Africans came under fire and casualties might occur. Sergeant Taylor of the carrier platoon had both legs broken when, under enemy artillery fire, an armoured car nearby reversed over his legs. He was brought back to safety and ultimately rejoined the Battalion. Wireless contact was maintained with Brigade HQ and the patrols passed back much useful information on enemy movements. In time, the men of the Battalion learned about the desert and its navigation and were able to pick out landmarks in what was, at first, considered to be a featureless landscape.

Another form of aggressive activity which the Battalion experienced was through the organisation of 'Jock' Columns. These were of full or half column strength and named after Brigadier 'Jock' Campbell VC who initiated hit and run raids against enemy positions to gain information or attack specific objectives. A full column was usually made up of a company of infantry, a section of carriers, two detachments of 3in. mortars, a battery of twenty-five pounder field guns, a battery of two-pounder anti-tank guns, a platoon of Vickers machine-guns and a troop of Bofors anti-aircraft guns, with some administrative and medical personnel. These columns, which were completely mobile, would move out into the desert in front of the Gazala Line and stay there for up to six days. At night these would laager as close as possible to the enemy lines and send out foot patrols to observe and pinpoint enemy positions and targets. The cool daring of the men who took part was a feature of these activities. A patrol would crawl forward on the desert floor to within a few feet of enemy troops who might be resting or working on defences, and try to ascertain their number or nationality. This information would be passed on to the Intelligence Section of the Brigade. Sometimes men got too close for comfort to the enemy parties. Private Jim Coglan remembered:

'On one patrol I crawled up to this one [gun emplacement] and heard whistling, "Who's Afraid of the Big Bad Wolf". I was hid just down below and he came over and nearly peed on me. I was

ready, I was going to give him the lot but he never saw me. If you were laid down [on the ground] you couldn't be seen, it was very dark. If you stood up you could be seen silhouetted against the skyline.'

On occasions columns came under heavy enemy artillery fire. Private Coglan was a member of one such column:

'The officer said, "Retire." So I got into the wagon and all of a sudden I saw the end truck go up in flames. So I dived off and there were lads getting off the portee and running towards us. The officer called after me, "Leave them. Leave them," and I shouted back, "I'm going back for them." So I went back for them and got two men off the portee. One had his back ripped open ... Out in the open they [the enemy] weren't half giving me some hammer. I didn't think I would get back, I'd had it. But I got them off ... and got back."

Jim Coglan was ultimately awarded a Military Medal for this action. Corporal Reg Haseley wrote of patrol activity he was involved in:

'While at Gazala, I went out on patrols every third night, sometimes to find out what regiment was in the German forward positions. Other times, to fire at them and cause them trouble and, at other times, to put explosives in some knocked out tanks they were using as lookout posts.'

The Battalion quickly settled into a routine in the Box. There was stand to each morning and evening. Positions were strengthened and camouflaged. With the enemy so far away, days remained fairly quiet except for occasional air activity by either side. The subject of an early lecture attended by company commanders on the 2nd March, was 'The Desert Patrol.' 151 Brigade instructions laid down that sandbags be placed under the front seats of all vehicles to give some protection from exploding anti-tank mines. On the 9th March, a demonstration on 'Disarming the German 'Teller' Anti-Tank Mine' was held and various enemy booby traps and anti-personnel mines were described to the Battalion. On this same day, Lieutenant Redway and twenty-two other ranks left for 'B' Echelon to attend an Anti-Tank Gunnery Course which lasted for three weeks. In a Battalion Exercise on the 10th of the month, a column under Lieutenant D.E.I. Thomlinson, Intelligence Officer, proceeded twenty-two miles into the desert to practice movement and use of the compass. The Army Commander, Lieutenant-General N.M. Ritchie, CBE, DSO, MC, visited the Battalion on the 13th and inspected the defences. Some changes occurred amongst the positions in the Battalion held by some of the officers. Lieutenant Thomlinson relinquished the position of Intelligence Officer to be succeeded by Lieutenant D.Y. Caldwell. Major P.B. Robinson was succeeded as second in command of the Battalion by Major M.L.P. Jackson of the 4th Green Howards. Major Jackson stayed with the Battalion only for a short time before taking over as Commanding Officer of the 8th Battalion The Durham Light Infantry. Major Bill Watson succeeded him as second in command of the Battalion.

On the 30th March, a 151 Brigade column set out to relieve the 150 Brigade column which had been operating west of El Cherima. The 151 Brigade Column included units of the 6th Battalion: 'B' Company (Major Bill Watson), 'C' Company (Major Mike Ferens), two sections of carriers, two detachments of 3"in. mortars, the anti-tank platoon, the Transport Officer with vehicle fitters and the Medical Officer and a few stretcher-bearers. From Brigade came a battery of twenty-five pounder field guns, a platoon of machine-guns, a troop of Bofors and a detachment from the Field Ambulance. The column was entirely mobile, everyone was carried on trucks whose cabs and hoods had been removed to bring them nearer the ground as possible, so making them less visible to any enemy observers.

How did such a force move across the desert? Major Bill Watson has left a description:

'The formation plan of so many vehicles is simple. It was, in fact, a square, far out in front of which ranged the carriers as a a screen, working their wireless sets in communication with the column headquarters. Along the front, behind the lone truck of the navigation officer marked by a black and white checked flag by day, and a red light at the top of the pole shining to the rear by night, was the battery of twenty-five pounders; down either side were the troops of Bofors and Anti-Tank guns with the trucks of each company of infantry, next to them inside the square. Along the back were ranged the Vickers machine-guns mounted and ready for action. In the centre of this quite formidable square were the administrative trucks. During daylight the distance between the vehicles was one hundred yards or more but as the short dusk turned to night, the vehicles closed in to almost touching distance and then stopped. The guns pointed outwards ready for instant action and then all would be silent. There would be no digging of slit trenches, for the ping of a pick or shovel carries far into the stillness of the desert. Listening posts and sentries would be put out to keep watch, while every man slept on the hard ground, close to his gun or truck...'

The column commanded by Lieutenant-Colonel Battiscombe, left the Box at 9.20 a.m. and formed up two miles west of the minefield. It proceeded by compass bearing to El Cherima, which it reached at 12.30 p.m. Contact was made with the 150 Brigade column and the relief took place. The column proceeded a further five miles westward and halted. Enemy strongpoints were known to be established at Ras Eleba, Rotunda Afraq, and Gabr El Aleima. A reconnaissance party under Captain Bill Proud went out during the night and succeeded in approaching within one thousand yards of Ras Eleba, at which point a compressor was heard in use in the construction of positions on the hill. No contact was made with the enemy and the patrol returned safely to base.

The following day, the 31st March, the artillery moved out to cover the approaches to Ras Eleba and El Aleima. Observation posts were established overlooking the ridge which the enemy used as observation posts. South African armoured cars patrolled the ridge used by the column's observation posts. Between it and the ridge used by the enemy was No Man's Land stretching across a valley of one thousand yards, a valley of deep sand. Little of note occurred during the day except for some harassing fire from the artillery. At night patrols were sent out to the areas of Gabr El Aleima, Ras Eleba and Rotunda Afraq but no contact was made with the enemy. At 9.30 a.m. on the 1st April, the enemy shelled the forward artillery post, no damage was sustained. Later in the morning the column was visited by Brigadier J.S. Nichols, Commander of 151 Brigade. During the afternoon a considerable amount of movement of enemy transport was observed. At 8.00 p.m. the column moved to a new night laager position. At night patrols were sent out. One, led by Lieutenant David Rome, had an exciting time. The patrol consisted of the Lieutenant, Corporal Allen and three other ranks of the 6th Battalion, with three sappers of the 505 Field Company, Royal Engineers. The sappers carried a mine detector and some dynamite charges. The objective was to ascertain whether the mound at El Aleima was occupied at night and, if so, whether they were German or Italian troops and to identify their unit. The valley was crossed in a truck under the protection of the armoured cars. Dismounting from the vehicle, the patrol crept forward towards the enemy positions. A bright moon shone and the men had to keep as close to the ground as possible. The enemy positions were reached at 11.40 p.m. Lieutenant Rome reported what happened next:

'Two members of the patrol went forward to investigate two dark objects. One man returned to say that two light machine-guns were mounted in a small trench, loaded and two men asleep in the trench. Decided to try and capture the two men - no other section positions could be seen in vicinity. Visibility about twenty yards. On approaching the position, the soldiers in the trench awoke and stood up. Myself and one other rank of the patrol were by this time five yards from the trench. The nearest German soldier repeated twice what appeared to be a question and sounded like, "Hoo Yah." He then screamed loudly and I gave the order for the patrol to open fire. A grenade was thrown into the trench and I fired three shots at point blank range with my revolver. One sapper who was also armed with a revolver opened fire as did one of the rifles close behind me. When the grenade had burst the scream from the trench ceased and one of the light machine-guns was blown into the air.

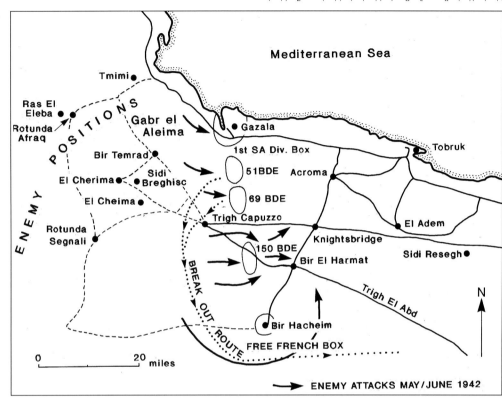

The Gazala Box, *February to June, 1942, showing the direction of Rommel's attacks of May/June and the route of the 50th Division breakout*

'By this time many automatic weapons had opened fire and shots were falling thirty to forty yards in front of the section position. I gave orders to withdraw. The sappers had by this time dismantled their detector and took it back with them, but failed to collect their satchels of explosives which they had taken off while searching for mines.

'The enemy opened fire very quickly after the German soldier screamed and, at first, most of the fire came from the vicinity of the Mound which was about one hundred yards away. Later more fire opened from the west at about two hundred yards range. The time then would be 00.05 hrs, 2nd April, and at this time a green Verey light went up from the centre of the Mound. Also a gun which sounded similar to our Bofors opened fire in bursts of five or six rounds. The flashes of this gun appeared to be green and it also fired green tracer. The direction of its fire was to the south-east. Fire continued till we were about six hundred yards from the section position. The light machine-guns in the section position were very similar to our Bren Guns and had the same type of magazine. All light machine-guns that opened fire appeared to be grouped in pairs in similar positions to the one which we had first encountered.'

Lieutenant Rome and his party returned safely to the column. The enemy certainly appeared very windy after this, as other patrols which went out later reported that the Germans kept up a continual firing at nothing. Lieutenant J.R. Ireland took a patrol to Rotunda Afraq on the same night. They came across three positions apparently held by Italians. For a while they lay watching the right hand position. The whole post and particularly the sentry were very relaxed and in no way alert to possible danger. The patrol shot the sentry and threw a grenade into the post and then beat a hasty retreat. Two of the patrol lost contact with the others in the retreat and were thought to be missing. However, forty-eight hours later, they were picked up by South African armoured cars and returned to the unit. It was not unknown for men to be lost on night patrol. Experience taught any man lost what to do. Private Jim Coglan recalled:

'If you lost your way you had to drop where you were, stop where you were, because everthing in the desert looks the same. Wait till next morning then crawl to the minefield and when you get to the minefield you had to lay outside ... They used to stand to [in the morning] and they would see you.'

The column moved position again at 7.00 a.m. on the 2nd April. Two enemy mobile guns appeared on the skyline of the far ridge and were engaged and driven off by the column's artillery. Patrols remained active throughout the night of 2nd-3rd April. On the 3rd the column's artillery shelled an enemy observation post and motor transport in the area south-west of Gabr El Aleima. At 7.45 p.m. the column again shifted its position and took up a new laager area. the tactic was not to spend too long in the same position, so keeping the enemy guessing.

On the night of the 3rd-4th April a detachment of 3in. mortars was taken out under the command of Lieutenant Maurice Kirby, with the object of attacking enemy motor transport west of Ras Eleba. The party consisted of the Lieutenant, four other ranks, one officer and five other ranks of the mortar detachment, and one driver. Lieutenant Kirby's report stated:

'Arriving just outside mortar range, infantry debussed, going forward on foot, truck following closely behind. Moon had risen by this time. Visibilty good. Officer in front reported enemy MT approximately one thousand yards ahead. Fired from this position. Twelve rounds fired, eight aimed at the transport and four at Ras itself. After the seventh or eighth bomb, several transport heard to start up, very close. Heard trucks revving up and thought it time to withdraw as mortar was giving position away by its flash.'

The eight mortar bombs which fell amongst the transport caused casualties as vehicles exploded and flames shot into the air.

On the morning of the 4th April, Lieutenant Freddie Cole and his carriers came into their own. Lieutenant Cole led his carriers like the dashing cavalry commander of old - at full speed in the charge at the enemy, a brief but savage engagement and then out and away before the enemy could recover. He took a section of carriers to look at a feature called the 'Pimple.' One hundred yards short of this feature he saw a large enemy working party. A quick command and the carriers drove at full speed towards the party, as yet unaware of the approaching danger. On a signal from their commander, the carriers swung broadside to the party and poured a withering fire into the astonished enemy soldiers. Then the carriers dashed for home with the shells from the opposing guns falling all around. Out again in the evening of the 4th with two anti-tank guns on portees and two machine-guns in trucks, Lieutenant Cole led the way in the leading truck, down Lancer Ridge and attacked another enemy working party. The machine-guns poured fire into the party and the anti-tank guns engaged enemy trucks and armoured cars. As they withdrew, German guns opened up. A tyre of Cole's truck was hit. Without stopping he waved the other vehicles to continue and followed them until the tyre dropped off. The truck stopped and the Lieutenant and crew dismounted, changed the tyre still under enemy fire, and drove off and back to safety. On his return to the column Lieutenant Cole received a ticking off from Lieutenant-Colonel Battiscombe who had wanted him, on spotting enemy armoured cars, to draw them onto the column's anti-tank guns and not to engage them himself.

Major-General W.H.C. Ramsden, GOC 50th Division, visited the column on the 4th April. On the following day, the column was relieved by one drawn from the 5th East Yorkshire Regiment of 150 Brigade and returned to the 151 Brigade Box. It could be well satisfied with the results of its work against the enemy and the way that personnel of all ranks had acquitted themselves. Valuable experience had been gained in moving around the desert, particularly at night, and the confidence of the men was now very high.

Soon after the return of the column there were clear signs that enemy tactics were changing. He had not shown a great deal of aggression in No Man's Land, which allowed British columns and patrols to gain and retain the initiative. Both sides had been working hard to build up their forces and so take the offensive. Rommel now made the first move to sweep the British columns and patrols out of No Man's Land prior to going onto the offensive. German elements began to operate more actively in these areas. British daylight patrols were attacked within eight miles of the Box. El Cheima, was permanently occupied by enemy armoured cars and tanks.

In an attempt to regain the initiative, a 151 Brigade column was ordered to sweep the desert and drive off any enemy columns which it met and, especially, drive the armoured forces from El Cheima. The 8th Battalion was given the task of providing elements for the column which was commanded by Major Ross McClaren, DSO, of the Battalion. 'Rosscol' moved out on the 8th April. Unfortunately it came under severe attack from enemy artillery and tanks and sustained heavy losses, including its commander who was taken prisoner. The Germans had truly arrived in strength.

A 151 Brigade column under the command of Major Fawkes of the 74th Field Regiment, Royal Artillery, left the Box on the 22nd April. It comprised 'A' Company, 6th Battalion, under Captain

George Leslie Wood, MC, Lieutenant Freddie Cole with two sections of carriers, a detachment of the mortar platoon and Lieutenants J. Cathcart, M.J. Kirby, A.S. Halse, J.M. Jackson and Second-Lieutenant G.W. Butler, together with supporting arms. The column moved to the area of Rotunda Segnali, known to be occupied by enemy forces. Patrols sent out by the column identified these troops as being the Italian Bersagliere, and Grenatier Regiments. The column remained in this area until the 25th of the month, carrying out patrolling and shelling enemy positions. At first light on the 26th April, the column moved north-west towards Sidi Breghisc. Here, the artillery of the column shelled enemy transport and armoured cars. The column returned to the Box on the 27th.

On this raid, two men of 'A' Company had a remarkable escape. They became lost whilst on patrol and decided to lie down until daylight. At daybreak they found, to their astonishment and dismay, that they were in the midst of an Italian working party. Trucks were parked all around them and soldiers were actively engaged digging positions. Both men lay still and quiet behind a clump of scrub hoping to remain undiscovered until nightfall or when the working party moved off. Assistance came from an unexpected quarter. A flight of Tomahawk fighter aircraft dived out of the sky and fired on the working party. The Italian soldiers dived for cover. Two of them flung themselves down on the other side of the bush which concealed the British soldiers. One of the Italians parted the bush and looked into the faces of the British. For a few seconds they stared at each other. Then, showing no surprise or recognition, the Italian released the bush which closed. No longer wishing to tempt fate further when the raid ceased, the two British soldiers crawled away on their backs. This proved to be too painful and, after moving a short distance by this method, they both got to their feet and walked steadily away from the enemy party. The Italians had obviously not recovered from the air attack as both men were not challenged and returned safely to the column.

On the 23rd April, the Battalion was reorganised into 'HQ' Company, three rifle companies and a 'Support' Company. The Support Company consisted of: Company HQ (previously 'B' Company HQ), anti-tank platoon, carrier platoon, and mortar platoon. Major Bill Watson was appointed to command this company, with Captain Tim Chamberlain as his second in command. Lieutenants Kirby, T.A. Redway and Second-Lieutenants C.F.Boy-Stones and F.L. Cole were transferred to Support Company. Personnel already in the anti-tank platoon were transferred to the Support Company. These were replaced by sixty five other ranks who were transferred from 'B' Company to 'HQ' and the rifle companies. The remainder of the month of April was spent in digging and improving defences, laying a subsidiary minefield west of that already in existence, additional wiring and carrying out specialist and company training.

On the 6th May, the intrepid Freddie Cole took out a Brigade patrol of three carriers and two anti-tank guns. The enemy was now fully alert and the patrol was heavily shelled and nothing was achieved. Major M.L.P. Jackson was appointed to command the 8th Battalion on the 9th of the month and was succeeded as second in command of the Battalion by Major Watson. During the course of the month the enemy became more and more aggressive, both on the ground and in the air. A night patrol led by Lieutenant Jackson, joined the 1st Royal Natal Carbineers, prior to moving out on the night of the 21st. It was heavily shelled and one other rank was killed, one wounded and a third suffered from shell-shock. On the 22nd of the month, information was received that Rommel would attack within the next forty eight hours and the Battalion was put on full alert.

The expected enemy attack came on the 26th May. The 1st South African Brigade, north of the 151 Brigade Box, was heavily shelled all day, the shelling directed by a spotter plane. Stukas dive-bombed and machine-gunned the South African and 8th Battalion positions. The Bofors of Lieutenant Howe-Browne's troop of Northumberland Hussars firing outside Battalion Headquarters Mess, shot down one plane and damaged another. Only odd shells and bombs fell among the 6th Battalion positions, the South Africans suffering by far the heaviest concentrations. Information was received from South African armoured cars positioned beyond Ambulance Post that enemy tanks were advancing all along the Brigade front. The armoured cars were forced to withdraw shortly afterwards. At about 3.00 p.m., enemy tanks were seen advancing on the 1st South African

Brigade lines accompanied by lorried infantry. The infantry debussed in front of the lines and commenced digging in.

Rommel's plan was simple and obvious and one he had used before and would use again later at Alam Halfa where, on that occasion, he came unstuck. It was to threaten and hold British attention by frontal attacks in the north and centre of the Gazala Line, whilst strong armoured and mobile forces hooked round the open left flank south of Bir Hacheim. This mobile force would attack the British tank formations to the east and defeat them on the first day. The Gazala positions would then be attacked from both west and east and Tobruk assaulted and taken by the 30th May. The Italian Brescia and Pavia Divisions were given the task of carrying out the frontal attacks against the Gazala Line, so holding the British forces in their Boxes. This was the plan. How did it involve 6th Battalion?

At 7.50 a.m. on the morning of the 27th May, the small garrison at Ambulance Post fired on an Italian truck which approached the position. The truck withdrew. The Battalion carriers reported that 8th Battalion's Strickland Post was under attack from a battalion of Italian infantry. A section of carriers and the Battalion's Armoured Observation Post was sent to assist the beleaguered platoon in Strickland Post. The Italians, now some five hundred strong, were heavily engaged by the Post's garrison and the artillery of the 151 Brigade Box. At 8.46 a.m. three British fighters machine-gunned the advancing Italian infantry. The enemy advance was halted about eight hundred yards short of the Post and the Italians retreated, having suffered very heavy losses. 9th Battalion on the right flank did not wait for an enemy assault. It carried out a very successful raid into the Italian lines and, amongst the casualties inflicted, captured a battalion commander.

At 9.40 a.m. on the 27th enemy shells began to fall between Ambulance Post and Auckland Gap. An enemy motor cyclist and truck advanced towards Ambulance Post and was driven off by the sustained fire of the garrison. By 11.30 a.m. reports were coming in that enemy tanks had failed to break through the minefield protecting Bir Hacheim and had skirted the southern edge of the minefield and had turned north. They were now being engaged by tanks of the 2nd Armoured Brigade. The British were being driven back towards Knightsbridge by strong enemy tank formations. At 2.45 p.m. an enemy car approached Ambulance Post and was engaged by anti-tank guns. The driver fled the vehicle which was approached by our carriers. It was a German Airforce car and contained many documents and a marked map which appeared to be of some importance. These were immediately forwarded to Brigade Headquarters. The map was found to have places ringed - probably immediate objectives such as Bir El Harmat, which had already fallen to the enemy, and arrows pointing to Acroma, Bir El Cuscia and Bir El Gubi. A fierce tank battle was reported to be taking place east of the Box around Knightsbridge. The immediate concern of the Battalion was the obvious signs of Italians digging in at night in front of Ambulance Post. Patrols were sent out to observe this activity and reported over the next two or three nights that the positions were moving closer to the Post. An Italian Macchie fighter plane was shot down in the minefield and the badly burned pilot was brought to the Regimental Aid Post. During the 28th May, a great deal of enemy vehicle activity was heard and seen. At 11.00 a.m. a German Mark III tank, spotted behind Ambulance Post, was hit by a captured 28mm Braum anti-tank rifle on a carrier. The bullet passed underneath the driver's seat. He and his companion surrendered and informed his captors that his tank was new and had only been in Libya for five days. Little damage had been done to the tank and Lieutenant Wiggins, acting Transport Officer, drove it back into the Box.

Rommel's plan was in danger of breaking down. Fierce resistance from the British had slowed his timetable. Losses were heavy on both sides. Of immediate concern to him was the long, tenuous supply line which stretched round south of the Bir Hacheim Box which was being held with great courage and skill by General Koenig and his Free French. His forces were in real danger of being bogged down for lack of fuel and supplies of food and ammunition. He now sought to shorten his supply lines by aiming to break through between 69 Brigade and the Free French by eliminating 150 Brigade and creating a direct route from west to east. To the east of the 150 Brigade Box, he concentrated his armour which, when supplied through the new corridor, would be launched to complete the final defeat of the British. This area came to be called 'The Cauldron' and the killing ground of the British armour and hopes of winning the battle. General Ritchie flung his forces against the Germans before any corridor could be opened but, failing to concentrate his armour for one surging attack, he was flung back with extremely heavy losses. On the 29th May, Rommel's engineers had started to clear two gaps through the British minefields on either side of the 150 Brigade Box. Cut off from any aid, 150 Brigade put up a fierce resistance but on the 1st June was compelled to surrender when ammunition and supplies ran out. Rommel had his corridor and much shortened supply lines and the depleted British Army faced defeat.

Meanwhile 'Apple Column' under the command of Major Bill Watson had been standing by at two hours' notice for the past two or three days, prepared to move out of the Box. The column comprised: 'D' Company (Major Ronnie Cummins, MC), detachments of the carrier, mortar and anti-tank platoons, 452 Battery and 1 Troop 258 Anti-Tank Battery of the 74th Field Regiment, Royal Artillery. In addition there was a detachment of 505 Field Company, Royal Engineers, a platoon of 'C' Company, 2nd Cheshire Regiment - machine-guns - and a detachment of 'B' Company, 149 Field Ambulance. At 7.20 a.m. on the morning of the 28th May, the column passed through Darlington Gap in the eastern minefield. His task was to go to Eluet et Tamar and hold it against the enemy. Eluet et Tamar was a slight eminence in the desert, from the top of which a distant view was obtainable of the Cauldron area. 'Applecol' reached its objective at 10.20 a.m. German and British tanks faced each other a mere five miles away from the column. At 11.15 a.m. enemy shells began to fall around the column's observation post. Applecol was ordered to remain where it was until relieved by the 44th Royal Tank Regiment, 7th and 8th Royal Tank Regiments and a South African infantry Battalion. On relief, the column was to withdraw into Divisional mobile reserve about six miles to the south-west. During the afternoon, the tank regiments arrived without infantry and German armoured forces approached the position, to be driven away by artillery fire.

On going into mobile reserve in the late afternoon, new orders were received that the column was to come under Brigadier O'Carrol of the 1st Army Tank Brigade. General Ramsden, 50 Division Commander, insisted that the artillery of the 150 Brigade column which was out at that time, be relieved by Applecol artillery, as the Brigade Commander urgently required it back in his Box. Major Watson with the artillery element of his column, set off at 7.05 p.m. to contact Brigadier O'Carrol and then 150 Brigade column. The journey meant crossing through the Cauldron area where fierce tank battles were taking place. It was soon obvious that, in spite of orders, it would be suicidal to attempt to reach the 150 Brigade column on the other side of the Cauldron. Fortunately, within a short time, orders were received from Divisional Headquarters that the column's artillery was to protect the 1st Army Tank Brigade Headquarters from where they were and were not to move forward. Major Watson was in a very difficult position. Part of his force was in Divisional reserve and the rest was at Bir Tamar. 150 Brigade column was awaiting news of its relief so that it could get back into its Box where it was urgently needed. Major Watson decided to try to reach 150 Brigade column and with this objective in mind, set off with his Intelligence Officer (Lieutenant Benthall), his Staff Officer (Lieutenant Poole-Hughes, Royal Artillery) and Major Cummins, in an attempt to reach this column, thought to be near Knightsbridge. Major Watson described the journey and its aftermath:

> 'All went well till the leading truck got to the foot of the ridge beyond Trigh Capuzzo, when suddenly a German tank appeared on the scene and gave chase. Swinging this way and that the truck dodged the bullets and eventually gained safety in a fold in the ground. It was a very close shave. The other trucks avoided the pirate and all three eventually reached Brigadier O'Carrol's Headquarters at Bir El Aslagh - merely a hollow in the ground which was continually being shelled.

> 'The Brigadier knew nothing of the whereabouts of the force to be relieved but thought it was still out beyond Knightsbridge; although the situation in that part of the desert was more obscure.

> 'Time was getting short if contact were to be made before dark so off set the trio of trucks once more, with the Intelligence Officer navigating. The little party slipped out of the hollow

then began to skirt the low ridge running south towards where it was hoped the company of the 4 East Yorks would be. They had not gone a mile when a sudden burst of tracer from a German tank, concealed in a slight re-entrance on the left, whipped across the bows of the second truck. Shouting to Private Parkinson who was driving to swing hard left, Major Watson seized the wheel and the 15 cwt vehicle took a lurch to port just as the second burst passed on the starboard side.

> 'Meanwhile the Intelligence Officer had gone gaily on. Majors Watson and Cummins continued to search until night-fall but without success so circled back to Bir El Aslagh and 1 Army Tank Brigade Headquarters. Again little news was forthcoming, except that the battle had gone badly so the two retraced their steps in the dark to the group of artillery left at Bir El Tamar. On arrival the Column Commander set off in the moonlight for Divisional Headquarters. He reached Divisional Headquarters just in time. It was 11 o'clock as he drove in.

> 'The moon showed a dismal spectacle; every truck was fully loaded and had its engine running. Standing conspicuously in his staff car was General Ramsden ... the General made it only too plain: that battle which at first had gone so well was now lost. German tanks were all around his Headquarters which was about to move into one of the boxes in the line. "Applecol" should also return as soon as possible.

> 'Tired and very weary the column drove through the Darlington Gap at 4 a.m. just as dawn was breaking. Throughout the day its members rested...but no one for a moment thought that 150 Brigade was being slowly annihilated or that the Free French in Bir Hacheim were in the midst of a life and death struggle.'

Throughout the 29th May, the enemy continued his attempts to creep nearer to the Box. Whenever he showed himself, he came under heavy artillery fire from the Brigade artillery. On the 30th of the month, six carriers and a mortar attacked two enemy guns six thousand yards west of Ambulance Post. All of the Bren guns came into action; one gun alone fired three hundred rounds and the mortar fired about a dozen rounds to some effect. Ambulance Post had played a vital role in the actions since the enemy attack started, both as a lookout reporting enemy movements and in breaking up many enemy probes towards its position and the Box. Since the enemy advance had commenced, it had been garrisoned by platoons of 'A', 'C' and 'D' Companies under the command of Lieutenants Farrel, Dennis and Cathcart respectively. The Post was continually in action and the platoons and supports distinguished themselves time and time again.

Applecol went out again through Darlington Gap on the 30th, and spent the afternoon shelling enemy trucks in the Cauldron. Some hits were recorded. On the 31st, the column was given a different task. The 8th Battalion had been carrying out a number of 'commerce' raids, with considerable success. These raids were made against enemy supply columns using a desert route marked as 'Many Tracks' on the map. The first of these raids was carried out by a patrol led by Captain Ian English on the 28th of the month. Others followed. The plan was to move out to the vicinity of Many Tracks, lie in wait and ambush enemy supply columns. At 8.00 a.m. on the 31st May. Applecol was ordered to return and assemble outside Stanley Gap in the western minefield opposite 8th Battalion positions.

8th Battalion had already sent out a raiding party under Lieutenant P.G. Hampson and this was lying in wait near 'Many Tracks' for any enemy supply column using the route. 'Many Tracks' was a series of tracks running parallel to one another, at least four hundred yards in width. The constant flow of enemy vehicles had churned up the sand of the desert to more than ankle depth. Applecol moved out from Stanley Gap to a point about one thousand yards west of Strickland Post - the 8th Battalion outpost. Captain Freddie Cole and his carriers and a Gunner Observation Post, set off to join Lieutenant Hampson's party, at a position on the map marked as B 12. Major Bill Watson, who was commanding Applecol records:

'For some time the patrol commanders watched the ceaseless activity on Many Tracks which the gunner was shelling from time to time. It was now late in the afternoon [31st May] and some columns of enemy vehicles were obviously returning from the field of battle. B 12 was a wonderful vantage point and as these good soldiers waited and watched, a small convoy came bumping along the tracks going in the opposite direction to the main flow of traffic. The Gunner OP ordered the familiar two rounds gunfire from Applecol's guns, the shooting was good and all the shells crashed on the convoy. Three trucks were instantly knocked out and the remaining three made straight for the two patrols, obviously not realising the danger that lay

ahead. The carriers waited until their prey were within three hundred yards before breaking cover, then dashing forward. Cole's party rounded up two and Hampson's one, with a total of 30 prisoners. Deciding not to tempt providence any further the two patrols parted company taking their spoil with them, Hampson returning to Strickland's Post while Cole was compelled to lie up to cool his carriers which were getting very over heated in the midday inferno.

'Once when he went northwards to B 15 a few miles from B 12 he was shelled but at 7 o'clock in the evening, he was again watching Many Tracks. Again another little convoy came bumping towards them but this time Cole's patrol used their own weapons - Bren guns and other fancy weapons mounted on their carriers. Two troop lorries full of troops were destroyed and one, a prize of all prizes, a ten ton lorry of lovely fresh Derna water, better than all the brackish fluid from the wells of Tobruk, fell into his hands. On the lorry was a surly Italian officer and five other ranks who showed an intense dislike to being ordered to drive back to Applecol nevertheless they did and once there one and all drank their fill.'

During the 31st May, activities in the Box followed a familiar pattern though with a gradual increase in intensity of effort from the enemy. The 6th Battalion was ordered to occupy Heinkel Ridge and 13 Platoon of 'C' Company under Lieutenant Dennis was ordered to carry out this task. On reaching his objective, Lieutenant Dennis and his men came under increasingly heavy shell fire but continued to hold on to the position. Heinkel Post - 9th Battalion's lookout post - was now also part of 6th Battalion's responsibilities and a platoon was put into this position. Both Ambulance Post and Heinkel Post continued to send back vital information on enemy movements, though subjected to enemy shelling. Lieutenant Dennis's platoon had lost contact with the Battalion and for a time there was some anxiety as to their safety. Contact was regained and the platoon withdrawn at 9.30 p.m. It was again sent out to occupy Ambulance Post at 11.00 p.m. A number of Stuka dive-bombers had appeared overhead during the day but no bombs were dropped on the Battalion's positions.

Applecol remained in position outside the western minefield on the 1st June. Carrier patrols were met by a more alert enemy who had taken up position on B 12 and would not be moved. The gunner OP asked for infantry support to hold B 13 now threatened from B 12 and a platoon of 'D' Company was sent forward from the column as quickly as possible. Their attack broke down as the enemy proved to be too strong since it included seventeen armoured cars and three tanks or self-propelled guns. The platoon pulled back whilst the guns of the Gunner OP held the enemy advance. Applecol came under attack from these same enemy units and pulled back into the 8th Battalion positions in the Box. In the late afternoon, Lieutenant-Colonel Jackson, the Commanding Officer of the 8th Battalion, ordered Applecol to send a small force of Bren carriers, two anti-tank guns on portees and a Gunner OP in his carrier, all under the command of Captain Cole, to retake B 13 and then push on to B 12. This order seemed to have been given although the enemy armoured cars and self-propelled guns which had just attacked Applecol were still in the vicinity and able to observe any movement out of the Box. Major Watson described the ensuing action:

'Captain Cole soon collected his little band and set off through Stanley Gap into "No Man's Land." No sooner had he got well out into the desert than eight heavy armoured cars and the remainder of the seventeen self propelled guns and lighter vehicles appeared on the skyline. The eight instantly opened fire while the others started to encircle the bren carriers and the two very naked portees. The latter started to retaliate but one received a direct hit and was soon in flames. Cole's carrier was also struck, his driver instantly killed and himself seriously wounded. Seeing it was obviously hopeless task he signalled the order to retire. He himself had not the strength to move the dead soldier so could only keep his vehicle going by pressing the dead man's leg on the accelerator. Realising that something was amiss the gunner officer in his own carrier gallantly dashed up to that of Cole's then jumped into the front seat, dragged the dead man out of the way and drove Cole to safety while his own driver continued to withdraw -a heroic action more reminiscent of the days of the galloping charger than a mechanical skirmish in the desert. All the time the armoured cars kept firing away at the fleeing carriers while the gunners of "Applecol" flung their shells at them...

'To add to the troubles of Cole's little force, someone closed the Stanley Gap with the result that the quick way to safety was

barred, and the gallant force had to drive hard for Pedro's Gap, another sally port on the front of 8 Battalion. Sergeant Hall not realising what had happened and the imminent danger that lay ahead, drove straight for Stanley Gap. Everyone could see the carrier coming but no one could stop it. There was a sickening explosion as the tracks went over the first mine. For a moment the billowing cloud of black smoke and sand blotted out the vehicle then mercifully the blackened figures of the whole crew staggered out carrying their weapons while the wrecked machine lay sprawled in the minefield.'

In addition to Captain Cole, another officer was wounded, one private soldier killed, three wounded and four missing. Captain Cole was awarded the Military Cross for this action and his leadership of the Battalion's carriers. Applecol returned to 6th Battalion's positions in the evening.

As the enemy dug in closer to the Box, they protected their positions with mines many of which were laid on the surface of the ground. Patrols were sent out over the next few days to try to catch enemy working parties laying these mines and to locate the positions of the new minefields. It was discovered that many of the mines were French Mark IV type. A 'game ' now ensued which the Battalion entered into with great enthusiasm. As quickly as the enemy laid the mines, Battalion patrols went out to lift them and bring them back to the Box. Mine lifting patrols were quickly organised. In the early hours of the morning of the 6th June, Lieutenant J. Farrel, 'A' Company, returned with his mine lifting patrol with a haul of two hundred mines. In the evening of the same day a patrol returned with two hundred and forty mines, though not without loss when a carrier was wrecked in the enemy minefield and one NCO and one man were killed. Lieutenant Boys-Stones commanded a patrol and later wrote:

"I took out a patrol from George Wood's Company with four sappers and we took a three tonner out in front - pushed it most of the way so as not to be heard - and brought it back full of mines. I rang up Eardley Wilmot [Lieutenant] from Strickland Post and he said he wouldn't believe it till he'd seen it. Redway [Lieutenant] had located the mines the night before.'

As the 6th Battalion lifted mines the 8th Battalion lifted prisoners. Ten officers and about one hundred and eighty other ranks, all Italian, were captured in an action around Gabr El

Fachri. The three Battalions of 151 Brigade were sending out aggressive patrols and raiding parties which were inflicting losses on both men and material. This activity continued for the first half of June. Battle Patrols attacked enemy working parties inflicting losses, not without occasional losses to themselves. A Battle Patrol led by Lieutenant J. Farrel on the 11th June to enemy positions in front of Heinkel Post, found an alert enemy and a corporal was killed and four men wounded. Three of the latter had to be left behind.

The situation to the east of the Box was becoming critical. Bir Hacheim, which the French had held against considerable odds, fell on the 12th June. The French defence of this southern bastion of the Gazala Line had been superb. Reviving memories of Verdun, albeit on a smaller scale, the French had delayed Rommel's advance, refused demands to surrender and in the end had fought their way out through the ring the Axis had flung round their positions. Rommel could now concentrate on much shortened lines of supply. 69 Brigade was now the southern most Box left in the Line. The final destruction of the British armour was about to begin.

Rommel's original plan to reach Tobruk and the coast by the end of May had failed. With his supply lines stretched and threatened in the wide sweep round Bir Hacheim, he had been forced onto the defensive to the east of 150 Box in the area known as the 'Cauldron.' Here the Afrika Corps defeated British attempts to destroy it and inflicted heavy losses on our armour. 150 Brigade was isolated and was destroyed on the 1st June and a direct supply line was opened to his Army, now badly in need of replenishment of food, fuel and ammunition. British attempts to cut the newly won supply routes and thus seal off the enemy in his positions east of the old 150 Box failed, with heavy losses. The fall of Bir Hacheim left the 1st South African and two brigades of the 50th Division holding the Gazala Line, with increasing enemy pressure from the west and a powerful Afrika Corps in the rear to the east. On the 12th June, fierce tank battles raged as the contest moved towards its final conclusion. The German and Italian forces were resupplied and concentrated and were directed northwards to the El Adam - Acroma line. Knights-bridge fell and the British armour took a beating from which it

never recovered. It was only a question of time before the enemy reached the coast and cut off the escape of the South Africans and the 69 and 151 Brigades to the west.

In the Boxes, morale remained very high in spite of the loss of 150 Brigade. Day and night patrols went out, enemy working parties continued to be located and attacked, vehicle columns were bombarded by our artillery and any movement of the enemy was shelled and driven back. There was a feeling that, if launched westward, the Division could cut Rommel's lines of communication. The Division was eager to come to grips with the enemy. The successes obtained by patrols and columns served to give each man the feeling that, given the opportunity, they could defeat the enemy, Italian or German. Events to the east ensured that such an opportunity was never available.

On the early morning of the 14th June, Major Watson and Captain Thomlinson visited the left hand company of the Natal Carbineers in the South African Box. Their visit was to reconnoitre the ground in that area to see if it would be possible to send out night patrols through a gap in a slight depression known as 'Tank Valley.' After carrying out the reconnaissance they reported to the headquarters of the Carbineers and listened to the interception of wireless messages. It was soon obvious that the situation to the east was desperate and that the end was near. Tank battles on the 13th July in the Acroma - El Adam area had gone against the British and losses were horrendous. Pleas for ammunition, which was running out, were coming in thick and fast. The Commanding Officer of the Carbineers informed the two officers that he had only a platoon per company in the Box. The remainder had been sent to the east to take part in the defence of Tobruk. The dispirited officers returned to the Battalion to find that Lieutenant-Colonel Battiscombe had been called to a conference of Battalion Commanders at Brigade Headquarters. Here, he was informed that orders had been received for the two Divisions in the Line to withdraw, as both were in considerable danger of being surrounded in their current positions. General Ramsden informed his commanders that, in view of the critical and confused situation to the east, he had decided that his two brigades would break out through the Italian lines to the west, turn southwards and continue until well clear of the enemy formations. A further turn eastwards would then be made and units would move to a concentration area around Fort Maddalena on the Egyptian frontier - a total distance of about one hundred and fifty miles; a plan which by its audacity and surprise element sprung on an unsuspecting enemy would, hopefully, bring success.

General Ramsden's orders were received with some astonishment and bitter disappointment by the Commanding Officers. Not being completely aware of the crisis in the rear and feeling they and their men were more than a match for the enemy, it was a blow to discover that they were faced by another Dunkirk. However, there was no alternative to withdrawal as the enemy had all but surrounded the Gazala positions. General Ramsden's decision to strike westwards, then south and east was taken in the knowledge that there was only one coast road running eastwards and this was allocated to the South Africans who had been given a twelve hour start to enable them to get clear before the 50th Division moved. Extensive minefields and large enemy forces lay directly east and south and to attempt to break through here would lead to certain disaster.

Both brigades would be completely mobile with men and essential supplies being carried on troop carrying trucks of the RASC. In addition to weapons and ammunition, sufficient petrol for three hundred miles and food and water for three days was carried. The 8th Battalion was given the task of attacking westwards and opening and holding the corridor to enable the rest of 151 Brigade to break out. All stores would not be destroyed but dug into the ground and covered in case the Brigade could not break out and had to return and fight it out to the end. The Battalion was divided into three independent groups:

First group commanded by Lieutenant-Colonel Battiscombe:

1 South African Armoured Car.

'C' Company (Captain R.B. Proud) less one platoon.

'D' Company (Major R.L. Cummins MC) less one platoon.

2 Sections of Carriers.

2 Detachments of Mortars.

3 Anti-tank Guns.

1 Detachment of 'B' Echelon.

1 Troop 452 Battery 74 Field Regiment, Royal Artillery.

1 Sub Section 505 Field Company, Royal Engineers.

1 Section 11 Platoon 'C' Company, 2nd Cheshire Regiment.

Regimental Aid Post.

Second group commanded by Major W.I. Watson:

1 South African Armoured Car.

'A' Company (Captain G.L. Wood).

Headquarters Company (Captain R.E. Ovenden).

4 Detachments of Mortars.

1 Section of Carriers. (Captain M.J. Kirby)

3 Anti-tank Guns

1 Detachment of 'B' Echelon.

1 Detachment of 505 Field Company, Royal Engineers.

1 Detachment 149 Field Ambulance, Royal Army Medical Corps.

Third Group commanded by Major M.R. Ferens, acting as Brigade Rearguard:

Outpost Platoon.

1 Section Carrier Platoon (Lieutenant Boys-Stones).

1 Section Anti-tank Platoon.

Platoon Headquarters.

1 Section of 'C' Company, 2nd Cheshire Regiment.

1 Detachment of 505 Field Company, Royal Engineers.

'F' Troop 452 Battery, 74 Field Regiment, Royal Artillery.

A dust storm blew up during the day and blinded the enemy to the preparations which were taking place for the breakout. The 8th Battalion was ordered to seize and hold a bridgehead west of

Gabr El Fachre in the area of Point 168 on 'Many Tracks.' The first of this battalion's columns crossed the starting line just before 9.00 p.m. on the 14th June and the battle commenced to form the corridor. The enemy quickly recovered from their surprise and heavy and accurate gunfire broke out from all sides. The 8th Battalion reached its objectives, opened the corridor and held the flanks, a success achieved in some places only after bitter hand-to-hand fighting in which Major Harry Sell and his column played a vital part as his was to be the last group of the Brigade to leave through the corridor.

The 6th Battalion completed its final preparations. The Battalion Intelligence Officer, Captain Thomlinson, visited Brigade Headquarters at 5.30 p.m. to receive final instructions. A final meal was eaten at 6.00 p.m. Unfortunately, Ambulance Post came under enemy artillery fire and at 6.30p.m. direct hits killed Lieutenant J. Cathcart, who was commanding the outpost platoon, together with another member of the platoon. Captain Thomlinson's roll as Intelligence Officer was of great importance as his truck was to lead and navigate Colonel Battiscombe's column through the corridor and beyond. Each group would move in single file and once clear of the bridgehead would travel independently south westwards for forty miles on a bearing of 190 degrees. Auckland Gap in the minefield had been widened to one hundred yards across by the 505 Field Company, Royal Engineers. By 7.30 p.m. the first group had passed through Auckland Gap and had formed up outside ready for the start. The second group just inside the Box, was ready to start. It had been impressed upon all drivers to keep hard on the heels of the vehicle immediately in front.

The Commanding Officer's column moved off followed by the second group.This group had an early mishap when a carrier of the 74 Field Regiment, Royal Artillery, swung out of line as the group left Ambulance Post and blew up on a mine. Major Watson described the journey:

'Despite this early mishap the remainder of the column managed to get past and continue the journey slowly forward but only very slowly. Yard by yard the line of vehicles crawled forward in the dark starlight night. There was no moon. Shells were bursting all round Strickland's Post to the North, but it still

seemed as if the Italians were unaware of what was taking place, indeed under their very eyes. Then about a mile and a half beyond this outpost of the 8 Battalion, there was another horrible explosion as the truck Captain Thomlinson was navigating for the Colonel, struck a mine. The driver Private Campbell was killed and Thomlinson stunned by the explosion (he was actually wounded by splinters), while the vehicle itself lay a torn wreck blocking all further movement.

'This was the signal for which the Italians were waiting. Flares were immediately sent up into the darkness, where they hung in the sky to light up the whole of the surrounding desert. Then bullets began to stream overhead as the Italians wildly fired at the naked vehicles. Feverishly the little party of Sappers in No. 1 Group worked to clear a passage round the derelict truck, while the occupants of the others lay flat on the ground; waiting , it seemed, for eternity. Occasionally a truck would be hit but still the firing was wild. Then came another column careering past on the right, regardless of the danger that lay ahead and in a matter of moments, six of its vehicles were blazing furiously. Other vehicles seemed to be burning far and near, turning night into day, and tracer shells were streaking through the darkness, but still these gallant Sappers calmly continued their job of lifting the mines - more French mines - a job made easier by the conflagrations all around. Eventually the task was done and once more the column began to move. The First Group got through. The head of the Second Group had got into the narrow lane when there was yet another blinding explosion as the South African armoured car, between the truck of the navigating officer and that of Major Watson, struck a mine. The crew were picked up and good fortune held to permit the remainder of the column to squeeze past the lurching hulk into the darkness beyond.'

Corporal Bert Davies remembered his experiences that night:

'It was getting dark as we approached the minefields, there was lots of shelling and machine-gunning in front and to our right there were five vehicles already hit and in flames, just like daylight. We kept advancing slowly about five miles an hour, following a Bren gun carrier. All the time shells were landing close and a machine-gun firing tracer bullets were just going over our heads and hitting the trucks already knocked out. The carrier in front suddenly ran into a deep shell hole and by going so slow had not got enough power to get out the other side and so it ran backwards. and in the confusion and the shelling and machine-gunning, my driver got too close and rammed the back of the carrier. After swearing like hell at him for not keeping his distance and eyes open I jumped down and found that the Portee steering wouldn't move as the crash had bent the bumper bar right into the tyre. The driver and the two crew knowing I was the very last vehicle and now immobilised grabbed what they could and ran like hell to catch up with the carriers in front leaving myself and, lucky for me, Sergeant Doug Rory standing there like mugs. After swearing a whole lot more about the crews going, we both sat down and had a smoke to discuss what we were going to do next. We couldn't go back or forward on foot and I had vowed I wouldn't be taken prisoner and so we started to look for a spanner or a hacksaw to take off the bumper but nothing was found. So, together, we tried levering the bumper with the gun lifting bar which was too springy. After throwing more of the kit off the truck, we did find a short piece of chain and so unhooked the gun and pushed it round to the front into the shell hole, tied it up (to the truck) and hoped that by giving the truck a quick jerk backwards it would pull the bar away from the tyre. Each time we tried it it simply pulled the gun out of the hole but it had eased it a little to partially move the steering wheel. It needed more leverage and looking round found a deeper slit trench and we upends the gun into it ... I gave the truck a mighty jerk backwards, righting the gun on its wheels again but it had eased enough to stear with a mighty pull for it was still stuck on the corners of the tyre ... We decided to take a chance and head off after the column who by now were at least 3 to 4 miles ahead. As I could not see the tracks through the minefield Dougie walked in front of me as a guide until we were through the minefield. We sounded like a tank with the corner of the tyre rotating on the bumper - perhaps to our advantage...'

This was not the end of the adventure:

'After about five miles we found ourselves heading straight for a German-Italian laager camp of tents, tanks and armoured cars. After passing a few I veered off to the right. Two armoured cars were heading our way. Although we had got two anti-tank guns and a Bren gun, the one on the Portee was incapable of firing because of all the equipment on top of it and the one on tow was suspect because of the rough handling and tugging it had and only two of us. Therefore, we sped off to put some distance between us and the armoured cars so as to give us time to get the gun ready to fire...'

The armoured cars did not follow and Davies and Rory made

it to Fort Maddalena. Captain Joy, the Battalion Medical Officer wrote:

'We moved through the enemy lines. There was some firing. Our navigator's truck was blown up in a minefield just outside an enemy position. The driver lost a leg. I dressed the wound and gave him morphia. As there were about one hundred and twenty miles of desert to cross next day it appeared to be best to leave him to be picked up by the enemy. Travel could have undoubtedly killed him. We afterwards heard that he was picked up next morning and given treatment but he died about a week later.'

The first two columns of the Battalion continued on their way across 'Many Tracks', clearly identifiable by the soft sand and the many deep ruts made by the constant stream of enemy vehicles who had passed that way. A small German convoy on the Tracks actually halted to let the head of Major Watson's column go by. In the darkness and confusion it was often difficult to identify friend from foe. Once out into the open desert beyond the enemy positions a halt was called and stock taken. The darkness and the thick dust thrown up by exploding shells and the vehicles had brought confusion to the columns and many trucks had become detached. There was nothing else to do but to continue with the journey and hope that such detached vehicles would either catch up or arrive at Fort Maddalena. Vehicles which broke down were destroyed or damaged by the simple expedient of dropping a grenade in the engine compartment. This did not always work. Lieutenant Boys-Stone recalled:

'Wood's carrier (a corporal I think) ... broke down and I put a hand grenade in the engine hoping to wreck it but it didn't go off. So I put another one in and that didn't go off either! And before you say it, I assure you I let the handles go or whatever they were called. I remember thinking that although I had thrown quite a lot of grenades in training I'd never held a live one with the fuse going and, obviously, I still haven't! There wasn't time to get more grenades and put fuses in.'

Occupants of vehicles which had broken down were picked up by other trucks and brought into the concentration area around Fort Maddalena. On the 17th June, this concentration area was moved to Bir Thalata about forty miles east of Fort Maddalena. Over the next few days a variety of vehicles limped in, many grossly overloaded with men of the Division.

The 8th Battalion's attack had opened up the corridor and enabled the 6th Battalion to pass through. The next battalion expected through was the 9th, to be followed by the Brigade rearguard under Major Mike Ferens. By 2.30 a.m. on the 15th June, Major Harry Sell of the 8th, on the right flank of the corridor, was faced with a very difficult decision. The number of vehicles which had passed through the corridor had dropped significantly. Neither the 9th Battalion nor Major Ferens' rearguard had appeared. The commanders of both of these units had been left with the option of coming out through the corridor or taking the coast road through Tobruk if, in their opinion, the situation called for it. By now the enemy was fully alert. The sky was lit with a profusion of flares and burning vehicles. Heavy losses could be expected, if not total destruction. 9th Battalion decided to move out via the coast road and through Tobruk and the rearguard decided to follow suit. Major Sell, unaware of this decision, hung on until an hour before dawn when he decided that the withdrawal through the corridor had been completed. He moved his party out through the corridor in vehicles, charging through German and Italian held positions at full speed and firing every gun into the strongpoints until the column broke free into the open desert. Casualties to Major Sell's party had been heavy but it had performed brilliantly and its commander well deserved the Military Cross, with which he was ultimately awarded for this action.

The rearguard had been waiting its turn to move watching the flares and fires and listening to the heavy gun fire and explosions ahead of them. Private George Iceton of the Motor Transport Section, with Major Ferens remembered that wait:

> '...Just the wait, that was the bad part about it because you could hardly see anything apart from the flares and gun bursts ... We set off, it was a relief to get on the move again, but just sitting there with shells falling all around you, we did get out and lay on the ground. Even so you still felt naked, because once an enemy gets wind of something like this there are flares all over the place. The sky is absolutely lit up ... You feel so naked. You daren't get too near the vehicle because that was obviously silhouetted against the skyline. Obviously they are going to have

> a go at anything they can see. If there is a truck there you can guarantee that there are some men around and pretty close...'

The 9th Battalion had been split into two columns, one commanded by Lieutenant-Colonel Percy and the other by the Second-in-Command, Major Slight. Major Ferens's rearguard attached itself to Major Slight's column. The rearguard consisted of:

1 Platoon 'C' Company, 6 DLI

1 Platoon 'D' Company, 6 DLI

1 Section Carriers, 6 DLI

1 Section Anti-tank Guns, 6 DLI

Platoon HQ and 1 Section 11 Platoon, 'D' Company, 2nd Cheshires

1 Detachment 505 Field Company, Royal Engineers

'F' Troop, 452 Battery, 74 Field Regiment, Royal Artillery

Detachment 149 Field Ambulance

At 2.00 a.m. the rearguard moved off to Strickland Post where it learned of Lieutenant-Colonel Percy's decision and joined Major Slight's column. At 7.00 a.m. the Gazala Pass was reached, which led down the escarpment to the coastal plain. It was found to be mined and impassable. The column moved on to the El Agheila Pass, which was also mined but had been cleared by South African engineers. Here the rearguard joined the queue to move in single file down the pass. It was shelled and bombed on the way down, though fortunately without casualties. The column crossed the coast road and continued east, moving parallel to the sea, by now mixed up with many South African troops and bombed and machine-gunned from the air. The enemy had already cut the coastal road with tanks about five miles to the east. A battery of German field guns in position on the escarpment strengthened the road block. The 9th Battalion and Brigade rearguard column crossed the coast road and moved on to a track which ran east between the road and the sea, hoping in this way to bypass the road block, only to find, as it approached M'Rassus that enemy infantry also blocked the track. The congestion of retreating vehicles and guns almost slowed to a halt and was a perfect target for the German tanks, artillery and airforce. Grasping the situation at once, Major Slight gathered a party of 9th Battalion infantry together and with the support of Major Ferens' carriers led by Lieutenant Boys-Stones and a South African 25 pounder gun and two South African armoured cars, attacked the enemy infantry block on the coastal track and brushed it aside. The danger was not over. Seven enemy tanks appeared from the south east and attacked the column. Bofors and anti-tank guns with the column were immediately brought into action and five of the enemy tanks were destroyed or damaged. The enemy artillery on the escarpment was bombarding the retreating troops and congested vehicles on the coast road and track below. Major Slight contacted a South African 25 pounder battery and pointed out the target up on the escarpment. The battery put down smoke to cover the retreating units and fired high explosives into the enemy gun positions. A major disaster had been averted by Major Slight's actions and the retreat continued until Tobruk was reached.

By this time, Major Ferens' column had lost contact with the 9th Battalion. On entering Tobruk, Major Ferens reported to the South African Command Headquarters where he was told that his column would come under its command and reinforce the town's garrison. Major Ferens objected and pointed out that his orders were to rejoin his own 50th Division as soon as possible. He was told he was under new orders and had to stay where he was. Major Ferens had no intention of allowing this to happen. On leaving the headquarters, he 'disobeyed' his new orders and moved his column to the defence perimeter where he told the Indian troops on duty there that he was going out on a reconnaissance. The column moved through the perimeter and rejoined the Battalion at Bir Thalata on the morning of the 17th June.

50th Division had carried out a remarkable feat and whilst the losses in men were not as great as expected - ninety six per cent of those who had started out from the Gazala Line reached the Egyptian frontier - the loss of equipment and materials was considerable. In addition to that left buried in the Gazala Line, a large amount had to be jettisoned during the journey to make room on the trucks for the men whose vehicles broke down or were damaged or destroyed. At this stage there was no hope of replacing these losses. The 6th Battalion had lost many vehicles and carriers but by late morning on the 19th of the month, twenty-one officers and six hundred and twenty eight other ranks had rejoined.

CHAPTER 21

MERSA MATRUH AND THE WITHDRAWAL TO EL ALAMEIN

1942

Tobruk, made famous by the months of siege of the previous year, was generally expected to repeat that defence and by so doing hold down around its perimeter a large portion of the German and Italian forces. This would make it possible for General Auchinleck to halt the enemy advance on the Egyptian frontier, receive reinforcements and, in due course, throw Rommel back as he had done at the end of 1941. Tobruk had supplies to last three months of siege and a large garrison mainly made up of the 2nd South African Division. Rommel had no intention of allowing this to happen a second time. As the British reeled back towards the frontier, he switched the major portion of his German and Italian Divisions to attack Tobruk.

The assault against the fortress perimeter commenced on the 20th June with a concentrated bombardment and heavy bombing of minefields and the forward positions of the defenders. The anti-tank ditch and minefield were breached and elements of the German 90th Light Division, tanks and Italian infantry poured through. The fortress surrendered on the following day, 21st June. The shock to Winston Churchill and the British people was considerable. In their minds, Tobruk would be held come what may. We now know that General Auchinleck was extremely reluctant to tie up a significant number of his already depleted army and supplies in Tobruk, a tactic he considered militarily unsound. In addition, the defences round Tobruk, since its relief in December, 1941, had been neglected and allowed to crumble. They were much weaker than the previous year. The tragedy of Tobruk was that the decision to get the garrison out came too late. Rommel moved too fast and took the town with its garrison

and enormous supplies, a great material loss to add to the psychological blow to the British people.

General Auchinleck, being a realist, could see no way of holding the line of the Egyptian frontier. He had suffered heavy losses in men and materials. Mersa Matruh, the next place to the east with some form of prepared defences, could only act to slow down the enemy advance, certainly not stop it. He had seen the possibility of building a strong defensive line at El Alamein, between the sea and the Qattara Depression capable of holding Rommel until new divisions, guns and materials arrived to reinforce his army and, therefore, once more take the offensive. In this position both flanks were secure; to the north by the sea and to the south by the Qattara Depression considered impassable to wheeled vehicles and tanks. It was towards El Alamein that General Auchinleck now directed his weary army.

With the fall of Tobruk, Rommel could now push his whole army towards the Egyptian frontier. He drove his men ruthlessly and to their limit. The British must not be allowed to regroup or make any stand which would appreciably delay the advance. The advance was led by his two German armoured divisions, the 15th and 21st Panzers; the Italian Ariete Division; the 133 Littorio Armoured Division - recently arrived in the desert - and the German 90 Light Division. Released by the fall of Tobruk, four Italian infantry divisions added to his strength. A British screen comprising the 7th Motor Brigade, 3rd Indian Motor Brigade, a battalion of the King's Royal Rifle Corps and the 29th Indian Infantry Brigade attempted to hold off the enemy but gallantly though they tried they were too weak for the task. Mersa Matruh was garrisoned by the 10th Indian Division and was joined by the two brigades of the 50th Division, 69 and 151 and a South African Brigade. To the south was the 5th Indian Division and General Freyberg's 2nd New Zealand Division, together with an armoured brigade made up from the remnants of the 4th and 22nd Armoured Brigades. It was here at Mersa Matruh that the 151 Brigade became involved in a fierce rearguard action.

On the 20th June, Major Bill Watson was taken to hospital and Major Mike Ferens became Second-in-Command in his absence. On the 21st, the Battalion left Bir El Thalata for Manquar Sidi Hamza, twelve miles south of Mersa Matruh. The move was made in two columns. The first under Major Ferens comprised 'B' and 'C' Companies. The second comprised 'D' and 'HQ' Companies under Lieutenant-Colonel Battiscombe. 'A' Company under Captain G.L. Wood had been sent to Divisional Headquarters as defence company. It was a painfully slow and weary journey in darkness over very rough desert. The columns travelled eastwards throughout the following day, the intense heat adding to the discomfort. Whenever there was a halt, the men sought shelter in what little shadow was afforded by the vehicles. The destination was reached at 6.30 p.m. The Battalion remained at Manquar Sidi Hamza on the 23rd June. The transport received much needed maintenance, the men cleaned themselves and their equipment and, in addition, began to dig and prepare defences. It was hard work under the unrelenting sun. On the 24th June, a move was made to a new area, Point 77, seven miles south east of Mersa Matruh, where defences were dug where possible and, in places where there was little or no soft ground, rocks were piled to make sangars. To the great annoyance of both officers and men who had sweated and toiled so hard to prepare the defences, another move was made. In the afternoon, an advance party left this area for Gebel Shaquaqa and a sector was allotted in and around Wadi El Kharuba. The main body of the Battalion reached this area at 9.00 p.m. 151 Brigade's task was to prevent the enemy reaching the escarpment which ran eastwards and overlooked the coastal plain. The urgent task was to prepare the area for all round defence and this work took precedence over the next two days. Work continued in shifts throughout the night of the 25th-26th June and the following morning. It is not difficult to imagine the anger and frustration when orders arrived, yet again, for the Battalion to be prepared to move at two hours' notice. It arrived at its new area, Bir El Hamam, about ten miles south of Wadi El Kharuba, at 11.00 p.m. and digging defensive positions commenced again and continued throughout the night. The escarpment at this point was very nearly one hundred feet high. The Battalion area was very wide and lay south of the Bir. The result was that the platoon and section positions were widely scattered. Orders were received for the Battalion to lay a minefield, found impossible to carry out as there were no mines to lay.

General Auchinleck took command of the 8th Army on the 25th June. The enemy forces had bumped into the Mersa Matruh defences and by the 27th June, Rommel's armoured units had bypassed the defences and cut the coast road east of the town. They continued to press the retreating British towards the Egyptian frontier. With the coast road cut, the 10th Indian and the 50th Division in and around Mersa Matruh were in danger of being surrounded. For the 50th Division, it was Gazala all over again. The enemy shelled the Battalion area on and off for most of the day. The British artillery was also busy replying and shelling targets to the south and south-west. The brunt of the enemy activity against the Brigade on this day fell upon the 9th Battalion. Heavy and powerful attacks were made against this Battalion's positions. By 9.00 a.m., communications with the 9th had ceased. For two hours, the Battalion put up an heroic resistance and stemmed the German attacks until it was completely overrun and the survivors taken into captivity. It was in this action that Private Adam Wakenshaw was awarded a posthumous Victoria Cross for courage and devotion to duty which has seldom been equalled and even more rarely surpassed.

With the 9th removed from the battlefield, the 8th Battalion in the centre of the Brigade's positions found itself with an open left flank. Fortunately a lull ensued as the enemy withdrew to lick his wounds and prepare for the next assault. The Italians were advancing on Mersa Matruh from the West. German forces were concentrating about eight miles to the south of the 151 Brigade positions in the Mingar Qa'aim area and were preparing to advance on Mersa Matruh from that direction. A further coordinated attack was expected from those German forces which had bypassed and lay to the east of Matruh. At 4.30 p.m. on the 27th, a warning order was received at Battalion Headquarters that a raid was to be made in transport with the objective of cutting and disorganising the enemy lines of communication some five miles to the south of the British positions. Units of the 10th Indian and 50th Divisions would form this raiding column. At 5.30 p.m. Lieutenant-Colonel Battiscombe joined other Commanding Officers at the Brigade Headquarters to discuss the plan. Colonel Dewing of the Royal Artillery had taken over temporary command of the Brigade when Brigadier Nichols had assumed command of the 10th Indian Division. He now gave out the orders for the attack. The 6th Battalion column was made up of 'C' and 'D' Companies and elements of 'S' Company. Unmounted detachments of 'HQ' Company were left behind to cover the Battalion rear. These were under the command of Captain Ovenden. It will be remembered that 'A' Company was at Divisional Headquarters as its defence company.

The order of march of the 151 Brigade column was: 8th DLI; Tactical Headquarters, 151 Brigade; 6th DLI with attached batteries of the 74th Field Regiment, RA. At 8.05 p.m. the Battalion column moved towards the start line in close desert formation. It was reached at 8.30 p.m. As the Brigade column formed, it was harassed by intermittent shelling from a German 105mm gun, which caused very little damage. The Brigade column moved off and bumped its way slowly over the desert in bright moonlight, too bright for comfort. Heavy enemy anti-tank gun fire was encountered, most of it from automatic weapons firing on fixed lines. The column's driving discipline was such that all vehicles kept station throughout the initial stage. The halt at the end of this stage allowed time for a short reorganisation to take place and vehicles which had driven into slit trenches to be pulled out and catch up. It was disconcerting to see solid tracer shot hitting the ground and bouncing over into the darkness. From time to time a shot would hit a target and a truck would go up in flames. To the west, similar fire indicated where the column

of the 10th Indian Division was moving south and to the east where the 69 Brigade column was moving in the same direction. It was almost impossible to identify friend from foe since the Germans were using many captured British vehicles. The whole night's activity was turning into a frantic 'free for all.' The column moved on. A picture of the drive forward was given to Major Watson:

'...Battalion experienced very heavy anti-tank fire and had to pass through a veritable cross-fire of projectiles that went hissing into the night. Trucks and other vehicles were going up in flames. The carrier platoon under Captain Caldwell and Lieutenant Boys-Stones respectively, working as a screen on either flank were, by now, inexorably involved in the hopeless melee. It was not long before Captain Caldwell's carrier was ablaze from a direct hit. Sergeant Hall seeing what had happened drove up to his aid in his carrier but before he reached the scene his carrier was also hit. He and his crew jumped out but before he could get away the carrier received another hit and burst into flames and Sergeant Hall himself was seriously wounded in the leg. Efforts were made to get him to safety but it was impossible, by now the Battalion had faded away in the dark, with the result that Captain Caldwell and the others were all taken prisoner.

'On the other flank Lieutenant Boys-Stones' servant was killed in the act of firing a Bren gun from the back of his carrier but despite this the carrier closed with an enemy anti-tank gun and crushed one of the crew before pulling out into the darkness once more. Amongst the trucks that were hit was that of Major Ferens, who was bringing up in the rear of the column, with the result that both he and the occupants were all slightly wounded.'

The final objective was reached. The carriers brought in a German officer and his truck. Orders were received to return via the same route to the Wadi El Zarga area. Once more the journey was retraced through an alert enemy, the same crossfire from anti-tank guns and machine-guns, with more destroyed trucks and casualties. Along with the German officer taken prisoner were two other ranks. The three of them were despatched to Brigade Headquarters. The Brigade moved down the escarpment on to the coastal strip where the morning was spent checking casualties, cleaning weapons and servicing vehicles.

What had happened to the Battalion rearguard under Captain Ovenden which we left at Bir El Hamam when the rest of the Battalion joined the raiding column? The force under Captain Ovenden's command consisted of:

1 troop 65th Anti-tank Regiment, RA.

2x2 pounder anti-tank guns - 6 DLI under Lieutenant Redway.

1 platoon anti-tank gunners without guns - Lieutenant Ireland.

1 platoon Signallers and odd details - Regimental Sergeant-Major Page.

1 platoon A/A gunners and Pioneers - Sergeant D'Auvergne.

1 platoon 3" mortar men without mortars - Sergeant Aylen.

On the 28th June, the Captain was ordered to return to the Battalion on the coastal plain, which it had just reached after the raid of the previous night. On arrival, Colonel Dewing ordered him, together with his mixed force back to the escarpment near Bir Hamam and hold this position until ordered to retire. Such order could be expected not later than 10.00 p.m. The rearguard returned to its previous positions. Let Captain Ovenden's report, written immediately after the action, tell the story:

'Shortly after 18.30 hours I was called to the head of the wadi in which I had established my headquarters, by a report of armoured cars and saw approaching from my left flank two self-propelling guns, a Bren carrier and other vehicles, including armoured cars. They were flying our pennants and gave an indefinite recognition signal. Covered by my men, they approached slowly to about 150 yards when I recognised them as German and at about the same moment, they put up their hands shouting, "Don't shoot." They were signalled to get out of their vehicles and the leading gunner started to do so with his hands still in the air. Suddenly, however, he jumped back into his turret and fired, scoring a direct hit on a 2 pdr gun near me, killing the two gunners and putting the gun out of action. At the

same time the enemy must have dealt similarly with the 2pdr guns on my left flank for no fire came from them. This meant that the position on my front which was being attacked was without anti-tank gun weapons: as something else seems to have happened to the gun which was in the wadi about three hundred yards to my right."

The enemy now opened up on the rearguard force with heavy machine-gun, cannon fire and shells. The defenders returned this with armoured piercing small arms fire to some effect. Anti-tank guns on the right began to fire from long range. The action raged on. Captain Ovenden wrote:

'My two left hand platoons were shot up by the self-propelling guns and were forced to surrender. Shortly after this one of those guns was put out of action but the remaining one compelled the surrender of the forward section of my right centre platoon also. By this time an enemy ammunition wagon was burning fiercely and two armoured cars appeared to have been hit. The Regimental Sergeant-Major worked round to the right a bit and finding the two pounder anti-tank gun there deserted, got it into action and hit the remaining enemy gun which caught fire. He also put the enemy commander's staff car out of action and killed the officer. A small party of enemy infantry next debussed from a semi-tracked vehicle, but this was hit and the men dispersed by fire. One vehicle which had been set on fire was cleverly recovered by the enemy about this time - I believe this to have been an armoured car - and it was uncanny to see the plumes of smoke moving away from our position. The enemy started to shell us with 105mm guns but only half a dozen rounds fell. All this time my left flank was being held by my reserve Bren gun belonging to the Troop Carrying Section, RASC, which I had pushed up to the left centre position. I had, however, sent my Company Sergeant-Major to withdraw two Bren sections from the right hand platoon which had not been engaged and the arrival of these appeared to settle things and the enemy withdrew, the action having lasted for about two hours, most of it at a range of 200 yards or less.'

On the withdrawal of the enemy the following were left behind:

1 staff car - engine destroyed.

1 self-propelled gun - on fire.

1 ammunition wagon - on fire.

1 semi-tracked vehicle - engine damaged.

The enemy were able to recover two damaged armoured cars and one self-propelled gun. Towards the end of the action Captain Maurice Kirby arrived with orders for the little force to withdraw and this was done successfully and the wounded brought out by 11.15 p.m. The rearguard's losses were: four killed; fourteen wounded and fifty-three missing. Captain Ovenden continued:

'It is difficult to estimate the size of the enemy force. My men are insistent that there were tanks in the background, but I was of the opinion that they were armoured cars to a probable total of five altogether who kept weaving in and out two at a time. The probable attacking force was therefore:

2 Self-propelling guns.

5 armoured cars.

1 Bren carrier - not seen after initial approach.

1 Semi-tracked armoured carrier.

'In addition there were, of course, the staff car and ammunition wagon and either two or three Troop Carrying Lorries in which our prisoners were taken away. These may or may not have contained enemy infantry.

'I wish to recommend the following for immediate award: Second-Lieutenant T.G. Stanley, No 14 Company RASC and No 4442194 Regimental Sergeant-Major Page, A.

'Second-Lieutenant Stanley was the officer i/c troop carrying transport attached to us and kept one Bren gun mounted on a truck for A/A defence. This I was keeping in reserve. After my two left hand platoons had capitulated I shouted to him to cover my left flank. He immediately rushed his gun to a somewhat exposed but very advantageous fire position and kept up a very accurate fire for the remainder of the action, using armour piercing bullets. After about ten minutes firing, the firing pin of

his gun broke and the gun was useless. Without hesitation, he went forward across bullet swept ground and brought back an abandoned gun from the A/A platoon and continued firing, although continually fired upon by both machine-gun and cannon. His general bearing was in the highest tradition and his action undoubtedly saved my left flank from being turned.

'Regimental Sergeant-Major Page was in command of the composite platoon on my right centre and from the very beginning of the action his bearing and conduct was of the highest order. Although commanding a very mixed force including clerks etc he put such heart into it that the two rear sections held on doggedly after the forward one had been captured. His personal bravery was beyond reproach and he was repeatedly standing up sniping the armoured car commanders who kept on trying to open their turrets - this at a range of 150 yards. Working round to the right he brought an abandoned two pounder gun into action and personally knocked out a self-propelling gun. He also put the enemy commander's car out of action and killed the officer. A large number of maps and papers were taken from the car. Although wounded in the leg near the beginning of the action, he bandaged himself and no one was aware of the fact until the following morning. I consider it entirely due to his personality and efforts that the right centre of my position was held.'

Private George S. Richardson of the Signal Platoon was with Captain Ovenden:

'There were two wadis stretching downhill from the escarpment. To the right of us in one wadi, the Company Sergeant-Major and Company Quartermaster-Sergeant Andel with cookhouse staff and other Battalion HQ staff, about twenty-five of them. In the other wadi was Regimental Sergeant-Major Page, about eight of us from Signal Platoon and some others from HQ Company; drivers, buglers, about thirty of us. One officer, Major Ovenden was with our Regimental Sergeant-Major. Our Signal Officer had gone along with our CO, Lieutenant-Colonel Battiscombe. It was about 1 p.m. and we had constructed heaped blocks about two feet high to give rifle cover, firing posts. We'd all been issued with armoured piercing rifle bullets with some tracer. We had our Bren gun. Suddenly the Regimental Sergeant-Major spotted an approaching armoured car. At first, after giving a flag signal of recognition and receiving one in return he said, "I think its South African." But as it got closer he shouted, "Bosche! Open fire!" We did. There were three armoured cars and one wagon load of infantry. The first armoured car got about one hundred yards away when I fired and shouted, "I got him," as one of the Germans slumped over his turret. My mate next to me, Herbert Latham from the Signal Platoon, said, "No you didn't, I got him." Lance-Corporal Jimmy Sixsmith who was at the left side of us said, "Shut up. You both got one." The German infantry dismounted and set up a Spandau machine-gun. They were about three hundred yards away but lying on the open sand. We killed quite a few and just when we thought we were winning a burst of machine-gun fire hit the top of our rock cover and splattered splinters down Herbert Latham's back through his battle dress jacket. He said, "I've had it George." I started saying, "Our Father who art in Heaven..." and those around, including Herbert carried on praying. There was a shout to stop firing and we watched Company Quartemaster-Sergeant Andel and the cookhouse party all marching out with a few Germans. The Germans decided to break off the action and went away leaving behind two armoured cars. We had a chance to bandage up the wounded including Herbert who had lots of 'pebble rash' on his back but not serious. As dusk came and it was quiet out front, Regimental Sergeant-Major Page who had a wound in one leg went out to examine the armoured cars and found some maps and that we had been fighting a section of the 21st Panzer unit.'

Padre Davies had helped with the wounded. He had crawled out with morphia to a member of the crew of the anti-tank guns. This man was seriously wounded and the Padre gave him an injection of morphia. He then removed the man's shattered arm with a bayonet and bound up the stump. Despite this aid the wounded man died. Padre Davies was awarded the Military Cross as was Regimental Sergeant-Major Page.

Whilst Captain Ovenden's rearguard party was denying their area of the escarpment to the Germans, the main body of the Battalion was preparing to move from its position on the coastal strip. At 12.00 p.m. news arrived it that the Germans had cut the coast road to the east and that the 50th Division was surrounded. At a conference of company commanders held at 3.00 p.m., Lieutenant-Colonel Battiscombe decided that the Battalion would attempt to break through the enemy lines in three columns: the first, 'D' Company under Major Cummins MC; the second, the composite force left at Bir El Hamam under Captain Ovenden; the third, 'C' Company under Colonel Battiscombe. The route to be taken was south, through the same area as the previous night's raid. Then the columns would turn east and make for Fuka.

At 8.00 p.m. twelve Honey tanks appeared to the west on top of the escarpment overlooking 151 Brigade. These captured British tanks manned by Germans began to make their way down the escarpment with the obvious intention of causing havoc amongst the closely packed transport. Lieutenant-Colonel Battiscombe was talking to Colonel Dewing, the acting Brigadier. Spotting the approaching tanks and realising the danger, the former raced across to a troop of 25 pounders of the 74th Field Regiment, RA, and got them into action immediately, directing the fire himself. The anti-tank gunners of the 8th Battalion and machine-guns of the 2nd Cheshires joined in. One tank was set on fire and two more were stopped, the crews of which were killed when trying to escape. The rest of the German tanks withdrew. It had been a narrow escape.

The danger in which the 50th Division now found itself cannot be overestimated, far more difficult than the Gazala breakout. There had already been heavy losses in vehicles and weapons. The enemy was in close contact and it would be extremely difficult to break away unseen. The Division was faced with German armour not infantry. There was a full moon on the night of 28th-29th June. The route led through ravines and wadis leading off the coastal plain before the open desert could be reached. Furthermore, the enemy was very alert following the raid carried out the previous night. The prospects were not good. The columns were kept deliberately small to improve the chances of slipping through the ring and limited to twenty-five vehicles, each column responsible for its own navigation. Lieutenant-Colonel Battiscombe was shocked to discover that his column had grown to one hundred and thirty vehicles, largely made up of anti-aircraft gunners, machine-gunners and many other leaderless groups that needed to be led if they were to survive. There was no alternative but to take them along.

At 10.30 p.m. the column led by the Intelligence Officer, Lieutenant F.S. Benthall, who was navigating, set off on its perilous journey. The column travelled south for about three and a half miles then turned south west and covered a further four miles. A halt was made and the column was reformed into the usual 'Box' formation for travelling across the desert, that is: vehicles in the middle, trucks with machine-guns and the infantry on the outside. A mile further on, the line of telegraph poles was reached and the column turned to the left to follow this well marked route. Unfortunately at this point, a column of South Africans drove into the 6ths and in the midst of the confusion the Germans opened up with anti-tank and machine-guns. Lieutenant-Colonel Battiscombe's truck was hit and set on fire. After travelling a short distance and with the flames creeping closer, the truck, which was being driven by Lieutenant Wiggins, had to be abandoned. In the darkness, the smoke and dust, the Lieutenant became separated from his CO. Trucks careered past without seeing the stranded officers. Eventually Lieutenant-Colonel Battiscombe scrambled aboard a South African truck loaded with kit and native troops. Lieutenant Wiggins got a lift on Lieutenant Boys-Stones' carrier, which later blew up on a mine and the former was wounded and taken prisoner. Boys-Stones got a lift on another carrier but again ran over a mine and was blown up a second time. He again escaped without injury and got a lift in a truck. He ran into a German unit of the 15th Panzer Division on the 29th June and was captured. Corporal Little's truck was hit and he and his passengers scrambled on to a towed 25 pounder gun. In the melee others who lost their transport scrambled on to anything they could.

The column broke free of the ambush and reformed about a mile south of the enemy position. A mile further on, the leading truck ran into a minefield. The column split up and trucks moved right and left to try to avoid these mines. The CO's truck got through safely, though his personal 8 cwt vehicle was blown up in the minefield along with the driver and his batman, Private Atkinson. The Intelligence Officer's truck also got through but Lieutenant Benthall was severely wounded in the shoulder. By this time vehicles belonging to many formations were mixed up and had stopped in or on the edge of the minefield. A Brigadier took control of the situation. Fit and wounded men were placed on the vehicles still in running condition and the convoy drove on without further mishap. The CO's and IO's trucks had lost contact with the main group and with the former navigating,

drove off into the desert. After twelve miles, the two trucks turned due east to avoid soft sand and travelled four miles on a new bearing. They came across a party of Indian troops of the 10th Indian Division whose truck had been wrecked on a mine. Surplus kit was jettisoned from both vehicles and this party taken on board. Several of the Indians were wounded. The trucks then moved on again. At 5.45 a.m. on the 29th, with an early morning mist, the trucks met up with a small column of the 8th Battalion which included four carriers, under the command of Lieutenant-Colonel Jackson, the Commanding Officer of this Battalion. As the mist lifted, the leading vehicles of the party saw ahead of them the welcome sight of 25 pounder guns with the crews cooking breakfast. Almost too late, it was realised that the crews were Germans of the 15th Panzers who had captured the guns. The trucks drove through the encampment with machine-guns opening up all around them. It was here that Lieutenant Boys-Stones' truck was hit and he and Lieutenant Harriman, who had suffered damage to his ear drums when his vehicle had blown up in the minefield, were taken prisoner. Vehicles in the rear were able to veer off and escape but many of the remainder were captured.

Lieutenant-Colonel Battiscombe, with three or four trucks escaped and moved off in a south-easterly direction. At 2.30 p.m. the column arrived at the 7th Motorised Brigade (South Africans) Advanced Dressing Station about thirty miles south west of El Daba and Lieutenant Benthall and one Indian soldier were evacuated to hospital. The column proceeded for a further seven miles to the east. At 6.30 p.m. the column halted for a meal but owing to reports of enemy units being in the vicinity, it was considered wise to continue travelling through the night. News had also been received that Fuka was now occupied by the enemy. Some difficulty was experienced in negotiating the numerous escarpments and patches of soft sand which were met from time to time. At 3.45 a.m. on the 30th June, the column halted in the region of El Daba. It moved on again, until at 5.00 a.m. it halted for breakfast outside El Daba wire. During the final stages of the drive, three 3 ton lorries had been found abandoned full of canned beer - a welcome prize indeed. At 8.00 a.m. the journey was continued northward for about thirteen miles, where 'D' Company under Major Cummins and part of a column from 151st Brigade HQ were contacted. Major Cummins' party had followed a route slightly westward of that taken by the CO in the journey south from Mersa Matruh and had been fortunate to pass through the enemy without detection. 'D' Company losses during the journey were slight - eight casualties in all. Major Watson described the conditions under which the journey was made:

> 'For those who have been spared the torture of travel in the desert in high summer, it is well nigh impossible to appreciate the exhausting discomfort the men experienced. Hour after hour the cruel sun beats down. The glare is intense. With little water and without shade the passengers are buffeted about as the trucks lurch to and fro. Occasionally on a pan of hard surface speed is fast enough to create a breeze, for the rest of the time clouds of choking dust swirl around each vehicle and cover its cargo, human or otherwise, with a thick layer of sand.'

The exhausted convoy reached the Battalion's collecting point a few miles east of El Haman Station at about 5.45 p.m. A small party of 'C' Company personnel had already arrived and shortly afterwards another small group under the Adjutant, Captain Eardley-Wilmot, joined them. There was precious little time to rest. At 7.30 p.m., a warning order was received from 151 Brigade HQ that the Battalion had to provide a column at two hours' notice, together with supporting arms. 'D' Company under Major Cummins MC was given the task. The company with the anti-tank platoon, under Lieutenant Redway and a small group of HQ personnel, reported to Brigade HQ at 9.00 a.m. on the 1st July. Here it formed part of the 50th Division No.2 Battle Group. Over the next four days this Group moved about from one position to another until settling in the area of Point 96 where it prepared defensive positions. The 6th Battalion personnel rejoined the Battalion at Mareopolis on the 5th July.

Meanwhile at 11.00 a.m. on the 1st July, the remainder of the Battalion, now joined by Captain Ovenden's party and a number of 'A' Company personnel under Captain Wood from Divisional Headquarters, left the area of El Haman and moved eastwards along the track which ran parallel to the railway line. It camped for the night two miles north of Amiriya. It moved again on the

3rd of the month to No. 3 Camp, Mareopolis. The Battalion had suffered very heavy losses since leaving the Gazala Line. About three hundred men were killed, wounded or missing. Casualties amongst the officers included: Lieutenant Cathcart killed, Captain Caldwell (Carrier Platoon), Lieutenants Boys-Stones (Carrier Platoon), Farrell, Harriman, Wiggins (Transport Officer) and Halse (Signal Officer) were missing. Major Ferens' slight wounds had turned septic due to lack of attention during the retreat and he went to hospital. Captain Thomlinson ('C' Company) was wounded but quickly recovered and rejoined the Battalion as Adjutant in place of Captain Eardley-Wilmot, who took over 'C' Company. In addition, Captain Proud ('B' Company) and Lieutenant Benthall were wounded. Captain Kirby took over 'S' or Support Company. The loss of equipment and vehicles was most serious. Only one company had Bren guns. There was in total: one anti-tank gun and two mortars and only four carriers in the Carrier Platoon. There was virtually no transport.

What of the men's morale? Since the beginning of the war they had suffered defeat in France and retreated through Dunkirk. In the desert they had been surrounded and had to fight their way out at Gazala. Within a fortnight they were surrounded yet again and had to break out at Mersa Matruh, this time with heavy losses. Were their superior officers at fault? In the 6th Battalion and this is no doubt true of the Brigade as a whole, the officers retained the faith and respect of the men. Were the Germans, man to man, better soldiers? Was Rommel a super leader, incapable of being defeated? Neither of these seemed to influence the views of the men in the Battalion. The superiority of the Germans as soldiers, the view that they were better than the British, was not recognised. The fault lay not in the lack of fighting qualities of the British troops but their almost complete lack of arms and equipment capable of matching those held by the Germans. Private Jimmy Coglan of the Battalion expressed the commonly held view:

> 'We were better when we got reinforcements and we saw a few tanks with better armourment. We got better guns, better equipment. That's when our morale was the best. What we were fighting with wasn't a patch on what the Germans had. They

were just like pea-shooters to what he had. That's what
demoralised us. Our tanks weren't good enough. They were
only small tanks, no match for the German 88 guns. We started
getting six pounders. We wanted something to fight with. That's
all we wanted.'

CHAPTER 22

THE COMPOSITE BATTALION ACTION - THE ALAMEIN LINE

1942

Mareopolis was not a pleasant place. A flat piece of desert, fly-ridden, it had been condemned long ago and resurrected in the emergency. A small number of huts served as the Battalion office and a mess for the officers. One or two corrugated iron shanties formed the cookhouses. Tents were few in number but were issued over a number of days. Nearby, there was an RAF landing ground. Every time a plane took off or landed a small sandstorm blew up which added to the discomfort of the camp. Its only saving grace was that Mareopolis lay about nineteen miles south-west of Alexandria and this city with its hotels, bars, clubs and shops could be easily reached. Officers and men could get a full day's pass to visit Alexandria and passes for four days' leave began to be issued. A Divisional Leave Camp was established at Sid Bishr, which lay closer to the city.

The 151 Brigade as a whole had suffered severely in the retreat and each Battalion was reorganised on a two company basis with specialist support. The 6th Battalion had 'C' Company under Captain Eardley-Wilmot and 'D' Company under Major Cummins. 'A' Company was now merely the Anti-tank Platoon. 'B' Company was no more having been reorganised to form the Support Company when in the Gazala Line. Support Company was now undergoing training at Mareopolis. Major Watson returned to the Battalion from hospital on the 7th July and brought with him a draft of one hundred and twenty men from the Duke of Cornwall's Light Infantry, The Essex Regiment, The Sussex Regiment and The Welsh Regiment, many of whom were placed in the Signal, Mortar and Carrier Platoons.

On the 11h July, an unexpected straggler turned up. Corporal Hall of the Motor Transport Section had been posted missing since the retreat. He had been captured by the Italians during the Mersa Matruh action. Fighters of the RAF attacked his captors and he and a number of other men got away in the confusion. The party found a portee which was well supplied with petrol, food and water and they drove it off into the desert. Having been told by the Italians that Alexandria had been captured, Corporal Hall and his companions took a wide detour almost as far as Cairo to avoid what they understood to be enemy occupied country.

Major-General J.S. Nichols, DSO, MC, until recently commander of 151 Brigade, succeeded Major-General Ramsden as 50th Division Commander on the 13th July. Brigadier J.S. Percy DSO, MC, was promoted from command of 9 DLI to 151 Brigade Commander. Both new commanders paid visits of inspection to the Battalion in the days that followed. The camp was cleaned up, improvements in the standard of dress and cleanliness of the men were introduced. A Battalion canteen was opened with sufficient supplies of beer for sale. Limited training commenced whilst the arrival of new equipment and vehicles was awaited. A number of officers left on the 24th July on training courses at the Middle East Tactical School.

On reaching the Alamein Line at the beginning of July, Rommel soon realised that his exhausted troops were in no condition to make a major attack on the defences. It was soon quite evident that the British would stand and fight. His lines of supply and communication were stretched and strained to the utmost and his tanks needed urgent attention and reinforcement. The German Commander decided to go on to the defensive and he withdrew his armour for rest, repair and maintenance, leaving the Italian infantry holding the line, supported by a strong anti-tank screen of 88s. His plan then was to strengthen his forces, launch an attack and break through to the Canal before the British, in turn, became stronger. General Auchinleck went on to the offensive, though his depleted and exhausted troops were in no shape to bring success. The counter-attacks which were launched gained little advantage and, it could be argued, only added to losses in men and equipment already in desperate short supply. This was certainly true of the attack which involved the battalions of 151 Brigade. This followed counter-attacks launched by the 9th Australian Division and the reorganised South African Division on the 9th-10 July and the 69th Brigade on the 20th of the month, neither of which achieved a great deal.

On the evening of the 24th July, a warning order was received from 151 Brigade that the Battalion was to supply a company which would be ready to move at two hours notice. 'D' Company, the one company which had survived the retreat virtually intact, was chosen for this operation along with supporting arms. Major Cummins MC was in command with Lieutenant Dennis as his second-in-command. A Composite Battalion from 151 Brigade was formed for this operation under the command of Lieutenant-Colonel Battiscombe of the 6th. The Battalion was made up of the following:

Second-in-Command:	Captain R. Ovenden (6 DLI).
Adjutant:	Lieutenant J.M. Jackson (6 DLI).
Intelligence Officer:	Second-Lieutenant C. Harker (6 DLI).
Signal Officer:	Lieutenant G.W. Butler (6 DLI).
'A' Company - 9 DLI:	Captain A. Hartnell.
'B' Company - 8 DLI:	Captain R. I. Pitt.
'D' Company - 6 DLI:	Major R.L. Cummins MC.
Support Company - 6 DLI	Captain M.J. Kirby.

Lieutenant-Colonel Battiscombe received his orders from Brigadier E.C. Cooke-Collis, DSO, of the 69 Brigade, on the morning of the 27th July. The attack was to be made by the 5th East Yorkshire Regiment, a Battalion of the 24th Australian Brigade and the Composite Battalion of The Durham Light Infantry. The 6th Green Howards was echeloned back on the left and as the attack progressed it would lay a minefield guarded by anti-tank guns to protect that flank. The Australian attack was planned to come in at right angles to that of the Composite Battalion and both battalions sent an officer to the other to establish contact with the objective of minimising the risk of either battalion firing on the other. Tanks and artillery would be in support.

The objective was Sanyet el Miteiriya in the central sector and the ridge running north-west from it. The Composite Battalion objective was a prominent ridge, known locally as 'Ruin Ridge' because of many failed attacks which had been made against it. This ridge ran roughly east and west and jutted out into the enemy defence line. It was strongly held by Italian and German infantry with well dug-in positions on the slopes and protected by an extensive minefield all round the foot of the ridge. The Battalion would attack the south-eastern slopes of the ridge whilst the Australians attacked the north-eastern slopes. If the ridge was taken and held, there was talk of a break through by armoured formations and the possibility of driving the enemy back out of Egypt and beyond. High hopes, but the reality of the current British situation was that there were never sufficient reserves available nor was the 8th Army in good fighting condition to make such an objective anything more than wishful thinking.

The Composite Battalion arrived at El Dakar, east of El Alamein Station, on the 26th July. The Commanding Officer held a conference with his officers at 5.30 p.m. and orders were given out. Each Bren gun would have fifteen magazines of ammunition. Each rifleman would carry one hundred rounds of ammunition, one hand grenade and four empty sandbags. The Battalion would attack with the forward companies of 6 DLI, on the left and 8 DLI on the right and that of 9 DLI in reserve. South African engineers were given the task of clearing a gap through the minefield. The gap would be marked with shielded lights.

By 11.10 p.m. on the 26th the Battalion had formed up in the assembly area, after one or two delays en route. These delays resulted in a postponement of the attack of thirty minutes and the men had to lie down on the start line for about an hour, becoming colder and more apprehensive as time passed. At 1.45 a.m. the artillery bombardment commenced and for fifteen minutes the most intensive barrage experienced so far by the men of the Battalion fell on the German and Italian positions. The noise was deafening. After fifteen minutes it stopped as abruptly as it had begun. It was 2.00 a.m. and in the silence the Australian infantry could be heard cheering as they stormed their objective. The advance of the Durham Battalion had been held back, probably by the delays experienced in moving up to the start line. It had lost the advantage of the barrage. The enemy now out of their holes in the ground were ready for them. The Battalion began its advance in open formation. Almost from the outset it came under machine-gun and artillery fire. The enemy minefield lay in a slight hollow but the approach to it lay over high ground which was exposed to enemy observation and fire. As a result some casualties were suffered before the minefield was reached. On reaching the minefield it was discovered that the South African engineers had not cleared a gap due to the fact that they had come under very heavy enemy machine-gun fire which pinned them to the ground. Second-Lieutenant Harker, the Battalion Intelligence Officer, went forward with some of the mine-lifting party to make a reconnaissance but was soon wounded and evacuated by the South Africans. Under a deafening retaliatory enemy barrage, the two forward companies advanced across the minefield led by Lieutenant-Colonel Battiscombe. They kept going as many men fell under the barrage until within two hundred yards of the enemy positions when, firing rifles, Tommy guns and Brens from the hip, they charged cheering and shouting into the enemy positions. The defensive fire lessened at this point and the enemy infantry was seen running back up the slope of the ridge. 'D' Company, 6th DLI, gave chase and rushed one post with the bayonet. A number of prisoners were taken.

At this moment in the action, 5th East Yorks having lost direction, blundered into the company of 9th DLI, causing some confusion. 'D' Company got separated from the rest of the Battalion and contact with it was never really regained. 'B' Company, 8th Battalion, had reached its objective with thirty-five out of the ninety-seven men who had started out. Some 9th DLI men joined them. They had six Bren guns with a few magazines, one 2in. mortar and one anti-tank rifle. Wireless communication had broken down with rear headquarters and Lieutenant Butler was sent back on foot to try to regain contact. After a long wait and with no sign of communications being restored, Captain Hartnell of 9th Battalion DLI was sent back. Neither of these two officers succeeded in reaching the rear nor were heard of again. There was no sign of the supporting British tanks and when German tanks ultimately appeared, the situation became desperate indeed.

The situation at the minefield gap was no better. The Brigade signal truck travelling with HQ Company and rear Battalion Headquarters attracted enemy fire and was, for a time, sheltered in a fold in the ground. At 3.30 a.m., Captain Ovenden the second-in-command, and the acting Adjutant, Lieutenant J.M. Jackson, together with a small party reached the minefield gap and were able to straighten out the confusion caused by the mix up between the East Yorks and the company of 9th DLI. The area of the minefield gap was under heavy fire from enemy machine and anti-tank guns. A corporal of 'D' Company returned to the gap with twenty-eight German and Italian prisoners and reported that the forward companies were attacking with the bayonet. In the heat of battle few prisoners were being taken. Captain Ovenden's party moved through the gap and in the general direction of the attack. A runner was sent back to bring up the Brigade signal truck. At 3.50 a.m. the signal truck, with a small escorting party of Headquarters' personnel under the command of the Company Sergeant-Major, together with an Australian patrol, passed through the minefield gap and moved to within a few hundred yards of the first road. On hearing a command to fire given in English and the sound of Bren guns firing, the group altered direction and travelled a further eight hundred yards before coming under very heavy machine-gun fire. The party retaliated with rifle fire. However, in the face of intense machine-gun fire and suffering some casualties, the party withdrew to the minefield gap. Captain Ovenden's party had experienced a similar situation. They had almost reached the first road but could see no signs of the forward companies. It was impossible to continue under intense enemy fire and it was forced to withdraw. Lieutenant Jackson was wounded. It was now obvious that the forward companies had reached their objectives but were surrounded by the enemy.

At daybreak a slight mist obscured visibility. Outside the minefield the Support Company awaited developments. Captain Kirby was ready to lead the anti-tank screen forward to the objective. Captain Ovenden, well aware of the strength of enemy opposition in the area of the minefield gap, ordered that carriers be sent forward to reconnoitre the situation before any other move was made. This was done but two carriers were quickly knocked out by enemy anti-tank guns. On the left, it could be seen that carriers of the East Yorks were also suffering casualties. At 10.00 a.m. Captain Ovenden was ordered by the Brigade Major of 69 Brigade, to collect his entire party, stragglers and the Support Company to go through the gap and reinforce the forward companies. This move would commence as soon as the British armour had mopped up the area. Captain Ovenden waited but the tanks did not put in an appearance until 12.30 p.m. Apparently, the tank commander objected to the width of the minefield gap which he considered too narrow for his tanks to pass through. At 2.30 p.m. the tank commander reported that there were three 88mm anti-tank guns covering the minefield gap which had knocked out two of his tanks and as a result the attack was held up. The tanks withdrew behind the start line and started shelling from there.

Without support, the three forward companies on Ruin Ridge had no hope of survival. The men were becoming exhausted under the heat of the desert sun and ammunition was running out. The few survivors of 'D' Company, still under Major Cummins, were on their own. About sixty men of the companies of 8th and 9th DLI, under Lieutenant-Colonel Battiscombe, with three Bren guns and one anti-tank rifle, held on and prepared to meet what must be the final enemy attack. At daybreak, two self-propelled guns had moved to within two hundred yards of their positions. These were engaged and both were knocked out. A captured British tank now manned by Germans appeared shortly afterwards. It was roughly handled and the crew wounded and taken prisoner. Small groups of German infantry were observed creeping nearer the British positions. By 9.30 a.m. the heat and lack of food and water were beginning to have an effect upon the survivors. On a number of occasions Germans had approached the Durhams, obviously unaware of the exact location of their positions. These lay on the reverse side of the slope and out of enemy observation. Away to the right, the men watched the enemy counter-attack against the Australians who were suffering heavy losses at the hands of the German tanks and anti-tank guns. The Australians were forced to withdraw under cover of the tanks of 50th Royal Tank Regiment, who also suffered severe casualties.

On the Durhams' front there were no signs of tank support. A captured jeep driven by a German officer appeared in front of the Battalion's positions. He stopped about four hundred yards away. On being fired on he quickly drove away and escaped. The Germans now knew where the British positions lay. Twenty minutes later a group of about thirty German tanks closely followed by infantry moved across the Battalion's front and commenced to circle round the flanks into the rear of the positions. The British had no anti-tank weapons to hit back with. The men lay flat on the sand hoping they would not be seen. Two Mark III tanks closed in to about a hundred and fifty yards and opened fire. In the hail of bullets many men were killed or wounded. There was no hope, no way of fighting back. After another burst of firing, men stood up and surrendered. Very few men returned through the minefield gap to safety. The three Durham companies had fought with considerable gallantry and the enemy had learnt that the fighting spirit of the British soldier was not exhausted. However, the action left a bitter taste in the mouths of officers and men of 151 Brigade. Experienced soldiers who had come through the Gazala and Mersa Matruh breakouts had been sacrificed in an action for which there appeared to be little object. They would have been better spared to fight at Alamein.

At 8.00 p.m. a general withdrawal was ordered, covered by smoke. At the same time enemy tanks appeared on the high ground beyond the minefield and began to shell the withdrawing forces. What was left of the Composite Battalion withdrew through the lines of the 1st South African Brigade and moved back to El Dakar where it arrived at 10.30 p.m. For the next two days the Battalion remained here collecting stragglers until on the 29th July, it moved back to No. 3 Camp Mareopolis.

Casualties had been very heavy. It was thought that Lieutenant-Colonel Battiscombe had been killed as he was seen to fall during the fighting. Fortunately a bullet had hit his belt buckle which had caused him to fall. It was later learned that he, Major Cummins and Lieutenant Dennis were prisoners. Lieutenant Butler was missing. As Major Watson, who succeeded Lieutenant-Colonel Battiscombe in command of 6th Battalion, was absent on a course, Major Ovenden assumed temporary command. Major Ovenden was promoted on the 30th July, the same day that he learned he had been awarded the Military Cross, along with Regimental Sergeant-Major Page, for the action at Mersa Matruh.

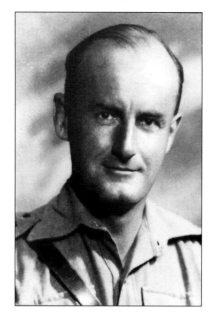

Lieutenant Colonel W.I. Watson.
Commanded the Battalion from July, 1942 to August, 1943. Colonel Watson's papers covering the history of the Volunteers and 6th Battalion form much of the basis of this book

For most of August the Battalion was refitting, receiving drafts and training. Fourteen new officers joined and drafts of NCOs and other ranks were received from The King's Own Regiment and elsewhere. Captain Cole received the immediate award of the Military Cross on the 12th August, this for his gallant leadership of the Carrier Platoon referred to above. Major Watson returned from his course and learned of his appointment as Acting Lieutenant-Colonel and command of the Battalion, an appointment his father had held from 1911 to 1914. The Battalion could only raise two rifle companies and a Support Company. Captain Graham Wood, commanded 'A' Company and Captain A.N. Eardley-Wilmot had 'C' Company. Major Ovenden commanded 'HQ' Company and Captain M.J. Kirby Support

Company. Padre Davies left the Battalion and was succeeded by Padre Garbutt. Captain Joy left to join the staff of a hospital and was replaced by Captain Gibson RAMC.

In August, important changes were made in the Middle East Command. General Auchinleck was replaced by General Alexander as Commander-in-Chief Middle East and General Gott was given command of the 8th Army. Tragically, General Gott was killed when the plane carrying him to take up his appointment was attacked and shot down by enemy fighters. He was replaced by Lieutenant-General B.L. Montgomery. The effect of General Montgomery on the 8th Army was considerable. All talk of further retreat was banned. The Army would stay where it was, fight where it was and if necessary, die where it was. However, with the promise of considerable reinforcements and new weapons and materials, General Montgomery told his troops that Rommel would be thrown out of North Africa. Of the expected attack from Rommel, he said that he would not be happy if it came within the next two weeks but after that he would welcome it. The enemy attack expected late in August would be defeated and then it would be the British turn to take the offensive but not until he was ready. The General visited his Army to talk to officers and men and tell them what was going to happen. Two new Corps Commanders were brought in. General Sir Oliver Leese CB, CBE,DSO, replaced General Ramsden commanding XXX Corps and General Sir Brian Horrocks MC to command XIII Corps. There was a strengthening air of purpose and confidence about this 'new' 8th Army.

As late August, approached the expectancy of a German attack grew. The 25th of the month onwards, when the moon would be full, were the critical dates. In the event that the Germans might use parachutists to seize landing grounds around Mareopoli, 151

Brigade was given the task of protecting a number of these air strips. 151 Brigade left the 50th Division on the 22nd August and came under the command of 12 Anti-Aircraft Brigade. The 6th Battalion had the task of looking after three landing grounds, 97, 98 and 99. Under command was 'A' Company, 5th East Yorks, as an immediate reserve and 'B' Company of the same Regiment as reserve for Landing Grounds 98 and 99. Support Company was 'dismounted' so as to become a temporary rifle company to enable the Battalion to provide a flying column for each landing ground. 9th DLI had a similar role whilst 8th DLI along with some RAF armoured cars, the 10th Hussars, Royal Warwickshire Yeomanry, Poona Horse and a battalion of Free French, made up a Brigade reserve, available to respond to any call for assistance.

There were enemy air attacks on the landing grounds on the nights of 28th, 29th and 31st August. The Battalion took part in a number of anti-parachutist exercises, some of which annoyed the RAF as they involved vehicles tearing across their precious landing strips in pursuit of the 'enemy' and causing some damage to the surfaces on which planes had to land and take off. However, relationships with the RAF were on the whole good and the Battalion's spirits were much uplifted as the increasing strength of the Air Force became apparent.

The expected attack by Rommel took place on the night of 30th-31st August and his plan of attacking through the southern sector of the front and turning north, much as he had done at Gazala, was exactly as Montgomery and his predecessor Auchinleck had predicted. The key to the defence was Alam Halfa Ridge in the rear of the Alamein Line. This ridge was put into a state of great strength and it was Montgomery's plan to draw Rommel's Afrika Corps on to these defences. The bulk of the British armour took up position in this area. During the night the 15th and 21st Panzer Divisions thrust between the New Zealand Division's positions in the extreme south of the Alamein Line and a conspicuous hill at the top of the Qattara Depression, known as Qaret el Hameimat. They were followed by the 90th Light Division and the Italian Ariete and Littorio Divisions and Trieste Motorised Division. The attacks on Alam Halfa were smashed. Now caught in a vulnerable position with fuel supplies running short and pounded by the RAF and British tanks and

Leave group in Egypt. *Private Jack 'Ginger' Avery, centre rear, Private Jim Coglan, MM, front left, Corporal Reg Haseley (awarded the DCM and MM), centre front.*

artillery, Rommel was forced to withdraw, having sustained heavy losses. On the night of 3rd-4th September, the New Zealand Division was launched southwards in an attempt to cut

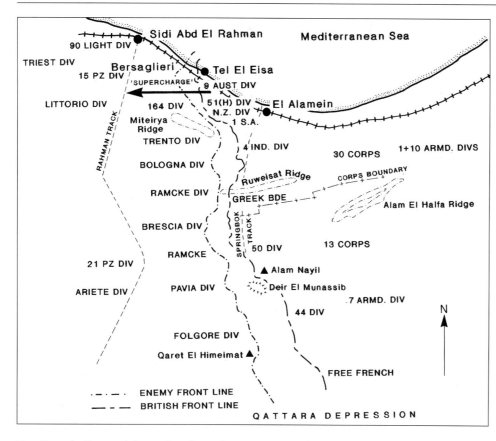

The Alamein Line and Operation Supercharge. *151 Brigade was moved North for Operation Supercharge which took place on the night of the 1st-2nd November, 1942.*

behind the Alamein Line proper just north of El Ruweisat Station, on some high ground called El Qasimiya. The move commenced on the following day and the positions when entered were found to be well dug. It was, however, a very dusty area on a prominent feature which could be easily observed by the enemy and subjected to shelling. On the 3rd, another warning order was received to the effect that the Battalion was to move into the Alamein Line on the following day. The New Zealanders launched their attack, referred to above, on the 3rd-4th September. The Brigade was to move into their vacated positions. Lieutenant-Colonel Bill Watson wrote in his diary:

'The NZ Division doesn't seem to know much about us. Two of their Battalions are to do a night attack, later that night and we are expected to come up and take their place in the line. All rather vague as no one seems to know exactly where. A distinctly unhealthy spot as there is little cover for practically no digging can be done as the ground is hard as iron.'

On the 4th, the Battalion moved into its new area. Fortunately a sandstorm was blowing all afternoon and the movement was made without enemy interference. The New Zealanders pointed out that the Durhams had been fortunate to move in under cover of the sand as the line was constantly under enemy observation and a very unhealthy place during the daylight hours. Some shelling took place later in the day and Corporal Williams of the Orderly Room was wounded. On the Battalion right was the 25th New Zealand Battalion, with 9th DLI on the left. A few days later, 8th DLI took over from the New Zealanders, on the elbow

off the retreat by closing the gap the enemy had come through. This attack failed and the enemy finally occupied in the south the line of Deir el Angar - Deir el Munassib - Himeimat. The British had won a considerable victory which would ensure that the enemy would be unable to launch any major attack before Montgomery was ready for his offensive.

On the 1st September, a warning order was received from 151 Brigade Headquarters that a move was to be made to an area

bend formed when Rommel had taken up his final positions after his retreat at the beginning of the month. Part of 8th DLI faced south-west, the remainder echeloned backwards to face south. 6th and 9th DLI faced south, a long frontage running along the top of a ridge. All three rifle companies were forward with

Dawn in the Alamein Line. *Early morning shave in a foxhole position*

platoon posts on the exposed slopes and Battalion HQ on the reverse. The Battalion still had two rifle companies with the 5th

East Yorks under Major Edgar making up a third. In the area of the right hand company was a small hill called Alam Nayil. Whilst heavily shelled, it afforded a good view of the surrounding desert. The minefield ran east to west along the foot of the ridge. Another ran southwards at right angles to the Italian positions some two thousand yards away. This was called the Don Minefield. A similar minefield ran southwards from the centre of the 8th Battalion's front. This one was called the Volga Minefield. Between these two minefields, the area was known as the 'Steppes' and this saw much patrol activity. A scattered assortment of damaged and destroyed vehicles lay out in No Man's Land, the result of the abortive New Zealand assault. Beyond the minefields protecting the enemy positions were the depressions of Deir Munassib and Deir Alinda with their almost perpendicular sides into which he had dug a system of strong trenches and dugouts. Only the most accurate shelling and mortaring could hope to damage any of these fortifications.

Captain (QM) Runciman with 'B' Echelon was well behind the front line about five miles from the sea. Each night he brought up food, water and mail, all vital to the welfare of the soldier. Rations at El Alamein were quite good. A NAAFI was established at Burgh el Anab and Alexandria was not far away. Breakfast was often bacon, eggs, sausages and beans, with tea. Bully beef and biscuits sufficed for the meal in the heat of midday. At night 'Maconochies', 'M & V' - tinned meat and vegetable stew - with tinned fruit and tea formed the supper. Water was plentiful and sometimes a can of American beer or a bottle of 'Stella' ale was available.

The Brigade came under the command of the 44th Division until the 10th October. General Horrocks and General Hughes, the GOC 44th Division, visited the Battalion on the 7th September. General Horrocks impressed everyone he met with his charming and friendly personality. He fully explained the reasons why Rommel lost the battle and impressed upon the officers that they must talk to their men and explain what was happening. He also impressed upon commanders the importance of fitness. General Montgomery himself visited the Battalion on the 13th September, when he made a considerable impression. He pointed out that he realised the Brigade needed training but

meanwhile it had a job to do to hold the line. General Horrocks followed again on the 26th of the month and impressed upon all commanding officers that they must try to train their battalions as much as possible. The visits of the great and small continued from time to time but one was of particular interest when two South African pilots spent a few days in the line with the Battalion. After experiencing the shelling and having gone on patrol through the minefield, they decided it was best to stay in the air - it was much safer.

Daylight carrier patrols were immediately organised under the alternative command of Captain Cole MC and Second-Lieutenant Pringle. These patrols found that minefield gaps were covered by enemy anti-tank and machine-guns. They also discovered that the Italians now facing them were made of sterner stuff than those met so far in the campaign. They were part of the Folgore Division of parachutists, tough and well trained. Air activity was quite considerable as the RAF gradually gained the ascendancy over the battlefield. Alam Nayil was bombed by Stukas on the 7th September and air raids were carried out from time to time until the Luftwaffe was driven from the skies. In addition to carrier patrols, reconnaissance and protective patrols were organised.

To meet the demands of training it was decided to withdraw each company at a time for a four day period. Each company would then leave the rear positions for a six mile march through the Heliopolis Gap in the minefields at the rear of the line and there on an appropriate strip of desert undertake training exercises. The company would return in the evening as the sun set to enable them to get back without attracting enemy shelling.

To describe every patrol action is beyond the compass of this book but one or two incidents will give the reader an idea of the type of activity which was going on day by day throughout the Battalion's stay in the line. Early in September, a figure was seen crawling into a slit trench near two derelict Valentine tanks in the minefield. A patrol under Captain J.H. Chapman of twelve other ranks and one sapper, investigated the two tanks. One was found to be carefully sandbagged and the light on the dashboard was on. The obvious conclusion was that the tank was being used as an observation post. The patrol commander placed explosive charges in the tank. An unpleasant surprise for the next enemy observers to use the tank. Our patrols ranged far and wide observing and attacking enemy working parties and probing for any weaknesses in their defences. Lieutenant-Colonel Watson wrote:

> 'Nightly we provided a protective patrol along the front of the 8th Battalion. I call it the Nursery Slopes and every junior officer had to do it. If he fails he does it the second night ... To show he has done it he has to bring in some of the weapons and salvage lying out...'

There were casualties. On the night of the 27th September, a protective patrol under Lieutenant Cox of the 5th East Yorks encountered eight enemy soldiers. Lieutenant Cox and one member of the patrol went forward to investigate and were greeted by the cry 'Surrender'. The patrol commander immediately ordered the patrol to open fire and grenades were thrown at the enemy. In the fire fight which followed, Lieutenant Cox was wounded and left for dead. A sergeant and another man of the patrol were also wounded. The patrol was ordered to withdraw by the sergeant and on reaching the Battalion lines it was found that one man was missing. This man was Lieutenant Cox's batman. Lieutenant Cox himself regained consciousness a few hours after the action and managed to walk and crawl to the 8th Battalion lines. Strong patrols were sent out to look for the missing man, one of them suffering more casualties. The missing man was not found.

No Man's Land contained the destroyed and damaged vehicles and weaponry of the New Zealand attack. Recovery patrols went out to save what they could. On the 23rd of the month for example, a carrier and a 2 pounder anti-tank gun were brought in though these were lying about two thousand yards from the front positions. On the 25th, Lieutenant Redway's patrol brought back three carriers, two Bren guns, two anti-tank rifles, one Besa, a 2in. mortar and ammunition. All types of patrol, which were active day and night, gathered important information which, when added to photographs taken from the air, helped to plot the layout and dispositions of the enemy. This information was of great value later when offensive actions commenced.

New drafts meant for the Brigade, who had little or no experience, were held for training at Dekheila, near Alexandria. Here, Major Ovenden and Lieutenants Bluitt, Fenton and Green, and Second-Lieutenant Dunlop, prepared for the line those drafts earmarked for the 6th Battalion. On the morning of the 3rd October, an electric storm, preceded by a heavy dust storm and followed by torrential rain and hail, flooded the slit trenches and dugouts. No one seemed to mind as it was a great relief from the fierce sun. On the following day, the new drafts arrived from the training area under Major Ovenden. 'A' Company was reformed from these drafts and this allowed 'A' Company, 5th East Yorks to return to its own Battalion. Three quarters of the draft were from the South Lancashire Regiment. On the night of the 4th, a protective patrol went out and moved down the Don Minefield to opposite the Washington Gap, where it found the body of Lieutenant Cox's batman. He had been shot through the chest and lay facing the enemy positions, gripping his sub-machine-gun, its magazine empty. He had died fighting. The following night, Padre Nesbitt, the Roman Catholic priest with the 8th Battalion, went out with a patrol and buried this soldier where he lay. A cross was erected over his grave. Active patrolling went on. There were occasional clashes with the enemy resulting in casualties on both sides. On one patrol on the 24th October, Captain T. ff. Chamberlain and one Sapper, the latter from 505 Field Company, RE, were reported missing following a clash with an Italian patrol which was lying in ambush. A patrol out on the night of the 25th/26th October found both bodies which were brought back for burial. Captain Chamberlain was a regular soldier who had joined the 6th Battalion before the war. Later he had left but had returned to the Battalion; a much respected officer and another sad loss to add to the many officers and men who had lost their lives since the war had begun.

CHAPTER 23
THE BATTLE OF ALAMEIN - OPERATION SUPERCHARGE
1942

By the middle of October the build up of the 8th Army had reached its peak. Reinforcements were pouring into Egypt. New tanks, many of which were the new Shermans from America, gave General Montgomery a superiority of nearly two to one over those of the enemy. Montgomery held a similar superiority in men, growing to nearly four to one if compared only with the German soldiers available to Rommel. His artillery was not only stronger in numbers but had been trained to a very high standard of efficiency. There were considerable reserves of ammunition. The Luftwaffe had lost control of the skies and the British troops were greatly heartened by the sight of Boston, Baltimore and Mitchell bombers streaming west to drop their lethal loads on the enemy positions and lines of communication. Rommel's army lay at the end of an exceedingly long and tenuous supply line stretching back to Tripoli. It was vulnerable to raids from the air and desert. A large proportion of his supplies were being lost attempting to cross the Mediterranean. He was particularly short of fuel. His army, however, though weary and short of many essential supplies, was still a potent fighting force. It was protected from the 8th Army by nearly half a million mines and a screen of what was still the most feared of all anti-tank guns, the German 88s. Rommel had been a sick man for some time and had been obliged to return to Germany to recuperate. He was away when the great blow fell and battle was joined on the night of the 23rd-24th October.

The British 8th Army was now organised in three Corps: XXX Corps was commanded by Lieutenant-General Sir Oliver Leese with the 51st Highland Division, 2nd New Zealand Division, 9th Australian Division, 4th Indian Division and 1st South African Division with Corps Artillery, armoured and supporting arms. XIII Corps was commanded by Lieutenant-General Sir Brian Horrocks with the 7th Armoured Division, 44th Infantry Division and 50th Infantry Division with the 1st Greek Brigade attached. Under command of the 7th Armoured Division were 1st and 2nd Free French Brigade and 1st Free French Flying Column. Corps Artillery and supporting arms completed the Corps structure. X Corps was commanded by Lieutenant-General Herbert Lumsden with 1st and 10th Armoured Divisions and artillery and supporting arms. XXX Corps held the northern part of the Alamein Line, XIII Corps the southern part and X Corps was assembled to the east behind XXX Corps.

General Montgomery's plan was to reinforce Rommel's belief that the 8th Army would attack on the south flank and then hook north to engage his armour. This is what Rommel had done at Gazala and Alam Halfa. It was very much the way that the armies had fought each other in the desert to date. The southern open flank was always considered the most vulnerable. The British, Rommel considered, would do the same. Montgomery strengthened this belief by building dummy tank formations, fuel and ammunition dumps, behind his southern positions in the days leading up to the outbreak of the battle. He intended to attack with XIII Corps in the south to draw the main German Panzers to the southern front. The real blow would come in the centre and north where it was planned that XXX Corps would breach the minefields and open up a corridor to enable the strongly armoured X Corps to pass through and engage

Rommel's armour in the open desert and there destroy it.

Gen Montgomery spoke to all officers down to Lieutenant-Colonel on the two days 19th and 20th October. He gave his listeners a remarkably clear and concise description of his plan of campaign, spoken without the aid of a single note. He stated that there would be a 'dog fight' or 'killing match' which would be severe and would last perhaps for ten days. He emphasised that everyone taking part must be fired with drive and enthusiasm and the main aim was to kill Germans. He left no one in doubt that his army would defeat the enemy. On the 21st and 22nd October the men of the 8th Army were told the plan and their part in it. Leave was immediately stopped. All that was left to do was to wait for Zero Hour.

The Battle of El Alamein commenced at 9.40 p.m. on the 23rd October, 1942, with the heaviest bombardment from British Artillery yet experienced in the Second World War. At 10.00 p.m. the infantry of the 9th Australian, 51st Highland, 2nd New Zealand and 1st South African Divisions of XXX Corps advanced to attack the enemy infantry positions behind their immensely strong minefields. Although the infantry took their objectives in a number of places the armour following ran into difficulties and were halted by the mines and the screen of dreaded 88s and other anti-tank guns.

In the south, XIII Corps attacked at the same time. 44th Division was to attack and break through the minefield connecting the Munassib Depression with the prominent hill called Himeimat, on the edge of the Qattara Depression. As soon as the bridgehead was secured, the 7th Armoured Division was to pass through, turn right and roll up the enemy defences in the rear of the Munassib Depression. At this point, 50th Division was to attack the Munassib Depression frontally with 69 Brigade on the south and 151 Brigade on the north, to a depth of about 1200 yards. 50th Division would not attack until 7th Armoured was established in the rear of the Munassib Depression. The 151 Brigade plan included sending 6th Battalion silently through the night to take up a position on the plateau north of the Munassib Depression and east of the main enemy minefield so as to able to dominate the Depression when dawn broke. A second Battalion of the Brigade was to be ready at dawn to mop up the enemy positions on the north side of the Depression in co-operation with the 69 Brigade. Further north beyond the 8th Battalion was the 1st Greek Brigade whose task it was to make a raid into the enemy positions to pin down enemy reserves in that sector. The Greek Brigade had already established a reputation for carrying out enthusiastic raids into the enemy lines.

During the night 23rd-24th October as the battle raged in the north, patrols from the 6th Battalion went out to find details of the enemy defences in the area the Battalion was to move to if the attacks of 44th Infantry and 7th Armoured Divisions were successful. British artillery put down a harassing fire on the east end of the Angar Depression and enemy positions on the northern tip of the Munassib Depression, between the Don and Volga Minefields. Lieutenant Pringle, out with carriers and 3in. mortars, put down a harassing fire on enemy positions on the northern tip of the Munassib Depression in order to create a diversion during a raid on North Point by 9th DLI. This raid failed as did one by 69 Brigade on the area known as the Twins. The Signals Officer, Lieutenant J.A. Wedgewood and the Intelligence Officer, Second-Lieutenant G.E. Mansell reconnoitred the position in No Man's Land which would be occupied by Battalion Headquarters in the event of the operation allotted to the Battalion being carried out. Signal cable was taken out and concealed in the desert, as were twenty-four hours' emergency rations. Sappers opened a new gap in the Don Minefield and the minefield in front of 'D' Company.

44th Division failed to breach the enemy minefields and the 7th Armoured Division was unable to break through and carry out its task. The 6th Battalion's action was, therefore, postponed. Throughout the 24th, fierce fighting could be heard from the area between the Munassib Depression and Himeimat as the 44th Division strove to break through. On the 25th October a patrol of two sections of carriers under Lieutenant P.B. Hodgson went out at first light to look for any signs of enemy withdrawal in the area of the Volga Minefield and to try to find the men missing from patrol which had gone out on the previous night under Captain Chamberlain, referred to above. The patrol moved to the Jarrow Gap, turned south as far as Barnard Gap and came under heavy enemy shell fire and had to withdraw. Over the next three days active patrolling continued until on the 28th news was received that the Brigade was to move out of its present positions and come into Army Reserve that night and move northwards. The Battalion relief by advance parties of the 2nd Free French Brigade began at 3.00 p.m. An evening meal was provided and as completed each section quietly moved back and formed up in darkness to await transport. This arrived and at 9.00 p.m. the convoy moved off via the Heliopolis Gap, 'C' Track, Beachy Head, down the Bombay Road to an area near the Mediterranean Sea which it reached at 3.00 a.m. on the 29th October.

Fierce and sustained fighting had continued in the north since the battle began but a final corridor had not been opened to allow X Corps to break out into the desert. 'Operation Supercharge' was planned to take place on the night of 31st October-1st November, later postponed for twenty-four hours and 151 Brigade was to play a vital role in this assault. The plan was for 151 Brigade attacking on the right and 152 Brigade, 51st Highland Division, attacking on the left, to punch a hole through the minefield and enemy positions as far as the Rahman Track, about five thousand yards from the starting line. The armour of X Corps would then be able to pour through the corridor into the open desert beyond. The Rahman Track stretched from the mosque at Sidi El Rahman on the coast to the oasis at Bahariya in the desert to the south-west. Its route was marked by a line of telegraph poles. The advance would be made in two phases; the first to an intermediate objective, three thousand five hundred yards forward of the Start Line. When this was reached the attacking Brigades would pause for half an hour to reorganise for the second phase advance to the final objective. The enemy opposing the Brigades were battered but far from defeated and fought tenaciously to hold their positions. They were the German 90th Light and 164 Divisions, the Italian Trento Infantry and Littorio Armoured Divisions.

The artillery support for 'Operation Supercharge' was an immense concentration of guns for such a narrow front of attack. There were thirteen field and two medium regiments of artillery, about three hundred and fifty guns, which would fire a creeping barrage, starting from the forward positions of the Australian infantry who would vacate their positions before the bombardment began. The bombardment was timed to move forward one hundred yards every two minutes in front of the advancing troops. Further support would come from the 8th Royal Tank Regiment with a squadron of Sherman Tanks. Each Battalion would also have the support of a platoon from the 4th New Zealand machine-gun Company and a troop of the Northumberland Yeomanry with their anti-tank guns. The terrain over which the advance would be made was flat and open with a very slight rise to the stony, barren waste of the Track. Sappers opened a corridor through the enemy minefield which had been identified but other mines immediately behind these minefields had been laid by the enemy and these were not marked. The mines were thought to be mainly for tanks and the infantry was ordered to advance straight through this unmarked minefield taking a risk that casualties would be light. The enemy positions were strong and supported by dug-in tanks and self-propelled guns. A strong 'Box' of 88s dominated the area to be attacked, which lay west of Tel el Eisa Station. The success of this operation was vital to the outcome of the Battle of El Alamein as it would open up the final corridor to enable X Corps, concentrated immediately behind the attacking Brigades, to carry out its tasks.

Bofors guns firing red tracer marked the boundaries between the two Brigades and assisted in keeping direction. 151 Brigade was now under the command of the 2nd New Zealand Division for this action. The 28th (Maori) Battalion of this Division was to put in a local attack to protect the right flank of the Brigade. Brigadier Percy's plan was for the 8th Battalion to attack on the right, the 9th on the left while 6th Battalion followed about five hundred yards in the rear mopping up any isolated enemy posts left by the two forward battalions. During the pause at the end of the first phase when the 6th should have advanced about two thousand five hundred yards, the Battalion was to make a right wheel facing north, whilst the other two Battalions faced west, so forming two sides of the bridgehead.

The Battalion arrived at the lying up area about 3.30 a.m. on 29th October, and quickly settled down for the rest of the night. On the following day, Lieutenant-Colonel Watson attended a

Brigade conference when the Brigade plan, as outlined above, was revealed. The Brigadier emphasised how essential it was for the leading Battalions to keep up with the creeping barrage. Meanwhile, the Battalion prepared for battle: ammunition, water and rations were issued; letters and papers which might disclose the identity of the unit were destroyed or parcelled up by their owners and left with 'B' Echelon. Weapons were cleaned and checked. At 9.00 p.m., the Battalion moved via Star Track, which ran parallel to the railway line, to a new lying up area, south-east of Tel El Eisa Station. It was a nightmare journey as the vehicles, without lights and visibility, almost totally obscured by the clouds of dust, lumbered along the Track only to find that the area allocated to them for the overnight stop was already occupied. The vehicles had to pull off the track and the men had to sleep where they were. On the morning of 31st October, Brigadier Percy held another conference with his Commanding Officers and informed them that the attack had been put off for twenty-four hours and would now take place on the night of the 1st-2nd November. This delay was welcome to the Battalion as it give it more time to make final preparations.

About midday, Lieutenant-Colonel Watson held an Officers' Conference and gave out his orders. The advance would be led by 'D' Company (Major Wood) on the right and 'C' Company (Major A.N. Eardley-Wilmot) on the left. 'A' Company (Major Ovenden) would be in reserve behind 'D' Company with Battalion Headquarters moving behind 'C' Company. The carrier Platoon under Lieutenant P.B. Hodgson and Second-Lieutenant R.W. Pringle would follow closely behind the Battalion. Captain Kirby would bring up the Anti-Tank Platoon (Second-Lieutenant B. Sagar), the Mortar Platoon (Lieutenant I. Daw), the New Zealand machine-gun Platoon and the Anti-Tank Gun Troop of the Northumberland Hussars. A squadron of Sherman tanks of the 8th Royal Tank Regiment would be in support of the Battalion.

In the afternoon, a general reconnaissance of the Start Line and the whole area was made by the CO, his Second-in-Command (Major D.J.R. Parker), Intelligence Officer (Lieutenant G.E.H. Mansell) and Company Commanders. On the way back, the CO's jeep was attacked by Stukas and he and his three companions had to dive off the vehicle and into the ditch for protection. An ambulance which passed them was destroyed and the driver, his companion and patients were either killed or wounded; a very narrow escape.

At 3.45 p.m. on the 1st November, the Battalion commenced its march to the assembly area near Tel El Eisa Station. The Quartermaster provided a hot meal and brought up the mail. Those men who received letters read them and then handed them back for safekeeping. Major Parker with the Intelligence Sergeant and the Seconds-in-Command of companies, reconnoitred the Forming Up Line and marked it with white tape. At 7.00 p.m. the Battalion set off on its seven mile march to the Forming Up Line. Major Parker was the guide followed by 'C' Company, 'D' Company, Battalion HQ, HQ Company (Captain J.M. Jackson) and 'A' Company in the rear. The route followed was along Diamond Track to the forming up positions which were reached at 10.00 p.m. The march was both long and dusty. Lieutenant-Colonel Watson remembered the march:

> 'It was about seven miles march from where we were and we had to pass the New Zealand gunners in the dark as we marched up. We had to be in position, I think I'm right in saying, about 10 o'clock at night and I remember passing the New Zealand gunners stripped to the waist and they were firing their guns up towards the Australian Lines as a diversion and they were just pumping in the shells ... You could see the flashes of the guns, of course. The smell was awful, dead bodies lying about and then we moved into the Line and just lay down.'

At 10.00 p.m. the Battalion reached the Start Line and the companies got into their battle formations and settled down to await Zero Hour. 8th and 9th Battalions were contacted five hundred yards forward. It was a long wait. The men were dressed in shorts, shirts and pullovers. Lieutenant-Colonel Watson continued:

> '...At that time of the year it can be intensely cold at night in the desert ... We lay down at about ten and it was about ten-to-one when the battle was due to start. We just rested there. Our actual line was marked out by white tape but, of course, the Sappers would do that under cover of darkness and it was also marked by large drums of oil, great big, high oil drums.'

Men tried to sleep but few could do so. Waiting, before a great battle, is not something that a soldier finds easy to do. The mind is assailed by thoughts: 'Will I get through? Will I be lucky?' The thought of what could happen to them kept recurring in their minds. The shell fire had lessened. Lieutenant-Colonel Watson remembered:

> '...There was a deathly silence. It was quite extraordinary. Deathly silence along the whole of the Alamein Line. Every now and then you would hear the odd shot way down in the south of the Alamein Line. We had an issue of rum. I should think it was badly needed and I remember the grey jars the rum was carried in being put on top of the drums, the oil drums and, I should think, they're probably still there to this day. It was absolutely dead silence.'

The rum ration was issued about midnight. At 12.40 a.m. on 2nd November, 1942, every one stood up, buckled his belt, put on his equipment and fixed his bayonet to his rifle. It was still remarkably quiet. At 0.55 a.m. the Battalion moved forward through the first minefield, each man with his rifle at the port, others with their Thompson sub-machine-guns at the ready and the officers with their revolvers drawn. The sounds of the men's boots swishing through the sand could be clearly heard. Silence - and then this terrific noise started up behind them, the thunderous sound quickly merging into a strange rhythm. The horizon behind the advancing troops was lit up, alive with thousands of dancing flashes. The shells roared overhead to burst somewhere ahead. The air became thick with dust and acrid fumes. Visibility was cut to barely fifty yards at best and often even less. Lieutenant Mansell and his Intelligence Section moved stolidly forward, keeping direction and counting the paces which would indicate when the Battalion had reached the point where it had to pivot through ninety degrees to face north.

The first sign of enemy reaction was from machine-gun fire from the front, probably directed at the advancing 8th Battalion. This was soon accompanied by desultory shell and mortar fire which caused a few casualties. After advancing about five hundred yards, scattered German minelaying parties caught in the open, dazed, with many wounded, stumbled out of the dust fog. Unresisting they were passed to the rear, often without escort. At one thousand yards the Battalion met heavy fire from machine-guns firing on fixed lines from the northern flank. Immediately to the south, the skirl of the pipes of the Highlanders could be heard through the noise of battle. With the terrific noise and with adrenaline in full spate, it was difficult to move at a slow pace and also maintain control. Enemy posts which had escaped the shells were rushed with the tommy-gun and rifle and bayonet. Retaliatory fire from the German gun positions was now coming down on the Battalion. Alarm flares were soaring up into the air as were tracers from Bren guns, the signal of recognition between units. The noise was terrific and signals had to be made largely by hand rather than voice. Germans in isolated dug-outs missed by the forward Battalions began to pop up and fire at the men of the 6th. Soldiers began to fall.

Regimental Sergeant-Major Page with Sergeant Bramwell and a few other members of Battalion Headquarters cleared out a German machine-gun post with the bayonet. A few prisoners were sent back and the gun turned on other enemy machine-gun positions which were hindering the advance. Enemy artillery fire began to fall on the small group and Regimental Sergeant-Major Page was wounded in the leg as he went to help Private Gough. Captain J. Gibson, the Medical Officer and Sergeant Fairley, the Medical Sergeant, were both killed whilst helping the wounded. Corporal Davies, one of the stretcher-bearers, dressed Regimental Sergeant-Major Page's wound. Under the impression that the position they occupied was that judged to be the final location of Battalion Headquarters, the party remained where it was. At first light it was found to be only thirty of forty yards from the nearest enemy posts. With very little protection the group was sniped at the slightest movement. In mid-morning Regimental Sergeant-Major Page was killed by a sniper's bullet. Sergeant Bramwell and Private Gough remained doggo until able to withdraw on the arrival of some tanks. With the death of Regimental Sergeant-Major Page, the Battalion lost an exceptional soldier, a man of courage and distinction. A County Durham man - he came from Crook - he was a strong disciplinarian but was always fair in his dealings with the other ranks and he was much respected by officers and men.

Major Ovenden of 'A' Company sent No. 17 Platoon under

Lieutenant T.H. Vickers to deal with enemy machine-guns firing from the right flank. One of these positions was dealt with by a section commander with a sticky bomb but the whole platoon became pinned down by heavy fire from other positions and suffered casualties. Lieutenant Vickers was killed. Another Durham County man from the village of Thornley, near Tow Law, he had impressed his Commanding Officer in the short time he had been with the Battalion. 'D' Company was in the thick of the fighting. Sergeant Albert Dunn was awarded the Military Medal for this action described in his citation:

'During the attack on the night of 1/2 November after his Platoon Commander had been wounded, L/Sgt. Dunn led his platoon throughout with great dash and enthusiasm. He himself set a fine example, closing with the enemy and personally bayoneting three men. Throughout the action he kept his platoon under control, although the advance was a long one, and showed leadership of the very highest order.

'During the next night his platoon was so thoroughly organised that it was able to quickly overpower and destroy an 88mm gun and tractor and crew which drove into the platoon lines. This was in great part due to the way Lance-Sergeant Dunn had organised and controlled his platoon.'

Corporal Reg Haseley also of 'D' Company was awarded the Distinguished Conduct Medal. His citation read:

"During the Battalion attack on the night of 1st/2nd November when a gap was formed in the enemy lines, 'D' Company was Right Forward Company of the Battalion. No. 4034189 Corporal Haseley, C.R. was in command of No. 3 Section of 16 Platoon and during this attack and throughout the entire action his dash and personal leadership were most outstanding. When the Company came under fire on fixed lines from enemy M.G's! Corporal Haseley, with complete disregard for his own safety moved about among the men of his own platoon, leading them through and giving them encouragement by his own personal example.

"Two enemy dug in M.13 Tanks which had been holding up the advance a short while previously were rapidly engaged and once again Corporal Haseley led his section with great dash, and he himself killed the crews of both tanks. Immediately afterwards, Corporal Haseley gave chase to a third M.13 Tank. Corporal Haseley was responsible for taking many prisoners

during the advance and whilst the Company was consolidating the position gained he led his section forward searching the ground and bringing in two more prisoners.

His leadership was of the highest order."

Corporal Bert Davies of the Anti-Tank Gun Section remembered the battle:

'The worst thing is waiting, waiting for Zero Hour. Everybody seems to get tensed up not knowing what to expect. But once you got going you sort of lost that bad feeling in your stomach. You just followed the crowd and kept going. It's that dusty as well, carriers, transport churning up dust, choked with the dust and it was very difficult to see which was German and which was our tanks. Many a time we ran right over German trenches with Germans in. Very often we came to a German trench with Germans in it. We just jumped off the vehicle, took them out and sent them back as prisoners. They got back on their own some of them, they didn't have an escort. They'd just had enough ... We had to shout at each other or beckon, use signs ... We had instructions that if anyone was wounded he was left. You hadn't time because the more men that stopped to look after wounded the less was going to the front...so if one was wounded he was looked after by the First Aid lads that followed up ... They heard the cries of the wounded. You wanted to go but orders were that you weren't to go. There's got to be some sort of discipline and when you come to think of it it's right because there's already First Aid lads to look after them. We knew they'd get treated alright.'

Amongst the wounded was Private Jim Coglan MM. He was driving a lorry filled with ammunition behind the advancing companies. He remembered what happened:

'As soon as the guns opened up they gave the order, "Advance! Advance 'A'Company! Advance D' Company! ... I'd never seen as many flashes in my life ... Like everyone else I was a bundle of nerves. "Would I get out of it? How am I going to get out of it?" ... I lost my wagon about 6 o'clock in the morning. I was advancing with the infantry ... The wagon was hit and we dived off. The officer shouted, "Jump! Get off!" We went right away from it ... It burst like a ball of fire ... I joined the lads. I'd dropped off with my rifle...We were advancing, we were getting mortars and a little small arms fire. I got wounded about 9 0'clock ... I'd dropped in with 'A' Company. We were in slit trenches because we'd taken Jerry positions ... We could see Jerry was firing at us and we were firing at him. He was giving us some stick and we were giving him some stick. I found a German rifle and began firing with that ... I was wounded in the back with a mortar. I felt a burning feeling in the back and was knocked forward ... blood was coming out of my mouth ... I felt I'd had it.'

The advance continued through the thickening dust which made it increasingly difficult to keep direction, control and identify friend from foe. Small numbers of prisoners were taken mainly from 115 Panzer Grenadier Regiment. The few Italians taken were from the Littorio Armoured and Trento Infantry Divisions, all very badly shaken by the barrage and glad to be out of it. After an advance of between two thousand five hundred and three thousand yards several Italian Semovente Self-Propelled Guns were encountered. Tommy-guns and grenades accounted for the crews of two of them and both guns were later set on fire by 'A' Company. Three more were found abandoned. 'C' Company dealt with an infantry position. A sixth Semovente Gun was about to be investigated by Lieutenant-Colonel Watson when he was ordered to stop and stand back by a corporal who had placed a sticky grenade on the gun which exploded almost immediately killing the crew. Sergeant D'Auvergne's platoon attacked another gun. Making little headway the Sergeant shouted, 'This is no good, give me that Bren gun.' He grabbed the gun and ran forward alone firing the weapon from the hip. He fell wounded but his platoon, following up, rushed in and finished off the crew and destroyed the gun. Sergeant D'Auvergne was awarded the Military Medal for this action.

After advancing a further five hundred yards the Battalion wheeled to face north. 'A' Company now much weakened with having sustained heavy losses, was on the right. 'C' Company, slightly enfiladed back, was in the centre and in reserve and 'D' Company was on the left in contact with the 8th Battalion. Battalion Headquarters was in a slight hollow in the ground. The companies feverishly dug in before daylight. At about 5.00 a.m. Captain Kirby arrived with the supporting arms. Three 2 pounder anti-tank guns were allotted to each of 'D' and 'C' Companies and two given to 'A' Company. In addition, a battery

of 6 pounder anti-tank guns, less one Troop, joined the Battalion. Two 3in. Mortars were given to each company and a platoon from 4th New Zealand machine-gun Company was positioned on the right of 'A' Company. Reserve ammunition was brought up. At dawn the Battalion was well dug in. The second phase of the advance had begun behind a tremendous barrage until it ceased at 4.00 a.m., with the 8th and 9th Battalions close to the Abed El Rahman Track. Silence fell on the battlefield. The Battalion carriers made contact with the Maori Battalion on the right flank and on their return brought in a dozen prisoners.

The mist cleared about 7.30 a.m. and revealed enemy infantry positions about three hundred yards north of the Battalion line. These were engaged by the New Zealand machine-gunners and the Battalion's light machine-guns. The enemy sniped from their positions during the whole morning. Captain Jackson of the 'HQ' Company was found to be missing. There were no Regimental Aid Post personnel with the Battalion except for two stretcher-bearers who worked manfully and heroically to help the wounded. Captain Jackson had lost his way in the dark and had been taken prisoner when he had stumbled into a manned German post. He was rescued by British armoured cars in the late afternoon.

Spasmodic enemy shelling continued all day, sometimes directed on the Battalion's positions, sometimes on the British armour passing through the corridor or the soft skinned vehicles which followed the armour. With the positions held and consolidated, the tanks began to pass through westwards attempting to make a final breakout into the desert and take on the German armour. It was not that easy. The Germans had quickly placed a ring of 88s around the western tip of the corridor and the British tanks began to suffer considerable losses attempting to break out. A 25 pounder concentration was laid down on the German positions. About the middle of the morning, groups of bombers began to fly over from the east to drop their loads on the German guns. The Germans were swamped by shell and bomb but continued to fight bitterly to contain the bridgehead.

On several occasions, enemy tanks and self-propelled guns

appeared on the ridge one thousand yards north of the Battalion positions. The supporting artillery chased them off. One enemy armoured vehicle and a signal truck ventured near and were destroyed by the 2 pounders. It was far from comfortable for the men lying in their slit trenches which had been hastily dug during the night. Movement was severely restricted by the enemy sniper fire. The flies and the smells of the battlefield were terrible. Communications with Brigade Headquarters were continually breaking down. Lieutenant-Colonel Jackson came over from the 8th Battalion to try to communicate with Brigade HQ which he could not reach from his own headquarters, only to find that 6th Battalion Headquarters were also out of touch with Brigade. The wireless sets had broken down and the telephone lines were being continually cut by tanks and shell fire. Brigadier Percy arrived and pronounced that he was quite satisfied with the way things were going.

During the afternoon, about thirty tanks, Grants, Crusaders and Valentines, moved through the Battalion positions northwards. They were met by very heavy anti-tank fire from German 88s. They were not popular with the infantry as they brought down retaliatory enemy shell fire on their shelters. The tanks stayed sometimes out in front sniping at distant German tanks. They had one marked success when, from out of the trenches immediately in front, a long row of German infantry appeared with their hands held high. Amongst the ninety Germans who surrendered was a German Colonel from a Panzer Grenadier Regiment and five other officers. Lieutenant Colonel Watson described his prisoner:

> 'He was unmistakably Prussian, in his long double-breasted regimental greatcoat and short cropped hair on a round bullet shaped head. When the CO asked him about his regiment, he properly refused to speak and countered by asking if he, the CO, spoke German, and then passed on to apologise for the dirty state of his troops. He himself was immaculate. Then he asked that aid should be given to those of his staff who were wounded. All his men were completely demoralised and when one or two shells came over, scattered in all directions...'

At 7.00 p.m., after a quiet period, a heavy German bombardment fell on the Battalion's positions. For twenty minutes the violent shelling continued whilst everyone crouched in their slit trenches expecting an enemy counter-attack at any time. However this never came and the shelling ceased as abruptly as it had began. The Quartermaster's lorries had just arrived at Battalion Headquarters bringing the men's greatcoats for the night. Whether the dust they raised brought on the shelling no one knows but one lorry was destroyed by a direct hit and Colour-Sergeant Robinson and Private Toes were killed and others wounded. After dark, the advance elements of the relieving Battalions arrived from the New Zealand Division. The distant sounds of vehicles starting up and moving were clearly heard and a feeling grew that the enemy was beginning to pull out. At about 1.30 a.m. on the 3rd November, there was a loud explosion in front of 'C' Company's position. A German 88mm gun pulled by a tractor had driven to within thirty yards of the Company Headquarters. When challenged the crew had refused to surrender and a tracer bullet was fired into the petrol tank which had immediately exploded. One of the crew ran off into the night, two were captured and the rest died in the inferno.

At 4.00 a.m., the Battalion was relieved by the New Zealanders and began the weary march back to Tel El Eisa Station. Quietness had again fallen over the battlefield. On all sides there were the signs of war, with knocked out vehicles and the dead lying all around. The men were desperately tired but marched stoically onwards. Only one man dropped out. The CO asked what was wrong with him and was told, 'He was hit in the shoulder yesterday and doesn't think he can make it.' This spirit of the 6th had already seen them through some tight spots and would continue to do so in the future. It was a tiring and dusty march. As they continued along the track, small groups of men clambered out of their shelters to watch them go by. At one halt, thoughtful Australians gave each man a mug of tea. The news of what the Brigade had done was already filtering back. At 7.00 a.m. the Battalion reached its previous lying up area near the Station. Breakfast was already prepared and waiting. It was eaten in silence, The reaction to the severe stress of violent action is invariably one of great tiredness. After eating, the men lay on the ground and slept. As they slept the British armour strove to break out through the corridor that the two Brigades had opened and the Battle of El Alamein went into its final stages as the enemy began his long retreat westwards.

Casualties were heavy:

Killed: Captain J. Gibson RAMC
               Lieutenant G.E. Green
               Lieutenant T.H. Vickers
               Regimental Sergeant-Major A. Page, MC
               14 Other Ranks

Wounded: Lieutenant L. Atkinson
               Lieutenant C.H. Lawrence
               Lieutenant P.G. Tyndale
               Second-Lieutenant S.M. Cutting
               47 Other Rank

Missing: 20 Other Ranks

The 3rd November was a day of severe fighting as Rommel's 88s and surviving tanks fought to hold the British inside the corridor and enable the German elements of his forces to drive off in retreat in the transport available, leaving the Italian infantry very much on its feet. On the 4th, the 5th Indian Brigade put in an attack which opened up the last enemy defences and the final retreat began.

On the 3rd November, 151 Brigade ceased to be under the command of the 2nd New Zealand Division and came under the command of the 9th Australian Division. Brigadier Percy arrived in the evening to congratulate the Battalion on the good work it had done. The next day two officers, Second-Lieutenant L.J. Godbold and Lieutenant W. Lyburn, with twenty-five other ranks, arrived from the Infantry Base Depot. On the 5th, a warning order was received from Brigade HQ for the Battalion to be ready to move at an hour's notice. Orders were given out to

the effect that the Brigade was to mop up the area from Tel El Eisa Station, westwards as far as El Daba. The 9th Australian Division had already pushed through the latter place. 9th DLI was to mop up the area between the sea and the coast road whilst 6th DLI mopped up between the coast road and the railway. At 10.30 a.m. the Battalion moved off with the Carrier Platoon in front followed by 'D' and 'C' Companies, Battalion HQ and 'A' Company on foot. It was not a pleasant march. Derelict tanks and the bodies of German and Australian soldiers lay on either side. After two hours' marching an angry General Leese, the Corps Commander, appeared and met Brigadier Percy, who was with Lieutenant-Colonel Watson, at the side of the road. Lieutenant-Colonel Watson described the incident:

> 'After going for about two hours General Leese, the Corps Commander, met the Brigadier who was with the CO on the road at the time, and appeared far from pleased at the slow progress. He explained that Daba was now clear of the enemy and that he was not in the least interested in clearing the ground between the Alamein Line and Daba and that the Brigade should be in Motor Transport getting to the latter place as quickly as possible to make the firm base there. So the Battalion was collected on the roadside to wait the arrival of the trucks which should have been provided by the Australian Division.'

The transport duly arrived and the Battalion reached El Daba at 6.30 p.m. and the companies got into position. Attached to the Battalion was a troop of Australian 6 pounder anti-tank guns. Behind the Battalion positions was a huge enemy dump of stores covering over a square mile and surrounded by a barbed wire fence. During the night an enemy aircraft dropped a few anti-personnel bombs on 'C' Company area and around Battalion HQ, with little damage and no casualties. On the morning of the 6th November, carrier and foot patrols were sent out and twenty Italian prisoners were brought in. Much useful equipment and supplies were 'salvaged' from the great supply dump but the Army Commissariat was already at work and they forestalled the collection of much booty. At 2.00 p.m. a warning order was received from Brigade HQ for the Battalion to be ready to move at short notice. The Brigade was in XXX Corps reserve. At 4.00 p.m. the Battalion moved to an area just south of Ghazal Station. It was now becoming obvious that the Brigade would not take

Christmas Card *drawn by Sergeant T. Cairns, 1942*

part in the pursuit and this proved to be the case. Losses had to be made up from drafts and training would then be necessary.

On the 8th November, Brigadier Percy visited the Battalion to give his farewells prior to taking up another appointment. It was a sad parting of a man steeped in the traditions of the Durhams. He was to die on his way home from the Middle East. His replacement was Brigadier D.W.M. Beak, VC, DSO, MC. After spending the 9th of the month back at Daba on guard duty, the Battalion returned to Ghazal Station on the following day. On the same day of the return, a NAAFI Mobile Cinema Unit put on a performance in the Battalion area and provided entertainment for the men. The first of the leave parties left for the Sidi Bishr Rest

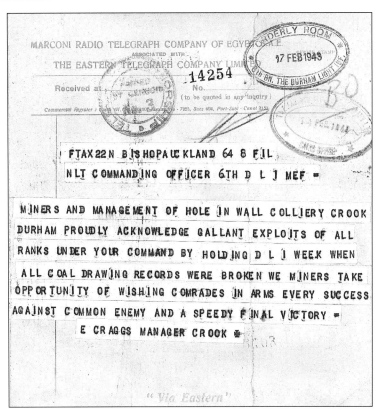

Many miners were serving in the Battalion at the beginning of the war. Subsequent battles and heavy casualties diminshed their number

Lieutenant A.G. Urwin.

The training continued, until on the 2nd December, when the Battalion left the area on the first stage of its long journey westwards to catch up with the rest of the 8th Army. It moved forward by day, camping at night, until at 7.00 a.m. on the 23rd of the month, the Battalion column advanced across the Trigh El Abd to the enemy supply dump at Giof Um El Ameied which was garrisoned by a Battalion of the Italian Folgore Division. The 151 Brigade mounted an attack and gave covering fire whilst 50th Division's Royal Engineers destroyed the dump. The Battalion returned to the El Adem area where it remained for the rest of the month. Christmas Day was celebrated with a Church Service in the morning and

Camp near Alexandria. On the 11th, the Brigade rejoined XIII Corps. The Battalion moved to a new area on the 13th November. This was back to the area it had previously occupied in the south of the Alamein Line where it was learned that it was to be used to clear up the battlefield in that area, a salvage operation which would last two weeks. However, these orders were changed and this period of time was to be spent in training. On the 25th November, a draft of one hundred and seventy men was received from the Infantry Base Depot, together with Lieutenants R.J. Bennett, D.J. Fenner, W. Middleton, R.H. Stabback and Second-

Christmas Dinner in the afternoon. On the last day of the year, the Battalion was preparing to move westward once more.

1942 had been a year of marked contrasts: the severe winter in Iraq, followed by the long journey to the Gazala Line and the torrid heat of the desert. Defeat and two desperate breakouts followed when surrounded by enemy forces and heavy losses were incurred as a result. Reformed behind the Alamein Line, the Line itself was occupied and this culminated in Operation Supercharge and the defeat from which Rommel would never recover.

The story of this eventful year ends with a personal though remarkable story. Captain Tim Chamberlain was killed when on patrol on 24th October, as referred to earlier in the narrative. He had lost his cigarette case during the evacuation of Dunkirk. His mother gave him another to replace it, made of silver and engraved with the family crest. Inside was engraved the Regimental Badge and the following words: "With love from Mum, Dunkirk 1940." He lost this cigarette case in the Gazala Line. On the 5th November, when 9 DLI reached El Daba, this same cigarette case was found on a table in an underground shelter. Lieutenant-Colonel Watson returned the case to Captain Chamberlain's mother.

CHAPTER 24
THE BATTLE OF MARETH
1943

Rommel had been chased out of Egypt and by the end of December had reached Buerat in Libya, a strong position where he was expected to make a stand. The position was assaulted by the Eighth Army on the 15th January, 1943, and carried. Rommel continued his withdrawal. Meanwhile 50th Division, now in X Corps and in reserve, began its move westward from the El Adem area on the 1st January. The route lay south of the Libyan Bulge, an area of pleasant hills clad in juniper trees and with fertile plains, passing Bir Hacheim and the Gazala Line across the desert to Agadabia and El Agheila. On the 3rd January, the desert was turned into a quagmire by heavy rainfall which caused trucks to bog down which had to be pulled out by use of the tow rope and spade. Conditions were so bad that the Battalion halted for the whole of the 4th. The next day the convoy had barely travelled seven miles when, again, conditions deteriorated and a halt was called.

At 8.00 a.m. on the 6th, the Battalion route was changed and it moved westward. At Sceleidima a further change of direction was made and it moved north-west. On the 7th January the column reached Benina and bivouacked south of the airfield on a rough but comparatively flat piece of ground. Italian colonists had built their attractive white-washed houses in the area and their work had made the countryside more fertile and attractive. The 8th January was spent cleaning equipment and weapons and on vehicle maintenance. A route march of ten miles was undertaken and small parties visited Benghazi to look at the town made famous in the desert war. Here they were able to able to take advantage of a bath at the Mobile Bath Unit. These visits became a daily occurance during the stay in the Benina area. On the 10th of the month, information was received that the Division was likely to stay in the Benina area for a number of weeks. The reason for this was due to a very serious situation which had arisen as a result of the recent storm which had caused enormous damage to Benghazi harbour. Seven supply ships had sunk during the storm. Supplies to the advancing divisions of 8th Army had been drastically cut and only one Corps could be maintained in the forward area. X Corps, which included 50 Division, was grounded so that its transport could be used to carry urgent supplies forward from Benghazi to the front line.

Lieutenant-General Horrocks encouraged the drivers of the lorries taking part by announcing a competition between the various Brigades based on good driving, vehicle maintenance and general efficiency. First prize for the winning company was £20, priority leave and a laurel wreath painted on the door of the drivers' cabs. At the end of the five weeks' emergency scheme 151 Brigade, which had made up a transport company from a platoon from each Battalion, gained third place out of sixteen entries. Early on arrival at Benina, the Carrier and Mortar Platoons, the latter also on carriers, were sent off to Castel Verde, eight miles east of Tripoli, where they stayed for some time with precious little to do. This move was the response to Divisional orders, though why they had been sent to stagnate at Castel Verde was not known.

Training commenced at Benina. The day started with physical training. Marches to build strength and toughness were undertaken at a fast pace up to the top of the escarpment and back. Various drills for gapping minefields were carried out with or without Scorpion tanks - tanks with flails of heavy chains in front which rotate and explode mines and so clear a passage through a minefield. Specialist training was commenced for signallers, anti-tank gunners and so on. In an uninhabited area of Benghazi, the Battalion held street fighting exercises over three or four days, training which was new to the officers and men.

Lieutenant-Colonel Watson returned from hospital on the 11th January, having recovered from jaundice. On the same day, Lieutenants T.O.M. Cranke and Atherton joined from the Infantry Base depot. On the 21st of the month, Second-Lieutenants A.E. Short, D.B. Isaac, A.R.W. Maddox and R.W. Bussen joined the Battalion. Football and basketball games were commenced with inter-battalion, company and platoon games. An ENSA Concert was performed which included that rarity in the desert, female entertainers. The Divisional Concert Party gave several concerts. Meanwhile the advance of the Eighth Army continued. After breaking through enemy resistance at Beurat, Tripoli fell on the 22nd January.

In mid-February it was announced that the 50th Division would join the 2nd New Zealand, 51st Highland and 7th Armoured Division in XXX Corps. On the 24th of the month, Captain Kirby joined the carriers and mortars and shortly afterwards took them to Ben Ghardane, which had just fallen. This area quickly became one huge supply dump for the Eighth Army and the carriers and mortars were given the task of guarding the area. The training given to the Brigade was quite intense and towards the end of the month Brigadier Beak ordered two days' rest. Officers were ordered to keep away from the men. The Quartermaster arranged a series of 'Try Your Luck' sideshows to keep the men interested. There was a singing competition in the evening won by 'D' Company which happened to have a number of Welshmen in its ranks. Major 'Crackers' May of the Regiment arrived on a visit and tried to interest some of the men in joining the parachutists. Only one man did so, Corporal Blackmore, an old Territorial soldier from Crook.

On the 2nd March, the Battalion set off and travelled towards Tunisia through a very pleasant landscape covered with many varieties of flowers - a change indeed from the desert. The Battalion still consisted of three rifle companies which were now at full strength. On the 5th of the month, it passed through Mussolini's Triumphal Monument called, 'Marble Arch.' On the 6th, the Battalion reached a position twenty miles west of Sirte, a very dangerous area. A warning on the walls of the town read, 'Sirte is dirty with mines and booby traps. Keep to the road and you'll survive. Perhaps!' On Sunday, 7th March, Buerat was reached. In the evening, wireless sets were tuned to home and hymn singing was picked up coming from the Regimental Infantry Training Centre at Brancepeth Castle. The programme ended with the singing of the Regimental hymn, *Abide With Me*, a most moving moment with many thoughts of home. Tripoli was bypassed and Castel Benito reached on the 9th of the month. The frontier into Tunisia was crossed the following day and camp made in an olive grove at Ben Ghardane. On the 13th, Djorf on the east coast, opposite the island of Djerba was reached, where Captain Kirby and the carriers and mortars rejoined. Here, training continued with exercises in breaching enemy minefields. These were carried out in co-operation with the 50th Royal Tank Regiment. Scorpion minefield clearing tanks were used in the exercises. In addition a new form of training was introduced which was to be of great help in the forthcoming battle. Practice was given in scaling cliffs followed by an assault on an enemy strongpoint. Various methods were taught: the use of rope ladders, rifle slings tied together to form a rope and, finally, a human ladder whereby one man would climb on the back of another until the top of the cliff was reached.

Following the enemy defeat at Medinine in early March, the Eighth Army closed up to the Mareth Line, a very powerful position built by the French before the war to protect Tunisia from any incursions from Italian Libya. It derived its name from the small village of Mareth which lay behind the Line. The Italians and Germans had spent some time strengthening the positions still further.

The Mareth Line was formidable indeed. It stretched for some twenty-two miles from the sea near the village of Zarat, to the

Mareth Line. *The formidable defences are clearly visible in this photograph with the anti-tank ditch in front of the concrete pillbox*

Imperial War Museum photograph No. NA 1470

Matmata Hills. The latter formed a barrier to any large force. They were almost impassable to wheeled vehicles as only the roughest of tracks crossed through ravines and defiles. These hills also dominated the western end of the Line and its approaches. It was in miniature a Maginot Line with concrete and steel pillboxes, blockhouses and gun positions and a network of deep, interlocking trenches with dugouts, capable of holding and protecting large numbers of men. That part of the Line nearest to the coast was further protected by the deep and wide Wadi Zigzaou, itself a natural barrier to tanks. It was here, between the coast road and the sea, that 151 Brigade was to attack.

Wadi Zigzaou was about fifty yards wide, even further extended in width nearer the sea, At this time of the year it held water and near the coast it was tidal. The bed of the Wadi was muddy. It had steep sides and the enemy had taken great care in accurately registering his guns and mortars to fire into the obstacle. In addition, the Germans and Italians had dug an anti-tank ditch, twelve feet deep and fifteen feet wide, between the Wadi Zigzaou and the fortifications. Minefields with Teller mines to damage and destroy tanks and anti-personnel and shrapnel mines to kill and maim men, had been laid on both sides of the Wadi. On the high ground overlooking the Wadi were a series of carefully sited gun positions which could fire down its whole length. One final natural obstacle was to be found in the coastal area which protected the enemy outposts in that sector and could not be used by wheeled vehicles. This was a large 'Sebkret' or mud flat running in from the sea. It was passable to marching men.

The Mareth Line had one weakness known to General Montgomery. It could be outflanked. The Long Range Desert Group had found a route, rough but passable to wheeled vehicles, through the Matmata Hills. This knowledge was reflected in General Montgomery's plan for the assault. The 50th Division and 23rd Armoured Brigade would carry out a frontal attack in the coastal sector of the Mareth Line. The 2nd New Zealand Division, 8th Armoured Brigade and General Leclerc's Free French would, at the same time, carry out a wide outflanking movement through the Matmata Hills. The intention was that the enemy's full attention would be taken up by the frontal attack which would draw in his armoured reserves and the left hook when delivered would fall upon his rear. The Mareth Line was held near the coast by the Italian Young Fascists' Division and the German 164th Infantry Division with the the 90th Light and 15th and 21st Panzer Divisions in reserve.

As 151 Brigade prepared for its assault, the enemy outposts were dealt with by 201 Guards Brigade and 69 Brigade. 201 Guards Brigade's attack on the Horseshoe feature failed but otherwise the attacks were successfully carried out on the nights of the 16th/17th and 17th/18th March and the ridge was taken overlooking the Wadi and the main enemy defences on the far side. Patrols could now creep down under cover of darkness into the Wadi itself. One very strong obstacle remained on the British side of the Wadi. Lying to the east, the 'Bastion' commanded an excellent view of the Wadi and surrounding country. It was wired in and well protected by minefields. General Nichols decided that it would be attacked by the 7th Battalion Green Howards at the same time as the 151 Brigade assault went in. This Battalion of 69 Brigade stormed this strongpoint and in bitter hand-to-hand fighting captured it, taking some two hundred prisoners. Lieu-tenant-Colonel Seagrim commanding the Battalion won the Victoria Cross in this action. He was killed shortly afterwards at Wadi Akarit.

The objectives of 151 Brigade were the little forts of Ksiba, Ksiba Ouest, Ouerzi, Zarat Sudest, Ouerzi Ouest and Ouerzi Est. The Brigade was to cross the Wadi and anti-tank ditch between Ksiba Ouest and Ouerzi. The advantage of this sector was that there were no enemy positions in front of the Wadi. A number of tracks crossed the Wadi to Zarat. The anti-tank ditch lay on the enemy side of the Wadi whereas higher up it crossed to the British side. It was believed that the tidal waters did not reach further than Ksiba Ouest.

On the 17th March, the Battalion marched up to Wadi Zessar, south of the coast road. The following day, it marched to the Wadi Zeuss. Brigadier Beak proposed to attack in two phases. In the first phase, 9th DLI on the right had Ksiba Ouest as its objective. The objective assigned to 8th DLI on the left was Ouerzi. In the second phase, 6th DLI would attack through these two battalions and seize Ouerzi Ouest and Ouerzi Est, enlarging the bridgehead at the same time. Both attacking battalions would have the support of two Scorpions who would beat a clear path through the large minefields which the enemy had laid on the slopes leading to the Wadi. It was a formidable task summed up by Captain G.L. Wood, MC, who wrote:

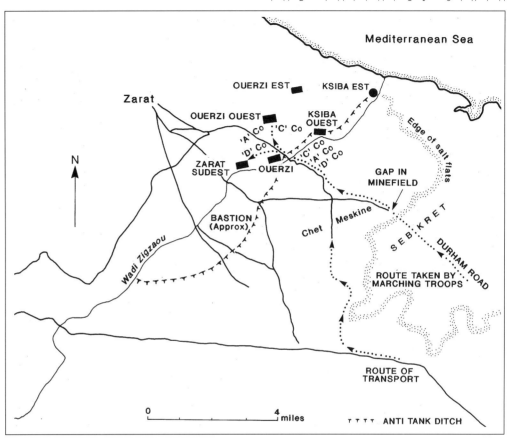

The Battle of Mareth, *21st to 23rd March, 1943*

'The task of 151 Brigade, under cover of the Artillery programme, was to breach a deep minefield, some 1000 yards in depth, cross the natural and somewhat formidable barrier - the WADI ZIGZAOU, scale the cliffs on the other side and storm the strong enemy posts, including pillboxes, which were all mutually supporting and protected by their own local minefields and wire defences, and finally to establish a bridgehead of some 4000 yards wide and approximately 2000 yards in depth.'

Between the two phases, tanks of the 50th RTR were to cross the Wadi to give support to the infantry. It was in this task and that of getting other vital tracked and wheeled vehicles across the Wadi to bring supplies and support to the troops, that a great problem presented itself and one which, we will see later, was to have a crucial bearing on the outcome of the battle. There was no bridging equipment available. A causeway would have to be built strong enough to take the heaviest Valentine Tank. Each tank going into the attack would carry a fascine of palm branches which would be dropped into the Wadi where the Royal Engineers would build the causeway. A number of lorries were also designated to carry fascines for this purpose. Brigade Headquarters was to control the forward movement of carriers and 15 cwt vehicles of each Battalion. The 'Sebkret' or mud flat being impassable meant that all of these vehicles had to go round the coast road then branch off down a rough track, given the name of 'Osborne Road' after the Commander of the REs of 50th Division. This track took the vehicles to the Chet Meskine, a slight hollow which was forward of the ridge looking across Wadi Zigzaou and was the Battalion Forming Up Place. The two leading battalions were ordered to cross the taped Start Line which would be laid between the Chet Meskine and the Wadi, at 10.30 p.m. on the 20th March. The 6th Battalion would form up at 9.45 p.m. that same night and cross the Start Line at 00.30 a.m. on the 21st, its vehicles having joined up with it at 11.15 p.m.

Captain Wood wrote:

'A large artillery programme, which, we were told, would be of such intensity that (1) The enemy infantry would be completely dazed and shattered and incapable of offering organised resistance; and (2) because strong counter battery programmes were included, would succeed in knocking out 60 to 80 per cent of the enemy's Artillery.'

On the morning of the 19th March, Lieutenant-Colonel Watson and his Company Commanders went up to the positions held by the 5th East Yorks, from which it was possible to observe the ground over which the attack was to be made. It was not possible to see into the Wadi itself due to the steep banks but the enemy fortifications beyond were clearly visible. There was no movement to be seen, all was ominously quiet. At 3.00 p.m. the Intelligence Officer took a number of officers from each company to the same positions to view their objectives. At 5.00 a.m. on the 20th March, Lieutenant Bell, the Intelligence Officer, proceeded to the Battalion HQ, 5th East Yorks and met Captain G.E.H. Mansell, Intelligence Officer, 151 Brigade and the Intelligence Sections of the 8th and 9th DLI, to stake out the position of the Start Line which was marked by white tape when darkness fell. During this day, with the attack going in that night, officers and men prepared themselves for the forthcoming ordeal. Twenty-four hours' battle rations were drawn and issued and an additional day's supply was loaded onto trucks. This included the precious water supply. An extra bandolier of ammunition was issued to each man. The Medical Officer and stretcher-bearers made sure they were well stocked with shell dressings and that the medical panniers were completely packed with the items required to tend the wounded. Letters and private papers were collected and tied up in sandbags and left behind at 'B' Echelon. It was essential to keep men busy and their minds off the battle due to start in a few hours. Most of the Battalion were about to face severe enemy fire either for the first time or were being reintroduced to violent conflict after a long period of quiet. Many of the officers were new and were faced with a night move and attack for the first time. It was to be a severe test for the Battalion.

During the 20th March, the Commanding Officer held a company commanders' conference and the Battalion Plan was explained. Captain G.L. Wood, MC, commanding 'D' Company wrote:

'Depending on the success of the other Battalions, the 6th Battalion's attack was to be a series of company attacks, each with its own objective. My company - 'D' - was to be leading company and by Z plus 30 had to be formed up on the Start Line, and there await instructions from Battalion Headquarters before moving forward to the attack.

'My task was to cross Wadi Zigzaou opposite Ouerzi and from that area to form up the company - attack and seize Ouerzi Ouest - an advance of some 1200 to 1500 yards.

'Upon my signal, 'A' Company, commanded by Major Ovenden, and 'C' Company, Major Wilmot, both killed in the battle, were to cross the Wadi at the same place, follow through and seize Ouerzi Est, 1000 yards further on.

'Apart from these orders which had to be carried out at night, we had been issued with marked maps showing in some detail the strength and dispositions of the enemy. These were issued down to and including Platoon Commanders. We also had a visit from a captain of the French Army who, prior to the war had been stationed in Mareth and who knew the system of defences fairly well. He was able to describe the ground and point out the advantages and disadvantages, the various landmarks etc. by use of a small sand model. Otherwise we had never seen the ground - reconnaissance was impossible owing to the fact that the enemy held the high vantage points overlooking the entire area. This was a decided disadvantage because nearly all the Platoon Commanders were new to battle and the task of map reading by night, particularly during action, added to the difficulty of controlling men during darkness, together presented quite a problem.'

The Battalion assembled in 'D' Company lines and moved off at 7.30 p.m. and proceeded to cross the 'Sebkret' by a track named 'Durham Road.' The transport under Captain Kirby used the 'Osborne Road.' The long snake of men marched across the mud flats feeling almost naked under the full moon and certain that the enemy reconnaissance planes overhead would surely see them. Flares were dropped a considerable distance away, so all seemed well. At the far side of the 'Sebkret' the Battalion began to climb the gradual slope in single file following the taped gap through the minefield. Lieutenant Bell, the Intelligence Officer, arrived with the worrying news that the Chet Meskine, which was to be the Battalion forming up place, was full of troops and transport and there was no room available. Battalion Headquarters and 'D' Company leading were almost on top of the ridge while the remaining companies stretched back through the narrow minefield gap. The order was to lie down where they were until it was possible to move into the Chet Meskine when the forward battalions moved forward. The ground was rock hard and it was impossible to dig in. There could be no going forward nor moving backwards. On either side of the very narrow gap in which the officers and men lay were the deadly mines. At 10.30 p.m. the terrific barrage began in support of 69 Brigade's attack on the 'Bastion' and the 8th and 9th Battalions'

attack across the Wadi. The enemy's retaliatory barrage fell and it was soon obvious that the ridge on which the 6th lay had been carefully registered and shells began to fall amongst the men. Casualties began to mount. A shell burst near Battalion HQ and a signaller was killed. Another broke under the strain and, screaming and sobbing, was restrained by the Adjutant or he would have rushed to certain death among the mines which lay so close. A third signaller was wounded. Private Joe Wear remembered the ordeal

'We got trapped in the minefield and they were firing into the minefield...we were lying in this area and they were just shelling it, and shelling it, and exploding mines. I don't think anyone knows how we got out. In my mind there was a lad, he stood up and he started singing, "Blaydon Races" and he walked out and I'm sure everybody followed him. It seemed as though you heard someone singing, "Blaydon Races" and after that everybody seemed to follow him ... to let you know where the path was. Under the shell fire you pray to your mother. "Mother help me." I remember we got the shock of our lives when they said we had to go back in tonight [21st March] and, of course, it was worse...'

For two and a half hours the 'Sixth' lay on the slopes under shell fire until at about 11.00 p.m. it moved forward along the top of the ridge to the junction with Osborne Road and then dropped down into the Chet Meskine with the head of the column about three hundred yards from the Start Line. Here, orders were received that it was to stay where it was until ordered to move by the Brigadier. The area was under enemy shell fire. Captain Wood described the confusion:

'We began to realise that we were well behind our programme and were somewhat relieved when, a little later, we were led forward by our Intelligence Section down to the area of some palm trees near Point 15, just behind our Start Line. Here the Battalion remained while I led my company down to the Start Line and formed up ready for orders to attack. Heavy shelling continued and further casualties were incurred here. There appeared to be a certain amount of confusion, odd vehicles pulling up and enquiring the way to such and such a Battalion Headquarters, one track completely blocked by our own Valentine tanks moving up the Wadi carrying their fascines.'

The air was thick with dust and smoke and visibility was

down to a few yards only. At about 2.45 a.m. on the morning of the 21st March, the Battalion and its transport was ordered to return to its original assembly area. Fierce fighting ahead had caused heavy losses to 8th and 9th DLI and progress was slow. Lieutenant-Colonel Jackson, commanding the 8th, had been killed. Major Lidwell later took over command. It was believed that their objectives had been taken but there was still some confusion as to the exact positions of their companies. It was considered too late for the 6th to carry out its tasks before daylight. In actual fact, the transport of the 9th DLI was only then moving forward to cross Wadi Zigzaou The delay was due to heavy shelling at the junction of the main coast road and Osborne Road and difficulty in building a causeway over Wadi. The 6th Battalion moved back after experiencing the great strain of spending five hours under continual enemy artillery fire and no opportunity to attack. One man had been killed and thirteen wounded. Captain Wood had a particularly frustrating time:

> '...orders were received from Brigade to return to our old assembly area. I hastened back to the Start Line [from Battalion HQ where he had been ordered to wait for orders] to collect my company but found them already gone - they had been given direct orders by Brigadier Beak VC, to return. However not knowing this at the time I and my batman spent a fruitless one and a half hours trying to locate their whereabouts, finally ending up in the middle of a minefield.

> 'Eventually we gave it up as a bad job and arrived back in the assembly area about 0900hrs to find that the Battalion, after a hearty breakfast, were sleeping soundly.'

During the morning of the 21st March, Brigadier Beak issued orders to the effect that a three phase attack would take place that night. In the first phase, 6th Battalion would attack and capture Ouerzi Ouest and Zarat Sudest. This attack would start at 10.00 p.m. In the second phase, 9th DLI would capture Ouerzi Est and this attack would commence at 1.30 a.m. on the 22nd. In the third phase commencing at 1.45 a.m., two companies of the 5th East Yorks would capture Ksiba Est. A concentration of three hundred guns would give support and the Battalion was ordered not to close up on their barrage for the first five minutes of concentrated fire. The 2nd Cheshire Regiment would give machine-gun support from Zero + 5 to Zero + 15 minutes, firing

on Zarat Sudest. The Brigadier also suggested that two companies should be directed to attack Zarat Sudest. The Battalion would leave its present position at the same time as it had done the previous night.

Captain G.T. Lindrea and representatives of each company were sent forward to contact 9th DLI to mark out suitable Start Lines for each company on the west side of the Wadi. Lieutenant-Colonel Watson gave the following objectives to his Company Commanders:

Right - 'C' Company (Major Wilmot) - objective Ouerzi Ouest.

Centre - 'A' Company (Major Ovenden) - objective to occupy the intervening high ground between 'C' and 'D' Companies.

Left - 'D' Company (Captain Wood) - objective with the left flank resting on the anti-tank ditch, to take Zarat Sudest.

Battalion Headquarters would be in a depression between Wadi Zigzaou and Ouerzi Ouest. The companies would move off in the order; 'C' Company, with the Commanding Officer and Intelligence Officer leading, 'A' Company, followed by 'D' Company; the transport following the coast road and Osborne Road. The Battalion again wound its way across the 'Sebkret' and up the slope to the top of the ridge to the junction with Osborne Road, then down to the Chet Meskine and to the Wadi. Some enemy shell fire was directed on it and sniper fire appeared to be coming from Zarat Sudest. The signs of battle were all around them with destroyed vehicles and the shell torn countryside. On reaching the Wadi, Lieutenant-Colonel A.B. Clarke, commanding the 9th Battalion, met the 'Sixth' and pointed out the crossing place and the positions of enemy snipers who had the crossing under observation and accurate fire. He strongly advised that the crossing should be made by parties of no more than ten at a time as larger groups might bring down mortar and shell fire. This advice was taken but in doing so the crossing of the Wadi took much longer than expected.

'C' Company led the way across the Wadi with a guide from the 9th Battalion. Lieutenant-Colonel Watson pointed out the Company's objective to Major Eardley-Wilmot and showed them a suitable Start Line for their attack. Snipers and machine-guns opened up on the Company as it moved between the Wadi and the anti-tank ditch. 'A' Company followed and dashed across the space. Some stragglers from 'C' Company were picked up by Lieutenant Galloway who was commanding the leading platoon. Again the CO pointed out their objective and Start Line and the Company moved into position. 'D' Company crossed the Wadi last. The Company was late in arriving due to the delay in crossing the Wadi by the forward two companies and confusion caused by heavy enemy shell fire directed on the Wadi. Battalion Headquarters crossed over and occupied an Italian dugout which had been used earlier by a company of 9 DLI as a headquarters. The location was in the entrance or neck leading from the Wadi into a cultivated depression in the surrounding high ground. 'C' Company's objective overlooked it.

Private Harry Wilkinson crossed the Wadi with 'C' Company:

'We were led down just below the skyline and then the word came to go forward. We went forward, I think it was more or less in extended line, told not to bunch together. I remember there was two or three of us, two or three yards apart each of us and then on our left there was - I don't know whether one or two had stepped on a mine in a bit of a dip - there was a helluva flash and screams and yells. We just shouted for stretcher-bearers and went on otherwise we may become too detached as things were starting to move then. The idea was to press on ... We came down this slope to the Wadi itself and waded through the water as I remember ... We got across the other side and hit the other wall of the Wadi which was much steeper than the one we had come down...'

The enemy shelling and mortaring of the Wadi and crossing place was now intense. When the British barrage opened up heralding the attack, the noise was terrific, the smoke and dust thick and choking. Early on, communications with Brigade and attacking companies broke down. The valves of the No.18 wireless sets were destroyed by the shelling. The rear link to Brigade functioned occasionally but it too was later destroyed by enemy shell fire. It became impossible to keep in touch with the three companies and much confusion was caused as a result. Runners and liaison officers who braved the appalling shell, mortar and small arms fire were the only means of getting messages to the units and many of these disappeared on their journeys. On reaching their objectives companies were instructed to fire off a Verey signal to convey their success to Battalion HQ. 'A' Company's signal was observed when it reached its objective and this was confirmed by Lieutenant Sandwith when on his way back to the Regimental Aid Post, wounded. It was thought that 'D' Company had reached Zarat Sudest but 'C' Company's exact position was not known.

What was happening to the companies? We have seen that 'C' Company (Major Eardley-Wilmot) led the way across the Wadi and took up its position on the Start Line. Some of its personnel straggled behind and were picked up by Lieutenant Galloway with the leading platoon of 'A' Company following behind. As soon as 'C' Company left the Start Line to attack Ouerzi Ouest it came under extremely heavy shell and mortar fire. No. 15 Platoon on the right was almost decimated and its commander, Lieutenant R.E. De Blabey, was mortally wounded. Confusion was great and control difficult. However, Lieutenant A.R.W. Maddox and thirteen men of No. 13 Platoon, led by Major Eardley-Wilmot, pushed forward to reach a point approximately half way between Ouerzi Ouest and Zarat Sudest. The Major ordered his party to lie down and take what cover it could whilst he reconnoitred the ground. Whilst the Major did this, Lieutenant Maddox and his small party, not satisfied with lying in one position under enemy fire, explored the maze of trenches they found themselves in. In doing so they came across an enemy machine-gun position. This was attacked by Lieutenant Maddox, his Platoon-Sergeant and three men with hand grenades. Two of the German crew were killed and the position destroyed. It was about 11.00 p.m. when Major Eardley-Wilmot reached some of the forward positions of Zarat Sudest held by Captain J. Chapman and men of 'D' Company. As he did so, he was shot through the neck by an enemy sniper. He was brought into the trench and, as there were no stretcher-bearers with the party, a man was detailed to take the Major back to the RAP. The Major had no sooner stepped onto the fire step in the act of leaving the trench than he was again hit by a bullet and killed. Shortly after this, Lieutenant Maddox and his party joined Captain Chapman.

The rest of 'C' Company was widely scattered and out of touch with Battalion HQ. Lieutenant Atherton with the survivors of his platoon, reached their objective where a little later they were joined by Company Sergeant-Major Watts. A number of stragglers, some wounded, came back to Battalion HQ where they regrouped under Captain G.T. Lindrea who, at first light on the 22nd March, led them back to Ouerzi Ouest which was found to have been evacuated by the enemy.

'D' Company, delayed at the crossing, lost the advantage of the supporting barrage and in the process of forming up came under heavy enemy shell and mortar fire. The Start Line had not been marked and the Company could only form up facing roughly in the right direction and move forward on a compass bearing. 'A' Company was on the right. As 'D' Company formed up, No. 1 Platoon on the left and Company HQ were hit by shell fire and many men became casualties, including the Platoon Commander, Platoon-Sergeant, Company Sergeant-Major, both signallers and the No. 18 set destroyed. Captain Wood ordered his reserve platoon forward to take the place of the stricken No. 1 Platoon. The Company moved steadily forward though suffering heavy casualties from shell and machine-gun fire. The darkness, smoke and dust made control difficult. The objective was the north sector of Zarat Sudest. When the advancing Company reached a point about twenty yards from the objective the positions were found to be surrounded by a barbed wire fence. The Company stormed through this slight obstacle and charged into the trenches, dugouts and pillboxes only to find that the enemy had fled. Evidently the Italian garrison of this sector had evacuated the positions the previous night when the British artillery bombardment had fallen on it. German troops were sent to take over and had just arrived at midday. They were not familiar with the ground and three prisoners were captured. They had become separated from the main body and lost in the maze of trenches. Several Germans lay dead or wounded in the trench. Captain Wood consolidated on the objective. He found that he had with him about fifty to sixty men of both 'A' and 'D' Companies. He took command of this force and organised the defence of the positions. Later he was joined by Major Ovenden of 'A' Company who took command of the group with Captain Wood as his second-in-command. Major Ovenden had with him Second-Lieutenant Dorman and the remnants of No. 17 Platoon and Lieutenant Burdett with a party he had found on the way up to the objective, lost and confused.

An enemy machine-gun post about one hundred yards away was becoming quite a nuisance and endangering the force. A number of attempts were carried out to try to put it out of action but it was some time before it was finally destroyed. Two gallant individual attempts in particular were undertaken. The first one was made by Second-Lieutenant Dorman of 'D' Company who, under very heavy fire, crawled forward with a Bren gun and engaged the machine-gun post. He was wounded through the head. This young officer was ultimately awarded the Military Cross for this action. Lieutenant Isaacs of 'A' Company made another attempt to destroy the machine-gun. He leapt over the top of his trench and raced towards the enemy post in an attempt to destroy it with hand grenades. He was, unfortunately, killed in the attempt. Just before dawn, accurate 2in. mortar fire was brought down on the post and the crew was killed by Bren gun fire as they tried to withdraw. Captain Wood described the trench system at Zarat Sudest:

> 'The trench system seemed unending. It was a maze of communication trenches and the whole complex system was most confusing. At intervals along the trenches there were circular recesses not unlike our Anti-Aircraft pits but, as these were sited to the east they offered no field of view or field of fire towards the enemy in the West. It was impossible, owing to the persistent enemy artillery barrage, this accurate sniping fire, to move into the open and dig fresh position, so the men lined the communication trenches and dug standing or lying positions on the parados.'

Movement in the positions was extremely limited due to the heavy retaliatory enemy fire, though fortunately the trenches were very deep and gave good cover. The main nuisance was the very accurate enemy sniper fire and many of the wounds suffered were to the head and neck. Neither 'A' nor 'D' Company had wireless communication, both of the No. 18 sets had been put out of action. Sergeant French volunteered to take a message to Battalion HQ but was forced back by the intensity of the shell fire and the constant sniper fire. It was not until dawn that a message was successfully delivered. In the appalling visibility and confusion, no one was certain that they had reached their correct objective and it took an hour since first arrival to ascertain this with any accuracy and fire the success signal. There were a large number of badly wounded and these were cared for by Private O'Keefe. All field dressings had been used and none of the larger shell dressings were available and there was no morphia. Private O'Keefe improvised a First Aid Post in the trench and kept the wounded warm with sandbags, German greatcoats and some of the clothing of their own comrades. When it became possible to remove the wounded in the morning, they were found to be comfortable and well cared for. To make matters worse, the Bren guns failed to work as they had become choked with sand and dust. They were stripped and cleaned time and again but, at best, could only be made to fire single shots.

'A' Company was on the right of 'D' Company. It, too, suffered heavy casualties as it moved off from the Start Line. Cohesion and control were equally difficult to maintain as they had been with the other two companies due to the darkness, smoke and dust. However, those who survived the heavy artillery and machine-gun fire reached their objective at Zarat Sudest at about 10.30 p.m. Lieutenant Galloway with about fifteen men of 'A' and 'D' Companies reached a forward position at Zarat Sudest. On the way this party had overrun a machine-gun post manned by five Germans of whom two were already dead. This officer was joined by Captain J.H. Chapman, Second-in-Command of 'D' Company, who assumed command of the party. A further five Germans were found in the captured position, one of whom was badly wounded. Lieutenant Sandwith and one man of 'A' Company had reached a position even further forward but had both received wounds and were forced back. They passed through Captain Chapman's positions on their way to the RAP

Front line first aid post by the side of **Wadi Zigzaou**, Mareth, the crossing of which was effected at night

Imperial War Museum photograph No. NA 1330

which had been established in the Wadi Zigzaou. At 11.10 p.m., Lieutenant Maddox of 'C' Company, with one section of men, joined Captain Chapman. This small force had to remain on the alert during the night as a group of six or seven Germans could be seen forward of the post. The time was spent building positions on the parados. At first light on the 22nd March, one of the Germans surrendered whilst the rest of the group made off. Captain Chapman and his men shot down most of this escaping group.

When the attacking infantry of the 8th and 9th Battalions, The Durham Light Infantry, had crossed the Wadi Zigzaou on the night of the 20th-21st March, the Divisional Engineers had immediately commenced work on the crossing, which was vital to the success of the battle. Tanks of the 50th Royal Tank Regiment and lorries carrying fascines had dropped their loads into the Wadi. Four Valentines had got across the first night. The crossing had collapsed under the fifth tank and nothing further could cross. It was impossible to repair and strengthen the causeway during the 21st due to the severe shell and mortar fire which fell into the Wadi. The work was recommenced on the night of the 21st-22nd and the Engineers worked under the most appalling conditions to complete their task. Artillery and mortars continued to bombard the Wadi and the men worked feverishly under constant machine-gun and sniper fire. At dawn on the 22nd, about forty Valentines of the 50th RTR, crossed the causeway but seriously damaged the crossing in the process. They moved into the bridgehead where the ability to move freely was hindered by the minefields and anti-tank gun fire. They were still a welcome sight to the tired infantry though it soon became obvious that the tanks' 2 pounder guns would be of limited value when German tanks appeared. The decision to put the tanks across the Wadi first before the Battalion's 6 pounder anti-tank guns and mortars began to look like a mistake.

The position early on the 22nd March was that 6th Battalion had reached its objectives at Ouerzi Ouest and Zarat Sudest, though not without heavy casualties. The 9th DLI had also reached its objectives at Ouezi Est and the unnamed strongpoint 1,000 yards to the north but only after severe hand-to-hand fighting and considerable losses, which left the Battalion possibly too weak to hold its positions satisfactorily. The 8th DLI still held Ouerzi. The bridgehead had been extended to about 1,200 yards in depth and a further 800 yards wide. However, the infantry was tired and beginning to run short of ammunition. Reserve supplies and particularly anti-tank guns could not be brought across. At midday, a cloudburst flooded the Wadi and wrecked the causeway.

The fighting during the night 21st/22nd March had been severe. Many acts of considerable courage went unrecognised.

Amongst those who received recognition were Sergeant Reg Haseley who had already won a DCM at El Alamein and Private Hudson. Sergeant Haseley was awarded a Military Medal. His citation read:

> '...this Sergeant has shown repeated disregard to his own personal safety and his leadership in Battle has been of the very highest order.

> '...during the operations in the Ouerzi area on the night 21st-22nd March Sergeant Haseley took part in the advance of his Company, leading his men with great bravery. At first light on the 22nd March Sergeant Haseley inspected his Platoon positions and not being satisfied with the field of fire of his Bren Guns climbed onto the parapet in order to determine the best positions for them. At this time the positions were under heavy shelling and intense MG fire and Sergeant Haseley fell back into the trench wounded. His wound was bandaged and although he was urged to make his way back he refused to do so and climbed back to direct the fire of his Brens against the advancing enemy who were then counter-attacking...'

Private James Hudson of 'C' Company was awarded a Distinguished Conduct Medal. His citation read:

> '...On sighting an enemy machine-gun post he immediately led a group of men forward with fixed bayonets and charged the position. The rifle bolt was damaged and the rifle could not be fired, but he still led on this party relying solely on the use of the bayonet. He succeeded in capturing the post, killing many of the enemy personally. This action of Private Hudson's enabled the rest of his company to move forward onto the position ... He showed outstanding courage and complete disregard for his own safety.'

Many wounded were lying in the trenches patiently waiting removal to the RAP. Captain Rumney, the Medical Officer, the Padre, Captain A. Garbutt and three NCOs, set up the RAP in the Wadi about twenty yards from the crossing. The only equipment available was a few surgical haversacks, a medical companion, some shell dressings and a stretcher. The remainder was with the medical truck which was due to come up with the 'A' Echelon transport. At 10.30 p.m. on the 21st March, the RAP personnel begin to dig slit trenches in the bank of the Wadi to protect the wounded against enemy fire which fell all around the position.

Men of the Battalion in dug in positions of the anti-tank ditch of their sector of the Mareth Line. It was at this point that they were fiercely counter-attacked by the enemy. Front group left: Lieutenant I.A. Daw. Front group right: Sergeant Bishop. Front group right: Private Meeks.   Imperial War Museum photograph No. NA 1453

Sergeant Davies, a stretcher-bearer and ex-bandsman, went round all the forward companies braving the shell, machine-gun and snipers swept ground, to ensure that his stretcher-bearers were in position and coping with the increasing number of wounded. For his gallant conduct throughout the action, Sergeant Davies received the Military Medal. His citation reads as follows:

> 'Sergeant Davies was in charge of the Battalion Stretcher-Bearers during the Battalion attack on the MARETH line on the night 21st/22nd March. after stretcher-bearers had brought in their first casualties from the Companies, he organised them into squads for the wholesale evacuation of casualties and personally led them to the very forward localities under heavy shell and M.G. fire. Later he carried stretcher cases across the wadi to ambulances under intense artillery and mortar fire. Sergeant Davies displayed throughout great coolness and set a fine example to all his men which was responsible for the safe evacuation of all casualties from the R.A.P. His conduct was of the highest order. Never once did he cease to work and there is no doubt that he very materially assisted in the safe evacuation of at least 100 cases from the R.A.P.'

The first casualties began to arrive at about 11.00 p.m. The wounded could only be given morphia and anti-tetanus serum. Their wounds were bandaged with shell dressings and, where appropriate, bound with rough splinting. No ambulances arrived until dawn on the 22nd. Blankets were scarce and the wounded were kept warm by covering them with sandbags. Some wounded were evacuated on two lorries that had brought up fascines for the causeway. Others walked back. The number of wounded greatly increased as the battle continued. Captain Garbutt, the Padre, organised the evacuation of the casualties. At dawn, an ambulance arrived on the opposite side of the Wadi and some serious stretcher cases were removed. The arrival of this vehicle of mercy was very much due to the excellent work being carried out by Captain Maurice Kirby, commanding 'S' Company.

'S' Company, together with 'A' Echelon transport, left the Battalion area at about 10.15 p.m. on the 21st March, and arrived at Chet Meskine at 11.30 p.m. Captain Kirby was instructed by Brigadier Beak that as the crossing was not yet constructed he was to remain at Brigade HQ and put Captain Redway in charge of the Company. During the night, Captain Kirby made several journeys to the crossing to see if it had been completed. Just before dawn, General Nichols, Divisional Commander, arrived at Brigade HQ and gave instructions that no wheeled vehicle was to cross the Wadi that day. When the causeway was completed, priority was to be given to tanks who would act as an anti-tank defence for the infantry. The Battalion carriers could then follow the tanks across.

About 5.30 a.m. on the 22nd, Captain Kirby was ordered to get his carriers and mortar carriers across the Wadi as soon as possible. He led the way down the now well worn track to the Wadi crossing only to find that the causeway was in a very poor condition after the tanks had crossed. The Bren carriers got across but the mortar carriers were less fortunate. One got stuck in the middle and four others behind were unable to cross. Captain Kirby reported the position to the Brigadier and was ordered to wait till the time came for the anti-tank guns to cross the Wadi. Captain Kirby, quite rightly, felt that the Battalion Commander should be acquainted with the situation, so at about 9.00 a.m. he went to Battalion HQ to speak to Lieutenant-Colonel Watson. Whilst at the HQ he arranged with Captain Thomlinson, the Adjutant, for food, water and ammunition to be brought up to the Wadi after dark. On his way back to Brigade HQ he arranged for more ambulances and the RAP truck containing the essential medical supplies, to move up behind the Wadi.

At about 8.00 a.m. on the 22nd, seventy-three enemy prisoners passed through Battalion HQ from the 9th Battalion positions. The hollow in which Battalion HQ lay was constantly under heavy enemy shell fire and communications with the forward companies and to the rear with the Brigade were constantly breaking down. These could only be maintained by runners. Ammunition was very low and beginning to cause great concern. The average company strength was about fifty men. In the middle of the morning, a runner arrived from Brigade HQ with the not unexpected news that the enemy was concentrating for a counter-attack. RAF reconnaissance planes had seen tanks, guns and lorries assembling in the palm groves around Zarat. What seemed like a perfect target for our planes could not be attacked as the cloudburst had grounded our aircraft. At first it was thought that the enemy attack would come in at about 11.30 a.m. but a later message from Brigade indicated that it might not take place till about 1.30 p.m.

At 8.00 a.m., Captain Wood, then Second-in-Command of the force holding the northern part of Zarat Sudest, contacted Captain Chapman. Ammunition was checked and redistributed on the scale of forty rounds per rifle and six magazines per Bren gun. Of the latter, only two out of the original four were working. Shortly after noon the enemy counter-attack began to develop. Lieutenant Spike Galloway described what happened:

> "Being in a position some one hundred yards forward of Major Ovenden's force, we were the first to see the enemy tanks at Zarat. At about 12.30 hrs the tanks could be plainly seen to the East of the village: they then went behind Zarat and appeared again at a short distance to the North East. From here they advanced in 3's. We watched their progress till they became hidden by the ridges in front of us. The infantry accompanying the tanks advanced in extended line, well spaced and making good use of all possible cover. They kept moving steadily forward in spite of our barrage. Unfortunately the W/T set in our trench ceased to function and accurate artillery fire could not be brought to bear on them. Some of the enemy succeeded in getting into positions on our left flank. We sent back to Major Ovenden for a 2in. mortar when this enemy force got to within two hundred yards of our position. When the mortar arrived it was used with good effect. As darkness fell we received the order to withdraw to the Anti-Tank Ditch and there joined the remainder of 'A', 'D' and 'C' Companies under Major Ovenden."

Lieutenant Galloway was later wounded during a bayonet charge to break through the enemy. He was one of the last to withdraw across the Wadi Zigzaou with about a dozen men of the 6th and 8th Battalions. They also brought back a wounded officer.

At 11.00 a.m., a troop of Valentines had moved behind the positions held by the men of 'A' and 'D' Companies under Major Ovenden and Captain Wood. The troop commander informed them that an enemy counter-attack was expected. At about 12.30 p.m. sounds of enemy tank fire could be heard from the direction of the positions held by 'C' Company on the right flank and

Ouerzi Ouest. Nothing could be seen but the tanks of 50th RTR began to move slowly in open formation in that direction. The 2 pounder guns of the Valentines were no match for the 75mm guns of the German Mark IV tanks and the British tanks suffered horrendous losses. They fought with great gallantry to protect the infantry but were hopelessly out gunned. During the course of the day thirty-two Valentines were destroyed with most of their crews and the loss of their Commanding Officer, Lieutenant-Colonel Cairns, MC.

It was becoming increasingly obvious that the main weight of the enemy counter-attack was falling on the survivors of 'C' Company in Ouerzi Ouest. Under heavy fire and with the enemy tanks creeping ever closer the Company tried to hold on to its positions. Captain Lindrea tried to reach one of the Valentines to ask for assistance and was wounded in the face and evacuated. The position at Ouezi Ouest was now under the command of Lieutenant Atherton of No. 14 Platoon, with Company Sergeant-Major Watts and a small number of men. Ammunition was now critically low. The German infantry had pushed between Ouerzi Ouest and Zarat Sudest and commenced an encircling operation. A fierce artillery barrage fell on the tiny force's position. Lieutenant Atherton called for a volunteer to try to reach Battalion HQ. The runner got through but by this time it was too late and, although smoke was laid down to assist the withdrawal, only a handful of 'C' Company got away. They had fought almost to the last round. Private Harry Wilkinson of 'C' Company:

> 'Ammunition was running very low and they said to Spendlove and I, "Go back down to the Wadi and see if you can get some ammo up here." We went down and when we got into the Wadi ... three [British] tanks appeared on the skyline. I don't know why instead of coming right down they were almost silhouetted, side on, and Jerry's guns opened up and they were just like clay pigeons. "Bang! Bang! Bang!" and there was three blackened hulks, burnt out wrecks ... Captain Rumney ... He was a swarthy little chap and MO. In actual fact he was a surgeon. Out of the line you got Aspirins and made the best of it. When you were in action he was busy with the knife, he was a marvel.. We'd been detailed, this other fellow and I, to take a stretcher through the water and go up to the tanks to see if there was any wounded

there to get out and get back. But while we were part of the way through the Wadi Jerry started shelling again and the shrapnel was flying between our legs and all around us and, all of a sudden, this lad got a piece in the thigh and that was it. I mean I couldn't manage on my own and we just had to drop the stretcher ... supporting him on my shoulder we got back ... and got a field dressing out and started to dress his wound. Then Spendlove and I contacted each other again and we got a box of ammo which was quite heavy and we were making our way back when Jerry started mortaring and shelling and we jumped into this - not a slit trench really - it was more of a square which had been cut to a depth of about 18 inches as though they were going to put a gun or something in there at one time. We laid there with bullets whistling over the top and a mortar burst and I got a small piece of mortar in my left leg. It didn't go too far and I managed to pick it out. It burnt a bit. That was it, we were stuck there, hardly dare move ... I happened to look up to the left and saw tin hats and I gave a shout. It was the sergeant who had detailed us to get the ammo. He said, "Christ!" he says, "I thought you two buggars had been shot." He says, "Howay, leave everthing." I said, "Wait till I get me pack and that back on," I'd just released me belt and dropped it low on me shoulders. He says, "Bugger that." He says, "Off! Leave everything. Come On." ... Me, daft, I don't know why I did it, I got me webbing back on and I was facing forward and Jerry was coming down firing from the hip, bayonets. So that was enough for me. I turned round and fled. As it happened the white tapes marking the minefield had been blown to bits. I was on me own and there was a group of chaps slightly forward and to my left. Maybe about twenty or so ... and a shell or something went off and there was corpses and God knows what flying about. Anyway I made it back to the Wadi.'

With 'C' Company position gone, the location of Battalion HQ was precarious. It had been overlooked from that position. The Germans now overlooked the Headquarters. Lieutenant-Colonel Watson ordered a withdrawal to the anti-tank ditch where a joint headquarters was set up with Lieutenant-Colonel Clarke of 9th DLI. His company at Ouerzi Est had also been overrun in the enemy counter-attack and the survivors of it and 'C' Company and the Carrier and Mortar Platoons of 6th DLI, prepared the new Headquarters position for defence. One unfortunate result of Lieutenant-Colonel Watson's order to retire was that it was misinterpreted as a general withdrawal by some of the Carrier Platoon and headquarters staff. They recrossed the Wadi and retired towards the rear but were stopped and sent back by Captain Kirby.

'D' Company front had remained quiet during the enemy attack on ' C' Company. At about 5.00 p.m., stretcher-bearers had arrived to take away the remaining casualties. The Signals Officer, Lieutenant Wedgewood, arrived with instruction to hold on as long as possible but should the situation deteriorate and become untenable, then, on their own initiative, they were to retire to the anti-tank ditch. Major Ovenden requested fresh Bren guns and ammunition as without these there was little likelihood of holding the position. As dusk set in, the enemy succeeded in infiltrating to within a hundred yards of the Company positions and heavy sniping was renewed. The order was given to fix bayonets and it was decided that if the enemy should attack they would go forward to meet them. However, shortly after dusk, Lieutenant Wheatley of the 8th DLI arrived and informed Major Ovenden that survivors of his Company, on the left of 'D' Companys positions, had received orders to withdraw to the line of the anti-tank ditch. With the right flank already gone and now the rear left flank open, with practically no ammunition left and the strong possibility that the enemy would surround them, it was decided to retire to the anti-tank ditch. This was done in single file, very quietly and without interference from the enemy. The survivors of the three battalions which formed 151 Brigade were now lining the anti-tank ditch. On the right was 9th DLI, centre 8th DLI and on the left 6th DLI with two or three medium machine-guns of the 2nd Cheshire Regiment dug in on the top of the anti-tank ditch.

For Captain Kirby, the 22nd March was another eventful day. At about 3.00 p.m. he saw a number of carriers approaching Brigade HQ from the direction of the Wadi. These were the parties who had misinterpreted the withdrawal of the Headquarters to the anti-tank ditch as being a general withdrawal. They were turned round and sent back to the front led by Regimental Sergeant-Major McMahon. Captain Kirby ordered Captain Redway to take the Anti-tank Platoon to the east bank of the Wadi and prepare to cross to the other side. With them went a platoon of the 2nd Cheshires who were to manhandle their guns across the Wadi as the crossing was effectively blocked. The balance of the carriers, under Company Sergeant-Major Taylor, had been able to cross earlier and report to Lieutenant Pringle. Captain Kirby now ordered that the anti-tank guns be dug in on the ridge overlooking the Wadi from the British side, so forming a second line along with any light machine-guns available. The ground was hard and it was extremely difficult for the guns to be dug in. Sergeant Bert Davies remembered the move:

> 'The anti-tank guns when we set them up were probably just out of range of his [German] smaller guns but the 88s they would hit them. In fact they hit one of our guns ... All you could do was lie there in case they tried to get over this side of the ditch ... I remember Captain Kirby and Sergeant Ingram lying on the edge of this anti-tank ditch and I remember him (Captain Kirby) shouting, "Davies! Over Here!" So I crouched, ran like hell for I knew it was under fire all the time and dived down alongside Captain Kirby. He said to me, "Well Davies, which would you rather have? This or Bullshit?" I said, "Neither." I said, "Just a little deeper trench." At the same time as we were talking the Spandaus were cutting off the top of the shrubs. He said, "I think you're right."'

Between 4.00 and 5.00 p.m., Brigadier Beak visited the combined headquarters of 6th and 9th Battalions and told the two Battalions Commanders that the line of the anti-tank ditch must be held to the last man, the last round. It was impressed upon the Brigadier that ammunition, small arms and mortar, was urgently needed and he promised to have some sent up. The crossing was now beyond repair and nothing could cross. However, it was discovered that at one point in the Wadi the floor was quite firm and the water not too deep. Carriers could cross over at this point and it was decided to use carriers to bring up the ammunition supplies which had been so urgently requested. The remaining eleven tanks of 50 RTR under Major Venn, had withdrawn behind the anti-tank ditch and were asked to remain and form part of the defence line although they too were running short of ammunition.

At 6.45 p.m. Captain Kirby visited the 6th and 9th DLI combined headquarters and told the two COs that a meal and ammunition would be brought up at 7.30 p.m. The Captain returned to Brigade Headquarters and ordered the Motor Transport Officer, Lieutenant A.E. Short, to bring up a meal. Brigadier Beak ordered Captain Kirby back to the combined headquarters to ascertain the strength of the Brigade. On his return, the Brigadier was informed that it stood at about three hundred men and a request was made for artillery fire to be brought down in front of the ditch in case any enemy attack developed. At 9.30 p.m. a hot meal was brought to the Wadi. It was dragged in its containers from the Wadi to the anti-tank ditch by three Company Quartermaster Sergeants, three drivers, the Motor Transport Officer and Motor Transport Sergeant J. Bruce, part of the journey having to be made through a minefield.

There was a continual stream of casualties during the day. Four ambulances, one of which was from the American Field Service, were making continuous journeys to and from the Advanced Dressing Station. The Medical Officer of the 50th RTR had collected his wounded in a jeep and brought them back to the 6 DLI, Regimental Aid Post, for evacuation. The casualties were carried across the damaged causeway under continual shell and mortar fire. A stream of bullets from an enemy machine-gun was falling on one of the forward slopes used by the stretcher-bearers. Fortunately no one was hit and the evacuation of the wounded continued.

During the night several attacks were made on the left flank held by Major Ovenden's mixed band of 'A' and 'D' Companies' men, supported by some of the carrier platoon and two tanks. He also had two mortars, part of Lieutenant Ian Daw's Mortar Platoon. The Mortar Platoon did sterling work throughout the night, continually breaking up enemy concentrations and frustrating attempts to attack in force. The Platoon fired over two thousand rounds in total during the battle. The enemy attacks were broken with heavy losses but the lack of ammunition was becoming critical and the Bren guns were so choked with dust that they would not fire. Major Ovenden made his way over the bullet-swept ground to Battalion Headquarters to obtain .303 ammunition. He was given the last box but on his way back he was shot and killed by a sniper.

The 6th Green Howards under Lieutenant-Colonel G.C.P. Lance, arrived in the anti-tank ditch to launch a counter-attack at 1.15 a.m. on the 23rd March. Their objective was the high ground between Ksiba Ouest and Ouerzi Est. It was obvious that the enemy was massing in some strength to begin another attack which was stopped by our barrage and the mortar and machine-gun fire that had kept up throughout the night. Only three Germans succeeded in reaching the ditch whilst nine others were killed in front of the Green Howards who had lined the ditch between the 9th DLI and Ksiba Est.

In the early hours of the morning, Captain Kirby was asked by Lieutenant-Colonel Clarke to contact Brigadier Beak and inform him that he proposed to attack with the 8th Battalion, with 6th and 9th DLI following behind. He requested that the Brigadier come forward and make a plan as the situation was very confused. Brigadier Beak refused to move forward until General Nichols made a Divisional plan. He also stated that he would not countenance any attack by 8th DLI and that on no account were 6th and 9th DLI to leave the anti-tank ditch. The Battalions Commanders were further informed that Sherman Tanks were to come forward to support them in their present positions. It must be said in all fairness to Brigadier Beak that the proposed attack had been thought up by the tank commander and the two infantry commanders on the spot and his first knowledge of it was when Captain Kirby arrived with the message.

At 3.45 a.m. on the 23rd, a German Mark IV Special tank moved into the old site of the 6th Battalion Headquarters, about two hundred and fifty yards from the anti-tank ditch. By this time the infantry had no weapon of sufficient power to damage this tank. The tanks of 50th RTR had run out of ammunition. These tanks, now in a suicidal position, somehow found their way back across the Wadi. Captain Kirby on yet another visit to the anti-tank ditch was pleaded with to make one last try to get the Battalion anti-tank guns across the Wadi. He managed to get two over, pulled by carriers. On his return to get two more of these guns, he was informed by the Staff Capt, 151 Brigade, that orders had been received to the effect that the Brigade was to be withdrawn at 5.00 a.m. and that this message was to be taken to Lieutenant-Colonel Clarke and then passed on to the 6th Green

Howards. The withdrawal was to be made to the ridge immediately to the west of the Chet Meskine. The message was delivered at 4.50 a.m. and almost immediately a tremendous barrage from the British guns came down in front of the anti-tank ditch to cover the withdrawal. At the same time the enemy guns pounded the Wadi and the crossing. Captain Kirby reported to the Brigadier who was ignorant of any orders to withdraw. He and Captain Kirby went to see General Nichols who confirmed that he had given the orders to withdraw as he now considered the opposition too strong to make any further progress.

Lieutenant-Colonel Clarke ordered The Durham Light Infantry to withdraw at once as there was only ten minutes to the deadline. Five minutes later the 6th Green Howards followed. The withdrawal of these very tired men was made through the minefields and the heavy shelling from the enemy guns. They assembled around Brigade Headquarters. It was not the end of the story. Lieutenant-Colonel Watson, Major Robinson, Second-in-Command of 9th DLI and the crew of the Bren gun carrier under Corporal Scott, which had sunk in the Wadi Zigzaou and who still carried their weapons, which included a useless anti-tank rifle, climbed out of the Wadi. They passed through the minefield, passed the Chet Meskin now under the most severe enemy bombardment, crossed the 'Sebkret' only to realise as dawn broke that there was no one ahead of them.

Unfortunately Captain Wood's mixed party of 'A' and 'D' Companies did not receive the order to withdraw. The same was true of 'C' Company, 8th Battalion, under Captain English on his right. Regimental Sergeant-Major McMahon was now with Captain Wood's party. With ammunition now perilously low he volunteered to go to Battalion Headquarters to see if he could get further supplies. Moving along the anti-tank ditch he found that the remainder of the Brigade had withdrawn and only Captain Wood's force and the small group under Captain English remained in position. He returned to Captain Wood with this information. To make absolutely certain that all had gone, he made a further two journeys along the ditch, which confirmed the situation they were now in. Captain Wood moved up the ditch to discuss the situation with Captain English. It was now 5.45 a.m. and about forty German infantrymen appeared in the rear. In the pale light of dawn these were first mistaken for the Green Howards but Captain Chapman of 'D' Company, also with the party, realised that this Regiment would not attack wearing greatcoats. The line of retreat through the gap in the minefield was now cut off and, with no ammunition left, the force had no alternative but to fix bayonets and attack the advancing enemy and break out through the minefield itself. This was achieved only with heavy losses. Harassed by enemy machine-guns the survivors passed over the ridge behind the Wadi and reached the assembly area.

Regimental Sergeant-Major McMahon's remarkable adventures had an even more remarkable ending and it is most opportune to record them here:

'He [Captain Wood] gathered his men together and crossed the Wadi. He called to me to join him but I wished to ascertain whether or not Battalion Headquarters ... were still in position. I crawled towards them, being sniped and machine-gunned the whole way. When I reached the area formally occupied by Battalion Headquarters, I found it in German hands and I was made a prisoner by two German officers who handed me over to an Italian officer. This officer made me understand that I was to be used as a decoy in an attempt to capture Ksiba Ouest, which was held by two companies of the 5th Battalion The East Yorkshire Regiment under the command of Lieutenant-Colonel R.B. James, DSO. I was to approach the position waving a white handkerchief with Italians in single file behind me. I was to tell the Commanding Officer to surrender otherwise 40 Panzers would pound the place to dust and the entire garrison would be killed. I refused to do this and they threatened to shoot me but when the threat was not fulfilled I concluded that they were bluffing. I then suggested that I go alone as only eight men were holding Ksiba Ouest: I insisted so much on this that they granted my request. They allowed me 20 minutes to return with the 8 men as prisoners. If I failed they added, I would be shot.

Arriving at Ksiba Ouest one of the Garrison pointed out the entrance: as I disappeared into the positions the enemy opened fire with a machine-gun. I reported to Lieutenant-Colonel R.B. James, DSO, and told him my story. True to their word, when the 20 minutes had elapsed, the enemy bombarded the position. One block-house was badly damaged. However, the East Yorkshire Regiment held out during the entire day of the 23rd and withdrew through the enemy lines under cover of darkness.'

Regimental Sergeant-Major McMahon rejoined his Battalion forty-eight hours later. He was awarded the Military Medal and Captain Wood a Bar to his Military Cross.

The Battalion suffered a loss of sixteen officers and one hundred and eighty-nine other ranks killed, wounded or missing in this most severe battle. The disadvantages under which the Brigade had fought included: poor wireless communications; a supply route to the infantry which could not be maintained; lack of an adequate anti-tank defence; the difficult ground over which the battle was fought and the lack of time for proper reconnaissance. Most of the advantages lay with the enemy in their powerful positions which commanded the ground. It was indeed a soldiers' battle, with higher authority not able to exert any great influence once the battle commenced. There were one or two disturbing instances of order/counter orders from Division and Brigade - note the withdrawal confusion. Both Brigadier Beak and General Nichols were to lose their commands shortly after the termination of the battle.

What did the Battle of Mareth achieve? Did so many officers and men suffer in vain? Montgomery's left hook, led by the 2nd New Zealand Division, was able to get round the left flank of the Line whilst the enemy's attention was rivetted on what was happening at Mareth. One of his two strongest Panzer Divisions - the 15th - had to come to the rescue of his infantry and was thus not available to counter the British outflanking movement which was reinforced by the 1st Armoured Division. On the 26th March, the New Zealanders commenced the advance towards El Hamma. The Germans tried desperately to reinforce the El Hamma area but failed though they did succeed in withdrawing their forces relatively intact. The New Zealanders by-passed El Hamma and moved on Gabes. The enemy retreated and by the 29th of the month, El Hamma and Gabes had fallen and the Eighth Army advanced on Wadi Akarit and the 'Gabes Gap' the final barrier before breaking out into Central Tunisia.

CHAPTER 25

WADI AKARIT - ENFIDAVILLE - RETURN TO THE CANAL ZONE

1943

The 24th March was spent in cleaning up and resting. The personnel left out of battle under the Second-in-Command, Major D.J.R. Parker, rejoined. On the 25th, orders were received that the Battalion was to relieve the 201st Guards Brigade in the Bir Bsir area. Before the Battalion left to do so, Brigadier Beak arrived to say his "Good-byes" because of his replacement as Commander of 151 Brigade by Brigadier R.H. Senior, DSO. Brigadier Senior was a Territorial Officer who had commanded a battalion of the 44th Division. The Corps Commander, Lieutenant-General Oliver Leese, also arrived and paid tribute to the part played by 151 Brigade in the Battle of Mareth. Relief of the Guards Brigade was carried out on the 26th March. Patrols out on the 27th saw movement to the rear which seemed to indicate that the enemy was about to retire. Lieutenant J.E. Bell, commanding one patrol, was killed when he trod on a mine. Patrols on the 28th discovered that the enemy had, indeed, gone. The Battalion moved forward on the 28th but did not get the opportunity of continuing the chase for long as it was soon withdrawn and sent back to Mareth Sud for rest and reorganisation. At the end of March a draft of one hundred and thirty-six men was received. Lieutenants D.A. ffrench-Kehoe, C.J. Long and D.J. Fenner and Second-Lieutenants L. Attenborough and J.C. Shaw also joined the Battalion. Lieutenant Fenner had just recovered from jaundice. He joined 'C' Company and recorded the state of the company and platoon as he found it on rejoining the Battalion and showed how casualties since the war had altered the Durham contingent. This had, of course, been almost one hundred per cent when the war started. This was also, to a greater or lesser degree, the picture in every company and platoon.

'I joined 'C' Company or rather what was left of it. The Company Commander and two officers had been killed, the other two officers wounded and prisoners of war. Company Sergeant-Major Watts, killed in action and all sergeants save one were casualties. Less than a third of the company had survived. The senior survivor was Sergeant Albert Dunn, MM, one of the original members of the Battalion. We had a new Company Commander, Peter Walton, who had rejoined the Battalion from ERE (Extra Regimental Employment). His father had commanded the Battalion during the spring of 1918 ... I took over 13 Platoon with Corporal Connel as acting Sergeant. Tony [Kehoe] with a new Sergeant, Moroni had 14 Platoon. Albert [Dunn] commanded 15 Platoon. The company was about 40/50 strong. 13 Platoon comprised myself, Connel and thirteen private soldiers including one Lance-Corporal from IBD [Infantry Base Depot] ... Composition of 13 Platoon: As well as the two Guernsey men there were two Londoners, 'Charlie' Elson and Whitwell; Ben Dickenson and Scott my batman/runner, were from Liverpool; Corporal Connel, acting Sergeant was from Birmingham; Walters from Wales; Moffat, Ritchie, Todd, Bowers and Cummings from Durham...'

Lieutenant Bennett and his platoon had a particularly harrowing task. They were detailed to search the recent battlefield to identify and bury those members of the Battalion killed in the battle. To make the task even worse, the enemy had scattered mines over the ground and booby trapped some of the bodies. One man was killed and two wounded carrying out this sad task.

The next defensive line prepared in considerable strength by the enemy was on the Wadi Akarit position, fifteen miles west of the Wadi Zigzaou. Wadi Akarit, a dry watercourse at this time of the year, had the sea on one flank and a large inland salt marsh - the Sebkret El Hamma which was impassable - on the other. Prominent hills behind overlooked the Wadi. These were strongly held by the enemy. XXX Corps was given the task of breaching the defences with X Corps in reserve ready to break through into the plain beyond. The Corps plan was for 51st Highland Division on the right to attack the hill called Djebel Roumana, five hundred feet high, very steep and impassable to wheeled vehicles. The 4th Indian Division on the left would assault Djebel Meida and Mesreb El Alig as far as the Djebel Tebaga Fatnassa Hills behind. On the night of the 5th/6th April, the Indian Division would make a silent night attack and the 51st Division would attack at 4.30 a.m. with artillery support. Between the Djebel Roumana and the Djebel Meida ran a low ridge connecting the two hills, with a track crossing it at the Roumana end. Along the front of the ridge ran an anti-tank ditch and minefield. The 69th Brigade of the 50th Division was given the task of assaulting this ridge. The 6th Battalion, The Durham Light Infantry, was placed in reserve to this Brigade. The 69th Brigade planned to attack in two phases and Lieutenant-Colonel Watson was informed that if these attacks failed the 6th would make a third attempt to break through.

The battle commenced in the early hours of the 6th April as outlined above. The speed of the early advance across the front slowed as enemy resistance stiffened. 69 Brigade could make little progress until the Djebel Roumana and Djebel Meida were taken by the Scots and Indians respectively. When progress was made on these two objectives, 69 Brigade began to move forward at greater speed. A gap of eleven hundred yards opened astride the track over the ridge between the 6th Green Howards of 69 Brigade and the Highlanders and General Nichols ordered 6th Battalion to fill it in case of an enemy counter-attack. As dusk fell, the Battalion began to move into position. It was not easy in the dark to find the positions on the ground it was to occupy, for the area was covered with slit trenches and emplacements. The companies felt their way forward, always aware that the enemy may counter-attack and catch them at a disadvantage. Lieutenant Fenner wrote:

'We were now in the gun line and it was very noisy...We set off in the dark to find our defensive positions which neither of us had seen...The platoon and I moved in bounds checking with Peter [Walton] from time to time. There was a certain amount of artillery noise, except where we were, where it was quiet. Then we heard a vehicle noise to our front and we could see vehicle movement on the skyline. Down the track towards me came a motorcyclist. He drove up to us and stopped to say something, then we grabbed him. One very surprised panzer grenadier...By first light we had made contact with 'B' Company on our left and they were in touch with 'A' ... Bobby Pringle took the Carrier Platoon through and rounded up about 300 Italians...'

It was quite obvious that the motorcyclist had not been able to find his friends because they had gone. The enemy was in full retreat once more leaving behind great quantities of weapons and equipment. Captain Kirby claimed a Lancia car ready to drive away. Between the 7th and 12th April, the Battalion was given the task of clearing up the battlefield. It collected: six hundred rifles, thirty-three light machine-guns, one 120mm anti-tank rifle, four 65cm field guns - 1917 models with wooden wheels. A further ten of these had to be left. Four smaller anti-tank guns were collected, five tons of ammunition and enormous quantities of equipment which included crates of biscuits and tons of bully beef. Private Parkinson persistently told everyone the latter was horse. One man picked up a bicycle.

On the evening of the 8th April, the Battalion reverted to 151st Brigade and moved off to the Divisional Concentration Area, five miles in the rear. It took with it its own legitimate loot: fifty-five automatic rifles with five thousand rounds of ammunition, ten motorcycles, twelve motor bicycles, one Lancia car and two lorries, binoculars, five lamps, an enormous cheese and large quantities of medical stores. General Nichols carried out a GOC's inspection on the 12th April. On the 13th of the month, the Battalion travelled seventy miles to a staging area six miles west of Sfax, through delightful countryside. The Eighth and First Armies had now linked hands and XXX Corps was closing on the Enfidaville defences. On the 17th, the small village of Hergla was reached, near the coast with enjoyable bathing in the sea.

Leave group in Egypt. *Private G. Iceton, MM, seated right, Corporal T. Russ, seated left*

enemy. The patrol linked up with one led by Lieutenant Hampson, the 8th Battalion's Mortar Officer. They came across three enemy positions and a working party laying mines. The four mortars each rapidly fired twenty rounds, causing considerable panic and casualties, before beating a hasty retreat as enemy guns opened up from the hills behind the town. On the 20th April, the Indian and New Zealand Divisions attacked the Enfidaville positions at first light. 201 Guards Brigade entered Enfidaville and moved into the hills beyond. The last party of 6th DLI to see the enemy in North Africa was a patrol led by Lieutenant Attenborough and Ian Daw who joined one led by Lieutenant Gardner, Mortar Officer of the 9th Battalion. They were unable to fire any bombs as they watched the enemy, too far away, retreating towards the hills. On this day, the Brigadier informed his officers that the Brigade would commence moving back to Egypt the next day. The 50th Division was being relieved by the 56th London Division. Rumour quickly had it that they would be going back to Kabrit on the Great Bitter Lake to train for amphibious operations. There was disappointment that the Division would not be in on 'the kill' which would end with the Axis surrender in early May and yet some relief also that there would be no more killing - at least for the time being.

The journey to the Delta began on the 21st April, 1943. The Bren gun carriers had been handed into XXX Corps Vehicle Park. One of the carriers had survived with the Battalion since Gazala. Named 'Bishop Auckland', the vehicle had assumed a special place in the hearts of the Carrier Platoon and it was with great reluctance that it was handed over. A journey in trucks of one thousand four hundred and fifty miles, was made to Tobruk which was reached on the 7th May. On the 2nd May, the Commanding Officer, Signals Officer and Company Commanders went on ahead to attend a course on combined operations at the Combined Operations Training Centre, Kabrit, at the southern end of the Great Bitter Lake. The Battalion continued its journey under the command of Major W.W. Harrowing, DSO, who had joined as Second-in-Command. Major Parker had taken over 'A' Company. The journey from Tobruk to the Delta was by train and in two groups. The groups reached Sidi Bishr on the 9th and 10th May. Four days' leave passes to

Enfidaville lay a short distance ahead. Patrols were sent out to note enemy positions and strength. On the 19th of the month, a mixed patrol of carriers and mortars led by Lieutenant Attenborough, followed a narrow sand dune out of sight of the

Alexandria were issued the next day. Alexandria was basking in its new found freedom from the close proximity of war. Civilians were back in the city in large numbers. Its hotels, bars and clubs attracted the soldiers with money in their pockets and following a long, uncomfortable and dangerous sojourn up the desert and an uncertain future, it was an ideal interlude.

On the 22nd May, the Battalion moved by train and motor transport to Mena camp near the Great Pyramids. The following day the journey continued to Kabrit, thirty miles north of Port Suez. Lieutenants Dorman, Holt, Sandwith and Urwin rejoined, having recovered from their wounds. Captain R.G. Atkinson, a regular officer with the Regiment, joined the Battalion. Kabrit was the location for HMS *Saunders*, a Naval Training Base. Combined operations training was immediately organised. On the 24th May, initial training commenced, embarking and disembarking on LCAs (Landing Craft Assault). Over the following weeks, the Battalion practised scaling operations using ropes, loading tables were drawn up and vehicles were water-proofed. On the 27th of the month, 'Exercise Dredger' was held which involved an early morning assault landing on the Sinai shore. This was followed by a Brigade Exercise, 'Duchess.' The training continued until the 6th June when the Brigade sailed on LCTs (Landing Craft Tanks) for Suez. On leaving, HMS Saunders sent the following signal to the Brigade, 'To 151 Brigade, from HMS *Saunders*, Good Luck.'

The next camp was at the foot of the Djebel Ataqa. At 4.15 a.m. on the following morning, companies climbed the Djebel - a very strenuous exercise. Early morning though it was, it was not too early for one local Egyptian to open for business selling his 'Good lemonade' at four piastres a bottle. New officers arrived at the camp: Lieutenants J.L. Bell, R. Bousfield. A.C. Copinger-Hill. W.T.A. Davey, J. Dennis MM and R.S. Loveridge. Major E.W.H. Worall DSO, MM, of 9th DLI, joined as Second-in-Command. On the 9th June, the Battalion embarked on HMT *Winchester Castle* as part of a convoy which was to take part in 'Exercise Bromyard.' The Gulf of Aqaba was reached on the 11th June. During the journey, the men learnt their way round the ship and to form at assembly and boat stations in daylight and in darkness. 'Exercise Bromyard' started on the 13th June. It was a full scale invasion exercise made as realistic as possible. The Battalion disembarked into LCAs in darkness. The landing on the shore was opposed by the 8th Punjabs. Bren guns fired into pits, barbed wire obstructions had to be dealt with and tremendous explosions were fired off. During the course of the Exercise, four men were injured, one man losing an eye. All this was observed by General Sir M. 'Jumbo' Wilson, Commander-in-Chief, Middle East Land Forces. On the 15th June, the Battalion reembarked, sailed for Suez and returned to Ataqa Camp. The Djebel was climbed and assaulted on a number of occasions. A new weapon arrived from England, the PIAT, a much improved and efficient personal anti-tank weapon.

General Montgomery spoke to the officers of the Brigade on the 24th June. The following day, he visited the Battalion and spoke to both officers and men with everyone gathered round his jeep. The Secretary of State for War, Sir James Grigg, came to the camp and on the 27th of the month, General Kirkman, now commanding 50th Division in place of General Nichols, was a visitor. The camp was sealed off. Something was in the air. Rumours were rife with the favourite objectives being the invasion of: Corsica, Sardinia, Italy, Greece, Crete or the Balkans.

CHAPTER 26
THE INVASION OF SICILY
JULY 1943

On the 29th June, the Battalion went on board the *Winchester Castle* lying in the Gulf of Suez, along with the Divisional Commander and his staff, the Brigade Commander and Brigade Headquarters. Nearby was the Netherlands ship *Ruys* with the 8th Battalion on board, the *Orantes* with the 9th Battalion and other vessels carrying the remainder of the 50th Division. The convoy sailed through the Suez Canal on the 30th June. Lieutenant-Colonel Watson wrote the following in his diary:

'Pass through Suez Canal for Port Said. Cheers and shouts of "Good Luck" from Kabrit.

'A Yank from the banks shouts, "Where are you going?" The reply, "Home." He answers, "Home! With those damned canoes strung alongside." Certainly LCAs do not look very like ships life boats.'

Port Said was reached and on the 1st July the Battalion was taken ashore and sent on a three mile route march. Then it bathed in the sea, had a haversack lunch and marched back to the ship. On the 5th July the convoy sailed and once at sea the troops were told that the destination was Sicily.

The planning of the invasion of Sicily was attended by much delay and controversy. The delay was due very largely to two factors; first, the continuing military activity in Tunisia which concentrated the attention of the higher command whose task it was to plan the invasion. Second, controversy raged over the submission of initial plans which were not acceptable to the ground commanders, Generals Montgomery and Patton. Montgomery struggled hard and long with his superiors and it

was his plan which was finally accepted.

Initially, the plan put forward was for landings to take place to capture the ports of Syracuse and Catania on the east coast of the island and Palermo on the west coast, together with the airfields in these areas. In addition several landings of Brigade strength would be made at various places round the island to dissipate the enemy's strength and confuse him as to where the main effort would be made. These landings in a variety of small parcels were not to Montgomery's liking and he pressed for concentrated landings on the south and south-east coasts of the island by divisions of the 8th British and 7th United States Armies, the latter under General Patton. After much debate, Montgomery won the day.

The new plan was for XIII Corps of the 8th Army to assault between Syracuse and Pozallo, the capture of the former port followed by those of Augusta and Catania. To do this, the 5th Division would land in the area of Cassibile and move north to take these ports and the airfields close by. Parachutists and glider-borne troops of the 1st British Airborne Division would assist by seizing and holding the Ponte Grande Bridge which carried the main coast road over the Anapo River, south of Syracuse, thus keeping the coast road open and blocking any enemy attempts to move south towards the bridgeheads. 50th (Northumbrian) Division would land in the area of Avola and protect the left flank of XIII Corps and later assist in the capture of Augusta and Catania. XXX Corps of the 8th Army was to seize Pachino Airfield, relieve XIII Corps in the Avola area and gain contact with the 7th US Army on the left. To do this, 231 Brigade would land at Marzamemmi. The 51st Highland Division would land astride the tip of the Pachino Peninsula and seize Pachino. The 1st Canadian Division would land on the Pachino Peninsula between Punta Castellazo and Punta di Formiche to capture Pachino Airfield and make contact with the 7th US Army near Comiso Airfield. Further west, the 7th Army would land and seize the vital airfields of Ponte Olivo, Comiso and Biscari and the port of Licata and its airfield.

The estimated strength of the island garrison was two hundred thousand Italians, many of them Sicilians, badly trained and armed, with the exception of the Livorno Division which was better trained and equipped. The other Italian Divisions involved were the Aosta, Assietta and Napoli together with GHQ and coastal defence troops. The latter were mainly Sicilian and of a very low calibre who, invariably when the bullets and shells began to land amongst them, made off to their homes. There were thirty-two thousand German Army personnel on the island. The two German Divisions were the Herman Goering Panzer and the 15th Panzer Grenadiers. A further thirty thousand German Air Force personnel were also there. In the south east area of the island where the 8th Army would land, there were the Livorno, Herman Goering and the 206 Italian Coastal Defence Division.

The terrain over which the armies must move was exceedingly rough. There were rocky mountains of which Mount Etna, a steep volcanic barrier, was the most well known. Narrow enclosed valleys and dry water courses were etched into the landscape. There were few roads in the main, most of them narrow and lined with dry stone walls. The state roads, one of which skirted the coast, were well built, all-weather, with a good macadam surface. Provincial roads varied widely, usually with a macadam surface and not more than nineteen feet wide. The communal roads were unsurfaced tracks, narrow and often unfit for military traffic. On the east coast, dominated by Mount Etna, over which 50th Division would move and fight and where the mountain came close to the shore, the coastal road was often clinging to the edge of the lower slopes of Mount Etna and in places it was even cut into its rocky sides. Numerous bridges

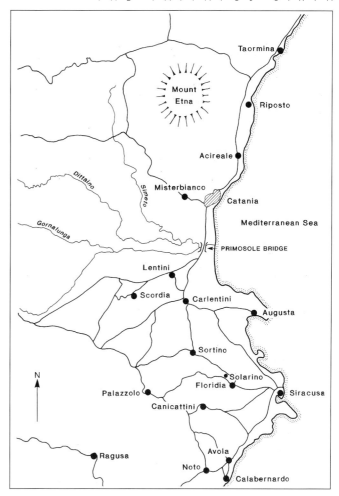

Sicily, *July to September, 1943. Avola to Taormina*

spanned the narrow valleys cut by the water courses from the mountain. It was a terrain ideal for defence and the Germans quickly showed considerable skill in using it to the full. Between Syracuse and Catania was a coastal plain measuring twenty miles long and eight miles wide. It was cut by the Dittaino,

Gornalunga and Simeto rivers and many drainage channels. A notable feature, the Catania Plain, held a major airfield and became an important objective of the advancing British.

50th Division was to land in the area of Avola, a town of about twenty thousand inhabitants, lying on the coastal plain which extends to an average three thousand yards inland. The town itself lies about one thousand yards inland from the coast. The coastal plain was, at the time of the landing, cultivated with vineyards, orchards and olives in small fields bounded by drystone walls. On the coast was a small fishing boat harbour known as Marina d'Avola and, immediately to the north, two concrete pillars and a circular concrete platform jutted out into the sea. This was called the Lido d'Avola. From the coast, the land rose slowly for about one to two thousand yards and then more steeply, with the top of the escarpment about one thousand feet above sea level. This high ground dominated Avola and the beach head. In addition to the coast road, one good road ran inland from Avola to Palazzolo Acreide, climbing the escarpment in a succession of hairpin bends. A railway ran parallel to the shore about one to two thousand yards inland. The enemy defences were a series of pill-boxes and entrenchments, on average about fifty yards apart. They were wired. There were only a few mines and no underwater obstacles, though neither of these facts were known at the time. As we have already seen, the defenders were the 206 Coastal Division, with the main Italian and German Divisions strategically placed inland.

Supporting units with 151 Brigade were as follows:

98th Army Field Regiment (Self-propelled guns - known as Priests).

107th Anti-Tank Battery, 102nd Anti-Tank Regiment (6 pounder guns).

Reconnaissance Party, 3rd Survey Regiment.

505 Field Company, Royal Engineers.

'A' and 'C' Companies, 2nd Battalion The Cheshire Regiment (MGs).

Detachment of 149th Field Ambulance.

34 Beach Brick - Beach organising unit - included 18th Battalion DLI raised in Egypt.

The Brigade plan was for the 9th DLI to land on No. 47 Beach as indicated on the map, in the Jig Green sector - the north end of the beach. 6th Battalion would land on the same beach in the Jig Amber sector between the Marina and the Lido. The two Battalions would then turn south and mop up all beach defences and establish themselves on the main coast road and at the eastern exits of Avola. This was to be accomplished before first light. At first light an advance would be made to the railway embankment. 8th DLI would then pass through and seize the hills behind Avola which dominated the beach area.

So much for the planning and the description of Sicily and the assault areas. Let us now return to the voyage itself and the landings. On the 5th July, the convoy left Port Said and sailed along the North African coast as far as the Gulf of Sirte when it turned north and sailed for Sicily. The slower moving convoy carrying transport sailed from Alexandria prior to the 5th July and LCTs, loaded with vital D Day transport and guns, sailed from Tripoli. Enemy interference from the air did not occur though there were rumours of a reconnaissance aircraft overhead at about forty thousand feet on the 6th July. Nothing materialised from it. A ship carrying motor transport in the slow moving convoy was sunk by a submarine on this same day.

The *Winchester Castle* was reasonably comfortable and the food was good. Unfortunately the ship was declared 'dry' by orders of General Eisenhower, which upset those officers and men who enjoyed a drink. There were air raid alarms but no enemy planes showed up. Time was spent in practising the loading and unloading of LCAs, both in daylight and in darkness and in assembling on deck at their LCA stations and boat drill. Weapons were cleaned and inspected. Officers and men were shown maps, models and photographs of the beachhead area and were fully briefed. The Commanding Officer spoke to the Battalion, explained the plan and described its role in the forthcoming invasion. On the 7th and 8th July, conditions at sea were ideal but on the 9th a strong wind got up and the sea roughened. There was even some discussion between the GOC and the Senior Naval Officer about a possible postponement if conditions did not improve. Towards the end of the day, the wind lessened but the sea retained a heavy swell which was obviously going to make disembarkation into the LCAs difficult.

Lieutenant-Colonel Watson wrote in his diary:

'At 8 p.m. against a stormy looking sunset, with the gale still blowing but with not quite the same force, we got our first distant views of Sicily. Very low on the horizon we could just see the outline with Mt. Etna towering above it all. Europe. Then darkness fell. Everyone was very quiet ... Got up shortly before 11 p.m. Ship proceeding slowly. Went out on deck. The wind still blowing in the rigging and an unpleasant sea. All very dark, except for flak from the shore, against the bombers and gliders of the Airborne Division. They passed over about 10 p.m. Nobody on deck. Certainly the black oily waters looked far from comforting. The moon had gone down. Perhaps the sea would be a little calmer when we got a little nearer land but it was not too good now ... Some of the thoughts that passed through my mind I can remember were whether we would get to the right place, what would our reception be. Would it be a terribly wet landing and would we survive the storm.'

The men assembled on deck just after midnight. It was the 10th July, 1943. Everyone was quiet, the only noises coming from the clump of boots and the occasional bang of equipment on a cabin door. Not a word was spoken. The boat was still rolling and

Men of the Battalion cleaning weapons on the ship carrying them to Sicily
Imperial War Museum photograph No. NA 4144

pitching in the considerable swell of the sea. The men moved onto their craft. At 1.00 a.m. the first wave was launched. Lieutenant David Fenner wrote:

'We had our final meal on board on the evening of the 9th. One wag called it "The Last Supper" and Padre gave a communion. At midnight, the assault troops paraded on the mess decks and we were called forward by LCA [Landing Craft Assault] loads to our boat stations. I had my platoon, 25 of us plus 3 sappers from 505 Field Company, RE. The sappers carried packs containing 2 anti-tank mines in sandbags, equipped with pull igniters and a short fuse. This equipment was for blowing gaps in barbed wire fences. We were to be very grateful for someone's foresight. The move to our boat stations was smooth and quiet, the fruits of much training. We reached our LCA and the heavily laden soldiers climbed aboard. The ship's engine stopped and the assault craft were lowered into a heaving sea. Falls were released and we pitched off into the night."

There were immediate problems. Lieutenant-Colonel Bill Watson wrote:

'Once we were in the water everything went wrong. In a very short time boats were all over the place. The normal drill is as a hen with chicks. We being the chicks. We circle the parent boat 3 times till all the 12 LCAs in the flotilla are in line astern. There seemed to be a mad rush with boats all over the place. We made a large circle but there was no other boats following us. Then we went in again and found ourselves going round the Orantes, with a few LCAs of the 9th. It was difficult to see for first we were on the crests and then in the troughs of the waves ... In no time breakers were coming over the craft and everyone was soaked ... Everyone was feeling terribly seasick ... Poor Derek T[homlinson] was in good heart but feeling wretched. Water poured over at intervals and we had to stand by to man the pumps. It was difficult to see much of the huddled figures in the darkness ... We passed other LCAs but a maddening conversation followed: Q:"Who are you?" A: "Who are you?" Q: "Who are you? I can't hear." A: "Who did you say you were?" Q: "Who are you? A: "We are 9 DLI!"'

Captain Reggie Atkinson was in another LCA with the Battalion Second-in-Command, Major Teddy Worrall. He wrote:

'I happened to be allocated a position near the front of the craft...I had more or less accepted the fact that I was bound to get my feet wet in the landing but I hadn't bargained for the thorough soaking I got every time the bows of the craft rose then went through the top of the waves. We appeared to be meeting the waves head on, and the result, in addition to getting extremely wet, was that we were subjected to a continual and very pronounced see-saw motion. The bows would rise up, hover a second in mid-air, and then plunge down into the trough between the waves making a loud thud as the flat bottom hit the water. I seriously began to wonder if we would ever reach land.

'Conditions like these made it quite impossible for the coxswains to maintain position, and soon there was a lot of shouting between craft as they tried to check up their positions. Teddy Worrall was standing up in the bows looking extremely well, but as I glanced round the boat I saw many doleful faces. I have never been seasick in my life before, but this eternal motion up and down, up and down, was beginning to do peculiar things to my tummy. I grabbed my pint mug and was violently sick into it.'

At times the situation bordered on the chaotic with the army officers in charge of the men in the boat having to come to the rescue of coxswains who were losing direction. Lieutenant Fenner had his problems in his boat:

'The coxswain of the LCA reported to me that his compass light was unserviceable. I told him he should have found this out before and he was to stick to our Battalion's own LCAs. By now the sea was full of rolling and pitching LCAs from both DLI Battalions and the assault element of 5 Div, who were attacking to our north. I realised that we were heading too far north because the coxswain was taking us towards Siracusa, which was under continuous air attack and easily identifiable. We pulled alongside an LCA of KOYLI (5 Div). I took a firm line with the coxswain and got him heading in the right direction. He then rammed another LCA. It contained 14 platoon of our company, so we set off together with various other shadowy shapes. By now most of the platoon were sick, there was about a foot of water in the boat in which well used vomit bags were swilling about. I decided to do a tour of my heroes with some rum. The first soldier, Cummings, sitting in the bow with me just didn't want to know. Only the old and bold made my journey necessary...'

Rum was in plentiful supply that night for those who wanted it. Private George Richardson, signaller:

'As soon as we were under way ... a large bottle of rum was passed down each side of the craft with orders to take a good sip and pass it on."

One error, not spotted at the time, was that the troop transporters had stopped about twelve miles from the shore and not seven miles as planned. This meant that in an unfriendly sea, bad enough in itself, the LCAs had to travel a much further distance to reach the coast and, in the prevailing conditions, more time for difficulties to occur and occur they did.

To show how these difficulties affected the landings of the companies of the 6th Battalion, let us first look at the tasks set by the Commanding Officer, Lieutenant-Colonel Watson. 'B' Company was carried in three LCAs, each with three sappers from the 505 Field Company, with demolition charges and mine detectors. Also travelling with the Company was a small group of the Assistant Beach Master's Staff. As part of the first phase of the attack, it was to land on the right of Jig Amber at 2.45 a.m., destroy all the beach defences along the coast to Lido d'Avola and make contact with the 9th Battalion. 'A' Company, with similar small parties of support units, was timed to land on the left, also at 2.45 a.m. and work southwards to Marina d'Avola, destroying enemy posts on the way and then to push on to the mouth of the River Mammaledi. On reaching the river, it was to take up positions along its banks to prevent any enemy interference from the south.

In the second wave, 'C' Company was to land behind 'A' Company at 3.00 a.m. It was carried in three LCAs, also with some sappers on board. Its task was to seize an important road junction on the south-east corner of Avola and seal all of the exits from the town on the south side, thereby preventing any enemy attempts at infiltration. Battalion Headquarters, also in three LCAs, was with the second wave and was to land behind 'B' Company. In addition to Headquarters personnel on the craft, there was Major Paine, Battery Commander, 98th Field Regiment (Surrey and Sussex Yeomanry), RA, the Signal Officer and the Forward Observation Officer who was to direct the gunfire from the gunboat HMS *Aphis* and the destroyer HMS *Tescott*. 'D' Company was to land last at 3.15 a.m. in an LCI (Landing Craft Infantry) - a larger boat which carried the whole Company. It had additional personnel with it, the interpreter and some of the Support Company for the carriers, mortars and anti-tank guns. This Company's task was to pass through 'C' Company to seize a

strong enemy position around yet another road junction on the south side of Avola with a nearby distillery which possessed a tall chimney. This was a convenient landmark. After completing this task, 'D' Company was to secure the line of the River Mammaledi on the right of 'A' Company, to the railway line. As part of this phase also, 'A' Company was to move from its positions on the River Mammaledi and seize and demolish all enemy positions southwards to Punta Giorgi, if possible before first light. 'B' Company was to push through 'C' Company and clear the enemy from the houses in the south-west corner of Avola, capture the railway station and seize the western exists from Avola. 9th DLI would deal with the town itself. 'C' Company was to be ready to form a mobile column to deal with any coastal batteries which were suspected of being concealed in the hills behind the town. In addition to the men of the Company, there would be four anti-tank guns, four carriers and two mortars from Support Company. Sappers, a troop of the 44th Royal Tank Regiment and an Observation Post from the 98th Field Regiment, RA, completed the column. In the third phase, the beachhead would be reorganised and vigorous patrolling commenced. The Battalion would then form one and a half sides of the beachhead on the southern and western outskirts of Avola, with 9th Battalion DLI completing the other section.

The difficult conditions outlined above greatly affected the neat planning. 'B' Company (Captain J.H. Chapman MC) was first ashore, arriving at 4.15 a.m., ninety minutes late. It landed, with one platoon missing, just north of Punta Giorgi, about three thousand yards south of Jig Amber. The beach defences were dealt with and then it soon became obvious that the Company was in the wrong position. Captain Chapman quickly identified his objective and moved across country towards the railway station. On the way, he was joined by a platoon of The King's Own Yorkshire Light Infantry (5th Division) which was about six miles south of its landing beach which lay north of Avola. The railway station was taken at 8.45 a.m. and the Union Jack carried by the Company was run up. To the great surprise of the British troops, they were joined by a number of American parachutists who had been dropped in the wrong position. They had spent some time fighting the enemy and trying to find out where they were. In all, some two hundred of these parachutists joined the Battalion, one of whom attached himself to the CO as a personal bodyguard until the whole group rejoined their own countrymen.

At 4.30 a.m. 'A' Company (Major R. Galloway) with 'B' Company's missing platoon, came ashore about four thousand five hundred yards south of Jig Amber, just north of the village of Calabernardo. As the craft neared the shore, a searchlight beamed in on them. It was knocked out by the Bren guns of No. 9 Platoon firing from the bows of the LCA. Considerable shell, mortar and machine-gun fire opened up on the approaching craft, fortunately most of it inaccurate. Once ashore, the wire obstacles were gapped and the defenders attacked. Most of them surrendered. Major Galloway, obeying his orders, turned south and began to mop up any enemy defence positions he encountered. Here again, most of them surrendered. At about 6.00 a.m., having advanced for about four miles, Major Galloway realised that he and his Company were heading in the wrong direction. He was out of wireless contact and uncertain as to where he was. He withdrew a short distance and took up a defensive position astride the railway line, facing south. He was soon joined by one platoon of 'C' Company who had also lost contact with the rest of its Company. They were found by the Intelligence Officer of the Battalion at about 11.00 a.m. and he brought them back to the line of the River Mammaledi. 'C' Company had taken over 'A' Company's role of holding the bank of the river and, on arrival, the latter was placed in reserve near Avola. 'A' Company had suffered some losses. Lieutenant Sandwith was wounded and ten other ranks killed or wounded.

'C' Company under Captain H.E. Walton in place of Major D.J.R. Parker who was landing with the 'Left Out Of Battle' personnel travelling with 'D' Company, landed just south of Calabernardo, about five thousand yards south of Jig Amber. On the run into the shore, Lieutenant Fenner's craft continued to have problems:

'We were alert. Cummings the seasick Bren gunner, sitting opposite me in the starboard bow position, checked his weapon and magazine. The platoon was quiet and waiting, seasickness forgotten. Small arms and mortar fire was directed at the LCAs on our right who were nearer the shore. A searchlight was switched on, fire from the LCAs switched it off! We were closing in on the beach, mortar bombs were exploding on the water and bursts of fire from Breda machine-guns were cracking past. The coxswain came forward to report he had dropped his kedge anchor too soon and lost it. This, he said, meant he could not beach the LCA because he had no means of winching the boat off the beach. The men began to comment freely on the Coxswain's ability. I told him to stop engines when the other LCAs to port and starboard did. The enemy fire continued, the door of the LCA went down and out we went into about three feet of water.'

Private Harry Wilkinson, 'C' Company, remembered the landing:

'We were going to land at a place called Avola. We had been told that much but the heavy swell had washed us about four miles down the coast at a place called Little Avola. I remember getting ashore from there and looking back over my shoulder as I got out of the water onto the sand. I could see our captain, Captain Walton and quite a few more who had been hurt. He was holding his belly and singing "Blaydon Races". That's the last I saw of him going down into the water.'

In addition to Captain Walton, one soldier was drowned, two were killed and one wounded. Captain Walton, who had joined the Battalion a year or so before the war, came from a Crook, County Durham, family. His father, Colonel F. Walton, MC, served with the 'Sixth' during the 1914-18 War and commanded the Battalion during the 1918 retreat.

'C' Company, now under Lieutenant D.A. ffrench-Kehoe, gapped the wire obstacles using the mines that the sappers carried in their sandbags. These were called Howard Grenades and proved to be very effective. The Company pushed inland, just missing 'A' Company who were moving south behind them. 'C' Company had lost contact with No. 15 Platoon, which joined 'A' Company. A platoon of 'A' Company similarly found itself with 'C' Company. Lieutenant ffrench-Kehoe quickly realised that the Company had landed in the wrong place and moved across country towards Avola. Progress was slow due to the thick orchards and vineyards encountered but no opposition was met and Battalion Headquarters was reached about noon. It was sent to take 'A' Company's place along the dry River Mammaledi from its mouth, to where 'D' Company was already in position.

'D' Company (Major Wood) landed as a complete unit from its LCI in approximately the same place as 'B' Company, just north of Punta Giorgi at about 4.30 a.m. They encountered shell and machine-gun fire but received no casualties. The Company advanced inland through the gap in the wire made by 'B' Company. Major Wood set up his headquarters on some high ground near Castello Palma. From this position, he was able to see the distillery chimney which marked the objective. He was joined here by the Battalion Second-in-Command, Major Worrall. The Company was moved out towards the objective, taking the Calabernardo - Avola road to the bridge over the River Mammaledi. One platoon was left here facing north. The remainder of the Company advanced along the dried up river bed. Closing in on the Avola - Noto road bridge over the river, sounds of firing could be heard. The password 'Desert Rats', with the answer, 'Kill Italians' was shouted. This was followed by a number of mortar bombs fired into the river bed. Major Wood moved his platoons back a short distance and sent one of them into Avola to contact Battalion Headquarters, to ascertain the position on his front. Joined by a self-propelled 105 mm gun of 98 Field Regiment, Major Wood attacked the enemy positions only to find that carriers of 9th DLI were also attacking the same objective from the north. This combined attack was too much for the Italian defenders, who surrendered. Needless to say, the carriers of 9 DLI were a long distance from their landing beach.

Lieutenant-Colonel Watson and part of his Headquarters came ashore behind elements of the 9th Battalion The Durham Light Infantry and not too far away from his planned landing place. His small party set off southwards along the beach and within a short time reached the pre-arranged site where the Headquarters was to be set up. A patrol was sent out into Avola and quickly returned with the news that Major Worrall was in the town and had organised a headquarters. By 10.00 a.m., with the exception of 'A' Company, the Battalion was concentrated and had carrier patrols out in front. During the remainder of the morning, more and more American paratroopers appeared - about two hundred in all. They were organised into a company and took up position in the Battalion perimeter between 'B' and 'D' Companies. They were very tired and some were wounded. They had been dropped, scattered and out of position, by inexperienced pilots, further confused by being fired upon by Allied ships as they passed over the invasion armada during the hours of darkness. They had fought their way through the Italian positions until they met up with the British. Both Allies were pleased to see each other and the Americans would have gladly stayed with the Battalion a little longer if it had been possible. However, the next day they were returned to their own lines.

Avola was quickly cleared. It had suffered from a little bomb damage and a number of dead Italians lay about; otherwise the town had come out of the ordeal quite well. Private George Richardson recalled:

'I was sent out with Lance-Corporal Weir of the Signals to contact a forward company and recce a route for running out a telephone line. We came into the town centre and an Itie who looked like the town mayor came up and surrendered a bunch of keys to my mate. They were the keys to his council offices which also contained the jail. We went in. There were about 6 prisoners in the cells. We opened the doors and told them they were free. They all flung their arms round our necks and we told them to get off in case we changed our minds.'

At first the civilians encountered showed great fear and in places came up to the troops pleading for mercy. They were soon put at ease by the men who gave them sweets and cigarettes.

The Battalion had taken about sixty prisoners. Later in the day, enemy aircraft attacked the ships at sea and these increased during the evening. Attacks over the next few days caused the loss of three ships carrying the 50th Division's motor transport with a loss of one hundred and twenty-five of its personnel. The loss of the transport was to have considerable effect upon the advance inland by the laden infantry who were faced with long and wearisome marches in the stifling heat. By nightfall on the 10th July, a firm beachhead had been established. The Allies were back in Europe.

CHAPTER 27
PRIMOSOLE BRIDGE
JULY 1943

The glider-borne troops of the 1st Airborne Division had landed and taken the Ponte Grande Bridge but only after suffering considerable losses, not only by the enemy. In the final approach, the inexperienced pilots of the towing craft had released some of the gliders over the sea and many men had been drowned. Others had been hit by the defensive anti-aircraft fire from the ships and beaches who had failed to identify the aircraft and their tows. Others, of course, had fallen to enemy fire. However, sufficient numbers had landed safely to enable the bridge to be taken and held against superior enemy forces until the arrival of the 5th Division. As a consequence, Syracuse had fallen by nightfall.

On the 11th July, orders were received that 151 Brigade would be relieved by a brigade of the 51st Highland Division and the former would, in turn, relieve the Brigade of the 5th Division. 69 Brigade of the 50th Division was ordered to move on Floridia and Sortino. At 1.15 p.m., the 6th Battalion marched off through Avola northwards along the main Syracuse road as far as Cassibile and then westwards, to take up positions in the high ground near Canicattini Bagni. Sergeant Tom Cairns, Intelligence Section, wrote of this first march in Sicily as follows:

'In the burning heat ... the men of the companies who march away envy more than ever the blokes of the carriers and Anti-tank who don't. The march north from Avola is long and gruelling and when the Battalion halts in the evening the marching troops are pretty well "all in".'

At night, two platoons with carrier screens were sent forward to give warning should any enemy attack develop from the direction of Canicattini Bagni. All remained quiet throughout the night.

The following day, the Battalion was on the march again. However, by using the carriers and portees loaded to capacity and used in a shuttle service, the majority of a company could be moved at one time. The other companies marched on until picked up themselves.

The terrain through which the advance was moving was in stark contrast to that experienced in the desert. A coastal plain about seven miles wide stretches between Syracuse and Cassibile. To the north of the road which connects Syracuse, Floridia and Solarino, there are many broken hills which extend to the Plain of Catania. Two good roads ran north: the coast road used by the 5th Division and an inland road which ran almost parallel to that on the coast. The two of them converged and met at Carlentini, then continued to the River Simeto which it crossed at Primosole Bridge and then ran on to Catania. The 50th Division was using the inland road as the axis of its advance. For the most part this inland road through Floridia and Sortino to Carlentini, followed narrow valleys or climbed over steep hills, admirable for defence.

On the morning of the 12th July, the Battalion moved out in the direction of Solarino where it was to relieve the 2nd Battalion The Wiltshire Regiment of 13 Brigade. This Battalion was in contact with the Italians of the Napoli Division outside the village of Solarino. This village lies west of Floridia, about a mile and three quarters away and at the end of the straight road which joins the two. West of Solarino, there are steep hills with slopes covered in olives and rocks and the road to Palazzolo is lined with stone walls and boulders. The Italians were well concealed on either side of the road. The Wiltshires held positions below those of the Italians who could observe every movement made by the British troops.

Lieutenant-Colonel Watson and his Intelligence Officer, Lieutenant Bell, went on ahead to reconnoitre the new positions. He returned to meet the Battalion column outside Floridia where it debussed and prepared to march along the straight road to Solarino, following the Battalion Headquarters and its transport which had gone on ahead. At 2.40 p.m., 'D' Company was about to march out of Floridia when Lieutenant-Colonel R.B. James, Commanding Officer, 5th Battalion East Yorkshire Regiment, came racing down the road on a motor cycle shouting, "Look out, tanks are coming." Quickly the anti-tank guns were put into position amongst houses and the street corners, the civilians disappeared and Major Wood placed his company astride the road on the outskirts of the town. A R35 light French tank with its Italian crew raced into Floridia with all its guns firing. It knocked down a telegraph pole and finally crashed into a Sherman tank. The crew were captured. The R35 was the sole survivor of four or five which had managed to break through the positions of the 2nd Wiltshires at Solarino and had gallantly continued its charge until stopped. Lieutenant-Colonel Watson's jeep had been hit shortly after Privates Parkinson and Gaunt had jumped into a ditch. One 15 cwt and three 3 ton trucks had been damaged. Two other ranks were killed and the Medical Officer, Captain Rumney, and two other ranks were wounded.

The Battalion continued on its way to relieve the Wiltshires and this was completed by about 5.30 p.m. The companies were dispersed as follows: 'A' Company on the right of the road, 'B' Company astride the road, 'C' Company on the left of the road, with 'D' Company in reserve. At 6.45 p.m., the Italians mortared 'D' Company's positions and followed this with an attack directed mainly against these and 'C' Company. An attempt was also made to infiltrate between 6th and 8th Battalions. These failed and a screen of carriers were placed out in front to forestall any further attacks. During the attack, Private Girvan of the Pioneer Platoon, who was manning a Bren gun was killed and one other man wounded. The Commanding Officer, in consultation with Brigadier Senior, arranged to attack the Italian positions on the following morning. A six minute artillery concentration would be fired by the 105 mm guns of the 98th Field Regiment and then 'A', 'B' and 'C' Companies with 'D' in reserve, would attack the high ground held by the enemy. Just before dark, an enemy aircraft crashed into the houses of Solarino and the Battalion's new Medical Officer, Captain Murphy, was soon busy attending the wounded civilians.

Following the extremely accurate initial bombardment, the attack went in at 4.45 a.m. on the 13th July. 'A' and 'B' Companies were the first to meet opposition from quite intensive machine-gun fire which was, fortunately, very inaccurate. The vigour of the attack drove the enemy out of their positions and shortly after 5 a.m. the companies were moving on to their second objective which was the open ground beyond. Captain J.H. Chapman MC, commanding 'B' Company, was hit by a sniper's bullet from close range and sustained wounds from which he subsequently died. Casualties on the whole were very light. The enemy experienced severe losses. 'C' Company met little opposition in taking their first objective. Lieutenant David Fenner described the action:

'Our objective was some 2000 yds away and we were to advance two platoons up. 14 (Tony [ffrench-Kehoe]) left and 13 [me]right, Company HQ, 15 Platoon and stretcher-bearers behind.The attack axis was a compass bearing with the distance to the objective measured in paces. This was standard desert procedure and quite appropriate under the circumstances. We had no time for reconnaissance before darkness fell ... I returned to give the good news to my three corporal section leaders. I then shared a tin of cold M & V with my sergeant. We split what was left of the night between us, to sleep. Reveille was 30 minutes before H hour. Just before H hour the whole company was in its attack deployment facing west. The sounds of pre-attack preparations were going on all around in the dark. Magazines clicking on to Bren guns, the snick of bayonets fixing. We deployed on the S[tart] L[ine]waiting for H hour. I gave out the last of the rum left over from the assault landing two days ago. It measured about a spoonful each and may have provided some comfort at this dreary moment. Some of us had been through this limbo period before an attack on one or more occasions. One feels low and fearful. The presence of your friends around you is the only comfort. It is a relief when the time comes to advance...'

The Company moved forward over the uneven ground. Lieutenant Fenner continued:

'...I recall the men puffing away at cigarettes as they advanced, rifles in the high port position. The guns had stopped firing. As we approached the objective (some farm buildings on a ridge) we saw the enemy. The two leading platoons swept forward whooping, until our progress was stopped by a low stone wall across our front. Beyond this were three lorries and a lot of Italians shooting at us. We stopped and returned the fire. Dominic (Parker) came up to speak to me and was hit in the chest ... Lance-Corporal Montgomery, our company stretcher-bearer [a splendid man] ran up to attend to him and some other casualties. We were shooting back at these Italians. Cummings who was standing next to me, was firing his Bren from the shoulder. I could see the tracer passing over one of the trucks. I said, "Shoot at the truck." His first burst [more by luck than by judgment] started an explosion followed by a fire with burning debris showering over the Italians lying by the vehicles. We broke through the dry stone wall and I found myself amongst a bunch of Italian soldiers. I started to shoot at them with my revolver when I realised they were surrendering and offering me cigarettes. I remember saying, "No thanks, I smoke a pipe," before realising how stupid it sounded. But the fighting here was over ... We settled on our objective, made some protection for ourselves, building up sangers by pulling down the dry stone walls. Tea was brewed, prisoners carrying casualties were moved to the rear. The dead were buried and the battlefield tidied up ... Tony sent me off again to contact D Company on our right. I set off with Ritchie, the pitman from Witton Park. On the way we put up a hare. We both opened fire at once, me with my rifle, Ritchie with his Thompson, fortunately missing. I don't think we meant the hare any harm. I suppose we were tense and it was an immediate reaction to being surprised.'

About sixty Italians had been taken prisoner. With Major Dominic Parker severely wounded, Lieutenant D.A. ffrench-Kehoe took over command of 'C' Company until the action was over when Captain W.D. Glass assumed command. Captain Reggie Atkinson took over command of 'A' Company following the death of Captain Chapman.

At 8.00 a.m. 'D' Company was ordered to mop up the area between the roads Solarino - Palazzolo and Solarino - Sortino. At first the Company encountered no opposition until it had passed through 'A' Company and was combing the higher but more open ground beyond. Mortar and machine-gun fire fell on Nos. 16 and 17 Platoons, fired from a wadi ahead. No. 18 platoon attacked the wadi and approximately sixty Italian prisoners were taken with large quantities of equipment. The Company continued searching the ground towards the main road where it contacted the carrier patrol. It continued down the main road, accepting the surrender of large numbers of Italians who came streaming down the from the surrounding hills. 'D' Company returned to Battalion Headquarters at 7.30 p.m., tired but exhilarated by the day's successes. Many prisoners continued to be brought in. A high proportion were wounded and these caused a problem due to the lack of transport to get them to the rear. The slightly wounded commander of the 54th Mortar Battalion was amongst the prisoners.

At 8.00 a.m. a mobile column was organised, comprising two sections of carriers. They were to act as scouts for one troop of Sherman Tanks. The column was under the command of Captain Pringle. Its task was to set off from Solarino to make contact with the 51st Highland Division at Palazzolo. The troop of tanks was commanded by Sergeant Hampson who was later awarded the Distinguished Conduct Medal for his exploits on this venture. Christopher Buckley, War Correspondent of the Daily Telegraph, was attached to what he described in his book, *Road to Rome* as 'an immense hunting party.' The column travelled westward along the winding road through very rough hill country with outcrops of rock, coarse grass and dry stone walls. A carefully sighted anti-tank gun could have held up any large force.

The first encounter with the enemy was when two R35 tanks were seen driving abreast down the road towards the column. The leading Sherman knocked these out with one well-placed shot apiece. The ram's head insignia painted on their turrets indicated that they belonged to the Italian Napoli Division. Soon afterwards, an ammunition truck was destroyed. This blocked the road but was pushed aside by one of the Shermans. Captain Pringle and his carriers led the way and he cautiously looked around each corner he encountered before moving on. It was a sensible precaution because as he approached one corner he saw three anti-tank guns well sighted to fire on any vehicle which came into view. The tanks were ordered up and they destroyed all three guns before either of them could get a shot off. On rounding the corner at Casa Rossa, the column came upon an Italian staff car containing General Julius Cesare Gott-Porcinari, the commander of the Napoli Division, together with some of his staff. He was, of course, taken prisoner and sent back to Battalion Headquarters on Sergeant Raine's carrier and ultimately to Brigade. About six hundred yards further on, a battery of field guns was observed on a flat piece of ground on the right hand side of the road. These were destroyed by the Shermans and those of the crews who had survived made off into the hills, with the exception of three who were taken prisoner. The next target to present itself was a group of sixteen R35 tanks stationary in a field to the right of the road. These were engaged by the Shermans and were knocked out or surrendered by their crews but not before the leading Sherman had been hit and had to be abandoned. The column moved on and at Metilli an ammunition dump was set on fire, a 75 mm gun and five trucks were hit and put out of action. Twelve Lancia 10 ton Diesel trucks were captured intact, a welcome addition to the Battalion's transport. At 12.30 p.m., the column met up with the 51st Highland Division just short of Palazzolo. At 4.00 p.m it returned to Battalion Headquarters. The total Battalion haul as a result of the activities of the 13th July was as follows:

Seven 150 mm Italian Field Guns.

Two 88 mm German Dual Purpose Guns.

Two 75 mm Italian Field Guns.

Two 28 mm Italian Anti-Tank Guns.

Two Braun German Anti-Tank Guns.

Thirteen Breda Italian Medium machine-guns.

Six 3 inch Italian Mortars with ammunition.

One Fiat Italian Ammunition Wagon.

Five Bianchi Italian Motor Cycles.

Six Bianchi Italian Motor Tricycles.

Twelve Lancia Italian 10 ton Diesel Trucks.

Three Fiat Italian 15 cwt Trucks.

Sixteen R 35 Tanks.

Four hundred prisoners of war.

Large quantities of small arms ammunition.

Sergeant Tom Cairns described the scene along the Palazzolo road:

'Two wrecked and abandoned 88's cover the road; a 75 hit by a shell heels over into the roadside ditch. Motor cycles and tricycles - some smashed, others burning - are strewn across the road, making passage difficult. Abandoned machine-guns, mortars, anti-tank guns are thrown along the walls and hedges bordering the road. Cartridges, bombs and shells are heaped amid the cactus. In the fields more guns, more trucks, more cycles stand unattended, left behind in the rush of a headlong retreat. An ammunition carrier, set alight by Bren tracer, blazes on the road, its cargo popping and whizzing into the neighbouring fields. Italian corpses, charred or mangled, some headless, some legless, are everywhere. Three dead Italians lie huddled around an anti-tank gun. In the roadside ditch a few yards away lies one of our Lance-Corporals.'

The Napoli Division had, in fact, almost ceased to exist.

The 69 Brigade ahead of 151 Brigade was encountering stiffening resistance as it ran into German troops of the Schmalz Battle Group, Herman Goering Division, which was advancing northwards towards Sortino. Ahead, ominous developments were taking place at Catania. On the 12th July, the first elements of the German 1st Airborne Division, transported by air from the Avignon area of southern France, were landing. These tough, highly trained, disciplined and experienced troops were formidable opponents. The first units to land were the 1st Parachute machine-gun Battalion, the 3rd Parachute Regiment and the 1st Parachute Signals Company of the 1st Parachute Communications Battalion. The 3rd Parachute Regiment joined the Schmalz Battle Group in opposing 69 Brigade's advance from Sortino to Carlentini causing a critical delay which was to have a

Primosole Bridge. *The scene of bitter fighting, July, 1943*

serious affect on what was happening at Primosole Bridge. This bridge across the River Simeto was the key to opening the Catania Plain to the advancing British, with Catania and its harbour and airfields seen as vital objectives which needed to be seized for the successful continuation of the advance towards Messina.

69 Brigade entered Sortino on the 13th July and the advance continued throughout the rest of the day towards Lentini. The

infantry pushed on with orders from General Kirkman, GOC 50th Division, to 'march, march and march!' But in the stifling heat and lack of transport the troops were tired. General Montgomery arrived at Divisional Headquarters and ordered General Kirkman to capture Carlentini and Lentini during the night 13th-14th July. During the same night, No. 3 Commando was to land from the sea and capture and hold the Malati Bridge across the River Leonardo about three thousand yards north of

Lentini. At the same time, the 1st Parachute Brigade of the British 1st Parachute Division, was to be dropped at Primosole Bridge to capture and hold it until the arrival of the 50th Division. The British commandos and parachutists took the two bridges and dismantled the charges laid by the enemy to destroy them. They lost their hold on the bridges but held off all enemy attempts to re-lay charges so that both remained intact. All this was achieved under extreme difficulties and savage attacks by far superior numbers of enemy infantry and tanks. The British fought with great gallantry always looking over their shoulders to catch a glimpse of the relieving force coming up from Lentini.

The Germans were also well aware that whoever held Primosole Bridge held the key to the Catania Plain. The British parachutists landed widely scattered but were able to concentrate sufficient numbers to take the bridge and, as we have seen, dismantled the explosive charges set to destroy it. Captain Franz Stangenberg of the German 1st Parachute Division, was in command of the advance party in the process of landing at Catania. He organised an immediate counter-attack against the British. He had available the 1st Signals Company under Captain Erich Fassl and a mixed force of air force ground staff, members of the Herman Goering Panzer Division and of the 1st Parachute Division. Amongst its number of two hundred men were clerks, mechanics and drivers as well as the signallers. Captain Fassl's Signallers occupied the sunken road just north of the bridge. It must be clearly understood by the reader that whether clerks, mechanics, drivers or signallers, these men of the German 1st Parachute Division were as highly trained and disciplined as any other troops in the Division and well versed in the use of their weapons. All through the 14th July, the battle for the bridge went on. The British parachutists, small in number and hopelessly outgunned, put up a tremendous fight. Ultimately driven off the bridge, they continued to fight off any attempts of the Germans to reoccupy it. On the night of the 14th-15th July the 1st Parachute Engineering Battalion of the German 1st Parachute Division arrived at Catania and reinforced the troops in front of Primosole Bridge. This was the position on the morning of the 15th July.

69 Brigade leading the advance was in trouble. As we have

seen, they were meeting first class German troops fighting ferociously. The terrain was ideal for defence. The road from Floridia was narrow, just wide enough to allow two lines of vehicles to pass each other. It was lined with dry stone walls approaching six feet in height. It wound its way through deep valleys, with steep rising hills on either side two or three hundred feet high and either covered with small walled olive groves or boulders and rock outcrops. Just before Sortino the road passes through a narrow gorge until about half a mile away it commences to climb in a series of hairpin bends to the little town on top of the ridge. Beyond Sortino, the countryside is more open until it climbs over another ridge and drops down to Carlentini and Lentini some ten miles on. Beyond Lentini, after crossing the River Leonardo at the Malati bridge the road runs along the top of a ridge and then drops steeply down to Primosole Bridge, a distance of ten miles from the town. Over the River Simeto, the road runs as straight as an arrow across the Plain to Catania with the backcloth of the dominating Mount Etna behind.

Just before dark on the 13th July, 69 Brigade bumped into a strong rearguard of infantry, tanks and self-propelled guns, about three miles from Carlentini. The road was dominated by Mount Pancali, a high conical hill which the enemy had turned into a strongpoint. Bitter fighting took place on its slopes until it eventually fell at about 1.00 a.m. on the 14th and the advance began once more. Carlentini and Lentini fell and four hours later the 5th Battalion The East Yorkshire Regiment linked up with No 3 Commando to find the Malati Bridge undamaged. The advance was well behind schedule. 69 Brigade's units were nearing exhaustion and the decision was taken to pass 151 Brigade through its positions to make the final push to relieve the rapidly dwindling numbers of parachutists at Primosole Bridge. 9th Battalion The Durham Light Infantry led the way, followed by the 8th Battalion with the 6th at the rear.

Lieutenant-Colonel Watson described the journey:

'At 8.30 a.m. on the 14th July, the 6th Battalion left its positions up the Palazzolo road and started out on its march to Sortino. It was the rearmost Battalion of the Brigade. The road was terribly dusty and congested and for some miles the bad hills and tortuous hair-pin bends proved a horrible nightmare for the drivers, after the flat wastes of the desert. The journey, too, was slow and wearying, due to the difficulties the 69 Brigade was experiencing ahead. By 10 a.m. the Battalion was at the cross-roads just outside Sortino, where the 5 East Yorkshire Regiment had had their engagement on the previous day.

'Halting and moving, the overburdened column, carrying most of the marching troops in bren carriers, anti-tank gun portees or captured lorries, ground its way forward.

'During the late afternoon the commanding officers of all three Battalions were called forward by Brigadier Senior. By now Carlentini and Lentini had fallen, so that he met them beside the road on the high ground overlooking the towns. On the other side of the road stood Mount Pancali, bare and gaunt, whilst strewn around on its slopes lay the blackened debris of the bitter fighting earlier in the day. The short stretch of straight road up to Mount Pancali was no place in which to linger; the Luftwaffe had given it a great deal of attention and now seven carriers of the 2 Cheshire Regiment were in flames with the scorched bodies of their former occupants strewn around, whilst sappers dug graves and hurriedly filled in the nearby bomb crater on the road; an ammunition lorry, too, was blazing further away, and the sickening stench of death filled the air.'

Brigadier Senior explained that 151 Brigade was now to take the lead and ordered 9th DLI to advance at all speed to relieve the airborne troops at Primosole Bridge. Once there, the Battalion was to make a bridgehead on the northern side. Lieutenant-Colonel Clarke told the Brigadier that his men were very tired but he would do his best to carry out his orders. 8th DLI would move behind this Battalion and stop at a selected site just short of the bridge. The 6th Battalion was to make a firm base at Mount Pancali.

The 9th Battalion, supported by Sherman tanks of the 4th Armoured Brigade, pushed on towards the Bridge and the beleaguered paratroops. When it reached them at 9.30 p.m. on the night of the 14th July, it had marched some twenty miles over hot, dusty roads. The paratroops had given up the bridge to superior numbers about two hours before but were able to stop any enemy attempts to replace the charges by shooting them down from the south bank as they tried to move onto the bridge. The 9th Battalion was in no fit state to put in an immediate attack

on the bridge, being almost exhausted by the terrible march it had just completed. The Brigadier decided, therefore, that the attack would go in at 7.30 the next morning, so giving the Battalion a night's rest, the opportunity for some reconnaissance to be made and to finalise the artillery support programme. It was a very disturbed night for the men of the Battalion. At 4 a.m. on the 15th, some Italian armoured cars, cut off from their comrades on the other side of the river, blundered into the Battalion camp and were stopped just short of Battalion Headquarters by the prompt action of the anti-tank gun crews. Many of the armoured cars were destroyed. The road Floridia - Sortino - Lentini, whilst held by the British had German and Italian forces on its west and east sides desperately trying to regain contact with their own units north of the River Simeto.

About seven miles south of Catania, the River Simeto is crossed by a bridge which looks not unlike a Bailey Bridge. Primosole Bridge carries the main highway over the river. The bridge, at the centre of a wide horseshoe loop, is about four hundred feet long and about eight to ten feet above the water. It lies about three thousand yards from the sea. On the south side of the river and looking westwards, the ground is flat and open, cut by a number of banks and dykes which afford some cover to troops approaching the river banks. The two which are larger than the rest are the Fosso Gornalunga and Fosso Dittaino which, when full of water, drain into the Simeto above Primosole Bridge. To the east and south of the river in the direction of the sea, the countryside is cultivated with olives and around the mouth of the river amongst the marshy reeds and tall grass, there is a small lake. In the middle of the bend in the river to the east of the bridge, a tower marked the country dwelling of the Duc di Misterbianco. This tower was used as an observation post by the artillery observation officers during the forthcoming battle. The road from Lentini, which winds down from the ridge south of the river, is joined by a subsidiary road. The junction was the scene of much destruction, with destroyed pillboxes, smashed signposts and telephone wires and seven or eight dead mules of an Italian pack train. The smell was dreadful and the place appropriately named 'Dead Horse Corner.'

North of the river, thick vineyards extend down both banks on both sides of the bridge and are about four to five hundred yards in depth. Olive trees are dotted about. Just north of the bridge are two stone built farmhouses, one on each side of the road. On the left of the road and on the far side of the vineyards is a sunken road running parallel with the river. It was like a wide, deep trench surmounted by a thick cactus hedge and a formidable defence position, out of sight and unknown to the attacking troops. The vines in front of the sunken road were from three to five feet high and only three feet apart, an excellent place of concealment for the defenders.

The attack by 9th DLI, commenced at 7.30 a.m. on the 15th July, supported by the guns of the 24th and 98th Field Regiments, RA. The companies advanced in open formation across the bare ground towards the river. From the vineyards on the other side, heavy machine-gun fire commenced and the companies lost heavily. Only the odd platoon was able to cross the river and in the fierce hand-to-hand fighting which followed, these were driven back to the south bank. The Battalion had lost over one hundred men, including nine officers. The survivors dug in on the south bank of the river and defeated any attempts by the Germans to lay charges to destroy the bridge. It was all they could do in the circumstances. Any movement brought down mortar fire and any attempt by armoured vehicles to cross the bridge was defeated by one or more 88s sited to fire down the Catania road.

The situation on the German side of Primosole Bridge on the morning of the 15th July was that Captain Fassl's Signals Company occupied the sunken road. Captain Stangenberg's group was in position on the river as far as the Dittaino. Here, it linked with the 1st Parachute machine-gun Battalion and, continuing westward, the Schmalz Battle Group. The 1st Parachute Engineer Battalion under Captain Paul Adolff had arrived in time to strengthen these forces and take part in holding off 9th DLI's attack early in the morning. The initial German reaction to the British attacks was to withdraw to the northern edge of the Catania Plain to a position called the Etna Line. Captain Stangenberg persuaded the elements of the Herman Goering Panzer Division and other units taking part in this withdrawal, that it was vital to hold the line of the Simeto to deny Catania and its airfields to the British. By doing this, the British advance up the eastern side of Sicily was blocked. The wisdom of this argument was not lost on the German command and it was decided to hold the line of the Simeto and units were ordered back to the river.

As the 9th Battalion moved into the attack, the 8th moved up to the area around 'Dead Horse Corner' and the 6th followed behind. General Kirkman arrived at Brigade Headquarters at about 10.00 a.m. on the 15th July. 9th DLI was now back across the river holding the south bank and denying all German attempts to destroy the bridge. It was decided that 8th DLI, with even heavier artillery support than that given to the 9th, would attack at 4.30 p.m. It was obvious that any daylight attack would be suicidal and, on the advice of Lieutenant-Colonel A.S. Pearson, DSO, MC, Officer Commanding 1st Parachute Battalion, the attack was postponed until the early hours of the 16th July. Lieutenant-Colonel Lidwell reconnoitred the bridge and its approaches. There were a number of problems not least the positions of the German defenders which could not be seen. They were totally concealed amongst the olives and vines and the sunken road, the existence of the latter still unknown to the British. The water in the river was thought to be too deep for heavily laden men to wade across. Lieutenant-Colonel Lidwell and his officers did not view the task with much optimism. Assistance came from an unexpected quarter. Lieutenant-Colonel A.S. Pearson whose parachutists had attacked the bridge, arrived at 8th Battalion's Headquarters. He had discovered a crossing place about three hundred yards above the bridge where the depth of the water would allow men to wade across. He volunteered to lead the assaulting companies across.

The 8th Battalion's attack was to start at 2.10 a.m. on the 16th. Prior to H hour, the artillery would fire an eighty minutes' barrage into the German positions, for the last ten minutes of which the whole concentration would fall on the bridgehead. machine-guns of a platoon of the the 2nd Cheshires, mounted on the flood bank, would pour its fire into the German positions and so thicken up the artillery barrage. A squadron of Sherman Tanks would move down on to the low ground by the river. Two companies of the 8th, led by Lieutenant-Colonel Pearson would

253

cross the river at the ford he had discovered. Once over, these companies would move through the dense vines and olives to the bridge and there create a bridgehead. Immediately this was achieved, the other two companies of the Battalion would cross the river and enlarge the bridgehead to about one thousand five hundred yards in depth and two thousand yards wide, with the flanks protected by the banks of the horseshoe bend of the river.

After dark the 6th Battalion moved up to lie alongside the companies of the 8th as they rested prior to the assault. Lieutenant-Colonel Pearson had been down to the crossing and had taped the route for the attacking companies to follow. He met the two companies shortly after 10.00 p.m. and led them to the river. At 1.00 a.m., the artillery barrage commenced. Ferocious in intensity it seemed impossible that anyone could survive as the shells and bullets saturated the ground north of the river. But many indeed did survive. The two companies led to the river crossed and moved to the far side of the bridge to form a bridgehead. A complete break down in communications occurred with the rest of the Battalion on the south side of the bridge and it, therefore, did not move. This threatened the success which had been gained initially in the bridgehead. Fortunately, Lieutenant-Colonel Lidwell, who went back across the bridge, met Major Wigram, a War Office observer, who was seen cycling over the bridge into the bridgehead and the latter turned about, retraced his steps over the bullet swept bridge and brought up the remainder of the Battalion. Bitter fighting then broke out and the 8th Battalion could only hold onto a bridgehead some three hundred yards deep and one hundred and fifty yards wide, which extended on both sides of the road. Casualties on both sides were heavy with dead and wounded lying in front of the positions of both sides. Captain Fassl, with the help of a captured British medical orderly, organised a temporary ceasefire to enable both sides to collect their wounded. Colonel Wilhelm Schmalz, commanding the Battle Group, commented later that he had experienced similar ceasefires during the war but only with British troops who had a 'chivalrous disposition.' The experience of the 6th Battalion on the following day was to be entirely the opposite.

The 8th Battalion, then, held a small bridgehead. The approach to the bridge itself was continually mortared, snipers were very active and two well sited 88s made it impossible for the Sherman tanks to pass over. Those who did try were either driven off or destroyed. The Brigadier met Lieutenant-Colonel Watson of the 6th Battalion during the morning of the 16th and proposed to launch the Battalion in a daylight attack with a view to enlarging the bridgehead. The Brigadier decided to cross the bridge to see the situation in the bridgehead for himself. He did this by carrier and then found he could not get back. General Kirkman arrived at Brigade Headquarters and ordered both the 6th and 9th Battalions to attack at night. Meanwhile, 'D' Company was sent south of the river and east of the Battalion's positions to comb out the dense reed-beds and orchards in which both Germans and Italians who had lost contact with their units were hiding, before attempting to cross over to the northern bank and join their comrades. This resulted in eight Italians and six Germans being taken prisoner.

At 7.00 p.m. the Commanding Officer issued his orders for the forthcoming attack. Both battalions taking part would cross the river at the ford and move to enlarge the bridgehead, the 9th on the right of the road to Catania and the 6th on the left of this road. The 6th Battalion's objective was the edge of the vines from the main road westwards to a bend in the river. This line lay just beyond the infamous sunken lane which came to be called 'Stink Alley.' By now its location was known. The Battalion was to advance, followed by the 9th Battalion, using what cover there was via farm buildings, ditches and tracks, until the crossing was reached. On crossing the river, the Start Line for the attack was along the track running north west and companies would form up on this with 'A' Company on the left, 'C' Company in the centre and 'B' Company on the right. 'D' Company would take up a position protecting the left flank. Zero hour would be 1.00 a.m. on the 17th July and this would be the time that 'A' Company, leading the Battalion, would enter the water to cross the river. After the three companies extended along the Start Line the advance would be made to 'Stink Alley.' Battalion Headquarters would be initially located in the river bank and then move forward to a site on the Start Line. Artillery support was a standing barrage on the Start Line, then a creeping barrage ahead of the advancing troops.

At 11.00 p.m. the relief by the 1st Battalion The London Scottish, was completed and the 6th moved off along the taped route towards the crossing. There was a clear moonlight sky. 'A' Company reached the river and waited for zero hour and then plunged into the water. Lieutenant David Fenner led his platoon in 'C' Company:

'The whole Battalion moved silently in single file to the attack. Rum had been issued before we left and was of some comfort at this time when we had little to do but occupy our thoughts with the grim and inevitable prospect ahead. We reached a dry ditch running towards the river and began moving through a battlefield where our parachutists and the German had fought. All around the vegetation had been burnt by phosphorous bombs and tracer bullets. Evidence of the fighting was everywhere. The ditch contained many burnt bodies. One completely blackened sat upright staring sightlessly at each member of the Battalion as he struggled past in the moonlight. The only sounds came from the burst of harassing fire from the Cheshire machine-gunners and the bull frogs croaking in the reeds. We paused before the leading company entered the river, bayonets were fixed, rifles and machine-guns cocked. Ben Dickenson, the platoon runner and oldest soldier in the platoon argued with Connel, the sergeant, about the need to fix bayonets. He said he had never found it necessary to use one. I cannot remember the outcome of this disagreement but I did appreciate the easing of tension it produced amongst us. Then we were on the move to the river, sliding down the bank into chest high water, again in single file, guiding ourselves by

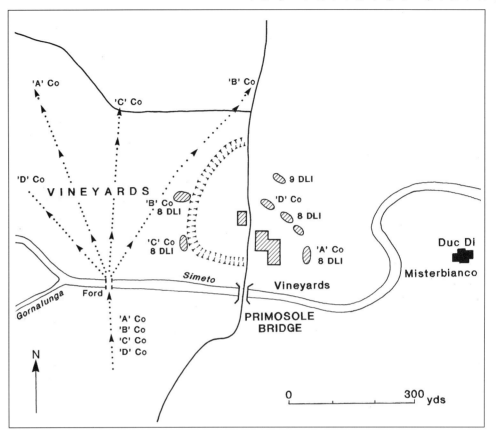

Sicily: *Primosole Bridge, 17th July, 1943. The battle for the vineyards and sunken road 'Stink Alley'*

hanging on to a wire stretched between the banks for this purpose.'

The water was deep, reaching the necks and shoulders of the smaller men. The bottom was muddy but each company waded over. On the far bank, they fanned out into their positions as ordered. Behind, came the two platoons of the 2nd Cheshires, carrying their heavy loads of twelve belts of ammunition per gun on their shoulders or above their heads. The initial enemy

Primosole Bridge. *The Sunken Road, named by the troops 'Stink Alley', flooded after heavy rain. German parachutists held this position, location unknown when the action commenced, and inflicted heavy losses on the attacking companies*

reaction was to direct heavy mortar fire on to the southern bank, by now well behind the Battalion. As soon as the companies climbed out onto the bank and through the tall reeds at the water's edge, a heavy and accurate fire hit them from well concealed enemy machine-guns sited in 'Stink Alley' and from spandau and rifle along the front and from the flanks. On reaching the Start Line, the companies were unable to advance as the artillery barrage had not moved forward and a number of shells appeared to be falling short. Casualties began to increase with the men virtually pinned to the ground. Battalion Headquarters was set up at the water's edge but wireless contact with the companies was never firmly established except in the case of 'B' Company. At last, the companies could move forward as the artillery barrage lifted and proceeded to creep ahead. 'B'

Company reached its objective astride the main road. 'C' Company reached its objective on the bend in the sunken lane but both companies had suffered heavy losses from the enemy firing on fixed lines along the track and down the rows of vines. Captain Reggie Atkinson and 'B' Company, broke through the cactus hedge and into the sunken lane near the main road and drove the Germans out of it. He then moved over the open ground beyond to a position in a shallow ditch to the left of the Catania road where he could cover the approach of any enemy coming down this road. The Company's losses, sustained in working its way through the vineyard and the sunken lane, were very heavy and it was a much depleted Company which reached its objective. At first light, some Germans managed to get back into the sunken lane, whilst others, supported by an 88 gun, moved down the Catania road in support. It was a critical situation for the survivors of 'B' Company, now under pressure from two sides. However, the Company held on until the Germans in front and those behind in the sunken lane withdrew, as British tanks began at last to move forward. The enemy in the sunken lane had to run the gauntlet between 'B' Company and the road and suffered heavy casualties in trying to do so. Many were shot down and others surrendered.

Captain Glass and 'C' Company also reached their objective, which was the bend in the sunken lane. In doing so, the three platoons were caught in the vines and suffered heavy losses. They were pinned down on their objective by persistent sniper and machine-gun fire which made movement of any sort virtually impossible. Captain Glass went out to contact 'B' Company on his right. The Company dug in as best it could and tried to make the wounded comfortable. At about 8.00 a.m., a party of twenty-eight German paratroops approached Nos. 13 and 14 Platoons along the sunken lane from the direction of 'B' Company positions. The two platoons opened up on this unsuspecting target, killing one and wounding two others. The remainder surrendered. Two oberleutenants were amongst the captured. Private Harry Wilkinson of 'C' Company described his own experiences:

> 'I think we crossed a river first and with me being small, about 5ft. 4ins. it came up to my shoulders but somebody had got a rope across and I think we nearly all managed to grab hold of that. It was a heck of a shock for me going into that icy water ... I believe that one or two of the chaps got swept downstream ... We came into this vineyard ... it was there that the barrage took over. There was quite a bit of fighting and shooting while we were laid among the vines, the barrage, I think we got some of our own to be truthful. Whether they were shells that were falling short or that, I know that the earth was literally heaving and I mean heaving. This chap and I just managed to make a scrape. It wasn't a trench at all, just trying to get a bit of cover and get our heads down and, somehow, a bit of protection. You scrape about maybe two or three inches deep and we were being bounced up and down. Anyway Sergeant Dunn had managed to get to us. He was slightly in front of us and there was a lull and he shouted for us to go forward so I was getting up and somehow my feet slipped on the bit of scrape I'd made. I fell more or less forward and I remember this little Irish laddie, I can't recall his name other than Paddy that he naturally got. He raised himself a little higher and I just heard him shout and he'd got a bullet through the neck and it had whizzed over the back of my neck and gone clean through him and he was gurgling and spilling blood from the mouth and he seemed to scramble up and turn round to go ... I was pretty hot on Sergeant Dunn's heels. I should think maybe about twelve yards behind him and slightly to his right and we came across the sunken road in front of us ... We had to break through a cactus hedge ... Because of the barrage and everybody being split up, chaps were shouting, "Where are you 11 Platoon?" and so forth and Jerries were answering us and as soon as a chap popped up they were getting shot. Anyway, as I say, we had got across the sunken road and broke through this cactus hedge and Sergeant Dunn shouted, "Look out!" I looked to my left and slightly to the rear and there was a big German Para just about to break through the hedge to go across the sunken road to the vines where we had come from. When he fired I fired ... Later on when we were clearing up a bit ... we saw him laid down in the lane with his pack on fire.

> '...There's quite a lot of noise in battle and as you go forward chaps shout to keep a contact with each other and let folk know you're there sort of thing ... The fact that it's a British voice it sounds a bit reassuring to know there is somebody fairly near you. You're not entirely on your own.'

On moving forward from the Start Line, Lieutenant Fenner, 13

Platoon, 'C' Company, recalled what happened:

'Firing began at isolated Germans seen running away, then from the direction of the road came a murderous fire from the Spandaus located there. The gunners were firing on "fixed lines", they could not see us in the dark. Bursts of tracer swept past at knee height. The lines of infantry kept on going in spite of men being hit until we were struck by heavy concentrations of artillery. Some of this was probably enemy DF (defensive fire) but in the opinion of those who had been shelled by our gunners on previous occasions we were in our own barrage. Ben Dickenson was clear on this point. He shouted, "When I get out of this I'll do those bloody gunners." He sounded a bit optimistic, shells were dropping all around, then it stopped, lifted, and groups of men got up, moved on through the cactus hedge into the sunken road. There was a lot of shooting, suddenly it was over and we had taken eight prisoners, all but two wounded. Mark [Glass] organised what remained of the Company into a defensive position astride the road. There were elements of two platoons and we started to provide some sort of protection for ourselves by scraping away at the ground with our pathetic entrenching tools. The older soldiers acquired the more efficient German article and were soon digging in at great speed. The place was littered with German equipment, Spandau machine-guns, belts of ammunition and corpses. Our prisoners were all parachutists, one spoke good English and told us that three days ago they had been in the south of France! A fierce battle was in progress on our right where the 9th were going in. Apart from the pop of small arms fire where we were was comparatively quiet. In the first light of the summer's day we dug while the stretcher-bearers attended to the wounded lying thick in the vines.'

'A' Company, under Major Galloway, was unable to reach its objective at the left hand corner of the vineyard. It was pinned down amongst the vines with intense enemy fire from both sides. Three Sherman tanks arrived later in the morning in 'A' Company's positions but stopped and remained stationary and contented themselves with firing towards any enemy targets which appeared and their presence had little or no effect on the situation. Major Galloway attempted to contact the tanks but with no means of communication other than climbing on the back of them and knocking on the hatches to gain attention, there was little he could do for some time. It was suicidal to attempt to climb onto the back of a tank.

'D' Company, under Major Wood, also failed to reach its objective on the west flank of the Battalion. It, too, suffered from enemy sniper and machine-gun fire, much of it coming from the area outside that bombarded by the British artillery.

Sergeant Tom Cairns described the horror of it all:

'The vineyard is continually swept by enemy fire. Red white and green tracer rips through the vines, scattering their leaves, tearing through their roots. Sometimes the bullets find a mark and a man drops, wriggling on the soft, sooty earth. But the companies keep on advancing, In spite of casualties, screams and groans of wounded and dying comrades, they advance towards the sunken road, towards the formidable line of spitting machine-guns, they advance so quickly and so determinedly that the forward elements are caught in our own barrage. Several are killed, others drop with smashed legs and ugly shrapnel wounds. And all this in darkness, when control is difficult and voices are scarcely audible and the bursting shells and malicious double-barrelled crack of German machine-guns. The dawn comes and the Germans are more active than ever, for now they can see. Men are killed and lacerated as they try to move among the vines. Wounded men lie helplessly near the sunken road, make feeble attempts to move and are shot dead. And the worst of it is the Jerry positions are so cunningly concealed that they defy detection. To move, to disturb a vine, is to ask for a deadly burst of Spandau bullets.

'The position is intolerable. Some men who cross the road are shot in the back. Others throw themselves on the ground and engage the Germans from the flank. But he has the advantage. He remains hidden and mercilessly snipes from behind the breastwork. No one, not even those wearing the red cross, is safe from the murderous fire. The Second-in-Command calls for tanks. The Shermans try to cross the bridge and two are immediately hit. The 88 that hits them is destroyed and three tanks roll in to the vineyard.

'But still the Germans hold out. Stretcher-bearers moving among the wounded, are callously shot. One man carrying a stretcher is shot from a distance of a hundred yards. He falls and expires almost immediately. Another has his finger tips shot away while carrying a wounded man.'

'A' and 'D' Companies were withdrawn to enable the tanks

who had arrived to have a clear run and shoot at the enemy. The Second-in-Command, Major F.W.H. Worral, DSO, MC, went forward to contact 'A' Company and bring them back to the Start Line. The withdrawal was made but not without more casualties. Major Worral, while trying to lift a wounded man onto the top of a tank, was shot through the thigh by a phosphorous bullet and severely wounded. With the two Companies back on the Start Line, the tanks began their shoot and enemy resistance quickly crumbled until by 12.30 p.m. the Companies were able to establish themselves on their final objectives, about a thousand yards beyond the bridge and river.

Whilst the rifle companies were battling for their lives, Battalion Headquarters had experienced problems. The original site for the Headquarters was the Start Line but this was found to be too vulnerable, continually under fire with personnel unable to move about with any freedom. It was, then, moved back to the reed area on the river bank where there was more protection. The Regimental Aid Post had been set up a little further upstream. Here, Captain Murphy, Sergeant Davies, Padre Garbutt and the rest of the staff, worked tirelessly to help and comfort the wounded and the dying.

At 6.00 a.m. Captain Redway was ordered to cross the bridge with his Anti-Tank Platoon of two 6 pounder and two 2 pounder guns pulled by carriers. He was accompanied by his two troop commanders, Lieutenant Hawkins with the 6 pounders and Lieutenant Sager with the 2 pounders. As soon as they appeared on the southern end of the bridge, the enemy opened fire and killed a corporal. The four carriers dashed across the bridge and got into cover behind the buildings immediately to the north. They then dashed down the road towards Catania, looking for the forward company ('B' Company) on the left hand side of the road. Lieutenant Sager and the two pounder guns following behind the two leading 6 pounders, spotted the company, pulled into the side and got their guns into position. Captain Redway and Lieutenant Hawkins failed to spot the company position and raced on down the road for about two miles towards Catania. At this point, the leading carrier with Captain Redway on board, was hit by an anti-tank shell. Lieutenant Hawkins in the following carrier saw this, spun round in the road and made off

in the opposite direction. The driver pulled off the road to avoid the anti-tank shells which were being fired at the carrier. Unfortunately, the vehicle got stuck in a ditch. The officer and his party of seven men, which included the crew of a carrier of 9 DLI which had also taken avoidance action, got into the ditch and lay there hidden for some time, as parties of Germans passed up and down the road only a few feet from them. At about 1.00 p.m., a grass fire started by our own artillery forced them out and they ran to another ditch and remained there until about 6.00 p.m. when, all being quiet, they made their way back to 'C' Company positions, which they reached about one hour later. Captain Redway was taken prisoner along with the surviving members of his crew. Two sergeants and a private were killed.

The 6th Battalion had not had the advantage of a local ceasefire to tend to their wounded as had 8th Battalion the previous day. The was no Captain Fassl to negotiate with. The Battalion faced Battle Group Walther consisting of: 1st Parachutist Engineers Battalion, 1st Parachute machine-gun Battalion and elements of the 1st Parachute Tank Destroyer Section and 1st Parachutist Artillery Section. They fought with great ruthlessness, stubbornness and gallantry. Lieutenant-Colonel Watson described the scene at the end of the battle:

'By the middle of the morning the Battle of Primosole Bridge was over and by 11 o'clock the 6 and 9 Battalions were in their positions on the perimeter of the bridgehead ... while within these comparatively few acres, was a picture of the most appalling carnage. Casa di Stefano, and the buildings on the other side of the road, stood in gaunt ruins, olive trees were torn to shreds and grape vines were crushed to the ground. Over all lay a pall of white dust, and the sickly smell of death hung on the still morning air. Soon flies and the sun's heat, added to the trials of the weary victors, as they set about their loathsome task of clearing the field of battle; a platoon of the London Scottish came in to help them. One hundred and fifty five Germans had been taken prisoner; while it was roughly estimated some three hundred were lying dead upon the ground.

'On the Catania road the telephone poles and wires were wrecked, and like the olives, the tall poplars had had their limbs and tops torn from the trunks. Not far away an 88 m.m. gun had received a direct hit, but burned Shermans and wrecked Bren carriers near the Bridge, showed that it had not fired in vain. The sunken lane, which wound its way along the edge of the vineyard, and from the shelter of whose banks, protected by the dagger sharp leaves of the cactus and the needles of the prickly pear, the German paratroops had put up such desperate defence, was a ghastly shambles. Cratered with shell holes throughout, it almost beggars description. Overturned ammunition boxes, smashed paniers and broken rifles, mingled with torn blood stained clothing and equipment of both sides, while the dead of Britain and Germany lay sprawled throughout its length - "Stink Alley" it was, indeed.'

What of the men of the Battalion who had fought the battle? Lieutenant Fenner wrote this record:

'...Men who had served in the Battalion since France in 1940, at Gazala, Alamein and Mareth had not seen so much slaughter and destruction in such a small space. The area around the 8th Bridgehead and along the sunken road where we and the 9th attacked was a shambles. 600 casualties had occurred in our three Battalions. Over 300 German dead lay there, torn trees, smashed guns, tanks and equipment were everywhere. Now little rough wooden crosses made from ration boxes began to appear as we buried our dead. For the survivors began a few hours' respite. We spent the day tidying up the battlefield. There was one grave of 20 men of the Battalion in our company area.'

Primosole Bridge, the door to the Plain of Catania had been

opened. Like most doors it was a bottleneck and into its narrow entrance the attacking 151 Durham Brigade had been funnelled to try to force a way through a narrow opening where all of the advantages lay with its resolute, highly disciplined and trained defenders. These qualities were also held by the Brigade's soldiers and in the infantry battle which followed, its Battalions ultimately won through but not without grievous casualties. The Brigade suffered over five hundred casualties of which the 6th Battalion lost one hundred and twenty men killed, wounded and missing.

At the junction of the sunken lane - 'Stink Alley' - and the Catania road, there stands today a memorial with the following words written on it:

This memorial has been erected
To keep fresh the memory of
the soldiers of 151 Durham Infantry
Brigade who gave their lives for their
Country
and the cause of the Freedom during the
Sicilian Campaign 10 July - 17 August 1943

It is placed here because it was
during the actions round the
Porte Primosole 14 - 17 July 1943
that the Brigade experienced the fiercest
fighting in which it took part during the Campaign

H.Q. 151 Durham Infantry Brigade
151 Durham Brigade Support Company.
6th Battalion The Durham Light Infantry
8th Battalion The Durham Light Infantry
9th Battalion The Durham Light Infantry

"WE WILL REMEMBER THEM"

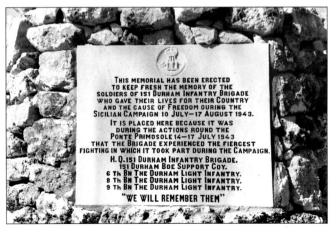

Primosole Bridge. *War Memorial erected after the battle*

CHAPTER 28
THE END IN SICILY - THE RETURN TO ENGLAND
JULY - OCTOBER 1943

The 18th July was spent in burying the dead and cleaning up the battlefield. About two and half miles north of Primosole Bridge, the main highway crossed the Fosso Bottaceto, a dry irrigation ditch and it was to this natural defensive position that the enemy retired. The bridge and its area continued to be shelled by enemy artillery which caused some casualties amongst the men of the battalions of the Brigade. For some time, the bridge remained a dangerous place to cross. It was hit and damaged by shell fire and had to be closed to traffic. Two Bailey Bridges, one above and one below the bridge, were built to take the traffic. They had the advantage of being low enough to be unseen by enemy artillery observers. At 8.00 p.m., 6th Battalion waded back across the Simeto - the water was no more than shin deep - to its southern bank and moved to a rest area between the road and the sea. The transport, which moved across the bridge, was shelled and Sergeant Kent, Transport Sergeant, was wounded. The rest area was not far to the rear and here amongst the lemon trees and with the Mediterranean on the doorstep, the Battalion enjoyed two or three days' relaxation. Kit bags arrived from B Echelon and clean clothes replaced the dirty, stained uniforms worn during the battle. The first eagerly awaited mail since landing in Sicily arrived on the 19th July. False reports of German parachutists landing in the Lentini area caused one platoon and one section of carriers to be put on alert to act as a mobile patrol.

It was obvious that the enemy had no intention of giving up the Plain of Catania without a fight. It was equally obvious that any advance up the east coast towards Messina would be slow and costly. The only road which followed the coast clung, in many places, to the edges of the mountains which came down almost to the shore. A number of road bridges, which spanned dried up river beds at this time of the year, would most certainly be blown up to slow down any advancing forces. The whole area was dominated by Mount Etna, affording perfect observation to the enemy. It was first class defensive country and the Germans could be expected to make the most of it. In addition, the infantry of XIII Corps, of which 151 Brigade was part, were tired and in need of rest. On the 21st July, General Montgomery decided, therefore, to switch the weight of the attack from the coast to the left flank. XXX Corps, strengthened by the arrival of the 78th Division from North Africa, was given the task of advancing round the west side of Mount Etna to threaten the rear of the enemy coastal defenders.

50th Division was placed on the defensive in front of the Fosso Bottaceto where the enemy were well dug in and almost immune from shellfire. The Division held a shallow ditch and dyke running parallel to the Fosso. It was a typical hot Sicilian summer. At dusk, mosquitos appeared and many soldiers contracted malaria. Nets, ointment and pills were available but it was impossible to enforce absolute discipline under the conditions in which the men lived.

At 10.00 p.m. on the 21st July, the Battalion moved across one of the Bailey Bridges and marched off to relieve the 6th Battalion Green Howards and one platoon of the 7th Battalion in the front line. The Battalion was on the left flank of the Divisional front about four thousand yards west of the main road to Catania. 'C' Company was on the extreme left astride the railway line at Massa Paterno. 'B' Company was on the right astride a secondary road which ran into the enemy positions. The enemy in the Fosso Bottaceto was about nine hundred yards away. 'A' Company was in the centre at Massa Pelacani and, here, the enemy was only four hundred yards away. 'D' Company was in reserve at Massa Paterno and Battalion Headquarters was behind a high bank nearby.

The enemy line was a series of section posts, liberally sprinkled with machine-guns and sited either in pill boxes, farm buildings or shell craters. There were many mortar positions behind the ditch, apparently quite mobile as they were constantly changing their positions. With the exception of a few 88s, there appeared to be no other artillery available to the enemy but their long range mortars included the Nebelwerfer, the multi-rocket mortar weapon. Usually, the enemy were very alert at night and frequently fired Verey lights. At first light or dusk, he opened up with machine-guns firing on fixed lines. The days were fairly quiet, with occasional mortar or machine-gun fire. It was thought that the forward positions were vacated during the day except for sentries.

The Battalion was in the line until the 26th July. Patrols were sent out at night to observe the enemy positions. These sometimes led to skirmishes, with losses to both sides. In the early hours of the 25th July, two sections of 'B' Company under Lieutenant J.B.S. Holt, occupied the railway bridge close to the enemy positions. The enemy fired on this party and three men were wounded. The sections withdrew but were unable to bring out Private Marrion, one of the wounded, who was left lying on the bridge. Several attempts were made by stretcher-bearers, accompanied by a covering party, to reach this soldier but failed due to intensive sniping from the flanks. Between 5.30 and 7.00 p.m., four separate smoke screens were laid down by artillery and 4.2in. mortars and attempts were made to reach Private Marrion. Unfortunately, the strong wind blew away the smoke which also drew heavy enemy retaliatory fire. No movement could be seen from the wounded man and it was finally presumed that he was dead or a prisoner. The end of this story

was that at 3.00 p.m. on the 28th July, a message was received from 151 Brigade Headquarters stating that Private Marrion had been picked up by a patrol of the 5th East Yorkshire Regiment at 5.00 a.m. that morning. He was still alive though suffering from multiple gunshot wounds and exposure. At 1.30 a.m. on the 26th July, a patrol led by Lieutenant Dennis MM, who had served with the Guards Squadron of the Long Range Desert Group, bumped into an enemy listening post. In the short action which followed, Lieutenant Dennis was wounded in the leg by an exploding grenade and was carried back to safety by the other members of the patrol.

Any enemy movement was shelled. The enemy, in turn, fired into the British positions with his Nebelwerfers. On one occasion, a stick of mortar bombs from one of these weapons fell on the 9th Battalion in a reserve position in the river bed and killed its commanding officer, Lieutenant-Colonel A.B. Clarke, DSO and Second-in-Command, Major W. Robinson. 6th Battalion Headquarters came under fire at times. On the 23rd July, a number of shells landed in its position. Lance-Corporal Alexander of the Regimental Police was killed and Lance-Corporal Booth, Officers' Mess waiter was wounded. On the 25th of the month, Captain Glass, commanding 'C' Company, was shot in the thigh by a German sniper when moving between two of his forward platoons.

Over the period of time the Battalion was in the front line, there were many signs that the enemy was planning to withdraw. During the afternoon of the 22nd July, a series of explosions were heard which caused dense clouds of black smoke. These came from the direction of Catania Airfield and were thought to be the destruction of bomb and fuel dumps. Further explosions and fires were experienced on the following days.

At 11.30 p.m. on the 26th July, 'A', 'B' and 'D' Companies with Battalion Headquarters, assembled and the relief by the 5th East Yorkshire Regiment commenced. Towards Catania Airfield a huge fire blazed, probably an incendiary bomb dump. The relief of these companies was completed just after midnight and they moved over one of the Bailey Bridges to the rest area previously occupied. 'C' Company found it much more difficult to get away.

Enemy sniper and machine-gun fire made movement difficult and the relief could only be completed by the exchange of section by section. This Company reached the rest area at 4.30 a.m. on the 27th. A reinforcing draft of fifty-one other ranks was received. This was followed by a further draft of forty-eight from the Welsh and North Staffordshire Regiments. Major P.H. Richardson from the Queen's Royal Regiment, joined the Battalion as Second-in-Command. A working party of one officer and sixty other ranks was sent on an all night task on the 29th of the month, to erect dummy tanks and vehicles to represent an armoured brigade. A section of carriers followed under Captain Pringle to add to the deception by adding tracks to the dummy tanks.

At 8.00 p.m. on the 30th July, the Battalion marched off to relieve the London Irish Rifles in the reserve area of the right hand forward brigade. This was to the right of the road south of the River Simeto. The 8th and 9th Battalions moved north of the river in front of the Fosso Bottaceto, where it crossed the Catania road, turned south east to Primosole Wood and joined the river near its mouth. 6th Battalion was in reserve and lay in the large horseshoe bend which bulged into the enemy positions. 'D' Company was on the bank of the river at the apex of the bend. The other companies lay amongst the thick rushes and scrub round the damaged Massa Duca di Misterbianco. This was the area cleared by 'D' Company on the day before the attack on Primosole Bridge. The enemy occupied a few posts at night between the wood and the river, one being a pillbox only two hundred yards from 'D' Company's positions. Enemy artillery and Nebelwerfers frequently shelled Primosole Bridge and Massa Duca di Misterbianco. The companies sheltered in the dense undergrowth during the day and patrolled at night.

On the night of the 2nd/3rd August, the Battalion relieved the 9th Battalion on the north side of the river in front of the Fosso Bottaceto where it crossed the main Catania road to where it swung south-east in the direction of the River Simeto. Two companies were astride the main road, one behind the other and the other two companies were astride a secondary road which ran parallel to the woods on the coast. 'A' Company had a particularly unpleasant position in and around a farm, with a number of dead cows lying about which could not be buried, as movement was restricted due to enemy spandau activity. Battalion Headquarters was in a ditch behind the two rear companies. It was a far from pleasant position as any movement was fired upon by a spandau in the woods on the right. The usual patrols were sent out but, with the exception of a few shots fired at one from an enemy position between two farm buildings, no contact was made. On the 3rd August, Major Wood, Regimental Sergeant-Major McMahon MC, MM, Corporal Dougan MM and Private Hobbley, had moved to a transit camp on being posted back to England. Captain A.C. Copinger-Hill took over command of 'D' Company.

Intelligence reports suggested that the enemy was about to withdraw from the Fosso Bottaceto positions and strong patrols were sent out in the early hours of the 4th August to ascertain whether the enemy was pulling out. This was found to be the case and, in accordance with plans already made, the Battalion advanced astride the main and the subsidiary road with 'B' Company on the right and 'C' Company on the left, each headed by a screen of carriers. 8th Battalion was on its right, pushing through the orchards and woods on the coast. 7th Battalion The Green Howards, 69 Brigade, was on the left. On reaching the Fosso Bottaceto, the crossings over the ditch were found to have been blown up by the retreating Germans. However, the carriers found a crossing about three hundred yards to the left and the advance continued. The scene where Captain Redway's carrier had met its end was reached and the bodies of Sergeants Raine and Redhead were found, with two carriers and a six pounder anti-tank gun. The second anti-tank gun was found a little later, with empty shell cases lying nearby, which indicated that it had been used by the enemy.

151 Brigade found the going a little easier than 69 Brigade on the left. The latter, crossing open ground and under fire from the airfield defences, failed to keep up with the 6th Battalion on its right. The left flank of this Battalion was exposed to enemy machine-gun fire which slowed all forward movement. This, in turn, exposed the left flank of the 8th Battalion advancing on the right. All attempts to close up were thwarted by heavy enemy machine-gun fire and, with dusk falling, it was decided to stop in

the present positions on the outskirts of Catania. Huge explosions rent the air during the night from the southern slopes of Etna where the enemy continued to destroy his dumps. Patrols sent out during the night found that the enemy had gone.

At 7.00 a.m. on the 5th August, the 6th and the 9th Battalions, the latter had relieved the 8th, moved forward into Catania. 'A' and 'D' Companies led the way with 'B' and 'C' Companies in reserve. No opposition was encountered. On the right, the 9th Battalion moved through the business and commercial centre of the city and the 6th, on the left, passed the railway station and, thence, into the city centre. The Battalions received a tremendous reception from the civilian population. Lieutenant-Colonel Watson described the scene in his diary:

> '...Shell holes, craters, bomb craters, smashed buildings all over the place but somehow as if by magic the poor people came out of their holes and hovels and gave us a royal welcome. Flowers etc. and nuts are thrown to us. I stop in the centre and up come the War Correspondents and reporters who start writing their experiences on the steps of the Tribunal. Then come film people ... Disarm some of the Carabinarie to the intense delight of the crowd who seize their rifles and smash them on the pavement...'

The Germans had blown down buildings and blocked routes through the city making it difficult for vehicles to get through. At 11.15 a.m. the two leading companies reached the village of Canalicchio on the northern outskirts of Catania. The road bridge here over a narrow ravine had been blown and its approaches covered by a strong pillbox on the higher ground beyond. The machine-gun operating from this strong point was engaged with fire from 3in. mortars and light machine-guns. This proved to be too much for the Italian defenders who quickly surrendered to 'B' Company. 'A' Company took up position lower down after crossing the ravine, with 'D' Company further down still and in contact with 9th Battalion on its right. 'C' Company was in reserve. On capturing the pillbox on Point 206, 'B' Company bumped into strong enemy posts on higher ground beyond and was shelled and mortared throughout the afternoon. An attempt by 'C' Company, commanded by Captain R. Bousfield, to drive off the enemy from the left flank failed. These two companies were now attacked by Germans, later identified as parachutists,

Battalion carriers held up by an obstruction on the outskirts of Catania
Imperial War Museum photograph No. NA 5374

but held firm until nightfall when the enemy withdrew.

At 7.00 a.m. on the 6th, Lieutenant Cranke of 'C' Company took out a strong reconnaissance patrol to locate the enemy position at a large castellated house. It was fired on from this position and had to withdraw leaving two dead and two wounded. Stretcher-bearers who went out to bring in the wounded were also fire upon. A patrol from 'B' Company, under Lieutenant Holt, went out to observe enemy positions at Villa Biondi. It came under heavy and accurate fire. Lieutenant Holt and two men were killed and the remainder taken prisoner. This was discovered later when a civilian delivered a note from a German Lieutenant, who commanded the post, which praised the gallantry of the patrol and informed the Battalion of the names of the men killed and the whereabouts of their graves. The note also stated that the wounded were being well cared for.

The day's misfortunes continued. Captain Pringle commanding the Carrier Platoon, went with six carriers and a detachment of sappers under Lieutenant Cossens, RE, to reconnoitre the San Gregorio road. The column moved off, three carriers leading with two sappers in each, followed by an armoured scout car with Lieutenant Cossens and six sappers. Behind these were three more carriers with two sappers in each. On reaching the bend in the road north of Pomaro, the leading carrier was fired on by an anti-tank gun sited on the slopes of Mount Catira. Captain Pringle gave the order to withdraw and turned his carrier into the track on the right of the road. The second carrier turned round and made off to warn the others. The shot had damaged the scout car and third carrier. Lieutenant Cossens had been seriously wounded. The second carrier with the crew of the third aboard joined the remainder of the column and got away. Under heavy anti-tank and machine-gun fire, Captain Pringle withdrew around the corner in his carrier where he stopped and dismounted to see if he could be of any assistance to the wounded officer. Before he could reach the scout car, he was challenged by a German standing in a drive entrance at the side of the road. The Bren gunner of the carrier heard the challenge, saw Captain Pringle walk towards the entrance of the drive with his hands up and heard him say, 'O.K. lads, we've had it'. As the gunner could see no one he dashed off and got away. The rest of the crew were taken prisoner. The total losses were one officer and two other ranks taken prisoner, two carriers lost and, amongst the REs, one other rank killed and one officer and four other ranks taken prisoner. One scout car was captured.

'B' Company continued to suffer from heavy mortar fire throughout the afternoon of the 6th August and a number of men were wounded. Point 206 was lost but later regained by a company of the 1st Battalion London Scottish which appeared in the Battalion's positions and was taken under command. Brigadier Senior arrived to inform Lieutenant-Colonel Watson that the 8 DLI would relieve the Battalion that night. This relief was completed at about 3.00 a.m. on the 7th August and the Battalion went into rest in a quieter area. At 3.00 p.m., two platoons established themselves on the high ground and at the crossroads in Ficarazzi and remained here until the 8th Battalion passed through on its way to San Gregorio. On the 6th, the Battalion moved to an area south of Aci San Filippo. As Captain Hawkins got his anti-tank guns in position, he was approached by a deputation of Sicilians from the town. He was handed a note which contained the following message:

> Englishmen
> We dwell at Aci S. Filippo and we have come
> here for telling you that the German soldiers
> have gone away from our country where still
> are mines at the road, for this reason we
> caution you to be attentive and to remove
> the mentioned above mines.
> All people are happy in receiving you and
> they pray you to respect them.
> Hurra Englishmen!
> England for ever!

San Filippo was shelled by the enemy throughout the 8th August and there were many civilian wounded who sought attention from the Battalion Medical Officer. By nightfall on the following day, the 9th Battalion in the lead had pushed through Acireale to the small village of Puzzilo. The 6th Battalion came up after dark and prepared to take the lead and give chase to the retreating Germans the next day. At 7.00 a.m. on the 10th, the Battalion passed through 9 DLI and became the right-hand Battalion. 'B' Company led the advance followed by 'C' with 'A' and 'D' Companies in reserve. Both companies crossed the River Leonardello at 8.45 a.m. Six Italian prisoners were picked up. Four were sappers from the 266 Autonomous Company and two infantrymen from the 102 Coastal Battalion. No contact was made with the enemy, though civilians reported that there were Germans in Giarre and Reposto. By nightfall, 'C' Company was in contact with the enemy who occupied Altarella. Private Worthington, batman to Captain Bousfield who commanded 'C' Company, decided to reconnoitre the village on his own. He entered the village posing as an Italian and approached a German sentry. The sentry showed him the hiding place of a number of Italian mortars. Private Worthington also noted the parking area of a number of motor vehicles and the position of a minefield. A German staff officer appeared, so Worthingon

General Montgomery *shakes hands with Private R. Robinson to whom he had just awarded the Military Medal*

Imperial War Museum photograph No. NA 6133

decided that his subterfuge had gone far enough. He shot the officer and sentry and made his escape. On returning to the Battalion, he informed the gunner Observation Post of what he had seen and helped in directing some accurate artillery fire into the enemy positions. He was later awarded the Military Medal for this exploit.

The next morning, the 11th August, the enemy had withdrawn leaving behind the usual mines and booby traps and considerable demolition. Altarella was heavily mined and booby trapped and it was here that yet another of the Battalion's stalwarts was killed. Sergeant Dunn MM, of 'C' Company, was killed as he tried to defuse a booby trapped mine from the road. A much respected NCO from County Durham, his face had appeared on a poster of the 'Salute the Soldier Week' as typifying the British Tommy, with his steel helmet on the back of his head, his rifle slung over one shoulder and a pick axe over the other. At 4.45 p.m., a patrol from 'B' Company reached the outskirts of Riposto. Standing patrols of 'B' and 'C' Companies were posted in the town during the night 11th-12th August. The German occupied the dried up bed of the River Macchia. A small number of enemy tanks were in Riposto during the morning of the 12th. Artillery fire was brought down on the area of the bridge over the river which, if destroyed, would trap the tanks in the town. This caused the tanks to make a hurried withdrawal. Lieutenant ffrench-Kehoe whilst leading a patrol in the town, turned a corner and came across a German. Both fired their pistols simultaneously at each other. The Lieutenant was wounded in the foot and evacuated. The fate of the German was unknown. By the afternoon, the enemy had withdrawn from the river bed and the advance continued. By 10.30 p.m. on the 12th August, the Battalion had been relieved by the 7th Green Howards and marched to the rest area at Schifazzo. The Sicilian campaign, as far as the 6th Battalion was concerned, was over. The Americans were now pushing eastwards along the northern coast of the island. On the 14th August, Taormina was captured. On the morning of the 17th August, the Eighth Army joined the Americans in Messina.

On the 13th of the month and over the following few days, the Battalion rested. Clothes were washed and bathing took place. On the 16th, 'D' Company was disbanded and its personnel distributed among 'A', 'B' and 'C' Companies with potential specialists selected for 'HQ' Company. The Companies bivouaced on the terraces of the vineyards. A swimming gala was held in 9 DLI bathing pool, known as 'Durham Rock.' 'B' Echelon rejoined the Battalion, having been separated from it since the landing in Sicily. On the 23rd, training was commenced. On the same day, the following awards were announced for gallantry during the Sicilian campaign:

Lieutenant R.S. Loveridge	Military Cross.
Lance Sergeant Critchley	Military Medal.
Corporal Worthington	Military Medal.
Private Robinson	Military Medal.
Private Saban	Military Medal.

On the 28th August, the Battalion moved to the area west of Giardini, just off the Kaggi road. Two companies were in the orange groves near Torre Venera with 'B' Echelon. 'A' Company was in a farmhouse in the same area. Battalion Headquarters was in a villa. General Montgomery visited the Battalion on the 30th August. The Companies were drawn up in a hollow square in a dried river bed. He presented ribbons to Lance Sergeant Critchley, Corporal Worthington, Private Robinson and Private Saban. He then spoke to the Battalion. He praised the 50th Division in general and the DLI in particular for the part they played in both Africa and Sicily. He spoke of the forthcoming invasion of Italy but announced that the Division would not be taking part in it. The troops waited with bated breath. Would he tell them they were going home? He ended by saying, 'And never forget, wherever I go, I shall send for my 50 Division.' The groans of disappointment were audible. The General quickly raised his hand and stated, 'You never know, I may go home.' This was greeted with cheers and laughter as he drove away.

Before the training could begin, orders were received for a move to the area of Syracuse where the Battalion would relieve the 7th Battalion Royal Marines and take over the guarding of the prisoner of war camps, the wireless station at Mellili and the petrol depot, the Banca d'Italia and the hospital. There were about six thousand Italians and fourteen German prisoners to guard. Lieutenant-Colonel Watson left on leave on the 6th September. Major Maurice Kirby assumed temporary command of the Battalion. Lieutenant-Colonel Bill Watson did not return to the Battalion and was replaced by Lieutenant-Colonel A.E. Green of the Middlesex Regiment. Lieutenant-Colonel Watson had commanded the Battalion since July, 1942, through three great battles, El Alamein, Mareth and Primosole Bridge. He had earned his rest.

Lieutenant-Colonel Green assumed command on the 16th September. On the 22nd September, the 1st Battalion Gordon Highlanders arrived to relieve the Battalion which moved to Augusta having been informed that it would be going home with the rest of the Division. Disappointing delays followed and time was filled with training. On the 7th October, Major Kirby assumed command of the Brigade Support Company. Captain W.J. Field joined the Battalion in his place. At 2.30 p.m., the first performance of the 6 DLI Concert Party, organised by Lieutenant D.A. Kirby, took place in the Citadel Theatre, Augusta. On the 9th of the month, twenty battle casualties reported back from hospital. The following awards for gallantry were announced:

Lieutenant ffrench-Kehoe	Military Cross.
Sergeant Connell	Distinguished Conduct Medal.
Private Duckworth	Military Medal.

At 4.00 a.m. on the 16th October, the baggage party under Lieutenant Rome left camp to embark on the Troopship *Sibajak*, a Dutch vessel. At 8 a.m on the following day, the Battalion embarked on LCI and were taken out to the Sibajak. 8 and 9 DLI were already on board.

Emergency boat stations were practised, areas of the deck were set aside for PT and various lectures and talks planned to keep the troops active and interested. Sports tournaments were organised. On the 23rd October, the convoy sailed for the United Kingdom. On the 25th, the *Sibajak* anchored in Algiers harbour. It sailed the next day. 'HQ' Company won the ship's tug of war competition. The following gallantry awards were announced:

Major R.G. Atkinson	Military Cross.
Captain R. Galloway	Military Cross.

Private Worthington	Military Medal.
Private Kay	Military Medal.

On the 3rd November, Khaki Drill was replaced with Battle Dress. In the late afternoon of the following day, the convoy entered the River Clyde and anchored off Gourock. After two and a half years, the 6th Battalion was home.

CHAPTER 29
PREPARATIONS FOR D DAY
1943 - 1944

Over the next two days, baggage was loaded onto lighters and taken ashore. Customs officials came on board to make the necessary checks and currency was exchanged from British Military Authority notes to stirling. At 7.45 a.m. on the 7th November, the first train party consisting of the rifle companies and 'B' Echelon, paraded and were taken ashore by lighters. At 8.45 a.m. the second train party paraded. This consisted of 'HQ' Company less 'B' Echelon and was taken ashore. At 11.15 a.m., the first train departed for Bartlow in Cambridgeshire via Carlisle and Crewe. The second train left at 11.50 a.m., for the same destination via Edinburgh and Newcastle. If there was any secret attached to the arrival of the Division, it was not well kept. At the station, the band of the Cameronians played and tea and buns were handed out by the WVS. As the trains sped through the Scottish countryside, messages of welcome were chalked on the gable walls of houses and bunting and streamers hung from the windows. By the railtracks, civilians cheered and waved. It was particularly difficult for those men of Tyneside and County Durham who were travelling on the train that went via Newcastle and Durham. They were so close to their families who, at this time, had no knowledge of the arrival of the Division in this country. A few of the men could see their street or home from the carriage windows. Yet after the heat of the Desert and Sicily, the colours of the English countryside, even in November, were a joy to the eye.

The first train arrived at Bartlow at about 3.00 a.m. on the 8th November and the party was taken to Shudy Camps, approximately three miles away. A hot breakfast was provided by the camp staff and huts were allocated. The second train party arrived to similar arrangements. The troops slept until midday. During the afternoon, the Regimental Band from the Infantry Training Centre at Brancepeth played and an ENSA show was given in the NAAFI in the evening. The overall arrangements made by the staff were excellent but the men were anxious for leave. Those who had left with the Battalion in May, 1941, had not seen their families and loved ones for over two and a half years. They had not long to wait, as leave was immediately organised for periods of fourteen to twenty-eight days, depending upon the length of service abroad. Key personnel were sent on leave on the 9th November. The first main leave party left Bartlow by special train on the 13th of the month, the remainder following over the next two days.

The Battalion had returned to England without equipment. The men had their rifles and other personal weapons but would need to be totally re-equipped to bring them up to war establishment. This began in December as the men returned from leave. New vehicles began to appear: 15 cwt and 3 ton trucks, Universal and Carden Lloyd carriers. Training was urgently needed. New battle training had developed in England over the period of the war and this differed in some aspects from that which the Battalion had experienced abroad. A training area close to Shudy Camps was required and on the 4th December, Lieutenant-Colonel Green and the Intelligence Officer, reconnoitred the area for a suitable company training ground. It was not very successful as most of the surrounding land was given up to the plough and pasture. However, in time, land became available and training was stepped up. Many members of the Battalion were sent on courses to bring them up to date with recent developments. These covered a wide variety of subjects and responsibilities such as: Pay and Administration, Vehicle Maintenance and Drivers' Courses, Junior NCOs Cadre, Company Commanders' Courses, Hygiene and Sanitation, Signals and many others. Weapon training took place at the Middlewick Ranges, near Colchester. A programme was introduced to get the Battalion back to peak physical fitness. Sport was central to this and the usual games were arranged at inter-platoon, company and unit levels. Cross country running brought to the fore Lieutenant Bateman and Lance-Corporal Last, who represented the Battalion in inter-Battalion, Brigade and Divisional competitions. The former won the inter-Brigade competition and both represented the Division in the Eastern Command Championship. Physical training started off each day's programme and regular route marches made their appearance once more.

Initially there were constant changes in duties, particularly affecting officers who were transferred from one duty to another until the team settled down. Much of this was due to the large number of training courses which took officers away from their Battalion duties for a period of time and replacements had to take over. The companies were under strength and reinforcements were required. These gradually appeared and were absorbed into the respective platoons and companies.

On the 13th December, individual training commenced and was to last for two weeks. The following day, a Battalion Pioneer Assault Platoon was formed and came under the command of Captain Field of 'S' Company. On this same day, Lieutenant-Colonel Green visited the DAAG (Deputy Assistant Adjutant General) at Divisional Headquarters to discuss the problems of reinforcement. On the 15th, he visited Major-General Wilson at the War Office to discuss developments in infantry training and weapons. On the 17th of the month, a demonstration of battle tactics was held and the CO and a number of officers attended. Work on an assault course was commenced on the 20th December. A 30 yds. Range near Bartlow was completed on the 24th December. Christmas Day was celebrated in the usual Army

fashion, with officers and senior NCOs waiting on the men. An ENSA concert was held in the camp entertainments hall in the evening. The end of the month and the year arrived, with the Battalion settled in to its new routine. The kindness and hospitality of the local population helped the process enormously.

On the 3rd January, 1944, the Battalion welcomed back Major G.L. Wood, MC, who rejoined as Second-in-Command and Unit Security Officer. Another long serving officer with the Battalion, Lieutenant (QM) Runciman, was promoted to Captain. Hardly a day went by without someone being sent on a course. Some of these and the conferences also being organised, were obviously aimed at future operations, for example: 'Infantry Co-operation with Tanks' and 'Advance from a Bridgehead.' On the 17th January, a farewell message was received from Major-General Kirkman, CBE, MC, who relinquished command of the Division. He had commanded the Division throughout the Sicily campaign. His successor was Major-General D.A.H. Graham, CBE, DSO, MC. On the 20th of the month, the Battalion Commanders of 151 Brigade were shown over the Thetford Battle Training Area. The companies of the Battalion carried out exercises with squadrons of the 9th Royal Tanks. The aims of the exercise were threefold:

(1) To instil into all ranks the importance of intimate co-operation between tanks and infantry.

(2) To train platoon and company commanders to work with their opposite numbers in an Army Tank Battalion.

(3) To practise an effective method of inter-communication which will ensure that rapid supporting fire is brought down by tanks against enemy opposition holding up infantry.

On the 23rd January, fifty-seven other ranks arrived as reinforcements to the Battalion. Thirteen were from the 1st Battalion The Durham Light Infantry and the remainder from the King's Own Yorkshire Light Infantry. The arrival of bicycles added a new dimension to the mobility of the Battalion. Sufficient for a company, they were to be used to create a mobile force. On the 24th of the month, 'B' Company, mounted on these veritable 'bone shakers,' rode through Haverhill, Clare, Stradishall and Great Thurlow on an exercise during which they were 'fired' upon. They immediately jumped off their 'mounts,' deployed and attacked the 'enemy' force. Increasingly over the next few weeks, longer and more demanding exercises were carried out on the Thetford Battle Range.

February was a month of visits by high ranking visitors. The Colonel of the Regiment, Colonel C.L. Matthews, came on the 10th of the month. Five days later, General Montgomery inspected the Brigade drawn up on Haverhill football ground. Once more, he praised the Division and the Brigade for the work they had done in the past. He announced that he would be giving the Division a leading role in future operations. This information was not received with much enthusiasm. The Division had been away from England for a long period of time and had travelled far. It had seen much action, fought in bloody battles and lost many friends who had not come back but lay in 'some foreign field'. The men were very much aware of the fact that there were several Divisions in the country which had never been abroad and had never fired a shot in anger. Wasn't it time that someone else led the way? Feelings such as these were to linger for quite some time and were only thrown off as the date of the invasion neared and training and experience came together to weld a strong fighting force, confident and ready to break into 'Fortress Europe.' At this time, however, with the knowledge that once more 50th Division was to be at the forefront of battle, men who had come through the horrors of Mareth and Primosole Bridge would have to face great danger yet again. 'The bloody Durhams again. It's always the bloody Durhams,' was an oft overheard remark at this time. There was a great need to see more of their families than the official leave allowed. A number of men of the Division, therefore, overstayed their leave for a day or so and became AWOL (Absent Without Leave). This was not desertion, for they all returned, to be dealt with by their Commanders who were not without some sympathy for them. When the time came for the invasion, however, the companies were at full strength.

On the 23rd February, His Majesty the King inspected the Brigade. Those units presented to the King were: 6th, 8th and 9th Battalions The Durham Light Infantry; 61st Reconnaissance Battalion, 151 Brigade Workshops and the 524th Company RASC. Demonstrations were arranged for the Royal visitor in addition to the inspection of the troops. There was a mortar firing demonstration, an assault by 'A' Company on the Battalion Assault Course and a demonstration of blowing anti-tank pits by the Assault Pioneer Platoon. The visit lasted from 11 a.m. to 11.45 a.m.

Much more demanding and realistic exercises were being introduced using live ammunition. Exercises Fox I and Fox II were carried out on the Stanford Battle Area. Accidents could and did happen and Lieutenant I.W. Spain, who had recently joined the Battalion, was wounded by the explosion of a 2in. Mortar. All of the rifle companies were given the opportunity to experience a mobile role on the heavy bicycles, with runs of up to forty miles. A Battalion Dance Band was formed with Lieutenant H.K. Muff in charge and it held its first practice on the 27th February. The daily round of courses and lectures continued unabated and, if anything, increased in number. The pressure increased. However, some release was obtained by playing football and rugby games against other companies and units, with varying success. On the 12th March, the Battalion moved to Lowestoft. The training programme now laid down was as follows:

(1) Concentration by all companies on breaching minefields, in preparation for exercises to be carried out in co-operation with flail tanks.

(2) Use of street fighting area in Lowestoft by all companies. This was carried out in the heavily bombed areas of the town.

(3) Company exercises to be carried out in the local training areas.

The flail tanks were not new to those members of the Battalion who had fought at Mareth. Then called 'Scorpions,' two had assisted the 8th and 9th Battalions to cross the minefields. These at Lowestoft were updated models initially called 'Crabs' but changed to 'flail tank.' Short chains revolved on a drum at the front of the tank and exploded any mines in the vehicle's path. Other strange vehicles were introduced to the Battalion for the first time, for example, 'AVRES' (Armoured Vehicle Royal Engineers) - an armoured bulldozer for crossing anti-tank ditches and sea walls. Others were armoured flame-throwers called Crocodiles, tanks which 'swam' and those armoured vehicles which threw a heavy mortar shell into strong concrete positions. On the 13th March, all officers of the Battalion went to Southwold for a lecture and discussion on cloth models regarding 'Exercise Bullshead.' On the 21st, the Battalion bivouacked for the night in Sudbourne Great Wood and the exercise was carried out the next day. It covered such tasks as attacking strong points and coastal defences. The Battalion arrived back at Lowestoft in the late afternoon and had enough energy to attend a dance in the new Drill Hall in the evening. Courses now included Street Fighting, Waterproofing of Vehicles, Sniper and Signal exercises and Minelaying and Lifting.

On the 2nd April, 1944, the Battalion moved from Lowestoft to Nightingale Wood between Romsey and Southampton to the tented Camp C 17, in a beautiful area of England. Bad weather throughout the previous few days, had made the camp area very muddy and conditions were difficult. Eighteen year old Private Ken Lodge, new to the Battalion, remembered the conditions:

> 'When we went in it was teeming with rain and it was a brand new site. They were pitching tents in this wood and the site hadn't even been cleared. They were pitching tents on top of wet grass, on top of brambles and we slept on the ground on ground sheets in these tents. There was no lighting facilities, just a candle. Even one tent had two grass snakes in it. One morning the squirrels were running up and down the guide ropes. Being there, coming from Lowestoft, God, it was terrible. This is what we called real soldiering...It eventually got better as the camp progressed. It was even better when the Americans moved in.'

The following two or three days, were spent in laying duckboards and tidying up the camp. Major Derek Thomlinson, with the Company Commanders, reconnoitred the training areas of Copythorne, Landford and Fritham. These were areas of open heathland and ideal for training infantry and tracked vehicles.

On the 11th of the month, Major Reggie Atkinson, MC, rejoined the Battalion from 2nd Army Headquarters and took over command of 'B' Company. Major Thomlinson carried out an exercise on the 14th April, to give troops practice in the role of a mobile column. Two platoons of 'D' Company on bicycles, the Carrier Platoon, Anti-tank Platoon, a platoon of the 2nd Cheshires and a detachment of the Assault Pioneer Platoon took part. The journey was from Romsey to Cadnam Common, quite a distance on those far from comfortable, nor easy to handle machines

On the 17th April, Exercise Smash III commenced. The wetshod troops of the Battalion, those who were to be conveyed by LCIs, left for Southampton and went on board their craft. The dryshod personnel of the Battalion left camp in TCVs (Troop Carrying Vehicles) and moved to the area of Corfe Castle where they bivouacked for the period of the exercise. On the night of the 17th-18th, the wetshod personnel sailed and landed on the beaches at Studland at 9.30 a.m. They then marched across heathland for a distance of four miles to the assembly area near Rempstone Hall where the whole Battalion was concentrated by 12.30 p.m. A mobile column under Major Wood, MC, moved off for the objective at 3.00 p.m. which was reached by 6.00 p.m. The marching troops left the assembly area at 4.00 p.m. and reached the objective, twelve miles away, at 8.00 p.m. It was considered that both the mobile column and marching troops had taken too long to reach the objective. It was thought that the reason for this was that the whole Brigade had advanced along the same axis, the first three miles of which were along moorland tracks. An important lesson had been learned. The objective was consolidated, positions dug and defensive patrolling carried out during the night. The exercise ended the following day and the Battalion returned to camp. On the 24th April, 'D' Company was out once more on its bicycles to exercise in the area of Plaitford Common. Two days later, the Company rode to Bournemouth and bivouacked at Sandbank for the night and carried out exercises in manhandling cycles in the sea. It returned to camp on the 27th.

The second major exercise commenced on the 1st May. The object of Exercise Fabius was to give experience in embarking troops and vehicles and landing on open beaches. The Battalion embarked at Southampton on the afternoon of this day on LCIs manned by American crews . The transport were driven onto LCTs (Landing Craft Tank). The Quartermaster and an advance party made their way by road to Leigh Park to await the arrival of the rest of the Battalion. The craft remained in harbour during the whole of the 2nd May. Drill parades and short route marches took place and the Royal Marines Band entertained on the dock side in the afternoon. The convoy set sail during the night of the 3rd/4th May. At 10.00 a.m. on the 4th, the Battalion landed on the beaches of Hayling Island, east of Southampton and waded ashore in waist deep water. On landing, the Battalion marched off to Leigh Park and a bivouac area in a wood. Rain made conditions uncomfortable. The men carried twenty-four hour ration packs. Everything possible was done to simulate war conditions. The 5th May, was spent in inspecting weapons and equipment and maintenance work on vehicles and wireless sets. A return was made to Nightingale Wood by road transport on the 6th May, to find that part of their camp had been occupied by American troops. Some improvements to the conditions were made, with the issue of camp beds to the men. The general environment of the camp was, by now, most pleasant with the trees in leaf and flowers blooming outside the tents.

On the 10th May, a 50th Division Signals Exercise was held to test the communications at Divisional and Unit Headquarters' level. Exercise Grab commenced at 1.00 p.m. and was completed by 9.30 a.m. on the following day. The Supreme Commander, General Eisenhower, visited the camp on the 13th May and spoke to the men. He emphasised how important it was for them to get to know the Americans who would be fighting alongside them. He reminded them of the good name of the Division, which was held in high esteem and hoped that they would enhance still further. His talk was extremely well received by the men. Corporal George Richardson remembered this visit:

'Ike came and started walking along our 6th Battalion line, now and then stopping and pointing to our Africa Star and saying, "You should be proud of that." He had just about got along to the end of the line, when he said, "Aw shit! This isn't what I have come here for. I want to talk to the men." So he walked over to the centre of the field and told us to move closer. Not an officer or man moved. Ike looked at our Brigadier who told the Commanding Officers to fall us out and move over in front of him, which we did. Then the General said how proud he was to have met men who had done so well in the Middle East. But we were now spoiling our records by fighting with the Yanks. We had a big war to win and you have to do it alongside Yanks, not fighting against them. He went on to say that next time we met a Yank in the Pub to go up to him, shake him by the hand and offer him a drink. So we all got on our transport and went into Cambridge that evening. The Yanks must have been told the same because we all finished up the best of friends with the Yanks paying and we had a good night.'

A party of men of the Battalion, who had won awards, attended an investiture at Buckingham Palace on the 16th of the month. The King presented awards as follows:

Sergeant Haseley	Distinguished Conduct Medal.
Company Quartermaster Sergeant Davies	
	Military Medal.
Quartermaster Sergeant Cant	Military Medal.
Sergeant Critchley	Military Medal.
Sergeant Grey	Military Medal.
Corporal Worthington	Military Medal.
Private Saban	Military Medal.
Private Worthington	Military Medal.
Private Coglan	Military Medal.
Private Robinson	Military Medal.

During the remainder of May, time was taken up with working out the details of and completing the loading of vehicles and the detailed planning and briefing for future operations. The latter included details of the considerable support for the invasion from the sea and air. A briefing centre for 6th and 8th Battalions was opened in the camp. Officers and men were briefed in this centre over the final days of May, using bogus maps and a cloth model - bogus for security reasons. Every man in the Battalion was briefed so that he knew the whole plan of the invasion and his role in it, together with the immense support from the Royal Navy and the Air Forces of Britain and America, which the infantry would receive both prior to and on landing on the beaches of Normandy. On the 26th May, the camp was finally sealed with the perimeter guarded by American soldiers. On the 29th, the Foreign Secretary, Mr. Anthony Eden, visited the camp and spoke with officers and men of both Battalions. The tremendous task to prepare the Battalion for the invasion was almost complete. All was ready. The spirits of the officers and men were high. On the eve of the invasion, the complement of the Battalion was over eight hundred and forty officers and men. Lieutenant-Colonel Green's officers were as follows:

Second-in-Command	Major G.L. Wood, MC.
Adjutant	Captain R.S. Loveridge, MC.

Headquarter Company:

Officer Commanding	Captain A.E. Short.
Intelligence Officer	Lieutenant N. Myers.
Signals Officer	Lieutenant J.A.W. Wedgwood
Motor Transport Officer	Lieutenant P.G. Tyndale.
Quartermaster	Captain J. Runciman.
Medical Officer	Captain J.W. Murphy, RAMC.
Padre	Captain C. Hawksworth, RAChD.

'A' Company:

Officer Commanding	Major R. Galloway, MC.

'B' Company:

Officer Commanding	Major R.G. Atkinson, MC.

'C' Company:

Officer Commanding	Major M.J. Kirby.

'D' Company:

Officer Commanding	Major D.E.I. Thomlinson.

Support Company:

Officer Commanding	Captain W.J. Field, BEM.
Anti-tank Platoon	Captain G.B. Hawkins.
Carrier Platoon	Captain I.A. Daw.
Mortar Platoon	Lieutenant E.V. Oldham.
Assault Pioneer Platoon	Captain A.H. Sandwich.

CHAPTER 30
D DAY - THE BATTLE FOR THE BRIDGEHEAD
1944

Full details of the Allied plan for the invasion of Europe are not a part of this book. They are available to the reader in other works. However, a brief outline of these plans is necessary to place the role of the 6th Battalion in context. The United States 4th Division was to land on Utah Beach, west of the River Vire, on the south-east corner of the Cotentin Peninsula. The US 1st and 29th Divisions were to land on Omaha Beach to the east of the River Vire, in the area of Verville-sur-Mer - St. Laurent - Colleville. 50th Division was to land on Gold Beach in the area between Le Hamel and La Rivière. The 3rd Canadian Division was on the left of the 50th, landing on Juno Beach on either side of Courseulles. Finally, the 3rd British Division was to land on Sword Beach in the area of Ouistreham. In the west, to assist the American landings at Utah by securing the crossings of the inundated areas behind the beachhead, the 82nd and 101st US Airborne Divisions would be dropped. In the east, to protect the left flank of the 3rd Division and to secure the crossings of the River Orne and the Caen Canal, the 6th British Airborne Division would be dropped. 50th Division of XXX Corps, would land on a two brigade front. 231 Brigade would land on the right and 69 Brigade would land on the left of the beachhead. Their task was to advance inland and establish the vital lodgement area which would enable the follow up units to pass through and rapidly expand and secure the bridgehead. The initial landing was timed for 7.25 a.m. on the 5th June but this was delayed by twenty-four hours due to adverse weather conditions. 56 and 151 Brigades were the follow-up brigades of the Division and were timed to land at 11 a.m. and move forward to take their places between 231 Brigade on the right and 69 Brigade on the left. In the hours prior to the landing the German defences would be pounded by the bombers of both the American and British Air Forces, culminating, as the invasion armada approached the beaches, in a combined bombardment by planes and ships which would saturated the beachhead area, destroy bunkers and gun positions and, hopefully, stun the defenders to the extent that they would be incapable of making effective opposition to the landings.

During the first two days of June, briefings continued and gradually the support plan for the invasion was revealed to the Battalion, although at this stage, no names or locations were revealed. Officers and men studied the models, maps and photographs of the invasion area, marked with bogus names. There were no illusions as to how difficult the invasion tasks would be but the spirits of the infantrymen were considerably uplifted as the knowledge of the tremendous support bombardment by air and sea was revealed to them. At 9 a.m. on the 3rd June a Church Parade was held in Camp 17 and at 1.30 p.m. the main body of the Battalion left the camp in trucks for Southampton. Major G.L. Wood, MC, Second-in-Command of the Battalion, described the scene and his own feelings:

'We marched out of our camp this morning and embussed beside the gates - It is June 3rd. There is a small boy standing just outside the gate - he attracts the attention of all eyes - on his jersey he is wearing our Regimental and Divisional signs - on his chest is pinned the ribbon of the North African Star with Eighth Army Clasp - I find myself thinking whether any of our men feel as proud of their North African Star as this little boy so obviously does. If so, they certainly don't show it - but then they always hide their true feelings - it is not always easy to know what the men are thinking.

'However, they are all cheerful this morning - smiling and whistling, waving and calling to the girls as we pass them en route for the Docks - People gaze from their windows, stand on the pavements and wave - Somehow one has the feeling that they know "this is it." Some are very cheerful and shout "Good luck, Get it over quickly" - Others look sad, some silently weeping - perhaps they have a husband, son or sweetheart whom they know will be on the move also.

'My thoughts are very mixed - what a grand set of men - Hope we don't lose too many of the old faces this time - already they've seen so much and done so much - they know what it's all about, what to expect, they've done it all before - No false illusions - War is not a pleasant pastime, besides we cannot possibly hope for such an easy landing as we had in Sicily.'

Private Ernest Harvey also remembered the journey:

'The most thing I can remember was we were all in these 3 ton trucks going down to the docks. All the money they had they were giving to any old pensioner. If the lorry had to stop and a pensioner happened to walk by, they would shout of them and pass any spare money they had to them. If they had any money they knew it was no good to them where they were going and I think the people of Southampton, if there were any kicking about at that time, they must have done very well.'

When the docks were reached, a marvellous spectacle was revealed. Row upon row of landing craft lay waiting for the troops and their equipment. A distinguished party was waiting on the pier. The Prime Minister, Mr. Winston Churchill, Field Marshal Smuts and Mr. Ernest Bevin, Minister of Labour, watched the embarkation and wished the CO and the Battalion, 'God Speed'. The Battalion moved on to its allotted LCIs (Landing Craft Infantry). Private Ernest Harvey described the quarters:

'Well, it was just like a big hold and you went down these steps and there was a big hold. There were these bunks, double bunks and we all made the best of it we could.'

On the 4th June, information was received that the invasion had been put back for twenty-four hours. During the day two craft loads in the morning and two in the afternoon, were allowed on to the docks to visit the Transit Camp set up in the large sheds on the quayside. Here, the men had the opportunity to have a good wash, were served with a hot meal and could write letters, play organised games, visit the NAAFI and enjoy various entertainments. The same facilities were made available during the 5th June. On this day, the Battalion experienced an unexpected and, in the circumstances an unfortunate blow, when the Commanding Officer, Lieutenant-Colonel Green was taken ill with malaria and was taken to hospital. Major George Leslie Wood MC, took over command in his absence. After the delay due to stormy conditions, a break in the weather was forecast and this was expected to last for some thirty-six hours. General Eisenhower grasped the opportunity and, in the early hours of the 5th June, made his momentous decision to go ahead with the invasion. During the night of the 5th-6th, the landing craft set sail for Normandy. Major Wood, thrown unexpectedly into the command of the Battalion, had much to do:

'There was still a lot to be done ... "Pass the order round. All ranks will wear their Mae Wests - Tonight we shall all sleep fully dressed".

'We hold a practice alarm. In the event of the ship sinking [enemy gunfire or mines - I understand we have a big stretch of minefield to get through] all ranks must know what is expected of them - How to use the Escape Hatches quickly. It's all simple enough - As you come on deck, you must rush to the side and jump clear, into the water. Simple? Very. But what an awful thought - the sea looks so cold and rough, already it's beginning to get dark. I hope the men understand this business ... unless they come quickly and jump immediately, many men will be trapped below deck. Anyhow, we have a good escort - we have been told that we are the centre group of five naval convoys - we ought to get away with it ... General Montgomery's message to the troops to be issued - We called them 'Montigrams' in the 8th Army. Issue maps to all officers, So far they have only had bogus maps - The new maps are scanned in silence - the only comment, "So, it is Cherbourg peninsula after all." There is a small descriptive booklet for each man - Full of useful information about the area we are going to...

'...we are due to land at 10.00 hrs tomorrow - better make sure of things - Reveille 06.00 - Breakfast 07.00 - all ranks to be dressed and ready to move from 09.30. "Tell the Adjutant to pass this information round." I visit the Ship's Captain - an all American crew - seem like good chaps - know their job alright. "If we land in deep water, will they run out Lifelines to the shore?" otherwise our men so heavily laden, may well be swept away and drowned. Back comes the answer "Sure Major - we'll do all we can to help your boys."'

The sea was rough and the journey, similar to the Sicily landing, was very unpleasant. Sergeant Bert Davies was amongst the many who suffered:

> 'We were all issued with two seasick tablets and I thought, Well, I'll not take mine yet. As soon as we set off, watching other people, seeing one sick then another, I thought I'd best take mine and within ten minutes I was seasick. The pills did no good at all. I should have taken them an hour before. It was very very rough. The boat reared up, right to the top of a wave and then the wave would disappear and then, flap, on to the sea again. Just like a bomb itself dropping onto the water. I was darned pleased when I got to the other side...'

The conditions did not make the tasks of the various Company Commanders easy. A good breakfast was to be prepared and given to the men before going ashore. Major Reggie Atkinson, MC, commanding 'B' Company checked on the preparations:

> '...On reaching the galley a very distressing sight met my eyes. Several tins of bully beef had been opened and their contents tipped into trays, but that is as far as the preparations for breakfast had gone. The cook now lay flat out on the galley table. I was furious and dashed off in a rage to find my CSM. My progress was most undignified though, as the craft was doing a sort of corkscrew motion through the water, and it was all I could do to remain upright. I eventually found the Company Sergeant-Major amongst the sprawling mass of bodies on the troopdeck, woke him up and told him to get breakfast laid on at once. Hardly had I finished doing this than I became acutely conscious of a peculiar feeling in my tummy, I shut my mouth and gave a gulp, and quickly made my way back to my bunk. Whether it was the motion of the ship, or the atmosphere of the crowded troopdeck, or both, I don't know, but there was no use denying it, here I was seasick for my second invasion running.'

Most officers and men looked and felt terrible. At reveille at 6.00 a.m. on the 6th June, the Battalion slowly came to life. They were dressed and ready by 9.30 a.m. though many had done without breakfast. The beaches they were to land upon, following the assault Battalions of the two brigades who had landed some two hours earlier, had been breached. The various obstacles, steel hedgehogs, steel ramps, wooden stakes with anti-boat mines attached, which had been erected at low water along the beaches, had been negotiated though not without some loss and some still remained to ensnare any unlucky or unwary landing craft. Tracks had been cleared through the minefields - both anti-personnel and anti-tank - by flail tanks and Royal Engineers who had gone in with the first assault troops. The crust of beach defences some two or three hundred yards in depth, the concrete pill boxes and bunkers and the infantry strong points, had very largely fallen to the assaulting troops. Behind the beaches which the 50th Division assaulted, ran a sea wall which had not been kept in good repair and was crumbling in many places. Behind this wall, which was not considered to be any great obstacle to infantry, ran the coast road. Marshy ground lay south of the coast road and this was considered an obstacle to tracked vehicles and motor transport. A minefield was laid in this area to a depth of between seventy-five and one hundred yards. It was marked with a wire fence. South of the marshy ground the land rose to the Meuvaines Ridge which dominated the area. Here the countryside was cultivated, with very few hedges or ditches and with isolated clumps of trees, especially near the villages. The bocage country of small fields, thick hedgerows and sunken roads lay further south.

A combination of events led to the Allies achieving complete surprise. The weather conditions were so bad that the enemy considered it unlikely, if not impossible, that any invasion fleet would put to sea. The Allies held complete command of the sea and skies. No German reconnaissance missions were flown and, with the one exception of the sinking of an Allied destroyer by enemy E Boats on the western flank of the invasion armada, there was no interference from the German Navy. Unknown to the Allies, several of the senior German Commanders were away from their units. Rommel was on leave at his home in Germany. The German 716th Division occupied the coastal defences on Gold Beach and, like the remainder of the coastal divisions in

Normandy, it was of low calibre, with many impressed foreigners in the ranks particularly from the conquered areas of Eastern Europe such as Russians and Poles. The 352nd Infantry Division had taken over a number of positions with its 914th, 915th and 916th Infantry Regiments. It was a mixed division of personnel from Russia, Alsace and Luxembourg. Also under its command was the 642nd Ost Battalion made up of Russians with German officers and NCOs. Morale in these divisions was not expected to be high and this proved to be the case. Though some units fought with considerable tenacity, the majority melted away and were pleased to surrender to the advancing troops. The 21st Panzer Division lay just south of Caen and moved quickly into action to blunt the British drive on Caen. The 12th SS Panzer Division was in the area of Bernay and Verneuil and the 130th Panzer Lehr Division was in the area of Le Mans - Laval - Chartres. This latter Division was arguably the finest of the German Panzer Divisions available to meet the invaders in the ensuing days of June. A training division, it was staffed with experienced officers and NCOs and had an almost full complement of tanks, vehicles and equipment. It was soon to prove a worthy opponent of 50 Division. Other Panzer Divisions were to appear in Normandy over the next few weeks as they made their way from lying up areas further afield, their journeys much hampered by Allied air strikes.

By 9.00 a.m. the French coast was visible. Information was received that the leading brigades were ashore and making progress, though slower than expected. A warning was received that Ver-sur-Mer had not been taken and the Battalion should be prepared to move to a different assembly area not so far inland. Coastal guns were firing in the distance but no shells came in the direction of the landing craft carrying the Brigade. Several naval craft were firing intermittently at targets inland. The sight which unfolded as the beach was approached, was quite amazing. A huge number of ships stood out at sea. Hundreds of landing craft were in the process of discharging their cargoes of men and materials on to the shore. Destroyers and frigates weaved amongst the ships, firing now and again at targets passed to them from naval observers ashore working with the troops. A variety of landing craft which had landed 69 Brigade could still be seen on the shore line. Some were empty with their ramps down, others lay damaged or destroyed by enemy gunfire, the beach obstacles, or the heavy seas. For most of the Battalion it was to be a wet landing. Major Wood's landing craft had its difficulties as he recorded:

'We touch down - the ship shudders as she touches the bottom. Down come the ramps into the water - Ron Simpson steps off into the water - He is a big strong chap, but it's no use the sea sweeps him away - He just manages to grab the rail in time to pull himself back on. One of the crew, starts swimming towards the shore - it is only a few yards away, but he doesn't seem to be making any headway - at last he makes the beach - curse it he's lost the lifeline. The Ship's Captain shouts to us to stand clear - up come the ramps again - He is going to put out to sea and come in again at a different place. Another half hour passes - we are terribly late - a small motor boat goes past towards the shore - It is the Brigade Commander - He spots us, smiles and waves - one feels so much better. In we go again, this time the ramps come down on dry land - off we walk without getting our feet wet - Good show.'

Private Harry Wilkinson, who had not boarded his landing craft at Southampton with the main body, needed some assistance as the boat sailed:

'A Yankee sailor said to me, he says, "Can you swim much?" I said, "Well, I'll make a bloody good try. It's the second invasion for me but I'm always glad to get ashore. It depends what the tide's like, with me being so small." He says, "Well look," he says, "I can swim." He says, "Have my lifebelt." It was one of those inflatables. He put it round me and it inflated.'

It was 11 a.m. when the Battalion waded ashore. Sergeant Bert Davies looked over his shoulder when he reached the beach:

'I looked round once and saw the ships, brief glimpse of the ships. Blooming hell! I could understand how the Germans felt. There were thousands of them. You thought you were part of something big. This was a change for us. We were dishing it out and they had to accept it. We knew they were more frightened than us. Once we got off the beach, I had another quick look round. A terrific sight. Aircraft above, ships, some with barrage balloons, all firing away, these heavy ships. Tanks being unloaded at a very early stage. That was a good sign. Flail tanks that soon left the beach and flailed a path through the minefields for us. Once we were through the minefields we had to spread out. Sooner you got off the beach and inland the better.'

The spirits of the troops were heightened by the sights and sounds around them. Private Ken Lodge was on the beach with a group of men with the heavy wireless batteries. He remembered:

'There was a German prisoner we had on the beach and the corporal in charge of us was an old soldier and he was making the German do some chores. He (the German) was shouting at us the German National Anthem. He was saying "Deutschland Uber Alles" and the corporal was saying, "Now its Deutschland UNDER Alles."'

Once on the beach a small number of enemy shells exploded but nowhere near the amount of gunfire the Battalion had expected. Lance-Corporal Joe Wear described his narrow escape from one near miss:

Major Derek E.I. Thomlinson, *served in the Battalion as adjutant and company commander*

'I had just got my waterproofing off when my wireless fell off my back ... [the straps] had been cut by a piece of shrapnel, went right through and I had to carry the wireless all that day ... There wasn't as much [firing] as we had expected ... personally I had expected a lot of small arms fire, it wasn't there. There was some shelling ... People, like myself, just running up [the beach]. There were tanks there, some were bogged down but some were moving. That was the first time the tanks had gone in before the infantry. That was something that pleased us actually ... They were firing, like dustbins at the concrete towers ... I don't think people realise that the infantry always went in before the tanks.'

Almost to a man, the Battalion was pleased to be on dry land again and, with the exhortations of the Beach Master ringing in their ears to move off the beach quickly and follow their officers, the companies moved off to the assembly area. Things had

improved since the last message and the original assembly area just north of Ver-sur-Mer was now available. This village had received a severe pounding and there was much destruction but even so, a few French civilians stood smiling in the street as the Battalion moved through. It was 1.00 p.m. when the Battalion finally assembled and a lunch, which included hot soup, was taken. It was hoped to move forward at 2.00 p.m. but the congested roads and narrow village streets slowed the advance down and the Battalion did not move forward until 3.00 p.m. some two hours later than planned.

The Brigade plan was for the 9th Battalion to advance on the right with the 6th on its left. 8th Battalion would follow in reserve. Each Battalion was headed by a mobile column. In the case of the 6th Battalion, the mobile column consisted of: the Carrier Platoon; Mortar Platoon; Anti-Tank Platoon; No. 4 Platoon 2nd Cheshire Regiment (machine-guns); 'D' Company on its bicycles; Sniper Section; Detachment of the Pioneer Platoon and the FOO (Forward Observation Officer), 86 Field Regiment, RA. In support, the mobile column was accompanied by a Squadron of the 4/7 Dragoon Guards with their Sherman Tanks, under the command of Major Bell. Originally, the column would have been commanded by Major Wood but, as he had to assume command of the Battalion on the illness of Lieutenant-Colonel Green, Major Derek Thomlinson took command. The mobile column, in turn, had an advance section under Lieutenant Tim Firth. This comprised: two sections of the Carrier Platoon; one section of the Mortar Platoon; one section of the Anti-Tank Platoon and a detachment of the Pioneer Platoon. A troop of Sherman Tanks was in support.

Lieutenant Kirk described the advance of his section:

'Although the country was open, we were not able to move as freely as we had appreciated from aerial photographs, because most of the hedgerows had tree trunks in them and were usually carrier obstacles.

'When we got to Villiers-le-Sec, we met a few pockets but, when we turned our not inconsiderable fire power on, they quickly left. I found the greatest difficulty in stopping the tanks once they had started firing as they were both blind and deaf. I tried rapping on the turret with my pistol-butt, but it did not have much effect...

'On our journey, we had encountered a troop of armoured cars from the Inns of Court. They seemed slow in getting along, so we left them. We reached Esquay-sur-Seulles and pushed on to the main Bayeax - Caen road, where the tanks indulged in an orgy of destruction, knocking telegraph poles for six. As this was the Battalion's first objective and it was now 20.00 hours, we stopped there to and dug in...'

The advance of the mobile column was slow. Again, congested roads and narrow village streets, which were difficult for Sherman Tanks to negotiate, were the chief problems encountered, rather than any opposition from the enemy. Some opposition was encountered on route but was easily dealt with and prisoners taken were found to be from the 642nd Ost Russian Battalion who quickly surrendered and were obviously pleased to be out of the war. Esquay-sur-Seulles, was reached at 8.30 p.m. and, after some delay, orders were received that the Battalion was to dig in for the night. A number of M10s, self propelled 17 pounder anti-tank guns of the Northumberland Hussars, joined the Battalion here. During the course of the march, Major Kirby, who had an eye for the confiscation of useful enemy material, came across a 10 hp Ford car, which was repainted and the sign TT 60 placed in a prominent position on the vehicle. It was to serve the Battalion for quite some time. Having dug in, patrols were sent out, but the first night in France was found to be a relatively quiet one for the 'Sixth'. News was received from Brigade Headquarters that Brigadier Senior had been wounded and taken prisoner. He had been wounded in the arm near Crépon, but had escaped capture by hiding up for some time. He had successfully made his way back to the British positions but his wound was such that he had to be sent back to England and Lieutenant-Colonel Lidwell of the 8th Battalion assumed temporary command of the Brigade.

At 5.00 a.m. on the 7th June, the advance continued to the second objective which lay in the area of Condé-sur-Seulles. The mobile column led the way, with Captain Ian Daw and part of the Carrier and Mortar Platoons ranging ahead. It was expected that the Germans would defend the line of the Bayeux - Caen railway. However, the carriers soon reported back that the line was undefended and the advance continued. The head of the mobile column turned south from the Bayeux - Caen road and moved towards Condé. Captain Sandwith, together with the Assault Pioneer Platoon, was in the rear of the column, acting as link between it and the main body. He ambushed a German column of vehicles which he spotted approaching the road junction, destroyed three enemy trucks and captured a Volkswagon car.

The mobile column reached the objective north-west of Condé at about 7.30 a.m. and took up defensive positions whilst waiting for the arrival of the main body. Captain Daw and his carriers, patrolling out in front of the positions, were suddenly and unexpectedly attacked by American 'Thunderbolts'. Two carriers were hit by rockets and destroyed. One of these was Lieutenant Kirk's 'Gazala' driven by Private Marsh. Fortunately, all the crews got out in time and there were no casualties. As the planes dived on the carriers, the yellow celenese recognition triangles carried by platoon and section leaders appeared but were too late to stop the attack.

Lieutenant Kirk described the attack:

'A squadron of American Thunderbolts appeared and started to circle round. "Good old air cover," I said, "but I'll just put up some recognition signals."

'That did it! Immediately, one of their number dived down and opened up at us with his guns. Naturally, we all hit the deck, which was just as well as our worthy ally hit the back of my carrier and set off a box of 77 grenades, which showered burning phosphorous all round the vehicle. Ian [Daw] got some on his Mackintosh, but no one was hurt, however my carrier was blazing furiously and, before we could put it out, back the swine came.

'We had a slight lull and Ian and the remainder swerved of to their various tasks.Then back came our intrepid and enthusiastic aviators, but by this time we had realised the impossibility of trying to extinguish the flames and were well hidden in a deep ditch. Still it was most unpleasant, although made humorous by my driver, Marsh, who thought "Gazala" the best carrier in the Battalion and was furious at her ignominious end. His comments on the Yankee Air Force were weird and wonderful, "You're not fit to be bloody allies of ours."'

The main body reached the objectives held by the mobile column at about 9.00 a.m. It was subjected to a certain amount of sniping and sniper-hunting parties were organised to deal with this nuisance. Captain Hawkins, in command of the Anti-Tank Platoon, had just completed siting one of his guns in position on the Battalion front when he observed a German 37mm. anti-aircraft gun behind a 5 ton truck standing stationary at a cross roads on the Tilly Bayeux road. He got his gun behind the hedgerow about two hundred yards from the target and shot and destroyed the German gun and vehicle. It was quite obvious that the enemy were not yet aware of the British presence in the area.

The boundary between two units, in this case that between 151 and 69 Brigades, is vulnerable to enemy infiltration. The boundary between the left of 151 Brigade and the right of 69 Brigade met on the River Seulles at Condé. The gap was to be filled by a Joint Post, made up of elements of both brigades and which was to be established where the road from Ducy-St.-Marguerite meets the minor road which runs south-east from Condé in the valley of the River Seulles. The aim was to stop the enemy creeping up the River Seulles unobserved. Within a few

Captain Fenner *commanded the Joint Post at Conde Sur Seulles, 7th June, 1944*

yards of the road junction, a railway viaduct crosses the road and the river. A strip of thick trees ran down to the road to the rear and thick hedges cut down the field of view. The position was out of sight and about twelve hundred yards from the main body of the Battalion. It was not an area which would be easy to defend. A further problem was that 69 Brigade had failed to come up on the left as it had been delayed by enemy resistance at St. Léger. The Joint Post was, therefore, out on a limb with an open left flank. The Post's garrison comprised No. 18 Platoon of 'D' Company less one section, a carrier section of three vehicles and nine men, and one six pounder anti-tank gun, under the command of Lieutenant David Fenner. The officer placed the two sections of No. 18 Platoon, on the viaduct and astride the railway line. Through the arch of the viaduct and on the left, was a small farmhouse and yard. Here the carrier section was deployed. Back under the bridge was a bank between the railway embankment and the road. Captain Fenner set up his small headquarters here. The six pounder anti-tank gun was sighted at the end of the strip of trees where it met the road. The garrison set about preparing its defences. Lieutenant Fenner described what happened:

'...While this was going on there was some shooting on the carrier section's side of the bridge. They had killed a young SS man, a panzer grenadier. But another had got away. I concluded that this could have been a two man reconnaissance patrol to examine our layout. Everyone was warned to keep a good look out...

'...Then a Frenchman from a farm just south of our position came to us and reported a party of Germans had passed west to east through his farm. Again our little force was alerted ... There was an outbreak of firing from the direction of the 6 pounder position, two or three men ran past the HQ in the direction of the carrier section under the bridge. These were, in fact, the 6 pounder crew survivors. I stepped from behind the bank into the road and charging down the road towards us was a bunch of angry Germans. I jumped back behind the bank and we all began firing through the hedge that topped the bank. A furious fire fight developed at very close range. One of our number was hit, but we seemed to have succeeded in checking the German attack temporarily. I yelled for the carrier section to come and support us and I lobbed one of the plastic 69 grenades I had in my pouches over the bank...

'...The Germans stopped firing and disappeared up the road followed by some of the carrier section, who had charged round to our support, and the HQ party. We ran past an abandoned machine pistol and a pair of binoculars. I surmised later we had probably hit the German commander. At the entrance to the wood we ran into another fire fight at close range. Probably a covering party to secure the withdrawal of the assaulting force. We took three more casualties including the brave carrier section commander [Corporal King] who was killed. These Germans ran back through the wood. They were shot up by 18 platoon from their position on top of the railway bridge. We found the 6 pounder intact, we also found the 6 pounder commander. He had been walking up the line of the wood when he surprised the Germans coming the other way. They shot him down, sprayed him as they ran past after the other gunners, whose arrival past our HQ was mentioned earlier. He was badly shot up but was able to walk. We found one wounded and two dead Germans ... The German patrol was skilfully handled and the young SS men pressed home their attack. The whole affair could have only lasted a few minutes but it was pretty savage while it happened.'

During the action, Lieutenant Fenner had contacted the Battalion and asked for support as he feared that the road between Condé and the Joint Post might be cut. Captain Daw, with four carriers, was sent out to protect the left flank of the Joint Post. It halted on the road to the Post and the crews dismounted. Lieutenant Fenner, meanwhile, had been wounded and was making his way back to the RAP when he met Captain Daw's party. He pointed out the whereabouts of the enemy and the carrier sections made an attack on and through the wood.

They drove the enemy off in the direction of Ducy-St.-Marguerite. Captain Daw reorganised the Post and assumed command of the position. Later in the day, enemy armoured cars were heard on the left flank coming from Ducy-St-Marguerite and these were engaged by Captain Daw's party and driven off. Captain Daw was ordered to withdraw so that artillery fire could be brought down on the Joint Post area and as he did so, the enemy occupied the Post. Major Cummings, the artillery FOO, directed the artillery shoot onto the railway bridge and its immediate area.

Meanwhile, the Carrier Platoon with 'D' Company under Major Thomlinson, secured Condé as a firm base. At 9.00 a.m. on the following day, the 8th June, Lieutenant Kirk was sent to re-occupy the Joint Post with one platoon of 'D' Company, one section of carriers and one anti-tank gun. The Post was found to be deserted by the enemy. An hour later, sporadic firing broke out from the enemy positions and shortly afterwards an armoured car was heard approaching the Post down the Ducy-St.-Marguerite road. It fired a few shells into the railway embankment close to the forward section. The enemy attacked with infantry and another armoured car. The latter knocked out a carrier but was then destroyed by our fire. A second German assault came in at 11.00 a.m. much stronger than the first. Lieutenant Kirk was told he could withdraw at his own discretion. The forward section over the railway embankment lost contact with the platoon and came under heavy fire as it attempted to clamber back over the embankment. The right forward section saw enemy infiltrating to the right. The garrison was in real danger of being cut off from the main body of the Battalion. Lieutenant Kirk decided to withdraw, covered by heavy artillery and mortar fire directed by Major Cummings from a farmhouse in Condé. Corporal George Richardson was a signaller with the garrison and described his role in the withdrawal:

'...We were in these slit trenches that had been occupied by our previous platoon and one or two dead bodies lying about which we hadn't time to see to. There was about twenty-four of us ... Suddenly coming up towards midday, there was a big battle going off to our right along the viaduct, at the other side of the viaduct ... I started sending broadcasts back giving, more or less, a running commentary - numbers of Germans and the action we were taking. Jerry was slowly closing in and we could see we were going to be overrun ... I said I could bring artillery down on this position ... He [the Lieutenant] gave me the map reference and I gave the old signal, "Murder" - eight figure map reference - "Three minutes, Now!" He had told Sergeant Cooper and the men to get ready to run back, which they were all too willing to do, as soon as he shouted, Up and go!" As soon as I sent the message, I turned the dials off our station, put a bullet through the top and a bullet through the bottom and put it out of commission ... and I ran like hell back about one hundred yards where there was a hedge and a ditch behind it. It probably took five to six minutes for the artillery to open fire and there must have been about twenty-four 25 pounders ranged on the one position and they all came down and shattered the whole of the wooded area...'

Private George S. Richardson, *Signal Platoon, played an important role in the defence of the Joint Post on the 8th June, 1944*

captors to the grounds of the Chateau d'Audrieu a few miles from Condé. On the 8th June, together with twenty-four Canadian prisoners, they were shot by SS troops. This atrocity was witnessed by members of the family who owned the Chateau at the time. A Court of Inquiry held a month after the event suspected that the killings were carried out by men of the 12th Panzer Reconnaissance Battalion of the 12th SS (Hitler Youth) Panzer Division. No hard evidence could be found to link any of the perpetrators to the crime. It was not until 1994, after an investigation by the Newcastle *Evening Chronicle*, that the Regiment discovered the true story about how these unfortunate young men lost their lives.

To complete the story of the Joint Post actions, on the 10th June, Captain Rome with a platoon of 'B' Company, plus carriers and an anti-tank gun, occupied the Post and was joined by a similar force from 69 Brigade. The next day, the Post took fourteen enemy prisoners.

On returning to the Battalion positions, the carriers had to cross an open hillside under heavy enemy fire. Private Davidson was driving one of the carriers when his engine stalled in the open and under the eyes of the German gunners. Cooly, though under enemy fire, he dismounted from the carrier, got his starting handle and cranked the engine until it fired. He replaced the handle and drove away unscathed. The forward section of the garrison had been cut off and had to find its own way back. A serious game of hide-and-seek was played in the wood on the left flank between themselves and the Germans. Two men rejoined 'D' Company at 2.30 p.m. and the section leader and one man at 5.30 p.m. Three men were reported missing. Two of these men were Privates Evan Hayton and William Barlow, aged twenty and twenty-one respectively. They were taken by their

They were part of a Pioneer Battalion which had been working on the coastal defences and had left the area as soon as the invasion commenced. Commanded by a lieutenant, most of them were aged between forty and forty-five years. Total casualties during the various actions were: one officer wounded, two other ranks killed, five wounded and three missing. One carrier had been destroyed. Captain Ian Daw was awarded the Military Cross for his gallantry shown during the action on the 7th June. Corporal George Richardson was Mentioned in Despatches for his part in the action of the following day.

The Battalion positions lay slightly north-west of Condé-sur-Seulles, with 'A' Company astride the main Bayeux - Tilly-sur-Seulles road. 'B' Company was on the left, with 'D' Company in

Condé, itself. 'C' Company was in reserve. During the course of the morning of the 8th June, 'A' Company destroyed a German four-seater staff car in which an officer of the 130 Artillery Regiment, Panzer Lehr Division and a private of the 195 Grenadier Regiment, 352nd Infantry Division, were found dead. In the late afternoon, a half-tracked vehicle approached the Company's positions and was fired on. Its two occupants jumped out and gave themselves up. They, too, belonged to the 130th Panzer Lehr Division. The half-track carried a full load of ammunition, grenades and mortar bombs. Shortly after 7.00 p.m. a three ton lorry, escorted by a motorcycle combination, came along the road and they were fired upon. The lorry was destroyed. The occupant of the sidecar gave himself up but the driver swung round and managed to escape. Until now, the exact whereabouts of the British had not been known. The escaped man would obviously change that situation.

On the 9th June, the 8th Battalion clashed with the German 130th Panzer Lehr Division in St. Pierre and in bitter fighting drove the enemy out of the village. The fighting raged for the next three days when the Battalion was withdrawn after a very gallant action. On the 10th June the 6th Battalion met the 130th Panzer Lehr Division for the first time. This division was, arguably, the finest German Panzer Division in Normandy. It was a training and demonstration division and extremely well equipped. Its officers and NCOs were highly trained and experienced men many of whom had already seen fighting in Poland, France and Russia. They commanded young, fanatical and highly disciplined troops. The division had incurred some losses, particularly amongst its soft topped vehicles, whilst moving up to the front - the result of Allied air attacks. However, it remained a formidable force with the aim of driving through to the beaches and threatening the success of the British landings.

In the morning, from the direction of Douet, a German Mark IV Special tank, with infantry, approached 'A' Company's positions, which were astride the Tilly - Bayeux road. Private Ken Lodge described what happened:

> 'We could hear them coming .. .but the tank was coming straight down the road ... Our officer issued sticky bombs ... We were supposed to run out and stick it on the side of the tank and that

used to knock the tank out. We thought, "There's no tank going to get that near." ... On the opposite side of the road, we had the Cheshires with their machine-guns and our own anti-tank 6 pounder. "Crack!" Our 6 pounder knocked the first one out ... I can just see, still remember the first one, because I was up with my rifle waiting for someone bailing out and there was nobody bailed out in this. The fellow next to me pulled me down and said, "If you don't want your head blown off, get down here".'

The tank was set on fire and was still burning at midday. Sergeant William Botterman of 'A' Company was awarded a Military Medal for his gallant conduct during this initial action. His citation read:

> '...Sgt Botterman's platoon was on a very exposed position, and was under heavy fire from light machine-guns, sniping posts and tanks. Sergeant Botterman with entire disregard for his own safety during the entire action went from one section post to another encouraging his men, pointing out enemy targets and directing the fire of his platoon to very good effect. By his courage and outstanding coolness under fire, his platoon was greatly encouraged - all snipers were eliminated and the enemy were eventually forced to withdraw.

> 'Later in the day, 'A' Company was again attacked by enemy tanks and infantry. Again Sergeant Botterman, by his personal courage and fearlessness compelled the enemy to withdraw. Throughout the whole action this NCO showed the most conspicuous gallantry and courage of the highest order.'

At 11.45 a.m. reports were received that enemy motor transport and armoured fighting vehicles were concentrating in the area of Bucéels and moving up the road towards Bayeux. This was confirmed by Lieutenant Kirk whose carrier patrol was fired on near Douet. At about 2.30 p.m. enemy armoured cars and infantry opened fire on 'A' Company's positions. The Company returned the fire and the enemy was seen to be carrying out a flanking movement to the right, under the cover of the hedgerows. The enemy was unaware that this movement was taking them towards 'B' Company. This Company, well-concealed, withheld its fire until the enemy was close and then opened up with medium machine-guns and Bren guns. The enemy was driven off and the small arms battle died down by about 4.00 p.m. During this action and for some time afterwards, the Divisional artillery had concentrated its attentions on Buceels where it was thought the enemy armoured forces were concentrating. At 5.20 p.m. it was reported that tanks were approaching 'A' and 'B' Companies' fronts and were engaged by artillery and mortars. Lieutenant R.D. Scott, commanding 'B' Company's forward platoon, reported that a tank was working its way under cover into the Company's area. Engaged by anti-tank guns, this tank was hit but not knocked out. One anti-tank gun, by firing, had revealed its position, was fired on by another tank and destroyed. Its commander, Lieutenant Dodshon and four of its crew were wounded. Sergeant Tommy Russ had his anti-tank gun with the forward platoon and continued to engage the enemy throughout the whole action. More tanks could be heard forming up in an orchard area about six hundred yards south of 'B' Company. A dangerous situation now developed. The FOO had been pinned down in 'A' Company's area and was unable to observe the artillery defensive fire. Six enemy Mark IV Specials were seen approaching 'B' Company's positions. Major R.G. Atkinson and Lieutenant Scott acted as observers for the artillery, directing the shelling from the map. The effect of this accurate artillery retaliation, much of it from naval ships out at sea, was to stop the tank attack about three hundred yards from the forward positions of the Company. Lance-Corporal Wear, Company Signaller, remembered the effect of the bombardment:

> '...this shell came over from the ships at sea ... We thought it was going to take our heads off ... The first shot was a direct hit on a tank. It was fantastic to see and then there was salvo after salvo fired after that. The infantry lads were standing up cheering. It was really fantastic what the navy did that day.'

For gallantry and devotion to duty in keeping his wireless

Private Wheatley *firing on an enemy position near Douet, June, 1944*
Imperial War Museum photograph No. B 5382

operating throughout the day whilst under heavy enemy fire, Lance-Corporal Wear was awarded the Military Medal.

Major Wood, still acting CO in place of the sick Lieutenant-Colonel Green, thickened up 'B' Company's defences by moving anti-tank guns from other Company areas. He also sent an urgent request for M10s and tank support. Two M10s of the Northumberland Hussars, moved into the area shortly after 8.00 p.m. One of the guns was hit and damaged whilst moving between 'A' and 'B' Companies. The second M10 knocked out the enemy tank which had done this damage and then moved into 'B' Company positions where it damaged a track on a Hawkins mine. These mines had been laid by 'B' Company as defence

A 6th Battalion patrol moves through Douet, June, 1944

Imperial War Museum photograph No. B 5381

against enemy tanks. By 9.00 pm the enemy had had enough and had withdrawn. Three Mark IV Specials had been destroyed. The Battalion losses were: one officer and five other ranks wounded and an anti-tank gun destroyed. Had the enemy broken through the Battalion's positions and driven up the road to Bayeux and the coast a serious situation may have developed. Whilst these were the advance elements of the Panzer Lehr Division, the main body would not have been far behind. Major Atkinson, who received a bar to his Military Cross for this action, wrote:

'...It was the naval gunfire which finally drove the enemy back in my opinion. We had two SP Anti-Tank Guns knocked out. The first I saw hit moving in rear of my orchard position between my company and 'A' Company, astride the road on my right. I've never seen men get out quicker! The other SP Anti-Tank Gun came rushing up into my orchard and had a track blown off by one of the Hawkins Anti-Tank Grenades my men laid to protect Company Headquarters! It was nice to see it worked but I received a mild reprimand from the Acting CO, George Wood, for putting it there without informing Battalion HQ. I suppose he had to say something.

'A crucial advantage we had over the attacking Germans was we were all dug-in in trenches they themselves [or their Labour Corps] had dug prior to the invasion. We only had to alter them so they faced in the opposite direction.'

Major Wood wrote in his report:

'The successes of the last two days were reflected in the magnificent spirit of the men. Some were under fire for the first time and had certainly been shaken by the appearance of at least a troop of tanks on our front, but the first class shooting of artillery and anti-tank guns soon restored confidence.'

Major Wood received the Distinguished Service Order for this action. His citation read:

'On 10 June 44 at Condé-sur-Seulles Major Wood was commanding 6 DLI when it was counter-attacked by both tanks and infantry. The position which HAD to be held was a difficult one owing to the thick nature of the country which allowed the enemy to get close up without being observed. For 4 hours the enemy made determined attempts to break through the position first at one place and then at another. On each occasion he was driven back with heavy loss. The enemy finally withdrew leaving 3 Mark IV tanks knocked out by A/Tk guns and considerable numbers of dead. This attack was a direct attempt to break through the bridgehead and that it was held is in no small measure due to the commanding officer Major Wood who was always at the most threatened sector of the front encouraging his men and personally helping to locate the enemy

tanks which were trying to work round the position. His complete disregard for his own safety and his fine powers of leadership were responsible for this vital position being held.'

The Battle of the Bridgehead had been won.

Four days of relative inactivity followed the actions at Condé. Keeping clean can be a problem in the field but at 'A' Echelon this problem was being solved. Lieutenant Peter Tyndale, the Battalion MTO, wrote:

'A few days after 'D' Day, 'A' Echelon were in a sloping field to the west of Jerusalem cross roads. We had all settled in again to living in "the Field."

'Winston Field noticed that there were several heavy brown canvas waterproof containers lying around. They had been used to bring the Signal platoon equipment ashore, [telephone, wireless sets, batteries etc.]. We also had captured a German Field Kitchen. It worked on the same principle as the old 'soya stove', but was rectangular instead of round, and was mounted on wheels.

'Winston decided that we should have our own unit Mobile Bath! The Equipment Repairer cut and joined the canvas containers as necessary. The Pioneer Pl. provided wooden slatted floors and wood stiffeners at the corners. We ended up with four, 4ft long x 18" deep canvas baths. The hot water came from the German Field Kitchen. The whole bath unit was set up at the bottom of the 'A' Echelon field beside the stream which provided the water.

'The company in reserve used to send one platoon back to the Bath unit in the morning, another in the afternoon; the third platoon the next morning and Company HQ, plus drivers, cooks etc. that afternoon.'

These days of calm quickly came to an end, and the Battalion was about to enter a period of fierce fighting against some of the best units in the German Army.

CHAPTER 32
THE BATTLE FOR NORMANDY
JUNE - AUGUST 1944

The 50th Division objectives were the capture of Tilly-sur-Seulles, Hottot and Villers-Bocage. 7th Armoured Division's advance on Tilly and Villers-Bocage had been halted. 151 Brigade was given the task of advancing to the main road Hottot - Juvigny. Initially, 9th Battalion was to take Lingèvres, a village lying on the main road three miles west of Tilly. 6th Battalion's first objective was the village of Verrières, which lay a short distance north east of Lingèvres. Both attacks were timed to take place together on the 14th June. At the same time, 231 Brigade was to attack on the right of 9th Battalion.

The 6th Battalion lined up on the main Tilly - Bayeux road and, with 'A' Company leading, moved down the road to Le-Pont-de-la-Guillette. On turning right at this point, the leading companies were almost immediately engaged by mortars and machine-guns from the area of nearby farm buildings. It was obviously a major enemy strongpoint and completely unexpected. All means of communication with Battalion Headquarters were quickly destroyed and Captain Sandwith was perforce to act as Liaison Officer under the most trying and dangerous conditions. 'A' Company suffered heavy casualties. Private Ken Lodge described what happened to him:

'All of a sudden the spandaus opened up. What a mess. That was probably the fastest I've ever hit the deck ... and we were just lying there taking it. We had no cover on either side of the road. Up on the right there was a bit of a building ... We were forward section and we were getting it. All I could hear was bullets thudding into the ground and the muck flying, the muck flying into my face. I could hear the bullets going into the ground, buzzing, buzzing and I said, "Good God, what am I going to do now?" The lads behind could get back behind the road and they were setting up the Bren guns and someone was shouting, "Fire into the Barn," or something. Anyway eventually they got them all except me, everyone in my section. I was the only one that wasn't hit. They weren't all dead, the first four was. I lost my mate, Eddie Fenwick. They got the officer, Lieutenant Bell. They got the corporal, got Eddie, got Bennett and then they got this other lad in his two legs and this other lad lying beside me, hit him through the wrist. And I was lying there. I said, "Good God, I'll never get out of this, I've gone down." I honestly thought I'd gone ... This went on for a while and I was just laid there and then it went quiet.'

Lieutenant R.D. Scott's platoon almost reached the farm buildings before he was himself hit and wounded and the rest of his men pinned to the ground. Major Wood decided to put in a Company attack on the right flank to try to work round to the enemy rear. Major Atkinson's 'B' Company moved out on this task and followed the line of a small stream. As the leading platoon under Lieutenant R.D. Busson moved up the stream bed, a salvo of Nebelwerfer bombs fell amongst it. Major Atkinson wrote:

"Busson was amongst the wounded in the Nebelwerfer attack on the leading platoon of 'B' Company as it commenced its right flanking movement from Le-Pont-de-la-Guillette when 'A' Company was held up. The salvo of bombs landed in the middle of the leading platoon as it made its way along a small stream. It was a horrific sight as you can imagine. I saw Bell [Lt] being carried back on the front of a tank of the 4/7 DG [Dragoon Guards]. I understand he actually requested permission to leave intelligence duties, and join a Rifle Company.'

Two men were killed and six wounded by the Nebelwerfer. Major Atkinson decided to push over the high ground towards the farm with his two reserve platoons. Meanwhile the enemy positions were being heavily engaged by both mortars and artillery and a troop of tanks was brought up to support the attack. The Germans, however, were well dug in and concealed behind hedgerows and the road running across the front. Major Atkinson reorganised his Company and with the support of a tank, attacked again but was again driven off by machine-gun and mortar fire. The Company withdrew slightly from the open ground and re-organised along a hedgerow two hundred yards from the farm. The remnants of 'A' and 'B' Companies made contact with each other and dug in astride the track up to the farm, 'A' Company left and 'B' Company right. 'C' and 'D' Companies were sent forward and dug in astride the main road to Tilly to link up with 'A' Company's left. At 8.30 p.m. the Brigadier ordered the Battalion to withdraw and move to Folliot. The casualties were: Captain L. Attenborough the Second-in-Command of 'A' Company who was wounded; Lieutenant J.L. Bell who died of his wounds and Captain David Rome, 'B' Company's Second-in-Command, who was badly wounded in the hand whilst helping to bring in the wounded. He was awarded the Military Cross for his gallant action. Lieutenants Busson and Scott of 'B' Company were wounded as described above, seven other ranks were killed and forty-two wounded. The Battalion stretcher-bearers did magnificent work. Sergeant Montgomery and Private Doodney set up an advanced RAP at Le-Pont-de-la-Guillette and covered by fire from the two leading Companies and the tank, evacuated all casualties. Sergeant Montgomery was subsequently awarded the Military Medal. At 11.00 p.m. the Battalion withdrew through the South Wales Borderers and bivouacced for the night at Folliot. The line Tilly through Lingèvres and west was obviously strongly held by the enemy and would not be given up easily.

On the morning of the 14th June, the Battalion was given the objectives of Hottot and the village of Verrières. The advance was to have the support of bombing and strafing by rocket firing 'Typhoons' of the RAF and a creeping barrage by the Divisional

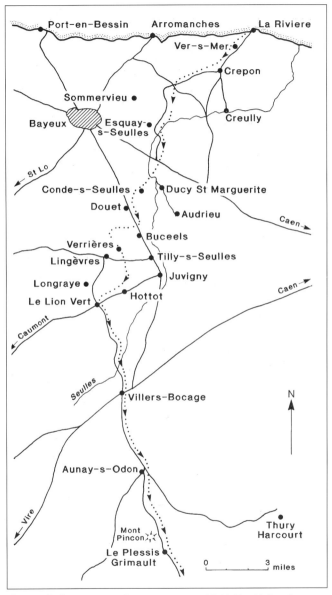

The Battle for Normandy, *June to August, 1944. The 6th Battalion advance through Normandy*

289

artillery. 'C' and 'D' Companies led the advance on either side of the road from Folliot to Verrières, with 'B' and 'A' Companies following up in reserve. A squadron of the 4/7 Dragoon Guards was in support. The advance commenced at 10.15 a.m. and the Companies crossed the open country in open formation. The advance went well for the first few miles. Immediately north of Verrières there was a field of standing corn. Running north-east to south-west along a track north of Verrières itself was a wood. Across the front lay a ditch which was strongly held by the enemy. On first entering the cornfield, the only sound was the swish of the corn and the men's feet as they pressed on in open formation with rifles and bayonets held at the port. At about one hundred and fifty yards away, the whole enemy line opened up with machine-guns and rifle fire. It was estimated that at least twelve machine-guns opposed the Battalion's advance. The fire was devastating and men fell all around. The advance was held up and a heavy artillery bombardment fell on the enemy positions but this failed to neutralise the opposition. The reserve Companies were pushed into the attack and though they, too, suffered heavy casualties, the enemy began to give way. At about 4.00 p.m. after five hours of fighting, the position was taken. machine-guns, large quantities of ammunition and other equipment were taken. Some machine-guns had been mounted on tripods and had been fired by men well dug in to the side of the ditch and protected from all but a direct hit by shell or mortar bomb. The Companies paused and reorganised in the ditch and turned the captured machine-guns on the retreating enemy. 'A' and 'D' Companies remained in the ditch and 'B' and 'C' Companies went forward to clear the village and try to reach the main road at Les-le-Gallois. Even to this day, veterans of the 6th Battalion remember the attack across the cornfield at Verrières. Private Ernest Harvey was one of them:

> 'We were all going into the attack and we were going across this cornfield. We got about 20 - 25 yards into this cornfield when Jerry opened up with spandaus. Well, [there was] a small groove in the ground where, fortunately, I got into it. I got down. The men were getting mown down left, right and centre. In fact the Company was being slaughtered, its as simple as that. As those were going down more men were coming up and these were getting knocked down. The cry then was, "Mother! Mother!" I

know it's a funny thing but everybody was crying for their mothers. Eventually there was two tanks came up behind us. This was after a long while and all the corn had been completely mown down as though it had been with shears, by the spandaus ... We couldn't move. If you moved you got shot. You had to stay down and, I remember, two tanks came up eventually and they blasted this hedge ... Eventually we took the position but the point was that nearly all the men had gone ... You'd think they'd expected us coming...I thought that only went on in World War I. I never thought that it would have happened in 1944 ... The sergeant says,"Ernie, go round and collect the ammo out of the pouches" ... and I started gathering the ammo from the wounded and the dead. Of course, the stretcher-bearers were coming up and tending the few wounded that was left ... Suddenly this voice said, "Leave that alone. Don't touch them." It was the Padre. The tears were streaming from his eyes. I went back to the hedge and this German was running across the field and someone started firing at this German and this chap knocked the gun out of his hands. It was the Padre again. He said,"There's been enough killing for one day." ... The sergeant and he had words.'

'B' Company advanced through Verrières without opposition, crossed the stream and paused on the left of the track to allow 'D' Company to come up to them on the right. One tank, commanded by Lieutenant S. Jenkins of the 4/7 Dragoon Guards, was in support. The Lieutenant spotted an enemy tank at the Les-le-Gallois cross-roads covering the track along which the two Companies were advancing. 'D' Company, now commanded by Captain Sandwith, was quickly pinned to the ground. 'B' Company continued to advance to within two hundred yards from the main road, where they came under intense fire from concealed machine-guns and the machine-gun from the tank. Major Atkinson sent his left hand platoon forward under the cover of the hedgerows and one section reached the road. This platoon came under fire from the left and the forward section was cut off. Four men were killed and two wounded. This section lay hidden in the ditch for two days and four survivors were picked up by 'B' Company when the Battalion reached the main road on the 16th June. Major Wood withdrew all companies to the line of the track just north of Verrières and dug in for the night.

The casualties had, indeed, been very heavy. Twenty-three other ranks had been killed, sixty-two wounded and fifteen were missing. Major R. Galloway MC, Major D.E.I. Thomlinson and Lieutenant W.T.A. Davey had been wounded. Known enemy losses were: fourteen prisoners from the 130th Panzer Lehr Division, two half-tracked vehicles with short 75mm close support guns; one troop carrying half-tracked vehicle in perfect condition; one 75mm anti-tank gun and one half-tracked motor cycle. The Battalion was reorganised, 'A' and 'C' Companies were combined, on a three company basis:

'B' Company - Commanding - Major R.G. Atkinson, MC.

'C' Company - Commanding - Captain R. Bousfield.

'D' Company - Commanding - Captain A.H. Sandwith.

From the landing in Normandy just over a week ago, total Battalion casualties were: ten officers wounded (one died of his wounds); thirty other ranks killed; one hundred and twenty-six wounded and twenty-six missing. Lieutenants T.O.M. Cranke and M.H. Norman joined the Battalion and were posted to 'B' Company. The 9th Battalion had distinguished itself in taking Lingèvres on the right, again, only after severe fighting and suffering considerable casualties.

The Battalion was now fighting in the bocage country. It was an area of small fields bounded by high banks with almost impenetrable hedges on top. Weaving throughout were narrow sunken roads, dotted with copses of trees, farmhouses and buildings and small hamlets and villages, which had been turned into strongpoints by the enemy. Observation was cut down to the length of the field in front. It was ideal defensive country for infantry. Cunningly concealed anti-tank guns in hedgerows and around the bends of the narrow tracks and roads, were a constant danger to any armoured vehicles. Snipers were everywhere, hiding in hedgerow, tree and building. Over the next few weeks, the strain on officers and men fighting in these conditions was considerable. Lieutenant Peter Tyndale wrote:

> '...During these long periods everybody progressively suffers from severe lack of sleep ... What sleep you do get is not as recuperative as it should be because you are always suffering from one or more of the following: too cold, or too hot, wet

Major 'Spike' Galloway, *MC, of Newcastle, wounded at Verrieres on the 14th June, 1944, goes to hospital after his wounded arm had been attended to at the Regimental Aid Post. On his return to the Battalion he was later killed in action at Le Plessis Grimault*

Imperial War Museum photograph No. B 5529

through, fully or nearly fully dressed complete with boots, uncomfortable, being bitten by mosquitos...

'When in the forward areas your senses and muscles are taut and on call at all times, including trying to sleep.

'It is when you are in this condition, a state of varying degrees of mental and physical exhaustion that various forces affect your conscious and unconscious thoughts. Self preservation pulls you one way, your self control and self discipline the other way; then military training and discipline take over and you are operating on a personal "Auto Pilot". When you are in this condition you have difficulty in thinking coherently and the memory part of your brain is on a low priority for mental energy and makes little effort to retain even major events.

'The various forces influencing you when you are on 'Auto Pilot' can vary from hour to hour and from day to day; sometimes for no apparent reason. These force affect every individual differently and in different ways.'

Private Ken Lodge recorded:

'...many times you couldn't see further than the fields in front of you. It was very rarely you actually saw a German. They were always behind a hedge and there was that many hedges to hide behind. We were the worst and were exposed because we had to come out of the hedgerows and attack them and they were sitting waiting for us. Very rare you saw a German. Apple orchards, very thick country, wooded areas, a lot of trees, a sniper's paradise ... Sniping us from hedgerows, church steeples, buildings, anything where they could get a good view of you.'

Snipers were deadly. Sergeant Bert Davies described one event:

'You may be walking around thinking it's so quiet, you know, so quiet before a battle, you wouldn't credit it. So, walking around in the open, exposing yourself more and more. Then, suddenly, "Ping!" There were so many snipers there. Snipers were - there were more snipers than anything. Sergeant Ingram - I'd been across the cornfield and back again in the attack but we didn't see the snipers at the top of the trees and they had proper wooden hideouts. They were chained to the trees, some of them. I came back from this cornfield, behind this hedge. Not much of a hedge and Sergeant Ingram said to me, "Eh Bert," he says, "Watch out, there's a lot of snipers about this area. I said, "I know there is, I've just come across that cornfield." Just as he said that it went, "Ping!" and they scalped him across the head. He just spun round and dropped on the deck and I said, "Get up you silly buggar, they haven't hit you yet." But they had hit him. Scalped him alright so he was whipped off to the First Aid tent ... You couldn't expose yourself. Sometimes you had to and if you did, did it quickly ... as long as you're a moving target you're difficult to hit but so long as you stand still ... that's when you're an easy target.'

Lieutenant-Colonel Green returned to take command of the Battalion on the 16th June. Major Wood, now relieved and reverting to Second-in-Command, had commanded the Battalion with considerable distinction during a very difficult period. Patrols were sent out on the 15th but no contact was made with the enemy. On the following day, the Battalion moved forward to the cross-roads at Les-le-Gallois and dug in. Major Atkinson and Lieutenant Kirk went forward to a chateau across the main road to recce the area, so that Sappers and Carriers could be brought forward to thicken up 'B' Company positions. Major Atkinson described what happened next:

'I decided that the best view would be obtained from the top floor of the Chateau. On entering through the front door on the north side, I found two private soldiers of my company in the hall. They had obviously been drinking sherry. A decanter and glasses lay on the hall table.

'Almost immediately the owner of the Chateau, a distinguished looking elderly French aristocrat, appeared from the drawing room and invited the officers in. They went into the drawing room which was magnificently furnished, offered sherry and introduced them to his wife and young daughter. After a few polite words in school boy French, they excused themselves saying they wanted to look out from the top floor to see what it was like on the south side. They climbed two flights of stairs, leaving the soldiers in the hall to watch the entrance. In one of the bedrooms which faced south, they pulled out a table and placed it below one of the high windows. Tim Kirk then climbed onto it, opened it and looked out. Almost immediately he bobbed back again saying that there was a party of German soldiers coming across the lawn towards the Chateau and that one had actually lifted his rifle and fired at him. They, the two officers, were down two flights of stairs, two at a time, before you could say, "Jack Robinson," but when they arrived at the front door there was a loud explosion in the front drive. They knew they were trapped inside the Chateau.

'They waited inside and made provision for all round defence of the hall and landing. The owner, his wife and daughter, took shelter in an alcove on the first floor landing.

'I then detailed off the smallest soldier to make a dash across the drive into the long grass, covered by the remainder. He was

stripped of all arms and equipment except his rifle and took a long run across the hall to obtain maximum speed by the time he emerged through the front door. He was ordered to crawl through the grass and go straight to his platoon headquarters and request assistance.

Sergeant Trevor Ingram *of Nantwich, wounded at Verrières on the 14th June, 1944, has a cigarette after his wound has been bandaged at the Regimental Aid Post*

Imperial War Museum photograph No. B 5524

293

'To our immense relief he was across the drive in a 'flash' and into the long grass. We then waited as patiently as we could. Eventually a party of our troops started making their way by fire and movement (and covered by smoke), up the avenue leading to the Chateau. They were fired on by the enemy on the right of the front door (as they, the officers, looked out of it). But our troops won the fire fight and the enemy withdrew.'

Sergeant Obadiah Stewart, of the Battalion Sniper Section, had moved into the Chateau grounds with three of his section. Leaving them in position, he had gone on to look for the enemy in the grounds. Unfortunately, he ran into the same enemy party hiding in the rhododendrons and was killed. On the evening of the 16th June, 'B' Company was mortared and sustained six casualties. At 5.30 a.m. on the 17th, an enemy patrol penetrated into 'C' Company's positions and inflicted one casualty. Half an hour later, a young German soldier of eighteen years of age gave himself up. He had been in the army for a year and had had no leave. He had been wounded in the ankle by our mortar fire on the previous day. The Battalion was relieved by the 9th Battalion at 3.00 p.m. and returned to Folliot. The 2nd Battalion The Essex Regiment was to make an attack on Tilly-sur-Seulles at 4.00 p.m. and the 'Sixth' was to follow on a different axis, with an objective south of the town and astride the main road Tilly - Juvigny.

At 5.00 p.m. the Battalion left Folliot and advanced across country to Marcel, five hundred yards west of Le-Pont-de-la-Guillette and along the tracks which had seen the encounter of the 13th June. 'C' and 'D' Companies led the way and met opposition from machine-guns, snipers and mortars from the farm buildings in the area of the stream and track running from Marcel to Le-Pont-de-la-Guillette. 'B' Company on the right, encountered sniper fire. Each section, by making good use of ground and cover, closed in on the farm buildings. The infantry was learning that the bocage would also assist an attacking force using the correct tactics of movement and infiltration. 'D' Company reached the second group of farm buildings and dug in on the left of the track. 'C' Company, under Major Kirby, reached the line of the Tilly - Lingèvres road. None of its wireless sets were working, making control difficult. It was in position behind the hedge on one side of the road, with the enemy behind the hedge on the other side. Both parties lobbed grenades at each other. Tanks were again in support but were of little use in the close countryside, with the enemy well-concealed. 'C' Company withdrew two hundred yards to the line of the second group of farm buildings. 'D' Company was on the left of the track with 'B' Company in reserve. The Battalion had only got halfway to its objective. Casualties were: Major Maurice Kirby and Lieutenant Cranke wounded and Captain Bousfield and Company Sergeant-Major Charlton wounded and believed to have been taken prisoner. Major Kirby, a Territorial Officer, had been with the Battalion since before the war. Lieutenant Cranke later died of his wounds. He had been with the Battalion only a few days.

At 10.00 a.m. on the 18th June, Lieutenant-Colonel Green went to a Brigade 'O' Group where the acting Brigadier, Lieutenant-Colonel Lidwill, had taken over from Brigadier Walton who had been wounded. The acting Brigadier informed the 'O' Group that the Brigade was to push on to the road running south-west from Tilly to Hottot. The attacking forces would be preceded by a creeping barrage put down by three regiments of artillery, moving at one hundred yards in five minutes, with tanks moving level with the infantry and shooting up all the hedgerows. machine-guns on carriers would take on the role of light tanks. The attack commenced at 2.30 p.m. when a terrific curtain of fire was laid down by the artillery. At 2.45 p.m. the Battalion moved off behind the creeping barrage. 'C' Company was on the right, now commanded by Lieutenant Tim Kirk. 'D' Company was on the left. The support given by both the artillery and tanks on this day was excellent. Tanks crashed through the hedges and the enemy was blasted out of his position by shell and small arms fire. It was heartening to see Germans leaving their positions and running away. At 5.00 p.m. the objective, the high ground south west of Tilly, was reached and everyone dug in furiously to await any enemy reaction. Later, two enemy Mark IV Special Tanks were knocked out. Casualties were light and the men's spirits were high. Captain Sandwith was among the wounded and Lieutenant Bateman took his place in command of 'D' Company. The day ended with seventy reinforcements joining the Battalion.

It rained all day on the 19th June, making conditions most unpleasant. Lieutenant Horne of 'C' Company was seriously wounded by enemy mortar fire and he later died of his wounds. This left the Company with no officers other than the Company Commander, no Company Sergeant-Major and three platoons of about ten men each, commanded by two sergeants and a corporal. A rum ration was issued at night. The 2nd Battalion The Essex Regiment broke into Tilly on the 20th June and completed its capture. Little remained of the town, which had been bombarded from land, sea and air, yet those inhabitants still alive welcomed their liberators.

The Battalion had been moving and fighting for two weeks with precious little relief and though spirits were high, officers and men were tired. In addition to those already mentioned who were awarded medals for their bravery were: Lieutenant Kirk, Military Cross and Sergeants Botterman and Fradley who were both awarded the Military Medal.

Over the next few days the Battalion remained where it was, actively patrolling and probing the enemy's positions. 9th Battalion was on the left and the 2nd Battalion The Devonshire Regiment, 231 Brigade, was on the right. As a gap had opened between the latter and the Battalion, a Joint Post was established. On the 22nd June, the first batch of men was sent into Bayeux for baths and some relaxation. A second party was sent the following day. On the 24th, Major F.C. Atkinson joined and took command of 'C' Company. On the 25th, about one thousand mortar bombs were fired by the Mortar Platoon in support of an attack by the 49th Division on the left. Aggressive patrolling continued to take place, to harass the enemy. Artillery and mortars engaged transport moving along the Juvigny - Hottot road. On the 27th of the month, patrol tactics were changed. Small patrols were sent out to lay in wait for the enemy. One patrol claimed to have killed a German soldier from its ambush position. At 2.00 p.m. on the 28th, a reconnaissance patrol of 'D' Company spotted an enemy tank. Later, a standing patrol watched this tank. Its commander was seen standing in the turret observing our forward positions through his binoculars. The slope of the ground made it impossible to bring up an anti-tank gun unobserved. The patrol closed in and shot the commander of the tank. The next day, a crew member of the tank was shot by a patrol. Total casualties for the month of June were: one officer

missing and eighteen wounded (three died of their wounds); sixty-two other ranks were killed, seventeen were missing and two hundred and thirty-nine were wounded, of whom eight died later of their wounds. 'A' Company had been reformed under Captain R.J. Bennett.

On the 1st July, the Battalion again lost one of its long serving stalwarts. Captain (QM) J.W. Runciman left for 205 Corps Reception Camp. He had served the Battalion well through many difficult situations and had earned the respect of all officers and men. The following day the 8th Battalion relieved the 'Sixth' which, due to the close proximity of the enemy, was not completed till 2.30 a.m. on the 3rd July. The 6th Battalion took over the positions occupied previously by the 8th Battalion, with Headquarters at Marcel. The Battalion took up a counter-attack role in support of the 2nd Battalion Hampshire Regiment and 8th Durham Light Infantry. The CO ordered two days' rest whilst arms and equipment were checked. At 3.30 p.m. on the 3rd, a party proceeded to the cinema in Condé. A second party went off to this cinema on the following day. The Battalion tailor visited each company in turn to sew 'TT' and Battalion Flashes on the battledress of all reinforcements. Company training commenced on the 5th July and a Tank Hunting Squad was formed in each company. This rest period would also give the new officers an opportunity to get to know their men. This had not been possible as on their arrival, they had gone straight out to platoons in the line. The CO asked his officers to look out for men who would become good NCOs as the need for such within the Battalion was most urgent.

On the 6th July, the Battalion suffered a real loss with the tragic death of Padre Hawksworth, the Church of England Padre. He was seriously injured whilst riding a motorcycle. He was taken to 149 Field Ambulance but later died of his injuries. He had been with the Battalion since the end of the Sicilian campaign and his loss was felt deeply by all officers and other ranks. His funeral was held the following day in the 50th Divisional Cemetery. At 6.00 p.m. on the 7th, the relief of the 2nd Dorset Regiment south of Lingèvres, was commenced. Again, it was a slow relief during which 'A' Company was mortared. One man was killed and another wounded. Battalion Headquarters was at Lieu Meslier.

The positions were adjusted on the 8th, with 'C' Company moving to Parc-de-la-Mare. The Battalion now had three companies in the front line, with one in reserve. Standing patrols were established at 'Bomb House,' 'Op House' and 'Twin Houses'. At 11.30 a.m. four prisoners were taken at the latter position. They were Poles belonging to No. 4 Company, 276 Fusilier Regiment, 276th Infantry Division. The Panzer Lehr Division had suffered considerably in the fierce fighting and had been withdrawn. The prisoners volunteered the information that the 276th Infantry Division had been stationed at Bayonne on the Franco-Spanish border and had made its way northwards, harassed by the French Maquis and the Allied airforce. The last one hundred kilometres of their journey had taken place at night. They confirmed that the grounds of the Chateau de Cordillon, which lay just behind the German positions, was heavily mined and booby trapped.

Brigadier D.S. Gordon, DSO, the new Brigade Commander, ordered more aggressive patrolling, particularly at night, to try to find the location and strength of the enemy in the Chateau area. It was thought that the enemy was thin on the ground but, even if this were so, his snipers and machine-gun posts were difficult to dislodge and he held on grimly to his ground. 'A' Company occupied 'Bomb House' and 'D' Company occupied 'Op House'. The left hand section of 'A' Company, moved off to make contact with the forward platoon of 'D' Company in the area of 'OP House'. The gap between the farm buildings at 'OP House' was covered by a German sniper in a hedgerow about two hundred yards away to the south. Attempting to cross this gap, one man in the section was hit and he was taken into the house for first aid and treatment. Stretcher-bearers were sent forward just before last light to bring out the wounded man and one of them was hit and killed as he crossed the gap and this in spite of covering fire from 'A' Company. The enemy positions were between one and two hundred yards in front of the forward defence locations of the Battalion and those of the 8th on the right. An attempt in the early hours of the 11th July by a patrol of 'A' Company to drive out the enemy opposite on the other side of the field failed and Lieutenant McKelvie and three other ranks were wounded. Two patrols sent out later at 7.30 a.m. to create a diversion in support

of the 231 Brigade attack on Hottot, were shot up by the enemy from the hedges. Lieutenant Gardner of 'B' Company with his patrol almost reached the German positions before he was killed by machine-gun fire. The rest of the patrol succeeded in returning to our lines. The Germans retaliated by putting down heavy mortar and artillery fire which caused heavy casualties to the forward companies. The enemy, concealed in hedgerows, were adept at waiting until patrols were almost on top of them before opening fire and invariably inflicting casualties.

The enemy was not having it all his own way by any means. The British infantry was learning the lessons of bocage fighting. Two inch mortars and PIATs, fired at a high angle, along with personal weapons and machine-guns, could make life difficult for the enemy. The PIAT, an anti-tank weapon, could fire a bomb and drop it just over the hedge a short distance away. The Battalion had its own sniper section, which experienced considerable success, though six of them had been lost and were being reinforced by men who had attended a sniper course in the rear. The tactical use of these weapons and snipers replaced that of sending out fighting patrols, which had little success in close country and suffered heavy casualties. 8th Battalion reported that enemy units opposite were converted infantry from air force units. These did not prove to be easy opponents and they soon made a reputation for themselves as tough fighting men. On the 14th July, the Battalion was relieved by the 61st Reconnaissance Regiment.

Two days of much needed rest followed. A fair allocation of seats at the cinema was made and the President of the Regimental Institute issued companies with libraries and sports kit. On the 16th, the Battalion moved back into positions almost in the same area they had left on the 14th of the month. 'C' Company, with two anti-tank guns, came under the command of the 8th Battalion around Longraye. At 5.00 p.m. on the following day, General Montgomery carried out an investiture ceremony at Divisional Headquarters attended by Majors George Wood and Reggie Atkinson; Captain Daw, Sergeants Montgomery and Fradley and Lance-Corporal Wear. The other four recipients of awards could not attend having received wounds in action and had been evacuated. These four were: Captains Kirk and Rome,

Company Sergeant-Major Howson and Sergeant Botterman.

On the 18th July, information was received that a prisoner captured by 231 Brigade had stated that the enemy was withdrawing from the Divisional front. Repeated thrusts and pressure from the Allied forces were proving to be too much. The major portion of the German Panzer Divisions had been held in the east of the Allied front and had lost heavily in their endeavour to hold onto Caen and stop any breakout by the British and Canadian Divisions. Enemy strength had been worn down along the whole allied line. The Americans in the west had taken St. Lo and were now poised to break out to the south. On this day, Operation Goodwood was launched by General Montgomery in the east, which resulted in the capture of Caen. At 9.15 a.m. 'A' and 'B' Companies started to move forward, section by section. By 12 noon, the line of the track running east - west across the edges of the Chateau de Cordillon, was reached. It was an advance of only four hundred yards and was carried out without opposition. However, it must be remembered that in such close country where every hedge and copse may hide an enemy machine-gun which could decimate any platoon or section, movement had to be carefully undertaken. In addition, roads and tracks were heavily mined. Large quantities of ammunition and grenades were left lying around by the retreating Germans. The enemy rearguard soon became active. At 8.00p.m. a reconnaissance patrol from 'B' Company was fired on. A sniper, concealed on a track on the west side of the Chateau de Cordillon, killed a sergeant and private and wounded another sergeant, all from 'B' Company. As night set in, some firing took place from various points of the Battalion front. This died down and during the night, patrols reached the main Hottot road, having met no enemy. 'B' Company suffered casualties from anti-personnel mines strewn thickly in the grounds of the Chateau de Cordillon. Major Reggie Atkinson wrote:

'The Chateau de Cordillon grounds were littered with 'S' mines when the Germans withdrew. A nice young platoon commander, Norman, was permanently blinded here. I lost a platoon commander called Gardner on patrol in this section. He only joined my company the day before. One young NCO and a private soldier couldn't take any more and had to be sent back

out of the line. At the time of the German withdrawal from Hottot the strain on the Rifle Companies was beginning to tell. However we were revitalised by General Horrocks (Jorrocks) who inspired us to further efforts which did not cease until we had crossed the Waal (or Rhine) at Nijmegen.'

On the 20th July, Lieutenant (QM) T.J.F. Jones joined the Battalion and replaced Captain (QM) Runciman. Two days later, the Carrier Platoon was at La Marmonnier where it came under the command of 9 DLI on its left. Movement across country was difficult as heavy rain over the last few days had made the ground very muddy. 'C' Company was also forward but the other companies were now in Battalion reserve. The next four days were spent in resting and training. The Battalion relieved the 9th Battalion on the 25th July. There followed a relatively quiet period. Battalion patrols and snipers were active and there were occasional brushes with the enemy rearguard, usually the odd sniper and machine-gun post left behind to catch the unwary. Captain W. Ferguson, RAMC, joined the Battalion on the 26th July, in place of Captain J.H. Murphy who was posted to the 48th Field Dressing Station. On the 30th of the month, 'A' Company fought a brisk action with the enemy who held a farmhouse. The Germans were driven out but the Company lost three men wounded. Total casualties for the period from 'D' Day to 31st July were: One officer killed, one missing and twenty-two wounded (of whom three later died of wounds). Seventy-seven other ranks were killed, nineteen were missing and three hundred and six were wounded (of whom ten later died of wounds). The roll of officers at the end of July was:

Commanding Officer:	Lieutenant-Colonel A.E. Green.
Second-in-Command:	Major G.L. Wood, DSO, MC & Bar.
Adjutant:	Captain R.S. Loveridge, MC.
Intelligence Officer:	Lieutenant N. Myers.
Chaplain:	Captain R. Anwyl.
Medical officer:	Captain W. Ferguson.
HQ Company:	Captain A.E. Short.
Signal officer:	Captain J.A. Wedgwood.
Motor Transport Officer:	Lieutenant P.G. Tyndale.

Quartermaster:	Lieutenant (QM) T.F.J. Jones.
'A' Company:	Captain R.J. Bennett.
'B' Company:	Major R.G. Atkinson, MC & Bar.
'C' Company:	Major F.C. Atkinson.
'D' Company:	Major J.C. Browne.
Support Company:	Captain W.J. Field, MBE.
Carrier Platoon:	Captain I.A. Daw, MC.
Anti-Tank Platoon:	Captain G.B. Hawkins.
Mortar Platoon:	Lieutenant E.V. Oldham.
Assault Pioneer Platoon:	Lieutenant H. Calder.

The slow German withdrawal continued. He had sown the area with countless mines and booby traps, which kept the Sapper Platoon very busy indeed. There were casualties. On the 2nd August, Lieutenant A.R. Harvey and a section of men went from 'D' Company Headquarters to contact the 2nd/5th Lancashire Fusiliers on the left. They stumbled into a heavily booby-trapped area and the officer and four other ranks were wounded. A 15 cwt truck of 'A' Company was blown up on a Teller Mine. The driver and a colour sergeant were wounded. Prisoners taken were still stating that the enemy was continuing to withdraw. The Battalion was ordered to probe forward to the Sermentot - Ingy road. By 11.30 a.m. both companies were dug in along this road. Major R. Galloway, MC, who had been wounded at Verrières, rejoined the Battalion and took over command of 'A' Company. On the 3rd, the Battalion was relieved and moved back to the area of Hottot.

On the 4th August, 151 Brigade was warned to be prepared to move west to the area of Mont Pincon, if called upon, to support, an attack on that feature which was being carried out by the 43rd Division. Mont Pincon lay to the south of Villers-Bocage. It was about one thousand two hundred feet high and dominated the surrounding area, giving the Germans a wonderful observation point which, on a clear day, could stretch over the Bridgehead to the north and to the valley of the Loire to the south. The Brigade was not called upon as the 43rd Division captured the Mount on the 5th August. 151 Brigade was then placed in support of the 7th Armoured Division which was operating in the area east of Mont Pincon and west of Thury-Harcourt. This order was also cancelled. On the 6th of the month, XXX Corps Commander, Lieutenant-General Horrocks, spoke to officers and senior NCOs. He outlined the present situation and future plans, which included informing the Battalion that they would be spending the next few days out of the line. He was his usual enthusiastic and bubbling self and never failed to raise the spirits of his listeners. The American forces were gathering momentum after the fall of St. Lo and by the end of July, had reached Avranches at the base of the Cherbourg Peninsula. The advance, which would lead to the German disaster in the 'Falaise Pocket', was underway. The Canadians were pushing south from Caen whilst the Americans were advancing towards Argentan. If these two Allied forces could meet, the remains of the German Seventh Army would be trapped. 50th Division's task was to capture Condé-sur-Noireau, which was an important town at the junction of a number of roads, through which any threatened German forces would have to move to escape encirclement.

The Battalion did not get its few days out of the line. On the 7th August it moved to a concentration area near Aunay-sur-Odon. The plan was to follow the attack being made by the 43rd Division. 6th Battalion was to lead the Brigade, followed by the 8th and 9th Battalions, with 7th Armoured Division pushing down the left flank and the Divisional Reconnaissance Regiment moving down the right. The final objective was Condé-sur-Noireau. At 12 noon, the Battalion climbed into motor transport to commence its journey. The route was La Vesque - Le Lion Vert - Villers-Bocage - Aunay-sur-Odon. The last two places had almost been obliterated by Allied bombing and shelling. The Battalion was warned to be ready to move on Condé-sur-Noireau at 3.00 a.m. on the 8th August but at 7.30 p.m. this was put back to noon on the 8th. Brigadier Gordon's plan was to attack southwards from Le Plessis-Grimault which lay south of Mont Pincon, with 8th Battalion on the right, the 6th on the left and 9 DLI in reserve, holding the village as a firm base. 6th Battalion's final objective was a prominent feature near the village of La Cannardière. Each Battalion would be supported by a squadron of 13/18 Hussars, preceded by a creeping barrage provided by five field regiments of artillery. The road to Le Plessis-Grimault lay over the top of Mont Pincon which was constantly shelled by the enemy.

At 7.00 p.m. on the 8th August, the Battalion moved to Roucamps and prepared to make a night advance with the rest of the Brigade. This was cancelled at 10.00 p.m. At 11 a.m. on the 9th, the Battalion left the assembly area and began its march over Mont Pincon and to the Start Line south of Le Plessis-Grimault. 8th Battalion followed and both Battalions were shelled and mortared all of the way. The bombardment grew to a crescendo as the marching troops came into full view of the German observers on the road leading down the southern slopes of the Mont. Le Plessis Grimault was also under heavy bombardment as the Battalions passed through. A German Tiger Tank, the largest and latest German tank, lay wrecked at the cross-roads in the centre of the town. The progress to the Start Line had been slow and there was little time to get organised for the advance. However, this was completed on time and at noon the forward companies passed over the Start Line. 'A' Company was on the right, inclusive of the road, 'B' Company was on its left with 'D' and 'C' Companies in reserve. 8th Battalion was on the right. Lieutenant P.D. White and four other ranks had already been wounded and evacuated.

Behind the creeping barrage, the companies moved steadily forward. The tanks moved with them in support, their guns adding to the barrage. At 2.30 p.m. La Cannardière was reached, with only slight casualties. Once on the objective and before the men could dig in, a very heavy German bombardment of the whole area commenced. As a result, there were many casualties. In 'A' Company, Captain R.E. Evans, Sergeant Fradley and Corporal Jenkins were killed and twelve men were wounded. Major Browne, commanding 'D' Company, was hit and later died of his wounds. Lieutenant R. Atkinson was wounded. This company's strength dropped to one officer and thirty-four other ranks. Three sections from the Carrier Platoon, on foot, were moved to thicken up the defences. Shelling and sniping continued until stand to. A standing patrol from the Carrier Platoon, again on foot, was sent to a bridge over a small stream

running through the village of Cauville on the left flank. Its task was to report on any enemy movements in the area. The patrol was shelled and the sergeant in command was wounded. Prisoners taken during the advance numbered about one hundred from the 276th Infantry Division. Mainly a collection of young and old men, their spirits had suffered considerably from the heavy bombardment and they gave themselves up in batches of twenty to thirty. Casualties were: two officers killed and two wounded. Seven other ranks had been killed and fifty-three wounded, of whom three died of their wounds. At 3 p.m. the 6th and 7th Battalions The Green Howards passed through and secured the road as far south as Le Tremblay.

The Germans fought stubbornly to hold on to St. Pierre-la-Vielle and the high ground on either side and 69 Brigade were unable to make progress. 231 Brigade was called forward to capture the town. The delay meant that 151 Brigade could not pass through and take the lead as had been planned. For the next two days it rested, though it was informed that it must be prepared to follow up behind 231 Brigade as it passed through on the 11th August. The 10th was spent in salvaging equipment from the battlefield. A German codebook was found and passed to Brigade. Total equipment salvaged was: five spandaus, twenty-five rifles and about ten thousand rounds of ammunition. The next day there was intermittent shelling of the Battalion area. Major R. Galloway, MC, and two other ranks were killed and Lieutenant J. Whitaker and eight other ranks were wounded, one of whom died later. Major Galloway, known as 'Spike' throughout the Battalion, was a fine company commander whose loss was a great blow. Private Ken Lodge described what happened:

'I was standing beside the hedge and he came walking up the hedge and he always took an interest in the youngish chaps like myself and he said, "How are you going on?" I said, "Oh fine, sir," and he said a few words, "Thank you all. Good work," and that sort of thing. My mate was across there in a slit trench and he shouted, "Get here," and I ran over to the slit trench and jumped in and there was the great almighty, ear splitting bang and it went quiet. Just for a second it was quiet and then the screaming started and this lad came past me and he had a huge scar across the calf of his leg which was like a burn. There wasn't any blood, just a burn. He was screaming ... Major Galloway was dead, I don't know whether Major Galloway died then or he died just after. He was lying and they picked him up. There were another four of them lying dead. The shell had hit the tree, by the way...otherwise it would have gone past. There was ever so many wounded. The thing was that these lads didn't have a mark on them ... We'd lost a good leader ... Major Galloway was a very good officer, anybody would follow him.'

Lieutenant-Colonel Green decided to disband 'A' Company and reorganise the Battalion on a three company basis of about sixty men and two officers in each. These were: 'B' Company (Major R.G. Atkinson); ' C' Company (Major F.C. Atkinson) and 'D' Company (Captain R.G. Bateman). The attack by 231 Brigade during the day had failed. The Germans were still fighting fiercely to retain this vital area around Condé-sur-Noireau. The high ground around St. Pierre-la-Vielle was still in their hands. The CO met his officers at 9.00 p.m. on the 11th and told them that two plans would have to considered for the following day. First, if 231 Brigade was successful the original plan for the capture of Points 249 and 262 - both prominent hills south-east of St. Pierre - would be carried out. If 231 Brigade was unsuccessful, 9th DLI and one battalion from 231 Brigade would attack and 6th DLI would follow. 8th Battalion would be ready to pass through.

By 10.00 a.m. on the morning of the 12th August, 231 Brigade was two miles south of St. Pierre but the enemy still held the high ground to the rear. At 1.30 p.m. the 9th Battalion, with two squadrons of tanks of the 13/18 Hussars in support, advanced to take Point 249, whilst the Carrier Platoon of the 8th Battalion, which was attached to the 9th, took Point 262. At 4.00 p.m. the carriers of the 6th Battalion advanced to occupy the orchard on the left flank of the 9th. They encountered spandau posts which they attacked and five prisoners were taken. However, they failed to clear the wood. The Brigade made a squadron of tanks available to support the advance. With these and 'B' Company on the left and 'C' Company on the right, the Battalion moved forward at 7.00 p.m. Owing to the close proximity of our troops to the enemy, no artillery support could be given. The advance went ahead with fire support coming only from the tanks. The objective was reached at 7.30 p.m. and contact made with the 9th Battalion. 'B' Company lost two men. 'C' Company captured two

prisoners and claimed to have killed five of the enemy. 'D' Company moved up with the Carrier Platoon, the latter on foot, moving to the right of 'C' Company. The Battalion was heavily shelled during the advance. Captain Hawkins and Lieutenant Myers were both wounded. The former subsequently died of his wounds. Four other ranks were killed, nine were wounded and one was missing.

On the 13th August, 151 Brigade was relieved by 129 Brigade, 43rd Division, and came into reserve. The Battalion moved by transport to a rest area at Maunay. It remained here for the next few days. Parties attended baths at 'B' Echelon and cinema shows were available in the afternoon and evening. Meanwhile, the gap at Falaise was closed and although many of the enemy had made their escape, particularly tank divisions, the Germans suffered enormous casualties and loss of equipment. Lieutenant-General Horrocks sent the following message to 50th Division:

'During the last week the Division has been fighting down towards Condé from Mont Pincon. Although the country was suited for defence, and although the enemy was fighting stubbornly all the attacks launched by 50 (N) Division have been successful and many prisoners have been taken ... I cannot give you higher praise than by saying that the most experienced battle-fighting Division in the British Army has once more lived up to its high reputation.'

CHAPTER 32

THE PURSUIT TO BRUSSELS

1944

At 10.45 a.m. on the 18th August, the Battalion moved off away from the Normandy beachhead with its many memories. Now clear of the bocage, which had tested even the hardiest and bravest of men, it moved through the valley of Condé-sur-Noireau and on to the first night's rest area at St. Honorine-La-Chardonne. 151 Brigade was to follow behind the 11th Armoured Division, with the 8th Battalion leading and followed by the 6th and 9th Battalions. Its task was to protect the left flank of the 30th Armoured Brigade. The pursuit was on. The Battalion advance party led by Captain Short and comprising the Intelligence Section Sergeant and one representative of each company, moved ahead to each staging place. Usually the first British soldiers to arrive at each halting place, they would receive a tremendous welcome from an overjoyed French population. On the 19th, the advance party contacted five other ranks from the 3rd British Division who had escaped from a retreating German Pioneer Battalion. They had been captured in the Vire area on the night 14th/15th August. They told of the low morale of the German troops who were travelling round and round in complete chaos and confusion. Roads were choked with horse drawn and wheeled traffic. Their treatment had been considerate and courteous, though the food was very bad. They claimed that but for the German officers, they could have marched off the whole Battalion back to our lines. The staging place for the 19th was reached at 11.30 a.m. In the afternoon two Germans were found hiding in a barn by 'S' Company. Captain Daw with some of the carriers and assisted by a French Gendarme went off to search a nearby wood for more Germans but none were found hiding there.

On the 20th of the month, the Battalion led the Brigade. It was split into two groups: an advance guard and main group. The composition of the advance guard under Major Wood was: the Carrier Platoon; one section of mortars on carriers; one troop of tanks of the 13/18 Hussars; one section 505 Field Company, RE; 'D' Company in trucks and an ambulance jeep. The main group moved in the order: Battalion 'O' Group; Battalion HQ; 'C' Company and 'B' Company in trucks; Mortar Platoon - less one section; Anti-Tank Platoon; 505 Field Company, RE - less one section and 'A' Echelon. The route lay through Courteilles to Occagnes, on the main road between Falaise and Argentan. The Battalion was ordered to clear the woods to the north-west of the rest area. Heavy rain made the conditions unpleasant. Seven prisoners were brought in. A small number of German dead were found lying in the woods, probably killed by artillery fire. On the following day, the Battalion continued to clear the woods in the Vorche area. No contact with the enemy was made, though a number of dead Germans were found. On the track between Occagnes and Vorche, Captain Attenborough and his driver, travelling in a jeep, were blown up by a prepared charge and the 505 Filed Company, RE, found a further two charges in the area. At 1.30 p.m. orders were received to proceed to Bon-Menil. The main body moved off at 3.10 p.m. and on arriving at Bailleu, it was found that the road from this place to Bon-Menil was impassable. The route passed through the area of devastation wrought on the Germans caught in the 'Falaise Pocket'. Destroyed vehicles and equipment littered the roads and tracks, with dead horses and men lying amongst the destruction. The rifle companies debussed and marched the rest of the way. The vehicles drove round via Le Tellier and Crennes.

The main body arrived at Bon-Menil at 6.00 p.m. It was to relieve units of the 80th United States Division, who were shelling Chambois and the surrounding forests. Shortly after arrival, the Battalion observed a number of white flags fluttering to the north and a stream of Germans appeared. More shells brought out more Germans and about three hundred prisoners were taken by the Americans. The Battalion itself took twenty-six prisoners before the end of the day. The plan for the 22nd August, was for the 8th Battalion to move to St. Eugenie, 9 DLI to move on to Chambois and 6 DLI to remain where it was and establish a POW cage. At 10 a.m. on this day, an American Army Captain arrived at Battalion Headquarters with a certificate in duplicate which he required the CO to sign to signify that he had taken over from the US Forces - evidently a customary procedure in the American Army. In the afternoon, the Battalion was relieved by the 9th Battalion Dorset Regiment and moved to an area north of Fougy. 69 Brigade now took the lead in the pursuit. Twenty prisoners were taken during the day, three of them from No 6 Company, II Battalion, 84th Nebelwerfer Regiment. At 5 p.m. news was received that Paris had fallen to the Allies.

At 5.00 p.m. on the 23rd, the Battalion arrived in the area of Le Pont-de-Thiboult, east of Bourth. Wood clearance was carried out but nothing was found. One prisoner from the 12th SS Division was brought in by the Military Police. The Battlion remained here for two days. Forty-seven reinforcements were expected on the 25th but did not arrive. The Battalion moved to Pacy-sur-Eure on the 26th August. The plan was to cross the Seine and XXX Corps which consisted of two Reconnaissance Regiments, the 2nd Armoured Brigade, 11th Armoured Division, Guards Armoured Division and the 50th Division, would be directed on Amiens. On the left would be XII Corps and the Canadians would advance along the Channel coast. The Battalion stayed at Pacy-sur-Eure for the next three days. On the 28th August, Captain C. Harrison, Lieutenant S. Seggie and one hundred and sixteen other ranks from the 10th and 11th Battalions The Durham Light Infantry, were received as reinforcements. 'A' Company was reformed under Captain D.M. Corbett. The following day, the Battalion crossed the River Seine at Vernon and arrived at Heubécourt at 7

.00 p.m. It then moved on to Tourny, arriving at 9.45 p.m. where it took up defensive positions around the village. The CO informed his company commanders that they would move forward the next day as part of the left flank protection to the armour. On the 30th, the Battalion reached Guitry. 'D' Company moved to Mouflaines, 'B' Company to Thil en Vexin where it took twelve prisoners. 'A' Company passed through Doudeauville-en-Vexin where it picked up a single prisoner. Battalion Headquarters moved up to this village and later moved on to Mesnil-sous-Vienne. The enemy was reported to be in Le Foret de Lyons. 'B' Company carried out a search but nothing was found.

At 8.30 a.m. on the 31st August, the Battalion was ordered to move in support of the armour, the objective being Amiens. Its task was to reach and defend two bridges which crossed the River Somme in the city. At 10.45 a.m. the Battalion moved off via Les Flamands - Neufmarche - St. Germer - Senantes - Hanvoile - Crillon - Beaudenne - Fleury and Drury. The Maquis was out clearing the woods and shots were frequently heard. At Conty, a small scale battle was taking place in a wood and 'C' Company was directed to assist the Maquis. Later, approximately fifty Germans were seen marching towards the main road, bearing a white flag. The Battalion arrived at Drury at 5.20 p.m. Here, news was received that the 7th German Army Commander, General Von Hauser, had been captured in Amiens. At 8.55 p.m. 'B' and 'D' Companies arrived at the main bridge and took over its defence with 'A' and 'C' Companies in reserve. As the population of the city became aware that this was truly liberation, they gave the Battalion a tremendous welcome. One hundred of the enemy who were holding out in the citadel surrendered after being shelled by artillery. They were marched through the city escorted by Military Police and the Maquis and French Police. The prisoners were a mixture of Mongols, Russians and Turks, not at all in good condition. A column of largely female collaborators were also marched through the streets, escorted by the Maquis, on their way to having their hair shaven. Casualties in the Battalion for the month of August were: three officers killed and eleven wounded - of whom one died. Twenty-three other ranks were killed, eighty-eight were wounded - of whom six died, and six were missing.

On the 2nd September, the Battalion moved to Doullens, which was reached at 1.10 p.m. The following day, the 8th Armoured Brigade pushed on to Alost; the 6th Battalion followed. Progress was slow, as a large amount of traffic was using the same road. A diversion had to be made at Pont-à-Vendin as the bridge over the canal at Wingles-Meurchin had been blown. A halt was called at 6.35 p.m. and the Battalion was ordered to remain where it was for the night. In the area, a number of small battles was going on between the Maquis and the Germans. The Maquis were holding Lille and requested assistance and the 8th Armoured Brigade pushed on to leaguer south of the city. Brigadier Gordon arrived at 8.30 p.m. with orders that next day, 'B' and 'D' Companies with one squadron of tanks, would clean up the town of Roubaix. 'A' and 'C' Companies would form a firm base in the rear. Patrols went out at night as far as the canal. On the morning of the 4th September, the move to Roubaix was postponed. The French were bringing in reports of enemy troop movements in the area, At 10.30 a.m. the Reconnaissance Regiment reported that the enemy was in Beauvin. Companies were ordered to take up defensive positions. 'B' Company and three sections of carriers were ordered to move to the area of Beauvin to support the 13/18 Hussars. The rest of the Battalion was ordered to move to the area between Beauvin and the canal and companies would picquet the roads and approaches. 'C' Company would move to Gondecourt with 'A' Company in reserve. At 12.45 p.m. the Battalion arrived in the area and companies began to move into their allotted positions. At 3.05 p.m. elements of 'D' Company were in Wavrin. Reports were received that there were enemy troops in the area with some guns and tanks. These were thought to be elements of an SS unit. The French were handing over many prisoners.

Reports arrived on the morning of the 5th September, that the enemy was withdrawing in a north-easterly direction. 'D' Company crossed the canal at Don. The bridge here had been slightly damaged and civilians set to to repair it to enable vehicles to pass over. The reception given to the Battalion as it entered Wavrin was truly tremendous. The populace crowded the streets cheering and crying at one and the same time. In 1940, the Battalion had been stationed in the area. This reception took place in spite of the fact that the enemy were only a short distance away and some were still in the north east edge of the town. The Germans began to shell the town at 9.45 a.m. French civilians reported that there was a battery of enemy guns in the town cemetery. 'D' company with the help of civilian reports and a party of French Resistance, cleared the town. The Resistance was very active, attacking German units north of the canal and producing many prisoners. Battalion casualties were one other rank killed and nine wounded.

At 8.45 a.m. on the 6th September, the Battalion moved off on what was to become a momentous journey, much of it through 1940s territory. In contrast to that retreat, this was triumph all of the way. The route taken was via Nerrin - Gondecourt - Seclin - Vendeville - Baisieux - Tournai - Bizencourt - Ninove - Shepdaal and finally to Brussels, itself. The France-Belgium border was crossed at 9.45 a.m. The route was lined with laughing, crying and cheering crowds who threw flowers, drink and kisses as the vehicles carrying the delighted troops passed by. At every stop, the people clambered on trucks, carriers and tanks, offering drinks and kisses. The Belgians, in particular, went wild with excitement. At 5.30 p.m. Brussels was reached. Captain Short was the first to have problems. He wrote:

> "...After the Falaise Gap, I was put in charge of the company guides for planning staging areas for the Battalion each day. It was a mad rush and the 6th Battalion was the leading Battalion of the Brigade and my job was to go ahead and select areas for that particular night whilst chasing the enemy. On arrival at Brussels it was very quiet, the Armoured Division having passed through and I placed out my guides. On returning to my first guide I was inundated with the public who had surged into the square to welcome the troops and all my guides were lost in the crowds. Eventually, we sorted ourselves out and the next morning proceeded on our way."

The streets were blocked by a mass of people. Getting through the city was extremely difficult. The crowds swarmed around the vehicles. Young and old, male and female, they poured into the streets and lined the pavements handing up small gifts to the soldiers. Again, as the transport was halted, they climbed onto the vehicles, embracing and kissing the troops irrespective of rank. Captain Loveridge MC, the adjutant, described the scene

'The city itself was a sight never to be forgotten: from every window or flag staff the Belgian national colours were once again freely displayed. For four years these delightful people had not given up hope of freedom from the Nazi domination and at long last were seeing their welcome liberators moving triumphantly through BRUSSELS. No wonder there was an air of gaiety in the City - every conceivable able-bodied person that day thronged the streets in order to pay compliments and cheer the column as it passed on its way. Never before have I seen such an ovation - and how the troops responded: their spirits too were high.

"Amidst all this excitement control was extremely difficult from the directional point of view. Eric Short, the Battalion Recce expert, had previously been sent ahead to sign the route and difficulty was foreseen in the maze of streets. On the arrival of the Battalion, however, not a single sign remained and what Regimental Police and guides there had been placed could not be seen or found - they were engulfed in the massing throngs of rejoicing townspeople. After what was nothing but a Commander's nightmare we did eventually arrive at our destination - although a few stragglers were left behind. On arrival I found the CO [Colonel Green] not a little distressed as he was under the impression that his Battalion was spread all over BRUSSELS. When informed that all Companys were satisfactorily settled in, then, and only then did he sit back with a sigh of relief...

'...One anecdote of our stay in Brussels is worthy of repetition here: Reg Atkinson ... was talking to the CO when the latter was heard saying, "Amazing - out of all the innumerable women in the population of Brussels, the only one to kiss me was an old woman of 70!" Reg Atkinson, in his dry manner, retorted: "Well colonel, you can consider yourself d____ lucky; the only one to kiss me was an old man!'

The Battalion moved through the city and into the Bois de la Cambre where the companies took up defensive positions. Carrier patrols were sent out and Captain Daw found intact an enemy ammunition dump south of the Battalion area. The Battalion remained here for three days. Headquarters was set up in the grounds of a palatial house. The owner gave a magnificent dinner for the Brigadier and his Brigade Major, Lieutenant-Colonel Green and his Adjutant and Intelligence Officer. Those soldiers allowed into the city were wonderfully entertained by the warm and friendly population.

CHAPTER 33
THE LAST BATTLE - GHEEL
SEPTEMBER 1944

It could not last. The hundreds of miles of triumphant advance through village town and city crammed with wildly excited civilians, with only scattered groups of demoralised enemy troops to be winkled out of woods and houses and the rare bouts of shelling, just could not last. As the Allies approached the frontiers of Germany, the enemy hastily reorganised. A widening gap had been created between the German Fifteenth Army in the West and the Seventh Army being pushed eastward towards the Meuse and Ardennes. The gap was filled by General Student's First Parachute Army. This army was made up of parachute regiments and air force ground and crew personnel. What it lacked in infantry training it made up in fanaticism and courage of a high order. The German armies were now close to home. They were fighting to save their homes and families from the advancing enemy, an enemy which was now demanding un-conditional surrender. The Allies were now entering a period when there would be no easy victories before the final collapse of German resistance. For 151 Brigade, the Battle of Gheel was to bring the weeks of easy success to an end and show that the German foe had still the will to fight back.

The fall of Antwerp did not immediately assist the Allies as the Germans clung to the Scheldt Estuary and the island of Walcheron and fought bitterly to retain them. Resistance was stiffening all along the XXX Corps front. The Guards' Armoured Division had forced a crossing of the Albert Canal at Beeringen and were locked in a fierce counter-attack by Student's parachutists. 50th Division was ordered to force another crossing of the Canal and on the morning of the 8th September, 69 Brigade crossed between Steelen and Herenthals, near the hamlet of Het Punt. The Divisional Commander then decided to make another crossing using 151 Brigade, with the object of capturing the town of Gheel. 8th Battalion was ordered to make the initial bridgehead near Steelen and the 6th would then cross the Canal and move through to capture Gheel.

The brief but pleasant stay near Brussels came to an end late on the night of the 7th September, when orders were received to move the next day. At 9.00 a.m. on the 8th September, the Battalion reached Ramsel, south of the Albert Canal. The 8th Battalion began its gallant crossing of the Canal in the face of stiffening resistance, to form the initial bridgehead. The 6th Battalion was ordered to send out two patrols to clear out any Germans found south of the Canal and to give the enemy the impression that a further bridgehead was about to be established. The left hand patrol comprised: one section of machine-guns (2nd Battalion Cheshire Regiment); one section of carriers, one section of mortars and one platoon from 'B' Company, all under Captain Davey. The right hand patrol comprised the same elements with a platoon from 'C' Company, all under the command of Captain Ian Daw, MC. The patrols moved out at 2.15 p.m. and set about their first task of clearing the woods at De Schootersche, Bosschen, Tessenderloo and Kerkensberg. This completed, the patrols moved up to the Canal. The embankments of the Canal were between fourteen and twenty feet high and protected the movement of the patrols from German observers. Stealthy observation by the patrols enabled enemy targets across the Canal to be identified and engaged. Sergeant Pickin of the

Cheshire Regiment was in command of one of the sub-sections of machine-gunners. He was met by a Belgian patrol which led him to the top of the embankment where, across the other side of the Canal, he could see the crew of a German anti-tank gun lying on their backs enjoying the summer sun. He got his gunners in position and opened fire on this perfect and unsuspecting target. The whole crew was killed. Several other targets were engaged by the patrols. Unfortunately, Captain Daw was hit by spandau fire and received wounds from which he died. The Battalion had lost another fine and popular leader who had served with great distinction in the Western Desert, Sicily and Normandy.

8th Battalion had successfully carried out its bridgehead task under fierce German resistance. The Royal Engineers had been able to span the Canal with a Class 9 Bridge. By the morning of the 9th September, the 6th Battalion was ready to move across the Canal. The bridge was under heavy shell fire, largely from air bursts. 61 Reconnaissance Regiment had crossed the bridge fifteen minutes previously and its 'C' Squadron was now heavily engaged near Doornboom. This delayed 'D' Company from crossing the bridge until the situation became clearer. A further and more serious delay was caused through damage to the pontoon bridge by enemy fire. It was 11.00 a.m. before 'D' Company got across the bridge and moved to Doornboom, encountering only slight machine-gun fire on the way. A patrol was sent out to Stokt where two of the enemy were killed and two captured, together with a small mortar. With the whole Battalion over the bridge, the companies were disposed south of Gheel, as follows: 'A' Company on the right, 'B' Company on the left and 'C' and 'D' Companies in the rear of Battalion Headquarters. The 3in. Mortar Platoon was placed in the rear of 'B' Company and prepared to fire as a battery. The anti-tank guns were disposed to cover the approaches from the north-west and north-east. The Carrier Platoon was in reserve west of Battalion Headquarters. 'C' Squadron, 61 Reconnaissance Regiment was operating on the right flank reporting on enemy movements.

At 11.30 a.m. four prisoners were taken and identified as members of the German Air Force units. They stated that they had been reinforced during the night and were preparing a counter-attack to commence that afternoon. 'B' Company

reported that a strong body of the enemy had been seen west of Gheel. These were shelled by our artillery and suffered many casualties. About fifty of this force were seen running into the woods about one thousand yards away. They were engaged by machine-guns of the 2nd Cheshires and five were killed. Two prisoners captured stated that they were reinforcements from the 4th Fleiger Ersatz Regiment. They had arrived two days previously from Holland and had gone straight into their positions. It was obvious that the enemy in the area was in considerable strength. At 2.15 p.m. 'A' Company was moved to Stokt. At 2.30 p.m. this Company overran an enemy mortar position and sent back ten prisoners. They were a mixed group from the 572nd Grenadier Ersatz Regiment and 101st Grenadier Regiment. Three of them were Poles. They reported that Gheel had been reinforced by two to three hundred men. Little happened during the rest of the day, and darkness fell with only sporadic spandau and machine-gun fire to disturb a peaceful night, except that 'B' Company reported being heavily shelled. Casualties during the day had been one other rank killed and four wounded.

During Sunday the 10th September, things began to hot up. An enemy tank was spotted near Gheel at 7.45 a.m. An enemy tank and infantry were also seen at 8.15 a.m. The pontoon bridge came under shell fire during the morning. Forward companies were coming under increasing shell and mortar fire and there was every sign that the enemy was preparing to counter-attack. 'B' Company on the left, reported an enemy advance with tank support against its positions. The exchange of fire lasted for an hour and a half before the situation eased. Lieutenant R. Allan, commanding the forward platoon, was killed in this action. During this period, Lieutenant-Colonel Green was ordered to attack Gheel with artillery and tank support. Meanwhile the forward companies continued to be heavily shelled and mortared. 'B' Company in particular, was heavily mortared and the enemy attempted to infiltrate into the company's positions. Casualties included Captain W.T.A. Davey who was wounded and the situation became so serious that Major Reggie Atkinson was unable to leave his Company for a Battalion 'O' Group. Captain D.H. Corbett, commanding 'A' Company, was also wounded on his way back from the 'O' Group. The plan for the attack on Gheel was that 'D' Company would attack on the left with 'C' Company on the right. 'A' and 'B' Companies would follow and enter the town to give support. 9 DLI would move up on the right. The attack was timed to begin at 1.30 p.m.

As the Companies moved to the Start Line, the enemy launched a strong attack against the right flank and succeeded in over-running the forward platoons of 'A' Company. It was a desperate situation, only relieved by the arrival of two sections of carriers rushed over to block the enemy advance. 'C' Company, which moved through 'A' Company to reach its position on the Start Line, came under heavy spandau and mortar fire and sustained casualties, including its Commander, Major F.C. Atkinson. Captain Bennett took over command of the Company. The hold up on the right flank, did not stop 'D' Company under Major Ken Wood, brother of the Second-in-Command of the Battalion, from moving off from the Start Line behind the artillery barrage and with the support of tanks. Major G.L. Wood, DSO, MC, was sent forward by the CO to restore the situation on the right flank and reform 'A' and ' C' Companies into one composite company and get the attack going again in that area. Tanks had now arrived in support and progress began to be made. At 2.10 p.m. tanks reported several of the enemy lining a hedgerow in a depression in the ground. They could not fire on them because they were unable to depress their guns low enough. 'D' Company was ordered to close in and deal with this group of enemy troops. Artillery fire was brought down on enemy troops reported to be withdrawing towards Elsum. At about this time, 9 DLI came up on the right of the composite company. Meanwhile 'D' Company had entered Gheel and

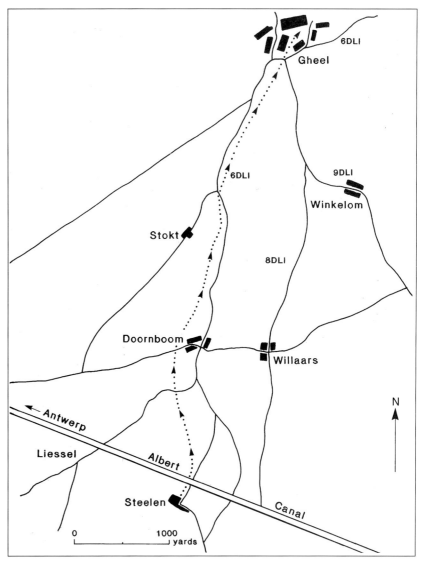

The Last Battle - *Gheel, 10th/11th September, 1944*

gained its objectives north of the church and south of the station. Fierce street fighting was now taking place as the enemy was driven out of the houses and yards of the town. Private Jim Coglan described how this was done:

'We were just throwing hand grenades sometimes. If we were in any doubt just a hand grenade went in through the windows, no messing ... If they were down in the cellars and we knew they were Germans, the hand grenade used to go down there. Sometimes the Belgian people would tell us, "Germans! Germans! Germans!" If we knew they were there we used to get round the house, surround it like. One would throw a hand grenade from the back and I'd throw one from the front ... and we'd go in and if there was nobody there, we knew they were down in the cellar ... We used to shout down like and if they didn't come up, we made sure they stopped down. They did the same with us...'

'D' Company was having a successful period. One hundred and sixty-five prisoners were taken during the advance and many dead were left lying on the battlefield. One armoured car, one 88mm gun, one mortar and two anti-tank guns had been knocked out. 'B' Company was sent through 'D' Company at 3.15 p.m. to consolidate the position on the right of Gheel. More prisoners came in during the late afternoon. At 4.00 p.m. a report was received that the bridge at Steelen was again out of action. The town of Gheel was suffering as so many towns had suffered in this war. Under heavy shelling, houses were being destroyed. The population sought shelter in the cellars or wherever they could. Some braved the shells and bullets to help the British. Private Ernest Harvey wrote:

'...As I was crossing this road into the town this young girl came towards me. She would be, I think 14 or 15. She had this large jar which contained peaches. She said to me in perfect English, "We have been waiting for you." Then she told me she was British and her father was a doctor in the town. She also informed me where Jerry was.'

Prive Ken Lodge also experienced the kindness and courage of some of the civilians:

'We were running down this street and civilians were still in the town and they were popping their heads out the doors to see what was happening. "Is Englander? Americano?" I was coming past this house and this chap pushed half a bottle of Cognac into my hand. I had a rifle in one hand and half a bottle of Cognac in the other, running down this street. We got so far down this street and we came under mortar fire. These mortars were crashing onto the cobbled stones ... there were shops and there was a woman straight ahead, waving ... I ran across there and I got to the shop and the whole of the windows went out. The glass was flying, this woman was screaming. She pushed me down the cellar. I rolled from the top to the bottom of this cellar with all my gear and this bottle of Cognac and I landed at the bottom of the steps in a heap. I could hear all the bombs crashing up a height and the cellar was full of people ... and this chap supped my half bottle of Cognac. I didn't drink in those days. I was down there about half an hour till it stopped and the lads were coming out of various positions and one or two of them had been hit ... Things calmed down and people came out of the houses, sticking flags up at the windows, had a few photographs taken ... This Belgian chap came flying back shouting, "The Bosche! The Bosche is coming!" And all their flags disappeared, disappeared off the windows...'

The squadron of tanks were giving wonderful support but, like the infantry, were suffering heavy casualties. Sergeant Bert Davies and his mortars were ordered forward. He wrote:

'...I was ordered to go forward with the leading sections and find suitable sites for the mortars who were to follow on later. The crossing of the Canal was OK but after advancing across and along the ridges of a spud field, Jerry opened up with shells and machine-guns hitting Sergeant Wilson on my right and two other lads on my left but we all had to keep going until we reached some cover and a farmhouse. Here we took some prisoners in the farm buildings. In the yard there was a small straw stack. Noticing pieces of straw falling off it one lad decided to prod it with his rifle and bayonet. There was a yell and out popped four Jerries, one after the other, all trying to hide until we had gone. I found a site to set the mortars up which hadn't arrived yet and so Geordie Whittaker and I decided to go forward to the next farmhouse in the hope of getting some eggs before anyone else got there. It was all very quiet. I shouted but no answer and so we went into the farmhouse. Cowering in the corner of the room, we found an old lady and a young teenage girl but everytime I asked them if there were any Jerries or eggs, they would both start crying and shaking. I sensed there were Jerries around but by now my mortars were arriving and so I had to get them set up for a counter-attack was expected...'

Enemy shelling of Gheel increased in intensity. Lieutenant-Colonel Green moved forward to ascertain for himself what the situation was. He was wounded by a piece of shrapnel and had to be evacuated. Major G.L. Wood, again, found himself in command of the Battalion at a critical time. At 8.20 p.m. an enemy counter-attack developed on the right flank and the Germans started to infiltrate behind the forward companies on the left flank. Colonel Watson described the scene in his unpublished manuscript:

> '...They [the Germans] could be seen dodging from street to street and through the houses and in the end they were successful in getting behind the forward companies. Two anti-tank guns of the Northumberland Hussars were over-run and the pieces captured. Nor did the night provide any relief. As darkness fell 'D' Company reported enemy patrols, as well as tanks, moving around their positions, and throughout the long hours during which every soldier stood alert at his post, machine-gun fire as well as the crump of mortar bomb continually broke the silence. Flares shot into the sky, and hung momentarily before falling to the ground to lighten the ghastly scene, while black oily smoke from burning tanks curled about the buildings. It was a night, too, full of scares and alarms. Nobody slept, every man just waited very tired but full of determination; patrols from both sides were crawling about the now deserted streets. One German patrol stumbled right into 'D' Company. There was a burst of machine-gun, a scuffle and some angry words and a German Officer and fifteen other ranks were unceremoniously hustled into a building as prisoners of war.'

The situation for the 6th Battalion was becoming more and more difficult. The Germans seemed to be all around it. Casualties were heavy and the companies were now weak in numbers. In addition to those officers already named as casualties in this account, Lieutenants Howell and Bateman had been wounded. Thirty other ranks had been killed, sixty-seven had been wounded of whom four died later and forty-two were missing. One of the latter was presumed killed.

The 6th Battalion was now close to being cut off from the rear. Late at night on the 10th, Brigade Headquarters moved acros the Canal and into the bridgehead. At 1.00 a.m. on the following day,

under the cover of a ground mist the enemy counter-attacked once more on the right flank. As the Battalion could not give infantry support, the tanks could not move forward to meet this attack. A further difficulty was that the companies were now cut off from Battalion Headquarters. The position became so serious that Brigade Headquarters was now threatened and moved back across the Canal. At 7.30 a.m. German infantry with tanks were reported south of Gheel and closing in on Battalion Headquarters. Captain Short wrote:

> 'We reached the Canal, Gheel, where we were held up and the Adjutant told me to hold the fort as he had to visit the CO. A message came through from a tank commander that a German tank was in the right of our position and when I said I would advise the company concerned, he replied, "No, on the right of you!" I felt completely naked high up on a tracked wireless vehicle with a canvas roof and any minute expected the worst, when one of our tanks engaged the German tank and it brewed up.'

The 8th Battalion, which had moved up its 'B' and 'D' Companies on the left of the 6th the previous evening, was also finding life very difficult. Germans were reported to be in the rear of this Battalion. The 9th Battalion had been under severe enemy pressure but had managed to beat off all attacks. Throughout the morning of the 11th September, the fighting raged in the streets of Gheel and along the front of 8th and 9th Battalions. At 8.40 a.m. 'D' Company was reported to be in good spirits though heavily pressed and stated it had knocked out one 150mm gun, one armoured car and a tank. At 10 a.m. a patrol was sent out with a PIAT to try to deal with an enemy tank on a road near Battalion Headquarters. This was later destroyed by one of the Shermans but it was towed away by another enemy tank supported by ten infantrymen. At 10.50 a.m. 'B' Company reported enemy tanks moving in the outskirts of Gheel. These were heavily shelled and a request was made for Typhoons' support. 'D' Company was cut off and medical attention could not be sent to aid the wounded. By 11.25 a.m. this Company reported enemy infiltrating the left rear of the town and it was finding it extremely difficult to keep them out. 'D' Company was urged to hold on as another squadron of tanks was coming to assist. Ammunition and food supplies in 'B' and 'D' Companies' positions had fallen to a dangerously low level. Jeeps were loaded with both of these items and, under the command of Captain Harrison, set off at 1.50 p.m. to reach these two companies which they succeeded in doing. As the jeeps had got through, this encouraged the CO to send reinforcements to 'D' Company. Major Field, commanding 'S' Company, collected about fifty men and, piling them onto six carriers, set off for the Company's positions. He recorded what happened:

'As we set off, the first carrier was heavily shelled when it had gone only 50 yards, and a nearby medical truck went up in flames. Apparently a Jagd Panther SP gun had the whole road in view and was actually in position on the road itself. However, another 17 Pounder Sherman moved slowly into position and set the enemy gun on fire with the 2nd shot.

'Although there was still some enemy infantry astride the road, we carried on cautiously and were not fired on, probably on account of our superior fire power, and eventually we reached the market square in Gheel. One carrier overshot the mark and was knocked out by an anti-tank gun, but the crew were unhurt.

'If we were thankful to reach Gheel, Major Ken Wood, of 'D' Company was even more glad to see us. His men had been fighting against heavy odds in the fields in front of the town, across dykes into the town and then from house to house inside the town, and now they were being heavily counter-attacked by the enemy, who were numerous, to cut off odd parties and sections in the street fighting. We loaded the wounded into 3 carriers and sent 40 POW off with them right away - just in time as we soon discovered - and that left one platoon, Company HQ, and my extra men.

'...the gunner OP in the Church tower called us up to show us a fair sized party of Germans advancing from hedge to hedge in the direction of 'B' Company. in the East of the town. Orders went back to the 25 Pounders: back came, "Guns Fired" - then the boom of discharge, the scream of the shells and the mushroom like explosions 200 yds beyond the grey figures, now digging furiously. A brief correction, and this time right amongst them; "repeat", and one more attack had been checked...

"We took our temporary abode in a café, whose owner told us the bar was ours and we were soon helping ourselves to a good glass of beer. However, the firing outside had been increasing, and suddenly, from a large white house on the other side of the

road where I had positioned some of my party, there was a rush to occupy some trenches in the square. This was serious for one of our two remaining anti-tank guns was overrun, so I collected the men together again, and we chased the Hun out, he had come up unseen and thrown grenades through the windows, and had then covered the street with Spandau fire. However, we were back in the house again and not a moment too soon, for heavy mortar fire began to fall outside and a Jeep was knocked out. Soon after this the enemy appeared on the road by which we had entered the town, and we could see them sheltering behind a disabled Ferdinand SP gun and one of our Sapper Carriers, which fortunately had a considerable amount of ammonal packed in it. Our tanks opened up at point blank range, blew up the carrier and all the Germans with it...

'...Then came word from Battalion HQ by wireless that we were to be relieved ... But perhaps the hardest thing for us to do was to leave behind in Gheel a pleasant looking girl, freckled and always cheerful who during the five years of war in Belgium had befriended, and helped with food and clothes and rest, 7 Allied airmen, all of whom had left letters of appreciation with her. Josephine, though only 17, had guided our men out of almost surrounded houses, and tended our wounded and had not flinched at the torn bodies of dying men. She told us she would look after those of our wounded in the town hospital, whom we couldn't take with us, until we came again, as she was sure we would...

'...When, two days later, we came back for our wounded ... The first person we saw was Josephine, and she told us where our wounded were, and that the Germans had treated them well and left them behind...

'We found a bottle of Burgundy wine, and drank to Josephine and the 6th Durham LI.'

Luck ran out for Private Ken Lodge. He described the events which led to his capture:

'We moved to the outskirts of Gheel and we dug in just in front of these houses, in this field. You couldn't see the back of the field because of the slope ... We spent the night [10th-11th September] where we were because it was pretty quiet. A woman came out next morning. There was a mist, a very heavy mist. She came out from one of these houses with this jug with coffee in it. It was very good of her ... The mist cleared ... Someone said, "Germans!" and there were these four Germans walking across the field...couldn't believe it. We fired at them. They went down and out of sight ... We must have hit them ... That was it, they knew we were there then. The mortars started and the machine-guns started ... it never ceased. We were getting a good pounding and they attacked up the field. We could see them first, see them waist high. We were firing and they were going down, firing was coming from all directions ... We got out of the trenches and into the houses. We were well and truly pinned down.'

Sergeant Bert Davies had finished up in the town square with Major Field's party minus his mortars. Eventually he made his way back to search for the mortars. He wrote:

'...suddenly I saw in front and to our right Jerries diving into a ditch. I gave a quick burst with my Sten and dashed towards them and with that they all came out with their hands up leaving their weapons behind in the ditch, 11 in all. One 6ft blond and very good looking said to me in perfect English, "Oh, I suppose you are going to hang out your washing on the Seigfried Line now." "No! But I'll hang you and the rest on that ... barbed wire if you don't get moving. So Schnell!"'

At 2.30 p.m. Major G.L. Wood received orders to withdraw the companies from Gheel to positions south of the town. The problem was to get the orders to the companies who were either almost surrounded or had the enemy as close as twenty to thirty yards away. Captain Peter Tyndale, Motor Transport Officer, was given the task of reaching 'B' and 'D' Companies. He wrote later:

'I had the job of taking the Order in the carrier. I could not get through by carrier because the road was blocked by a burning Sherman Tank. There were snipers about so I got through to 'D' Company on foot. I felt happier on foot than in the carrier. As I had taken longer than expected (however long that was) - the Orders were going out over the radio as I reached 'D' Company HQ. I therefore still have 'B' Company Orders. Incidentally before I left Battalion HQ with these orders I heard George Wood saying, "Good Bye" to his brother Ken (OC 'D' Company) as he did not expect the two coys would get out - anyway as coys.'

The Companies withdrew. 'D' Company being almost surrounded, fought its way out with bayonet and Sten. 'B' Company withdrew in spite of the fact that the enemy was so close. The composite company of 'C' and 'A' did not get out and

it was thought it had been taken prisoner. However, two days later it was learned that Lieutenant Seggie had brought out his remaining men, having fought from street corner to street corner through the town. On the 12th September, 151 Brigade was relieved in the bridgehead and a brigade of the 15th (Scottish) Division of XII Corps took its place. When the latter launched an attack on Gheel on this day, it was to find that the enemy had gone. The Germans had failed to carry out their orders to drive the Durhams back over the Albert Canal.

It was a fierce struggle, to rank with Mareth and Primosole Bridge. Casualties were heavy. Every officer and man who survived was close to exhaustion. Casualties were: one officer killed and six wounded. Thirty four other ranks were killed, four died of wounds, eighty-five were wounded and fifty-one were missing. After a brief stay at Vorst on the evening of the 12th, the Battalion moved to the area Ryssels - Pael on the following morning. Sixty-six reinforcements joined the Battalion. On the 15th, the XXX Corps Commander, Lieutenant General Horrocks, visited the Battalion and congratulated it on its stand at Gheel for thirty-six hours and denying the enemy the Canal which was their objective. A party attended an ENSA Variety Show, 'Irish Follies' held at Diest. Baths were available at 'A' Echelon.

CHAPTER 35

NIJMEGEN - THE ISLAND

1944

The rest, after the fierce exertions of Gheel, was soon over. At 11.25 a.m. on the 16th September, the Battalion moved off and, crossing the Albert Canal at Beeringen, travelled via Leopoldsburg - Kerkhoven to an area south of Lommel. In the afternoon, 'C' Company was sent forward just south of the Escaut canal to prevent any enemy infiltrating over this water course. Six new officers joined the Battalion: Lieutenants R. Quickenden and Withenshaw who went to 'B' Company, Lieutenant Kamofsky and Second-Lieutenant Hunt who went to 'C' Company and Lieutenants Lyms and Sykes who joined 'D' Company. 'C' Company returned to the Battalion on the 17th on being relieved by a company of the Royal Welsh Fusiliers.

On the 17th September, the plan for the airborne operation to seize the crossings of four major waterways was released to all units. Field Marshal Montgomery's plan was for three airborne divisions to be dropped with the object of securing the crossings over the Wilhelmina Canal at Eindhoven, the River Meuse at Grave, the River Waal at Nijmegen and the Lower Rhine at Arnhem. The Allied Airborne Corps would provide the troops for this hazardous enterprise which promised so much if successful. The airborne troops consisted of the 1st British , 82nd and 101st American Airborne Divisions and the Polish Parachute Brigade. XXX Corps would advance along the corridor from the Escaut Canal through Eindhoven, Veghel, Grave, Nijmegen to Arnhem. The right flank of this Corps would be protected and widened by VIII Corps to the east and XII Corps to the west. Once this was achieved, the Ruhr and the industrial heart of Germany would lie at the mercy of the advancing allies and the end of the war would quickly follow. The Guards' Armoured Division would lead the XXX Corps advance up the corridor, followed by the 43rd Division with the 50th Division in Corps Reserve. As the armour advanced, the infantry would hold the flanks of the corridor against any enemy attempts to cut this lifeline. 50th Division advance would be led by 231 Brigade with the 151 Brigade in reserve.

At 1.00 p.m. on the 18th September, the Battalion was part of a Brigade move into the bridgehead over the Escaut Canal to relieve 231 Brigade. It remained here for five days. Two officers and seventy other ranks joined the Battalion. The two officers were Major D.F. Crossthwaite and Second-Lieutenant Hall. Lieutenant-Colonel J.M. Hanmer joined the Battalion and assumed command. At 7.10 p.m. enemy aircraft bombed the bridgehead over the Escaut Canal and, though no damage was done, Captain Loveridge was slightly wounded. After treatment, he returned to duty. Lieutenants J.A. Young and R.M. Berry joined the Battalion on the 19th of the month. The following day, was spent on cleaning up and maintenance work. Forty-eight reinforcements arrived and 'A' Company was reformed under Major Crossthwaite. At 4.30 p.m. on the 20th, an armada of Dakotas carrying airborne troops went overhead. These were thought to be carrying reinforcements to the parachutists and glider forces of 'Operation Market Garden' which had landed previously. A draft of thirty-seven other ranks was received on the 21st, with Lieutenant W.S. Carr and a further seven other ranks arrived on the following day.

On the 23rd September, the Brigade, now under VIII Corps,

moved into Holland. Information was received that the airborne troops were fighting fiercely to hold the crossings, with the bridges at Veghel, Grave and Nijmegen in our possession. The position at Arnhem was more critical, with the British airborne troops almost surrounded and fighting against heavy odds. The Battalion order of march was: 'D' Company; 'B' Company; 'O' Group; Battalion Headquarters; one platoon, 2nd Cheshire Regiment; detachment of Northumberland Hussars (anti-tank guns); one detachment 149 Field Ambulance; 'A' and 'C' Companies. Vlokhoven Ekkart was reached at 2.45 p.m. The task was to protect the right flank of the armour spearhead and secure and hold all approaches to the corridor in its area. On the 24th of the month, the Battalion was again on the move, this time to the area of Breugel on the Wilhemina Canal, north of Eindhoven. The corridor, ever lengthening and in places little wider than the axis road along which the Guards Armoured Division was travelling, was cut by the enemy for the second time since the advance had begun. This road was terribly congested and each time it was cut, traffic piled up for miles. The passage of supplies to the airborne troops was delayed and it was extremely difficult to move reinforcements up to strengthen the flanks of this slender lifeline. 'C' Company occupied Lieshout and carrier patrols were sent out to the areas of Beek and Donk to ascertain if the bridges over the Canal were still intact. The carriers reported that three of these were blown and standing patrols were established in the area to prevent the enemy from infiltrating across the Canal. Patrols were active on the 25th and many reports of enemy troop and tank movements came into Battalion Headquarters. Covering parties were provided for Sappers who were building bridges at Beek and Donk. One prisoner was handed over by the Sappers at Beek. He had been found hiding in a barn and was from No. 4 Company, 1st Pioneer Ersatz Battalion. No other contact was made with the enemy.

Following a quiet day on the 26th September, the Battalion was on the move again on the following day. It moved northwards to Volkel, a village near Veghel, where patrols were sent out but no contact was made with the enemy. On the 28th, a draft of five officers and fifteen other ranks was received from the Divisional Reinforcement Pool. The officers were: Captain Moveley and

Lieutenants N. Wilkinson, A. Moody, D.F. Barclay and P.C. Capstick. Later in the day, a further four men arrived, all of whom had recovered from wounds received in Normandy. The last two days of the month were quiet. Parties attended 50th Division concerts at Gemert and short route marches were organised.

East of Nijmegen, the River Rhine divides into two, forming the Rivers Waal and Neder Rijn (Lower Rhine). West of Nijmegen, the two rivers come close together but don't quite meet. This area between the two rivers became known to the 50th Division as 'The Island'. The area was mainly pasture land with orchards and scattered villages and a few canning factories producing tinned jams and fruit. The two main villages in this salient were Elst and Bemel. The ground beyond, towards distant Arnhem, was flat. This enabled artillery and mortar shoots to be carried out by observation, always considered easier than shooting from the map. Every building roof top was a potential observation post, particularly church steeples, a favourite target for both sides. The land was intersected by broad and flowing dykes, a natural obstacle to all armoured vehicles. These dykes were blocked in places by dead cattle. The countryside being so flat, rain tended to stay where it fell and dykes quickly filled to overflowing. As the winter approached, the conditions became quite appalling in the sodden and squelching landscape. Many of the roads ran along the top of embankments and these, along with the main road to Arnhem, were littered with burnt-out wrecks of tanks of the Guards Division which had made the gallant race for Arnhem, to reach the 1st British Airborne Division, which proved to be in vain.

At 7.50 a.m. on the 2nd October, the Battalion moved off to relieve the 6th Green Howards north of the River Waal. The trucks were driven as far as the road bridge over the river at Nijmegen. Here the troops debussed and crossed the bridge on foot as quickly as possible as it was under enemy artillery fire. A Canadian Military Police notice on the bridge summed up the danger, 'If you are going fast - go faster.' The relief was completed and strong patrols were sent out to ascertain the strength and positions of the enemy and to try to take a prisoner. Battalion Headquarters and 'B' Company area were shelled and the Signals Officer, Captain Wedgwood, was wounded. A fighting patrol which returned in the early hours of the 3rd October had been heavily shelled but reported seeing a German soldier near a factory. Two snipers were sent out and these returned in due course to report having seen fifteen enemy and a half-track vehicle in the factory area. Artillery fire was brought down on this area. The weather and conditions were so bad that a rum ration was issued in the evening. More patrols were out at night. The Germans were also active. Colonel Watson described the conditions under which the patrols worked, in his unpublished manuscript:

> '...patrols went out each night and many a clash of arms took place in the dark. Once more the Germans were close at hand, and they too sent out their own picked patrols, down flooded ditch and dyke; they too watched the movement of the British and made their deductions, and they too made determined efforts to creep into the British lines. Patrolling had always needed clear thinking and steady nerves and never more so than on 'The Island'. On this flat marshy countryside all forms of patrolling were extremely difficult. The orchards provided good cover but once in the open, the flat country gave one an uncomfortable feeling that every movement was being watched from all the enemy positions on the comparatively high ground near Arnhem. As soon as darkness fell, the little bands would set off on their nerve racking missions through squelching countryside. As likely or not some brim full dyke would have to be crossed and a plank or ladder would be carried for the purpose. This movement was both difficult and noisy; the crossings would probably be followed by a crawl through mud and marsh which would beat the courage of the bravest soldier, little wonder the nightly tot of rum was always so welcome. When each task was finished the patrol leaders would bring in their information and in such a way a complete picture of the activities of the Germans, who themselves were by no means dormant, was built.'

There were three divisions in the line: the 101st United States Division and the British 50th and 53rd Divisions. The 50th Division was on the right with the 6th Battalion on the extreme right where the line swung back to the River Waal. The 307 US Parachute Brigade lay south of the river and contact was quickly made with this unit.

On the 4th October, 231 and 151 Brigades were ordered to assault, with the aim of enlarging the bridgehead to the east and capturing the eastern edge of the village of Haalderen. 231 Brigade attacked first on the left, followed by 151 Brigade, with the 8th Battalion on the right and the 9th Battalion on the left. The attacks were successful and the objectives gained with quite heavy losses to the enemy in both dead and prisoners. The attacks were preceded by artillery bombardments and Typhoon attacks. 6th Battalion sent out patrols that night. The reconnaissance patrol under Lieutenant Moody, returned at 1.45 a.m. on the 5th with an excellent description of the factory area and the route to it. No enemy was seen. At 3.00 a.m. 'A' Company reported a small craft similar to a rowing boat moving along the river towards the Nijmegen bridge. Searchlights were turned onto the boat and Bofors guns defending the bridge opened fire. Another attempt by the Germans to blow the bridge failed. During the rest of the day, various enemy movements were observed and on two occasions artillery shelled targets. Thirteen other ranks rejoined, all of whom had served with the Battalion in Normandy. On the 6th of the month, the Battalion relieved the 6th Battalion The Highland Light Infantry in order that the latter could make an advance on the factories at Haalderen. 'D' Company was attached to the Highlanders for this local action. A further sixteen reinforcements joined the Battalion. The 1st Battalion The Oxford and Buckinghamshire Light Infantry, of the 53rd Division, relieved the Battalion on the 7th October and the companies marched to Nijmegen and into billets in the town.

The Battalion's task was to defend the vital bridges across the river. It now passed under the command of the 100th Anti-Aircraft Brigade. The defenders had to be constantly on the alert for enemy attempts to blow the bridges. It was thought that there were a variety of methods open to the Germans to enable them to do this: midget submarines, human torpedoes, floating mines or frogmen. 'A' Company was responsible for the defence of the main road bridge. 'B' Company was responsible for a Class 40 bridge, 'C' Company for the railway bridge and 'D' Company had one platoon patrolling the river in DUKWs with two platoons in reserve. Lieutenant-Colonel Hanmer's mixed command included: two batteries of anti-aircraft guns, one west and one east of the town; one anti-tank gun troop from XXX Corps Anti-Tank Regiment, Royal Artillery; four DUKWs for river patrols; four searchlights for illuminating the area of the bridges; one section of Royal Engineers with DUKWs; a section of Field Security Police; Dutch Civil Police; a few M 10s (self-propelled 17 pounder anti-tank guns) and four explosive experts. This force was to deal with any enemy airborne landings in the bridge area, prevent sabotage and guard both the north and south approaches to the bridges. It was an area which received a good deal of attention from enemy artillery. However, the billets were good and the officers and men enjoyed hot baths, cinema shows and ENSA concerts in the Dutch Colonial Barracks.

At 9.45 a.m. on the morning of the 9th October, some objects were seen floating in the water six miles west of the bridges. They were thought to be one man submarines and the defences were put on the alert. No attack on the bridges materialised. The enemy shelled the area of the bridges throughout the day. One man was killed in 'B' Echelon area and a store truck damaged. 'C' Company had one man killed and one wounded. One despatch rider was wounded while crossing the bridge. Telephone wires were frequently cut by shell fire. Infantry of the 53rd Welsh Division searched a factory and discovered two cases containing 'Human Torpedoes', twelve feet long and two and three quarter feet wide. One of these was missing! The shelling continued on the 10th, the bridges were hit several times and three men of 'A' Company were wounded. On the 12th of the month, the Battalion relieved the 1st Battalion The Dorsetshire Regiment west of Elst. Once in position, the usual patrols were sent out at night. On the 14th, the first party granted forty-eight hours' leave in Brussels left from 'A' Echelon.

The Battalion relieved the 9th Battalion on the 15th October, north of Elst and about five miles south west of Arnhem. 'A' Company was on the left astride the Nijmegen - Arnhem railway with the right hand platoon dug in below the embankment on the main road. 'B' Company, east of the road embankment was echeloned back some seven to eight hundred yards, which left 'A' Company in an isolated forward position between road and railway. Heavy shelling by the Germans took place during the

evening and three other ranks were wounded. Patrols were sent out during the night 15th/16th October. A contact patrol supplied by 'A' Company was given the task of contacting the 6th Green Howards on the left and to give an immediate warning of any enemy attempt to infiltrate between the two Battalions. This patrol made three contacts with the enemy during the night. A standing patrol was given the task of reporting on any enemy attempts to infiltrate down the road. A second contact patrol from 'C' Company was to contact a patrol of 'B' Company and together to give warning of any enemy attempts to infiltrate between 'C' and 'D' Companies. The positions now occupied by the Battalion were far from pleasant and gave any enterprising Germans the opportunity to infiltrate down the road embankment and between the companies' positions.

At 8.45 a.m. on the 16th October, 'A' Company reported that a few Germans had worked their way along the road embankment to a ditch close to its forward positions and had opened up with heavy spandau fire. A party from 'C' Company and a sniper were sent forward to deal with them. At 9.15 a.m. 'C' Company reported that six of the enemy had tried to surrender but were mortared by their own troops and had suffered casualties. Two prisoners taken, belonging to the 37th Festung Battalion, gave useful information regarding the strength and morale of their unit. The enemy group in front of 'A' Company continued to give trouble throughout the day. PIAT bombs were fired at a high angle over the embankment to try to dislodge them. The Germans replied by throwing grenades which knocked out two of the Company's Bren guns. On the 17th, Lieutenant Berry and a small party tried to make a counter raid but were spotted and came under enemy machine-gun fire. Berry was wounded and one of his men taken prisoner. Stretcher-bearers went out to bring the wounded officer, who was lying on the enemy side of the canal, back to safety and eventually succeeded in doing so despite the attention of the Germans nearby. A section of 'A' Company led by Corporal Ferguson climbed the embankment unseen under the cover of the morning mist and rushed the Germans. Four prisoners were taken, two of whom were wounded. Four others were claimed as being killed. One of the German prisoners who had been wounded in the ankle was a tennis player and was concerned that his wound might affect his game. Corporal Ferguson was wounded in the raid. He subsequently received the Military Medal for his gallantry. 'A' Company's isolated position continued to give concern and it was decided to bring it back to conform with the other companies of the Battalion. This was done when night fell. It was a dreadful night with heavy rain and a strong gale. Patrols had nothing to report.

The conditions in 'The Island' deteriorated rapidly. The farmers had left the area and the dykes unattended were becoming blocked. The land was flooding and areas turning into a quagmire. Units were now spending ten days in the lines followed by three day's rest. The Battalion also sent one platoon at a time back to 'B' Echelon, to rest for a couple of days. At night, the rum ration warmed many a frozen body and was almost an indispensable commodity in the line.

The shelling and patrolling continued during the Battalion's stay in the line. The Battalion snipers were active and causing the enemy some casualties. On the 19th October, one other rank from a 9th Battalion post came into the positions, having escaped after being captured by the enemy in a raid. On the 20th October, Captain W.W. Teggin, the Brigade Intelligence Officer who had served in the 6th Battalion, came up to make a propaganda broadcast to the enemy opposite the Battalion front. Instead of arriving at 'C' Company which was in the rear of 'D' Company, he drove his massive vehicle straight to the latter company's Headquarters. Major K.M. Wood, commanding 'D' Company, suggested that it would be best for all concerned if the vehicle was removed forthwith as the enemy were only two hundred yards away! After a short discussion, Captain Teggins removed himself and his vehicle and returned to 'C' Company from whose positions the broadcast was made at 11.15 p.m. Early the following morning, four prisoners entered 'C' Company's lines. Impressed by the broadcast, they had decided to give themselves up and told their captors that it had been well received. Many more of their comrades would be willing to surrender but were afraid, as they were being watched continually by their senior NCOs and officers. They did give valuable information on the strength, positions and morale of their unit. Enemy shelling and machine-gun fire continued to cause casualties.

The Battalion was relieved on the 22nd October by the 6th Green Howards and moved back into schools in Nijmegen. Baths and entertainment were organised. Football matches were arranged for each day. Officers, sergeants and other ranks held dances in the gymnasium. Since the arrival of the Allies, the civilian population of the town, in spite of the great difficulties of living under constant enemy shelling and disruption to their lives, were full of kindness towards the soldiers. Private Ernest Harvey wrote:

'We reached Nijmegen ... I was going to sleep in the garage of this house but the occupier would not hear of it ... For the first time for quite a while I had a smashing bed. What a shock I got when I got up in the morning. All my uniform had been cleaned. I thought, "What a shock the lads will get when they see me," but they had all just about received the same treatment. This poor couple had more or less little food. I managed to scrounge some jam and marg. etc. and soap. You should have seen their faces, tears streaming down their faces.'

On the 25th October, Major G.L. Wood left the Battalion for the 50th Division Battle School as an instructor. On the 28th, the Battalion relieved the 508 RCT, an American unit, east of Elst. The 29th was a quiet day. The following day, the Sappers lifted two hundred mines from the Battalion front. Lieutenant R. Purdy, a Canadian, joined the Battalion under the Canloan Scheme. On the last day of the month, the 7th Green Howards exchanged positions. Casualties for the month were: two officers wounded, three other ranks killed, twenty-three wounded and one man was missing, believed a prisoner of war.

Over the next two days, the shelling and mortaring by both sides continued. Patrols were active. A free issue of beer from Mitchell and Butlers of Birmingham was issued on the 2nd November. On the night of the 3rd, Lieutenant P.J.G. Hunt and Corporal Hair both took out patrols. The former led a fighting patrol and the latter a reconnaissance patrol. The fighting patrol was spotted and had to withdraw. Corporal Hair's patrol remained unseen and watched the enemy for some time. It was discovered that two enemy posts were occupying this section of the line and this information was conveyed back to Battalion

Headquarters and recorded on the situation map. Captain D. Rome, and Lieutenants R.G. Bateman and E.V. Oldham, together with two sergeants and a private, rejoined the Battalion. On the 5th of the month, the Battalion was relieved by the 9th Battalion and commenced three days' rest out of the line. On the following day, a party of two officers and ten other ranks went on forty-eight hours' leave to Antwerp, followed by another party on the 8th of the month. On the 9th November, the Battalion relieved the 8th Battalion in the Bemmel area. The enemy was very active in this area and immediately began to make his presence felt. At 10.30 p.m. 'A' Company reported a German patrol of twelve men advancing south from the direction of King Post. This post was occupied by a handful of the Company during the hours of darkness, to prevent enemy infiltration south of the canal. At 11.05 p.m. Hampson Post was engaged by the Germans. This post was held at the time by the Carrier Platoon. A few minutes later, artillery defensive fire was brought down onto the German attackers. At 11.30 p.m. King Post reported that the enemy could be heard moving about in the rear. Ten minutes later, 'D' Company reported that Hampson Post had been rushed by the enemy and all but one man wounded and taken prisoner. Colonel Watson described what happened in his manuscript:

'...Private Wakefield was the survivor, and he told how the post was manned by one NCO and eight other ranks of the Carrier Platoon, the positions being four trenches. He went on to say that the Carrier Platoon Commander had just left the position after ensuring that his men were properly settled in, when a Spandau opened up with rapid fire a little to the right. Every man was alert but visibility was bad owing to torrential rain and the dark night. The post held its fire waiting for further events. Shortly after, hand grenades were thrown into the trenches from the front. Realising the enemy was close at hand the line of the dyke in front was engaged by Bren gun fire. Simultaneously some ten Germans rushed in and scuppered the post. Private Wakefield fell backwards out of the trench, rolled clear and lay low until the enemy had taken the others away as prisoners, one, possibly two, of whom were wounded. One of the latter was found later when the Carrier Platoon went out to reoccupy the post.'

Lieutenant J.A. Wedgwood completed the episode when he wrote:

'...But Lieutenant P.L.F. Capstick retrieved the situation by taking out another section to occupy the post, patrolling forward and restoring confidence on that part of the front. He himself brought back a wounded man. The CO personally congratulated this officer and also Lieutenant D.V. Sykes for taking out, "The finest recce party he had ever known," and "D" Company built up for themselves a fine reputation in this respect...'

For the following nine days, the pattern was familiar, namely: patrols, shelling and mortaring by both sides, bitterly cold nights, warmed a little by the rum ration. On the 16th, Major Reggie Atkinson, went to hospital with acute fibrositis. He was not to return to the Battalion until it had left the salient. There was considerable concern at Corps Headquarters that the Germans might take advantage of the forthcoming high tide and flood 'The Island' to a depth of three feet and, at the same time, make a full scale attempt to blow the bridges at Nijmegen. Elaborate plans were made to meet this possibility. However, the period of high tide passed without further alarm. On the 18th November, the Battalion moved back to Nijmegen. The Durham Light Infantry Band had arrived in the town and on Sunday morning the 19th, a Church Parade was held, followed by a March Past at which the Divisional Commander took the salute. The Service was held, with the Band playing. Thirty-two reinforcements were received.

There are always amusing or irritating stories about equipment or materials returns, demanded at the most inappropriate times by administrative staff at Higher Command Headquarters. Captain Peter Tyndale wrote of one such demand:

'The Brigade was in the Island between Nijmegen and Arnhem. Everyone was very tired - we were well under strength, and very damp if not wet all the time.

'One day Jim Loveridge [Adjutant] or George Wood told me that the Battalion had had a demand for about £400 because we were overdrawn on our Jerrycan (Petrol cans) account to the extent of 700 odd cans! In other words, the RASC reckoned that we had drawn something like 700 more full petrol cans than we had returned empties - presumably since 'D' Day!

'I was told to do something about it, or else! I was worried - a Captain's pay was 18 shillings a day [90p]. I took my trouble back to the MT lines.

'Needless to say someone (probably Sergeant Bailey, Bruce or Lance-Corporal Hall) quickly came up with the easy answer.

"It so happened at that time the 3 Tonners were not very busy; so Higher Authority ordered us to send about 4, 3 Tonners, once or twice a week to take salvage back into Belgium from a large Dump to the west of Nijmegen. When the detail came through we were given a letter of the alphabet to be cut out of white paper, 8ins. high, and stuck onto the windscreen of each 3 Tonner. The letter indicated to the MP on the Dump gate what load that lorry was to pick up. The letters and loads were changed daily.

'The loads we were taking back included empty shell cases, ammo boxes, ration containers, miscellaneous equipment and "EMPTY JERRYCANS."

'One day when we were not on the salvage run, two of the MT Section paid an early visit to the exit gate of the Salvage Dump and noted which letter the vehicles carrying empty Jerrycans displayed.

"Back in the MT lines the appropriate letter was cut out and stuck to the windscreen of four 3 Tonners and off they went to the Dump.

'Surely enough, they were directed to the field that contained enormous stacks of Jerrycans. Very quickly they were completely loaded. There was no paper work in this job, the Drivers were asked if they knew where to go - "Yes" they said, they had done this run several times before.

'So off they went, straight back to our lines! During the afternoon after the white letter had been taken off their windscreens ... they went back to the RASC Div Supply Point, and got the 108 [form] signed by them. After all they were the people who had raised the charge against us in the first place ... They innocently asked where to go as they were returning empty Jerrycans. They were directed to the field they had been to that a.m.'

On the 22nd November, the Battalion returned to the line. The usual shelling and mortaring from both sides took place. Patrols were sent out. The conditions were appalling. On the 27th, Lieutenant-Colonel Hanmer left the Battalion to take command of the 4th Battalion Royal Welsh Fusiliers. Major G.L. Wood returned from the Battle School to take command. On the 29th of the month, Major Wood was promoted to Lieutenant-Colonel. Lieutenant (QM) E.T.F. Jones was transferred to the 9th Battalion, The Durham Light Infantry. On the 30th November, the Battalion was relieved by the 2nd Battalion The Essex Regiment and, at the same time, completed its last operational task against the Germans in the Second World War. Casualties for the month were: two other ranks killed, six wounded and six missing, all believed to be prisoners of war.

CHAPTER 36
THE RETURN TO ENGLAND
1944 - 1945

Towards the end of November, rumours were circulating that the 50th Division was to return to England. There were very few officers and men left who had been with the Battalion throughout the whole of the war. They had a war record which few, if any, could surpass. From the wild hills of Iraq, the heat of the Desert and Sicily, the bocage of Normandy and the cold, squelching ground of 'The Island', few soldiers had experienced the widely contrasting conditions in which these men had served and fought. As the rumours grew, there is little doubt that most, if not all, were silently crossing their fingers and praying that the violence of their war was coming to an end. The well of courage is not bottomless. The more one draws on it, the less there is available for the next battle. Friends and comrades had succumbed in each action. Would it soon be their turn to fall?

When the news did arrive, it was to the effect that the 50th Division would become a Home Service Division. The Division which had done so much for victory would not, therefore, be in at the final fall of Nazi Germany. It would be broken up. Men who were considered fully trained would be moved to other rifle units. A number of these from 151 Brigade went to the 9th Battalion, The Durham Light Infantry, which was transferred to 131 Brigade, 7th Armoured Division. Men who required further training would receive this then be transferred to other infantry units. Others would return to the United Kingdom with the Battalion and finally, a group of men would remain on in Belgium and Holland on garrison duties. It was expected that those men who had served longest in the Battalion would return to England. Most, indeed, did but a number were retained for

garrison duty, amongst them Sergeants Bert Davies and Tom Russ and a handful of men who had served through all of the campaigns since 1939.

The reason for the withdrawal of the Division was the shortage of well-trained reinforcements for front line units. This had been obvious for some time. Drafts being received by the Division to make up losses during the North West Europe Campaign had included men from non-infantry backgrounds, for example, anti-aircraft units who were not needed as the German air threat diminished. Some of these turned out to be first class infantrymen but others did not take kindly to the infantry role, particularly in the desperate conditions of 'The Island'. There was an urgent need for better training and it was decided that the Division, or more accurately what was left of it, would return to England to train personnel of other arms as infantrymen.

On the 1st December 1944, the Battalion made preparations to move on the first stage of its journey back to England. Five officers and sixty-two other ranks joined the 9th Battalion. At 5.15 p.m. the Battalion moved off to Rousbrugge via Nijmegen - Grave - S'Hertogenbosch - Tilburg, bypassing Antwerp, Coutrai and Ypres. On arrival at Rousbrugge at 1.45 p.m. on the 2nd, the companies were dispersed: 'A' Company to Watou, 'B' and 'S' Companies to Proven, and 'C' Company to Haringe. 'D' Company along with Battalion Headquarters and 'HQ' Company were in Rousbrugge. The Divisional Commander spoke to the officers and men in the school room at Rousbrugge on the 6th December and explained to them why the Division was being broken up and of his sorrow that such a fine unit would not be in

Lieutenant Colonel G.L. Wood, *DSO, MC & Bar (left) and* **Major Ken Wood**, *MC. Two brothers receive their medals at Buckingham Palace*

at the end. On the 8th December, Field Marshal Montgomery visited the Brigade to present ribbons to those who had won awards. He, too, spoke of his regret that he had had to order the Division back to England but that there was much vital work for it to do there. Award winners who had ribbons presented to them were:

Major K.M. Wood	Military Cross.
Lieutenant S. Seggie	Military Cross.
Sergeant J. Swithenbank	Military Medal.
Sergeant W Horrocks	Military Medal.
Lance-Sergeant T. Vaulks	Military Medal.
Lance-Corporal M. Morgan	Military Medal.
Private G. Davison	Military Medal.
Private M. Cambridge	Military Medal.

Lieutenant-Colonel G.L. Wood, DSO, MC, who had served with distinction with the Battalion, had the unenviable task of saying goodbye to many of his officers and men. His farewell message follows:

'The time has now come when all of us must go our separate ways.

'It is a very sad moment for all of us.

'I would like you all to remember in these final days before the Battalion breaks up, certain facts which I consider of great importance.

1. The 6 Battalion has built up during the course of this war, a very fine reputation second to none in the British Army. It has taken part in many battles - It has never failed to get its objective or in any other task which it has been given. This is a very fine record.

2. A Battalion is judged by the behaviour and the achievements of the men in the Battalion. So it is with us and I would like each one of you always to bear in mind that you have played a great part in making this Battalion what it is, and for helping to build its record of War service.

3. Soon many of you will be joining many other regiments for service. When you get there, remember that your behaviour, discipline and smart turnout will reflect on the Battalion. I know that you will all do your best to ensure that your every action will reflect creditably upon this Battalion.

4. Finally, I wish you to remember always that you are an integral part of the 6th The Durham Light Infantry and not to forget your old Battalion.

'In conclusion I wish to thank each one of you for all that you have done for the Battalion. I know you will all realise how extremely sorry I am to lose your services.

'Au Revoir and Good Luck to every one of you.

G.L. Wood

Lieutenant-Colonel.

On the 8th December, two hundred and twenty-one other ranks left for the 9th Battalion The Royal Warwickshire Regiment, Northern Ireland District, for retraining as infantrymen. On the 10th of the month, over three hundred other ranks and seventeen officers were posted to various units. The remainder of the Battalion was formed into one Company. The move to the United Kingdom commenced on the 14th December. The Battalion was taken by truck to Poperinghe Station. It arrived at Ostend at 10.15 a.m. and marched to a transit camp for dinner at 12.15 p.m. At 2.00 p.m. it marched back to the docks, boarded the *Queen Emma* and sailed at 3.00 p.m. The Battalion arrived at Skipton in the West Riding of Yorkshire on the 16th, where meals were provided by the WVS. Among the long serving members of the Battalion who were now back on English soil were: Regimental Quartermaster Sergeant Barnes, Colour Sergeants D. and S. Kitching, Corporal Humble and Private Parkinson. Christmas leave was given for the majority of the Battalion. The remainder went on leave at the New Year. On the 27th December, six Companies were formed. Officers and NCO instructors began to arrive from the Infantry Training Centres up and down the country, many of them veterans who had spent long periods abroad or who were unfit for overseas service. All began to settle in. One officer wrote, 'although the Yorkshire Moors are not ideal places in winter time, at least there are no Spandaus and 88s up there!'

A draft of eight hundred men of the Royal Army Service Corps arrived early in the New Year. These were to be retrained as infantrymen. Some were of excellent quality, others resented their change in status. A number were men who had given the RASC difficulties, were now passed on to the Battalion. They continued to give both civil and military authorities problems. However, the majority settled in well once the training started. Training included the usual subjects: drill, weapon training, bayonet practice, firing on the ranges at Skipton, work on the assault course and so on. Street fighting was practised in Hull. 'Operation Craven' took place during the ten week course. This was an endurance test which entailed a forced march and an assault to secure a bridgehead over the River Wharfe. Intense though the course was, time was found for some football against units in the neighbourhood. Dances were held each week in Skipton Town Hall. Concerts were organised and the kindness of the people of the area was reflected in the many invitations to their homes. Many officers left the Battalion, to be replaced by others. Captains Sandwith and Wedgwood rejoined and Major Reggie Atkinson, MC, the redoubtable commander of 'B' Company, left in March to take up an appointment at the Australian Staff College.

The second course of training commenced in mid-April, 1945. The quality and enthusiasm of the trainees were a great improvement on those in the first draft. They were young soldiers who had already completed their primary training and their behaviour and discipline were very good. By the end of their course, they had completed their street fighting in Newcastle, had been taught about enemy mines and practised assault boating on Garthwaite Reservoir. Swimming instructions had been given in the Skipton Municipal Baths and live ammunition was fired in the Forest of Bowland. News of the end of the war in Europe on the 7th May came with great national excitement. VE Day was celebrated on the 8th May, 1944. The Battalion paraded for a Thanksgiving Service in the Skipton Parish Church and another was held in the open in front of the Town Hall. On the 16th May, two hundred and forty officers and men went to York Minster for a Thanksgiving Service. A few days later, a start was made in clearing away the encumbrances of war when two companies were sent to Tranby Camp near Hull to commence clearing away wire defences on the east coast. In the early summer, a platoon of men of the 50th Division was required for guard duties at the British Army Exhibition in Paris. The 6th Battalion had its representatives in the platoon which set a very high standard of turnout and drill in front of the many thousands of visitors to the Exhibition.

However, the war was not yet ended. An enemy remained in the Far East and men were being drafted to go to that theatre.

These had to be prepared for overseas service. This work did not go on for long. The 15th August was VJ Day and another round of celebration and thanksgiving followed. By now, the Battalion role as a training unit was diminishing as fewer and fewer drafts arrived. Demobilisation commenced, first for those who had served the longest. A great deal of sport filled the final days at Skipton. On the 26th October, 1945, two officers and twenty-five other ranks were part of a Guard of Honour provided by the 6th and 8th Battalions, for Field Marshal Montgomery when he received the Freedom of Huddersfield. Major Ian English, MC, of the 8th Battalion, commanded the Guard. Most of the men were long serving soldiers who had served under the Field Marshal in the Desert, Sicily and North West Europe. On a wet and stormy day, the Field Marshal somehow missed the Mayor of Huddersfield and the welcoming party at the town boundary and arrived ten minutes early and, of course, without his host. The Field Marshal, in good form, proceeded without concern to inspect the Guard of Honour and spoke to many of the men who wore the ribbons of the campaigns in which he had commanded them. He expressed his great pleasure at being with them.

On the 17th October, Lieutenant-Colonel G.L. Wood, DSO, MC, was released and he handed over to Lieutenant-Colonel H.M. Vaux, MC, a regular soldier who had been adjutant to the Battalion for three years prior to 1938. In November, Major K.M. Wood, MC, and Regimental Sergeant-Major Greening were amongst those released. Quartermaster Sergeant Barnes was commissioned as a Quartermaster. Early in the month, Major-General D.M. Wimberley, Director of Infantry, visited the Brigade and gave out the information that the 6th and 8th Battalions would go into suspended animation early in the New Year. Though numbers were small, many men had been released by now, Christmas and New Year celebrations were carried out to the full and those left had a wonderful time. As 1946 dawned, there was little to do but to make final preparations for the end. Many of the barrack rooms were empty. The sound of trampling feet and cheerful voices had gone. On the 16th January, 1946, the camp was closed and the last of the officers and men left. Captain W.E. Short wrote:

'...I was left as the only person in the Battalion and signed the memo to the War Office indicating the Battalion having gone into suspended animation. For me it was the most heart rending moment having served with the finest of men, both officers and ORs during the past three years and I was left with many vivid memories of their loyalty, comradeship and kindness.'

The war was over. The officers and men of the Battalion who had survived had gone their various ways with new challenges to meet, not least those of settling down to civilian life. Some did it quickly, many took much longer but in the end they became civilians again, got work and raised families. They picked up old roots or put down new ones. For those who fell in this war against Nazism, there are the beautifully tended graves in some foreign soil and the memories of them in the hearts and minds of their comrades and families.

CHAPTER 37
PRISONERS OF WAR AND ESCAPEES

This can only be a brief description of prison camp life but it does not lessen the awareness of the courage and suffering of prisoners of war, nor the fact that, even if behind the wire, they continued to have a role to play in the successful prosecution of the two World Wars. A number of men of the 6th Battalion were taken prisoner in both wars and spent the rest of the period, until the enemy capitulated, in prison camps. The conditions of life and the treatment of the prisoners in the wars of 1914-18 and 1939-45, were very similar. As a rule the Germans treated their British prisoners fairly well, certainly within the terms of the Geneva Convention which laid down minimum standards of treatment. The Italians in World War II, ran prison camps which appeared to have varied widely in the treatment of their prisoners. Some as good as the Germans, others where conditions were much harsher. However, in all situations, it was not an easy life and the fact of being confined behind barbed wire for a long period of time had its effects, not only on a man's physical health but his psychological and emotional health also.

Once captured, the treatment of British prisoners in both wars followed the same pattern. The inevitable search of the person and invariable removal of personal items such as binoculars, revolvers, watches and other souvenirs. This was an activity followed by the troops of both sides. With some exceptions, such as the shooting of the Canadians and the two 6th Battalion men at Condé, the treatment of prisoners by those who had captured them was usually good, certainly better than the second line troops to whom they were handed over after the first day or two. There was often an empathy between opposing front line troops in both World Wars who faced the same dangers and fears, which was lacking in second line soldiers. The majority of the latter were made up of older men, those unfit for front line service and very young and inexperienced soldiers. Pushing, a lot of shouting, and the occasional use of the rifle butt were used on prisoners.

The prisoners of both wars faced the long march into captivity, deep into Germany and certainly in the Second World War, into Poland and Czechoslovakia. Little food and water was provided for the first few days. Marching across France, many civilians left buckets of water by the roadside from which the men drank as they shuffled past. Attempts by these people to feed the long columns of hungry and tired men were not encouraged by the guards. Captain Lyon, captured in May, 1918, wrote:

> '...Many of the French peasants try to give us water and food, but are driven off. We find that they are not even allowed to speak to us...'

This was not an uncommon experience of POWs in World War II. Near to the German frontier or just inside the country, the prisoners were usually placed onto trains. The other ranks were in cattle trucks. The long journey to the large reception camps then commenced. Officers had their own camps and were not expected to work. NCOs down to the rank of corporal in their own camps, were not expected to work but could find themselves supervising the lower ranks in their working parties and a number worked alongside these as it helped to break the boredom and kept them fit. From these large camps, men were sent out to smaller working camps. The work could be on farms, down coal mines, on road building or repair and, later as the bombing raids by the Allies increased and reached out deeper into enemy territory, on clearing and repairing bomb damage. Most of the large camps were a collection of wooden huts holding quite large numbers of men, very cold in the winter but warmer in the summer. They were surrounded by wire fences with watch towers and a guard room at the main gate. The working camps depended on where the work took place. They ranged from a barn or empty storehouse or hut on a farm, to substantial accommodation for workers at large coal mines. The camps were occasionally visited by representatives of the Red Cross to ensure that the camps retained minimum standards of care and accommodation.

Food remained poor in the camps with a repetitive and boring diet. Bartering quickly became an important activity in all camps. The exchange of cigarettes, chocolate and soap from Red Cross parcels for eggs and other delicacies took place between the prisoners and local civilians and even some of the guards. The receipt of Red Cross parcels, once they began to arrive at the camps, was a keenly anticipated event. The contents supplemented the boring diet and did much to retain a basic standard of health amongst the prisoners. The Red Cross also supplied musical instruments, games equipment, books and even educational and training courses for men who wished to obtain some qualification for a career after the war. Men played football and other sports. 'International' games were held between the various country representatives. Concerts were organised to which even the guards could be invited. Talks and lectures were arranged and given by men who had specialist knowledge and skills. Many and varied were the activities organised to try to keep monotony at bay.

It was the duty of every soldier to try to escape, if possible. Many did so in both wars, though most were only free for a very short time. A few got away and escaped into neutral countries such as Holland (neutral in WWI), Russia (neutral until her entry into the war in 1941), Sweden, Switzerland and Spain. They found their way back to the United Kingdom, some to continue the fight in the forces. Any escapee, for whatever period of time he was free, was a nuisance to the enemy and tied down enemy troops in the search. Men of the 6th Battalion were amongst those who sought to escape and return to England. A handful succeeded. Due to lack of space only one or two can be mentioned here but they represent those of the Battalion who made the effort. This, in no way, is being critical of the majority who did not try to escape. In every way possible they supported those who did make the attempt. It must be remembered that many of the other ranks camps were located in Poland and Czechoslovakia, hundreds of miles from a neutral country and many deemed it impossible to succeed in any attempt to escape to freedom. However, prisoners in these camps did create problems for the Germans by escaping for short periods of time.

Corporal Tommy Jarvis, of the 6th Battalion, for example, was captured at Mersa Matruh in June, 1942. He was a prisoner of war in camps in Sicily and Northern Italy before he escaped and joined the partisans with whom he stayed until the Americans arrived in 1945. He took part in a number of partisan raids against the enemy. Lieutenant W. Wiggins was captured on the 29th June, 1942 and imprisoned in Italy. He escaped and returned home in November, 1943 and joined the 9th Battalion The Durham Light Infantry, in which he served until the end of the war. Captain R. Bousfield was captured near Tilly-sur-Seulles on the 16th June, 1944. He was wounded after capture by a machine-gun of the attacking British forces and ultimately moved back to the Stalag Hospital at Rennes. He escaped by hiding in bushes in the medical compound and then in the air raid shelter in the camp itself whilst the Germans searched the huts and outside the camp. He, with two other officers of another regiment, moved into the middle of the camp to hide and remained there until American forces arrived on the 4th August.

The amazing escape of Corporal Jack Horsman of Howden-le-Wear, County Durham, must be told. He was with a party which reached Boulogne in late May, 1940. He and his party of officers and men from a number of units were cut off in the Marine Station in the harbour. Corporal Horsman volunteered to swim down the harbour basin out to sea and try to reach the beach north of the town in the hope of contacting any British units there who could break through to the trapped party. He did this, swimming a distance of over two miles to reach the beach close to the wireless station. The wireless station proved to be occupied by the Germans and there were no signs of British troops. On making his way to the North Pier, he met a French Marine who was very much drunk at the time. On sobering up, the two men played cat and mouse with the Germans in the Old Town area of Boulogne. This lasted for a number of days as they eked out an existence as best they could on food found in damaged shops and bins. On parting company with his French friend, Horsman bumped into a captured British ambulance unit run by Captain Heslop, 6th Battalion's Medical officer. Captain Heslop was successful in passing off the Corporal as a member of his unit and for the next week Horsman helped to bury the dead and to look after the wounded of both sides. At the end of the week, he and others of the unit were moved to Camiers, south of Boulogne, whilst Captain Heslop was sent to Lille. Now, without his protector and in a medical unit commanded by a very suspicious Major who doubted his credentials, the Corporal decided to leave. Dressed in German fatigue clothes he walked past the guards and headed in the direction of St. Omer and the area he had been stationed in prior to the German invasion on the 10th May. He succeeded in walking into the very village he had been stationed in and the kindly French people who recognised him took their 'le corporal Jack' under their protection.

Dressed in civilian clothes, he worked openly amongst the French people of the village. In the café, he actually served German soldiers, who gave him tips. One German who guessed he was English, challenged him, to which Horsman replied that he came from Ireland. This satisfied the German, for he laughed and gave him a packet of cigarettes. After three weeks, the intrepid Corporal set off to try to reach Marseilles and, hopefully, get on a boat to take him to safety. His village friends were reluctant to see him go but gave him as much assistance and advice they could. They helped him to plan his route via Rouen, Evreux and Chartres and gave him one hundred and fifty francs. He was warned to stay clear of the French Police, especially the Gardes Mobile, who were already co-operating with the Germans. Over the next few weeks, a special prayer was said for him in the vilage church. No name was mentioned only a prayer

to 'our friend who has just left us and who is facing many dangers.' Dressed as a French workman, Corporal Horsman set out on his long and remarkable journey. He moved through St, Omer and Amiens. At a village, two German sergeants hired him to drive them to Rouen to deliver the British army truck they had with them, for which they agreed to pay him fifty francs. He was able to satisfy the Germans that he came from Northern France, hence his particular accent. He swam the river outside Rouen and passed through Louviers towards Evreux. Almost exhausted and with his feet badly swollen, he hid in an abandoned cottage for a number of days. He moved on to Evreux and joined a French working party, clearing up and burying the dead. A friendly Frenchman advised him to head for Spain as he was unlikely to get a boat at Marseilles.

He took a train to Limoges. His fellow passengers in his carriage were all Belgians. They spotted his accent and recognised him as English. They did not give him away and the Corporal reached Toulouse and then Marseilles. Here he got into a fight with three drunken French sailors and was arrested by the police and placed in a dungeon near the Old Port. He now found himself in the French Foreign Legion and teaching eight recruits British arms drill. He escaped, after a few days of this, with a young Scottish boy called Billy Brown and headed for Spain. They got into this country but at the village of Agullana, were arrested by the Fascist Police. While in Spanish hands, he was treated in an appalling manner. He was severely beaten by his warders day after day. He tried to escape and received more beatings for his pains. The food was very poor and his health deteriorated alarmingly. Finally, transferred to a prison in Madrid, a Spanish Officer of Republican sympathies got a message to the British Embassy and Horsman and his fellow Britons, who included Lord Cardigan, a Second-Lieutenant in the RASC, were freed and sent home. Corporal Horsman ultimately joined the 16th Battalion The Durham Light Infantry but it appears that he did not go abroad with this Battalion.

Of all of the men who returned home at the end of both wars, those who had experienced a long confinement - about five years for example for those taken prisoner in May/June 1940 - found it most difficult to settle down to civilian life. There was no counselling, which is available today. The prison camps left a long term scar on many men but, with few exceptions, they had conducted themselves throughout their long confinement in such a way as to be a credit to themselves and their Regiment.

CHAPTER 38
THE LAST CHAPTER
1945 - 1968

The 50th (Northumbrian) Division was re-formed as part of the Territorial Army in 1947. The Regimental Battalions which formed the Division came from: The Durham Light Infantry, The Royal Northumberland Fusiliers, The King's Own Yorkshire Light Infantry, The Yorkshire Regiment (Green Howards), The East Yorkshire Regiment, The West Yorkshire Regiment and the Duke of Wellington's Regiment. The Northumberland Hussars formed an armoured car element for reconnaissance purposes. The Royal Artillery element was drawn from Newcastle, South Shields, Darlington, Scarborough and Sheffield. The Divisional Signals and Royal Army Service Corps were at Darlington. The Royal Army Ordnance Corps and Royal Electrical and Mechanical Engineers were based on Middlesbrough. Divisional Headquarters was at Darlington.

There was some debate as to whether the 6th or the 9th Battalion, The Durham Light Infantry, should become part of the Parachute Regiment. It was finally decided that the 9th Battalion should make the change and they became the 17th Battalion, The Parachute Regiment (9 DLI). Recruitment to the 6th Battalion commenced on the 1st April, 1947. Posters and articles appeared in the local newspapers in the recruiting area along with letters signed by the new Commanding Officer, Lieutenant-Colonel W.I. Watson, appealing for men to come forward and join the Battalion. Lieutenant-Colonel Bill Watson was assuming command of the Battalion for the second time. The first Adjutant was Captain R.J. Hyde-Thompson, MC, who had served with the 1st Battalion The Durham Light Infantry during the recent war. The Quartermaster was Captain J.W. Runciman (QM), who had

also served with the Battalion during the war. The Regimental Sergeant-Major was RSM Rafferty. Many pre-war and wartime members were amongst the first recruits. Headquarters was established at the Drill Hall, Union Street, Bishop Auckland. The companies were located as follows: Battalion Headquarters, 'HQ' Company, 'A' Company and 'S' Company (Medium machine-guns, Anti-Tank Guns and 3in. Mortars) at Bishop Auckland. 'B' Company was at Barnard Castle, Birch Street Drill Hall. 'C' Company was at the Badcock Drill Hall, Spennymoor and 'D' Company at the Vane Armoury, Crook. By the end of the year the strength of the Battalion was nine officers and one hundred and thirty-one other ranks. The men were largely drawn from industrial and commercial employment in the area, such as: miners, factory workers, farm workers and office workers. Many of the officers were school teachers and sales representatives with, increasingly from 1948 to 1963, those who had completed their National Service and joined the Territorials. In the last years of its existence the Battalion had to select and train its own officers.

The highlight of each year from 1947-1967 was the fortnight's annual camp. The following is a list of the camps held during this period:

1947	Boulmer Airfield, Northumberland.
1948	Farnley Park, Otley.
1949	Stobs Camp, Hawick.
1950	Bodney Camp, Norfolk.
1951	East Wretham, Norfolk.

1952	Westwick Camp. Barnard Castle.
1953	Tilshead Lodge Camp, Salisbury Plain.
1954	Fylingsdale Camp, near Scarborough.
1955	Windmill Hill, Tidworth.
1956	Fylingsdale Camp, near Scarborough.
1957	Ollerton, near Nottingham.
1958	Otterburn Camp, Northumberland.
1959	Borrey Camp, near Carnoustie.
1960	Bodney Camp, Norfolk.
1961	Borrey/Buddon, near Carnoustie.
1962	Millom, Barrow in Furnace.
1963	Garelochmead, north of Glasgow.
1964	Sennybridge, South Wales.
1965	Devizes, Wiltshire.
1966	Bodney Camp, Norfolk.

Major General Lord Thurlow, *Commanding Officer Northumbrian District 50 Division (TA) meets miner Tom Harrison, a sergeant in the Battalion. The strong mining connection continued after the Second World War until the decline of the mining industry in the County affected recruitment from this source*

The camps from and including 1962, were increasingly concerned in training the Battalion for its role in support of the civil power. Civil defence, fire fighting and first aid training took place, skills required if a nuclear attack took place. The activities at annual camp were based on the lessons of the recent war, with manoeuvres in various types of countryside, initiative courses, mobile and crossing water obstacle exercises. Camouflage of men and positions was carried out and courses for the specialist platoons and sections were organised. There were undoubtedly, greater and more demanding training programmes than those carried out before the war. However, the Territorials went back to the end of the queue when it came to equiping with up-to-date weapons and materials. The .303 rifle remained with the Battalion for some years. On average, it took up to three years for new equipment and materials to arrive.

The challenge which Lieutenant-Colonel Watson and his staff faced in 1947, was a difficult one. The success of the Battalion in the future, depended on how successful they were in recruiting the best type of recruit and officer and on laying down the foundations of a well run unit. It was a very busy time.

Fortunately, officers and men of experience and quality became available in the years following the end of the war and the Battalion soon began to make its mark.

Captain W. Alder joined in February, 1948, after seeing service with the 1st Battalion of the Regiment in Greece. He was to become the last of the Lieutenant-Colonels to command the Battalion. Lieutenant G.C. Bartram, a future Second-in-Command, joined from the 1st Battalion and Greece in September. Captain (QM) T.H. Bewick, MBE, who had seen service with the 2nd DLI in Burma and Malaya, replaced Captain (QM) Runciman in November.

The impressive record of the Battalion on the shooting ranges began with the selection of Company Quartermaster Sergeant A.E. Williams who in February, was selected for the Army .22 Rifle Team. In May of this year, 'Exercise Fencible' was held in Northumberland. This was an amphibious exercise for 151 Brigade. The following represented the Battalion at the Territorial Army shooting championships held at Bisley in July:

Captain Patullo	Sergeant Brown
Company Sergeant-Major Loyn	Sergeant Pears
Colour Sergeant Williams	Lance-Corporal Conlon
Sergeant Alderson	Lance-Corporal White
Private Rymer	

On the 31st October, 1948, three officers and twenty-five other ranks, under the command of Lieutenant-Colonel Watson, took part in the Territorial Army Review held at Hyde Park before His Majesty The King and Field Marshal Montgomery. The Battalion strength at the end of the year was fourteen officers and one hundred and ninety-seven other ranks.

The movement of people in and out of the Battalion continued in 1949. Captain R.A.G. Birchenough, MC, succeeded Captain Hyde-Thompson as Adjutant in March. Captain Lockington and Lieutenants Phillips and Sampson joined in the same month, being posted to 'HQ', 'C' and 'D' Companies respectively. Major Reggie Atkinson, MC, of 'B' Company fame, joined as Second-in-Command in July. In the same month Major O.H. Pearson MBE, succeeded Captain Bewick, MBE, as Quartermaster. The Battalion football team was defeated by the 50th Division Column RASC in the final of the Divisional Cup: 6th DLI 1 RASC 3. In the Brigade Rifle Meeting at Whitburn, Sergeant Kitchen won the rifle competition and Lieutenant F. Phillips was best shot with the light machine-gun. Battalion strength at the end of the year was sixteen officers and two hundred and twenty-two other ranks.

The main event of 1950, was the long argument with the War Office over the uniform to be worn by Light Infantry units. Changes were announced in the Territorial Army in July, 1950. After completing their eighteen months, all National Servicemen would spend three years in the Territorial Army Supplementary Reserve. The War Office pressed for all Territorial Battalions to wear No. 1 Dress of the same colour as that worn by the Regular Battalion of their Regiment. The Battalion became very close to losing its black badge and buttons and rifle green uniform. The Honorary Colonel, The Rt. Hon The Lord Barnard, CMG, MC, TD, DL, supported by Lieutenant-Colonel Bill Watson took on the War Office. The following is part of a letter dated the 26th July, written to the War Office by Lord Barnard:

'1. I understand that it has been agreed in principal that when No. Dress is issued at some future date to T.A. Battalions, they are to wear No. 1 Dress authorised for the Regular Battalion of the Regiment.

2. It is perhaps not realised that this Battalion, and possibly other T.A. Battalions which were originally Rifle Volunteer Regiments, has never worn the uniform of the County Regiment. This Battalion has worn the uniform, except for minor details, of the King's Rifle Corps, that is green with red facings...

5...a very direct association with the old Durham Rifle Volunteers, who were the true forbears of this Battalion, can be closely traced, and a link such as this which has been built up over so many years naturally holds a very high place in this district and is one that should never be broken.

6. This very unique distinction has always had a great influence on the esprit de corps within the Battalion, particularly as the NCOs wear distinctive chevrons, and one that is held with highest regard by all ranks.

7. It is a distinction which helps to foster and maintain the spirit of volunteer service which, in all truth, was the greatest asset of the Volunteers.

8. I believe that this privilege is shared with a few other Battalions in the Territorial Army.

9. The wearing of a distinctive uniform in no way lessens the loyalty of all members of the Battalion to the Regiment, for clearly the origin of the privilege is an added incentive...

11...In view of the tradition attached to the wearing of this green uniform, a decision that this Battalion is now to change its complete uniform to that of The Durham Light Infantry would override this tradition which I consider, for the reasons set out above, extremely important. I am not, therefore, prepared to accept any such decision...'

In December, the War Office gave way and permission was given to retain the traditional uniform.

Major Maurice Kirby, rejoined the Battalion in April, 1950 and Captain (QM) John Jones replaced Major Pearson as Quartermaster. RQMS Andell retired after thirty years service with the Battalion. Majors A.D. Scotson and J. Widdas were awarded the Territorial Decoration in June. Major Reggie

Atkinson, MC, moved on to Headquarters, 50th Division. In December, Lieutenant-Colonel Watson relinquished command and was succeeded by Lieutenant-Colonel Lyster Todd, OBE. From this time onwards, each Territorial Army Battalion had either a regular CO, of a Training Major and regular staff of an Adjutant, Quartermaster, Regimental Sergeant-Major and one Warrant Officer Instructor for each company.

In July, Major Maurice Kirby commanded a party of two officers and sixty men who paraded for the laying up of the old colours of the 1st and 2nd Battalions of the Regiment and the dedication of the DLI Memorial Garden. Strength at the end of the year was sixteen officers and two hundred and fifty other ranks.

In January, 1951, Captain Birchenough was succeeded as Adjutant by Captain P.L. Rome MC, formerly 2nd Battalion. Regimental Sergeant-Major E. Thomasson was replaced by Regimental Sergeant-Major H. Thompson who had served with the 1st Battalion. The following month, Major Kirby was appointed Second-in-Command. The Battalion reached the Semi-Final of the Territorial Army Cup only to experience defeat at the hands of 471 (M) HAA. The score was 6th Battalion 2,471 (M) HAA 5. It reached the final of the 50th Division Football Competition, where it lost 2 - 1 to the 7th Battalion RNF. The TA Cross Country Championship was won in March. Lieutenant G.C. Bartram was the individual winner. It was second in April, 1952, when Lieutenant Bartram came in fourth. The Battalion's success on the sporting field was to continue in the years to come.

The 1951 camp saw the first of the 'Z' Reservists arrive to be incorporated into the Battalion for the fortnight's training. Its strength soared to over eleven hundred men but it took only twenty-four hours to get over the teething problems such an influx brought. Lieutenant-Colonel Lyster Todd, a regular officer who had succeeded Lieutenant-Colonel Watson in command of the Battalion wrote:

'...Our problem was to accept, kit out, train and keep in good spirits about 800 'Z' Reservists, who for some reason the Politicians had decided it was necessary for them to undergo fourteen days training. Our not very strong TA volunteer

element, bolstered up by National Servicemen doing their annual training, reacted magnificently and we had a most successful camp...'

In the January of 1952, Sergeant Majors Whittingham and Sykes joined the permanent staff, both came from the 1st Battalion. Exercise 'Forewarned' was held in May at Humbleton Camp, Northumberland. This was a mobile exercise organised by Northern Command.

1953 was a very busy year. It was Coronation Year and between February and May, rehearsals went on apace to prepare the Battalion party for its involvement in this event. The Procession Party comprised: Captain Alder, Regimental Sergeant-Major Thompson, Sergeant Gray, MM, Lance-Corporal Dinsley and Lance-Corporal Morgan. The street lining party was: Captain F. Phillips, Colour Sergeant Singlewood, Bugle Major Fallon, Sergeant Atkinson, Corporals Dixon, Dunn, Bradwell and Pennick, Lance-Corporals Swanston and Garrett, Privates Harle, Campbell, French, Hilary, Penna, Pirt, Young, Walker and Grayson. Superbly turned out, these officers, NCOs and men represented the Battalion at the Queen's Coronation in London In June. On the 14th January, Field Marshal Montgomery received the Freedom of the City of Durham. In his speech he made the following remarks about the Division:

'The 50th Division was the veteran fighting infantry division of the war; they did more fighting than any other infantry division ... I never knew the 50th Division fail to do anything I asked them to do and the men from the North of England were the hard-core of the division.'

The progress made by the Battalion was described by Lieutenant-Colonel Lyster Todd when writing about the 1953 camp:

'The third annual camp was on Salisbury Plain. The training area included a deserted village which enabled us to practice house clearing and attacking a built up area, as opposed to ordinary open country warfare. At the end of this camp the Battalion, which consisted of several good middle rank officers, some excellent junior officers, a first class NCOs and Sgts' Mess, many reliable National Servicemen, and above all superb TA volunteers, was in my opinion as good a fighting force as any regular Battalion.'

Coronation Party, *1953*

In August, Captain Rome was succeeded as Adjutant by Captain J.J. Percy. At the end of the year, Lieutenant-Colonel Lyster Todd was succeeded by Lieutenant-Colonel C.R.W. Norman, OBE, from the 1st Battalion where he was Second-in-Command. The highlight of the annual camp at Tilshead Lodge Camp, was the visit of the Chief of the Imperial General Staff, General Sir John Harding. The score in the 50th Divisional Football Competition final was 6th Battalion 1 7th Battalion RNF 3. However this disappointment was offset by the success of the Medium machine-gun Team which won the Northern Command

MMG Shooting Cup.

In October 1954, the Battalion formed the street lining party at Cleadon, on the visit of Her Majesty The Queen to the Sunderland area. It was defeated yet again in the final of the Divisional Football Competition. The score was 6th Battalion 2, 8th Battalion 4. The MMG Team won the Territorial Army Rifle Association Cup and the Northern Command Cup in January, 1955. Captain Percy was succeeded as Adjutant by Captain J.B. Thomkinson, MBE and Regimental Sergeant-Major C.H.J. Gibbens, MBE, replaced Regimental Sergeant-Major Thompson.

More ceremony followed in 1956. In June, Captain Alder commanded the street lining party in Stockton for the visit of the Queen and Duke of Edinburgh to that town. In November, the MMG Platoon provided the street lining party for the Queen Mother's visit to Barnard Castle. The Battalion provided the escort to the laying up of the colours of the 3rd and 4th Militia Battalions of the Regiment at Barnard Castle. Work started on the new Drill Hall at South Road, Bishop Auckland. The Eden Armoury, as it was called, replaced the old Battalion Headquarters in Union Street. This year saw the emergence of a remarkable rifleman. Lance-Corporal Jack Meynell of Barnard Castle, was third in the Queen's Medal Competition at Bisley. He was soon to make an even greater mark in the future. Lieutenant-Colonel Norman was succeeded by Lieutenant-Colonel R.B. Humphreys who came over from the 1st Battalion. Annual inspections of Territorial Army Battalions were carried out. The report by the inspector, Brigadier R.G.W. Melsome, for 1956 was typical:

'I am satisfied with the training of this Battalion. All exercises are well organised and attended. This is a very well administered unit in every way. Great care and keenness is taken by everyone to see a high standard is reached and maintained. There is a fine team spirit.'

Lieutenant Colonel C.R.W. Norman, *OBE, with members of the Sergeants' Mess, Scarborough Camp, 1954*

Lieutenant Colonel C.R.W. Norman, *OBE, with his officers, 1955*

The structure of the Battalion which prevailed until 1966 was:

Battalion Headquarters - including Band and Bugles - 'HQ' Company, 'A' Company at the Eden Armoury, Bishop Auckland.

'B' Company at the Larchfield Street Drill Hall, Darlington.

'C' Company at the Badcock Armoury, Spennymoor.

'D' Company at the Vane Road Armoury, Crook.

'S' Company at the Birch Street Drill Hall, Barnard Castle.

The highlight of 1957, was the success of Lance-Corporal Meynell in winning the Queen's Medal at Bisley. It was another Barnard Castle Volunteer, Edward Ross of Whorlton, who won the first Queen's Medal in 1860. Captain J.A.G. Arnot became Adjutant in August. On the 24th December, it was officially announced that Her Royal Highness The Princess Alexandra of Kent was to be the new Colonel of The Durham Light Infantry. This was the beginning of a very close relationship of Her Royal Highness with the Regiment which lasts till today.

The strength of the Battalion reached twenty-five officers and four hundred and thirty other ranks in 1958. It was the bicentenary year in the Regiment's history and was marked by a parade before HRH Princess Alexandra. Held at Brancepeth on the 17th May, one hundred and nine men of all ranks represented the Battalion. A Mobilization Exercise took place between January and May. Another defeat was experienced in the final of the Divisional Football Competition, again at the hands of those old adversaries the 7th Battalion RNF.

The Battalion held a farewell parade at the 1959 camp at Borrey, for Colonel T.H. Miller TD, DL, who retired as Honorary Colonel, a position he had held since 1953. Colonel Miller had commanded the Battalion from 1934 to 1940 and had also served with it in the 1914-18 War. He was succeeded as Honorary Colonel by Colonel W.I. Watson TD, DL.

The new Commanding Officer appointed in 1960 was Lieutenant-Colonel J.W. Kelley. On the 27th May, HRH The

Machine Gun Section, *runners up in the TA Medium Machine Gun Competition, 1957*

Queen and the Duke of Edinburgh visited Newton Aycliffe and the Battalion mounted a Guard of Honour under Major G.W. Lear, with Captain D.L. Bowron and Lieutenant R. Barrass. On the 29th July, a detachment paraded at Bowes Museum on the occasion of the visit of the French Ambassador His Excellency M. Chauvell. A Battle Efficiency Exercise was held at Catterick on the 10th July. It entailed crossing water and infantry obstacles, firing platoon weapons, moving across country by day and at night, patrolling and endurance marching. Corporal Davis of 'A' Company broke three ribs when he fell off an assault course obstacle. The MMG Platoon continued its successes in the TARA Cup which it again won. Final scores were as follows:

1st Team 195 score Winners

3rd team 142 score Sixth

4th Team 127 score Ninth

2nd Team 120 score Tenth

At the end of 1961, Lieutenant-Colonel R.E.G. Scott MBE, MC, became the new Commanding Officer. Major G.C. Bartram succeeded Major A.D. Scotson as Second-in-Command. Regimental Sergeant-Major Hey, MM, replaced Regimental Sergeant-Major I.J. McDowall. It was a highly successful year for the Battalion's various sporting teams. The boxing team, under Major R.E. Marsden, beat the 4/7th Dragoon Guards by ten bouts to one. Privates J. Short and I.R. Lowther represented the North of England against Scotland in an amateur boxing competition. The team won the 50th Division Boxing Competition and eight members fought in the TA finals. Private Lowther became the TA Light Heavyweight Champion at these finals. Private Thatcher was third in the Northern Command Cross Country Competition. The football team, at last, beat the 7th Battalion RNF to win the Divisional Competition. The greatest success on the football field was victory in the Territorial Army Cup Final. The score was: 6th Battalion 3 4/6th Royal Berkshire Regiment 1, so emulating the successes in this competition prior to WWII. The Battalion beat the 4th Royal Welch Fusiliers by four goals to one, in the final of this competition in 1962. In July of this year, Sergeant Meynell shot against the Regular Army at Bisley and attained the highest score in the Light machine-gun Competition.

An intense recruiting campaign was initiated in February, 1963 and fifty new members joined the Battalion. Major C.W. Alder succeeded Major G.C. Bartram as Second-in-Command. A party from the Battalion went to Norway for ski training. In the final of the TA Football Cup the Battalion lost to the 4th Battalion Royal

Corporal Jack Meynell *won the Queen's Medal in 1957*

Welch by two goals to one. The Battalion team was:

Goal:	Craftsman R. Robinson (REME)
Right Back:	Private T. Furness
Left Back;	Corporal Clarey (Capt.)
Right Half;	Private G. Peareth
Centre Half:	Private T. Whitfield
Left Half:	Corporal B. Lee
Outside Right:	Private F. Raw
Inside Right:	Private G. Thatcher
Centre Forward:	Private G. Brown
Inside Left:	Lance-Corporal G. Brewis
Outside Left:	Private J. Naylor
Reserves:	Privates G. Robinson and T. Brown.

In 1964, Lieutenant-Colonel D.J. Fenner became Commanding Officer. Sergeant Jack Meynell won the Queen's Medal at Bisley for the second time. He was only the fourth man in the history of the competition to win it on two occasions. He also won the Earl of Scarborough Cup, the TA Jubilee Cup and five medals. In the competition he used the new 7.62 self-loading rifle. He scored three hundred and thirty-five out of four hundred points and won by twenty-one points. In April, Corporal Mills became the Army Flyweight Boxing Champion. A party under Major F. Phillips went to Holland to take part in the Nijmegen Marches. A four day gruelling marching event, it was held annually and attracted ten thousand entrants including civilians and children. All of the men completed the course, which seems to have been the object of the exercise.

1966 was the year of the National Defence Review which led to the amalgamation of the 6th and 8th Battalions the following year. Major F. Phillips was the new Second-in-Command and in

September, Lieutenant-Colonel David Fenner was succeeded by Lieutenant-Colonel C.W. Alder. On leaving the Battalion, Lieutenant-Colonel Fenner received a letter from Brigadier A.E. Holt who was in command of the 151 Brigade. In it the Brigadier stated:

> '...Each year I have told the Divisional Commander that in my view 6 DLI was fit to undertake any role in an emergency with very little further collective training after embodiment.'

Her Majesty The Queen *inspects the Guard of Honour on her visit to Newton Aycliffe in 1960*

At the annual camp held at Bodney, Norfolk, from the 14th to the 27th May, 'A' and 'D' Companies and 'C' and 'B' Companies were amalgamated as part of the reductions in size taking place

Relaxed group of officers in No.1 Dress. Garelochhead Camp, 1963

due to the run-down. In August, a party of twenty-one had two weeks with the Royal Sussex Regiment at Sennelager, Germany. During this period, the group were able to use the most modern equipment available to the infantry, including the AFV 432 armoured personnel carrier. As the year ran its course, the disbandment of the 6th Battalion as an individual unit approached. Almost one hundred and ten years of Volunteer and Territorial service was about to end. On the 26th February, 1967, the 6th/8th Battalion Amalgamation Parade was held on the College Green, Durham City. A local newspaper carried the headline; 'Twin Excellence Merge In DLI Farewell And Hail At Durham.' The 'Hail' was not to last for long for the amalgamated Battalion was disbanded the following year.

Regimental Police *at the last camp at Bodney, Norfolk, 1966. Sergeant Dixon, Lance Corporal French and Corporal Holmes*

On the second Sunday of September of each year The Durham Light Infantry Association holds its annual reunion at Durham Cathedral, followed by a lunch, usually at Bede College. Survivors of all of the Battalions of the Regiment attend. Amongst them, are those of the 6th Battalion The Durham Light Infantry. The Burma Band and Bugles play at a somewhat slower

Men of the Battalion leave for Germany, 1965

pace now as the veterans march into the Cathedral for their annual service. They include men who joined the Battalion as Territorials between the wars, the conscripted of the Second

A unique group of former commanding officers of the Battalion covering the period WWI to 1968, left to right: Lieutenant Colonel F. Walton, MC, TD, DL, Lieutenant Colonel H. Miller, TD, DL, Brigadier P.J. Jeffreys, DSO, OBE, DL, Lieutenant Colonel W.I. Watson, OBE, TD, DL, Lieutenant Colonel G.L. Wood, DSO, OBE, MC, TD, DL, Lieutenant Colonel G.K. Lyster Todd, OBE, Lieutenant Colonel C.R.W. Norman, OBE, Lieutenant Colonel R. Humphreys,DL, Lieutenant Colonel C.W. Alder, TD.

The Band and Bugles lead the Battalion on its final parade, 1967

World War and those who joined after the war. As they are inspected by the Lord Lieutenant, their pride in Battalion and Regiment is clearly seen. Many of them wear the medals of World War II and the Territorial Decoration for years of loyal service. They inherited the Volunteers motto, 'Defence Not Defiance' and in two World Wars added to it 'Courage and Victor..' They are truly, 'The Faithful Sixth'.

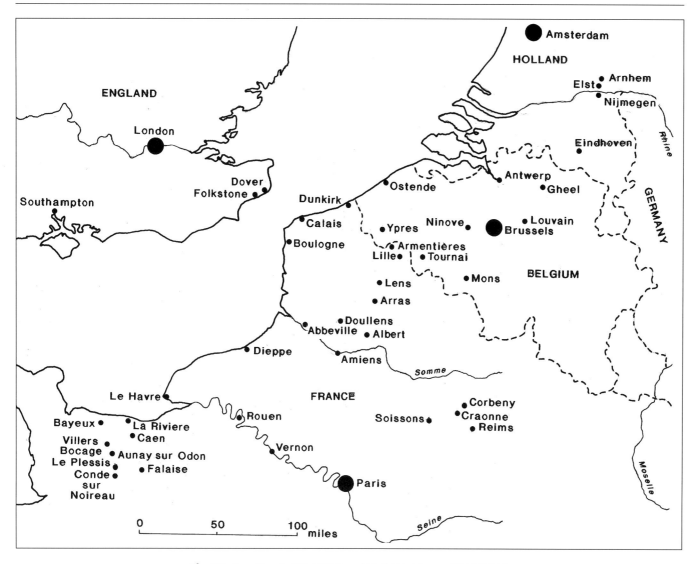

The Western Front, 1914-1918, and North West Europe, 1944/1945

BIBLIOGRAPHY

Archives of The Durham Light Infantry Regimental Museum:

The Watson Papers

Lieutenant-Colonel W.I. Watson's Unpublished Manuscript

The Diary of Captain P.B.H. Lyon MC

Whizz Bang 6th Battalion Trench Magazine - World War I

Northern Volunteers: Their Rise and Progress: *George Ogilvie, !888.*

A Few Notes on the 6th Battalion DLI: *W.L. Vane, 1910*

The Regimental Journal of The Durham Light Infantry

6 DLI Digest of Papers. 1947-1967.

The Story of the Sixth Battalion The Durham Light Infantry From April, 1915 to November, 1918: *Captain R.B.Ainsworth MC. 1919*

A Short History of the Sixth Battalion The Durham Light Infantry: *W.I. Watson.*

The Durham Light Infantry: *Lieutenant E.W. Short.*

The Eighth Battalion The Durham Light Infantry 1793 - 1926: *Major E.H. Veitch, MC.*

A History of the 50th Division: *E. Wyrall, 1939*

The DLI At War: *David Rissick., 1952*

Faithful: The Story of the DLI *S.G.P. Ward.*

Into Battle With The Durhams: *Majors I. English and P. Lewis. 1990*

The Story Of One Green Howard In The Dunkirk Campaign: Green Howard's Gazette, 1966: *Gen. Sir Harold E. Franklyn KCB, DSO, MC.*

The Path of the 50th: *Major Ewart W. Clay MBE, 1950*

The Journal of the Old Comrades Association: 6th Battalion DLI

The Shadow of Vimy Ridge: *Major K. Macksey, MC.*

Operation Victory: *Major Gen. Sir Francis de Guingand KBE, CB, DSO, 1947*

Overlord - 'D' Day and the Battle for Normandy: *Max Hastings, 1984*

Military Operations France and Belgium, 1915, 1916, 1917

History of The Second World War: *HMSO*

The Age of Reform 1815-1870: *Sir Llewellyn Woodward. OUP*

Riflemen Form: *F.W. Beckett ,1982*

The Territorial Battalions - A Pictorial History 1895 - 1985: *Ray Westlake 1986*

War Diaries 6th Battalion DLI, WWI & WWII: *Public Records Office*

HONOURS AND AWARDS

WORLD WAR I

DISTINGUISHED SERVICE ORDER:

Lieutenant-Colonel T.B. Heslop.
Lieutenant-Colonel J.W. Jeffreys.
Captain J.F.G. Aubin.

MILITARY CROSS:

Lieutenant-Colonel F. Walton.
Captain J.F.G. Aubin.
Captain R.B. Ainsworth.
Captain A.N. Brown.
Captain G.E. Cardew
Captain A.B. Hare.
Captain R.S. Johnson.
Captain P.H.B. Lyon.
Captain T. Rushworth.
Captain H. Walton.
Captain T. Welch.
Captain R.H. Wharrier.
Captain (QM) W.M. Hope
Lieutenant G.R. Angus.
Lieutenant H.T. Bircham.
Lieutenant W.P. Gill.
Lieutenant B.J. Harvey.
Second-Lieutenant R.A. Wilson.
Second-Lieutenant J. Woodhead.
Regimental Sergeant-Major J. Taylor.
Acting Regimental Sergeant-Major T. Sordy.

BAR TO THE MILITARY CROSS:

Captain J.F.G. Aubin
Acting Regimental Sergeant-Major T. Sordy

CRIOX DE GUERRE:

Company Sergeant-Major T. Sordy.
Colour Sergeant B. Neiled.
Corporal S.J. Betts.
Lance-Corporal J.J. Robinson

DISTINGUISHED CONDUCT MEDAL:

Company Sergeant-Major P. Finn.
Company Sergeant-Major H. McNair.
Company Sergeant-Major G. Perry.
Sergeant H. Henderson.
Sergeant S. Maddison.
Sergeant J. Malpass.
Sergeant C. Welsh.
Corporal J. Greenwood.
Lance-Corporal J.J. Robinson. Croix De Guerre.
Private F. Davies.

MILITARY MEDAL:

Sergeant R. Bell.
Sergeant A. Bowran.
Sergeant F.M. Britton.
Sergeant J.J. Cooke.
Sergeant T.C. Fairless.
Sergeant P. Finn.
Sergeant W. Gibson.

Sergeant R. Hall.
Sergeant R. Hancock.
Sergeant E. Horsfield.
Sergeant E. Huggins.
Sergeant J. Malone.
Sergeant C. Malpass.
Sergeant N. Sayers.
Sergeant W.R. Smith.
Sergeant A.L. Walters.
Sergeant J. Younger.
Lance Sergeant T.W. Simpson.
Corporal S.J. Betts.
Corporal J. Dixon.
Corporal T.D. Hann.
Corporal G. McKay.
Lance-Corporal J. Armstrong.
Lance-Corporal C.C. Bonner.
Lance-Corporal H. Cruddace.
Lance-Corporal H. Ellis.
Lance-Corporal H. Gartland.
Lance-Corporal H. Golightly.
Lance-Corporal J.W. Hamilton.
Lance-Corporal R. Hilton.
Lance-Corporal G. McPherson.
Lance-Corporal G.R. Nesbitt.
Lance-Corporal F. Ripley.
Lance-Corporal J. Robinson.
Lance-Corporal J.J. Storey.
Lance-Corporal E.G. Thomas.
Lance-Corporal C. Wilson.
Private I.W. Allison.
Private A.E. Alderson.
Private T.C. Allen.
Private D. Bainbridge.
Private E. Blankley.
Private A.J. Dinsley.
Private M. Doughty.
Private D. Ede.
Private A. Gash.
Private J.L. Hammond.
Private G.B. Jardine.
Private R. Logan.
Private B. McLindon.
Private J. McNeille.

Private A. Moss.
Private J. Murphy.
Private C. Neasham.
Private R. Parker.
Private R.W. Pearson.
Private O. Rushford.
Bugler N. Scrafton.
Private W.M. Sinclair.
Private E.P. Smith.
Private G.J.W. Vasey.
Private T. Tindall.
Private R. Tiplady.
Private W. Turnbull.
Private T. Vickers.
Private A. Walton.
Private W. Ward.

BAR TO THE MILITARY MEDAL:

Acting Company Sergeant-Major P. Finn.
Sergeant F.M. Britton.
Sergeant H. Cruddace.
Lance-Corporal H. Gartland.

MERITORIOUS SERVICE MEDAL:

Quartermaster Sergeant W. Lowes.
Company Quartermaster Sergeant T.A. Noble.
Sergeant P. Sturt.
Corporal S. Wear.
Private H.W. Hall.

MENTIONED IN DESPATCHES:

Company Sergeant-Major J. Taylor.
Corporal J. Dixon.
Private C.C. Bonner.

2ND/6TH BATTALION THE DURHAM LIGHT INFANTRY

DISTINGUISHED CONDUCT MEDAL:

Sergeant G.H. Dowdall.
Sergeant J.R. Griffith.
Private J. Murphy.

MILITARY MEDAL:

Sergeant P.F. Spraggs.
Sergeant C. Towers.
Corporal F. Clowes.
Corporal J.R. Miller.
Corporal R. Russell.
Private R.B. Bailey.
Private W.H. Baines.
Private B. Benson.
Private A. Brown.
Private J.L. Cawthorne.
Private. T. Clarke.
Private W. Cook.
Private F. Cowburn.
Private A. Dowling.
Private H. Harker.
Private W.H. Jeffries.
Private W. Jeffreys.
Private W. Kohler.
Private A. Liverski.
Private W. Paisley.
Private A. Richardson.
Private A.E. Richardson.

MEDAILLE MILITAIRE:

Company Sergeant-Major J. Field.

MENTIONED IN DESPATCHES:

Acting Regimental Sergeant-Major J. Field.
Sergeant L.T.C. Cooper.
Sergeant J.H. Purser.

Sergeant V.M. Raw.
Private C.A. Salt.

WORLD WAR II

FRANCE AND BELGIUM 1940

MILITARY CROSS:

Captain R.L. Cummins.
Captain J.R. Heslop (*RAMC attached 6 Battalion DLI*)
Second Lieutenant D.W.W. Blackman.

MILITARY MEDAL:

Sergeant T. Pallas.
Corporal J. Cant.
Lance-Corporal J. Boustead.
Private G.C. Dean.
Private G.E. Iceton.
Private R.L. Puddle.

NORTH AFRICAN CAMPAIGN 1942 - 43

MILITARY CROSS:

Captain J.H. Chapman.
Captain F.L. Cole.
Captain R.E. Ovenden.
Captain The Rev. L.L.J. Davies BA (*R.A.Ch.D. attached 6 Battalion DLI*).
Second Lieutenant R.A. Dorman (*Commissioned in Border Regiment*).
Regimental Sergeant-Major A. Page.

BAR TO THE MILITARY CROSS:

Captain G.L. Wood, MC

DISTINGUISHED CONDUCT MEDAL:

Sergeant C.R. Haseley.
Private J. Hudson

MILITARY MEDAL:

Sergeant C.R. Haseley DCM.
Sergeant F.C. D'Auvergne.
Sergeant W. Davies.
Sergeant A. Dunn
Sergeant R.M. Grey.
Corporal S. Lishman.
Lance-Corporal J.O. McFarlane.
Private W.W. Capon.
Private J.E. Coglan.
Private J. Dougan.
Acting Regimental Sergeant-Major J. McMahon

SICILIAN CAMPAIGN 1943

MILITARY CROSS:

Captain R.G. Atkinson.
Captain R. Galloway.
Lieutenant D.A. ffrench Kehoe *(Commissioned in Northampton Regiment).*
Lieutenant R.S. Loveridge

MEMBER OF THE BRITISH EMPIRE:

Captain W. Field.

DISTINGUISHED CONDUCT MEDAL:

Lance-Sergeant J. Connell.

MILITARY MEDAL:

Lance Sergeant C.R. Critchley.
Lance Corporal G. Worthington.
Private H. Duckworth.

Private P. Kay.
Private R. Robinson.
Private D.H. Saban.

MENTIONED IN DESPATCHES:

Company Sergeant-Major J.N. Howson.
Corporal H. Lord.

NORTH WEST EUROPE CAMPAIGN 1944

DISTINGUISHED SERVICE ORDER:

Major G. L. Wood MC & Bar

MILITARY CROSS:

Major K.M. Wood.
Captain I.A. Daw.
Captain D. Rome.
Captain J.M. Murphy *(RAMC attached 6Battalion DLI).*
Lieutenant T.M. Kirk
Lieutenant S. Seggie *(Commissioned in Middlesex Regiment).*

BAR TO THE MILITARY CROSS:

Major R.G. Atkinson MC.

DISTINGUISHED CONDUCT MEDAL:

Company Sergeant-Major J.N. Howson

MILITARY MEDAL:

Company Sergeant-Major J. H. Harrison
Sergeant W.F. Botterman
Sergeant W.H. Fradley
Sergeant W. Horrocks
Sergeant J.H. Swithenbank
Sergeant E.P. Boyd
Lance-Sergeant D. Montgomery
Lance-Sergeant T. Valks.

Lance-Corporal J. Wear
Corporal J. Ferguson
Private J. Redman
Private G. Davison

Major R.S. Loveridge MC
Staff Sergeant W.H. Davies
Sergeant F.W. Scott
Lance-Sergeant L N Shipley
Corporal J. Redman, MM
Lance-Corporal R. Peters
Private R. Hepple
Private G.S. Richardson

CROIX DE GUERRE:

Major R. S. Loveridge
Regimental Sergeant Major E. J. Greening

ESCAPING FROM FRANCE 1940

MILITARY MEDAL

Corporal J. Horsman

(Ranks are those held at the time of the Award)

ROLL OF HONOUR
WORLD WAR II

This list of men killed and died of wounds, has been collated from information available. It may not be complete and apologies are made for any missing names. The Roll of Honour can be viewed in the Regimental Chapel in Durham Cathedral. The Roll of Honour of the dead of World War I can be found in 'Soldiers Who Died In The First World war - Volume 62 - DLI.'

Private	J.R.	Atkinson	1. 5. 40
Private	J.L.	Carrigan	19. 5. 40
Private	T.E.	Hall	21. 5. 40
Private	H.A.	Lewis	21. 5. 40
Private.	M.	Nichol	21. 5. 40
Private	S.B.	Roberts	21. 5. 40
Private	T.	Robinson	21. 5. 40
Private	J.	Sullivan	21. 5. 40
Private	H.A.	Williams	21. 5. 40
L/Corporal	J.	Nicholson	22. 5. 40
Private	W.	Nevison	22. 5. 40
Corporal	W.M.H.	Jarvis	27. 5. 40
Private	H.E.	Reid	28. 5. 40
Private	G.	Dunn	29. 5. 40
Sergeant	H.	Waterworth	30. 5. 40
Private	G.	Allison	30. 5. 40
Private	R.	Ramm	30. 5. 40
L/Corporal	W.K.	Goodall	31. 5. 40
Private	L.W.	Whing	31. 5. 40
Private	F.A.	Tate	1. 6. 40
Private	R.W.	Ellis	2. 6. 40
Sergeant	G.W.	Todd	4. 6. 40
Private	R.J.	Robson	4. 6. 40
Private	R.	Hay	6. 6. 40
Private	R.W.	Carr	11. 6. 40
L/Corporal	T.	Docherty	14. 6. 40
Lieutenant	J.	Cathcart	14. 6. 40
L/Sergeant	T.	Wadley	16. 6. 40
L/Corporal	E.	Bramhald	16. 6. 40
Private	J.W.	Dinsley	16. 6. 40
Private	R.S.	Kirkup	16. 6. 40
Private	P.	McCulloch	16. 6. 40
Private	J.R.	Simpson	16. 6. 40
Private	J.T.	Wright	16. 6. 40
Private	H.	Pitt	25. 6. 40
Private	F.N.	Rooks	26.11. 40
Private	R.M.	Smith	7. 2. 41
Sergeant	F.	Chatt	26. 4. 41
L/Corporal	J.T.	Robertson	18. 8. 41
Private	T.	Flatley	4. 9. 41
Private	G.	Hinds	6. 4. 42
Private	P.	Flood	7. 4. 42
Private	J.E.	Walker	14. 4. 42
Sergeant	H.	Wilsher	10. 5. 42
Private	D.P.	Roche	21. 5. 42
Sergeant	H.L.	Dawson	29. 5. 42
Private.	A.	Banks	30. 5. 42
Corporal	A.T.	Robertson	1. 6. 42
Private	P.	Brown	1. 6. 42
Private	C.	Osolin	5. 6. 42
Corporal	H.	Aston	6. 6. 42
Private	T.B.J.	Flockhart	6. 6. 42
Private	A.	Rose	8. 6. 42
Corporal	H.B.	Scott	10. 6. 42
Private	G.	Balfour	11. 6. 42
Private	J.P.	Brown	11. 6. 42
Private	F.	Hutchinson	11. 6. 42
Private	J.	Campbell	12. 6. 42
Corporal	T.	Snowdon	15. 6. 42
Private	N.S.	Campbell	15. 6. 42

L/Sergeant	F.	Johnson	28. 6. 42	Private	A.J.	Coles	2.11. 42
L/Sergeant	W.	Robinson	28. 6. 42	Private	W.S.	Fowles	2.11. 42
Private	J.	Pears	28. 6. 42	Private	T.	Gallop	2.11. 42
Private	J.	Stephenson	28. 6. 42	Private	A.	Griffin	2.11. 42
L/Corporal	J.R.	Newstead	29. 6. 42	Private	J.	Higgins	2.11. 42
L/Corporal	G.S.	Walker	29. 6. 42	Private	J.	Jones	2.11. 42
Private	G.K.	Dawson	29. 6. 42	Private	F.	Kelly	2.11. 42
Private	R.	Dewar	29. 6. 42	Private	H.	Longstaff	2.11. 42
Private	W.	Marshall	29. 6. 42	Private	T.H.	Longstaff	2.11. 42
Private	W.	Sproat	2. 7. 42	Private	W.P.	McDonald	2.11. 42
Private	T.W.C.	Wooten	8. 7. 42	Private	T.W.	Morris	2.11. 42
Private	A.	Young	10. 7. 42	Private	G.	Palfreyman	2.11. 42
Private	T.C.	Chandler	13. 7. 42	Private	H.G.C.	Pape	2.11. 42
Corporal	L.C.E.	Townsend	27. 7. 42	Private	A.T.	Robertson	2.11. 42
L/Corporal	R.	McDuff	27. 7. 42	Private	E.W.	Robinson	2.11. 42
Private	G.	Edmundson	27. 7. 42	Private	J.	Robson	2.11. 42
Private	J.	Hall	27. 7. 42	Private	C.W.	Selley	2.11. 42
Private	R.	Lee	27. 7. 42	Private	T.	Tasker	2.11. 42
Private	F.H.	Reynolds	27. 7. 42	Private	P.	Taylor	2.11. 42
Private	J.	Vallely	27. 7. 42	Private	N.F.	Thomas	2.11. 42
Private	J.	O'Hara	17. 8. 42	Private	R.	Toes	2.11. 42
L/Corporal	C.P.	Burdis	7. 9. 42	Private	W.	Travis	2.11. 42
Private	R.L.	Puddle, MM	23. 9. 42	L/Corporal	T.A.	Waller	4.11. 42
Private	J.	Jones	27. 9. 42	Private	A.	Barnfield	6.11. 42
Private	W.	Burn	27. 9. 42	Private	T.W.	Jackson	8.11. 42
Private	F.	Goodwin	12.10. 42	Private	J.	Dawson	10.11. 42
Private	H.A.D.	Andrews	13.10. 42	Private	W.H.	Buckle	13.11. 42
Captain	T.F.	Chamberlain	24.10. 42	Private	J.	Appleyard	14.11. 42
Private	J.	Smith	24.10. 42	Private	W.	Colwell	14.11. 42
Private	G.	Adams	26.10. 42	Private	R.	Leng	14.11. 42
Sergeant	N.	Kay	1.11. 42	Private	A.	Lowe	14.11. 42
Private	A.	Carroll	1.11. 42	Private	N.	Pedelty	14.11. 42
Lieutenant	T.H.	Vickers	2.11. 42	Private	E.	Reilly	14.11 42
WO 1	A.	Page MC	2.11. 42	Private	P.	Soutar	14.11. 42
C/Sergeant	J.N.	Robinson	2.11. 42	Private	J.F.	Davidson	16.12. 42
Sergeant	T.E.	Morris	2.11. 42	Private	J.C.	Davies	16. 1. 43
L/Sergeant	R.H.	Fairley	2.11. 42	Private	R.	Peart	28. 1. 43
Corporal	A.	Hewson	2.11. 42	Private	J.	Barrett	7. 2. 43
Corporal	A.	Moffit	2.11. 42	L/Corporal	E.	Walton	19. 2. 43
Corporal	A.F.	Whittle	2.11. 42	Private	W.	Cringan	26. 2. 43
L/Corporal	T.W	Sewell	2.11. 42	Corporal	R.L.	Green	1. 3. 43
Private	B.	Bates	2.11. 42	Private	F.H.	Gough	1. 3. 43
Private	R.	Brown	2.11. 42	Private	D.J.	Greenslade	1. 3. 43
Private	R.N.	Bull	2.11. 42	Private	J.W.	Mitchinson	2. 3. 43

Private	A.E.	Willis	2. 3. 43
Private	E.	McNally	4. 3. 43
Private	J.	Lynch	6. 3. 43
L/Sergeant	R.S.	Pigg	8. 3. 43
Private	J.	Plant	8. 3. 43
Private	S.	Anear	10. 3. 43
Private	J.	Craighill	11. 3. 43
Private	H.	Chandler	15. 3. 43
Private	G.	Davison	16. 3. 43
Private	G.	Wall	17. 3. 43
L/Corporal	L.	Bassett	18. 3. 43
L/Corporal	W.	Holden	21. 3. 43
Captain	J.M.	Jackson	22. 3. 43
Corporal	J.	Shand	22. 3. 43
L/Corporal	F.C.	Gwynn	22. 3. 43
Private	A.	Bradshaw	22. 3. 43
Private	A.P.	Brown	22. 3. 43
Private	L.A.	Cole	22. 3. 43
Private	B.J.	Gildea	22. 3. 43
Private	J.H.	Howarth	22. 3. 43
Private	J.L.	Scott	22. 3. 43
Private	N.	Waugh	22. 3. 43
Sergeant	T.	Butler	23. 3. 43
Sergeant	J.	French	23. 3. 43
Corporal	F.	Allen	23. 3. 43
Private	E.A.H.	Bell	23. 3. 43
Private	M.H.	Darker	23. 3. 43
Private	N.G.	Denton	23. 3. 43
Private	A.R.	Dix	23. 3. 43
Private	G.H.	Heslington	23. 3. 43
Private	A.	Millward	23. 3. 43
Private	W.H.	Rainford	23. 3. 43
Private	J.	Riley	23. 3. 43
Private	H.D.	Riordan	23. 3. 43
Private	J.T.	Rouse	23. 3. 43
Private	N.	Thomas	23. 3. 43
Private	W.L.	Wright	23. 3. 43
Private	J.T.	Yates	23. 3. 43
Private	J.	Nichols	25. 3. 43
Corporal	T.D.	Harris	28. 3. 43
Private	D.B.	Collins	30. 3. 43
Private	G.W.	Evans	1. 4. 43
Corporal	R.	Edwards	15. 4. 43
Captain	H.E.	Walton	10. 7. 43
Private	G.H.	Barr	10. 7. 43
Private	J.	Matthews	10. 7. 43
Private	J.T.	Shimmen	10. 7. 43
Private	W.	Spearman	10. 7. 43
L/Corporal	H.	Bell	12. 7. 43
Private	G.A.	Bramwell	12. 7. 43
Private	L.	Girven	12. 7. 43
Private	H.F.	Pursall	12. 7. 43
Captain	J.H.	Chapman MC	13. 7. 43
L/Corporal	J.J.	Lowther	13. 7. 43
WO 11	T.	Pallas MM	17. 7. 43
Sergeant	J.	Monaghan	17. 7. 43
Sergeant	W.	Raine	17. 7. 43
Sergeant	H.	Redhead	17. 7. 43
L/Sergeant	J.W.	Burks	17. 7. 43
Corporal	A.E.	Joyner	17. 7. 43
Corporal	S.	Lishman MM	17. 7. 43
Corporal	W.	Pipe	17. 7. 43
Corporal	H.P.	Prior	17. 7. 43
L/Corporal	E.	Berry	17. 7. 43
L/Corporal	A.	Clarke	17. 7. 43
L/Corporal	E.	Luty	17. 7. 43
Private	F.	Armitage	17. 7. 43
Private	C.	Brown	17. 7. 43
Private	E.	Collins	17. 7. 43
Private	A.	Cosgrove	17. 7. 43
Private	M.D.	George	17. 7. 43
Private	J.	Glover	17. 7. 43
Private	J.	Heeps	17. 7. 43
Private	R.	Laybourn	17. 7. 43
Private	J.E.	Milner	17. 7. 43
Private	F.	Seddon	17. 7. 43
Private	H.	Shaw	17. 7. 43
Private	M.L.	Wilkinson	17. 7. 43
Private	J.	Wilson	17. 7. 43
L/Corporal	E.	Jenkins	18. 7. 43
Private	F.J.	Dell	18. 7. 43
Private	R.M.	Gormley	20. 7. 43
Private	R.	Murray	21. 7. 43
L/Corporal	W.S.	Alexander	23. 7. 43
Private	C.W.	Stephan	27. 7. 43
L/Corporal	E.	Comer	31. 7. 43
Sergeant	J.	Hodgkiss	4. 8. 43
Private	T.P.W.	Crates	4. 8. 43

Sergeant	G.T.	O'Bryant	5. 8. 43
Private	T.	Noone	5. 8. 43
Private	R.	Stanley	5. 8. 43
Private	W.H.	Boardwell	6. 8. 43
Private	F.G.	Cole	6. 8. 43
Private	R.F.	Elvin	6. 8. 43
Private	T.J.	Jones	6. 8. 43
Private	S.J.	Sharp	6. 8. 43
Lieutenant	J.S.B.	Holt	6. 8. 43
L/Sergeant	W.	Moroney	6. 8. 43
Private	A.	Tinling	10. 8. 43
Sergeant	A.	Dunn MM	11. 8. 43
Private	J.	Butler	11. 8. 43
Private	J.	Walker	14. 8. 43
Private	M.N.	Allen	12. 9. 43
Private	H.	Starr	23. 9. 43
Private	W.	Robertson	8.12. 43
Private	J.	Swales	7. 4. 44
Private	J.	Burns	4. 6. 44
Corporal	L.J.	King	7. 6. 44
Private	A.G.	Lockwood	7. 6. 44
Private	W.H.	Barlow	8. 6. 44
Private	E.	Hayton	8. 6. 44
Corporal	W.	Brown	13. 6. 44
Private	H.T.	Crumpton	13. 6. 44
Corporal	E.M.	Firth	13. 6. 44
Private	E.	Baker	13. 6. 44
Private	C.F.	Bennett	13. 6. 44
Private	W.A.C.	Causley	13. 6. 44
Private	E.A.	Fenwick	13. 6. 44
Private	T.	Garvey	13. 6. 44
Private	E.	Sterio	13. 6. 44
Private	L.T.	Webb	13. 6. 44
Private	J.	Wilkes	13. 6. 44
Sergeant	A.	Dawson	14. 6. 44
Sergeant	A.	Moralee	14. 6. 44
Corporal	R.	Davies	14. 6. 44
Corporal	G.K.B.	Dewar	14. 6. 44
Corporal	J.W.S.	Gibson	14. 6. 44
L/Corporal	R.A.	Hale	14. 6. 44
L/Corporal	R.A.	Layfield	14. 6. 44
Private	C.F.	Alderman	14. 6. 44
Private	P.L.	Arnold	14. 6. 44
Private	N.	Barrett	14. 6. 44

Private	A.B.	Bradley	14. 6. 44
Private	I.	Dickinson	14. 6. 44
Private	E.	Ford	14. 6. 44
Private	J.C.	French	14. 6. 44
Private	T.V.	Humphries	14. 6. 44
Private	J.A.	Jackson	14. 6. 44
Private	T.H.R.	Jenkins	14. 6. 44
Private	H.T.	King	14. 6. 44
Private	H.	Oakley	14. 6. 44
Private	R.J.	Oliver	14. 6. 44
Private	V.	Pearson	14. 6. 44
Private	D.H.	Saban, MM	14. 6. 44
Private	G.G.	Spendlove	14. 6. 44
Private	G.	Thornton	14. 6. 44
Private	H.J.	Williams	14. 6. 44
Private	A.	Mycock	15. 6. 44
Sergeant	O.M.	Stewart, MM	15. 6. 44
Private	A.	Campin	16. 6. 44
Corporal	A.G.	Taylor	17. 6. 44
Private	H.	Biott	17. 6. 44
Private	A.H.	Burton	17. 6. 44
Private	P.R.	Davies	17. 6. 44
Private	C.V.	Egglestone	17. 6. 44
Private	L.F.	Jenkins	17. 6. 44
Private	H.	Kay	17. 6. 44
Private	G.W.	Lee	17. 6. 44
Private	E.A.	Trott	17. 6. 44
Private	G.W.	Whaley	17. 6. 44
Corporal	H.J.	Morris	18. 6. 44
Corporal	E.J.	Pugsley	18. 6. 44
L/Corporal	J.	Grady	18. 6. 44
Private	A.	Gentle	18. 6. 44
Private	J.	Glasper	18. 6. 44
Private	W.	Pears	18. 6. 44
Private	H.W.	Rankle	18. 6. 44
Private	J.W.	Sharpe	18. 6. 44
Private	A.A.	Tanner	18. 6. 44
Sergeant	J.	Crombie	18. 6. 44
Lieutenant	J.B.	Horn	19. 6. 44
Private	L.C.	Elmes	19. 6. 44
Private	J.	Hawkins	19. 6. 44
Private	D.R.	Jones	19. 6. 44
Private	F.	Leatherbarrow	19. 6. 44
Private	T.B.	Clough	21. 6. 44

Private	C.N.	Garrard	24. 6. 44
L/Sergeant	W.	Williams	25. 6. 44
Private	N.	Booth	25. 6. 44
Private	G.	Hesp	25. 6. 44
Private	W.A.	Gaunt	26. 6. 44
Private	C.G.	Henderson	27. 6. 44
Private	G.F.	Lawrenson	27. 6. 44
Private	T.	Vallely	30. 6. 44
L/Sergeant	E.	Payne	1. 7. 44
Corporal	G.F.	Lewis	1. 7. 44
Private	J.	Longson	9. 7. 44
Private	A.B.	Farthing	11. 7. 44
Private	J.	Hayes	11. 7. 44
Private	F.E.	Jones	11. 7. 44
Private	E.J.	Mahy	11. 7. 44
Private	R.E.	Pattison	11. 7. 44
Private	J.	Sankey	11. 7. 44
Private	J.R.E.	Ralph	12. 7. 44
Private	H.K.	Hosking	12. 7. 44
Private	H.	Bayliss	13. 7. 44
Private	R.E.	Prosser	13. 7. 44
Sergeant	N.	Macklam	18. 7. 44
Private	J.	Cook	18. 7. 44
Sergeant	V.	Martlew	23. 7. 44
Private	F.	Ratcliffe	24. 7. 44
Private	J.A.F.	Ades	26. 7. 44
Private	T.	Ansell	29. 7. 44
Private	W.G.	Arkless	29. 7. 44
Private	R.	Blundred	31. 7. 44
L/Corporal	H.	Wilson	1. 8. 44
Private	A.G.	Arthur	1. 8. 44
Private	T.W.	Crawford	1. 8. 44
Private	A.	Hill	2. 8. 44
Sergeant	T.	Pease	3. 8. 44
Corporal	J.	Dewsbury	3. 8. 44
L/Corporal	J.T.	Brookes	3. 8. 44
Private	C.H.	Whitwell	3. 8. 44
Private	M.M.	Symonds	7. 8. 44
Sergeant	W.H.	Fradley MM	8. 8. 44
Major	J.C.	Browne	9. 8. 44
Captain	R.E.	Evans	9. 8. 44
L/Sergeant	F.A.E.	Maddocks	9. 8. 44
Corporal	A.	Jenkins	9. 8. 44
L/Corporal	F.C.	Sully	9. 8. 44
Private	M.	Butcher	9. 8. 44
Private	F.J.	Churston	9. 8. 44
Private	B.C.	England	9. 8. 44
Private	J.R.	Maddison	9. 8. 44
Corporal	G.	Marsh	9. 8. 44
Sergeant	J.F.	Chappell	10. 8. 44
L/Sergeant	J.L.	Jarvis	10. 8. 44
Corporal	R.J.	Blanche	10. 8. 44
Private	W.W.	Holt	10. 8. 44
Private	L.	Butler	11. 8. 44
Private	K.	Credland	11. 8. 44
Private	R.	Edwards	11. 8. 44
Private	A.	Robson	11. 8. 44
Major	R.	Galloway MC	12. 8. 44
Sergeant	W.H.	Greygoose	12. 8. 44
Private	W.	Lewis	12. 8. 44
Private	A.	Robbins	12. 8. 44
Private	W.	Smith	15. 8. 44
Private	T.C.	Hulston	16. 8. 44
Private	T.J.	Wheeler	20. 8. 44
Private	L.	Tyler	21. 8. 44
Corporal	R.	Walker	22. 8. 44
L/Corporal	A.D.	Kibble	31. 8. 44
Private	D.G.	Brookes	31. 8. 44
Private	J.D.	McVittie	31. 8. 44
Private	L.C.	Newell	4. 9. 44
Major	G.M.	Norman	6. 9. 44
Corporal	R.C.	Allen	6. 9. 44
Private	W.E.	Gilbride	9. 9. 44
Sergeant	E.P.	Boyd MM	10. 9. 44
Sergeant	W.A.	George	10. 9. 44
Corporal	S.	Cree	10. 9. 44
Corporal	R.J.	Harland	10. 9. 44
Corporal	J.	Stephenson	10. 9. 44
Corporal	G.E.	Stones	10. 9. 44
Corporal	J.A.	Thompson	10. 9. 44
L/Corporal	R.	Black	10. 9. 44
L/Corporal	F.	Goddard	10. 9. 44
L/Corporal	J.S.	Newson	10. 9. 44
L/Corporal	J.	Richardi	10. 9. 44
Private	R.	Barnes	10. 9. 44
Private	W.H.	Barrick	10. 9. 44
Private	K.R.	Brown	10. 9. 44
Private	W.L.	Burnell	10. 9. 44

Private	J.	Butler	10. 9. 44
Private	J.R.	Charlton	10. 9. 44
Private	L.C.	Devereux	10. 9. 44
Private	F.C.	Gladwin	10. 9. 44
Private	F.	Haddon	10. 9. 44
Private	F.	Haycock	10. 9. 44
Private	J.	Hutchinson	10. 9. 44
Private	J.R.	Jopling	10. 9. 44
Private	G.	Kell	10. 9. 44
Private	G.J.	Lancett	10. 9. 44
Private	A.	McCluskey	10. 9. 44
Private	C.W.	Parish	10. 9. 44
Private	R.	Robinson MM	10. 9. 44
Private	A.	Roden	10. 9. 44
Private	W.R.R.	Savage	10. 9. 44
Private	V.H.	Scott	10. 9. 44
Private	H.	Stephenson	10. 9. 44
Private	W.	Williams	10. 9. 44
Private	W.O.	Wright	10. 9. 44
Private	F.	Harker	11. 9. 44
Private	W.M.	Peake	11. 9. 44
Private	T.	Robinson	11. 9. 44
Private	C.E.	Pugh	13. 9. 44
Sergeant	C.R.	Critchley MM	15. 9. 44
Private	A.	Nichols	21. 9. 44
Private	J.F.	Hipgrave	1.10. 44
Private	J.J.	Brownless	6.10. 44
Private	A.	Molyneux	9.10. 44
Private	T.F.	Stephenson	9.10. 44
Private	J.W.	Hampson	10.10. 44
Private	J.	Walton	17.10. 44
Private	K.	Saxelby	21.10. 44
Private	J.R.	Dalby	11.11. 44
Private	D.F.J.	Young	14.11. 44
Private	A.	McGregor	16.11. 44
Private	T.P.	Quill	21.11. 44
Private	F.	Richardson	14. 1. 45
Private	J.	Donaldson	8. 2. 45
Private	T.	Anderson	4. 3. 45
Private	J.H.	Gibson	20. 3. 45
Private	R.	Johnson	24. 6. 45
Corporal	A.E.	Elson	29. 6. 45
Private	A.	Rowley	13.11. 45
Private	A.G.	Tate	28. 6. 46

GLOSSARY

The following are the English translations of the Arabic place names which appear in in the Chapters 20 - 24.

Alam
Landmark such as a cairn or small natural feature.
e.g. Alam Halfa   *Place of the esparto grass.*

Bir
A well, also ancient underground cistern for collecting water.
e.g. Bir Hacheim *Well of the wise man or doctor.*

Deir
Depression in the desert's
e.g. Deir el Munasib *The raised depression.*

Eluet
A height.
e.g. Eluet Aleima *Hill of the learned man.*

Gabre
Grave.
e.g. Gabre el Fachri *Grave of 'al Fachri.*

Gebel or **Jebel**
High hill or mountain
e.g. Gebel Roumana *Pomegranate Hill.*

Got or **Chet**
Saucer like depression, cultivated in peaceful times by the native Arabs.
e.g. Chet Meskine *The poor (miserable) depression.*

Qaret
Isolated flat topped hill.
e.g. Qaret el Himeimat *Hill of the little doves.*

Minqar
A ridge, escarpment.
e.g. Minqar Sidi Hamza *The ridge named after a holy man called Hamza.*

Ras
Headland or small mound.
e.g. Ras el Ali *The high headland.*

Sebkret
Salt Marsh.

Sidi
My Lord, term of respect for holy man, distinguished persons.
e.g. Sidi Abd el
e.g. Sidi Breghisc   *Local holy men.*
e.g. Sidi Rezegh

Tel
Small hill or mound.
e.g. Tel el Eisa *The hill of Jesus.*

Trigh
Desert track.
e.g. Trigh el Abd *The way of the slave.*

Wadi
Water course, generally dry.

ACKNOWLEDGEMENTS

The result of several years research, this book could not have been completed and produced without the encouragement and assistance of a number of people. My thanks to the Regimental Trustees for asking me to write the book and for their support throughout the period of time it has taken to write it. Major I.R. English, MC, TD, DL, Chairman of the Regimental History Sub Committee has given freely of his time and advice and, along with Brigadier P.J. Jeffreys, DSO, OBE, DL, read the draft and checked its accuracy. Major D. Bower, Secretary of The Light Infantry Association, spent several hours checking my word processor disks and preparing them for the publisher and the final draft owed much to his patience and tolerance of my many errors. Mr. H. Finlay of the North East TAVRA photocopied the final draft.

My grateful thanks must go to Stephen Shannon, BA, Museum Assistant at The Durham Light Infantry Regimental Museum who allowed me access to Regimental Archives, was patient with my many visits often at busy times of his day and who read the proof of the book. I was always able to call upon him for advice and assistance which he readily gave. Mrs. Geraldine Auton, a former colleague of mine, corrected the many grammatical errors in the first draft, a process which took up a great deal of time on her part. I am indebted to Mr. George Fraser who spent so much time extracting the list of awards and honours for both World Wars.

I also wish thank the Staff of the Sound Records Department of the Imperial War Museum, particularly Mrs. R. Tudge and Mr. P. Hart, for their permission to use recorded experiences of veterans of the Battalion, part of the Museum's The Durham Light Infantry Sound Records Project. My thanks to Mr. P. Kemp and his staff of the Photographic Records Department of the Imperial War Museum for permission to use those of the Museum's photographs which appear in the book.

I am grateful to Mrs. Elinor Wright for permission to use the diary and photographs of her father Captain P.H.B. Lyon, MC. I wish to thank the family of Major T.B. Heslop, DSO, for permission to use the photographs of this officer. Mr. George Harwood helped with the selection of maps.

My grateful thanks to the following officers and men of the Battalion who contributed to the successful completion of the book by making readily available to me their experiences, records, photographs and so on: Brigadier P.J. Jeffreys, DSO, OBE, DL, Major D.E. Thomlinson, Captain P. Armstrong, Major R. Wiggins, Major A.D. Scotson, TD, Major P.G. Tyndale, Lieutenant-Colonel C.W. Norman OBE, Major A.E. Short, Lieutenant-Colonel D.J. Fenner, Major M.A. Lockhart, Captain C. Boys-Stones, Captain D. Joy, RAMC, Major G.C. Bartram, Lieutenant-Colonel C.W. Alder, Major R.E. Marsden, Sergeant A. Davies, Sergeant T. Russ, Corporal J. Avery, Private J. Coglan, MM, Private K. Lodge, Corporal G.S. Richardson, Sergeant H. Wilkinson, Private E. Harvey, Lance-Corporal J. Wear, MM, Corporal T. Jarvis, Corporal G. Iceton, MM, Private J. Foster and Private Lowson. I also received considerable assistance from the following before their deaths: Colonel W.I. Watson, OBE, TD, DL, Lieutenant-Colonel R.G. Atkinson OBE, MC, DL, Lieutenant-Colonel M.R. Ferens, MBE, TD, Captain V. Ferens, Major M.J. Kirby, TD, Sergeant E. Huggins, MM, (World War I), Sergeant A. Bailey and Sergeant R. Haseley, DCM, MM. I am also indebted to the family of Lieutenant-Colonel H. Miller. TD, DL. for material assistance. I apologise for any names missing from this list which is not due in any way to lack of recognition of their support and help.

Finally I must acknowledge the patience and support of my wife who has had to put up with my absence for very many hours and, in those moments when I was tempted to relax from my task, chased me off to my study and supplied me with copious cups of coffee to sustain my efforts. I was, thus, able to meet the deadline.

INDEX

Except for the entry under its name Durham Light Infantry is referred to as DLI.

Individuals have been allotted their most senior rank mentioned in the text, even though they may have subsequently reached a higher rank.

Page numbers for illustrations are shown in bold print.

The Author

Harry Moses from Tow Law, a village in South West Durham now living in Aycliffe Village, was educated at Wolsingham Grammar School from 1941 - 1948. On completing his National Service in 1950 he commenced employment with Durham County Education Committee. He worked for this Authority from 1950 until 1963. In1963 he entered Teachers' Training College and in 1966 commenced his teaching career at Eaglescliffe Junction Farm Primary School until his appointment as Head Teacher at Aycliffe Village County Primary School in 1972. He retired on 31st December, 1993.

In the 1980s he renewed his research into Military History, particularly the First and Second World and the experiences of the County Regiment, The Durham Light Infantry. the result is this first book. Harry is a member of The Western Front Association. Since 1988 he has been a part-time interviewer with The Imperial War Museum.

He lives in retirement at Aycliffe Village with his wife Audrey. They have two children and three grandchildren.